# The 100 Greatest Days in New York Sports

**Books by Stuart Miller**

*Where Have All Our Giants Gone?*

*The Other Islands of New York City: A History and Guide* (with Sharon Seitz)

*Blue Guide: New York,* 3rd edition (with Sharon Seitz and Carol Von Pressentin Wright)

# The 100 Greatest Days in New York Sports

**Stuart Miller**

Houghton Mifflin Company · Boston · New York · 2006

*For my boys: Caleb, whose kickball exploits deserve a chapter of their own, and Lucas (a.k.a. Dookie, which rhymes with Mookie), who always wants one more turn at bat.*



Visit our Web site: www.houghtonmifflinbooks.com.

*Library of Congress Cataloging-in-Publication Data*

Miller, Stuart, date.
The 100 greatest days in New York sports / Stuart Miller.
p. cm.
Includes index.
ISBN-13: 978-0-618-57480-3
ISBN-10: 0-618-57480-8
1. Sports — New York (State) — New York — History. I. Title. II. Title: One hundred greatest days in New York sports. III. Title: Hundred greatest days in New York sports.
GV584.5.N4M54 2006
796.09747'1 — dc22 2006009768

Book design by Lisa Diercks
The text of this book is set in Celeste.

Printed in the United States of America
DOW 10 9 8 7 6 5 4 3 2 1

# Contents

# Introduction

New York City sports history, like the city itself, is noisy, self-important, and endlessly fascinating.

Go on, admit it: if you live or have lived in New York for any length of time, there is deep inside of you at least a touch of that New York arrogance, a sense that for an event to truly matter it has to happen in New York. Well, when it comes to sports, that self-imposed myopia has historically been somewhat justified.

Pick a sport — baseball, professional or college football or basketball, horse racing, boxing, or tennis — and in every case New York has consistently had front-row seats for every major development and many of the most memorable events in sports history.

The most prominent example is baseball: New York was home to the first well-formulated baseball rules, the first ballpark, the first paying customers, the first fastball, curve, and bunt, the creation of "Take Me Out to the Ball Game," Babe Ruth, the first televised games, the first racially integrated game, the first free-agent signing, and on and on. But it holds true for the other sports as well.

Sure, other cities have teams with rich and storied pasts (the Boston Celtics, the Green Bay Packers, the St. Louis Cardinals, the Montreal Canadiens); the Yankees alone, however, are more dominating, important, and influential than any team in any sport, and New York City's overall depth, breadth, and success blows everyone else away. And it's not just about "firsts" and historical developments: beginning in 1921, local teams captured 41 championships in a 58-year span, with all four major league teams, two pro football teams, one pro basketball and one hockey team, along with several college basketball teams, winning their respective big ones. It's not just the titles themselves — from Bobby Thomson's homer to Mookie Wilson's grounder, from Louis-Schmeling to Ali-Frazier, from Knute Rockne to Joe Namath, from CCNY to Pat Riley, from Bill Tilden to Jimmy Connors — but the fact that no other city can match this one for sheer sports drama.

And because New York is the nation's media capital, almost any great sports moment here has gotten extra amplification that guaranteed it was heard round the world. Would the 1958 New York Giants–Baltimore Colts NFL Championship have been seen as the watershed game in the league's history if it had pitted Baltimore against Green Bay? Would "Broadway Joe" Namath have become as large an icon playing in St. Louis?

So, while all the world may be a stage, New York has the audience and the media to make it the grandest, most important arena of all.

This book features the top 100 days in New York City sports, including not just team sports but great fights, tennis tournaments, marathons, track meets, horse races, and even a bicycle race. It also highlights the 25 greatest moments our home teams have experienced on the road. There were, however, so many worthy candidates for both lists that I've added 100 honorable mentions for the former and nine for the latter. Then I expanded my view and drew up lists for the greatest performances against New York teams as well as the worst moments, from blunders to painful injuries to bad behavior to brawls.

This list drew to some extent on my years of writing about both sports and the life and history of the city, as well as on my own deep local roots — my family has lived in Brooklyn for 100 years; my 96-year-old grandparents still live here, as does my mother; I even married a native Brooklynite, and we are raising our two boys here. I grew up on my dad's stories of Dixie Walker and Dolf Camilli (and knew the '41 Dodgers' starting lineup by heart at age eight) and my grandfather's tales of watching everyone from Babe Ruth to fellow NYU student Ken Strong and of the day Jackie Robinson came to the house for a business meeting.

Beyond my own experience, I picked the brains of numerous sportswriters, historians, and other experts. But ultimately it was the days, weeks, and months of endless research—watching videotapes, studying stats online, reading through hundreds of books and literally thousands of newspaper and magazine articles and even blogs—that provided the basis not only for what I wrote but for what I included and how I ranked each event.

That was the tricky part, of course. How do you weigh the relative merits of such wildly diverse sports and time periods, of great comebacks versus dominant performances, of championship moments versus classic wins in a season that ended in defeat?

There is, of course, no objective way to do it—I changed my list daily, sometimes every hour (and would be tinkering still if not for my deadline), and every argument you could make I've probably already had in my head . . . at least twice, since I took each side as I shifted and slid every entry around. Still, as the book evolved I tried to follow certain criteria.

First, the basics. I started with geography. This book is a tribute to New York City as much as to its teams and athletes—it is the city that gives us our identity first, that makes us root for New York teams—so I drew the line along the boundaries of the five boroughs. (Yes, I know I'm stubborn. My family has been telling me that since I was a kid.) So I tossed out Dr. J's Nets, LT's Giants, Mike Bossy's Islanders, the Devils, the Belmont Stakes, and other events beyond the periphery, though they do get their own top 10 list in the book. By contrast, I included events that took place in Brooklyn, Queens, and the Bronx before 1898 even though these boroughs were not part of the city at that point. Although some Brooklynites still rue the consolidation, now that all five are joined together, those events are part of our shared heritage.

The other catch is that many of baseball's greatest moments—Bobby Thomson's homer, Sandy Amoros's catch, Don Larsen's perfect game—came at the expense of another hometown team and could be seen as absolutely awful from that perspective. But they brought glory to at least part of New York, and that's the way I measured them.

(One other geographical note: there have been four Madison Square Gardens to date. The first, in Madison Square, lasted from 1879 to 1890; another in the same location lasted until 1925; the third held court at Eighth Avenue between 49th and 50th Streets through 1967, when the current version, above Penn Station, was built. For simplicity's sake, I refer throughout the book to all of these structures simply as Madison Square Garden.)

Next, I had to think about what to leave out. I rejected mythical tales (many propagated online), like the story floating around about Giant outfielder Red Murray getting struck by lightning while catching a fly ball to end a 21-inning game in Pittsburgh in 1914. It never happened, although apparently Murray had made a great catch in the same ballpark on a stormy day five years earlier.

To pick the ultimate survivors I pitted noteworthy moments against each other. Two dozen no-hitters or perfect games have been pitched against New York teams, but I reasoned that Cy Young's (at age 41) in 1908 and Jim Bunning's (on Father's Day) in 1964 were diluted by the deadball era (19 total no-nos from 1905–1910) and by expansion (17 from 1962 to 1965), while Daffy Dean's (in a double-header with his brother Dizzy, who pitched a three-hitter) in 1934 stood out (only three from 1926 to 1933).

Each Yankee game was held to a higher standard because it competed against so many other great Yankee moments: constant winning becomes a bit numbing. The Bombers' 1937 and 1938 and 1939 World Series didn't make the list because there was little suspense as the Yankees won 12 of 13 games. Even the seventh game of the 1952 World Series, a true nail-biter, didn't crack the top 40. After all, it was less historically significant than two other thrillers in that same dynasty: the final game of the 1949 regular season against Boston and the final game of the 1953 World Series, when the Yankees won their unprecedented fifth straight crown. (The same was largely true for the greats in other sports: Muhammad Ali's fight against Ken Norton doesn't compare to Ali-Frazier; Jimmy Connors's U.S. Open wins in 1976, 1978, 1982, and 1983 paled next to his 1974 triumph and his 1991 comeback.)

By contrast, singular seasons create multiple memorable moments. Titles for teams like the Mets, the Knicks, and the Rangers are so few and far between that each one stands out. And because these teams lack the Yankees' imperial air, their championship runs seem infused with more close calls and narrow escapes. So the top 100 and the top 25 "On the Road" include three wins from the Mets' 1969 World Series and four from the 1986 postseason, two from the Knicks' 1970 NBA Finals and three from their 1973 championship run, and three from the Rangers' 1994 Stanley Cup surge. The exception is the Brooklyn Dodgers' 1955 World Series — they'd been so close so many times in one generation that winning the final game was all that mattered.

The top five moments all transcended sports and had an impact on society beyond the game itself. The next five were pretty easy too — Bobby Thomson's homer, Brooklyn winning in 1955, Willis Reed limping onto the court in 1970, the Mets winning in 1969, Don Larsen's perfect game. These would be near the top of lists covering sports, or even popular culture, across the entire nation's history. (The only tough call was choosing Larsen over Game 6 of the 1986 World Series — Larsen achieved perfection, while the Mets won because Boston blew it.)

Most of the other top 25 entries are equally obvious — the Rangers winning after 54 years, Willie Mays making "the Catch," Jimmy Connors taking the 1991 U.S. Open by storm — but a few need explaining. Obviously Babe Ruth's 60th homer in 1927, Roger Maris's 61st in 1961, and Joe DiMaggio's hitting streak in 1941 rank among baseball's greatest achievements. And so they made the top 25. But why aren't they higher? Because these individual accomplishments ultimately had less impact than an NFL Championship or a Game 7 of the Stanley Cup, the World Series, or the NBA Finals. (The Yankees would have won the Series in 1927 if Ruth had hit only 55 homers; DiMaggio's streak also ranks lower in this book because it is measuring singular days, while his streak was impressive because it was a seemingly endless string of games.)

After that, I weighed a number of other factors. If a season was already represented near the top of the 100 or the 25 "On the Road," then the second or third entries from that team's season — the Mets in 1969 or 1986, for example, or the Knicks in 1970 or 1973, or the Rangers in 1994 — would get bumped further down; no matter how exciting those secondary games were, they did not define the season.

And if the game in question was a classic but occurred in a season that failed to produce a championship, in the end it ranked lower than a similarly great event that helped lead to a crown. For instance, the Yankees' Game 7 win in the 2003 ALCS may have been as dramatic as the finale of the 1953 World Series, but the 2003 season ended with a World Series loss while the latter ended in the Yankees' record fifth-straight title. Taking that reasoning one step further, great games in which the home team didn't win the series — think Robin Ventura's grand-slam single or John Starks's dunk over Michael Jordan — ended up even further down the list.

(Still, this book gave me more of an appreciation for the near-misses — the years the home team came up short. Finishing second seems so frustrating at the time; in retrospect, however, not only can it be hailed as an impressive accomplishment, but we ultimately cherish the great moments from those seasons more than we stew over the disappointment of the aftermath. In 1951 the Giants lost the World Series, for instance, but we remember only that they won the pennant.)

Those comebacks demonstrate another point worth making — the flawlessly played game is admirable but often less memorable. In the 1970 Knicks-Bullets playoff series, the Knicks played a masterful Game 7 and cruised to their 127–114 win, sapping that game of much of its drama; by contrast, in Game 1 of that series they fell behind early and needed two overtimes and some great defense by Walt Frazier to finally vanquish Baltimore. So it was Game 1 that made the honorable mention list, and Game 7 isn't in the book at all.

It's important to note that the honorable mention categories are not necessarily the ones I'd rank just below the ones on the lists. Most would fit in as numbers 101 through 200, but some made the list only because they fit a specific category. For instance, there are only three Ranger games in the top 100, but there were many others that came close. So I put the three next most memorable games in one category — an old-time classic against the rival New York Americans, Wayne Gretzky's playoff hat trick, and the Smurfs' 1983 dismantling of Philadelphia. But I also created a category that looked at "Building Blocks" to their Stanley Cups; some of the games on that sublist might not have made a top 200 list. Ranger fans might rank the triple-overtime win over Chicago in the 1971 playoffs higher, but since the Rangers lost that series, it didn't fit in anywhere.

Honorable mention was also a place for me to celebrate many of the individual achievements that didn't make the top 100. But even there, tough choices abounded. The Yankees have had numerous no-hitters that were dramatic beyond the accomplishment itself: in 1951 Allie Reynolds became one of only three people to pitch two in one season; in 1993 Jim Abbott pitched a no-hitter with just one arm; in 1996 Dwight Gooden briefly returned from his path of self-destruction to pitch gloriously. A strong case could have been made for putting all three no-hitters on a straight 101-through-200 list. But in a category that could fit just three items, they came up just short (in my view) when competing against the masterpieces of Steinbrenner's Davids — Wells, Cone, and Righetti.

In sorting through all the brawls, blunders, painful plays, and heartbreaking losses, I tried to use similar criteria, looking for a loss that was more than a loss but also historically significant (Bill Mazeroski's 1960 homer in the ninth inning of the seventh game), or at least a defining moment for a particular team (the passing of an era with the Yankees' 2001 World Series loss in the ninth inning of the seventh game). Some of those events are actually remembered favorably (the Buddy Harrelson–Pete Rose fight), while some are truly tragic (Thurman Munson dying in a plane crash), but I think that all of them, in their own way, are as compelling and memorable as the greatest moments.

There are always, of course, exceptions to just about everything I've laid out here: the quirks of the list are what make it interesting and, I hope, will make you want to argue one way or another. And I'd love to hear your arguments. Send me your version of the list (with explanations) to nycsportstop100@verizon.net. By the time this book comes out, I hope to have a Web site where I can post some of the more intriguing suggestions . . . and, of course, my own responses.

# Foreword

When professional baseball voided my original contract with the Atlanta Braves and made me a free agent, available to any team willing to match Atlanta's $50,000 offer, three teams put their names into a hat: the Cleveland Indians, the Philadelphia Phillies, and, of course, the New York Mets. There's no way to know how playing in Cleveland or Philadelphia would have affected my pitching and, ultimately, my career stats, but when it turned out to be New York that was pulled out of that hat, I was excited, because I knew that with a developing franchise I'd get a chance to pitch in the majors in a hurry. I also knew that pitching in New York would be a dramatically different experience than pitching for any other team: I'd be performing on a stage and in a spotlight unique in America.

This was the city of Babe Ruth and Lou Gehrig, of Jackie Robinson and Frank Gifford; this was the city where Jack Dempsey and Joe Louis and Sugar Ray Robinson had fought some of their biggest fights. With the departure of the Dodgers and Giants and the steep decline of the Yankees and the football Giants, New York was ripe for new stories and new stars. For a young athlete in the 1960s it was the land of opportunity. For Willis Reed and the Knicks, Joe Namath and the Jets, and for the Mets team that I played on, it was a magical moment, one in which our adventures and exploits captured the attention of the city and the nation, providing a thrilling, often hopeful backdrop in an

***Right*: Seaver displays his classic pitching motion, with his back knee nearly touching the ground. *Facing page*: Seaver attended the 1974 Welcome Home Mets dinner, where he made a young fan's night (and year) by posing for a picture. That fan grew up to be the author of this book.**

increasingly turbulent time. Our 1969 World Series win was even credited with giving John Lindsay's mayoral reelection campaign a needed boost across the finish line. And while it's impossible to truly measure the impact we had, the story is a reminder of how deeply sports resonate in New York.

This book is another reminder of how important sports are to the life of this city, but also of New York's preeminent place in the American sports landscape. Plenty of books have been written about the Mets—and about the Yankees, Knicks, Rangers, and other local teams—but no other book has undertaken a task with the breadth and depth of this one, covering the vast terrain from horse racing to tennis to baseball to marathons to football and on and on.

For those of us who lived through these moments, the book stirs up plenty of nostalgia. In my case, there was the thrill of pitching in the World Series at Shea Stadium; just two years earlier I began to understand that I really belonged in the big leagues and could compete on that level. (That moment came in the 1967 All-Star Game, when I realized that I was no longer in awe of the big stage.)

And then there are the events I remember as a fan. The first years of the U.S. Open, with Rod Laver, Arthur Ashe, and later Jimmy Connors, were when I became a tennis fan (my wife, Nancy, had long been one). I followed the meteoric career of Secretariat, whom I thought of as one of the great athletes of our time. And for me, as a longtime basketball fan, it was an especially great era to be in New York. The winter after we won the Series was the first time I didn't return home to southern California, and I went to see a couple of Knicks games. I loved to watch Dave DeBusschere and Willis Reed; they were pro's pros who headed a very good defensive team that played basketball the old-fashioned way. (I became good friends with DeBusschere, and later Jerry Lucas.)

Those Knicks and their coach, Red Holzman, shared a philosophy with our Mets, managed by Gil Hodges. Both men had a similar vision of the right way to play the game. Both the Knicks and the Mets were great *teams* that emphasized the importance of fundamentals.

But beyond evoking pleasant memories of bygone days, this book takes us beyond our personal experiences, back through time, stripping away lingering myths and providing incisive historical perspectives that add depth to the retelling of the events themselves. And because it is also a book of lists, it is bound to spark debates, although ultimately the book is like an umpire: you can argue as much as you want, but you're not going to change anything. But in the end, the rankings are secondary to the stories themselves, and those belong at the top of any list of the best New York sports events.

A book like this one about sports in New York is invariably also about the life and culture of the city. Being in the center of it all, with the enthusiasm of the hometown fans, and especially with the extensive media coverage of professional sports from so many different outlets, is truly amazing. When I played with the Mets I had to learn to withstand all that, because it could be overwhelming. Sports events in New York are amplified across the nation, but they loom particularly large among the locals, for whom these teams and these athletes are an integral part of daily life.

*Tom Seaver*
*May 2006*

**Tom Seaver became the face of the Mets and one of the biggest stars in New York in the 1960s and '70s, winning three Cy Young Awards and leading the Mets to their first World Series title.**

# Greatest Days The Top 100

GREATEST DAYS

## The Top 100

1. *Jackie Robinson shatters the color barrier, April 15, 1947, Ebbets Field*
2. *Joe Louis annihilates Max Schmeling, June 22, 1938, Yankee Stadium*
3. *Lou Gehrig proclaims himself the "luckiest man," July 4, 1939, Yankee Stadium*
4. *The Fight: Ali-Frazier I, March 8, 1971, Madison Square Garden*
5. *Babe Ruth christens the "House That Ruth Built" with a homer, April 18, 1923, Yankee Stadium*
6. *The Giants win the pennant, October 3, 1951, Polo Grounds*
7. *"Next year" finally arrives for Brooklyn, October 4, 1955, Yankee Stadium*
8. *Willis Reed hobbles to the rescue, May 8, 1970, Madison Square Garden*
9. *The Amazin' Mets win the World Series, October 16, 1969, Shea Stadium*
10. *Don Larsen achieves perfection, October 8, 1956, Yankee Stadium*
11. *Mookie Wilson hits a ground ball to first in Game 6 of the World Series, October 25, 1986, Shea Stadium*
12. *Fifty-four years later, the Rangers finally win the Stanley Cup, June 14, 1994, Madison Square Garden*
13. *The Giants crush the Bears in the NFL Championship, December 30, 1956, Yankee Stadium*
14. *CCNY wins its second national championship . . . of the month, March 28, 1950, Madison Square Garden*
15. *Willie Mays makes "the Catch," September 29, 1954, Polo Grounds*
16. *Jack Dempsey outslugs Luis Firpo, September 14, 1923, Polo Grounds*
17. *Reggie, Reggie, Reggie, October 18, 1977, Yankee Stadium*
18. *Matty shuts out the A's, October 14, 1905, Polo Grounds*
19. *Jimmy Connors defies Father Time, September 2, 1991, National Tennis Center*
20. *Roger Maris beats the Babe, October 1, 1961, Yankee Stadium*
21. *The Babe hits 60, September 30, 1927, Yankee Stadium*
22. *Joe DiMaggio hits in his 45th straight game, a new record, July 2, 1941, Yankee Stadium*
23. *Army and Notre Dame shut each other out in "the Battle of the Century," November 9, 1946, Yankee Stadium*
24. *The Yankees and the Dodgers both win on the season's final day, October 2, 1949, Yankee Stadium and Shibe Park*
25. *The Marathon expands to all five boroughs, October 24, 1976*
26. *Arthur Ashe wins the first U.S. Open, September 9, 1968, West Side Tennis Club*
27. *The Yankees win a fifth straight World Series, October 5, 1953, Yankee Stadium*
28. *The Giants win 1–0 to finish the first "Subway Series," October 13, 1921, Polo Grounds*

29. *The Subway Series rides again, October 21, 2000, Yankee Stadium*
30. *The Jets avenge their "Heidi" loss and win the AFL title, December 27, 1968, Shea Stadium*
31. *Notre Dame wins one for the Gipper, November 10, 1928, Yankee Stadium*
32. *The sky falls on Grady Little and Aaron Boone sinks the Sox, October 16, 2003, Yankee Stadium*
33. *Patrick Ewing lifts the Knicks into the NBA Finals, June 5, 1994, Madison Square Garden*
34. *Cookie Lavagetto ruins Floyd Bevens's no-hitter, October 3, 1947, Ebbets Field*
35. *Every match goes the distance on Super Saturday, September 8, 1984, National Tennis Center*
36. *The Giants win the NFL Championship in the "Sneaker Game," December 9, 1934, Polo Grounds*
37. *The Brooklyn Atlantics hand the Cincinnati Red Stockings their first defeat, June 14, 1870, Capitoline Grounds*
38. *Man o' War comes back to beat Grier at the Dwyer Stakes, July 10, 1920, Aqueduct Race Course*
39. *The Yankees win their first World Series, October 15, 1923, Polo Grounds*
40. *Willis Reed goes down, but the Knicks come back to win in Game 5, May 4, 1970, Madison Square Garden*
41. *The Mets come back once more to win Game 7, October 27, 1986, Shea Stadium*
42. *Billy Martin saves the Yankees, October 7, 1952, Ebbets Field*
43. *Stephane Matteau scores in double overtime in Game 7 of the Eastern Conference Finals, May 27, 1994, Madison Square Garden*
44. *Tommie Agee saves the day . . . then does it again, October 14, 1969, Shea Stadium*
45. *John McEnroe gets revenge against Bjorn Borg, September 7, 1980, National Tennis Center*
46. *Tony Zale drops Rocky Graziano, September 27, 1946, Yankee Stadium*
47. *Carl Lewis lifts off at the Millrose Games, January 27, 1984, Madison Square Garden*
48. *Bill Tilden becomes the first tennis superstar with his revenge win over Bill Johnston, September 6, 1920, West Side Tennis Club*
49. *Pat Summerall kicks a field goal in the snow, December 14, 1958, Yankee Stadium*
50. *Chris Chambliss homers the Yankees back into the World Series, October 14, 1976, Yankee Stadium*
51. *The Rangers beat the Islanders to reach the Stanley Cup finals, May 8, 1979, Madison Square Garden*
52. *Sugar Ray Robinson melts against Joey Maxim, June 25, 1952, Yankee Stadium*
53. *Fred Lebow and Grete Waitz run side by side, November 1, 1992, New York City Marathon*
54. *Joe Louis comes back to KO Billy Conn, June 18, 1941, Polo Grounds*
55. *The U.S. Open crowns two unique but very different champions, September 9, 1974, West Side Tennis Club*

GREATEST DAYS

56. *At the All-Star Game, Carl Hubbell strikes out Babe Ruth, Lou Gehrig, Jimmie Foxx, Al Simmons, and Joe Cronin . . . in a row, July 10, 1934, Polo Grounds*
57. *Seabiscuit wins the Brooklyn in a photo finish, June 26, 1937, Aqueduct Race Course*
58. *Columbia ends Army's winning streak, October 25, 1947, Baker Field*
59. *Ingemar Johansson's "Toonder and Lightning" strikes Floyd Patterson, June 26, 1959, Yankee Stadium*
60. *Larry Johnson shocks the Pacers with his four-pointer, June 5, 1999, Madison Square Garden*
61. *In a match for the aged, Pete Sampras beats Andre Agassi one last time, September 8, 2002, National Tennis Center*
62. *Jim Corbett has his finest hour in a loss against Jim Jeffries, May 11, 1900, Greater New York Athletic Club, Coney Island*
63. *Steffi Graf, struggling with her father's arrest, battles Monica Seles, struggling to overcome her stabbing injury, September 9, 1995, National Tennis Center*
64. *Tony Lazzeri, Joe DiMaggio, and the Yankees make a statement against the Giants and start a new Yankee dynasty, October 2, 1936, Polo Grounds*
65. *The Giants hold off the Packers for the NFL Championship, December 11, 1938, Polo Grounds*
66. *Graig Nettles flashes his leather and saves the World Series, October 13, 1978, Yankee Stadium*
67. *Ned Irish launches college basketball with the first double-header, December 29, 1934, Madison Square Garden*
68. *New York gets its first glimpse of a sports-mad future, May 27, 1823, Union Course*
69. *St. John's revs up the Big East, March 12, 1983, Madison Square Garden*
70. *The "Four Horsemen of Notre Dame" triumph over Army, October 18, 1924, Polo Grounds*
71. *Chris Evert becomes the "It Girl" with her comeback win, September 4, 1971, West Side Tennis Club*
72. *Robin Ventura hits a grand slam single, October 17, 1999, Shea Stadium*
73. *John Starks dunks over Michael Jordan in the Eastern Conference Finals, May 25, 1993, Madison Square Garden*
74. *Bernard King scores 44 in Game 6 to keep the Knicks alive against the Celtics, May 11, 1984, Madison Square Garden*
75. *Mike Piazza picks up New York with his post-9/11 game-winning homer, September 21, 2001, Shea Stadium*
76. *Brooklyn goes bonkers for its "Bums," September 29, 1941, Brooklyn*
77. *Baseball returns to Brooklyn, June 25, 2001, Keyspan Park*
78. *Dykstra rolls a homer in NLCS Game 3, October 11, 1986, Shea Stadium*
79. *The Mets sing the praises of their unsung heroes, October 15, 1969, Shea Stadium*
80. *Dave DeBusschere saves the NBA Finals, May 8, 1973, Madison Square Garden*

*81. St. John's gives Joe Lapchick a going-away championship, March 20, 1965, Madison Square Garden*

*82. NYU topples Fordham's "Seven Blocks of Granite," November 26, 1936, Yankee Stadium*

*83. Althea Gibson wins the U.S. National Championships, September 8, 1957, West Side Tennis Club*

*84. Carmen Basilio and Sugar Ray Robinson go to war, September 23, 1957, Yankee Stadium*

*85. Rocky has to go the distance, July 17, 1954, Yankee Stadium*

*86. Rod Dixon surges past Geoff Smith in the Marathon, October 23, 1983, Central Park*

*87. Salvator and Tenny go down to the wire, June 25, 1890, Coney Island Jockey Club*

*88. The Knicks beat the Celtics in double overtime in the Eastern Conference Finals, April 22, 1973, Madison Square Garden*

*89. Willie Pep gets revenge against Sandy Saddler, February 11, 1949, Madison Square Garden*

*90. Eamonn Coghlan breaks Glenn Cunningham's record by winning his seventh Wanamaker Mile, January 30, 1987, Madison Square Garden*

*91. Rod Laver wins the Grand Slam . . . again, September 8, 1969, West Side Tennis Club*

*92. Jack Elder leads Notre Dame to victory with a 98-yard interception return, November 30, 1929, Yankee Stadium*

*93. Monica Seles and Jennifer Capriati introduce power to women's tennis while Martina does her best Jimbo, September 6, 1991, National Tennis Center*

*94. Henry Armstrong collects another title as Barney Ross hangs on, May 31, 1938, Madison Square Garden Bowl*

*95. Harry Greb bests Mickey Walker amid a cavalcade of fists, July 2, 1925, Polo Grounds*

*96. Pete Sampras shows his guts against Alex Corretja, September 5, 1996, National Tennis Center*

*97. Secretariat shows his stuff, April 7, 1973, Aqueduct Race Course*

*98. The Giants beat Knute Rockne's Notre Dame All-Stars, December 14, 1930, Polo Grounds*

*99. Marathon mania reaches its peak, April 3, 1909, Polo Grounds*

*100. Charles Miller rides (and rides and rides) into the record books, December 10, 1898, Madison Square Garden*

GREATEST DAYS

## On the Road: The Top 25

1. *Broadway Joe makes good on his guarantee, January 12, 1969, Orange Bowl, Miami*
2. *Bucky Dent tops the Green Monster, October 2, 1978, Fenway Park, Boston*
3. *Babe Ruth calls his home run, October 1, 1932, Wrigley Field, Chicago*
4. *The Mets finally vanquish Houston in the 16th, October 15, 1986, the Astrodome, Houston*
5. *Columbia pulls off a stunning upset, January 1, 1934, the Rose Bowl, Pasadena*
6. *This time around Ralph Terry finds success and happiness in the ninth inning of a Game 7, October 16, 1962, Candlestick Park, San Francisco*
7. *Mark Messier backs up his guarantee, May 25, 1994, Brendan Byrne Arena, East Rutherford, New Jersey*
8. *The Knicks finally beat Boston in Game 7, April 29, 1973, Boston Garden, Boston*
9. *The Giants win but the Dodgers come from 6–1, 8–5 down on the final day against Philadelphia in 14 innings to force a playoff, September 30, 1951, Shibe Park, Philadelphia*
10. *Babe Ruth hits three homers to finish off St. Louis, October 8, 1928, Sportsman's Park, St. Louis*
11. *The Yankees resurrect themselves with a 10th-inning win, October 8, 1958, County Stadium, Milwaukee*
12. *The Rangers win the Stanley Cup after a six-year void, April 13, 1940, Maple Leaf Gardens, Toronto*
13. *Allan Houston sinks Miami, May 16, 1999, Miami Arena, Miami*
14. *Jim Leyritz powers a Yankees comeback, October 23, 1996, Fulton County Stadium, Atlanta*
15. *The Jets intercept the Raiders, January 15, 1983, Los Angeles Coliseum, Los Angeles*
16. *The Silver Fox saves the day, April 7, 1928, Montreal Forum, Montreal*
17. *Mel Ott homers to win the Series, October 7, 1933, Griffith Stadium, Washington, D.C.*
18. *Baseball's best team wins its 125th game, October 23, 1998, Jack Murphy Stadium, San Diego*
19. *Bernard buries the Pistons, April 27, 1984, Joe Louis Arena, Detroit*
20. *The Mets finally come out on top, October 1, 1973, Wrigley Field, Chicago*
21. *The Knicks win at the buzzer in double-overtime in the deciding playoff game against the Celtics, March 26, 1952, Boston Garden*
22. *The Rangers win their forgotten Cup, April 13, 1933, Maple Leaf Gardens, Toronto*
23. *St. John's wins down south, March 22, 1952, Reynolds Coliseum, Raleigh, North Carolina*
24. *The Mets outlast Atlanta, July 4–5, 1985, Fulton County Stadium, Atlanta*
25. *The Jets beat the Giants in the biggest preseason game ever, August 17, 1969, Yale Bowl, New Haven*

# 1. Jackie Robinson shatters the color barrier, April 15, 1947, Ebbets Field

The ninth-inning home run. The two-minute touchdown drive. The jump shot at the buzzer. In life, such exhilarating successes are exceedingly rare; for many people most days follow a relatively predictable routine—comfortable perhaps, but sometimes disquietingly mundane. The heart of our insatiable passion for sport is that vicarious ride on an emotional roller coaster, never knowing what will come next, the adrenaline rush of a stunning victory or the heart-stopping blow of a devastating defeat.

And yet the most magical, memorable, monumental day in New York City's sports history was, in that sense, a non-event: a man walked out to play first base. When Jackie Robinson took the field as a member of the Brooklyn Dodgers on April 15, 1947, his one small step was a giant leap, shattering the long-standing color barrier in a moment so inherently dramatic it transcended sports. It was a turning point in history, a moment crucial to the civil rights movement, and thus one of the most important days of the 20th century.

There was, of course, an inevitability to the breaking of the color line, but there was no guarantee it would happen here, although the city's relative liberalism and central place in baseball history made it fitting. (It's inconceivable it would have happened in most other National League cities, like Cincinnati and St. Louis, which were essentially southern in temperament, or in Boston, where segregation would long remain a problem on the field and in the schools.)

And there was no certainty it would be done right—the right team, the right player. Had Dodger boss Branch Rickey picked the wrong man, someone lacking both Robinson's baseball skills and inner strength, baseball's integration might have been derailed for years, and opponents of integrated schools, buses, and lunch counters would have had ammunition to delay the entire movement. When Robinson proved that he and all the black men who have followed truly deserved to share the playing field with whites, he laid the groundwork for everything that followed—from Harry Truman's integration of the Army to Rosa Parks's refusal to go to the back of the bus, to the March on Washington and Martin Luther King's "I Have a Dream" speech. (Indeed, Jacques Barzun's famous quote, "Whoever wants to understand the heart and mind of America had better learn baseball," was coined right when the Supreme Court was deciding *Brown vs. Board of Education.*)

Robinson did not take his role lightly and did not view himself as merely an athlete, although he was one of the century's finest. At UCLA he became the first person to letter in four sports—he was a revolutionary, fast-breaking point guard, an unparalleled broken-field running back, and a champion long-jumper. (Baseball was his weakest sport.) But he had a quick and fierce temper, especially when he believed whites were insulting or exploiting him. In the Army he successfully faced down court-martial charges after refusing to move to the back of a bus, and in the Negro Leagues he led his team, the Kansas City Monarchs, to prod gas stations, restaurants, and hotels to open their doors to blacks. But Rickey, in offering Robinson the chance to change history, persuaded the combative competitor to transform himself. "Mr. Rickey, do you want a player who is afraid to fight back?" Robinson famously asked at their first meeting when Rickey tested Robinson by baiting him with horrible insults.

"No," Rickey said. "I want a player with guts enough *not* to fight back."

Brooklyn signed Robinson on October 23, 1945. He became the first black in the minor leagues in 1946, making a sensational debut with the Dodgers' Montreal farm club and leading them to a 14–1 win over the Jersey City Giants with a three-run homer, three singles, and two stolen bases; twice he teased opposing pitchers into sending him home on balks. His .349 average that year set a team record. But obstructionist owners, skeptical sportswriters, and balking ballplayers still stood in his way. That off-season, baseball's owners met with commissioner Happy Chandler—who had replaced unrepentant segregationist Judge Landis—and voted 15–1 against integration. But Chandler bravely gave Rickey the go-ahead in private, knowing the owners were too image-conscious to protest publicly.

In spring training a rebellion broke out among the southerners on the Dodger team. Popular right fielder Dixie Walker organized a petition to persuade Rickey that his plan to promote Robinson by Opening Day was ill conceived. But Rickey and Dodger manager Leo Durocher stood firm. After learning of the insurrection, Durocher woke the players in the middle of the night to set them straight. "Well, boys, you know what you can do with that petition. You can wipe your ass with it," Durocher reportedly said. "I'm the manager of this ball club, and I'm interested in one thing. Winning. . . . This fellow is a real great ballplayer. . . . He's going to put money in your pockets and money in mine." Rickey then brought the full force of his personality down, lecturing each player individually and smashing any plans for organized action. (When Kirby Higbe still seemed discomfited, Rickey traded him.)

Just before Rickey officially announced Robinson's promotion came a stunning distraction. Chandler suspended Durocher for the entire season, citing his association with gamblers and other unsavory behavior. (The reality was far more complicated and stemmed in part from Durocher's public accusations that his former Dodger boss, Larry MacPhail, now running the Yankees, had himself consorted with gamblers.) But the resulting media frenzy provided some cover, diverting attention from Robinson's call-up.

On the day of Robinson's debut, the *Daily News* sports headline was not about integration but about the search for a new manager, while the *Baltimore Sun* editorialized: "This year sees a Negro, Jack Robinson, having his first chance in the big leagues, but the really big change, of course, is the absence of [Durocher], the most colorful personality in recent baseball history." (Coach Clyde Sukeforth served as interim manager for the first few games until Burt Shotton took over.)

Tuesday, April 15, 1947, dawned wet and cold. More than half the Ebbets Field crowd was black, many proudly wearing I'M FOR JACKIE buttons. Robinson was nervous but ready. Fifteen photographers hovered around the new first baseman snapping pictures beforehand. "I'll be number forty-two," he'd joked to his wife Rachel that morning. "Just in case you have trouble picking me out."

All eyes were on number 42, the second hitter in the bottom of the first, when he stepped in against the Boston Braves' Johnny Sain. Robinson made solid contact and tore down the line. He just beat the throw—or so he thought—but umpire Al Barlick called him out. Robinson whirled, ready to argue, before abruptly reining in his emotions and returning to the dugout. After popping out his second time up, Robinson hit into a double play in the fifth, but what the box score didn't reveal was that his grounder back through the box was stopped only by shortstop Dick Cullen's diving play.

Then, in the seventh, Robinson demonstrated those intangibles that would make him the

**Jackie Robinson ends baseball's policy of keeping out blacks when he crosses the threshold of the Brooklyn clubhouse.**

Dodgers' catalyst for the next decade. Trailing 3–2, with a runner on first, Robinson laid down what the *Daily News* called "one of his deft bunts"; Robinson's speed forced Earl Torgenson to hurry his throw, and the ball glanced off Robinson's shoulder, ricocheting into the outfield. Suddenly there were Dodgers on second and third. Pete Reiser, the game's hitting star, slammed a double, and Robinson sprinted home with the go-ahead run in what became a 5–3 win.

Robinson later wrote of his Opening Day performance, "If they expected any miracles out of Robinson, they were sadly disappointed," but no miracles were needed on that first day of a new nation.

Robinson's most famous quote — later his epitaph — was "A life is not important except in the impact it has on other lives." He'd affected people from his first days in the organization. In 1946 his minor league manager, Clay Hopper, had initially asked Branch Rickey, "Do you really think a nigger is a human being?" yet by year's end Hopper was telling Robinson, "You're a great ballplayer and a fine gentleman. It has been wonderful having you on the team."

In the majors Robinson's impact spread far and wide. Black papers covered the game like a new Emancipation Proclamation: the *Afro-American* devoted seven stories, seven photographs, an editorial, and a cartoon to it. While Robinson's debut gave blacks hope that a better, fairer day was coming, the change he inspired in whites was equally significant. On Opening Day, when Robinson left the clubhouse an hour after the game, he was sur-

**Jackie Robinson gets ready to take the field with his fellow Dodgers on April 15, 1947.**

rounded by 250 fans hoping to see, speak to, or touch him. Most were white. "By applauding Robinson, a man did not feel that he was taking a stand on school integration, or on open housing," Roger Kahn later wrote in *The Boys of Summer.* "But for an instant he had accepted Robinson simply as a hometown ballplayer. To disregard color, even for an instant, is to step away from the old prejudices, the old hatred. That is not a path on which many double back."

Robinson became baseball's biggest draw since Babe Ruth. The Dodgers set a road attendance record of 1.8 million, propelling the NL to its highest attendance figure ever. "Jackie's nimble, Jackie's quick, Jackie makes the turnstiles click," wrote Wendell Smith in the *Pittsburgh Courier.*

The racist taunts, talk of strikes, and even death threats that haunted the start of the season mostly abated while Robinson found acceptance in the clubhouse; after just a few weeks, he became, at least during meals and card games, just another Dodger to most of his teammates. (His on-field impact helped—as Durocher had predicted, Robinson was worth money, leading Brooklyn to the World Series.)

Even the influential white press transformed itself. On Opening Day they'd been skeptical about his chances and about integration in general, most writers seeming to believe that blacks might not be smart or skilled enough for baseball—or that their readers felt that way—and so the *Washington Post* devoted one paragraph to Robinson, the *Pittsburgh Post-Gazette* two, the *Baltimore Sun* three. As a result, many whites did not initially appreciate how momentous that game was.

But as Robinson emerged as undeniably, unstoppably a star, writers gave him more ink and more respect. That fall *Time* put him on its cover. *The Sporting News,* which had long maintained a public segregationist stance and had doubted

Robinson's chances in the spring, named him its first Rookie of the Year. That year marked the first televised World Series, and as television's reach grew, more and more people could see blacks and whites playing side by side, hugging each other after victories, consoling each other in defeat.

Fifty years after Robinson's first game, baseball commissioner Bud Selig—who had gone to see Robinson play at Wrigley Field in 1947—honored Robinson by retiring his number from all of baseball and declaring April 15 an annual Jackie Robinson Day. Robinson's legacy was not built simply on this one day, of course. Besides leading the league in stolen bases that year and winning the MVP in 1949, he propelled the Dodgers to the World Series six times in his ten-year career. He also infused the entire sport with a spark and an aggressiveness that was common to the Negro Leagues but had all too often been absent from the plodding white version. True integration came slowly, but the NL owners adapted first, and as its new wave of stars—Willie Mays, Roberto Clemente, Hank Aaron, Frank Robinson—built upon Robinson's style, it became the game's dominant league.

Still, all those accomplishments ultimately trace back to a hitless afternoon at the ballpark, an Opening Day that was truly an opening, the birth of a new era. "Whenever I hear my wife read fairy tales to my little boy, I'll listen," Robinson wrote about that first game in a column for the *Pittsburgh Courier.* "I know now that dreams do come true."

## 2. Joe Louis annihilates Max Schmeling, June 22, 1938, Yankee Stadium

Two friends strolled along the Harlem River on a June evening. "How you feel, Joe?" Freddie Wilson asked.

This was no idle question. His buddy was Joe Louis, set to fight a rematch against Max Schmeling at nearby Yankee Stadium that very night. At stake were personal pride and a heavyweight crown, as well as the hopes and dreams of a race and a nation.

"I'm scared," Louis replied.

Timidity was not what one expected from the heavyweight champion.

"Scared?"

"Yeah, I'm scared I might kill Schmeling tonight."

Louis's barrage of blows didn't kill Schmeling, but the attack did demolish the challenger with an abruptness and ferocity rarely seen in heavyweight title fights. And in leveling Schmeling at just 2:04 of the first round, Louis delivered a short jab to Germany's Nazi nationalism and a more telling blow to America's deeply bred racism, thus earning his place in the pantheon of American heroes.

"Ali-Frazier was a bigger event and a better fight but Louis-Schmeling was more important and changed the course of history," says Ali biographer Thomas Hauser.

Joe Louis Barrow was born in 1914, the grandson of slaves and the seventh child of an Alabama sharecropper. His father Munroe died when Joe was four; his mother Lillie remarried and in 1926 took the children north to Detroit. Louis built his muscles carrying blocks of ice at work and spent the money his mother gave him for violin lessons on a locker at a gym where he took up boxing. He had to wear sneakers instead of boxing shoes and endlessly reused the wrappings over his knuckles, but he was virtually unbeatable even as an amateur, making it to the Golden Gloves finals in 1933 and winning the National AAU light-heavyweight championship soon after.

Louis turned pro in 1934, his career steered by an array of blacks—including wealthy entrepreneur John Roxborough, nightclub owner and numbers runner Julian Black, and trainer Jack "Chappy" Blackburn—who were determined to forge a new black heavyweight champion. They carefully crafted his persona as the antithesis of Jack Johnson, whose flamboyance, gloating, and public dalliances with white women stirred up racism and even violence.

To get a title shot, they taught Louis to aim for knockouts so that judges wouldn't get the chance to favor white foes, and also to avoid drinking, smoking, boasting, being photographed with white women, or being "too black." They taught him to be flawless, and he nearly was—he not only floored his opponents but became a role model for many, including Jackie Robinson. (Louis was not so much flawless as discreet—he actually had numerous affairs with women, black and white, from Lena Horne to Lana Turner.)

Although Louis's team refused to bow to Michigan boxing authorities and hire a white co-manager, they became more flexible as Louis's star ascended, hiring Mike Jacobs, a savvy New Yorker looking to break Madison Square Garden's tight-fisted control of the fight game in Gotham. Jacobs got William Randolph Hearst's newspapers on his side, which proved integral to building Louis's celebrity. Louis made his New York debut in 1935 against the Italian Primo Carnera, right when Benito Mussolini was preparing to invade Ethiopia, and the press touted this matchup as American democracy versus Italian fascism, just as they would later make political hay with the Louis-Schmeling fight. Louis floored Carnera in six to become as big a star in black America as Satchel Paige.

In his first 18 months as a pro, Louis scored 23 knockouts in 27 straight wins, earning $371,645 when the average yearly salary was $1,250. Many thought him invincible, and destined for the heavyweight crown held by James Braddock. He had one more obstacle: former champion Max Schmeling.

Schmeling, a German nearly nine years older, was nicknamed "Moxie" Schmeling for daring to fight the dangerous Bomber, but he'd scored one of the biggest upsets in New York boxing history, defeating Louis at Yankee Stadium in June 1936 in a bout that reverberated around the city and the world.

Schmeling, Europe's first German champion, had conquered America in 1930 when he beat Jack Sharkey, although his title was both tainted and short-lived—he won only when Sharkey was disqualified for low blows and, after one defense, lost the rematch to Sharkey on a controversial decision. But Schmeling, who wore opponents down while he searched out their weaknesses, trained hard and diligently studied footage of Louis. "I saw something," he cryptically told the press. What he had seen was Louis briefly dropping his defenses between lefts. If he could take the pounding, Schmeling knew he'd find an opening for his big right.

He found it in the fourth, dealing Louis his first-ever knockdown. Louis, expecting another quick knockout, had devoted himself to golf, eating, his marriage, other women, and spending his winnings and thus was in no shape to recover. Taking control, Schmeling ground down Louis before finally punching him out in the 12th. White America did not yet feel it had much at stake, but blacks were distraught—there was rioting in Harlem and even reports of suicide and depression attributed to Louis's loss.

"I walked down Seventh Avenue and saw grown men weeping like children and women sitting on the curbs with their heads in their hands," Langston Hughes said afterwards. More than a fighter, Louis symbolized hope for blacks. But he had been reduced, Lena Horne said later, to "just another Negro getting beaten by a white man."

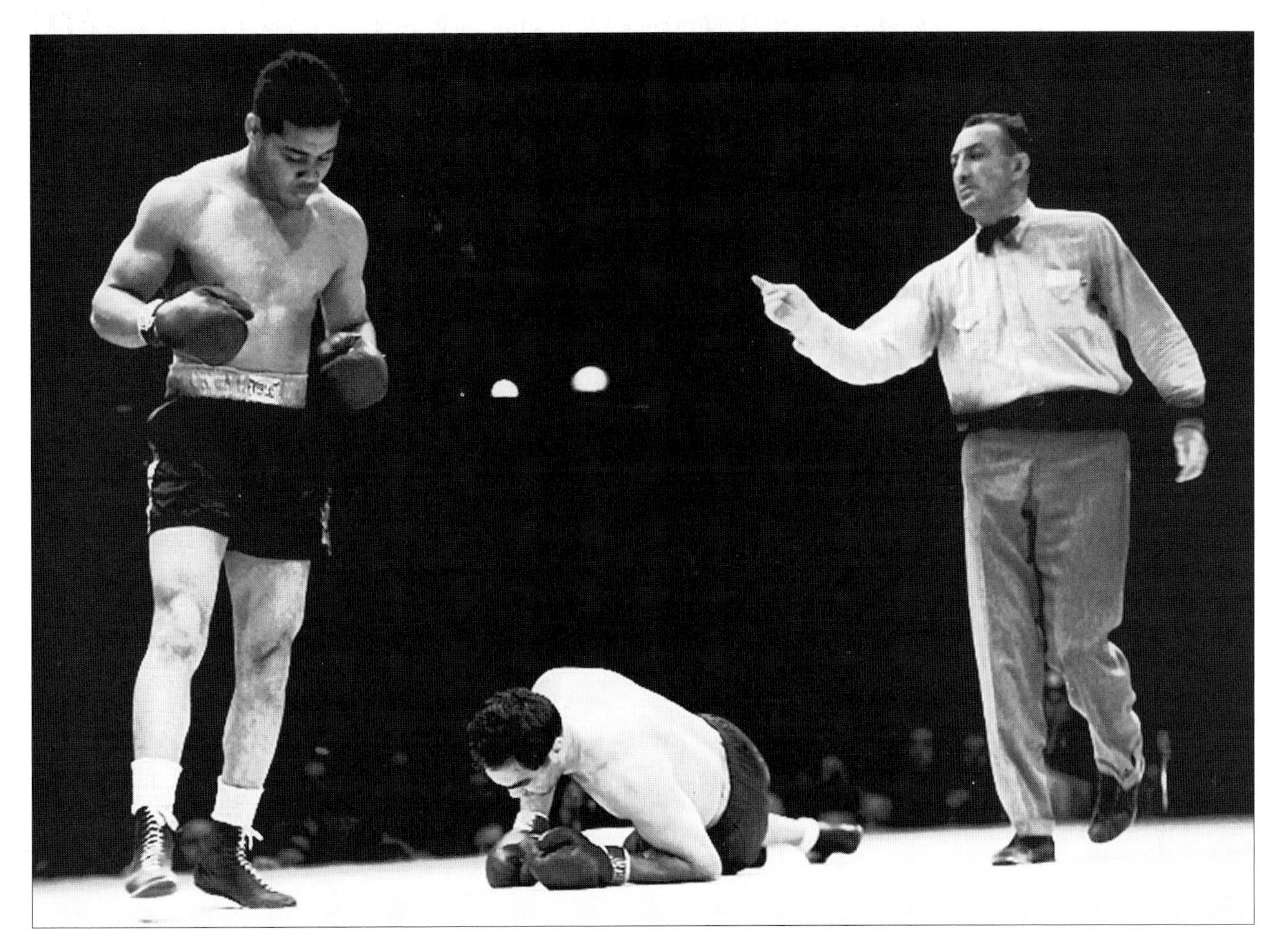

**Joe Louis annihilates Germany's Max Schmeling in the second round of a fight that has sociopolitical implications far beyond the ring.**

The Nazis were ecstatic. After having ordered the press to minimize the fight in case Schmeling lost to a black man, they now flew him back home on their new airship the *Hindenburg* (talk about bad omens), feting him at a dinner with Adolf Hitler and propaganda minister Joseph Goebbels and releasing the fight as a feature film (*Schmeling's Victory: A German Victory*).

Having bested Louis, Schmeling was next in line for a shot at Braddock. But while he desperately wanted his title back, Schmeling also loved his celebrity at home—once part of Berlin's robust nightlife, circulating with playwrights, actors, and other artists, many of whom were Jewish, he allowed Hitler to use him for propaganda purposes. He never joined the Nazi Party, although that may have been because Hitler thought him more useful outside of it.

With Schmeling viewed as a Nazi tool even more than he had been before he beat Louis, Mike Jacobs capitalized on growing political pressure and boycott threats by playing up fears that Schmeling would win, take the title to Europe, and refuse to defend it. He effectively made the case that Louis deserved the fight with Braddock, sweetening the deal by promising Braddock 10 percent of Louis's earnings for the next decade. Madison Square Garden, which handled Braddock, went to the Supreme Court asserting its right to determine Braddock's next foe. Like Braddock, it was doomed. It was Louis against Braddock, and Louis flattened the crown-holder in eight. But his victory felt hollow. "I've got to beat Schmeling before I'm the real world champion," he said.

On June 22, 1938, Louis got his shot at redemption.

By then Hitler had flexed his muscles, annexing Austria and threatening Czechoslovakia. The

Nazis touted Schmeling (whose manager, Joe Jacobs, was Jewish) as a representative of Aryan superiority, and he earned the enmity of the American public by going along, singing the Nazi anthem and doing the Sieg Heil at fights held in Germany while continuing to shill for Hitler. He also lied to the American press, pretending there was no persecution of Jews, and promised that Hitler had no grand designs.

There was genuine concern now among whites about what it would mean if "our guy," the American, lost to "one of them." Protesters outside Schmeling's hotel in Manhattan harassed the German, and the press heaped extra pressure on Louis, portraying him as the protector of American values. It's hard to fathom how sudden and shocking a transformation this was in public perception—Louis, whom the white press had routinely called things like "a wild animal," was transformed from a near-savage to democracy personified, a beacon equal to the Statue of Liberty. President Franklin Roosevelt dined with the champ at the White House, publicly squeezing his biceps and pronouncing, "Joe, we need muscles like yours to beat Germany."

Louis disliked the Nazis and was offended by the rumors that Schmeling's trainer, Max Machon, wore a Nazi uniform, but this fight was mainly personal—Louis was riled by reports that Schmeling said he wasn't smart enough to change his style and desperate to avenge his sole loss.

For their first fight, a day's delay for rain, a threatened boycott by local Jews, and the presumed lack of suspense had meant plenty of empty seats, but this time Yankee Stadium was packed. The whole country stopped to listen—70 million people, more than half the population, tuned in, and movies and dances around the nation were interrupted for the broadcast. The fight played throughout the Western world in English, German, Portuguese, and Spanish.

On top of the race and nationalism story lines, Louis's up-from-poverty saga and his comeback after losing to Schmeling made him a symbol of hope against the odds for Depression-era America. This night, everything was on the line. As Dave Kindred put it in *The Sporting News* decades later, "Lose, he's just another guy. Win, he's Joe Louis forever."

The hostility toward Schmeling was palpable. He entered the ring protected by 25 cops but was still bombarded by apples, cigarette butts, and banana peels.

Louis, who had run out of steam in their first fight, had no plans to pace himself this time. "For three rounds I was going to let it all go out," he said. "I was going to stay on top of him."

He didn't need one round, much less three. Schmeling was not expecting such aggression, and Louis snapped off two sharp left hooks to the face and a right to the chin before the German could set himself. Schmeling, who would manage only two ineffectual punches the whole fight, stepped back. Louis pursued immediately, drilling him in the head and body, slamming him to the ropes. Louis threw every punch in his arsenal, and they all connected . . . hard.

Schmeling was "a man caught and mangled in the whirling claws of a mad and feverish machine," wrote Bob Considine for the International News Service.

Louis sent Schmeling to the canvas twice. Then Schmeling, trapped against the ropes, turned away to escape yet another right but took the blow near his kidney, fracturing a vertebra. His high-pitched howl tore through the crowd. Soon after, Schmeling's handlers threw in the white towel, but that was against the rules in New York, so referee Art Donovan paid it no heed. He could not, however, ignore the beating that Louis was delivering. After just 124 seconds, Donovan stopped the fight.

The entire nation, black and white, celebrated with a giddy mixture of joy and relief, but it was a particularly wondrous night for black America. "Joe was the concentrated essence of black triumph over white," Richard Wright said later. The police commissioner closed off 30 blocks in Harlem for the revelers, and 100,000 people poured out onto the streets and into the bars.

"There was never a Harlem like the Harlem of last night. Take a dozen Christmases, a score of

New Year's Eves, a bushel of July 4ths and maybe —yes maybe—you get a faint glimpse of the idea," the *Daily News* wrote.

Back in Germany the reaction was quite different. The Nazis cut off radio transmission once they realized what was happening, and afterwards Machon portrayed Schmeling as the victim of illegal hits. He even doctored the film, blending in footage from 1936 to make it seem as though Schmeling had put up a fight.

In the long run, of course, Louis's victory may have embarrassed and infuriated Hitler, but it did little to slow his evil machinations. The us-versus-them mentality encouraged by the triumph did, however, eventually help Roosevelt when making the case for entering the war.

More lasting was the effect on the home front. While numerous sports icons had dominated the 1920s—Babe Ruth, Red Grange, Jack Dempsey, Knute Rockne, Bobby Jones—no national sports heroes had yet emerged in the 1930s. Louis's triumph over Schmeling was the biggest event in black America at the time, especially because black writers had just begun getting boxing credentials. In the days before major civil rights victories, it was white Americans rooting hard for a black man that started the process of breaking down racial barriers. Louis won even more white loyalty during World War II when he joined the Army and donated more than $100,000 in proceeds to the Army and Naval Relief Funds. (He also helped get blacks —including Jackie Robinson—into officer training school.) Jesse Owens had anticipated some of these accomplishments in the 1936 Olympics, but that performance happened overseas, was not a mano-a-mano matchup, and was in track, which lacked boxing's clout in public perception. The heavyweight champion was The Man.

"Louis definitely changed perceptions for a lot of people—certainly in the northern half of the country—about the status and accomplishments of the black man," says New York sports historian Bill Shannon. "The racial implications of this fight set the stage for Jackie Robinson."

# 3. Lou Gehrig proclaims himself the "luckiest man," July 4, 1939, Yankee Stadium

Words like grace, courage, and heroism often find their way into sportswriting, but the finest and truest display of those traits on a ball field came from a simple speech by a once-proud physical specimen who could no longer display them through athletic exploits. With just a few words before the Yankee Stadium crowd on July 4, 1939, Lou Gehrig not only touched the fans there that day but provided all of us with a poignant and powerful reminder not to take life and its joys for granted but instead to savor all that is good in our world. The speech has lasted as more than an athlete's farewell—it has stood the test of time as a piece of great American oratory, a testimony to Gehrig's dignity and humanity and to that potential in everyone.

Ironically, those brief moments ensured that Gehrig would be remembered not for his remarkable home run power, nor for his superior work ethic, but for how he handled himself when he was deprived of that which had made him famous.

Gehrig had lived the fairy-tale version of the American Dream. The child of immigrants had proved himself to local bullies by playing ball and then had achieved, by dint of a relentless work ethic, unimagined success even in the nadir of the Great Depression: he was twice voted the Most Valuable Player and was eventually baseball's highest-paid player. Yet Gehrig never got the accolades he truly deserved. Playing first base is an unflashy job requiring a solid, anchoring force more than a dynamic presence, and Gehrig was a quiet, colorless guy obscured by Babe Ruth, the loudest, most colorful player in history. After the Babe's departure, Gehrig watched, uncomplaining, as the press anointed another soft-spoken, colorless immigrant, Joe DiMaggio, as the second coming of Ruth, conflating his elegant playing style with his personality.

Gehrig's numbers were . . . well, no one ever called anything Gehrig-esque, but they were the closest thing to Ruthian outside of the Babe himself: Gehrig became a superstar in 1927 when he smashed 47 homers, frightening pitchers into giving Ruth more hittable balls. Ruth, of course, smashed 60 long balls as the duo demolished the American League and led one of the greatest teams in history. In 10 of 12 years from 1926 through 1937, Gehrig placed in the top three in home runs, RBIs, runs scored, and total bases. (He was first in those respective categories three, five, four, and four times.) He was also in the top three in batting average seven times, winning the crown once.

But Gehrig's remarkable consistency gradually allowed people to take him for granted — especially because what he did during each game took a back seat to the fact that he never missed one. Gehrig's consecutive-game streak started generating press in 1930 when Joe Sewell, owner of the longest active run, missed one game. It began earning headlines in 1932, the year before he broke Everett Scott's record of 1,307 games, and it defined him until 1939, when he was felled by amyotrophic lateral sclerosis (ALS). (His streak had begun on June 1, 1925, when he pinch-hit for Pee Wee Wanninger, who, ironically, was playing short for Scott, whose streak had only recently ended.)

The streak and the quiet dedication that created it invited admiration, not adoration or adulation. As Jonathan Eig wrote in *Luckiest Man,* Ruth's nicknames fit him perfectly — the Babe or Bambino was a beloved child, and the Sultan of Swat or King of Clout implied revered royalty — but so did Gehrig's, the Iron Horse, which was inspired by a train. "Most people don't appreciate a train's strength and reliability until they're standing on the platform one day and it doesn't show up," Eig wrote.

Gehrig endured sporadic criticism that he was hurting himself and the Yankees by refusing to rest. Enamored of the record, Gehrig played through a broken thumb, a broken toe, back spasms, lumbago, and numerous other injuries, sometimes to the detriment of the club. Yet Gehrig's relentless devotion and pride as a Yankee was the core of his very being, and without it he would never have become the great player he was. Gehrig approached every game as if he were just thrilled to be there — down eight runs in the ninth inning, he'd run hard to first on a weak grounder, and he also diligently transformed himself from an atrocious fielder into a solid, even strong one.

In 1938 Gehrig struggled, falling below .300 for the first time since 1925 as balls that would have once cleared the fence fell into outfielders' gloves. The calls for taking a day or two off to get his strength back grew louder. Even his wife Eleanor asked him to stop the streak at 1,999; Gehrig refused and played in his 2,000th game — before a crowd of just 7,000 fans who, as Eig noted, cheered DiMaggio louder. As the season progressed, manager Joe McCarthy refused to bench his star, saying it was Gehrig's decision, but he did drop Gehrig in the batting order. Gehrig, meanwhile, compensated for his loss of strength by ordering lighter

**Lou Gehrig, dying of ALS, declares himself "the luckiest man on the face of this earth."**

bats and guessing more on pitches. Clearly exhausted, he twice pulled himself out after one inning that September, maintaining the streak on the slightest of technicalities. This brought a fresh round of criticism, with some fans calling the hardest-working man in sports a phony.

In the off-season Gehrig began falling and dropping things with increasing frequency. By spring training it was apparent to all willing to let themselves see that something was seriously wrong with the Iron Horse. His muscles had withered, his body ached, and his balance was wobbly. Easy grounders rolled through his legs, and once he missed 19 straight pitches in batting practice. Gehrig started the exhibition season 3-for-35 as writer after writer called him washed up, speculated on the cause of his demise, and wondered when he would bench himself.

The season started, and it was painfully obvious that Gehrig wasn't going to shake off the winter's rust. The fans, who had occasionally booed him in 1938, realized this was no normal slump and began cheering Gehrig with all their might even after strikeouts, letting him know they appreciated his efforts. On April 30, in the ninth inning of his 2,130th consecutive game, Gehrig fielded a routine grounder but realized he couldn't beat the runner to first base, so he flipped to the pitcher for the out; when his teammates congratulated him for something so basic, Gehrig realized he had been reduced to a pitiable creature.

On May 2, 1939, in Detroit, Gehrig took himself out of the lineup. McCarthy gave Gehrig the honor of delivering the lineup card to the umpire so that as he headed back to the dugout after handing over the card the public address announcer could ask the crowd, "How about a hand for Lou Gehrig, who played 2,130 games in a row before he benched himself today." Gehrig tipped his hat to the roaring fans, went into the dugout, and wept.

Though he continued practicing, he would

never play again. On June 13, Gehrig checked into the Mayo Clinic in Minnesota, where specialists diagnosed his illness. He was 36.

The modest Gehrig downplayed the disease, implying that he might someday be crippled without letting on that ALS's progress is usually rapid and eventually fatal. In the following weeks it seems that only Eleanor Gehrig, Yankee executive Ed Barrow, and a few others learned the truth. Still, in Philadelphia on June 29, Athletics owner-manager Connie Mack requested that Gehrig come onto the field, and the fans gave him an eight-minute ovation. Gehrig didn't like such attention, so his teammates chipped in for a trophy they could present to him in the clubhouse. The writers, however, promoted the idea of a Lou Gehrig Appreciation Day, and Barrow agreed, scheduling the event between the games of a double-header with Washington.

And so, on July 4, 1939, a dozen members of the 1927 Yankees crowded into the clubhouse, including Bob Meusel, Waite Hoyt, Mark Koenig, Joe Dugan, Herb Pennock, Bob Shawkey, and Tony Lazzeri. Everett Scott and Wally Pipp, whom Gehrig had replaced at first base back in 1925, were also on hand. Gehrig was so nervous and so moved by the presence of his ex-mates that he hid out in McCarthy's office.

Before the game, the 1927 stars raised their old championship pennant in center field. The Yankees dropped the opener, 3–2, a desultory affair that everyone seemed anxious to be done with. Everyone but Gehrig, who said to McCarthy in the dugout, "I'd give a month's pay to get out of this."

Then, as a brass band played, the Yankees and Senators lined up on either side of the mound, and the 1927 squad — including Ruth, who had not spoken with Gehrig since a petty feud that dated to 1934 and who, operating on his own personal schedule, had finally arrived — gathered near home plate. Barrow and Gehrig walked out together. Mayor Fiorello La Guardia, U.S. Postmaster General James Farley, McCarthy, and Ruth all spoke glowingly of him. The Yankees retired number 4, the first time that had ever been done. Gehrig was presented with gifts from the Senators, the New York Giants, the Yankee beat writers, the office staff, Yankee executives, and, of course, his teammates. Gehrig, who spent the entire ceremony with his head down, said nothing, wiping tears away as the inscription from his teammates' trophy was read aloud.

Finally it was Gehrig's turn, but as the fans chanted, "We want Lou! We want Lou!" Gehrig shook his head at emcee Sid Mercer. No. It was too much for him. Afterwards, Gehrig told reporters that it was the only time in his life he was ever frightened on a baseball field, saying, "I'd have rather struck out in the ninth with the score tied, two down, and the bases loaded than walk out there before all those grand people."

Mercer apologized to the crowd, explaining that Gehrig was "too moved to speak," and the crew prepared to dismantle the microphones. But he had always been one to follow his manager's orders, and when McCarthy asked that he give it a shot, Gehrig stepped forward. The stadium fell utterly, deafeningly silent.

> Fans, for the past two weeks you have been reading about the bad break I got. Yet today I consider myself the luckiest man on the face of this earth.
>
> I have been in ballparks for seventeen years and have never received anything but kindness and encouragement from you fans. Look at these grand men. Which of you wouldn't consider it the highlight of his career just to associate with them for even one day? Sure, I'm lucky. Who wouldn't consider it an honor to have known Jacob Ruppert? Also, the builder of baseball's greatest empire, Ed Barrow? To have spent six years with that wonderful little fellow, Miller Huggins? Then to have spent the next nine years with that outstanding leader, that smart student of psychology, the best manager in baseball today, Joe McCarthy? Sure, I'm lucky.
>
> When the New York Giants, a team you would give your right arm to beat, and vice versa, sends you a gift — that's some-

thing. When everybody down to the groundskeepers and those boys in white coats remember you with trophies—that's something. When you have a wonderful mother-in-law who takes sides with you in squabbles with her own daughter—that's something.

When you have a father and a mother who work all their lives so you can have an education and build your body—it's a blessing. When you have a wife who has been a tower of strength and shown more courage than you dreamed existed—that's the finest I know.

So I close in saying that I may have had a tough break, but I have an awful lot to live for. Thank you.

The band played a German folk song, "Du, Du Liegst Mir im Herzen" ("You Are Always in My Heart"), and Ruth threw his arms around his former slugging partner; Gehrig's teammates, the press, the fans, and his family wept and cheered.

Since few knew how dire Gehrig's prognosis was (there were even plenty of empty seats that day), the event felt more like a valedictory celebration than a living memorial—the front page of the *New York Times* called it "as colorful and dramatic a pageant as ever was enacted on a baseball field."

But even without the fans' knowing that Gehrig would be dead in less than two years, his speech had a powerful, indelible impact on all who witnessed it.

"I saw strong men weep this afternoon, expressionless umpires swallow hard and emotion pump the hearts and glaze the eyes of 60,000 baseball fans in Yankee Stadium," Shirley Povich wrote in the *Washington Post.* "Yes, and hard-boiled news photographers clicked their shutters with fingers that trembled a bit."

And in the *Herald-Tribune,* Richards Vidmer noted that this reaction was not merely sentimentality or pity but a deep understanding that Gehrig was more than a mere jock, that he "stood for something finer than merely a great baseball player—that he stood for everything that makes sports important in the American scene."

When Gehrig died, subsequent viewings of the film clip of his speech and the somewhat altered climax of the popular biopic *Pride of the Yankees* added a layer of heartbreaking poignancy.

By avoiding self-pity and focusing on our better nature, Gehrig transcended sports, providing an eternal reminder of what really matters. For that, Gehrig—a stouthearted, hardworking, and honest man, a caring son and loving husband who faced the worst life had to offer with determination and optimism—truly was a hero.

# 4. The Fight: Ali-Frazier I, March 8, 1971, Madison Square Garden

It was simply "the Fight," but there was nothing simple about it. The heavyweight championship fight between Muhammad Ali and Joe Frazier at Madison Square Garden on March 8, 1971, had enough twists and turns—personal and political, in the ring and on the streets—to justify the endless articles, books, and documentaries that have explored its lingering echoes.

**Joe Frazier puts the finishing touch on "the Fight" when he floors Muhammad Ali in Round 15.**

Strip away the backdrop—the specter of the Vietnam War, the dazzling display of celebrities and outrageous fashion statements at ringside—and Ali-Frazier I is still, hands down, the greatest fight in New York City's history. For a display of sustained suspense, brilliant athleticism, and sheer human spirit, it at least equals any other event in any other sport on this list.

The Fight also symbolized the end of New York as boxing mecca. Although Ali would subsequently stage notable bouts here with Frazier, Ken Norton, and Ernie Shavers, the biggest fights moved to more exotic locales, and then the sport itself began a seemingly irreversible decline, brought on by shoddy and seamy management and the dwindling interest in most basic sports. (Track and horse racing also lost favor to more complex games like football and basketball.)

A case can thus be made for ranking this fight above Joe Louis's slam-bang, rapid-fire annihilation of Max Schmeling in significance. But the Ali-Frazier story line is so battered by mythology and misperception that its legacy may always be unsatisfyingly ambiguous. The Louis-Schmeling fight wasn't perfectly tidy as a political drama either: Schmeling wasn't personally anti-Semitic and did help individual Jews, while Louis was motivated more by personal drive than politics. But their fight was far cleaner than Ali-Frazier I (Schmeling did knowingly represent Hitler; Louis laid a foundation for Jackie Robinson and the civil rights movement) and thus had a nobility that transcended what transpired in the ring.

Ali-Frazier, by contrast, revolved around the outsized personality of Ali, a symbol of antiwar activism and black pride whose political views appear to have been skillfully manipulated by the Nation of Islam, a hateful and hypocritical cult of personality. Additionally, his portrayal of Frazier as the establishment bad guy and an Uncle Tom was cruel and inaccurate.

Still, those comparisons shouldn't diminish this electrifying event, which meant so much to so many millions of people and which lived up to and even surpassed the mind-boggling hype, producing 15 blood-tingling rounds the world will never forget.

The path to the Fight began in 1967 when Ali famously declared, "I got no quarrel with them Viet Cong," was convicted for refusing induction into the armed forces, and stripped of his world heavyweight title. Ali had earned the crown as Cassius Clay in his stunning upset of Sonny Liston. As Mark Kram argues in his book *Ghosts of Manila,* Ali, who'd converted to the Nation of Islam, was politically naive and allowed himself to be played by the group's leaders, the morally corrupt Elijah Muhammad and his son Herbert. (Ali even cut off Malcolm X to stay in their good graces and spouted their fantastical beliefs about a "Mothership" that would whisk blacks away to outer space.)

Still, once cast in this role, Ali played it bravely even as everything he'd single-mindedly striven for was taken away. In 1967 criticizing the war was not fashionable, and everyone from Joe Louis to Sugar Ray Robinson to Red Smith slammed Ali. Old-school whites who'd disdained the brash loudmouth's rhyming boasts now loathed him as a traitor.

Into the void strode Frazier, who had grown up dirt-poor in a Gullah community in South Carolina and earned a living in a Philadelphia slaughterhouse before turning pro. He captured the New York heavyweight title and the world title with knockouts of Buster Mathis (1968) and Jimmy Ellis (1970), but many regarded him as the illegitimate king, with Ali biding his time in exile.

Frazier initially liked, even admired, Ali. The first time he met the champion, he seemed to his manager Yank Durham too starstruck, too soft. Behind Durham's back, Frazier befriended Ali during his years in the boxing desert.

But the manic showman perplexed the soft-spoken warrior. Once Frazier drove Ali from Philadelphia to New York, chatting about the millions they'd reap together. "He was a brother," Frazier recalled later. But in Manhattan, Ali commandeered the sidewalks, shouting, "He's got my title! I want my title! He ain't the champ, he's the chump."

Still, during Ali's years in limbo, Frazier—knowing that to be the true champion he had to beat Ali—did what he could, talking on his rival's behalf to the press, influential people like Joe Louis, and even boxing officials. He reassured Ali that his day would come and even occasionally loaned him a couple of hundred dollars.

So it's no surprise that Frazier felt wronged when Ali, facing jail and desperate to whip up pressure for a boxing license, showed up at Frazier's gym, rabid crowd in tow, and challenged him to a fight then and there. The police, unable to cope with the throngs, ordered the two to a nearby park. Durham wouldn't let Frazier go, figuring he might get beat or hurt with no payday, so Ali badmouthed Frazier in absentia before 20,000 blood-hungry voyeurs. After that, Ali picked a fight with Frazier in the street, and Frazier went to Ali's house to issue stern words of challenge. It was a beautiful friendship no more.

After 1968, with Martin Luther King and Robert Kennedy dead and the antiwar movement surging, Ali became an iconoclastic voice that blacks and the alienated counterculture could rally around. Bowing to relentless pressure in this changed environment, boxing authorities finally let Ali back in the ring. He made short work of Jerry Quarry in October 1970, then bested Oscar Bonavena six weeks later. He was still rusty but felt ready for the fight he wanted—against the man wearing his crown.

The Houston Astrodome and Madison Square

Garden each offered a $2.5 million purse for an Ali-Frazier fight, a tantalizing total. But Jerry Perenchio, a show biz manager with no boxing experience, swooped in with $5 million (courtesy of backer Jack Kent Cooke). To earn it back, he not only booked the Garden—which bumped a James Taylor gig (giving Taylor balcony seats for the fight)—but sold the closed-circuit TV rights regionally for a fortune. (He also demanded ownership of the fighters' gloves, trunks, and shoes, understanding that they'd have value in the same way as Judy Garland's Dorothy shoes or Marilyn Monroe's dress. After the fight, however, Ali's handlers would chase away the man who came to collect.)

Understanding that the eyes of the world were likely to be riveted on his return, Ali went to extremes to attract attention. Were it a fight, Ali's low blows would have disqualified him. It was entertaining enough when Ali proclaimed himself "the People's Champion" and rhymed, "This might shock and amaze ya, but I'm gonna retire Joe Frazier." But Ali quickly crossed the line, calling Frazier "too ugly" and "too dumb to be champ," a vicious insult that played on white America's prejudice but also on one between lighter- and darker-skinned blacks. He further isolated Frazier by declaring, "Ninety-eight percent of my people are for me. They identify with my struggle. If I win, they win. I lose, they lose."

There was some truth there. Though nearly contemporaries, Ali seemed to represent a different generation than Frazier. In this era, outsiders—the young, blacks, women, and antiwar activists—were demanding that people take a stand. Ali had thrived in this new society, but Frazier found it utterly alien. Frazier provoked Ali back by stubbornly calling him Cassius Clay. (Ali had tortured Floyd Patterson and Ernie Terrell in the ring for that offense.) But Ali, who may have genuinely convinced himself that Frazier was a symbol of the establishment, knew no boundaries: in *Jet* magazine he even called Frazier "the unheralded white-created champion for the primary enrichment of two white businessmen: Jack Kent Cooke and Jerry Perenchio." Those same men were paying Ali, who'd also risen to the top with the backing of wealthy whites.

The worst came when he called Frazier and any black who rooted for him an "Uncle Tom." For the straightforward Frazier, this was an outrage. "I swallowed a lot of razor blades," he said years later. He'd been forced to leave home after talking back to whites; he had migrated north and taken a low-paying dangerous job; and he was a Baptist who read the Bible, worked diligently, and took quiet pride in his achievements. In a way he personified black America. "I tommed for him," Frazier cried out, since he'd appealed to white power brokers to help Ali. "He betrayed my friendship."

The countdown to this fight was unlike any other. At a prefight photo session, photographer George Kalinsky put the men in a ring to simulate action. Ali started teasing and testing Frazier, who snarled, "Let's go at it," and soon drove a real left hook into Ali's stomach, surprising and frightening Ali.

The hordes flocking to Ali soon grew so great that he fled New York to prepare in Miami. Meanwhile, Frazier was alienated in his own community: his children were taunted at school, and he received enough death threats and bomb threats to warrant constant protection. Ali so stained Frazier's image that months after the bout the editor of *Black Sports* sneered in print, "Is Joe Frazier a White Champion in a Black Skin?" That editor, Bryant Gumbel, later admitted that he was terribly wrong but said that it seemed Frazier "was one of them and Ali was one of us. We weren't interested in the fairness of it all."

The training and pressure left Frazier fatigued and burdened with high blood pressure, but if Ali thought he could unnerve Frazier, he'd badly misread his opponent. For Frazier, Ali's "sadistic" attempt to "de-blacken" him made him ready to kill or die in the ring.

Finally March 8 arrived. The Fight.

Durham insisted on separate weigh-ins to avoid another incident; the police, afraid of the surging crowds, wouldn't let Ali leave the Garden after his weigh-in, making him a prisoner of his own creation, left to restlessly prowl the building.

There were 700 press credentials issued, and 500 more turned down. There would be more than 300 million viewers across 35 nations, but everybody who was anybody was at the Garden:

Joe Louis, Jack Dempsey, Sugar Ray Robinson, Willie Pep, James Braddock, Gene Tunney; Coretta Scott King, Jesse Jackson, Andrew Young, Ralph Abernathy, Julian Bond; Count Basie, Aretha Franklin, Bing Crosby, Miles Davis, Diana Ross, Sammy Davis Jr., reportedly Elvis Presley, and one or more ex-Beatles; Dustin Hoffman, Barbra Streisand, Bill Cosby, Hugh Hefner, Senator Ted Kennedy, Mayor John Lindsay, Joe Namath, and Walt "Clyde" Frazier, along with thousands dressed even more flamboyantly than the dandyish Knick guard.

Frank Sinatra worked as a photographer for *Life* magazine, while Burt Lancaster handled broadcasting duties.

But all that mattered were the two men in the ring:

Ali: age 29, 6'3", 215 pounds, 31–0 with 25 knockouts, dressed in red.

Frazier: age 27, 5'11", 205½ pounds, 26–0 with 23 knockouts, dressed in green.

Before the opening bell, Ali danced in circles wide enough to accidentally-on-purpose bump Frazier's shoulder. But when Frazier glared into Ali's eyes, it was Ali who was "shaken" and unable to fight the fight he'd envisioned. Frazier never deviated from his plan—let Ali protect his pretty face by leaning back, then pound, pound, pound the body and arms until Ali came down to his height, exposing his head.

Frazier rushed right at Ali, who was surprised by Frazier's immediate intensity and his quickness. But after missing jabs and struggling with his timing, Ali settled in, looking like the young Cassius Clay, flicking his fists and dancing away or standing in and throwing long hard blows. He set the tempo early, scoring points, winning rounds.

But bobbing and weaving is a tiring business, and Frazier didn't care how much he had to take. Stamina wouldn't have mattered to the Ali of the 1960s, whom Kram called an "action poet," but after years out of the ring Ali was not as spry and couldn't dance with his old speed and endurance. By the third, Ali's feet were flattening, his back searching for ropes to lean on; he was fighting on Frazier's terms. Even as he waved away Frazier's best attacks, telling everyone he couldn't be hurt, the fight was shifting.

Ali's flurries were ineffective, and Frazier pushed the pace, unceasingly driving lefts and rights to the body. In the fourth, Frazier stunned Ali with a left hook to the jaw, then avoided the clinch and punished Ali's ribs, sending pain shooting down to his hips. Frazier never let up, pinning Ali against the ropes, landing another hook to the head.

As the fight moved toward the middle rounds, Frazier was in control. When Ali taunted, "Do you know I'm God?" Frazier growled back, "God, you're in the wrong place tonight. I'm taking names and kicking ass."

In the fifth, Frazier played Ali's game, aping his wounded foe by dropping his hands to his sides and laughing derisively when Ali hit him. Frazier wobbled a bit afterwards, but Ali's ribs were hurting. "I have a new respect for Joe," he wrote later of that round. "Sometimes his timing, his rhythm, is uncanny."

Knowing Ali had predicted a sixth-round knockout, Frazier came out aggressively in that round, bashing him against the ropes, while Ali resorted to pitter-patter punches as if he were playing games. Everyone from the ref to Ali's handlers said later that he simply gave away too many rounds with tactics like this. If he thought he'd distract Frazier, he misjudged his opponent, but perhaps he wasn't playing to the crowd or trying to con the scorers—perhaps Ali merely had nothing more to offer and was just holding on, hoping his second wind would arrive.

Ali staggered through Round 7. In the eighth, the crowd's chanting Ali's name fueled Frazier, who connected with lefts and rights to the head; by round's end, it was his name being cheered. And it was his name that the scorers were penning in.

Suddenly, however, Ali emerged from his shell. In the ninth, he whipped Frazier with a series of rights to the head and then combinations, leaving Frazier bleeding from his left nostril. Although Frazier retaliated with devastating force, striking Ali with eight unanswered punches, Ali had made his statement. After the 10th, ref Arthur Mercante had Ali winning 6–4, judge Arthur Aidala had Frazier 6–4, and Bill Recht had Frazier 7–3. Either fighter could have won a decision at that point.

Round 11 changed the equation. With under a minute left, Frazier trapped Ali in a corner, then left the ground to detonate a deadly hook. It just missed the jaw, but still, Ali's knees buckled and he fell into the ropes. He stumbled away, arms at his sides, shoulders slumped, seemingly out on his feet. No one had ever seen Ali like this. But Frazier didn't immediately close for the kill and warily watched his opponent instead, not completely sure this wasn't some Ali trick. Ali survived the round, and the next one too, but Frazier clinched a decision, meaning Ali needed a knockout.

Again, Ali somehow rejuvenated himself, landing long-range shots in Round 13 and drawing blood from Frazier's mouth. But just as Frazier—who earlier had asked his handler, "What is keeping this motherfucker up?"—couldn't fathom how Ali survived, Ali was stunned by the depths of Frazier's will. Ali had more energy than Frazier, but not enough to finish him off.

The 15th round provided the Fight with the perfect exclamation point. Both men were tired but still punching hard. Then suddenly, with both fighters in the middle of the ring, Frazier leaped and launched a bomb with his left. Ali pulled back but not quickly enough, taking it on the jaw. He toppled backwards to the canvas, his feet in the air. Frazier was surprised when Ali rose up, but he had accomplished his mission. Ali had nothing left and had to simply endure more punishment until the bell.

Frazier won a unanimous decision and heard the sweetest words in his life when Ali—who didn't live up to an old promise that he'd crawl to Frazier if he lost—came over and said, "You're the champ."

In the dressing rooms afterwards, Ali's jaw grew obscenely swollen, while his supporters were distraught. But there was little celebrating by the other side. A depleted Frazier spent weeks in the hospital, which he found embarrassing, knowing Ali would eventually brandish this against him. Rumors even circulated at one point that Frazier had died.

Having given his all, Frazier lost some of his grit and drive: in 1973 George Foreman flattened him in Jamaica, and the following January Ali handily bested him in their rematch, a 12-round nontitle fight at the Garden. When Ali pulled off his momentous upset over Foreman in Zaire that year to take back the title, he was again king of the world. He gave Frazier a shot at regaining his glory, and their final go-round in Manila was another visceral display of magnificent cruelty as the two men hammered each other literally to the edge of death until Frazier's trainer, Eddie Futch, stopped him from coming out for the final round.

For years afterwards, the rivalry simmered and occasionally boiled—in 1988 Ali mocked Frazier for laughs in front of a celebrity crowd, and Frazier got drunk and tried attacking Ali, stopped only by the physical intervention of Foreman and another ex-champ, Larry Holmes. Frazier had to content himself with numerous verbal blows; after Ali lit the 1996 Olympic flame, he said, "If I had the chance, I'd have pushed him in."

It took until the 21st century before the two men made peace with one another, but they have always had to live with each other because they truly need each other: without beating Ali, Frazier would not have been a genuine champion, and without surviving Frazier, Ali's claims to being "the Greatest" would have rung hollow.

And it all started with the Fight, which has resonated for decades because of the sociopolitical mess that ensnarled both men and because their skill and will elevated the event itself above all those outside forces.

# 5. Babe Ruth christens the "House That Ruth Built" with a homer, April 18, 1923, Yankee Stadium

The hero had fallen and fallen hard. But with one dramatic swing, Babe Ruth knew he could set things right again. "I'd give a year of my life if I can hit a home run in the first game in this new park," the Sultan of Swat said just before inaugurating Yankee Stadium.

Ruth's exploits often seem lifted not from the sports pages but straight out of American folklore. The story surrounding the first game at Yankee Stadium is a pivotal chapter in the saga of this larger-than-life figure, but it also is a turning point in modern America: Ruth and the Yankees were creating a new world, birthing an affluent society's obsession with sports and celebrity, and the Stadium, like the city's skyscrapers that would soon follow, was unlike anything America had ever seen, a New York blend of arrogance and accomplishment that produced a stunning landmark. Owing a great deal to the events of that day are the narrative arcs of both baseball—the Yankees' dominance, the endless love of the long ball, the hunger for stadium building—and New York as it defined itself with major real estate deals and ostentatious architectural monuments.

Beginning in 1920, Ruth had transformed baseball and transfixed the nation with his home run bashing, becoming the living, breathing postwar symbol of the American Century, of New York's grandeur and the large-living, fast-flying Jazz Age. The Stadium was to be a physical representation of Ruth's power, New York's supremacy, and baseball's magnificent future. At least that's the way it seemed when the Yankees hatched their magnificent plans in 1921. But by the time the Stadium opened on April 18, 1923, Ruth seemed washed up, a tragic symbol of American hubris, and it was possible the Stadium would become baseball's *Titanic.* Thus, when Ruth smashed a home run in that first game, it was no ordinary four-bagger. It reversed the tide and set the Yankees and baseball history back on course.

The Yankees had been born in 1903 as the Highlanders, playing in Hilltop Park in Washington Heights, just as John McGraw began creating a Giants dynasty that defined baseball. The small-ball, nitty-gritty, back-to-the-19th-century Giants finished first or second 19 times in 23 years and led baseball in attendance 10 times (despite local blue laws barring Sunday home games).

When the Hilltop lease expired in 1913, the team, renamed the Yankees, signed a 10-year lease as the Giants' Polo Grounds tenants, playing home games when the Giants were on the road. As long as the Yankees seemed harmless, the Giants were happy to collect rent money. But in 1920 Yankees owners Jacob Ruppert and Til Huston bought Ruth from the Boston Red Sox and everything changed.

Ruth's 1920 statistics remain truly shocking: he smashed 54 home runs when no other *team* hit more than 50, scored 158 runs, drove in 137, and set a record with an .847 slugging percentage. McGraw disdained this new home run fad, but one number particularly galled the Giants manager: the Yankees' attendance more than doubled, reaching almost 1.3 million—400,000 more than the Giants.

The Giants wanted the upstarts out, and not just because of McGraw's growing jealousy over Ruth. With Sunday blue laws repealed in 1919, the Giants wanted every big Sunday gate for themselves. The Giants couldn't evict the Yankees immediately because a secret deal with Red Sox owner Harry Frazee had given Ruppert and Huston the mortgage to Fenway Park—they could move the Yankees to Boston, throwing baseball into utter chaos. But they could publicly say it was time for them to find a permanent New York home. McGraw boasted that the Yankees would never find enough open space in Manhattan, declaring, "They'll have to move to the Bronx or Long Island. The fans will forget about them and they'll be through."

The Yankees looked at various lots, including one just a mile from their old Hilltop Park, one in Long Island City, and one over the railroad tracks on Manhattan's West Side that foreshadowed more recent debates over that land. (The War Department would grab it for antiaircraft gun placements.) Finally, in early 1921, Huston and Ruppert forked over $675,000 to the Astor estate for 10 acres in the South Bronx.

The Yankees were not the first to build a modern ballpark—in the previous decade Detroit's Navin Field, Boston's Fenway Park, and Chicago's Wrigley Field had arisen. But "The Yankee Stadium," as it was originally called, was different—no other ballpark had ever been so grandiose as to call itself a stadium.

Before television and merchandising, team revenue stemmed largely from gate receipts, so the Yankees wanted space for the anticipated masses, especially as Ruth topped himself in 1921 with 59 homers and 171 RBIs, leading the Yankees to their first World Series... which they lost to the Giants. Having the biggest ballplayer in the biggest stadium in the nation's biggest city would give the Yankees a tremendous advantage in revenue that would enable them to pay for the best scouts, front-office executives, and athletes. In other words, it was not just Ruth but the combination of Ruth and the new coliseum that laid the groundwork for baseball's dominant franchise.

The original plans, calling for a triple-deck enclosed stadium with 70,000 seats, had to be slightly scaled back to ready the stadium for Opening Day, but everything else was breathlessly announced: the 15-foot copper facade, the 950,000 board feet of Pacific Coast fir shipped via the Panama Canal, the 2,200 tons of structural steel, the one million brass screws bolted into the seats, the 16,000 square feet of sod. Overseen by Huston, an engineer, the $2.5 million ballpark was completed in only 284 days. (Soon after, Huston sold his Yankees' share to Ruppert.)

"From the plain of the Harlem River it looms up like the great Pyramid of Cheops from the sands of Egypt," gushed awestruck writer F. C. Lane in *Literary Digest.*

This majestic stage was clearly built for Ruth—some folks even suggested calling it Ruth Field. In most ballparks, right field was "the sun field," but since Ruth played right, left fielders would have to wage that battle. Center and left-center were impossibly deep ("Death Valley" was 490 feet), but right field was a mere 295 feet, eminently reachable for a left-handed pull hitter. (Ruth, however, later said, "I cried when I left the Polo Grounds," because it was only 256 feet down the line and had a better visual background for hitters.)

But as the Stadium was rising, Ruth was self-destructing. He drew a six-week suspension to start the 1922 season from commissioner Kenesaw Mountain Landis for 1921's rule-breaking postseason barnstorming tour. Signed to an eye-popping new $52,000-a-year contract, Ruth spent much of his time off at the racetrack, then slumped through his first games before throwing dirt in an umpire's face during an argument; upon his ejection, he was booed by Yankee fans and charged into the stands after one particularly vociferous heckler. American League president Ban Johnson kept Ruth out only one game and fined him only $200, but he demanded that the Yankees end Ruth's new role as captain of the team. Dur-

**On Opening Day, New Yorkers flock to the Yankees' new digs to see the Stadium and the superstar Babe Ruth. Both live up to the hype.**

ing the season, Ruth earned several more suspensions for arguing with the umps and got into a fistfight with teammate Wally Pipp. The Yankees won the pennant despite Ruth managing only 406 at-bats and finishing just third in home runs with 35. But the ultimate humiliation came in the World Series when McGraw ordered his pitchers to throw Ruth nothing but off-speed pitches out of the strike zone, and the Yankee slugger pressed harder and harder, going just 2-for-17 with no homers as the Giants took the crown yet again.

The press called Ruth "an exploded phenomenon" and a "tragic figure" who had "flashed like a comet." The *Sporting News* declared, "The baseball public is on to his real worth as a batsman and in future, let us hope, he will attract just ordinary attention." Knowing Ruth needed motivation, his agent, Christy Walsh, organized an off-season banquet where New York's press and powerbrokers called on the Babe to reform. State Senator Jimmy Walker, in a brilliant melodramatic touch, struck Ruth's soft spot, saying that Ruth had "let down the kids of America . . . on the vacant lot where the kids play baseball, and in the hospitals too, where crippled children . . . look up to you, worship you. . . . You carouse and abuse your great body, and it is exactly as though Santa Claus himself suddenly were to take off his beard to reveal the features of a villain. The kids have seen their idol shattered and their dream broken."

A repentant Ruth began sobbing, almost uncontrollably. As Walker comforted him, Ruth apologized and promised to both behave and play better in the future. Indeed, he largely abstained from partying that winter and arrived at spring training in formidable shape. Yet things quickly derailed when a 19-year-old girl sued Ruth for $50,000 in a paternity suit. She later admitted it was a hoax, but Ruth seemed distracted, striking out often during exhibition games, even against minor league pitchers.

As the team headed into the season, it seemed quite possible that Ruth would wash out completely, the club would collapse, fans would stop coming, and Yankee Stadium would be sneeringly called "Ruppert's Folly." As the *New York Times* wrote, "The Babe was on trial, and he knew it."

Opening Day finally arrived, a windy day that topped out at 49 degrees. Setting a pattern to be followed by certain other Yankee owners, Ruppert and Huston had shown little interest in promoting the health of the surrounding neighborhood, so the roads remained unpaved, and the crowds pushing forward against the phalanx of policemen nearly choked on all the dust kicked up. Newspapers estimated that 25,000 fans were turned away. Landis was swept up in a wave of people, and the police had to pull him inside.

Yankee general manager Ed Barrow announced the attendance at 74,217, shattering the sport's old record (47,000 at a 1916 World Series game involving the Boston Red Sox, whose star pitcher, it must be noted, was Babe Ruth). The figure was an active bit of mythmaking — soon after it was reported that the Stadium held only 62,000 seats. The real attendance for the standing-room-only crowd remains uncertain, but in keeping with everything about the slugger and his city, it was undeniably gargantuan. Just call it Ruthian.

In addition to Landis, an impressive array of generals and other military men were on hand, as well as Governor Al Smith, who threw out the first ball. The two managers, New York's Miller Huggins and Boston's Frank Chance, pulled a rope to raise the flag deep in center field. The Yankees' American League pennant was run up the flagpole, and Ruth was presented with an oversized bat in a glass case. John Philip Sousa led the Seventh Regiment Band in a parade and "The Star-Spangled Banner." Finally, at 3:35, home plate umpire Tommy Connolly shouted, "Play ball."

Fittingly, the foe that day was Boston, from whom the Yankees had purchased Ruth. Bob Shawkey's first pitch to leadoff hitter Chick Fewster (an ex-Yankee) was a ball, but he quickly retired the side. Howard Ehmke, who'd win 20 games that year, retired Ruth easily in the Yankee first. But in the bottom of the third the Yankees pushed a run across and had two men on when Ruth again strode to the plate.

Ehmke worked the count to 2–2. Following McGraw's World Series strategy from the previous year, he threw yet another off-speed pitch. This time, however, there would be joy in Mudville. Ruth anticipated it and crushed a line drive eight rows into the bleachers.

"As the crash sounded, and the white flash followed, fans arose en masse . . . in the greatest vocal cataclysm baseball has ever known," Grantland Rice effused in the *New York Tribune*. As the grinning Ruth reached home he lifted his cap and waved to the crowds. Shawkey scattered three hits, and Ruth botched a fly ball, but his home run would be the difference in the Yankees' 4–1 triumph — and would also, for all intents and purposes, seal the outcome of the season and even, arguably, the century.

The next day, Fred Lieb of the *Evening Telegram* dubbed the ballpark "the House That Ruth Built." Ruth kept rolling, belting 41 homers en route to another pennant. In the 1923 Fall Classic, the Yankees finally had their own home, their own turf, their own crowd, and it made a difference. Ruth batted .368 with three homers, helping to defeat the hated Giants. It was the first Series carried nationwide on radio in its entirety; Ruth's appeal had hastened the market for this new technology.

And 1923 was only the beginning. Swiping the mantle from the Giants, Ruth remade the Yankees into baseball's preeminent franchise, leading them to four more pennants and three more World Series titles while establishing Yankee Stadium as sport's most hallowed ground.

Although Ruth's home run that spring day was, statistically, just one of his 714 regular-season roundtrippers, it has always retained a magical aura. In 1998 the home run ball was auctioned off for a then-record $126,500, and in 2004 the bat Ruth used was auctioned off for $1.27 million, the second-highest-priced baseball item ever. (Fittingly, some of the proceeds were pledged to an orphanage.) And in 2005 a new children's book called *Babe Ruth Saves Baseball* builds to that home run as the climactic moment.

Ruth, of course, knew it from the beginning. In 1948, dying rapidly from throat cancer, Ruth came to Yankee Stadium one final time, putting on his uniform to celebrate the 25th anniversary of the ballpark. Barely able to speak, he slowly approached the microphone and told the fans, "Ladies and gentlemen, I just want to say one thing. I am proud I hit the first home run here against Boston in 1923."

# 6. The Giants win the pennant, October 3, 1951, Polo Grounds

October 3, 1951.

"The Giants win the pennant . . ."

No matter when you were born or whether you follow baseball, Bobby Thomson's playoff-ending home run for the New York Giants over the Brooklyn Dodgers has probably insinuated itself into your life. Now part of our collective unconscious, this seminal moment in the national pastime came in America's greatest city during the nation's glorious postwar boom.

For the first time that newfangled box in the living room united the nation for a magical, spontaneous moment. No one outside Wrigley Field had seen Babe Ruth's called homer, few people owned sets when Joe DiMaggio hit in 56 straight games and Ted Williams reached .400 on the last day of 1941, and only local viewers could see the Yankees overcome the Red Sox and the Dodgers squeak by the Phillies on the final day of 1949. This was different. President Harry Truman had made the first coast-to-coast telecast of any kind in September, but this game was the first sports event broadcast nationwide. Although television was still in its infancy, so many people in so many states saw Thomson's home run, and so many had a more intimate, visceral stake in the creation of this generational memory. This was the moment when sports and television became intertwined, when popular culture strengthened its hold on the American psyche.

"The Giants win the pennant . . ."

Maybe you read Yale historian J.R.H. Hexter's 1968 scholarly essay "The Rhetoric of History," which elevated the Giants' stretch run and triumph over Brooklyn to a lofty analytical plane.

Maybe you tuned in to Curt Gowdy's 1975 *The Way It Was* episode devoted to Bobby Thomson's heroics, or one of the numerous other nostalgic rehashings and celebrations since.

Maybe you saw the clip and heard the shouting on a 1980 episode of *M*A*S*H* when Dodger rooter Charles Winchester took a knife to the newsreel replaying the famous scene.

"The Giants win the pennant . . ."

Maybe you purchased Don DeLillo's opus *Underworld* in 1997 just to read his elegiac prologue, "Pafko at the Wall," or mailed a letter using the 1999 postage stamp commemorating the homer.

Maybe you followed the front-page news in 2001 and subsequent media brouhaha about the Giants' sign-stealing of a half-century earlier, or maybe you preferred the original story line, clean and neat, and bought your child or grandchild the 2005 picture book called *The Shot Heard Round the World.*

Or maybe your tie remains clear and direct. You, your father, or your grandfather was from New York, was a Giant fan or a Dodger fan, and the moment remains a potent stew of folklore, American history, and personal passion: where were you when Franklin Roosevelt died, when John Kennedy was killed, when Neil Armstrong took one giant step . . . when Bobby Thomson did the impossible?

"The Giants win the pennant . . ."

October 3, 1951. The Polo Grounds. The ninth inning. Find your thesaurus, for this was the most blood-tingling, hair-raising, mind-boggling, breathtaking, heart-stopping moment in New York team sports history. New York's major league teams played about 40,000 games in the 20th century, and the Knicks, Rangers, Jets, football Giants, and college teams like CCNY, Fordham, and St. John's played thousands more. This game, this inning stands above them all.

The facts are simple yet nearly impossible to believe. When Red Smith wrote, "The art of fiction is dead. Reality has strangled invention. Only the utterly impossible, the inexpressibly fantastic, can ever be plausible again," he aptly summed up not just the ninth-inning action but also the seasonlong narrative.

On May 25, the Giants were foundering in fifth place at 17–19 when they called up center-field phenom Willie Mays from Triple A. Mays went 1-for-25 before finding his stroke, but his impact was immediate—his infectious charm loosened up the club while his fielding firmed up a mediocre defense. The team went on an 18–8 run to keep pace with Brooklyn, which was burying the rest of the league, and the Giants moved from fifth to second place in under a month. Mays's presence also allowed manager Leo Durocher to move Thomson from center to third and lock Monte Irvin in left; both had been struggling, but the two men carried the offense after that, with Irvin finishing at .312 with 24 homers and 121 RBIs and Thomson ending at .293 with 32 homers and 101 RBIs.

Still, anything the Giants did, the Dodgers did better. They swept the Giants in Manhattan in July and in Brooklyn in early August. After snatching the August 8 double-header, Brooklyn manager and former Durocher protégé Charley Dressen boldly decreed, "The Giants is dead." The next day the Dodgers won again and celebrated as if they'd reached a great mountaintop. Jackie Robinson yelled, "Eat your heart out, Leo," and he, Pee Wee Reese, Carl Furillo, and others pounded bats on the wall separating the two teams' clubhouses, loudly singing, "Roll out the barrels, we got the Giants on the run."

The Giants and Dodgers had rarely been good the same year, yet a palpably bitter rivalry coursed through New York's NL fans. The mutual loathing dated to 1889, when the Giants beat Brooklyn (then the Bridegrooms of the American Association) in the "World's Series" despite Brooklyn's manipulation of the rules and umpires, and it remained so vivid that when Durocher, the longtime Brooklyn skipper, jumped to the Giants in 1948, it was considered heresy by fans of both teams. Against that history, the Dodgers' postgame revelry looms as 1951's turning point. The Giants were not humiliated but infuriated and thus, in keeping with Durocher's fiery persona, inspired. After one loss to Philadelphia dropped them 13½ games back, the Giants tore off 16 straight wins, including a three-game sweep of Brooklyn. The Giants finished 37–7.

(Although the Giants were stealing signs at home, the stats make it clear that this had little impact. They began pilfering pitch calls July 19 but didn't get hot until three weeks later; then they went 20–3 at home but were also 17–4 on the road, where they had no illegal help. Stan Jacoby noted in the *New York Times* after the controversy broke in 2001 that the Giants' run-scoring at home declined during their hot streak while improving on the road—thinking they knew the pitch may have hindered their offense—and it was stellar pitching that made the difference . . . along with the Dodgers' choke job.)

Brooklyn discovered that after the peak what's left is the descent—they had nothing but time for their long slide down. As the standings tightened, so did the Dodgers, going 26–22 after August 11. Brooklyn catcher Roy Campanella was banged up in the August 9 game; the 1951 MVP was injured again and again in September, and his diminished capabilities hurt badly. Meanwhile, everyone else stopped hitting. Dressen deserves much of the blame for the collapse: he acted panicky, not confident, particularly with his pitchers. When he started Ralph Branca on two days' rest, the pitcher's triceps acted up, and he struggled the rest of the way. Dressen's ego compounded the problem: a September dispute with red-hot rookie Clem Labine would turn into a season-sabotaging grudge.

Furious when Labine ignored his instructions to pitch from the full wind-up with the bases loaded (to gain more velocity), Dressen utterly ignored the pitcher the rest of the season. As the season ended, Dressen burned up his exhausted and diminished starting rotation—and his bullpen too—while Labine languished in the doghouse. Labine might have won one game or at least eaten enough innings to let Don Newcombe and Preacher Roe rest. "His vindictiveness cost him the pennant," Labine said later of Dressen.

The Giants and Dodgers started the season's final day tied. The Giants beat Boston; the Dodgers, down 6–1 in Philadelphia, forced extra innings, and Robinson made a game-saving catch and blasted a game-winning home run. The season was over, but the teams were still tied. It was time for a best-of-three playoff, a format invented in 1946 for Brooklyn and St. Louis.

At Ebbets Field, the first game, won by the Giants 3–1, turned on one pitch: a pitch thrown by Ralph Branca and belted into the stands by Bobby Thomson for his 31st homer of the season. It was as if the fates were taking a basic writing seminar and leaning heavily on the foreshadowing. Branca had already yielded eight homers to the Giants, including two by Thomson and four by Irvin, who slammed another for New York's third run.

The Giants went to the Polo Grounds with two chances to win one game.

Out of options, Dressen finally relented and gave the ball to Labine, who pitched a six-hitter in a 10–0 shutout. In the third with the bases loaded, Labine, pitching from a full wind-up, struck out Thomson on a 3–2 curve that was low and outside. Afterwards Dressen boasted that he was too smart to let the Giants' leading slugger beat him. "One run is better than four. That guy wasn't going to get the chance to hit one in the seats."

October 3, 1951.

The deciding game: Sal Maglie, who had beaten the Dodgers five times, against Newcombe, who had rescued Brooklyn in the season's final weekend. It was a last-minute weekday game on a cold, gray day—the lights would be needed by the third inning—and with televisions showing it everywhere in New York, 22,000 seats went empty. Filling other seats were General Douglas MacArthur, Toots Shor, Jackie Gleason, Frank Sinatra, J. Edgar Hoover, and many of the AL champion Yankees.

Maglie, so sharp over his two previous starts, promptly walked Reese and Duke Snider. Robinson's hard single produced one run. But with Campanella and his big bat sidelined, Maglie escaped.

The Giants had been coming back all season, and in the second Whitey Lockman singled and Thomson extended his hitting streak to 15 games, stinging the ball down the left-field line for a double. Well, Thomson thought it was a double, but Lockman had stopped at second, and Thomson was caught scrambling back to first. Rally over.

Maglie retired 13 of 14, but Newcombe was equally majestic, his scoreless inning streak reaching past 20. In the seventh, Newcombe—in his 31st pressure-filled inning in eight days—faltered. Irvin doubled. When Lockman bunted, Brooklyn's backup catcher, Rube Walker, threw unsuccessfully to third. (Would the sidelined Campanella have made that choice? Would he have succeeded?) Lockman screamed for time. Durocher's men played sneaky baseball, so they recognized it elsewhere: Lockman had spotted Billy Cox pulling the hidden-ball trick on Irvin.

Thomson up. Who else? A sacrifice fly to center tied the game, 1–1.

Not for long. In the eighth, Reese and Snider singled. Maglie, losing it fast, flung a wild pitch, scoring Reese. Robinson was walked intentionally, but Andy Pafko hit a ball that the third baseman—Thomson—couldn't handle. 3–1. With two outs, Cox hit another ball past Thomson: 4–1. Neither were errors, but a lifelong third baseman like Cox would have had one or both. Thomson had gone from goat to savior to goat again. The Dodgers were six outs from rendering the Giants' monumental effort meaningless.

On the bench, Newk, who knew his own limits, told Reese, Robinson, and Dressen he was done. Reese encouraged him to keep going, while Robinson said, according to various reports, "God-

**Bobby Thomson's ninth-inning homer off Ralph Branca soars over Andy Pafko and into American folklore.**

dammit, get in there and pitch," or, "You keep pitching out there until your fucking arm falls off." Newcombe zipped through a couple of pinch-hitters, and the eighth was gone. Having a competitive leader like Robinson had saved the Dodgers on the season's final weekend. But combined with Dressen's sudden paralysis, it worked against them in the ninth, when the Dodgers should have brought in a reliever right away: the Giants had their best hitters coming up, and it's always better to let relievers start an inning rather than inherit runners, especially when the reliever is a starter on emergency duty, which was what Brooklyn had in its bullpen.

Durocher, heading to coach third base, shouted final optimistic words to his team.

Alvin Dark hit a two-strike pitch off the end of his bat that Gil Hodges couldn't snare. Inexplicably, Dressen had Hodges hold Dark on first.

Right fielder Don Mueller, a master of bat control, sent the ball through the expanded hole. First and third.

Dressen went to the mound but made no change. After the breather, Newcombe got Irvin to foul out.

In the press box, Brooklyn announced, "The Dodgers will hold a victory party tonight at the Hotel Bossert, beginning at 6:00 P.M., and all members of the working press are invited."

With the right-field wall 254 feet away, the lefty

Lockman was thinking homer. Newcombe was too, and pitched him away. Lockman went with the pitch, knocking it to left for a double: 4–2. Then everything stopped. Mueller was on the ground at third, in agony—he'd torn tendons in his ankle. As he was carried off on a stretcher and Clint Hartung came in to replace him, Dressen got a free trip to the mound.

Always a know-it-all—he'd tell his team, "Just stay close, I'll think of something"—Dressen had been reduced to an indecisive wreck. He'd constantly phoned his bullpen for updates, yet hadn't made a move. He asked his pitcher and infielders what they thought. Reese, the captain, told him to make a change.

In the last phone call, coach Clyde Sukeforth had told Dressen that Branca had finally loosened up and was throwing hard while Carl Erskine had just bounced a curveball. Never mind that Thomson was a fastball hitter and owned Branca. Never mind that Erskine wanted his curve diving downward. Never mind that Labine, a curveball-sinkerball specialist who had mastered the Giants, sat nearby, ignored yet again.

Dressen signaled for Branca, who charged in confidently. Normally the manager would discuss the situation, but this time he nervously flipped Branca the ball from five feet away, said, "Get 'em out," and scurried to the dugout. One thing Dressen didn't do was tell Branca to walk or pitch around Thomson, which would have meant putting the winning run on base. Yet behind Thomson were the slumping rookie Willie Mays and the bottom of the order.

It was the Glasgow-born, Staten Island–raised Thomson against Branca, the youngest of 17 kids from Mount Vernon. Everyone and everything else receded, creating the head-to-head confrontation that makes baseball unique among team sports.

Branca's first pitch was a nice, fat fastball. Thomson took it for a strike and immediately chided himself for letting it pass. He wouldn't let another go by. Thomson's hits had all been to left or center, so Branca hoped to imitate Labine and get him on a curve away. First, he'd set Thomson up with a fastball up and in. (With hindsight, Branca admitted that if he wanted to get Thomson on a curve, he should have thrown the curve.)

The pitch zoomed toward the plate, high and tight but not up enough or in enough. Thomson whipped the bat around. He rotated his hips. The wood connected with the ball. A hard, spinning line drive. The fence was only 315 feet away in left, but 16 feet high. Pafko was at the wall. The ball might not have gone out at Ebbets Field, just as Thomson's Game 1 homer in Brooklyn might not have gone out at the Polo Grounds. But that's baseball, that's life. This time, in this place, the ball made it. Pandemonium erupted as Thomson floated around the bases and the Giants and their fans poured onto the field.

"Thomson settled a five-month argument in just seconds," Grantland Rice noted.

Branca trudged off the field and sagged, inconsolable on the clubhouse steps, moaning, "Let me alone, let me alone. Why me?" He was the last man to leave that night. In Brooklyn, number 13—Branca's unlucky uniform number—hung in effigy. (Brooklyn switched Branca to number 12 in 1952; he promptly suffered a freak injury from which he never fully recovered.) In the fallout, Dressen deftly pinned the blame on Sukeforth, who was fired. It may not have mattered, Labine later mused: "He could have brought Erskine in, he could have brought me in, the home run still would have been hit because that's the way it was supposed to be in history."

Thomson appeared on Perry Como's television show, took a taxi to the Battery, paid a nickel for the Staten Island ferry, hopped another cab to the firehouse where his brother worked, then went to dinner with his family.

The World Series, which the Yankees won (for the third straight year), seemed almost anticlimactic. "We didn't feel that badly let down," Irvin said later. "We were still thinking about the playoff against the Dodgers. That was our year, right there, when Bobby hit that ball."

When the pain subsided, even Branca ultimately realized that he, like Thomson, had achieved an immortality that most good-but-not-great ballplayers never attain (including a lucrative cottage industry signing autographs with his ex-nemesis). But it wasn't just television that gave this historic home run extra cachet—it was also the old-fashioned radio. On television, announcer Ernie Harwell simply said, "It's gone," and let the images speak, but on radio Russ Hodges had to paint a word picture for his listeners. He let his own deliriously giddy excitement convey the emotions of the moment.

But radio stations did not tape broadcasts in 1951, and this classic call at Coogan's Bluff would have rapidly faded—draining the moment of much of its staying power—if not for "the Miracle of Larry Goldberg" (and his mother Sylvia).

Goldberg, a Giants fan living in Brooklyn, showed his mother how to use his reel-to-reel tape recorder. Then he left for work in Manhattan, asking Sylvia to tape the ninth inning on WMCA 570-AM, the Giants' station. Afterwards, realizing what he had, Goldberg sent the tape to Hodges. The Giants' sponsor, Chesterfield, gave him $100 and box seats for 1952, then put Hodges's call out on a promotional record that still sends chills through its listeners more than a half-century later.

"The moment is still vivid today because of that call," says ESPN play-by-play man Jon Miller. Although he says Vin Scully criticized Hodges for being too caught up in the moment, he thinks that "it lasts because it encapsulated the whole panorama of that entire story in one call."

*Branca throws.*
*There's a long drive.*
*It's gonna be.*
*I believe.*
*The Giants win the pennant!*
*The Giants win the pennant!*
*The Giants win the pennant!*
*The Giants win the pennant!*
*Bobby Thomson hits it into the lower deck of the left-field stands.*
*The Giants win the pennant!*
*And they're going crazy.*
*They're going crazy.*
*Wheyyyywhoooooo!!!!*

# 7. "Next year" finally arrives for Brooklyn, October 4, 1955, Yankee Stadium

It was a routine roller to Pee Wee Reese, the easiest and most wonderful task in the world. Time stood still in the bottom of the ninth as an entire borough prepared to explode with delirious joy.

Reese, the 37-year-old shortstop and captain of the Brooklyn Dodgers in 1955, had been a rookie in 1941. That year the Dodgers and their fans celebrated reaching their first World Series in over two decades, even excusing Mickey Owen's dropped third-strike fiasco in the ninth inning of the crucial fourth game with the hopeful cry of "Wait till next year."

"Next year" was 1942: the team won 104 games but blew a nine-and-a-half-game lead over St. Louis in under a month.

"Next year" was 1946: closer still, losing to St. Louis in baseball's first tiebreaker playoff.

"Next year" was 1947: Jackie Robinson inspired a magical season, but the Yankees stopped them in the World Series' seventh game.

"Next year" was 1949: the Yankees . . . again.

"Next year" was 1950: the Phillies broke their hearts on the season's final day.

"Next year" was 1951: in case you hadn't heard, the Giants won the pennant.

"Next year" was 1952: *Herald-Tribune* reporter Roger Kahn wrote, "Every year is Next Year for the Yankees."

"Next year" was 1953: those Damn Yankees.

"Next year" was 1954: watching the Giants—the only rivals Brooklyn hated more than the Yankees—win it all.

Now it was Game 7 of the 1955 World Series, and there couldn't have been more on the line. There are perennial losers, like the Chicago Cubs or the pre-2004 Boston Red Sox, who probably think they understand that level of suffering, but they're wrong. No other team, especially one with the same core of players, has ever come so darn close so many times in one generation—ten times in fourteen years, eight in the last nine—and this bittersweet success was especially excruciating because most of the pain was inflicted by the teams of New York, a distressing reminder of Brooklyn's second-tier status since losing its independence at the turn of the century.

So in the ninth inning, having navigated through perilous territory clinging to a 2–0 lead, Pee Wee Reese gathered up the grounder and threw across the diamond to Gil Hodges. And finally it was done. On October 4, 1955, "next year" finally arrived.

In the beginning, it hadn't seemed like "next year." The start of 1955 saw the folding of the *Brooklyn Eagle,* the only daily paper devoted to a borough, and the youthful Milwaukee Braves, not the aging Dodgers, were the National League favorite. In spring training, sophomore Brooklyn manager Walter Alston clashed heatedly with veterans Jackie Robinson, Roy Campanella, and Don Newcombe, among others. Then opening day was postponed for bad weather, and the game, played on an unscheduled day, drew only 5,000 fans.

But when the baseball began, distractions fell away. The Dodgers won their first 10 games and 22 of 24. They clinched the pennant on September 8, the earliest date in league history. Still, waiting in the World Series were the New York Yankees. After the Dodgers dropped the first two games, it seemed time to dejectedly look ahead, once more, to "next year"—no team had ever won the Series after losing the first two games.

Back at Ebbets Field for Game 3, a desperate Alston turned to 23-year-old Johnny Podres. He'd finished below .500 after an injury-plagued second half and had nearly been left off the World Series roster, but Podres responded with an 8–3 win. Duke Snider hit three homers in games 4 and 5 as the Dodgers pounded Yankee pitching for 13 runs. But in Yankee Stadium for Game 6, another inexperienced (and injured) lefty, Karl Spooner, was raked for five first-inning runs; after Whitey Ford finished off an easy 5–1 win, the momentum had swung back to the Bronx Bombers.

For Game 7, Alston turned again to Podres. With Robinson suffering an Achilles tendon injury, Alston put Don Hoak at third and added Don Zimmer at second base, moving Junior Gilliam to left and Sandy Amoros to the bench. Yankee manager Casey Stengel returned to Tommy Byrne, who had stopped the Dodgers at the Stadium in Game 2.

Podres scattered eight hits, but Byrne, along with relievers Bob Grim and Bob Turley, allowed only five. It was the first time in the last 32 World Series games that a team held its opponent to two runs but lost. It was a game in which every out, every base, loomed large, especially considering the clubs' history.

The Yanks had the first opportunity, but this year was different: the little things broke for Brooklyn. With two out and two on in the third, Gil McDougald's slow roller seemed a sure infield hit, but as Phil Rizzuto slid into third, the batted ball hit him and he was automatically out, quashing the rally.

"That play gave me a sense of 'Hey, this may be a different finish,'" Dodger Carl Erskine said later. "Nothing like that ever happened to the Yankees before."

In the fourth, by contrast, Campanella doubled with one out, and when Carl Furillo grounded to short, Campanella read how slowly the ball was hit and surprised everyone by advancing to third, even though the play was in front of him. Stengel then inexplicably let Byrne pitch to slugger Gil Hodges instead of walking him for the weak-hitting Hoak. With two outs and two strikes, Hodges fisted an inside curve to left for a single, bringing home Campanella . . . who would not have scored from second.

Brooklyn nearly reverted to its heartbreaking self with a defensive gaffe in the Yankee fourth — Snider and Gilliam let Yogi Berra's pop fall between them for a fluke leadoff double — but Podres was unfazed by history and bad luck and retired three straight hitters. In the sixth, the Yankees again made a fundamental mistake. After Reese singled, Snider surprised everyone with a bunt. Byrne grabbed the ball and flipped toward first baseman Moose Skowron. But Skowron was off the bag; he swiped his glove at Snider, who knocked the ball loose. After a sacrifice and an intentional walk, Grim came on, but Hodges's fly to center was deep enough to score Reese for a 2–0 edge.

To replace Zimmer — who was pinch-hit for in that rally — and strengthen the defense, Alston moved Gilliam back to his natural spot at second, returning Amoros to left. After Billy Martin walked and McDougald bunted for a hit, that defensive maneuver saved the Series.

With the lefty pull hitter Berra up, the Dodger defense shifted toward right. Amoros set up behind Reese. Podres drove Berra off the plate on the first pitch, then pitched him away on the second. But it wasn't away enough from Berra, a notorious bad-ball hitter, who stung a slicing liner toward the left-field corner.

As Amoros ran and ran and ran there was enough time to imagine headlines proclaiming Berra the hero and the Yankees the champions. Then Amoros ran out of room. In the corner he stopped short, stuck out his glove, and caught the ball. Using his left hand to brace himself on the fence, he whirled and made a perfect throw to Reese, who relayed to Hodges at first. McDougald, unable to imagine the ball being caught, was past second and easily doubled off.

It's impossible to make an objective comparison of Amoros's catch with other classic World Series catches — but even if Al Gionfriddo made a more difficult play in 1947, its impact was muted when the Dodgers lost the Series, and even if Willie Mays's 1954 catch was more spectacular, it was in Game 1, not Game 7, and his throw, however astonishing, did not yield a double play. Amoros's heroics matter more, not because he made a better catch but because this was Brooklyn at the precipice, and Brooklyn had never before made the leap into the promised land. Had Amoros not gotten there in time, the Dodgers might well have gone once more into the abyss. Had Gilliam, a righty, still been in left, he'd have had to reach across his body to backhand the ball, he probably would not have made the catch — and "next year" might never have arrived.

Amoros's play crushed the Yankees' hopes but did not kill them — there was still a runner in scoring position. But Podres got Hank Bauer to escape; in the seventh, with two out and one on, he retired Mickey Mantle (limited by injury to pinch-hitting duty) with a runner on; in the eighth, Podres again faced Berra with two on, but the Yankee catcher popped harmlessly to right, and Bauer then fanned.

In the ninth, Podres easily retired Skowron and Bob Cerv. It was up to Elston Howard. After relying heavily on his changeup in Game 3, Podres had thrown more fastballs in Game 7, especially as the late-afternoon shadows grew longer. Against Howard, he fired four straight heaters, running the count to 2–2. Once more he tried blowing the ball by Howard, but the Yankee fouled it off. Campanella called for yet another fastball, but Podres, afraid Howard had timed it, shook off his battery mate for the first time all day. He returned to his changeup, and Howard, off balance, hit that final grounder toward Reese.

Reese, the only player ever to have lost five World Series to the same opponent, scooped the ball and fired. In his excitement, he threw off tar-

**In the seventh inning of Game 7, Sandy Amoros's running catch in the corner helps Brooklyn finally fulfill its World Series dreams.**

get, low and wide. But this was not another Mickey Owen moment. Hodges, the *New York Times* reported, "would have stretched halfway across the Bronx for that one." He reined in the throw, Podres leaped into the air, and up in the broadcast booth Vin Scully announced, "Ladies and gentlemen, the Brooklyn Dodgers are the champions of the world."

Then Scully was silent. Everyone else, however, let loose—the players, the fans, the entire citizenry of Brooklyn. Over the next quarter-hour, the telephone company reported the highest call volume since VJ-Day; the system was so overloaded that most callers couldn't get a dial tone.

The day was an endless celebration of honking horns, impromptu block parties, and a borough-wide swelling of exhilaration and relief. Red Smith wrote that the fans stayed in Ebbets Field long afterwards, "reluctant to leave the scene where the deed was done." On Court Street, someone put a jukebox outside for dancing in the street along with a keg of free beer; on Smith Street, a candy-store owner handed out free cigars; on Utica Avenue, a deli set up a hot dog stand outside and gave the franks away.

Erskine later eloquently recalled that heady mixture of emotions bubbling to the surface when the team reached the clubhouse. "To go to their park and beat them, after all those frustrating years, just added a dimension to it," he said. "There was a quietness when we first walked in that clubhouse, almost a spiritual feeling, gratitude for this accomplishment. Then someone popped a bottle of champagne, and the lid blew off."

That night, 2,000 fans partied in the street outside the Bossert Hotel while the Dodgers and their families whooped it up inside.

It was a moment to be savored. Those who experienced it can recall the emotions vividly, because as tremendous as this triumph seemed, it grew more so in retrospect. If not for 1955, there might never have been a "this year," a shining moment to recall. The Boys of Summer were entering the autumn of their careers, especially Robinson and Reese, the spark and soul of the team. And though few realized it at the time, the team itself was not long for Brooklyn.

The year 1956 would be Robinson's final season and Reese's last as an everyday player; in the Series the team would succumb again to the Yankees. In 1957 the Braves finally surpassed the Dodgers. And just as the Yankees were winning yet another Series, the final blow came when the Dodgers confirmed what everyone had been dreading: the team was leaving its home for sunny southern California. There would be no "next year."

Brooklynites were left with no one to root for but plenty of memories to cherish. And no game spoke louder about their underdog outlook and their perpetual "wait till next year" optimism than Game 7 of the 1955 World Series, when Gil Hodges, Johnny Podres, and Sandy Amoros grabbed the future and held on, finally corralling it back into the present.

# 8. Willis Reed hobbles to the rescue, May 8, 1970, Madison Square Garden

The Captain to the Rescue. The heroic saga of Willis Reed and Game 7 of the 1970 NBA Finals is so well known that even New York Knick fans who weren't born yet can visualize the wounded leader limping out of the Madison Square Garden tunnel, can hear the din of the crowd building to a frenzied roar, can sense the sagging in the psyche of the Los Angeles Lakers.

But the mythologizing has obscured the reality in ways that both understate and overstate the great center's inspiring performance. The story has been rubbed so smooth that all we hear about is Reed's remarkable physical courage and how he won the opening jump and scored the Knicks' first two field goals, sparking the stunning win over Los Angeles and their Goliath, Wilt Chamberlain.

It's all true, but it's not enough. This is a story not just of one man but of a remarkable team, one unique in its cohesiveness, one so deep and talented it could win even without its biggest star.

Reed truly was the soul of that team, but he did more than just lift his teammates' spirits. Many people, thinking he left shortly after his second basket, say, "He only played about five minutes, right?" Actually he played into the second half, with an impressive physical game on offense and defense that prevented Chamberlain from taking over. But still, he contributed just four points and three rebounds. The ultimate hero was New York's most skilled all-around player, Walt "Clyde" Frazier. Because of Reed's superhero appearance, Frazier once quipped, "People don't even know I was in the game," but he was the central figure at Madison Square Garden on May 8, 1970. It was his swishing and dishing, as it were, his 36 points,

19 assists, and 7 rebounds, that carried the Knicks to their elusive first championship.

The Knicks were a charter member of the National Basketball Association—having helped to form its forerunner, the Basketball Association of America—and they were nearly its first dynasty. They reached three consecutive NBA Finals, beginning in 1951, yet were thwarted each time, the last two times by the Lakers and the sport's most dominant player, although that team was still near actual lakes in Minneapolis and the player was George Mikan. The Knicks remained a winning team for several more years before disintegrating. By the early 1960s, they were the league's laughingstock, losing on Christmas 1960 to Syracuse by 62 points and having not one but two players break the NBA scoring record against them—first Elgin Baylor, with 71 in 1960, and then, most memorably, Wilt Chamberlain (on the Philadelphia Warriors) when he threw down 100 in one night.

Gradually, however, failed-coach-turned-front-office-wizard Eddie Donovan pieced together a contender. The first component proved to be the foundation, the little-known Reed, drafted out of Grambling in 1964. The 1964–65 Rookie of the Year was tough (taking on the entire Laker bench in a fight in 1966), talented (averaging over 20 points and 14 rebounds per game in four years leading to the championship), and team-oriented (moving to power forward when Donovan acquired fellow center Walt Bellamy).

In 1965 Donovan traded for Dick Barnett and drafted Dave Stallworth and Bill Bradley (who went to Oxford on a Rhodes scholarship before donning his uniform); the next year he picked Cazzie Russell. In 1967 he snatched Phil Jackson and a guard from tiny Southern Illinois University by the name of Walt Frazier, who'd caught the attention of Knick scouts with his dazzling play at the Garden in the National Invitation Tournament (NIT), where he'd helped upset Marquette in the finals. At SIU, Frazier had been declared academically ineligible after one season, but coach Jack Hartman allowed this reticent, conservatively dressed youth to practice with the team three days a week—only on defense. This "punishment" transformed Frazier into one of the game's top defenders. After his NIT showcase, Frazier had a year of eligibility left, but the Knicks drafted him sixth and brought him back to Gotham.

Donovan's next move was hiring scout Red Holzman as coach; it was Holzman who would mold these disparate talents into a unified, balanced team: what they lacked in size and superstars they made up for with intelligence, versatility, unselfishness, and crisp ball movement. But the Knicks still needed one final trade to make them a champion. In 1968 Donovan traded the inconsistent Bellamy and Howard Komives to Detroit; this addition by subtraction allowed Reed to shift back to his natural position and truly take control of the team, while Komives's departure yielded playing time for Bradley. But there was a genuine addition as well: Dave DeBusschere, whose outspokenness and hard living had worn out his welcome in his hometown of Detroit, gave the Knicks a rugged power forward who could defend and rebound like few others.

In 1969 the Knicks were nearly flawless, reeling off a then-record 18 straight victories and finishing 60–22. They attracted new fans to professional basketball and a media swarm as well. They bounced two tough rivals, Earl Monroe's Baltimore Bullets and Lew Alcindor's Milwaukee Bucks, to reach the finals. There they encountered an immensely talented Laker squad led by the indomitable Chamberlain, the incomparable Jerry West, and an old but dangerous Elgin Baylor.

The Knicks waltzed through Game 1, 124–112, behind Reed's 37 points—Reed exploited Chamberlain's recent return from a leg injury by running and by shooting from the outside—but Chamberlain blocked Reed's shots at the start and end of Game 2 as the Lakers toughed out a 105–103 win.

Out in L.A., New York showed its resilience in Game 3: although West tied the score with a 63-footer at the buzzer, the Knicks prevailed in overtime. Then the Lakers again evened the series with an overtime win of their own behind West's 37 points.

The series took a shocking and, for New York,

seemingly devastating turn early in Game 5, but this misfortune ultimately elevated this series from a memorable one to an all-time sports classic. Eight minutes in, Reed collapsed to the floor, clutching his hip and writhing in agony. Already playing on battered knees, the league's MVP had badly hurt his right thigh muscle and the tensor muscles around the hip. Reed was done, at least for the night, possibly for the series. That meant the Knicks were done too, for how could they possibly contain Chamberlain without their own big man? But with the 6'6" DeBusschere filling the void and a total team effort, New York shut down a surprisingly passive Chamberlain, implemented an innovative offense to negate their disadvantage in the middle, and came back from 16 down for a memorable 107–100 win.

Once again, however, the Lakers responded, and this time they did it so forcefully that it seemed the Finals had shifted for good. In L.A. again for Game 6, Chamberlain scored 45 points on 20–27 shooting and grabbed 27 rebounds in a 135–113 rout that was so emphatic it made the notion of a "decisive" seventh game seem a mere formality . . . unless, of course, Reed could play.

Reed had skipped Game 6 completely, returning home for intensive treatment, including massages, whirlpools, and ultrasound. "I'll play if I have to crawl," he'd vowed.

He arrived early on May 8 for more treatment. On the court he tested his leg and found that he could drag it but couldn't pick it up without extreme pain. Still, by his pregame meal Reed knew he'd try to play.

Holzman wanted Reed out for pregame warmups for moral support, but Reed had to stay behind as team physician Dr. James Parkes searched for the right spots to inject the half-dozen shots of cortisone and Carbocaine that would numb Reed's leg. This inadvertent break in the game plan ended up enhancing the boost Reed gave his teammates.

It was past 7:15 when Parkes finally began. Because Reed's legs were so huge, the doctor needed six-inch-long spinal needles to reach the muscles; Reed was in agony during the 20-minute process.

As the Knicks and Lakers loosened up, the sold-out crowd scanned nervously for Reed. A wild roar went up when a latecomer emerged but quickly died down when it proved to be Cazzie Russell, who'd stayed behind to check on Reed. The game was late in starting, and Laker officials began grumbling.

Then, slowly emerging from the dark tunnel, came the personification of desire, of determination, of hope. As Reed dragged his right leg onto the court, the fans, the vendors, the security guards, all let loose a sustained and deafening ovation that shook the Garden. The Lakers looked deflated, nakedly watching Reed as he took a few shots (doing the bare minimum to hide how crippled he was). He had to shoot flatfooted instead of jumping, but at least he was out there shooting.

After all that drama, the action finally began. Reed couldn't jump for the opening tap, but Bradley stole a pass and got the ball to Frazier, who decided to maximize the Knicks' psychological edge. He found Reed open at the top of the key and fed him the ball.

Reed drained the shot for the first basket of the game. There were still 47 minutes and 42 seconds to play, but the game and the championship were essentially over. "People always talk about last shots that win games, but I think the first shot won a game," Reed has said.

The Knicks believed themselves a team of destiny, while the Lakers sensed impending doom. Moments later Reed hammered home those themes by hitting another shot for a 5–2 lead. He'd miss his three other attempts that night, but it didn't matter—the Lakers played like laid-back Angelenos, while the Knicks displayed the killer instinct of stereotypical New Yorkers. Chamberlain said later that the players on both teams had the "inescapable feeling . . . that no matter what the Lakers did, individually and collectively, the Knicks would find a way to win, and we would find a way to lose."

Realizing his limitations, Reed dedicated himself to setting screens and picks. In the first 14 minutes a trio of sharpshooters—Bradley (who'd finish with 17 points), DeBusschere (who'd end up with 18 points and 17 rebounds), and Frazier—

**Though unable to jump or run, Willis Reed scores the first two field goals of Game 7 for New York, inspiring the Knicks' climactic win.**

pumped a fatal barrage of bullets into the Lakers, going on a 15–21 spree that helped the Knicks build a 30–17 lead. After that, as the *Los Angeles Times* noted, the Lakers "surrendered meekly."

Though his face was often contorted in pain —especially after he hurt his hip again going for a first-quarter rebound—Reed managed to be a force on defense, keeping Chamberlain as far from the basket as possible, while the slick Frazier led an aggressive ball-hawking effort that flustered the Lakers and disrupted their game plan. Knowing he wouldn't last the whole game, Reed didn't hesitate to foul Chamberlain, keeping the sport's most dominating player from getting comfortable. While Reed was on the floor, the Lakers got Chamberlain the ball 17 times, but he shot just 2–9. He'd finish with only 21 points and 16 shots, while going just 1–11 from the line.

The Knicks led 69–42 at halftime. Reed got another injection during intermission, made another late entrance, and played six more minutes in the third, departing after picking up his fourth foul. He'd played 27 minutes—far more than the Knicks ever could have expected.

The Knicks' insurmountable lead had, in true New York fashion, been an all-around team effort—in addition to Bradley and DeBusschere, Barnett added 21 points and hounded Jerry West (who'd also needed injections, for his wounded shooting hand) into a 9–19 night. But Barnett, Bradley, and DeBusschere shot a combined 25–53, and in addition to the appearance of their wounded superhero, it was Frazier, with his superstar performance—widely considered among the greatest Game 7 showings in any NBA Finals—that carried the day. At the start of the playoffs, Holzman had asked Frazier to pass more and shoot less, and Frazier had averaged just 14.9 points, 6 below his season average. In this game, however, New York needed his scoring: in 44 minutes, Frazier shot 12–17 from the floor and a perfect 12–12 from the line, where his aggressive play got him more often than his teammates. Yet Frazier never betrayed Holzman's "hit the open man" credo—his 19 assists not only tied a playoff record (shared by Bob Cousy and Chamberlain) but was 2 more than the entire Laker team.

After building a 94–69 lead at the end of three, the Knicks coasted to a 113–99 win. The Knicks had their first championship and New York had its third since the Jets pulled off their own stunner in January 1969; on May 8, 1970, the defending World Series champion Mets were playing at Shea Stadium, and most of the fans were listening to the Knicks on transistor radios, chanting, "We're number one."

While the Jets had been roguish underdogs and the Mets lovable losers turned miracle workers, the Knick championship was not an upset—they were an elite team from day one, and before Reed got hurt, the Knicks and the Lakers were considered even. But the Knicks had their own identity, representing basketball at its most cohesive and most artistic—a true team game. After the NBA's bush league days of the 1950s and the Boston Celtics' dynasty of the 1960s, this Finals resonated in part because it featured the nation's two most important and glamorous cities, which fueled both fan and media interest in the sport, but also because in a time of great disharmony for both New York and the country the notion of a group of individuals, black and white, hitting the right notes, perfectly in tune with one another, was a wonderful and much-needed symbol. "We exemplified an ideal," Frazier said.

## 9. The Amazin' Mets win the World Series, October 16, 1969, Shea Stadium

There are no words.

October 16, 1969, ranks among the greatest days in New York sports history, not because of a particular run, hit, or error, but because of the cumulative effect, the crowning moment: at 3:17 P.M., when this game ended on an ordinary fly ball to left field by Baltimore's Dave Johnson, the improbable New York Mets, baseball's longtime lovable losers, were, of all things, World Series champions.

Since Cleon Jones caught that fly ball, thousands upon millions of words have been spilled about "the Miracle Mets," about their ascension to David, with a heavy fastball and a nasty slider, slingshotting Goliath, about what their World Series victory meant to the city, its mayor, baseball, and underdogs everywhere. But the emotions were best summed up in the moment itself by the most renowned of the team's banner-bearing fans —when Jones caught the ball, Karl Ehrhardt, known as "Sign Man," whipped out a placard decreeing: THERE ARE NO WORDS.

By using words to declare language insufficient, he succinctly and eloquently captured both the rapturous explosion about to erupt from Shea Stadium and the implausible absurdity of the notion that the Charlie Browns of major league baseball had won it all.

(The other option is to choose one word, uttered repeatedly by the ancient "Professor," Casey Stengel, who served as reporter and baseball ambassador during the Series and delivered this loopy verdict: "Amazin', amazin', amazin', amazin'.")

At their birth in 1962, the Mets linked themselves to New York's grand National League past through colors (Dodger blue and Giant orange) and players (Gil Hodges, Duke Snider). Or at least, they tried. They lost their first 9 and a record 120 that first season. They would lose at least 109 games in each of their first four seasons, yet with Stengel at the helm through mid-1965 and players like Marv Throneberry raising baseball ineptitude to a comic art form, the Mets would also become a unique hit with fans—in 1964 they drew 1.7 million faithful, more than the American League champion Yankees.

What would happen when the novelty wore off? What would happen when the losers stopped seeming lovable? Evolution is a long and painful process, but the Mets, besides gradually stocking up talent (Tug McGraw and Ron Swoboda in 1965, Jerry Grote and Cleon Jones in 1966), transformed themselves with three Big Bangs.

First came Tom Seaver. A controversial commissioner's decision about his contract and college eligibility handed the Mets this intelligent, powerful righty, who made an instant impact as the 1967 Rookie of the Year, winning 16 games with a 2.76 ERA. Then the Mets hired retired Brooklyn star Gil Hodges as manager. The former marine's air of quiet authority earned respect and occasionally even fear from his young charges.

Despite the influx of talent, and despite the fair but firm presence of Hodges, no one expected more than baby steps toward respectability. In 1968, with lefty Jerry Koosman joining Seaver, the team won 73 games—which, sadly, was a franchise record.

In 1969 Hodges's stated goal was reasonable: 85 wins.

Without their third Big Bang, the Mets would have graduated from joke to contender in 1969 without making the jump to winner. On June 15, 12 days after reaching .500, they acquired Donn Clendenon, a third big bat. The first baseman fit well into Hodges's masterful lineup manipulations (he platooned four of eight positions) and pumped out 12 homers in 202 at-bats, complementing Tommie Agee (26 homers overall) and Jones (who hit .340).

But for true believers who don't subscribe to evolutionary theories, the Mets also provided plenty of evidence that destiny or divine force was in play.

- In July, when Ferguson Jenkins, ace of the first-place Chicago Cubs, took a one-hitter and 3–1 lead into the ninth inning, center fielder Don Young misplayed Ken Boswell's pinch-hit blooper into a double, then made a running grab of Clendenon's smash to left-center but dropped the ball upon crashing into the fence. The Mets won the game.
- The Mets swept a double-header from Pittsburgh, winning both editions 1–0 when their pitcher drove in the sole run.
- In the 13th inning of a game against the San Francisco Giants, Hodges employed a four-man outfield against Willie McCovey, putting Jones in left-center. McCovey hit one right there, and

Jones made a leaping catch at the fence, taking away a homer. Agee hit a dinger the next inning to win it.

- Against Los Angeles, the Mets won in the ninth when three Dodgers watched Jerry Grote's high pop fall between them.
- In a September rematch with the Cubs, a black cat darted at Chicago's first batter, Don Kessinger, ran in front of the Cub dugout, and hissed at manager Leo Durocher. The Mets won, 7–1.
- St. Louis Cardinal Steve Carlton set a major league record by striking out 19 Mets. But New York won 4–3 because Swoboda, following tips from Hall of Fame slugger and Met announcer Ralph Kiner on how to hit the talented lefty, blasted two two-run homers with two strikes on him.
- That same week Bob Moose pitched a no-hitter against New York, yet the Cubs lost too that day so the Mets did not lose ground.

Still 9½ games out of first in mid-August, the Mets won 38 of their last 49 to finish first with a 100–62 record. Everyone felt giddy: a *Daily News* headline declared, "The Moon: Astronauts Took 9 Years, Mets 8," the *New York Post* wrote a tribute poem parodying Milton's *Paradise Lost* as an editorial, and the *New York Times* adapted Shakespeare to the '69 Mets. (For Seaver: "'And put the world's whole strength into one giant arm'— *Henry IV*.")

But many experts dismissed the Mets as lucky—expansion had forced the creation of a new two-division alignment, and finishing first in a six-team division was easier than it would have been in the ten-team league of recent years. Hank Aaron's Braves would set matters straight in the playoffs. Trailing 5–4 in Game 1, the Mets built a five-run eighth on looping hits, seeing-eye bounders, a stolen base, and a throwing error. They swept Atlanta. "We ought to send the Mets to Vietnam—they'd end the war in three days," Atlanta general manager Paul Richards said.

Next up, the World Series and the Baltimore Orioles.

"The feeling persisted that the Mets had really done it with mirrors, magic, mesmerism, or even divine intervention," wrote Joe Durso, author of *Amazing: The Miracle of the Mets.* "Like the Marx Brothers at the opera, they scarcely belonged on the scene with the lordly Orioles."

The Orioles were a great franchise, a team that would win at least 90 games in all but two full seasons from 1965 through 1983, a team beginning a run of five postseason berths in six years.

Baltimore won 109 games, capturing the American League East by 19 games. They featured future Hall of Famers at the plate (Frank Robinson), in the field (Brooks Robinson), on the mound (Jim Palmer), and on the bench (Earl Weaver). Their top four hitters—the Robinsons, Boog Powell, and Paul Blair—out-homered the Mets; the O's scored 147 more runs than New York, and with two 20-game winners (Mike Cuellar and Dave McNally), they allowed 24 fewer runs. "They're so good that I wouldn't mind managing their bench," quipped Kansas City manager Joe Gordon.

In the anything-goes year of Joe Namath, Neil Armstrong, and Woodstock, Met fans believed anything could happen. But most experts expected the old-school O's, with their no-nonsense players, to annihilate New York. "We're here to prove there is no Santa Claus," Brooks Robinson sneered before the World Series.

New York had more than mystique and good fortune. They had two starters, Seaver and Koosman, who were equal to anyone the Orioles could offer (and they'd pitch four times in five games), as well as a team that was smart (22 players had gone to college) and opportunistic—they'd score just 15 runs in 5 games yet almost always produced on offense or defense with the game on the line.

Game 1 satisfied the conventional wisdom when Don Buford smacked a homer on Seaver's second pitch of the game and Cuellar stifled the Mets 4–1. And the Mets didn't get any lucky break—in their sole threat in the seventh, Rod Gaspar hit a slow topper with two on, but Brooks Robinson snuffed the rally with a nifty barehanded play. The magic returned, however, in Game 2 when

**The Mets, losers of 737 games in their first seven years, win the World Series in their eighth season. Amazin', amazin', amazin'.**

Koosman pitched six no-hit innings and the Mets won in the ninth on three two-out singles, and in Game 3 when Agee hit a homer and made two spectacular catches. The next day Seaver redeemed himself, retiring 19 of 20 Orioles before running into trouble in the ninth. Ron Swoboda bailed him out with a diving, tumbling catch, and the Mets found a new way to win in the 10th when the Orioles' throw to first on J. C. Martin's bunt ricocheted off his wrist and Rod Gaspar scored from second.

Suddenly, finally, everyone believed. The Mets were for real. When Game 5 began on October 16, the Mets had allowed just two runs over the previous 32 innings. Even when Koosman had a shaky third inning, giving up three runs on homers to pitcher Dave McNally and Frank Robinson, the Mets exuded confidence. Koosman backed it up by going the full nine and retiring 19 of the last 21 batters.

To make up the three-run deficit, the Mets conjured up one amazing Mets moment after another. In the sixth, Koosman busted leadoff man Frank Robinson inside with a slider; the ball drilled Robinson hard on the right thigh, but the umpire called it foul, mistakenly believing the ball first hit Robinson's bat. After an extensive argument and treatment from Baltimore's trainer, Robinson whiffed on a curve. Powell then singled, but there was no rally and Brooks Robinson flied out.

In the bottom of the inning, McNally pitched inside to New York's leadoff man, Cleon Jones, snapping a curve at his feet. The umpire called a ball, but Jones argued that the pitch had nicked his foot before caroming toward New York's dugout. Hodges strode out of the dugout displaying the ball with a telltale black shoe polish smudge. Faced with hard evidence, the umpires reversed their call and awarded Jones first base. The ball might have actually hit Jones—equipment manager Nick Torman became a mini-celebrity for his shine job—but many have speculated that Hodges had someone mark up the ball on his foot in the dugout. (One account says Koosman later admitted to the deed.)

So the Orioles were deprived of a deserved base runner, and the Mets were handed one. As broadcaster Curt Gowdy noted, "The Amazing Mets even win their verbal arguments." The Mets, who'd won all year by relentlessly capitalizing on such gifts, struck immediately. Clendenon, soon to be Series MVP, blasted a pitch off the loge section in left field for his third Series homer. The gap was just one run.

They tied the score at 3–3 in the seventh in an even more unlikely fashion when Al Weis led off with a roundtripper. Yes, Al Weis—whom the Mets had acquired largely because he was too old to be called for Vietnam duty, who batted just .192 in two seasons with the Mets and had just 6 homers in 1,446 career at-bats; who had never hit a homer at home. He was batting .444 in the Series, a miracle itself, but that meant four singles, nothing more. So no one, not even Weis, expected a long ball when he ripped McNally's fastball toward the 371-foot mark in left-center. Weis put his head down and ran hard, only realizing when he was at second base that the boisterous cheering meant the ball had cleared the fence.

In the eighth, after Jones doubled to the wall, Hodges made a rare mistake and asked Clendenon to bunt. He botched two, then bounced to third. Swoboda, a .235 hitter who hit .400 for the Series, lined a ball that Buford could only trap, and the Mets had the lead. With two out, they padded it on an error and some heads-up running: Boog Powell misplayed Jerry Grote's low liner but still had time to make a play—except reliever Eddie Watt was too late covering first. When Watt dropped the throw, Swoboda, hustling all the way from second, made it 5–3.

Koosman was so nervous and excited before the ninth inning that he couldn't control his warm-up tosses. He walked Frank Robinson, bringing up the tying run in Powell, who'd hit 37 roundtrippers that year and was second in the AL with 121 RBIs. But Koosman got Powell to ground into a force. (Blair, Frank Robinson, and Powell batted a combined .163 with one RBI.) Brooks Robinson flied to Swoboda. Two outs. Dave Johnson, who would manage the next Mets championship team, lifted a fly to left.

"Keep dropping down to me, baby," Jones said. "Keep dropping down." He caught the ball and went down on one knee. Then the Mets ran for their lives as Shea Stadium imploded in a frenzy of turf-tearing fans. Joe DiMaggio, the regal and aloof Yankee Clipper, who'd thrown out the first ball, said, "I never saw anything like it," but the Mets understood. It was, Swoboda said, "the most appropriate loss of institutional control I can ever recall."

In the locker room, after the ecstatic explosions of champagne, some Mets became so emotional they couldn't even speak. Everywhere else in the city strangers were talking to each other, shouting and hugging. In Manhattan fans dancing in the street at 34th Street stopped traffic for an hour, and a spontaneous outburst of ticker tape and other impromptu confetti poured out of windows downtown (1,000 tons of paper were dropped, more than during the formal Apollo 11 parade).

Back in the clubhouse, Mayor John Lindsay joined the Mets. His handlers had for months been trying to make the elegant WASP seem like just another New Yorker during his struggling reelection campaign. Then they shoved him into the celebration. When Tom Seaver doused Lindsay with champagne in a front-page photo op, their problems were solved. When Lindsay feted the team at City Hall after an official ticker-tape parade, New York acquired a Fun City flavor that helped mask its divisions and problems. On election day the Mets picked up, if not a win, then a save.

Long after that glorious autumn slipped away, long after the Mets entered the dark winter of the mid-1970s and went through similar changes of seasons in the decades to follow, 1969 retained its unique glow, with that year's Mets becoming the patron saints of underdog dreamers in all sports and all walks of life.

"A lot of things were separating people then—Vietnam, campus unrest, the generation gap, race riots—and at times like those, people look for a fairy tale to soothe them," Seaver once said. "We were that fairy tale."

# 10. Don Larsen achieves perfection, October 8, 1956, Yankee Stadium

Imagine this scenario: The defending World Series champions, a powerful club that has played in three of the last four Series, win the first two games of the Fall Classic. Their archrival evens it up in Games 3 and 4 but uses two of its best pitchers in the process.

The fifth game is critical to the defender's hopes for back-to-back titles, for a shot at the coveted word "dynasty." The champs send out their Game 1 winner, a veteran with one of the best winning percentages of all time.

Their foes have only a middling muddle of mediocrity—a hard-partying big righty who had a decent season but lost 21 games two years before and was rocked by the champs not only in the previous World Series but just days earlier in Game 2 of this one.

That was the setup before Don Larsen took the mound at Yankee Stadium on October 8, 1956.

From this side of history, most Yankee World Series crowns have an aura of inevitability, and it's often the truth—think 1927, 1950, or 1998. But in 1955 the Bums from Brooklyn had finally reversed their curse to beat the Bombers. With the Yankees' aura stripped away, the World Series would finally be battled on equal footing, and Game 5 tilted the Dodgers' way, with Sal Maglie, the quintessential gamer, starting against Larsen, a total nobody. By day's end he'd be somebody, all right.

Most no-hitters are flukes, aberrations that often say little about a pitcher's dominance, but Larsen's perfect game—while certainly a bolt of lightning in a lackluster career—earns its top 10 ranking not just because it was a singular achievement but because it came at a crucial moment in baseball history.

Before Game 5, the situation looked grim for the Bombers. Larsen had stunk in Game 2's 13–8 loss. Had he fallen on his face in Game 5, the Dodgers would have wielded a tremendous advantage, going home to Ebbets Field for Game 6 with momentum and the pitching matchup in their favor. And had the Dodgers won the 1956 World Series, we'd look back at those years very differently. The Yankee reign would have seemed less imposing, and a domino effect is imaginable—

# Honorable Mention: Yankee No-Hitters

### 1. The imperfect man hurls a perfect game, May 17, 1998, Yankee Stadium

One of baseball's saving graces, especially in an era of inflated contracts and inflated muscles, is that a man as patently imperfect physically as David Wells can attain perfection on the diamond. Surely there'd be no place for a "Boomer" in basketball, football, or hockey.

Wells's game par excellence symbolized general manager Brian Cashman's perfectly assembled 1998 Yankee team. Even in a year when the team's linchpins—Derek Jeter, Mariano Rivera, and Andy Pettitte—were all slightly below par, the Yankees went 114–48. It was a deep team without a weak link, and each player was capable of greatness in any given game.

For the portly Wells, that game came May 17 against the Minnesota Twins. In his first year in New York, Wells had broken his pitching hand in a bar fight and missed spring training time because of gout; in this second season, he had pitched poorly through early May and was entering this game with a 5.23 ERA. He was also reportedly still half-drunk from partying with the cast of *Saturday Night Live* after appearing on the show. But he knew from his bullpen warm-ups that he had electric stuff.

Unlike most no-hitters or perfectos, this one didn't require any great defensive plays—from the third through the fifth, Wells fanned seven Twins and the biggest threat was a hard one-hopper in the eighth that second baseman Chuck Knoblauch knocked down, then recovered in time. Wells went to three balls on only four batters, though he labored toward the end, falling behind on eight of the final nine hitters, requiring 121 pitches overall.

On the bench, Wells was feeling consumed by the tension and his teammates, in traditional baseball superstition, were avoiding him. But one fellow Yankee broke the ice before the eighth inning. "I think it's time for you to break out your knuckleball," David Cone joked, cracking Wells up and helping him relax. After the inning, Cone confronted Wells again: "You ain't shown me nothing."

Nothing is exactly what the Twins finished with. It was the first perfect game by a Yankee since 1956, and Wells, it turned out, had graduated from Point Loma High, Don Larsen's alma mater. A perfect coincidence.

### 2. David Cone catches some perfect karma, July 18, 1999, Yankee Stadium

July 18, 1999, was called Yogi Berra Day, but it could just as easily have been named Good Karma Day.

When George Steinbrenner fired Berra as Yankee manager early in 1985 without having the guts to call him personally, Berra vowed never to return to Yankee Stadium. But in 1999 a dying Joe DiMaggio reportedly urged the Boss to suck it up and apologize, and WFAN's Suzyn Waldman brought Steinbrenner out to the Yogi Berra Museum in Montclair, where the two made up. Berra threw out the first ball at the Yankee home opener, and Steinbrenner then organized a day in the great catcher's honor.

The 18th was also current manager Joe Torre's birthday. As a teen, the Brooklyn native had journeyed to the Bronx one day in 1956 to cheer on his beloved Dodgers in the World Series. Instead, he'd witnessed history in the form of Don Larsen's perfect game.

On hand to throw out the first pitch for Berra's big day was Larsen himself. On Berra's hand to catch Larsen's pitch was Joe Girardi's mitt. Girardi then donned the mitt to catch David Cone, the aging All-Star who had just shaken Larsen's hand. Cone, it turned out, had caught an armful of good fortune.

Cone's fastball-slider combo overmatched the Montreal Expos from the start. An early 5–0 lead let Cone relax, and so (ironically) did a blast of Amazonian weather—despite a 33-minute rain delay, the heat and humidity helped keep him loose. He zipped through the fourth with just seven pitches and the sixth with just five, changing his T-shirt after each inning. He required saving just twice—Paul O'Neill made a circus catch in the second, and in the eighth Chuck Knoblauch, despite a recent freakish inability to throw to first—made a nifty backhanded stop in the eighth and successfully nailed speedy Jose Vidro.

Cone began the ninth with a strikeout, then went 2–2 on Shane Andrews for just his fourth two-ball count before Andrews lined the ball to left. Rickey Ledee lost the ball in the sun but zigzagged in and corralled it at the last second. On Cone's 88th pitch, Orlando Cabrera lifted a pop foul. Scott Brosius snagged it, and Cone put his hands on his head and sank to the ground. But he couldn't stay down on this day, and

*(continued on page 50)*

**Don Larsen bears down on the final strike on the final out of his masterpiece.**

would Casey Stengel have survived after the Yankees lost again in 1957? Would a new manager have won in 1958? Larsen's win also fortified the Dodgers' place in history: they were not a dynasty but rather the ultimate victims of a Yankee machine that cranked out big plays and big games from the unlikeliest of sources. That elevated their 1955 triumph to the holy grail stature it has retained for 50 years and ironically gave the club a more sharply defined identity after it left Brooklyn in 1957. "A Dodger win in 1956 would have changed the whole vision of the rivalry," says New York sports historian Bill Shannon.

History is, of course, often written in broad strokes. The Dodgers symbolized falling short, when in reality they'd dominated the National League for a decade. And Larsen was better prepared for historic success at that one moment in time than one might think. He'd won nine games in the minors and nine in the majors in 1955. Heading into 1956, manager Casey Stengel said that Larsen could "be a big man in this business—any time he puts his mind to it." Admittedly, his mind often wasn't there—Gooney Bird, as he was called, crashed his car into a telephone pole at 5:00 A.M. during spring training, and he was maddeningly inconsistent on the mound, often getting bumped to the bullpen. Still, when he was on, he had electric stuff. And in September he'd had an epiphany: he'd abandoned his full windup for an abbreviated version that steadied his control, conserved his energy, and disrupted the hitter's timing. He'd reeled off four straight wins to finish 11–5 before his Game 2 fiasco, when he walked four and didn't last through the second.

With no travel days in a "Subway Series," the teams churned through more pitchers, and so Larsen got his shot at redemption. In the first three innings, however, it seemed just as likely that Maglie would make history—both he and Larsen reeled off nine straight outs. But Maglie, who had thrown a no-hitter in the final weeks of the season, could not keep pace with Larsen.

In the first inning, Pee Wee Reese worked the count to 3–2, but it would be the only time Larsen

## Yankee No-Hitters (CONTINUED)

soon Girardi, Knoblauch, and other teammates hoisted him in the air and carried him off in triumph.

Cy Young had pitched the first perfect game of the 20th century; on July 18, 1999, the 1994 Cy Young Award winner registered the final one.

**3. Dave Righetti doodles a dandy Yankee no-hitter, July 4, 1983, Yankee Stadium**

Dave Righetti was supposedly the next Ron Guidry, the Yankee ace of the 1980s. When the fireballing lefty was 1981 Rookie of the Year, comparisons seemed natural. But the burden wore "Rags" down, and he struggled in 1982 until getting shipped out to Triple AAA Columbus.

In 1983 Righetti climbed back on track, winning 10 of 13, and on a sunny Fourth of July, when the 24-year-old fanned seven Boston hitters in the first three innings, it seemed like he might pass the master; Guidry held the club record with 18 strikeouts. But Righetti finished with just nine Ks. Instead of breaking Guidry's record, he struck out on his own path and achieved something no Yankee hurler had accomplished since Don Larsen in 1956: Righetti pitched a no-hitter . . . and he did it against the Red Sox on George Steinbrenner's birthday.

Boston had 25 runs in its previous three games, but Righetti was hardly threatened—there was a slow roller in the fourth, a sixth-inning bloop, and a long foul drive that Steve Kemp snared against the wall. The game remained tight until the eighth, when the Yankees doubled their 2–0 lead. Righetti's final obstacle in the ninth was Wade Boggs, the league's top hitter.

Catcher Butch Wynegar set Boggs up brilliantly. On 1–2, Righetti busted Boggs up and in with a fastball that Boggs fouled off. Boggs wouldn't bite on a low slider. 2–2. The sequence called for another fastball, but Wynegar suddenly changed his mind and signaled for a big breaking slider. Looking fastball, Boggs ended the game with a feeble half-swing.

His moment of greatness seemed to liberate Righetti from the expectations, and the next year New York converted him into a stopper; he became the best Yankee closer prior to Mariano Rivera.

In the turbulent year of 1983—Dave Winfield killed a seagull, George Brett hit a "pine tar" homer, and Steinbrenner was fined for smearing umpires and fired Billy Martin yet again—and in all those years without the postseason from 1982 to 1994, there were few days more memorable than that Fourth of July when Dave Righetti provided Yankee fans with a Rags-to-riches story.

went three balls all day—a vital indicator that his on-and-off struggle with command was under control. Reese struck out looking. In the second, Larsen got an extraordinarily lucky break: Jackie Robinson smacked a liner that third baseman Andy Carey couldn't handle, but the ball ricocheted toward shortstop; Gil McDougald alertly grabbed it and threw hard to first, nailing the 37-year-old former speedster by a half-step. In the fourth inning, Larsen survived another scare after falling behind slugger Duke Snider 2–0. He had to come in with a fastball, which Snider ripped . . . a home run for sure . . . until it bent foul by inches. Snider struck out looking.

Larsen, staked to a 1–0 lead on a Mickey Mantle home run, gave up two more long balls in the fifth but survived both: first Mickey Mantle made a superb backhanded grab of Gil Hodges's 400-foot blast in deep left-center, then Larsen watched Sandy Amoros hit another shot that hooked just foul. Suddenly there was that nervous energy that flows through the stands and dugouts when a no-hitter is a serious possibility.

When Maglie disposed of the Yankees in the bottom of the inning, the two pitchers had retired 30 men while yielding just one hit. But the Yankees eked out another run in the sixth—Larsen helped himself with a sacrifice, setting up Hank Bauer's RBI single. An even bigger rally was cut short one hit later when Hodges fielded Mantle's grounder, stepped quickly on first, then threw home to trap Bauer in a rundown. Robinson put the tag on him, completing the unusual double play. It was brilliant execution, the kind of rally-killer that often hurts the other team. But this was no ordinary game.

By the seventh inning, Larsen was a bundle of

nerves—his hands shook in the dugout as he tried lighting his cigarette. Still, he breezed through the inning, retiring Junior Gilliam on a grounder that McDougald backhanded, Reese on a fly to center, and Snider on a fly to left. He had made it this far. Others had too—the Yankees' Herb Pennock in 1927, Monte Pearson in 1939, Red Ruffing and Cardinal Burleigh Grimes in 1931—but none had made it out of the eighth. Back in 1954, Larsen, then with Baltimore, had had a no-hitter against the Yankees ruined in the eighth by Andy Carey.

In the dugout Larsen said to Mantle, "Wouldn't it be funny if I pitched a no-hitter?" Afraid of baseball's no-hitter jinx, Mantle moved away.

The fans at Yankee Stadium were bordering on hysterical, reaching decibel levels no one had imagined. Dodger manager Walter Alston asked Robinson to ruffle Larsen. Larsen cared only about beginning the inning with a strong statement, a first-pitch strike. He got it with a fastball. When Robinson backed out of the box before the next pitch and went to talk to Hodges on deck, the fans, knowing Robinson was looking to disrupt the pitcher's rhythm, belted out lusty boos, but Larsen was not rattled. Robinson bounced back to the mound.

To Larsen, Hodges "looked like he stood seven feet tall," he wrote later in *The Perfect Yankee.* Larsen faltered briefly at 2–2, offering a flat nothing of a fastball. Hodges zinged it, but right at Carey, who snagged it just off the ground for the out. Not wanting to risk the umpire mistakenly calling a trap, Carey threw Hodges out at first. When Amoros popped to center, Larsen was three outs from perfection.

Larsen led off the bottom of the eighth and received a thunderous ovation. He received another one on his way back to the dugout after striking out.

"Let's all take a deep breath as we go to the most dramatic ninth inning in the history of baseball," Vin Scully announced.

There were nearly 70,000 regular-season major league games from the American League's birth in 1901 through 1956. Before October 8, there'd been only three perfect games, and none in 34 years. Before Larsen, of course, no one else had ever thrown a no-hitter, much less a perfect game, in the Series. Only ex-Yankee Floyd Bevens, now watching on television at home in Oregon, had reached the ninth, back in 1947, but he'd handed out 10 walks along the way and eventually lost the no-hitter, the shutout, and the game with two outs.

For Larsen, the crowd was so loud that he couldn't hear the encouragement of his teammates as they trotted out. He was just concentrating on reaching the mound, since his legs felt as though they'd turned to rubber. "My fingers didn't feel like they were on my hand," he later recalled. He wasn't the only one feeling a bit shaky—Billy Martin was so full of nervous excitement that he botched a grounder during warm-ups.

Time slowed down. Larsen fired a slider that Carl Furillo fouled off. And again. 0–2. After a ball, Furillo fouled off two more pitches. It was excruciating. Finally he lifted a slider to right. Campanella, perhaps anxious, chased a 1–1 slider off the plate and grounded to second. Martin fielded it cleanly. Two outs.

Larsen had thrown 92 pitches, 66 for strikes. He had one batter left, a pinch-hitter for Maglie, veteran lefty Dale Mitchell. For the first time in several innings, Larsen felt a calm wash over him. He walked around behind the mound, waiting.

"Yankee Stadium is shivering in its concrete foundation right now," Scully said.

A fastball. Catcher Yogi Berra just wanted the basics, figuring Mitchell would be especially flustered because he had never batted against Larsen's no-wind-up motion, which made pitches seem to arrive extra quick. Larsen missed, low and outside, just the fourth time all afternoon he'd fallen behind a hitter.

Another hard one caught the outside corner. No one could hear umpire Babe Pinelli over the screaming fans, but "strike" was the word he yelled. 1–1.

Larsen returned to his slider. It was low, but Mitchell eagerly chased it. Way too late. Strike two. One more to go.

Back to the fastball. Larsen nearly blew it by Mitchell, who fouled it back at the last second. He would have to try again.

Larsen needed a break. He took off his cap. He picked up the rosin bag. He was ready. Berra called for another heater, low and away. Babe Pinelli had been umpiring for 22 years and was retiring after the season. This was his final game, his final inning behind home plate. He was so tense that he could barely breathe. Everyone in the Stadium was standing.

The pitch came in. It was close. Mitchell started his swing, then checked. He definitely thought it was outside. Pinelli disagreed. His arm went up. The game was over. Larsen had achieved the unthinkable. Yogi Berra leaped into his arms, and the Yankees began celebrating.

The Dodgers managed to win Game 6, but their offense never recovered. Bob Turley's no-wind-up delivery stymied them until the 10th, when they scraped together one run. And as the Yankees exploded for nine runs in Game 7, Brooklyn posted nothing but zeroes. Larsen was named World Series MVP.

Larsen never regained that day's magic, and he flubbed his starts in Game 7 of the next two World Series. But his performance of October 8, 1956, was more than unique — it was influential. Before Larsen, few people differentiated between no-hitters and perfect games. Larsen himself knew he had a no-hitter but never thought about a "perfect game." This game made people appreciate the distinction between a no-hitter and retiring 27 straight batters, something that has happened only 11 times in the 50 years since Larsen did it (nearly half in the expansion-riddled, muscle-bound, free-swinging chicks-love-the-long-ball years since 1990).

But it did more than that. The 10 years from 1947 through 1956 were the greatest in New York City baseball. The Yankees, Dodgers, and Giants won all but one World Series and made history in every way imaginable. Although no one knew it then, this Series marked the last hurrah for that magical era. Larsen provided a finishing touch that was — in a word — perfect.

# 11. Mookie Wilson hits a ground ball to first in Game 6 of the World Series, October 25, 1986, Shea Stadium

Disbelief rapidly gave way to despair. You knew in your heart you shouldn't feel so despondent — this was a baseball game, there were far graver problems, much larger injustices. Still, as the Boston Red Sox scored one run in the top of the 10th inning and then a second, your body slumped. As your New York Mets made one out, then a second, in the bottom of the 10th, your soul shrank. It was Game 6 of the World Series, and the Red Sox led three games to two. No team had ever come back to win a Series from two down with two outs while facing elimination.

The Mets' scoreboard congratulated Boston on breaking their curse. How could it have come to this? After enduring the Tom Seaver trade, the Mike Vail hype, the disappointment of George Foster, after excusing 1984's close call and 1985's heartbreak as learning experiences, how could it have come to this for one of the best, most dominating baseball teams ever?

A single. It meant nothing, merely delaying the inevitable.

A second hit started a stirring. Ah, if only there weren't already two outs . . . and then an 0–2 count. No team had ever come back to win a Series when down to its final strike.

Then something happened. Call it ghosts, call it history, call it the irresistible force of greatness. Whatever. It happened in slow motion and all at once—an avalanche that you rode atop, full-throated in your cheering. A weak looping single cut the lead to one. An eternal at-bat, forever fending off strike three, elicited a wild pitch. The game was tied, but its fate, indeed the entire Series, was tilting in New York's favor. Then the clincher: a slow roller, just a trickler, but the batter's blazing speed and the first baseman's fragility and the most beautifully ugly play of all. And there you were in midair, hovering in the sky, flying, delirious. Someone bring back Red Smith: on October 25, 1986, fiction took another deadly beating.

Those heartbreaking-to-heart-stopping bombshells make Game 6's 10th inning perhaps the most riveting, thrilling inning in World Series history, particularly in the 51 World Series featuring New York City teams.

The 1986 Mets—a ferocious combination of talent and ego, pitching and hitting, youth and experience, All-Stars and bench depth—were built for history. After an ugly, despairing stretch that began when management devastated fans by trading Seaver in 1977, the Mets started rebounding in 1983 when general manager Frank Cashen promoted Darryl Strawberry from the minors and swiped Keith Hernandez from the St. Louis Cardinals. They finished a strong second in 1984 and nearly won the National League East in 1985. Each year brought more talent from within and without—from Dwight Gooden to Bobby Ojeda, Lenny Dykstra to Gary Carter. By 1986 the pieces were in place. They were great, and they knew it.

In spring training they left T-shirts declaring, NEW YORK METS—1986 NL EAST CHAMPIONS, in the locker room of St. Louis, the defending NL champs. Manager Davey Johnson boasted, "We don't want to just win. We want to dominate." They did, reeling off streaks of eleven, seven, and six straight . . . in just the first two months. After one-third of the season, Cardinal manager Whitey Herzog conceded.

Their endless curtain calls, rally caps, endorsements, and "Let's Go, Mets" irked opponents, who provoked four bench-clearing brawls with New York, but no one could stop those damn Mets—their 108 wins tied the 1975 Cincinnati Reds for the NL record. They clinched the East on September 17, the earliest date in divisional history, and won by 21½ games, the largest margin since 1920.

The Mets weren't typical bullies, collapsing when someone stood up to them. They were tough as Nails—as in the sparkplug Dykstra, of the perpetually dirty uniform—and proved their resilience in a scintillating playoff against Houston, winning Game 3 on Dykstra's bottom-of-the-ninth, two-run home run; Game 5 on catcher Gary Carter's slump-breaking 12th-inning single; and Game 6 when they rallied from being down 3–0 in the ninth and prevailed in the 16th inning of a raucous affair.

Standing between the Mets and the crowning honor they knew that they and the city so richly deserved was Boston. The Mets had traveled there back on September 4, an off-day, for a charity exhibition game at Fenway Park. It was a possible World Series preview, but no one knew what it meant when Rick Aguilera foreshadowed his Game 6 role by giving Boston a two-run lead (albeit in the third inning), when Bill Buckner booted a ball to set up a Mets rally (albeit in the fourth), or when the Mets came back from two down with two outs to win thanks to a Boston error (albeit by third baseman Ed Romero in the eighth inning).

The Red Sox had not won the Series since

1918, allegedly cursed after selling Babe Ruth to the Yankees. The Mets were a stronger, more dynamic club, but Boston was armed — Roger Clemens was 24–4, and "Oil Can" Boyd and Bruce Hurst had combined for another 29 wins — and they had their mojo working too, having made a dramatic comeback to beat California in the ALCS. The Series offered Boston a chance to end its awful spell in the city responsible for its most anguished memories, a city that had given many Bostonians an inferiority complex. Of course, the Mets, with their arrogance and the unseemly success that backed it up, symbolized New York's reputation to the nth degree and thus inspired animosity coast to coast.

The early going provided Met-bashers with a delightful schadenfreude. Boston won the opener 1–0 when Jim Rice scored on a terrible gaffe: Rich Gedman's grounder rolled through second baseman Tim Teufel's legs. Game 2 featured the best pitching matchup in a generation: Clemens versus Gooden. Clemens was shaky, but Gooden was far worse as the Mets tumbled to a 9–3 loss.

The previous year Kansas City had become the first team to win the Series after losing the first two at home. But these Mets were uninterested in precedent. They won 7–1 in Game 3 as Ojeda, a former Red Sox, became the first lefty victor at Fenway Park in the postseason since 1918, and 6–2 in Game 4 behind Carter's two homers. But Gooden faltered again in Game 5, and the Mets came home facing elimination.

In this perilous situation, Ojeda started shaky, yielding a leadoff single to Wade Boggs and allowing one run in each of the first two innings. But in that first inning the Mets received a sign from above . . . literally. With Buckner coming up, unknown soap opera actor Mike Sergio earned instant fame and 21 days in jail by parachuting onto the field, displaying a banner cheering GO METS. Buckner applauded, Dwight Evans grinned, and Ron Darling high-fived Sergio as he was led away through New York's dugout. Still, the Mets needed more than a brave and ardent fan as Clemens fired a no-hitter through four.

In the fifth, the Mets tied it by scraping together two runs on a walk and a steal, two singles, an error, and a double play. Boston regained the lead in the seventh thanks to a throwing error by Ray Knight, although the Mets caught a break when Mookie Wilson played the hero nailing Rice at home. Going two runs down would have been disheartening so late in the game.

In the eighth, the season again almost slipped away, but Boston manager John McNamara outbungled Davey Johnson and delivered the Mets the raw material for victory. With a man on second and one out, McNamara pinch-hit for Clemens, who had popped a blister on his index finger and then torn a fingernail on his middle finger (both times while facing Wilson) and had thrown 135 pitches. Still, Clemens was baseball's best pitcher, and McNamara ditched him in search of an insurance run and despite his shaky and weary relief corp. Pinch-hitter Mike Greenwell whiffed.

Then Roger McDowell loaded the bases with two walks, so Johnson called on southpaw Jesse Orosco to face lefty Bill Buckner.

The perpetually aching Buckner had endured nine cortisone shots in 1986 and strained his Achilles tendon in the playoffs. An inspiration but also a liability, he was seeking support from hideous hightop sneakers that served as a visual reminder of his decrepitude. In all seven postseason wins, McNamara had removed Buckner at game's end for defensive purposes. Dave Stapleton was ready to once again play the final six outs. Buckner wasn't contributing offensively anyway, with just a .216 OBP in the postseason, and McNamara wanted to send up righty Don Baylor, who'd smashed 31 homers that year and had a .381 OBP in the postseason. (He wasn't playing because a designated hitter could not be used at Shea Stadium.) But as Jeff Pearlman reveals in *The Bad Guys Won,* his account of the Mets' 1986 season, Buckner, just 3-for-19 lifetime against Orosco, persuaded McNamara that he could hit him. Then he flew out on the very first pitch.

Johnson, meanwhile, had failed to make a double switch at the pitching change, so Orosco was due up first in the Mets' eighth and had to be pulled for a pinch-hitter.

**Bob Stanley's pitch heads inside, and Mookie Wilson jackknifes out of the way as the ball gets away—along with Boston's championship.**

Running short on time, the Mets reached back to their ignoble past for Lee Mazzilli. The Brooklyn-born Maz had been hailed as a hunky savior in 1977 but eventually traded after failing to live up to the hype. He had been brought back in 1986 to replace another old favorite, Rusty Staub, the retired pinch-hitter extraordinaire.

Fortunately for the Mets, Boston also reached back to the Mets' ignoble past, for closer Calvin Schiraldi. Way back when, the Mets had drafted Clemens out of high school, but Clemens had chosen instead to go to college at the University of Texas, where his teammate was Schiraldi. The next time around Boston got Clemens and the Mets got Schiraldi, who had equally impressive stuff. But the Mets soon decided that Schiraldi lacked mental toughness and gladly dumped him to pry Ojeda loose.

Schiraldi buckled immediately, allowing a single to Mazzilli, then rushing a throw into the dirt at second on a bunt. Soon he'd loaded the bases with one out, then pumped three straight balls to Carter. Given the green light, Carter smacked a long fly, scoring Mazzilli with the tying run.

The Mets threatened in the ninth, but with two men on, Johnson inexplicably sent slugger Howard Johnson up as a pinch-hitter, then asked him to bunt; after one feeble attempt, he was allowed to swing away, but he whiffed. Mazzilli's subsequent outfield out was the sacrifice fly that wasn't. Still, despite being out-hit 10–5, the Mets were alive after nine innings.

Or so it seemed. On the second pitch of the 10th, Rick Aguilera, the less experienced reliever brought in after the Mets had pinch-hit for Orosco, yielded a home run to ALCS hero Dave Henderson, who rubbed it in New York's collective face with an annoying hop and infuriating backwards jog down the line as he watched his death blow sail on. "It's so quiet in New York you can almost hear Boston," Scully said.

It would get darker before it got any lighter. With two outs, Boggs doubled and Marty Barrett singled him home, making it 5–3. An extra run is often called a cushion, and this one seemed capable of suffocating the Mets, down to three last breaths.

"It is tough enough to lose, but when you make a decision that will stick in your craw, the long winter is interminable," Scully intoned. He was talking at that point about Johnson, not McNamara.

Despite Schiraldi's tentative performance and creeping fatigue, McNamara left him in.

Wally Backman flied out to left. Hernandez flied out to deep center. History dictated that the Mets could not revive themselves this time. The scoreboard, ready for the inevitable, inadvertently flashed: CONGRATULATIONS BOSTON RED SOX. Clemens, showered and freshly shaved, sat in Boston's dugout, while most players were on the top step or edging onto the field, ready to burst into celebration. In the clubhouse, bottles of bubbly waited along with Bob Costas, who would provide historical perspective on a team that had waited forever but finally won in the town where it counted most. As the game wound down, NBC announced Barrett as Player of the Game and Hurst as World Series MVP.

But Gary Carter had caught Schiraldi. He believed he could hit him: "I knew that he was gutless." He lined a single.

Kevin Mitchell, who was undressed and on the clubhouse phone making plane reservations for the flight home, dashed out to pinch-hit for Aguilera. Schiraldi, his roomie in the minors, once claimed he'd get Mitchell out with a fastball in, then a slider away. Remembering that conversation, Mitchell fouled off the fastball, then hit the slider for a single. No one wanted to make that final out. In the clubhouse all the dejected and downcast souls—Hernandez, Orosco, Darling, Ojeda, McDowell—either froze, afraid to change what they were doing, or donned rally caps. They felt something now.

Knight, seeking redemption for his error, fell in the hole, 0–2. One more strike and Schiraldi could escape into the loving embrace of a grateful Red Sox Nation. But he was too eager and forgot to waste a pitch; Knight looped a soft single, scoring Carter. Throughout the postseason the Mets had scored more than half their runs after the sixth inning. Could they get one more big hit?

McNamara brought on veteran Bob Stanley, who had lost his closing job to Schiraldi that season but had not allowed a run in the Series. Stanley faced Mookie Wilson. Neither scrub nor superstar, Wilson was a solid but flawed player and a fan favorite, beloved for his work ethic, team spirit (he had accepted Dykstra's arrival without much grumbling), and exhilarating speed. He was the longest-tenured Met (he'd been around since the 95-loss year of 1980) and a low-key voice of sanity in this rowdy crew.

The first pitch was high and away, but Mookie's hitting philosophy was, "Thou shalt not pass at thy offering." He fouled it off. He took two pitches well out of the strike zone before fouling off another. Again the Mets were down to their final strike.

Wilson stayed alive with another foul ball. And another. Stanley was desperate to finish things. Knowing Stanley was working him away, Wilson crept closer to the plate. Perhaps Stanley saw that and changed his location at the last minute, but whatever the reason, the next potentially final pitch of 1986 burst inside, dusting Gedman's glove as Wilson jackknifed away. The ball rolled to the backstop, and Mitchell tore home with the tying run. Red Sox fans have debated ever since whether Stanley or Gedman deserved more blame. Met fans don't care. They credit Wilson for keeping the at-bat going.

With the game 5–5, the momentum was all New York. Wilson fouled off two more pitches. On the 10th pitch, Wilson hit a grounder to first. The day before *Washington Post* columnist Thomas Boswell had wondered whether Buckner was selfish rather than inspiring in his "willingness to endure any amount of pain and any potential for embarrassment or failure just so he can say he played the game."

McNamara had blithely left Buckner in to be on the field for the celebration. A healthy first baseman, like Stapleton, would have charged in to make the play, but the mangled Buckner now stayed back, letting the ball play him.

Wilson knew he hadn't hit the ball well, but he tore down the line nonetheless. He had played every moment hard since 1981 when he hadn't hustled in the outfield on a single dumped in front of him—the Chicago Cub veteran who poked that hit was someone who never loafed, and he took advantage of Wilson's laxness to snatch the extra base, embarrassing the Met youngster. The Cub who inadvertently taught Wilson the lesson that his speed was inextricably linked to his effort was Bill Buckner.

Wilson's grounder headed toward Buckner, who knew how fast Wilson was, who must have suspected Wilson would probably win a race to the bag unless he hurried. In a Boston television interview before the Series, Buckner had said he hoped to be a hero but knew a dark side lurked out there. He didn't fret about striking out or hitting into a double play: "The nightmares are you're gonna let the winning run score on a ground ball through your legs."

As the ball skipped through Buckner's legs and his personal nightmare began, Knight bounded home with the winning run. After steamrolling baseball for the entire season, the 1986 Mets had saved themselves by returning to their Mets roots, to the defining character of the 1969 and 1973 clubs, which won the games no one expected them to win, in ways nobody imagined.

But you gotta believe that this Met miracle was the most "amazin', amazin', amazin'" of them all.

# 12. Fifty-four years later, the Rangers finally win the Stanley Cup, June 14, 1994, Madison Square Garden

In the early 1990s, New York City was suffering. From the crack epidemic to racial strife, things seemed tough all over. That tough run even extended to rooting for the home team.

From 1979 to 1993, Gotham had only one winner, the 1986 Mets, although the Giants, who like so many residents had fled the city in the 1970s, had won two Super Bowls and the Islanders had won four Stanley Cups out in Nassau County. Even with those six suburban titles, the tally was relatively low for a city used to winning. This was the worst dry spell since Babe Ruth arrived . . . and it hurt.

No one hurt more than Rangers fans, haunted by the merest mention of the year 1940, the last time their team had won it all.

World War II came and went, as did the Korean War, the Vietnam War, Watergate, Iran-contra, and Operation Desert Storm. Ten new presidents entered the White House. The civil rights movement, women's lib, the antiwar movement, the explosion of AIDS. Sinatra, Elvis, the Beatles, the *Saturday Night Fever* soundtrack, and Nirvana. Television,

**The 54 years were tortuous, but the joy on Mark Messier's face makes it worth the wait.**

cable television, *SportsCenter*. The world changed and changed and changed over 54 years.

And still, despite reaching the finals in 1950, 1972, and 1979, the New York Rangers could not win a single Stanley Cup.

From 1941 through 1993, the Yankees won 14 World Series, and the Dodgers, Giants, and their replacement, the Mets, a total of four; the Knicks won two NBA crowns; the football Giants won one NFL Championship and two Super Bowls, and the Jets one Super Bowl. Worst of all, those upstarts from Long Island, the New York Islanders, weren't born until 1972, yet they captured Lord Stanley's trophy four straight times in the 1980s. And still the New York Rangers could not win a single Stanley Cup.

Things were so bad that Rangers fans explained the problems away not with one curse, like the Boston Red Sox or Chicago Cubs, but with two. After winning the 1940 trophy, the Rangers' owners, who'd just paid off their mortgage, celebrated by burning the paperwork in the Cup. Such desecration was naturally frowned on by the hockey gods. Then Red Dutton issued a personal hex. Dutton had run the New York Americans, the first hockey team to play at Madison Square Garden. But Garden management created its own hockey team, the Rangers, in 1925; years of high rents and inadequate ice time badly damaged the Americans, who folded in the early 1940s. Dutton decreed that the Rangers would not win the Cup either in his lifetime or until the Americans played the Garden again (depending on the story). Terrible management was, of course, far more damaging than any curses, but in 1993 Rangers general manager Neil Smith tried exorcising one curse by creating an award honoring Dutton through the NHL.

Smith had done more than honor the past, of course; he had built for the future in 1991 by signing Adam Graves and trading for Mark Messier, both stars in the Edmonton dynasty. Messier was not just a great talent but a leader who seemed capable of imposing his formidable will on his team and lifting them to victory. After a 50-win season in 1991–92 was followed by a setback the next year, owing largely to Brian Leetch's injuries, Smith also hired the hard-edged Mike Keenan as coach for 1993–94.

Before the season the coach showed his new team a video of New York ticker-tape parades. "All this can be yours," he seemed to say, before forcing them to endure Pat Riley–esque torturous training to make sure they'd be the most physically fit team around.

After a slow start, the Rangers went on an 18–1–3 tear and moved into first, where they'd finish with a team-record 52 wins. Keenan and Smith loathed each other, but Smith listened to what Keenan wanted and got him plenty of talent in midseason deals, including Stephane Matteau, Craig MacTavish, and Glenn Anderson.

In the playoffs they blew out the New York Islanders and Washington Capitals before stumbling against the New Jersey Devils. Down 3–2 in games and heading to New Jersey, Messier guaranteed a victory, then backed it up with a hat trick to force a Game 7. Back at the Garden, Stephane Matteau blasted in the game-winner in double-overtime, and the Rangers had returned to the finals for the first time since 1979.

The Rangers were favored against the surprising Vancouver Canucks, but in Game 1 New York let a 2–1 lead slip away with a minute left and then fell in overtime. They bounced back, winning the next three games with relative ease, 3–1, 5–1, and 4–2. Up 3–1 in games, the Rangers were just one win away from eradicating 54 years of futility.

But disaster struck as the Rangers got slapped 6–3 at home, then 4–1 in Vancouver. The Finals were tied at 3–3, but the Canucks had all the momentum. (NHL officials were probably thrilled, however, since the drama captivated America in a way hockey rarely does.) Keenan was losing control of his team, but before Game 7 on June 14, despite knowing that many of his players despised him, he delivered a pregame speech that Messier called the best ever. "Go out and win it for each other," Keenan urged them. "If you do, you will walk together the rest of your lives."

The Rangers had fallen behind in each of the previous five games, but in the finale they seized the lead and never relinquished it. With the first period about halfway done, Messier burst past Canuck star Pasha Bure, then dumped the puck to Sergei Zubov. As the Canucks followed the action to the right side, Leetch was wide open on the left. Zubov found him, and Leetch angled in a wrist shot for his eleventh goal of the playoffs and his fifth of the finals (the latter number tying a record for defensemen). While Leetch had been riding high, Graves had seemingly vanished—he had not scored since Game 3 of the Devils series. But three minutes after Leetch's success, Graves found himself wide open, the puck heading his way from Alexei Kovalev via Zubov, and smacked it home for a 2–0 lead.

In the second period, the Canucks halved the lead when Trevor Linden came off the bench on a delayed penalty, took the puck at center ice, stayed a stride ahead of Leetch, and knocked in a goal. It took eight minutes (and a Mike Richter skate-save against another Linden shot), but at 12:46 the Rangers built their lead back up. It wasn't pretty, but it counted: Brian Noonan's pass to Graves was blocked, but Noonan recovered and shot. No good. As the puck rebounded away it either hit a Vancouver defender or was hit by a diving Graves or a swiping Messier. The scorer gave the goal to Messier, and since the Rangers made it stand up as the winning goal, that was, symbolically anyway, the perfect call.

The third finally arrived. The Rangers were 20 minutes from heaven. But Vancouver played aggressively, and New York found itself in a fight to hold on. On a power play at 4:50, Linden struck again: 3–2. There was plenty of time left, too much time for Ranger fans who'd watched so many leads vanish in the closing minutes.

Over the next two-plus minutes, Richter kicked away a Nathan LaFayette shot, Leetch struggled to crack down on a 2-on-1, then Linden nearly snuck a shot in from the corner. Heart attacks all around.

With seven minutes remaining, Vancouver's Martin Gelinas nearly tied it, but the puck hit the outside of the post and ricocheted off Richter. A half-minute later, Richter blocked a shot, but Vancouver recovered and LaFayette missed by a half-inch on Richter's glove side. Could one period last an eternity?

Time ticked slowly away, but in the final minute, when Vancouver pulled its goalie for an extra scorer, the Rangers smothered every desperate Canuck attempt. Finally, Zubov controlled the puck and found Steve Larmer, who backhanded the black disk away and down the ice, out of danger. The final seconds drained away . . . but wait. The ref called icing, halting any premature celebration with 1.1 seconds left . . . and the refs added a half-second back onto the clock. One last chance. All in.

The puck dropped. MacTavish tied up Bure and slid the puck harmlessly into the corner. At 10:59 P.M., the Rangers were NHL champions, and "1940" was just a year, not a taunt.

Messier, who notched 12 goals and added 18 assists in 23 playoff games, leaped in the air and the party began. Moments later, commissioner Gary Bettman held the coveted silver hardware and stated, "Captain Mark Messier, come get the Stanley Cup."

To the tune of Tina Turner's "Simply the Best," Messier, in a Rangers sweater, posed for photos with Bettman, then took the Cup and lifted it over his head. The team passed it around, skating across the ice with it, while the fans chanted, "We got the Cup!" and "1994!" Up in the stands, one sign read, NOW I CAN DIE IN PEACE.

There'd be no peace that night or in the days ahead. Only wild, giddy, prideful fun. The Rangers took the Cup to a party on the Upper East Side, and so many fans flocked there that the police had to block off the street. Esa Tikkanen carried the Cup out to show the crowd, then late into the night (or early into the morning), Messier and others began its tour by taking it to the strip club Scores. Then it was on to David Letterman's show, Gracie Mansion, Belmont Park, center court back at the Garden during the NBA Finals, Yankee Stadium, and, of course, down Broadway for a ticker-tape parade . . . just like the video finally come to life.

# 13. The Giants crush the Bears in the NFL Championship, December 30, 1956, Yankee Stadium

On November 25, 1956, the New York Giants led the Chicago Bears 17–3 after three quarters. Feeling confident, offensive coach Vince Lombardi ordered his men to play conservative and start killing the clock. Fifteen minutes is a lot of time to chew up, especially against an elite team. Chicago's Harlon Hill made two superb end zone grabs as Chicago came back to snare a 17–17 tie. Lombardi was furious with himself. Never again would he keep such a tight rein on his offense for such a long period. "From then on, we played every game like the score was nothing to nothing," Lombardi said later.

On December 30, 1956, the Giants and Bears met again, this time for the NFL Championship. The story of this title game is one of lessons learned — the lessons not only of that November tie but also of the Giants' 1934 championship win over Chicago, when they discovered the benefits of sneakers on an icy field. It was also a story of lessons taught — lessons about the power of this burgeoning sport to attract the attention (and the dollars) of a nation.

The 9–2–1 Bears were slight favorites — they scored 363 points in 1956, 63 more than the second-best team and 100 more than the 8–3–1 Giants. Ed Brown was the league's most effective quarterback, Rick Casares was second in rushing, and Hill was tops among receivers in yards and touchdowns.

But these Giants were a balanced, well-coached, and smart team with the fifth-best offense and the fourth-best defense, both overseen by future legends — the former by Vince Lombardi, the latter by Tom Landry. In addition to the five eventual Hall of Famers in their lineup (Sam Huff, Andy Robustelli, Roosevelt Brown, Frank Gifford, and Em Tunnell), there were a half-dozen NFL head coaches-to-be (such as Bill Austin and Harland Svare) as well as coordinators-in-waiting (like Bob Schnelker). Everything gelled that year — from the preseason trade bringing Robustelli to anchor the defense to the move from the decrepit Polo Grounds to Yankee Stadium, a first-class ballpark with a tradition of winning. The stadium switch gave a seasonlong boost: attendance jumped to 45,000 from 25,000, and Giants games suddenly became the place to be in New York, much the way Knicks games would be in the early 1970s and 1990s.

The team hadn't played for a championship in a decade, yet the players were loose and confident. "I smell something," Lombardi said the week before the game, implying that the assuredness, the overall aura guaranteed a win. Dick Modzelewski, Huff, and others played poker the night before, and in the locker room before the game they all clowned around. Perhaps they believed in themselves, or perhaps their understanding of the past had led them to know they were better prepared than their opponent.

There's a long-standing myth about "Mara weather," the supposedly balmy temperatures that blessed the Giants in big games. It's a fallacy. Many of the Giants' most notable wins were played in arctic conditions. This one would be no different — after a night of sleet, the temperature hovered in the low teens while winds rattled at 30 miles per hour. But Giants team owner Wellington Mara remembered well the 1934 "Sneaker Game" and was ready this time. He asked Robustelli, who owned a sporting goods store in Connecticut, for 48 pairs of thick, rubber-soled sneakers. The sneakers arrived right before game time. Gifford, who had tested cleats earlier on the frozen dirt surface, knew how hard and slick it was and how difficult it would be to make cuts and move aggressively without sneakers.

The first play set the tone: Gene Filipski charged the opening kickoff back from his eight-yard line 53 yards, while the Bears, who were trying shortened cleats, shimmied around, uncertain of their footing. Don Heinrich connected on a third-down, 21-yard pass to Frank Gifford, then Mel Triplett churned out 17 yards, lugging several Bears into the end zone.

Blink and you missed it: the Giants led 7–0. The Bears were stunned.

Less than two minutes later, Casares coughed up the ball near Chicago's 15, and Robustelli scooped it up. After Ben Agajanian lofted a field goal, Jimmy Patton picked off Brown's pass and, thanks to a perfect block by Svare, ran 26 yards to Chicago's 37, setting up another Agajanian field goal.

Blink and you missed it: the Giants led 13–0. The Bears were essentially beaten.

Recalling Lombardi's dictum, there was no letup. The Giants stopped the Bears on fourth-and-one near the end of the first quarter, then pounded

**Frank Gifford plows through Chicago's overmatched defense as the Giants rout the Bears.**

home 21 more points in the second, including a five-play, 71-yard drive helmed by Charlie Conerly and another clutch defensive effort: Ray Beck, who had lost playing time to the younger, more talented Huff, blocked a Chicago punt in the Bears' end zone, and rookie Henry Moore fell on the ball for another touchdown.

Blink and you missed it: the halftime score was 34–7. The Bears were buried alive.

The Bears finally switched in the second half to flat-soled sneakers, which helped a bit, but it was too late. Or perhaps on this day the Giants—especially that defense—was too much to handle no matter what the footwear. As Casares, who was held to 43 yards on 14 carries, said afterwards, "The Giants hit you hard on one play, harder on the next."

The Giants tacked on another touchdown in the third and another in the fourth; it's notable that they scored both from the air—the first on a nine-yarder from Conerly to Kyle Rote, the second an eleven-yarder from Conerly to Gifford—when they could easily have stuck to running plays. In this game, Lombardi played everything full steam ahead.

Finally, at 47–7, the Giants finished scoring. The Bears were just finished.

The game was not front-page news in New York—football hadn't yet earned such prestige—but it helped blaze the trail. Everything was coming together for the NFL: attendance was rising; CBS and NBC—which had earlier rejected football—had begun televising games in 1956, and NBC carried the championship; and *Sports Illustrated,* which had just started a weekly pro football section that year, called the championship a "sporting thrill to match the drama" of

Don Larsen's perfect game in that October's World Series.

In the aftermath, the nation's top communicators, both in newsrooms and on Madison Avenue, took a new look at football and now saw it as an action-packed drama with charismatic stars, a game America might be ready to tackle. Players like Conerly and Gifford suddenly had an air of glamour, landing endorsements and radio and television gigs. This in turn paved the way for the excitement surrounding the 1958 title game between the Giants and the Baltimore Colts. Later known as "the Greatest Game Ever Played," it catapulted the NFL toward where it is today: a supremely lucrative sport with its deciding game not just front-page news but a national holiday.

"We won in Madison Avenue's backyard," Rote said later. "These admen were young guys—bright and sharp—but they'd never had an NFL champion in their own backyard. This propelled football far beyond what it would have been had a Green Bay won the title or a Cleveland."

## 14. CCNY wins its second national championship . . . of the month, March 28, 1950, Madison Square Garden

Before the fall came the last days of innocence. For New York and for college basketball, those days were in 1950, a transcendent moment when the city was still the center of the basketball world, college players were still hardworking, upstanding young men, and CCNY's basketball team rocked the rafters of Madison Square Garden as it bathed its hometown in sports glory.

For now at least erase all that followed: the 1951 revelations that CCNY's stars were deeply enmeshed in a widespread point-shaving scandal that would stun the sports world and haunt the city hoops scene for generations. Instead, live in the blissful ignorance that prevailed in much of the city during that dizzying 18-day run in March 1950 when the Beavers won both the National Invitational Tournament (NIT) and the NCAA tourney. CCNY's timing was perfect: the NFL and particularly the new NBA were still small-fry (the Knicks played at the 69th Street Armory or shared Madison Square Garden bills with teams from Gimbel's versus A&S), college football's season was long over and largely irrelevant in New York schools, and baseball—the city's other true love—was lounging down in spring training. All eyes were on Madison Square Garden, which had been college basketball's mecca since the first successful double-header staged there in 1934.

CCNY had never reached the finals of the prestigious NIT nor its less-heralded rival, the smaller NCAA tourney. As this season opened in 1949, few expected greatness; coach Nat Holman's charges, mostly sophomores, seemed at least a year away from contention. The team looked immature in its wild unpredictability, blowing through lesser opponents like Brooklyn College, losing to elite Oklahoma, toppling top-ranked St. John's, then falling to unheralded Niagara. With five losses before season's end, CCNY nearly was shut out of the postseason before beating Manhattan College and NYU to snatch the final NIT slot. As the 27th-ranked team, with no All-America stars, CCNY seemed destined for the sidelines. How could these erratic kids beat the defending NIT champs from San Francisco, third-ranked Kentucky, sixth-ranked Duquesne, and Bradley, the nation's numero uno? Only a strong showing in the NIT would earn them an NCAA slot.

"I hope we can justify the invitation," said Holman. For those interested in gambling, Bradley was the favorite at 3–1, then Kentucky at 7–2. CCNY was the long shot at 9–1.

The roster was mostly blacks and Jews who had a difficult time gaining admission to a private university and who commuted from around the city without the benefit of a full athletic scholarship.

At center was sophomore Ed Roman, the big man, 6'6" and 220 pounds, from Taft High School in the Bronx. The forwards were Irwin Dambrot, the only senior and only married starter, who'd also gone to Taft, and Ed Warner, an orphan from Harlem who had perfected his no-nonsense work ethic at De Witt Clinton High in the Bronx. The guards were Floyd Layne, also an outstanding lefty pitcher, from Benjamin Franklin High in Manhattan, and playmaker Al Roth from Erasmus High in Brooklyn, who'd turned down numerous scholarships because his immigrant family wanted him close to home. Key players off the bench were sixth man Norm Mager, now a senior, from Lafayette High in Brooklyn, and Roth's Erasmus teammate Herb Cohen.

Some disliked the cold, imperious Nat Holman, but they bought into his coaching style. One of early basketball's greatest players, Holman put an emphasis on team basketball that not only led CCNY to unexpected heights but would reverberate a generation later when his protégé, Red Holzman, taught the same fundamentals to the New York Knicks. The Beavers were undersized but quick, and they excelled at rotating on defense, helping out and clogging the middle. At season's end, Holman occasionally shifted Warner into the low post, a new wrinkle that freed Roman to shoot from outside and kept teams guessing.

When the tournament began, CCNY suddenly went from inconsistent to invincible. The team gelled at the right time, challenging foes with a New Yorker's swagger and an aggressiveness on both ends of the court that reflected childhoods spent playing rough-and-tumble half-court games on warped rims. (As the world would later learn, they also stopped taking gamblers' bribes in the postseason.)

CCNY's other edge, as long as they didn't play other local schools like St. John's, was the hometown crowd, which virtually shook the Garden's walls and rattled opponents with the strange but unforgettable chant, "Allagaroo-garoo-garah, allagaroo-garoo-garah; ee-yah, ee-yah; sis-boom-bah." ("Allagaroo" was most likely a corruption of the French phrase "allez guerre," meaning "on to war.")

In the NIT, CCNY demolished their opposition. They shredded San Francisco by 19 points. Then came Kentucky, headed by legendary Adolph Rupp, a hard-core segregationist, who provided the New Yorkers with unintended inspiration, especially when some of his players refused to shake hands with CCNY's starters. (It was the first time Kentucky faced blacks in an official game.) Upping the ante, Holman shrewdly put in his backup center, 6'7" Leroy Watkins, for the opening jump against Kentucky's seven-footer Bill Spivey. Holman wanted his black player to rattle the Wildcats. Watkins controlled the ball, and though he was quickly replaced, CCNY raced out to a 13–1 start. They led by 25 at the half and won 89–50. "We were sky-high for Kentucky," Layne said later. It was the worst loss Rupp ever suffered; the Kentucky legislature proposed flying the state flag at half-mast.

CCNY's 10-point trouncing of sixth-ranked Duquesne put them in the NIT finals and earned them a spot in the NCAA tournament. Facing a team as middle America as it gets in the finals—Bradley from Peoria—CCNY was motivated to

**CCNY hoists up coach Nat Holman in celebration after winning their second championship . . . of the month.**

prove that city kids were best at the city game. Holman had a 103-degree fever, and the Beavers looked frazzled early, trailing the Braves 29–18; after Mager calmed them down, however, the Beavers didn't allow a field goal in the half's final six minutes, gnawing away to 30–27 at intermission. In the second half, the lead changed hands seven times. Bradley led 56–55 with less than five minutes to go when Warner—soon to be the first black tournament MVP—poured in several crucial buckets, sparking a 14–5 run. CCNY finished pulling away, 69–61.

The Beavers were NIT champs and the new darlings of New York. Classes were canceled, and 6,000 students attended a celebration; the team was also called to City Hall for honors. These players were embraced because they were not carpetbaggers seeking fame and fortune in the big city but part of the city fabric—they'd starred at your high school or grown up down the block from your cousin. The day after the finals, Ed Roman was playing pickup games at Claremont Park.

Within days the quest was on for a second championship. No one had ever won both, and CCNY got a quick lesson in why: CCNY was not nearly as fresh as they'd been, and making three more matchups with elite teams was going to be a daunting task. In the first game, the Beavers trailed second-ranked Ohio State by 52–49 before escaping with a 56–55 win. Against North Carolina State, the lead ping-ponged back and forth 14 times before CCNY pulled out a 78–73 victory.

One game remained, a rematch against Bradley. On March 28, the Garden was jammed with

CCNY rooters. Bradley had played man-to-man defense in the NIT, but Braves coach Forrest Anderson, knowing his team was tired too, started in a zone. (The Braves had an even longer road back, having to fly to Kansas to win a special playoff before topping Baylor and UCLA.)

The Beavers were undeterred. Ed Roman spread the zone by shifting from the pivot to the outside and pouring in 12 points in the first 12 minutes. The rest of the team shot well, and the Beavers led at the half 39–32. Just before halftime, Mager collided with Bradley's Aaron Preece, but in the locker room he bit down on a piece of balsa wood as the team doctor sewed five stitches so he could return in the second half.

Bradley returned to man-to-man, but their players hit foul trouble while CCNY built a double-digit lead. Then Roman fouled out with nine minutes left, and the Beavers tired and turned sloppy. Bradley choked off their less experienced opponent with a full-court press, and with two minutes left the CCNY lead was down to 66–61.

Still, in the days before shot clocks, five points seemed fairly safe. And it would have been, except for Bradley's 5'8" whirlwind of a guard, Gene "Squeaky" Melchiorre.

Melchiorre swiped a pass and dribbled half the length of the court to score. 66–63.

Mager hit a free throw, and Dambrot scored a bucket. It was 69–63 with a mere 57 seconds left. Now that had to be safe.

But the press had CCNY rattled, and Melchiorre revved: after Brave Joe Stowell sank a foul shot, Melchiorre grabbed a loose ball and drove for a lay-up, then intercepted a pass and converted again. In 17 seconds almost the entire lead vanished: 69–68.

With 30 seconds remaining, the smallest player did it again. Melchiorre nabbed a CCNY pass and burst full tilt for the basket. Dambrot desperately raced back and used the angle to cut Melchiorre off. The Brave pulled up instead for a short jumper and. . . .

Well, if you lived in Peoria, you thought Squeaky was fouled and the Braves cheated of their shot at victory. But in the Garden, it looked for all the world like Dambrot cleanly blocked the shot. There was no call. Dambrot grabbed the ball and fired to Mager, downcourt by himself. Mager laid it in, and it was all over. CCNY 71, Bradley 68.

The Beavers were the first squad to ever wear two crowns. And they'd done it as a team — that night Dambrot scored 15 points, Mager and Warner 14, Roman 12, and Layne 11. (They were also the first NCAA champ with black starters.)

If the city was excited by the first win, they were practically delirious after the second. Floyd Layne said CCNY was to New York what the Dodgers were to Brooklyn, a strange approximation but accurate in its sense of intimacy. And these were real students — you had to be to go to "the poor man's Harvard." During the tournaments, while the visiting teams concentrated on basketball, CCNY students attended class.

In his superb rumination on that championship season and the scandal that followed, *The Game They Played,* Stanley Cohen writes that this team seduced the city, even people who didn't follow basketball, because they were true New Yorkers, underdogs who made good through determination and hard work. "The national champions were kids like us — Jews and blacks mostly, sons of immigrants and grandsons of slaves — and they had taught us, demonstrated, that we could share equal footing with the best that America could offer."

This time around the whole nation toasted the team — newspapers across the nation touted this unique feat, and Holman earned an appearance on Ed Sullivan's television show. Heady times indeed.

A year later, of course, it all crashed down. Worst of all was the revelation that the 1949–50 narrative was false: at least two regular-season losses were games in which the team shaved too closely. Seven key team members were implicated, and the team and school were accused of doctoring transcripts to ensure eligibility. The school never played at the Garden again, and the NCAA soon moved all its games away from this den of iniquity.

Had CCNY stood alone, perhaps the shame

would have been so great that it would still be impossible to forgive, to separate out what they did, the great from the terrible. But the scandal permeated all college hoops, and even LIU, Bradley, and Kentucky were caught up and pulled down. "I don't condone what they did or give it a pass, but I don't think you can take away from the fact that in spite of what they did during the regular season, they were able to accomplish something unique," Cohen says today.

The much-repeated American myth is that life was simpler, more wholesome in the 1950s. It is, of course, patently false. It only seemed so on the surface. Yet while it's healthy to demythologize our heroes and see their human flaws, sometimes we also need to celebrate their achievements. Let's freeze this moment then: a time when the smiles, the laughter, the chants and cheers, the proclamations and celebrations really were pure and wonderful.

# 15. Willie Mays makes "the Catch," September 29, 1954, Polo Grounds

A kiss is just a kiss, went Bogie's song in *Casablanca.*

Sometimes a cigar is just a cigar, Sigmund Freud famously insisted.

But a catch is not just a catch. Not when it's "the Catch."

Willie Mays's over-the-shoulder haul of Vic Wertz's long, long, long fly in Game 1 of the World Series at the Polo Grounds on September 29, 1954, is the greatest defensive play in baseball history even though Mays himself made catches that were more athletically spectacular. What made this catch so much more memorable was a confluence of factors: the growing stature of the man who made the play, the number of people who saw him do it, and the events that followed, from "the Throw" to a pipsqueak pinch-hit home run to a World Series sweep to a sudden tilt toward the National League that lasted more than a decade.

First, consider Mays himself.

Mays had been the first young black player nurtured through the minors by a major league club (earlier stars like Jackie Robinson, Don Newcombe, and Larry Doby had been older, more established Negro League players), and his astonishing skills and smarts, combined with his great showmanship and joy in playing (he wore an oversized cap so it would fly off to make plays seem extra thrilling), seduced anyone who saw him play. Unlike Robinson, Mays didn't have to be a pioneer, so he could be an idol, a superstar. His enthusiasm was so contagious that fans used to come to spring training workouts to watch him play pepper. As major leaguer Ted Kluszewski once said, "I'm not sure what the hell charisma is, but I get the feeling it's Willie Mays."

As a rookie in 1951, he helped propel the Giants to the National League pennant. When he left for the Army in 1952, they were in first. Without him, they finished second, then fifth in 1953. A mythology built up around him. When *New York Herald-Tribune* writer Roger Kahn was assigned to the Giants in 1954, he had never seen Mays play but heard so much in spring training that he satirized the breathless descriptions: "Willie Mays is 10 feet 9 inches tall. He can jump fifteen feet straight up. Willie's arms extend roughly from 157th Street to 159th Street. . . . Willie can throw sidearm from the Polo Grounds to Pittsburgh. . . . The best evidence indicates he is a step faster than electricity."

Then Kahn watched Mays play and realized the hyperbole had been an understatement. "This is not going to be a plausible story, but then no one ever accused Willie Mays of being a plausible ball player. This story is only the implausible truth."

In that implausible 1954 season, Mays hit 36 homers in 99 games and had a shot at Babe Ruth's 60, but when manager Leo Durocher asked him to hit for average to help the team, Mays hit just five more homers but raised his average to .345, winning the batting title on the season's final day. Though the Giants were inferior to National League rivals Brooklyn and Milwaukee in many regards, Mays carried his team to the pennant.

By the time the World Series rolled around, everyone around the country had heard about Mays, but like Roger Kahn that spring, they needed to see him to believe him. Thanks to television, everyone could. Bobby Thomson's "Shot Heard Round the World" had brought sports to nationwide television in 1951, but just three years later (thanks largely to *I Love Lucy*) the total number of television sets had more than doubled to 32 million from perhaps 15 million. This may be hard to fathom in today's multichannel, fragmented universe, but with very few channels, television really did bind the nation together in a new way. When Wertz hit the ball, it wasn't just the ticket-holders watching—an entire nation turned its eyes to Mays. This up-close look at genius in action provided instant proof that live television could capture the immediacy and intensity of sports. "The game that changed the way we watched baseball was the first game of the 1954 World Series," Peter Gammons once wrote. (Ironically, just as Thomson owes much of his stature to a radio call, Mays's "Catch" derives much of its impact from a series of four still photos that froze this fleeting moment forever.)

Then there's circumstance. Timing is everything in life: a great catch in a World Series accrues more weight than one during a pennant race, which matters more than one in late May, which counts more than a spring training eye-opener, which lines up ahead of plays in the minors.

Mays made dozens of seemingly impossible plays at all times of the year. The stories have taken on a distinctive John Henry–esque folktale flavor, told as if sitting around a woodstove in winter, baseball men topping each other with their tales of the greatest play they saw Mays make. Many cite a play on August 15, 1951, in a 1–1 game against Brooklyn when Carl Furillo flew to medium-deep right-center with Billy Cox tagging from third. Mays couldn't throw across his body on the dead run, so he improvised a new move, coming down hard on his left foot, spinning counterclockwise away from the infield and back around, letting fly a bullet to the plate that stunned Cox. The late broadcaster Jack Buck spoke of watching Mays in Minneapolis in the minors run to the fence in left-center, catch the ball while climbing the wall, somersault, and then throw on target to second. Branch Rickey was awed by a play in Pittsburgh when Mays raced to deep right-center and, seeing the ball hooking less and sinking faster than he'd anticipated, reached behind and barehanded it on the dead run.

Mays has cited different favorites in different interviews: in the minor leagues he reached over the center-field fence, caught the ball barehanded, landed, and fired a strike on the fly to home plate 405 feet away; in the ninth inning at Ebbets Field in 1952, he ranged into the left fielder's territory to make a diving catch at the fence, knocking himself unconscious but holding on to the ball; and at the 1955 All-Star Game he robbed Ted Williams of a homer with a leaping catch in right-center.

All were miracles in their own right, but only one came in Game 1 of the World Series, and only one turned the tide against a heavily favored Cleveland team that had won an unimaginable 111 games, ending the Yankees' reign and possibly starting a new dynasty. In the bottom line of history, that one counted most.

The first game's excruciating tension made Mays's play even more dramatic. Wertz tripled in two runs in the first off Sal Maglie. Desperate to avoid getting in a deep hole against Cleveland's Bob Lemon, Durocher had reliever Don Liddle start warming up immediately. Would the Indians annihilate the Giants, as many had predicted?

Mays popped up in the bottom of the first with two on, but walked in the midst of the Giants' third-inning rally that tied the game. In the sixth, Wertz singled for his third hit and was on third with two out when Jim Hegan smashed a grounder at third baseman Henry Thompson, who couldn't handle it. It seemed that Wertz would score the go-ahead run (in which case, Mays's eighth-inning catch might have been moot), but Thompson recovered, grabbed the ball, and barely got Cleveland's catcher to preserve the 2–2 tie.

It was still tied in the top of the eighth when Larry Doby walked and Al Rosen got an infield hit. Alvin Dark's hustle at shortstop prevented the ball from going through, and Doby from going to third, which again would have altered history. With the lefty Wertz wielding his dangerous bat, Durocher brought in the southpaw Liddle.

Liddle threw one pitch. Wertz crushed it. The ball hurtled through space, heading hard and fast and not terribly high to center. Given enough space and a high enough arc on the ball, Mays could run down anything, but this was more a deadly liner, its harsher trajectory slicing off its hang time. Mays always played a shallow center field, but with a ground-ball pitcher and the go-ahead run on second hoping to score on a single, he'd crept in extra close.

This was no single. Mays, shaded slightly toward right-center, raced head down toward the spot where he and only he knew the ball would land. That spot was about 460 feet from home plate. Yet when it fell to earth, Mays was there to intercept it. Joe DiMaggio and Hank Leiber each made longer catches in the Polo Grounds during the 1936 World Series, but on much higher flies. In his classic book *A Day in the Bleachers,* Arthur Hano pointed out that Mays surely would have made those plays, but no one but Mays could have made this one.

If "the Catch" was the picture-perfect demonstration of Mays's speed and grace, "the Throw" that followed was a dynamic display of his brains and brawn.

Mays, knowing his own speed and uncanny judgment, never doubted he'd outrun Wertz's smash, but, as he told Roger Kahn, "that wasn't the problem."

Unless the throw was as perfect as the catch, Doby could easily tag and score from second. Mays knew his flat-out run posed a major problem. "Suppose I stop and turn and throw. I will get nothing on the ball, no momentum," he told Kahn. "To keep my momentum, to get it working for me, I have to turn very hard and short and throw the ball from exactly the point I caught it. The momentum goes into my turn and up through my legs and into my throw."

Mays slowed almost imperceptibly before catching the ball. He stopped, whirled, and hurled the ball back to second baseman Davey Williams in the infield without looking. His hat flew off, and his momentum spun him around and carried him down so that he landed on his stomach facing the wall. Many of his teammates were actually expecting him to make the catch, but no one was prepared for this throw. Even if another center fielder somehow had the speed and mental dexterity Mays did, no one else had the calculation, coordination, and strength to pull it off. The play made "all other throws ever before it . . . appear the flings of teen-age girls," Hano wrote. "This was the throw of a giant, the throw of a howitzer made human."

Rosen, thinking he was going to score on a triple, had already rounded second and had to scramble back to first. Doby, who had tagged up anticipating the catch, still could advance no farther than third. The rally crashed in Mays's glove

Back, back, back . . . Willie Mays runs down Vic Wertz's eighth-inning blast, then whirls and makes an astonishing throw.

and died with his throw. Liddle was lifted for Marv Grissom, who escaped the jam when the wind kept Hegan's long fly in the park. "Maybe the whole Series turned around on Mays's play," Rosen said later.

The game went into extra innings, and again Mays and Wertz found themselves on center stage. In the 10th, Wertz walloped one in the gap in left-center. This ball should have slithered through to the wall, either a leadoff triple (likely doom for New York) or an inside-the-park homer (near-certain doom). Mays, playing Wertz to pull, was annoyed with himself for not realizing Grissom was pitching Wertz away but made up for it by bending, scooping the low bounce barehanded on the run, and firing an impossibly powerful and accurate peg to third base, halting Wertz at second. Mays called this play more difficult and critical, yet it's usually overlooked. "At this point, I think, the Indians quit," Hano wrote. "When Mays again indicated he was not Mays, but Superman—they must have known they were through."

Indeed they were. Grissom quashed the rally. After using pinch-hitters, the Indians inserted backup catcher Mickey Grasso. Mays, ever alert, noticed that he didn't throw to second in warm-ups. Covering up a sore arm perhaps? Mays wanted to know. He drew a one-out walk, then lit out for second. Grasso's throw bounced well before the base. Mays's steal provoked the Indians into walking Henry Thompson, giving Durocher the opportunity to send up pinch-hitter extraordinaire Dusty Rhodes.

On a hanging curve from the righty Lemon, the lefty Rhodes pulled a soft pop toward the right side. Indian second baseman Bobby Avila started going back for it. But the wind or the fates or something carried it to the short porch 257 feet away in right. Hit some 200 feet less than Wertz's eighth-inning out, Rhodes's shot was a game-winning three-run homer.

In the clubhouse, Durocher walked toward Mays, his hand outstretched. One-pitch Liddle intercepted him, mockingly accepted the congratulations, and quipped, "I got my guy." (The following year, when Don's son Craig needed a glove for Little League, Mays tossed him his leather from 1954, saying, "Take care of this." Craig later loaned the Rawlings glove that had made "the Catch" to the Baseball Hall of Fame.)

Over the next three games Wertz produced eight hits, double Mays's total, but he couldn't compete—Charles Einstein, author of the memoir *Willie's Time,* pointed out that the Giants scored in eleven different innings and Mays was involved in eight of those. Rhodes too was unstoppable: in the first three games he drove in seven runs in just six at-bats; the Indians scored just five in that span.

The Indians were not as great as their record indicated: they'd beaten up on weak teams and were just 11–11 against the Yankees and Chicago White Sox, the only other AL teams to win more than 70 games. Having coasted for weeks, Cleveland was unprepared for a stiff challenge and collapsed after Mays's Game 1 performance as the Giants swept the Series, the first time an AL team had been swept since 1922. The loss was devastating. Yankees general manager George Weiss's dread about a new rival for AL supremacy evaporated. "I thought we would have a long, tough struggle to get back up there," he said afterwards. "I don't see how the Indians are going to recover from this." They didn't, becoming an awful team for four decades. They have not won the World Series since.

This World Series and Mays's performance demonstrated just how much the game had changed since Jackie Robinson's arrival. Cleveland—the first AL team to integrate—was the only non-Yankee AL team to reach the Series since then (they'd won in 1948), while Brooklyn and New York had dominated the NL. But in 1954, Mays, the ultimate mix of dramatic flair, superior talent, aggressive style, and a keen understanding of the game, was heading a new class of black and Latino superstars developed by the more welcoming National League. The AL had won 15 of the previous 19 World Series, but the NL, led by Mays, Hank Aaron, Roberto Clemente, Bob Gibson, and Lou Brock, would reel off 8 titles in 12 years. Only when Frank Robinson went from Cincinnati to Baltimore in 1966 would things even out.

A convincing case can be made that Mays's persona and performance throughout 1954, but particularly in his defining moment in this Game 1 classic, paved the way for this second wave of integration, encouraging owners and fans alike to open their eyes and their hearts to these players.

When Indians manager Al Lopez said, "Willie Mays made that great catch and we were never the same," he was talking about his club in that World Series, but he could have been talking about us all.

# 16. Jack Dempsey outslugs Luis Firpo, September 14, 1923, Polo Grounds

Boxing is the "sweet science," a complex sport with layers of nuance involving footwork, psychology, and strategy.

Aw hell, let's be honest, what fight fans really want is a damn slugfest. And for a feast of flying fists, no bout can top the fast and furious Jack Dempsey–Luis Firpo punch-a-thon at the Polo Grounds on September 14, 1923. It lasted less than two rounds and was marred by rule violations and poor refereeing, yet it's commonly hailed as the most thrilling fight of all time.

Jack Dempsey's mother told him he was fated to be a boxer because during her pregnancy she read and reread a book about heavyweight champ John L. Sullivan. Dempsey was the ninth of eleven children in a poor family and had left home to work an array of jobs while living in "hobo jungles" out west. He began boxing in saloons and mining towns. Although his ducking and sidestepping techniques were influential, he was best known for the ferocity of his attacks. In 1919 he overcame unfair accusations about draft-dodging during World War I to become a popular champ, winning five straight first-round knockouts before capturing the heavyweight title by flattening champ Jess Willard in the third. In his third title defense, "the Manassa Mauler" firmly established himself as boxing's biggest draw with the sport's first million-dollar gate, for which he punched Georges Carpentier senseless in the fourth.

The only other top-flight contender was Harry Willis, who was black, and promoter Tex Rickard wouldn't let Dempsey fight him because Rickard was afraid of another potential black champion so soon after the flamboyant and turbulent reign of Jack Johnson. But questions remained about whether Dempsey was a true great, whether he'd respond if hit hard, and with worthy foes hard to come by, Dempsey barely fought in 1922 and for much of 1923. Rickard decided if he couldn't have quality, he'd get somebody who would be a good draw. He settled on Argentinean Luis Angel Firpo, who had the exotic but decidedly inappropriate nickname "the Wild Bull of the Pampas."

The 6'3", 216-pound Firpo was big, tough, and phenomenally strong, but, man, was he raw. Nat Fleischer, founder of *The Ring* magazine, wrote that Firpo had "only a vague idea of the finer points of pugilism." He'd grown up poor and worked as a laborer, butcher, and drugstore clerk before he began boxing for exercise and soon for money. He was not a wild bull but a reticent miser—he wore cheap clothes and refused to pay for trainers, managers, or sparring partners, preferring to train simply by fighting more bouts. (After becoming wealthy thanks to this fight, he turned quite generous, and once gave Dempsey a gift of $20,000.)

When Firpo made his deal with Rickard, he shrewdly insisted on foreign film rights to his bouts leading up to and including the Dempsey fight. While Dempsey trained near Saratoga Springs, Firpo went low-rent in Atlantic City and initially demanded payment from the press for interviews or photos. The night before the fight,

**Jack Dempsey is down and out . . . of the ring. Despite this astonishing first-round turn of events, Dempsey returns to KO Luis Firpo.**

wrote W. O. McGeehan in the *New York Herald,* Firpo sat in his hotel room "stark naked with a pencil in his hand," calculating how much he'd owe in taxes for his take.

That night fans, armed with food, binoculars, and extra clothes, camped out at the Polo Grounds to get bleacher seats. Fight night was crisp, in the mid-50s, as over 80,000 packed the ballpark and tens of thousands were turned away. (When a van arrived containing 3,800 tickets for last-minute sales, it was attacked by fans who were forcibly removed by cops wielding nightsticks.)

The best seats were filled with society names like Astor, Belmont, Morgan, Gould, Vanderbilt, Rothschild, and Whitney, entertainment figures like Flo Ziegfeld and John Ringling, and former champs Jim Corbett and Jess Willard. The New York Yankees and visiting Chicago White Sox were all there, as well as Giants manager John McGraw; Babe Ruth attracted all the buzz as he walked to his eighth-row seat.

What these people didn't know was that the fight was nearly called off. At weigh-in, Dr. William Walker thought Firpo's left elbow was dislocated and fractured and was set to cancel the fight when Firpo demonstrated his fitness by smashing his fist hard onto a table, gritting his teeth and forcing a smile through the agony. New York Medical

Commission chairman William Muldoon deemed the limb dislocated but not broken and jerked it sharply back into place. Firpo sweated profusely but didn't utter a sound. His swollen arm was bandaged until the fight.

The fisticuffs began at 10:02. Firpo looked somber, while Dempsey, giving away 24 pounds, waved to the crowd. Then the ring exploded with a purposeful violence no one could have imagined. The action was so frenetic that every newspaper account differs about what actually happened.

Dempsey rushed Firpo instantly, but for one brief moment Firpo showed surprising agility and technique, sidestepping the champ's first blow and delivering a quick left that sent Dempsey to one knee and the fans to their feet. They would not sit down again. (In the eighth row the bench toppled over, taking down Ruth, who angrily came up swinging at the nearest target, who happened to be middleweight Mickey Walker.)

Dempsey was more surprised than hurt and was up without a count. He roared in, but the two men got tangled and clinched. When the ref shouted, "Break," and Firpo naively let his hands drop, Dempsey, uninterested in decorum, floored the challenger with a right to the body. Firpo too popped right back, but he didn't stay upright for long.

The two were doing a vicious tango in the clinches when a Dempsey left to the top of the head sent Firpo to the canvas. In a move that altered this fight and boxing history, Dempsey did not retreat to a neutral corner, and referee Johnny Gallagher failed to make him. Firpo rose quickly, but Dempsey attacked, and a left to the body slammed Firpo back down. Again, Gallagher was lax. Encouraged, Dempsey continually stalked Firpo like prey, knocking him down, then lurking nearby and pouncing as soon as Firpo pulled himself up. The fourth knockdown came with a left to the body. Firpo was up by nine, but Dempsey was right there, drilling him with a big right that immediately floored him again.

Somehow Firpo hoisted himself up again and dropped Dempsey to all fours briefly with an overhead right. Then they traded blows, and Dempsey soon landed a right cross that scored his sixth knockdown. He hovered over Firpo, who tried getting up and covering up simultaneously, but Dempsey left no room and thrashed him once more. After this record seventh knockdown, Dempsey nonchalantly stepped over his fallen foe and lounged in the corner with his arms against the ropes, surveying the havoc he had wreaked. Amazingly, however, the bell still had not rung. Dempsey later admitted, "I just relaxed. I didn't think the man would get up again."

Firpo not only hauled himself up once more but escaped the corner for the center of the ring and started firing away. Catching Dempsey off guard, he backed the champ into the ropes, then fired a remarkable volley of rights. Just before the biggest right of them all, he stung Dempsey with a left uppercut that raised Dempsey's face right into the path of the crashing right overhead. Firpo's heavy punch seemingly stayed connected to Dempsey's head as he went down and out, through the ropes, completely out of the ring. (Some say the ropes weren't strung tightly enough.)

George Bellows's classic painting, which now hangs in the Whitney Museum, commemorates this notorious moment. Dempsey was lucky to escape—if he'd stayed upright, another blow would have knocked him out. He tumbled into the press row, jamming his hip on a wooden board and banging his neck and head on the typewriters of *New York Tribune* writer Jack Lawrence, Hype Igoe of the *New York World,* and Western Union telegraph operator Perry Grogan.

It was almost impossible for Dempsey to resurrect himself before a 10 count. But the referee reacted slowly, and the writers shoved Dempsey up and back into the ring. They claimed later that they were not unfairly abetting the American but merely removing an intruder, an obstacle to their writing, although they also claimed that Dempsey—despite being dazed and semiconscious—snarled in a rage, "Get me back in there. I'll fix him."

Gallagher should have disqualified the champ

but instead remained a passive bystander. Dempsey—who wouldn't remember leaving or climbing back in the ring—was groggy, swaying with his chin unprotected, yet Firpo was so surprised to discover the fight was still on, and so weakened himself, that he was unable to land the final big blow. The brief letup allowed Dempsey to tie Firpo up until the round ended.

After the bell, Dempsey prompted some boos when he threw a few extra weak punches, but he was unaware of the bell, unaware of the chaos around him, unaware of pretty much everything.

This fight was so action-packed that even the scene in the corner was exciting. Dempsey's manager Jack Kearns yelled at everyone, asking where the smelling salts were; he couldn't hear trainer Jerry Ludvadis shouting back that the salts were in Kearns's own pocket. Kearns instead tried rousing the fighter with a bucket of cold water over his head, and when Ludvadis reached for Kearns to pull the salts out, Kearns, not understanding the trainer's actions, punched Ludvadis. Kearns finally found the salts, and they helped Dempsey snap to . . . kind of: thinking he'd been through a war, he innocently asked what round it was, only to find out he'd made it through only one.

"I was seeing double," Dempsey said later. "When the bell rang, I went out and hit every Firpo I saw."

Firpo seemed revived, at least enough to rear back for another right. But Dempsey had that move read and stepped in with a left. They seemed to wrestle a bit, but soon Firpo was back on the canvas. Again he got up, this time with blood gushing from his face.

Firpo missed a wild right, then desperately tried clinching, but Dempsey was the very definition of relentless. He tore free and fired a left uppercut to Firpo's jaw and a right to his face. The mighty Argentinean toppled. This time it was for good. Firpo rolled over onto his stomach but couldn't pull himself up. At 58 seconds of Round 2, the count reached 10.

The fight raised a hue and cry from preachers and editorials denouncing the primitive blood lust it incited, and Dempsey (who rushed over to help Firpo up afterwards) was ripped for unethical, even treacherous behavior. (Ironically, in the aftermath the rules would be strengthened to force boxers to return to the neutral corner during a knockdown; in 1927 Dempsey would lose the famous "Long Count" fight to Gene Tunney because he forgot to retreat after flooring Tunney and the ref refused to count until Dempsey moved, giving Tunney at least an extra four or five seconds. Though Dempsey lost that fight, he gained new stature for his dignity in defeat.)

Yet many prominent writers, like Grantland Rice and Nat Fleischer, lambasted Dempsey's tactics while gushing effusively about the fight itself: Rice called it the "most sensational" fight he had ever seen, while Fleischer wrote that neither "Shakespeare nor Shaw could have constructed a greater drama."

By bravely withstanding such an assault, Firpo became a hero, and his tour of Latin and South America with his film reaped a fortune for him when it created demand for Firpo's Fedoras, Firpo's Fantasy Perfume, and other products. Streets and soccer teams were named for him throughout Latin and South America. He retired soon after, a millionaire. Meanwhile, despite the criticism of Dempsey's tactics and the fact that even he admitted that Firpo rightfully should have won when he flew out of the ring, his stature was enhanced by the bout too. Dempsey had responded to his greatest challenge with undeniable greatness, and he became nearly equal to Babe Ruth as an American hero of folktale proportions.

From Dempsey through Muhammad Ali in the 1970s, boxing would flourish for five decades—paralleling the heyday of its working-class fan base—and New York would be the venue for more memorable and important fights than any other city. Dempsey's appeal had been growing since the Willard fight, but it was the Dempsey-Firpo fight that made the champ an icon and hauled boxing up near baseball at the top of the sports heap.

# 17. Reggie, Reggie, Reggie, October 18, 1977, Yankee Stadium

*One swing. One homer.*

By 1977 the New York Yankees had not won a World Series in 14 years, three times as long as any other drought since Babe Ruth arrived in New York.

*A second swing. A second homer.*

The missing ingredient: a superstar slugger so dynamic he could be a household name, no last name necessary. A ballplayer, one might say, who was famous enough to have a candy bar named after him.

*A third swing. A third homer.*

The Yankees had won with the Babe, Joltin' Joe, and the Mick. Finally, in the 1977 World Series, a new king of the hill brought New York to the top of the heap.

*Reggie! Reggie! Reggie!*

Reginald Martinez Jackson became a superstar in 1969 by clouting 47 homers for Oakland. Two years later, he blasted 32, helping the A's win the AL West. He was perhaps the most colorful and talented of that rambunctious and unbeatable crew, which won three straight World Series beginning in 1972; Jackson won the 1973 MVP and landed on the cover of *Time* in 1974. He led the league in homers in 1975, but a contract dispute and impending free agency prompted maverick (and cheap) owner Charlie Finley to trade him to Baltimore in 1976. Then the man who once said, "If I played in New York, they'd name a candy bar after me," passed up more lucrative offers to bask in the spotlight of the nation's media capital, where George Steinbrenner had become the Yankees' unlikely savior, resurrecting the franchise and revolutionizing the game with his headfirst slide into free agency.

The Yankees had reached the World Series in 1976 but were swept by the powerful Cincinnati Reds, so Steinbrenner imported the big bat and defining presence he thought the Bombers needed, even though his manager, the fire-breathing Billy Martin, a tactical genius with no people skills, vehemently objected.

And thus "the Bronx Zoo" was born. Jackson wasted no time in shining the light on himself at the expense of any team concept. "I didn't come to New York to become a star," he said upon his arrival. "I brought my star with me."

Martin did his best to antagonize Jackson and refused to bat him cleanup, even though this decision hurt the club. His teammates—jealous over Jackson's salary and celebrity—did their best to alienate him, and the fans and the media poured on more pressure. Some of this reaction to Jackson was racism—baseball's old school (which certainly included Martin and perhaps catcher and captain Thurman Munson and much of the press) still couldn't handle a commanding and outspoken black man. Martin, whose alcohol problems only fueled his nasty disposition, was a hero among the blue-collar New Yorkers in full "white flight" for the 'burbs in 1977. But Jackson, with his massive ego and a mouth to match, deserved his share of blame. In June, *Sport* magazine quoted Jackson as calling himself "the straw that stirs the drink" while also badmouthing Munson.

In *Ladies and Gentlemen, the Bronx is Burning,* Jonathan Mahler noted that the Yankees' turmoil was a reflection of a city in disarray and possibly out of control that summer of the perilous finances, the frantic crescendo of the Son of Sam saga, the blackout, and the looting and subsequent damage to the city's psyche and its reputation. Even the once lovable Mets turned ugly when the detestable general manager M. Donald Grant planted negative stories with the vitriolic newspaper columnist Dick Young as a prelude to running Tom Seaver, the franchise's most popular and talented player, out of town.

The South Bronx may have been consumed by flames, but the Yankees' most notorious conflagration took place in Fenway Park when Martin yanked Jackson from the outfield in the middle of an inning for failing to hustle, inciting a heated in-your-face shouting match that NBC's cameras showed to a nationwide audience. At a reconciliation meeting, Martin then called Jackson "boy," igniting new flames.

Finally, in August, with the Yankees 5 games out and only 53 games remaining, Steinbrenner told Martin he'd be fired if he didn't bat Jackson cleanup. Soon Jackson began hitting, the fans began cheering, "Reg-gie. Reg-gie," and the Yankees began winning, all the way to the AL East title.

Jackson went 1-for-14 in the first four games of the playoffs against Kansas City, and Martin benched him for the deciding Game 5, but Jackson responded with a crucial pinch-hit single in the eighth inning. Still, Jackson's slump extended into the World Series against the Los Angeles Dodgers, and his ego took another blow in Game 1 when Paul Blair replaced him for defensive purposes and then singled home the winning run in the 12th inning. Game 2 was the notorious affair when ABC's cameras showed the South Bronx self-destructing with one of that year's many five-alarm fires. At the Stadium, fans ran across the field while others threw bottles, firecrackers, and beer—Dodger Reggie Smith was hit in the head with a hard rubber ball. Amid the chaos, the Yankees lost 6–1, and Jackson fell to 3-for-22 in the postseason.

Away from New York, Jackson found his stroke, picking up a hit in Game 3 and a double and homer in Game 4 as the Yankees took a 3–1 edge. Los Angeles routed them in Game 5, but Jackson homered in his final at-bat.

The Series and Jackson returned to New York for a big finish. Before Game 6 on October 18, Joe DiMaggio—at the Stadium to throw out the first ball—made a point of visiting Jackson at his locker and heaping compliments on him. Inspired, Jackson put on a Ruthian batting practice display that had players stopping to stare. Dodger starter Burt Hooten, who had whiffed Jackson twice in Game 2, was among those witnesses and walked Jackson on four pitches in his first at-bat. But when first baseman Chris Chambliss homered, scoring Jackson, the Dodgers were forced to throw Jackson strikes the rest of the night.

In the fourth, with the Dodgers hugging a 3–2 lead, Munson got on base. Hooten had to come over the plate. Jackson suspected that Hooten would try tying him up inside, so he surreptitiously backed six inches off the plate. The first pitch did come in, but Jackson smacked it right out, a low hummer that landed in the first row of the bleachers in right. The Yankees led 4–3.

When Jackson arrived at home plate in the next inning, Hooten was gone, replaced by the hard-throwing Elias Sosa. Jackson had called scout Gene Michael on the phone for a quick report. He decided to look for a fastball. Again there was a man on base. Again the Dodgers tried a fastball down and in. Again Jackson clouted the first pitch into the right-field bleachers. Back on the bench, Jackson looked into the television camera and gleefully held out two fingers and mouthed the word "two." But he wasn't through yet.

In the eighth, with New York winning 7–3, Jackson got a rousing ovation from the Yankee Stadium crowd. No one had ever hit five homers in a six-game Series, and only the immortal Babe Ruth had homered three times in one Series game. (He'd done it twice.) Jackson had one shot at history. It was all he'd need.

On his first try, Charlie Hough tried his signature pitch, a knuckleball. Dancing to the plate, it was a stark contrast to the fastballs Jackson had walloped earlier. Yet he calmly waited before turn-

After a tumultuous first season in New York, Reggie Jackson relishes the headlines and the adulation at the ticker-tape parade after winning the World Series with his three-homer outburst.

ing on the ball so hard and quick that even his jaded teammates were impressed. On each of his first two home runs, the trajectory had been so low that Jackson ran hard to first, unsure whether the ball would clear the wall. This time, after whipping his bat through the strike zone with astounding force, Jackson stood and watched with everyone else as his final masterpiece climbed into the night sky before coming to rest some 475 feet away in dead center. As Jackson trotted around the bases blowing kisses, the chants of "Reg-gie" were deafening, and Los Angeles first baseman Steve Garvey silently applauded in his glove. Even Ruth had required more than three swings to wreak his damage.

"Oh, what a beam on his face! How can you

blame him," Howard Cosell declared on ABC. "He has answered the whole world."

Jackson had won the game and the Series for New York, and with his unprecedented display he had won over the city. In the ninth, fans chanted his name and showered him with confetti. (Afraid they might throw heavier artillery — this was the bleachers after all — he ran in for a batting helmet.)

From this night, Jackson built his Mr. October persona, embracing his image so wholeheartedly that it distorted the historical lens. The nickname was a hype job. Jackson had been inconsistent with Oakland, and when he came to the Yankees in 1977, he was a career .271 hitter in the postseason with just 5 homers and 15 RBIs in 118 at-bats. After his dismal 3-for-22 start against K.C. and L.A., it's easy to imagine Steinbrenner fuming in his owner's box, calling Jackson "Mr. May." (In fact, his moniker was first bestowed upon him by Munson during the ALCS with a heavy dose of sarcasm.)

After heisting the end of the 1977 World Series, Jackson, who also homered in his first swing of 1978, then cemented his reputation by smashing a crucial home run in the famous one-game tiebreaker at Fenway Park, batting .462 in the ALCS and .391 in the rematch against Los Angeles, totaling 4 homers and 14 RBIs in the postseason. But subsequent Octobers were remarkably unremarkable: from 1980 to 1982, Jackson batted just .200 in 45 at-bats with 2 homers and 4 RBIs. There are other players who equally deserve the title Mr. October (including, ironically, Billy Martin, who batted nearly 80 points above his lifetime average in the postseason and banged 12 hits in the 1953 Series), but few wore the mantle of greatness more comfortably than Jackson.

"Jackson does not live a life in the conventional, everyday sense," *Washington Post* columnist Thomas Boswell wrote later. "He manufactures a legend, a personal history with himself and his exploits at the center."

And of all his exploits in his Hall of Fame career, the centerpiece was his historic slugging display on this one October night, when he brought the championship back to the Bronx after a 15-year absence and slammed three exclamation points on his debut season in New York.

# 18. Matty shuts out the A's, October 14, 1905, Polo Grounds

With each zero, the young man's stature grew. After accumulating 27 frames of remarkable nothingness, the 25-year-old known as "Matty" or "Big Six" became an instant icon, America's real-life Frank Merriwell.

In Christy Mathewson, baseball found a new hero for a new age. Sure, Cy Young, baseball's biggest winner, was still a top pitcher, but he was just *so* 19th century. When Mathewson — the tall, blond, impossibly clean-cut college man — laid those golden goose eggs over three shutouts in the 1905 World Series, he ascended to the baseball throne and simultaneously helped transform the New York Giants into baseball's flagship franchise.

From the start, Mathewson had displayed impressive wares with his fastball, big overhand

# Honorable Mention: A Giant of a Pitcher

**1. Carl Hubbell and Roy Parmelee stifle St. Louis, July 2, 1933, Polo Grounds**

The St. Louis Cardinals were closing fast on the first-place New York Giants, snatching two of three games at the Polo Grounds. Then, in a crucial double-header, the Cards sent Tex Carleton and Dizzy Dean—who'd combine for 37 wins that year—to the hill. Carleton and Dean allowed just one run over 24 innings, normally enough to win three games, much less two. On this day, the Cardinals left winless.

In the opener, Carleton faced Carl Hubbell, nicknamed "the Meal Ticket" for his unflagging ability to provide for the Giants. Hubbell was on his way to leading the league in wins, ERA, innings, walks and hits per nine innings, and shutouts. Yet this performance was astonishing even by those high standards: the future Hall of Famer yielded six hits and no walks . . . over 18 innings. He pitched the equivalent of two full games, with just one Cardinal runner reaching third and three more making it to second. Carleton's 16 shutout innings were for naught as the Giants finally won in the 18th, 1–0.

Against Dean, erratic Roy Parmelee—who'd lead NL pitchers in hit batsmen and wild pitches and finish fifth in walks—pitched like his name was Hubbell. Dean surrendered just five hits, but one was Johnny Vergez's homer, while Parmelee struck out 13, giving up four hits and no walks. Another 1–0 win. The two Giant hurlers pitched 27 innings and allowed only 10 runners. By year's end, Hubbell had won the Most Valuable Player Award, and the Giants had captured their fourth World Series.

**2. Marquard goes from bust to boom, July 3, 1912, Polo Grounds**

Think of John McGraw's New York Giants and you invariably think of Christy Mathewson. But the Giants couldn't have won five pennants in ten years with just one pitcher. McGraw always had another ace in the hole, and for the 1911–13 run he had two: Jeff Tesreau and Rube Marquard.

The Giants signed Marquard late in 1908 for the then-outrageous sum of $11,000, but he pitched poorly in his one start in the heat of the pennant race. His confidence rattled, Marquard struggled badly for two years, earning the derisive moniker "the $11,000 Lemon."

But he blossomed in 1911, winning 25 games, and in 1912 he outdid himself: the winning streak he started on Opening Day stretched all the way to the record books. On July 3, Marquard won his 19th straight game in one year. He didn't have his best stuff, permitting nine hits and five walks, but he deftly sidestepped each quandary as the Giants came from behind to beat Brooklyn 2–1. (It was also his record 21st straight win over two years.)

Marquard finished with a league-leading 26 victories to help the Giants win the pennant. But that wasn't all. His fame propelled him into a movie called *19 Straight* and onto the vaudeville stage (where he'd performed previously) for a new dance called the Marquard Glide, which featured headliner Blossom Seeley. Then he capped his great run by winning Seeley's hand in marriage.

**3. Joe McGinnity shows his mettle, August 31, 1903, Polo Grounds**

Some guys will do anything to contribute. None top Joe McGinnity. Nicknamed "the Iron Joe" because he worked in a foundry during the off-season, he had given that moniker a new meaning in 1899 when he pitched five times in six days for Brooklyn. And in 1903 the Giant hurler earned his appellation all over again. On August 1, with the slumping Giants in danger of falling out of the pennant race, McGinnity volunteered to pitch both ends of a double-header. He won both. A week later, he did it again.

On August 31 against Philadelphia, McGinnity—who'd finish with a 20th-century record 434 innings—offered to perform the feat for the third time in one month. Staked to an early lead, the ultimate innings-eater scattered seven hits in his 4–1 win. He fell behind 2–0 in the nightcap, then shut the Phils down, striking out nine, as the Giants roared back for a 9–2 win.

McGinnity looked sharp till the end; the *New York Times* noted: "He seemed fresh enough to tackle the visitors for a third contest if that were necessary."

curve, and baffling fadeaway (today known as a screwball). Mathewson, at 6'2", was big for that era (hence "Big Six") and, as a former Bucknell University student, a rarity in a nation where most men didn't graduate from high school. He was impeccably virtuous and quite perfectly acceptable to the WASPy press and American mainstream, especially compared to some of baseball's other stars, like the German Honus Wagner, the malignant Ty Cobb, and the fiery Irishman John McGraw. But the Giants were awful in 1901 and 1902, and it wasn't until McGraw took over as manager in the latter half of 1902 that Matty's star really began to rise.

With the Baltimore Orioles as a player and manager, McGraw had been a pugnacious infielder and prime perpetrator of "inside baseball," the shrewd, sneaky small-ball style of play that he undertook with an aggressiveness that bordered on criminal. But the founder of the new American League, Ban Johnson, sought a wholesome public image, so McGraw—who umpire Arlie Latham famously said "eats gunpowder every morning and washes it down with warm blood"—was most unwelcome there. And so, in 1902, forever contemptuous of Johnson and the Junior Circuit, McGraw left Baltimore and landed in New York. Though starkly different in temperament and playing style, McGraw and Mathewson got along fabulously off the field, renting, with their wives, an apartment together on Columbus Avenue and West 85th Street.

By 1904 McGraw, with aces Mathewson and Joe McGinnity, had fashioned the Giants into 106-game winners and National League champs. The previous year had featured the first modern World Series between the two leagues' winners, which Giant owner John T. Brush and McGraw had sought to stop in court. In 1904 the Giants refused to play the American League champion Boston Pilgrims. But by 1905 agreements had been hammered out guaranteeing an autumnal confrontation.

The Giants again won the NL pennant that year, and Mathewson was baseball's best hurler. He won 30 games for the third straight year in a year when no other NL pitcher won more than 23. He struck out 206 while no one else in the league topped 175. His ERA was 1.28; only one other NL pitcher was under 2.00. Matty also hurled a no-hitter among his league-leading eight shutouts.

So everyone expected Mathewson to be a focal point of the World Series against Connie Mack's Philadelphia A's—especially with Mack's ace Rube Waddell out with an injured shoulder. Before Game 1, A's starter Eddie Plank was largely ignored, but Mathewson, wearing one of McGraw's dandy new black uniforms with white lettering, was surrounded by photographers. Still, no one could anticipate the impact that Big Six would actually have.

Mathewson seized control of the Series immediately, retiring the first six batters on just ten pitches. Crowds gathered in New York to watch the results get posted on large blackboards as Mathewson, relying most heavily on his curve, iced the A's, allowing just one runner to reach third. Philadelphia didn't know it then, but that runner—Ossee Schreckengost, who was thrown out at home—would constitute their crowning achievement against Mathewson. New York's hurler also started the winning two-run rally in the fifth with a single. The Giants won 3–0.

Philadelphia's Chief Bender returned the favor in New York for Game 2, beating McGinnity 3–0. Mathewson retaliated in Game 3, heading a 9–0 rout, with nine strikeouts. Then McGinnity avenged his earlier loss, with yet another shutout, 1–0.

Shutouts were relatively common at the turn of the century—the five other pre-1910 Series had yielded nine. So one or two such games were to be expected, and perhaps even three would not have been extraordinary. But with four straight, fans were abuzz. When Mathewson took the mound at the Polo Grounds on October 14 for Game 5, he was facing the AL champions for the third time in five days; to pitch another complete game shutout, by any era's standards, would be a unique accomplishment.

An overflow crowd of perhaps 27,000 stacked up behind the ropes in the outfield. Mathewson

**Christy Mathewson shuts out the Philadelphia A's not once, not twice, but three times in one classic World Series.**

was the last man to appear, earning a raucous minute-long ovation. He sauntered over to McGinnity and doffed his friend's cap; McGinnity, as if in some vaudeville skit, lifted the lid off Mathewson's dome. This was a loose, relaxed team.

Again, offense was scarce on both ends. Mathewson and Bender each permitted a meager five hits. But while Mathewson walked just one man over three starts, Bender issued three free passes in this game alone . . . and all three scored. In the fifth, Sam Mertes and Bill Dahlen both walked, Arthur Devlin bunted them over, and Billy Gilbert brought Mertes home with a deep fly to left. One run on no hits—vintage McGraw. In the eighth, Mathewson—who hit .250 for the Series while the team batted only .209—walked, advanced to third on catcher Roger Bresnahan's ground-rule double into the crowds, and scored on George Brown's grounder.

That second run was superfluous, of course. Here's what qualified as a Philadelphia threat: in the sixth, they managed two base runners in one inning . . . but not at the same time. Briscoe Lord was picked off first by Bresnahan just before Harry Davis singled. Mathewson allowed no one else to reach first, plowing through the final 10 batters, allowing only one ball out of the infield. In the ninth, with the crowd bursting with excitement, he got two weak grounders back to the mound and one to short. Just 95 minutes after the first pitch, 10,000 fans swarmed the field as the World Series champions celebrated their triumph. Soon after, Bresnahan and Mathewson reappeared with a banner proclaiming, THE GIANTS, WORLD'S CHAMPIONS, 1905. In response, the crowd unleashed an explosion of exultation that the *New York Times* declared "lifted Manhattan's soil from its base."

New York had been home to great sporting events before, but horse races, heavyweight fights, and six-day bicycle races conferred glory solely on the participants—only a team sport brought with it those hometown associations that enabled the rooters to feel a powerful kinship with the athletes and burnished the reputation of an entire municipality. There were only two such sports worth mentioning back then, college football and particularly baseball. The big college football games had featured out-of-town Ivy League schools, and their swells had done most of the cheering. This was different. This was New York's moment. The 1905 World Series established the primacy of America's biggest city as America's sports capital, with Mc-

Graw as its master and Mathewson—endorsing Coca-Cola ("He's proof of its wholesomeness"), sweaters, pipe tobacco, and other products—as its hero.

The Giants would be baseball's dominant team for a generation, and Larry Doyle's famous 1911 quote, "It's great to be young and a Giant," captured the aura in New York and in baseball surrounding McGraw's men, who, over 21 years, won the National League pennant 10 times, finishing second another seven. (As late as 1957, when the Giants departed for San Francisco, they were second to the Yankees in league pennants won.)

As for Mathewson, he'd finish with 373 wins; Frank Deford argues rightfully in *The Old Ball Game* that the Cy Young Award should probably instead be named for him. At the end of that third World Series shutout, Mathewson had pitched 27 innings in five days, struck out 18, and allowed just 14 hits, one walk, and one hit batsman, prompting the *Times* to breathlessly declare him "the pitching marvel of the century" just five years into the 1900s. Ninety-five years later, it turned out they were right.

# 19. Jimmy Connors defies Father Time, September 2, 1991, National Tennis Center

Jimmy Connors won five U.S. Opens on three different surfaces at two different places, yet he's best remembered for a tournament in which he didn't even reach the finals. That 1991 performance was the third and final act for Connors, who had won as the brash bully of the 1970s and as the curmudgeonly craftsman of the 1980s. This time Connors, seemingly washed up, transformed himself into a feel-good story for a society built on both a Peter Pan complex and the worship of true grit. This aging inspiration captivated even the most casual sports fans, attaining a new level of celebrity and forging an unforgettable legacy with his classic American blend of tenacity and showmanship.

That tournament, Connors said later, was "the most memorable eleven days of my career. Better than the titles."

And he gave his growing legion of fans not one but three classic matches.

So which is your favorite? Bet you can't choose just one.

*You could select the first-round comeback against Patrick McEnroe on August 27.*

Because it seemed incredible that Connors was even there. His iron man records—109 pro titles, 159 straight weeks at number one, 12 straight Open semifinals, and 16 straight years in the top 10—were in the past. Connors had played and lost three matches in 1990 before submitting to wrist surgery. He'd plummeted to 936th in the world, defaulted at the French Open in 1991 owing to a cranky back—the defining symbol of old age—and lost in the third round of Wimbledon; he was ranked just 174th by Open time and needed a wild-card berth just to gain entrance to his "home court."

Because he beat a McEnroe. Sure, Patrick, ranked just 35th, lacked the skill and artistic temperament of his famous older brother, but he was an Australian Open semifinalist and had beaten Boris Becker that summer.

Because this was the first time we saw Connors's vibrant Estusa racket flashing through the night, proclaiming the return of the king.

Because he overcame the greatest deficit of all, dropping the first two sets to the steady McEnroe 6–4, 7–6, then falling behind 0–3 in the third. Connors was limping (an act, perhaps, lulling his prey or laying groundwork for an alibi), and the stadium was emptying, everyone writing Connors off. By the next game there'd be perhaps 6,000 loyalists from the original sellout crowd. According to Joel Drucker's biography-memoir *Jimmy Connors Saved My Life,* even Connors's staunchest supporter, his mother and first teacher Gloria, turned away from the television.

Then, at 0–40, one mistake from oblivion, Connors finally turned it on. And once he did, McEnroe could not finish off tennis's Rasputin, who drew his lifeblood from the screaming, stomping, bowing fans that remained. Connors held, saved two more break points at 2–3, won five of six games for the third set, then snared the fourth set 6–2 and finished McEnroe off 6–4 in the fifth. The 4-hour-18-minute epic ended at 1:35 A.M. "The crowd won it for me," Connors said. "The crowd was an awful heavy burden for Patrick."

*You could choose the fourth-round marathon against Aaron Krickstein on September 2.*

With three wins already notched, Connors had people paying attention—Becker stopped practicing to come over and congratulate him after the McEnroe match; defending champion Pete Sampras's third-round press conference included a run of 12 out of 16 questions about Connors before Sampras snapped that he wanted questions about his own tennis; Nuprin rushed its new Connors commercial onto the air; and even Ted Koppel explored the Connors phenomenon on *Nightline.*

The fans greeted Connors, 39 on this day, with a rousing rendition of "Happy Birthday." Connors soaked up the spotlight's warmth and converted it to energy and power. He had always used the crowd better than any other player, first when they booed the strident young outcast and then, after 1978, when he started earning respect and adoration. And no crowd connected better with Connors than the New York crowd, which fed off his working-class humor, his defiant stances, his drive, his urgency.

Never before had Connors so perfectly played and played to his audience, exulting, exhorting, slapping his thigh, pumping his pelvis, thrusting his fist, for 4 hours and 42 minutes. Although he also still resorted to base tactics—calling an umpire "an abortion"—he mostly oozed charm, even as he used the ovations as a stalling tactic to catch his breath and psych out Krickstein. At one point he directly addressed the nation, turning to a courtside television camera and boasting, "This is what they come for. This is what they want."

Although he'd fallen further behind against McEnroe, beating Krickstein was no simple task. Krickstein, who had idolized Connors growing up and become a friend and occasional hitting partner, was fresh off a win over 1990 finalist Andre Agassi.

Connors lost the first set, then clawed back to win the second in a tiebreaker. Worn down, he tanked the third, 6–1, while waiting for his second wind, which enabled him to win the fourth. In the fifth set, after a 17-minute, 23-point game, Connors found himself trailing 5–2. Then he crushed Krickstein with another miraculous comeback, winning one game with a touch backhand volley and another with an overhead, while Krickstein remained pinned to the baseline, unable to slow the attack.

Tennis writer Peter Bodo was in the press box near Arthur Ashe, who had once loathed Connors for his refusal to join the players' union, his selfish unwillingness to play for America's Davis Cup team, and his on-court behavior. Witnessing Connors's voodoo magic, Bodo asked Ashe if he thought Connors was still an asshole. Ashe paused, then replied, "Yes. But he's my favorite asshole."

As the crowd screamed and shrieked at previously unimagined decibel levels, Connors finally flattened Krickstein 7–4 in the fifth set tiebreaker.

**Jimmy Connors exults for the fans after feeding off their energy in his stirring comeback against Aaron Krickstein.**

When Jimbo finally pulled it out, the stands—still full this time—echoed with thousands of fans singing a "Happy Birthday" encore. Even nemesis John McEnroe was impressed enough to search out Connors in the locker room to congratulate him. "I've just got to go in there and touch him and see if he bleeds," McEnroe said.

*Or finally, you could select Connors's win over Paul Haarhuis in the quarterfinals on September 5.*

Well, not the entire match, but one point. Fast-forward through the first set, with Connors looking his age and Haarhuis winning 6–4; fast-forward through most of the second too. Stop right after Haarhuis broke Connors for a 5–4 lead. There was no way Connors could endure another five-setter, so if he couldn't solve Haarhuis here, it would be all over. Haarhuis grabbed a 30–15 lead. Two points for the set.

Connors snatched two quick points and then, after stoking the crowd, pulled off his final miracle on break point. Back in his prime in 1978, Connors had pulled off perhaps the greatest shot in Open history, up 6–5 in the fifth set against Adriano Panatta, running down a ball past the doubles alley, and hitting a one-handed backhand around the net-post for a winner. Now, as an old man, he managed to win what was perhaps the Open's most memorable rally.

Haarhuis approached the net with a superb deep backhand. Connors flung a lob skyward. Haarhuis slammed an overhead. Connors, back literally against the wall, lofted another backhand lob. Another overhead from Haarhuis smashed to the backhand corner. Connors, refusing to give in, threw up one more lob. The crowd was electrified by his hustle, his perseverance. This time Haarhuis rifled the overhead toward Connors's forehand. Scampering like a young Michael Chang, he hurled another lob—Connors had turned tennis's most defensive shot into a statement of aggression and defiance, thrusting his jaw out and saying, "Hit me again, I won't ever go down."

Haarhuis, still not letting the ball bounce, was exhausted, mentally if not physically, by Connors's display. His last overhead was his weakest, and Connors, the game's finest opportunist, whacked a crosscourt forehand. Haarhuis reached it, but his backhand volley was weak and Connors raced in, driving a backhand winner up the line. The crowd, on its feet, roared for Connors—for this point, for nearly two decades of unsurpassed thrills. Connors and Haarhuis returned to playing, but the match was essentially over. Connors won that set 7–6 and the next two 6–4, 6–2.

Although Connors lost to Jim Courier in the semifinals, he was clearly the tournament's biggest winner—make that 1991's biggest sports story. In Eliot Berry's book *Tough Draw,* he quotes a stranger exclaiming about the Krickstein match: "I never really liked tennis, but I was in a bar yesterday with about a hundred people. And that Connors! We were all cheering."

Indeed, the aura surrounding this comeback gave Connors the leverage two years later to launch his "seniors" tour, which lured Bjorn Borg, John McEnroe, Guillermo Vilas, and others back to competitive play and gave the fans the show everyone wanted—even if it was just for show—for the rest of the decade.

"F. Scott Fitzgerald once commented that there are no second acts in American lives. Jimmy Connors would probably tell Fitzgerald exactly where he could shove that remark," Drucker once wrote in a magazine piece.

So there you have it: the first and toughest match, the birthday present when the spotlight shone brightest, or the greatest point.

The McEnroe match featured the longest road back at a time when no one expected anything, and it served as a reminder that Connors was more than just a great talent and mesmerizing entertainer: he had succeeded so often and for so long because of his intense dedication to the game and to the idea of competing. But for the history books, choose the Krickstein match—although Connors always thrashed Krickstein, this confrontation marked the apex because it put Connors back in the spotlight he loved and because he always preferred facing the pressure of high expectations and somehow exceeding them.

# 20. Roger Maris beats the Babe, October 1, 1961, Yankee Stadium

**Sometimes I think it wasn't worth the aggravation. Maybe I wouldn't do it over again if I had the chance.** ***— Roger Maris, on hitting 61 home runs in 1961***

Put a big fat asterisk next to the 61st home run of the season that Roger Maris hit on October 1, 1961. No, not the one with a negative connotation that then-commissioner Ford Frick had in mind, but more of a star, a positive symbol indicating that this is the true home run record, that Maris is the only person to hit more home runs than Babe Ruth without the aid of andro, creatine, cream, clear, and the other substances being swallowed, injected, and rubbed on in the modern muscle era.

To top it all, Maris faced more stress and pressure than Ruth in 1927, Mark McGwire and Sammy Sosa in 1998, or Barry Bonds in 2001.

When he hit 60 homers, Ruth was trying only to break his own mark of 59, which he had set in 1921. That 59 topped his 54 from the previous year, which shattered the high-water mark of 29 he'd attained in 1919. In other words, Ruth existed in his own universe. Every record was his, and had he finished 1927 with 53 or 57 or 59 four-baggers, he would have remained baseball's most important, popular, and successful star.

McGwire and Sosa faced a media brigade unlike anything Ruth or even Maris ever saw, but most of the interviews were friendly, even fawning. It would be years before these two shamed themselves in front of Congress and the nation. In the summer of 1998, McGwire and Sosa were being credited with saving baseball, not accused of betraying it. And they were chasing Maris, not Ruth, so there was no sense of a hero being demeaned. If Bonds didn't get such a lovefest, it was only because of his lifetime of surliness; besides, he didn't seem to care. And even though his overall 2001 performance was a marvel unlike anything baseball had ever witnessed, the record was only three years old and long-ball totals were so inflated that the chase did not resonate the same way.

Maris, by contrast, was chasing the ghost of Ruth while racing alongside superstar teammate Mickey Mantle and being harassed by the commissioner, the press, and fans who all felt this precious record should not fall into the hands of a mere mortal . . . and a bland one at that. (Only Hank Aaron would have it worse, being subjected to vicious racial hatred when he broke Ruth's career home run record.) By season's end, Maris's hair was falling out in clumps, and he was surviving on coffee and Camels, unable to think straight, feeling trapped inside the swirling media vortex.

Maris had never faced anything like it before. He'd grown up in Fargo, North Dakota, and was heading to the University of Oklahoma on a football scholarship when the Cleveland Indians offered him $15,000. In the minors, he learned to pull for power, and by 1957 he was in the majors. He was streaky and injury-prone but showed promise both in Cleveland and then in Kansas City, hitting 28 homers in 1958.

The Yankees—who treated the cash-poor Kansas City A's like their farm team, making 15 trades for 59 players from 1955 to 1960—snatched up Maris, whose hitting style they knew would be perfect for the House That Ruth Built, with its short right-field porch, and who could thus offer protection for Mickey Mantle in the lineup. In 1960 Maris hit 25 homers by June 30; he finished with 39 and won the Most Valuable Player Award, helping the Yankees reclaim the American League crown.

The next year new manager Ralph Houk flipped Maris and Mantle, batting Maris third, where he'd see better pitches, and Mantle, a superior all-around hitter, fourth.

Maris got off to a horrific start, batting below .200 and failing to homer until the 10th game, by which point Mantle already had 7 dingers. After 27 games, Maris had just 3 roundtrippers to Mantle's 10. Then Maris went on a tear, bashing 12 long balls in the next 16 games and 23 in the next 36. That hot streak would make the difference. He'd have short spurts after that—5 homers in 5 games in early July and again at month's end, 7 in 6 games in August—but he was never again superhuman, and as he attracted attention he endured more droughts.

In June Joe Trimble of the *Daily News* asked Maris if he might break the record. The reluctant star, who, despite his vanilla image with the public, already had a rep in the press for being surly, hated such speculation and was surprised that it was starting so early. "How the fuck should I know?" he responded.

By July 2, Maris had 30 homers—8 ahead of Ruth's pace—and Mantle 29. Mantle had been a shy hick when he first came to New York, and despite his popularity, the high expectations that accompanied him had caused perpetual disappointment in some fans and writers, his biggest flaw being that he wasn't Joe DiMaggio. But with Maris threatening Ruth's record, Yankee followers coalesced around the idea that Mantle, the 10-year-veteran, was the pure Yankee, their true love and the deserving one. As he gamely struggled to stay in the homer race, even when his body broke down at season's end, Mantle attained new stature in the eyes of the writers and fans . . . at the expense of his good friend and roomie Roger Maris.

On July 17, with Maris at 35 and Mantle at 32, Frick, a former ghostwriter for and buddy of Babe Ruth—and a classic "back when men were real men" guy—issued a decree. "Any player who may hit more than 60 home runs during his club's first 154 games would be recognized as having established a new record," Frick wrote, referring to the fact that the American League had just added two teams and expanded its schedule from 154 to 162 games. "However, if the player does not hit more than 60 homers until after . . . there would have to be a distinctive mark in the record books."

*Daily News* columnist Dick Young referred to Frick's proposed mark as an "asterisk," and the word stuck. Although Maris replied, "A season's a season," most baseball writers in a *Sporting News* poll backed the commissioner, and so did many players, at least publicly. Stan Musial, Warren Spahn, Yankee Whitey Ford, and the Mick himself supported the asterisk. "If I should break it in the 155th game, I wouldn't want the record," Mantle declared. (That same day Maris and Mantle each had a crucial home run erased when an incomplete game was rained out.) Then, while Mantle homered almost daily, Maris's bat went quiet but for a brief spurt in late July.

It wasn't just Frick, of course. You can't spell "pressure" without the press, and the television, radio, and newspaper sportswriters all piled on. Television's growth forced newspapers to go beyond game reports and seek quotes, color, analysis, and, of course, controversy. In many ways this journalism was better and more truthful than the gee-whiz mythmaking of Grantland Rice and his 1920s comrades, but in many ways it was a malevolent force, birthing the permanent tabloidization of all media. And as Glenn Stout noted in *Yankees Century,* because many Yankee beat writers

**Finally! Roger Maris passes the Babe with his 61st homer, hit off Tracy Stallard in the fourth inning on the season's final day.**

weren't Yankee guys but NL writers who had shifted over only after the New York Giants and Brooklyn Dodgers left town, the tone became "increasingly critical and mean-spirited."

Some writers chastised Maris for his low batting average or his inability to hit lefties; others pointed out that expansion had diluted pitching talent to the point that perhaps all AL records that year should be considered suspect. (They didn't analyze whether the advent of night baseball, West Coast travel, and relief pitchers and the influx of talent accompanying integration made life harder for Maris than it had been for Ruth.)

Just as Mantle hadn't been DiMaggio, now reporters held Maris accountable for not being his aw-shucks, life-of-the-party teammate. Maris didn't help his cause with comments like, "I'll be glad when the season is over."

By August 2 "the M&M Boys" both had 40 homers, and ever more reporters attached themselves to the race, asking the same questions over and over or tossing out personal queries or curveballs; Maris's inability to play along cost him badly, with headlines like "Maris Sulks in Trainer's Room" (*New York Times*) and "Maris Fails" (*Daily News*) shading public perception. Even in New York fans booed him.

After 125 games, Maris had 50 homers, still ahead of Ruth's 154-game pace. But then Mantle got an infection in September from a cold treatment, and an abscess followed—he'd finish with 54 homers, languishing in a hospital watching Maris on TV. Mantle's departure left Maris more exposed both in the lineup and in the race against Ruth (and Frick).

Stuck at 58, he ran into a rainy double-header in games 152 and 153 and was blanked. Before the fateful 154th, he told Houk, "I can't stand it anymore. All those goddamn questions. I'm at the end of my rope." Then he hit his 59th—beating Hank Greenberg and Jimmie Foxx, who were second to Ruth with 58 apiece—and hit another long shot that the wind held up. The Yankees clinched the pennant that day, but while his teammates celebrated, Maris got the third degree from the media about what would happen if he "belatedly" passed Ruth.

In the *Milwaukee Journal,* Oliver Kuechle gloated over Maris's failure, saying the record should be broken "by someone of greater baseball stature and greater color and public appeal. . . . Maris . . . is not more than a good big league ballplayer. He is colorless . . . and is often surly. There just isn't anything heroic about the man."

Maris hit number 60 off Jack Fisher in Baltimore on September 26 and then, utterly drained, was attacked for taking the next game off with just four to go.

October 1 arrived, the season's final day. Maris was stuck on 60. That was Ruth's number. To come so far but to end there hurt. Maris wanted the record.

That morning he went with his wife Pat to St. Patrick's Cathedral. At the ballpark, just 23,154 fans showed up. One has to wonder how high the attendance might have been if Maris had been hospitalized and it was Mantle going for 61.

In the first, Boston Red Sox pitcher Tracy Stallard—who'd yielded Mantle's 29th homer in July—started Maris with a high fastball, then went down and away. Maris swung late and popped the ball to left, where rookie Carl Yastrzemski caught it.

The game was scoreless in the fourth for Maris's next turn. Stallard missed, high and away, then missed low and inside. The fans, mistakenly thinking he was pitching around Maris, started booing.

2–0 is a hitter's pitch. A walk can be deadly in a 0–0 game, so the man on the mound must stop nibbling. Stallard's 2–0 was fat, not down and away like he'd intended. Maris whipped his 35-inch, 33-ounce lumber through the strike zone, his weight shifting into the ball. Then he watched it soar through space, not returning to earth until it was 365 feet away, six rows deep in right field.

This was the Yankees' 240th home run of the year, a new record. It was Maris's 132nd run scored, tying him (with Mantle) for the league lead, and his 142nd RBI, giving him that crown. And since the Yankees' 109th triumph would finish with no other scoring, it marked the only time in Maris's career that he won a 1–0 game with a home run.

Nobody cared. Only one number mattered.

It was 61.

Briefly, the number flashed through Maris's mind—the first time he thought specifically of a number as he hit one—then his mind went blank. He circled the bases "in a complete fog." One fan ran out and shook his hand near third base, and his teammates not only congratulated him upon his return but refused to let the modest Maris disappear into the dugout until he had waved his cap to the crowd, which cheered so long that the game was delayed even after Maris sat down. "It was," he admitted, "the greatest thrill of my life."

A local teen named Sal Durante caught the ball and was brought down to meet Maris and pose for pictures. In the sixth and the eighth, Maris, taking home run cuts, whiffed and popped up. Still, he had 61. And still, the media mob didn't let up, grilling him afterwards with queries like, "As you were running around the bases, were you thinking about Mickey Mantle?"

Frick never backed down, but the numbers legitimize Maris: he hit 61 home runs in 698 plate appearances; Ruth hit 60 home runs in 691. The last eight games did not make the difference. No one claimed Maris was Ruth's equal—Ruth's 1927 average was nearly 100 points higher than Maris's in 1961, he belted nearly twice as many doubles and twice the triples, drew 44 more walks, scored 26 more runs, and drove in 22 more. The big man even stole six more bases. But Maris's home run mark was fairly earned.

(One odd trivia note: A week later Whitey Ford set a new World Series record by pitching 32 consecutive scoreless innings. The old mark of 29⅔ belonged to a long-ago Boston Red Sox hurler: Babe Ruth.)

The record behind him, Maris found the pressure even worse. In 1962 columnist Jimmy Cannon called him "the Whiner," and Maris, who stopped talking to the media, was taken to task for mustering "just" 33 homers and 100 RBIs. He didn't find peace until he was traded to St. Louis in 1967, but he found appreciation a decade later when new Yankee owner George Steinbrenner cajoled him into returning to Yankee Stadium for Old-Timers Day, where Maris was loudly cheered.

By the time he died of cancer in 1985, the reevaluation had begun in earnest. When McGwire and Sosa began their assault in 1998, Maris's mark had lasted longer than Ruth's, earning him the stature he finally deserved. His mark was eradicated, of course, but the recent steroid controversy has only enhanced the aura around Maris's all-natural 61. The record books no longer call him the single-season home run king, but in the ultimate irony, the press and the fans are on his side. Maybe if Maris could know that he'd decide it was worth the aggravation after all.

# 21. The Babe Hits 60, September 30, 1927, Yankee Stadium

On September 5, 1927, Babe Ruth had 44 home runs to his credit but found himself deadlocked in the race for the crown with teammate Lou Gehrig, who would finish the season with the most home runs hit to date by someone not named Ruth. With the pennant race long since decided in the Yankees' favor, this dynamic duo had generated most of the ink devoted to baseball: at Fenway Park that day more than 70,000 people—twice the capacity—had tried for a glimpse of the "Great Home Run Derby."

Still, with just 23 games left, contemplating an assault on Ruth's 1921 record of 59 homers seemed absurd.

Then the "Sultan of Swat" reclaimed his royal throne by swinging his hefty Louisville Slugger as if it were Excalibur yanked from a stone. He clouted three homers on the sixth, walloped two more on the seventh, and hit another two on the eleventh, ending the back-and-forth with Gehrig and beginning a new home run race with his only true competition: himself.

By then, Ruth, who put a notch in his bat commemorating each new blast, was openly musing about 60 despite having just 17 games left, and soon the press was also championing the charge to baseball's Camelot.

The 1920s was the Golden Age of Hero Worship. America's press and public mythologized great talents, transforming them from stars into superstars into icons. As Bill Tilden, Jack Dempsey, and Red Grange had begun to fade, Ruth—the "Master Mauler," the "Big Bam"—would prove in 1927 that he remained first among equals. From the wide-open West to the skyscrapers sprouting in New York to folk heroes like Paul Bunyan and John Henry, America had long been infatuated with the grand and gargantuan. So nothing seemed more American than Ruth, his appetites and his feats—as Robert Creamer points out in *Babe,* from 1918 through 1921 Ruth had proudly upped his home run total each season, until he'd reached 59. Since then, he'd been frustrated by the notion that he too had peaked. Some even believed the 32-year-old slugger was heading downhill.

In the spring of 1927, America had crowned a

**The Sultan of Swat smashes his own record as he crashes his 60th homer in the eighth inning of the penultimate game off Tom Zachary.**

new celebrity king when Charles Lindbergh flew across the ocean in the *Spirit of St. Louis,* and in the summer Gehrig had challenged Ruth's supremacy on the Yankees and throughout baseball. Ruth had only one homer and one RBI in his first nine games before smacking out seven in nine days at the end of May. Still, he didn't think seriously about hitting 60, even turning around to bat right-handed on May 31 after swatting two homers.

But it was Gehrig's emergence that received the most attention. On June 30 both men hit their 25th homer. For Ruth, who had won seven home run titles in the previous nine years (falling short only when he'd missed at least 40 games), this was a challenge.

By mid-August, Gehrig—in just his third season—led 38–35 and had become a favorite subject for the mighty scribes of the day, who called him "the Buster," "Slambino" to Ruth's "Bambino," and "the Prince of Punch." But while those titles implicitly deferred to Ruth as "King," some columnists began predicting as early as July 4 that Gehrig would wear the crown by season's end. (Meanwhile, the excitement of the race was so great that more radio stations began broadcasting baseball games, prompting more people to buy this new entertainment device.)

Ruth freely credited Gehrig's fearsome presence behind him in the cleanup slot with forcing teams to pitch to him more often, although he still walked 138 times. But by September 22, when Ruth blasted his 56th roundtripper—carrying the bat around the bases to stop people from stealing it—few were paying attention to the young first baseman anymore, even though that day he broke Ruth's RBI record of 170.

Then Ruth skidded into a four-game dry spell. With just four games remaining, the record again seemed to be slipping out of Ruth's grasp. But in Game 151 Ruth swatted a grand slam for number

57 (no other *team* would top 56), and in Game 152 Ruth outdid himself, crushing a solo home run and another grand slam for 58 and 59 (along with a long triple and a fly-out to the fence). He had tied his record, stopping the presses from coast to coast: the *New York Times* talked about Ruth having the "palpitating world in suspense" and dismissed the Washington Senators as the team on the field merely for "scenic effect" in Ruth's grand production. Out west, the *Los Angeles Examiner* gushed over those "two luscious home runs" with a generous spread of photos, charts, graphics, and text.

That left two games for one blast. The opposing starter at Yankee Stadium on September 30, Washington Senator lefty Tom Zachary, had already yielded two dingers to Ruth that summer and was determined not to allow another. "I had made up my mind that I wasn't going to give him a good pitch all afternoon," Zachary said later. Not surprisingly, he walked Ruth on four pitches in the first. The fans let Zachary have it. Ruth managed to get his bat on pitches his next two times up for singles, which was wholly unsatisfactory.

Letting Ruth reach first, however, was dangerous too: Ruth had scored after each single, creating a 2–2 tie in the eighth inning. When shortstop Mark Koenig tripled with one out, Zachary knew that walking Ruth with Gehrig and Bob Meusel waiting would not solve anything.

He came after Ruth with a fastball for strike one. His next pitch was high for a ball.

Zachary broke off a curve at Ruth's knees to back him off the plate. "I don't say it was the best curve anybody ever threw, but it was as good as any I ever threw," he'd later recall. But Ruth somehow waded right into the pitch, reaching down and jerking it deep to right, well inside the foul pole. By the time the ball landed, it had hooked close to the line, prompting a protest by Zachary that fell on deaf ears.

"What Dempsey couldn't do with his fists, Ruth has done with his bat. He came back," *New York Times* columnist John Kieran wrote. "Put it in the book in letters of gold. It will be a long time before anyone betters that home run mark and a still longer time before any aging athlete makes such a gallant and glorious charge over the comeback trail."

The fans tossed their special "Homer 60" hats in the air and shredded paper to create instant confetti for Ruth, who took what the *Times* called a "triumphant almost regal tour of the paths." Even the sportswriters were on their feet applauding. When he returned to the field for the ninth, the fans waved their handkerchiefs in celebration, and Ruth in turn saluted them. The Yankees won 4–2, their 109th win, and when Ruth trotted in after catching the final out, fans jumped down from the bleachers to congratulate him.

In the clubhouse afterwards, Ruth was jubilant and almost defiant in his pride, boasting, "Sixty, count 'em, sixty! Let's see some other son-of-a-bitch match that!"

In the 34 years until the 162-game schedule came along and Roger Maris finally matched and passed Ruth, 60 was baseball's preeminent magical number as Hack Wilson, Jimmie Foxx, Hank Greenberg, Ralph Kiner, and Willie Mays all fell short. It was a more potent symbol than Cy Young's 511, Joe DiMaggio's 56, Ted Williams's .406, or even Ruth's 714. Although Ruth had better overall numbers in 1921, his 1927 homer mark captured the imagination: 60 became shorthand for baseball's love affair with the home run and for the Yankees' dominance of baseball in a year in which they set an AL record with 110 wins, captured the pennant by 19 games, had the unsurpassed clout of the league's top three home run hitters (Ruth, Gehrig, and Tony Lazzeri, way down there at 18), dazzled hitters with their oft-obscured pitching staff (no AL team would equal its 3.20 ERA until 1942), and then blew away Pittsburgh in the World Series for their first crown since 1923.

But most of all, 60 symbolized Ruth's greatness. Yes, Gehrig, Lazzeri, Earle Combs, and Meusel constituted a true "Murderers' Row," but Ruth had proved once and for all that this was his team, his sport, his nation of worshipers.

"Succumb to the power and romance of this man," Paul Gallico effused in the *Daily News*. "Feel the athletic marvel that this big, uncouth fellow has accomplished."

# 22. Joe DiMaggio hits in his 45th straight game, a new record, July 2, 1941, Yankee Stadium

The number 56 is among the most celebrated in all sports, yet this most hallowed statistic is an accidental icon. When Joe DiMaggio's hitting streak—what *The Sporting News* called back in 1941 "the greatest one man swat soiree in the history of major league ball"—reached its 56th game, no one knew it had reached its furthest point, and the number itself is bittersweet, symbolizing the end of the line, the return to normality. Back when "the Yankee Clipper" had America singing his song, the numbers that mattered most were 42 and 45: the marks he reached to break George Sisler's modern record of 41 and to surpass Wee Willie Keeler's all-time skein of 44 straight.

The day DiMaggio broke Sisler's record was more dramatic because his bat was stolen between the games of a double-header and he went hitless in the first three at-bats of the record-breaker with a new bat. The day he broke Keeler's record, however, July 2 at Yankee Stadium, was more important, particularly with the gift of hindsight: in 1978 Pete Rose equaled Keeler's 44-game streak, so if DiMaggio had not reached 44, he wouldn't even be the modern record-holder today. (This distinction between 42, 45, and 56 explains why DiMaggio's streak, so astonishing and enthralling, is not ranked higher up—this book is about singular days, but what makes DiMaggio's record so remarkable is that it required consecutive days of sustained greatness.)

When the streak started, DiMaggio was more concerned with shaking off his and the Yankees' slumps than with making history. The previous year had been the first in his five-year career when the club had fallen short of the World Series. Early in 1941 things looked even bleaker: on May 15 the fourth-place Yankees fell to 14–14, 5½ games out of first after a 13–1 loss to Chicago. DiMaggio made a crucial error but managed one single and two solid outs, a good day considering he'd batted .194 over the previous 20 games. Headlines belittling the weak Yankee offense laid much of the blame on DiMaggio, who had carried them for so long.

There were plenty of reasons for him to be distracted: his wife Dorothy was pregnant; his manager Joe McCarthy was shuttling newcomers in and out of the lineup, trying to resuscitate the team; Lou Gehrig, so crucial to the first three pennant-winners in DiMaggio's career, was dying; and the country was slowly, inexorably headed toward war. (Big leaguers like DiMaggio were getting draft numbers at that time.)

That 13–1 stomping was the first day of "the Streak." DiMaggio's hitting steadily improved, although what was more noticeable early on was that the Yankees started winning. (Catcher Bill Dickey carried the club too, batting .391 in his own 21-game hitting streak.) DiMaggio's streak garnered its first press mention at 14 games, but interest was negligible until a Memorial Day trip to Boston, where Red Sox star Ted Williams had started his own streak on May 15. (It ended at 23 games.) When DiMaggio reached 20, local columnists and headline writers began taking note—DiMaggio

**The Yankee Clipper poses with his lumber after breaking the all-time hitting streak mark.**

had hit in 61 straight in the minors and was seen as having a legitimate shot at Roger Peckinpaugh's and Earle Combs's club record of 29. Inspired by DiMaggio, the Yankees caught fire and on June 1 began a streak as a team, homering in a record 25 straight games (with 40 roundtrippers, 10 jolted out by DiMaggio) as they ascended the standings.

DiMaggio tied the Yankee record in a game against Cleveland (managed by Peckinpaugh) and reached 30 thanks to a bad-hop single off Luke Appling's shoulder and the generous decision of sportswriter and official scorer Dan Daniel. By then attention was spreading from New York to the national press, from the sports pages to the front pages, and was now focused on Sisler's 1922 record. But Daniel, the old man of the *World-Telegram,* started hyping Keeler's 1897 streak as the ultimate goal.

Records set before 1900 are generally dismissed as ancient history . . . with good reason. Back in 1897 a crucial rule favoring slap hitters decreed that foul balls did not count as strikes. If Keeler's ancient accomplishment hadn't been discovered until years later, no one would have given it much thought even if DiMaggio hadn't passed him, but once it was dug up, the record became a challenge DiMaggio had to meet. (Perhaps Keeler's old teammates would have otherwise lobbied for an asterisk.)

By the time DiMaggio set the righty record with 34 straight games, the streak had captured the attention of even the general public; radio stations were interrupting their regular programming to announce that DiMaggio had gotten his hit. *New York Times* columnist Dave Anderson, who as a boy wouldn't go to bed at night until he'd heard whether the streak had lived another day, notes that the lack of television in those days enhanced the excitement. "We never saw him except on newsreels, so there was a mystique surrounding this," he says. Adding to the suspense was the fact that Yankees games were not being broadcast on radio because no sponsor had been willing to shell out the $75,000 rights fee (although Don Dunphy provided 15-minute highlight re-creations on WINS each evening).

The Yankees moved into first place after the 37th game on June 26, and the streak nearly ended the next day: struggling against St. Louis submariner Eldon Auker, DiMaggio was 0-for-3 in the eighth. (Marius Russo had pitched seven no-hit innings, but no one had noticed.) With the Yankees winning 3–1, this would probably be their last ups. DiMaggio was up fourth. With one out, Red Rolfe walked. Tommy Henrich, terrified that he'd hit into a double play and kill the streak, went back to the dugout and asked McCarthy if he could bunt. McCarthy approved, and with two outs and Rolfe on second, DiMaggio drilled a fastball into the left-field corner to keep the streak alive with a double.

June 29 was DiMaggio's chance to both tie and pass Sisler, in a double-header in Washington. The Yankees, as Richard Ben Cramer notes in *Joe DiMaggio: The Hero's Life,* needed an extra train car for the trip to jam in all the writers now traveling with the team. The writers went on and on about the great DiMaggio and his nerves of steel, but privately he fretted away. In the opener, after fans rushed the field to shake his hand and ask for autographs, DiMaggio rammed a double on a 1–1 fastball in the sixth, but between games a fan swiped DiMaggio's bat from the bat rack.

DiMaggio was unnerved, because of superstition and because that bat had been just right—a 32-inch, 36-ounce bat with a half-ounce personally sandpapered off at the handle. Using an unfamiliar new bat, DiMaggio went hitless in his first three trips. The record was on the line. Henrich, who had earlier borrowed some of DiMaggio's lumber, thrust one of those sticks into DiMaggio's hands in the seventh, and DiMaggio singled to pass Sisler. (The fan who stole the bat went home to Newark and boasted about it; DiMaggio's mob-connected friends found him and got the stick back for the streak's last stretch.)

All that was left was Willie "hit 'em where they ain't" Keeler. More than 52,000 fans, including Mayor Fiorello La Guardia, turned out for a Tuesday afternoon double-header on July 1 caring only about whether DiMaggio could get hits in both games and tie Keeler. He did, reaching 44 in the second game with a first-inning single, which was well timed because the sky grew so dark and ominous that the umpires halted play after five innings.

One more hit and DiMaggio would stand alone.

The next day, July 2, was a scorcher, nearly 95 degrees in the midst of a brutal heat wave that would cause at least five fatalities. Boston's 41-year-old Lefty Grove—scheduled to go for his 300th win—bowed out at the last minute; the Red Sox put in Dick Newsome in his stead. DiMaggio got a good read on Newsome with his first at-bat, crushing the ball deep to right-center, but Stan Spence, after an initial misjudgment, made a fine running catch. In the third, DiMaggio jumped on another pitch, but this hard, long drive hooked foul. Then he grounded out to third. He'd probably have just two more chances.

On a 2–0 fastball in the fifth, DiMaggio looked overeager when he swung at a fastball up out of the zone, but the harmless foul pop landed in the stands. Newsome tried another high fastball. This one DiMaggio turned on: whipping his quick, compact swing from his wide stance, he lashed a hard liner over Ted Williams's head (a perfect location given DiMaggio's disdainful feelings for his peer) and over the fence in left field for a home run, giving him at least one hit in 45 consecutive games.

Teammate Lefty Gomez quipped that DiMaggio had broken the record of Keeler, a singles hitter, in perfect style. "Joe hit one today where they ain't."

As the fans realized what had happened, they stood and cheered, and even the sportswriters joined in the ovation. His teammates, who had long held back, afraid of pressuring or jinxing the great man, rushed out to greet him.

"My teammates never mentioned the streak, they'd never say, 'Come on, Joe, get that base hit,'" he said later, so seeing their excitement "was a real thrill."

Afterwards, DiMaggio acknowledged that 45 had been the magic number. Breaking his pose as Mr. Unflappable, he also admitted that the pressure on and off the field was getting to him. "I'm glad it's over," he said. "It got to be quite a strain over the last ten days. Now I can go back to swinging at good balls. I was swinging at some bad pitches so I wouldn't be walked."

Finally able to relax, he would hit safely in the first inning of each of his next five games (plus a double in the All-Star Game), and in the final 11 games of the streak he hit .545, going 24-for-44 and leaving baseball fans slack-jawed in awe. When Ken Keltner made two great stops to end the streak at 56, DiMaggio had tallied a .408 average, 15 homers, 55 RBIs, 56 runs scored, and just 7 strikeouts. Then he hit safely in his next 16 games.

By that time, the Yankees were cruising to another pennant and DiMaggio had graduated from baseball star to American idol. Back on July 2 he'd needed a police escort to get past the fans to Lefty Gomez's car, and every subsequent day added luster to his legend. Les Brown and his band recorded a new song that streaked up the charts. The lyrics to the chorus, "Jolting Joe DiMaggio, Joe . . . Joe . . . DiMaggio . . . we want you on our side," took on extra significance after America entered World War II that winter; Cramer points out that people looked back at the streak as a symbol of American might and excellence and at DiMaggio, the immigrant's son, as a "poster boy for valor, victory, and God-given grace."

Although those were overwrought exaggerations created by the press and the public, the record DiMaggio set in 1941 would prove unique. More than 60 years after the fact, only Rose has broken the 40-game barrier, leaving DiMaggio's streak intact as baseball's most remarkable mark.

# 23. Army and Notre Dame shut each other out in "the Battle of the Century," November 9, 1946, Yankee Stadium

Army didn't win. Army didn't even score.

Notre Dame didn't win. Notre Dame didn't score either.

But on November 9, 1946, before 74,000 screaming fans, a 0–0 tie added up to much more than nothing. This grudge match, the culmination of a storied and long-standing rivalry, was one of the most breathlessly hyped sports events of its generation. Although the game was far

**Notre Dame's Johnny Lujack hunts down Army's Doc Blanchard in the open field in the third quarter to preserve the scoreless tie between these two rivals.**

from flawless—it was filled with turnovers and questionable coaching moves—in dramatic terms it exceeded expectations.

The relationship between the old foes had undergone a seismic shift. Their annual contests had begun in 1913 with Knute Rockne catching passes in Notre Dame's 35–13 upset of undefeated Army. After Rockne became coach, his team pretty much owned Army, racking up historic wins in 1924 and 1928 along the way. The matchup drew such a following that it had moved to the big stage of New York City in 1923, helping to elevate college football to its central place in the American sports landscape.

Eventually, Notre Dame's dominance somewhat diminished anticipation for the game—Army didn't even score off the Irish from 1938 through 1943, losing 26–0 to the national champs that last year—but World War II changed everything. College rosters were depleted as star players and coaches entered the service; West Point was one of the few exceptions, and the Cadets assembled one of the most fearsome teams ever, headed by "Mr. Inside" and "Mr. Outside," Doc Blanchard and Glenn Davis. In 1944 Army humiliated a severely weakened Notre Dame squad, intercepting eight passes and running up a 59–0 score. The following year Army slapped the fight out of the Irish in a 48–0 walloping.

By the time Army and Notre Dame faced off in their annual Yankee Stadium showdown in 1946, the West Pointers, though no longer as deep as they were during the war, had racked up 25 straight games without a loss; meanwhile, Notre Dame had returned to form, winning its first five games by a combined score of 177–18 and climbing to number two in the rankings.

The press churned out proclamations about "the Battle of the Century." Beyond the long history and recent routs were inevitable comparisons between quarterbacks Arnold Tucker (Army) and Johnny Lujack (Notre Dame), competing for All-America honors, and between coaches Earl Blaik, an Army lieutenant colonel who stayed on the sidelines during the war, and Frank Leahy, who missed two years at Notre Dame to serve in the Navy. Leahy and Blaik, who had both taken over their team in 1941, actively disliked each other and would not share game films with each other.

Notre Dame, in particular, was riled up. *Time* magazine declared that the school was on a "holy crusade." Students created SPATNC (Society for the Prevention of Army's Third National Championship), chanted "59 and 48, this is the year we retaliate," and sent off pestering postcards to Blaik.

Ticket sales created mayhem—reportedly one million requests were refused, and Notre Dame alone had to return $500,000 to people who had sent in money for ducats that vanished the moment they were available. Tickets with a face value of $3.30 were scalped for $200—the equivalent of paying $6,000 for a $100 seat today.

Notre Dame closed practices to reporters and even parents. The team was so fearful of Army spies that they'd run only the most basic plays when planes flew overhead. "We all know Army picked on our youngsters," Leahy told his team in reference to the war-year losses. "What will happen on Saturday when they face men?"

At game time, in addition to the stadium full of fans (mostly Irish rooters, thanks to New York's huge Catholic population and their decades of success), there were 20 photo news syndicates, 5 newsreel companies, 4 radio and television teams, and 95 print reporters in the press box from 20 states and places as far away as Australia and Sweden.

On the field were four past or future Heisman Trophy winners—Blanchard, Davis, Lujack, and Notre Dame's Leon Hart—and more than a dozen All-Americans, an assemblage never again equaled. Given the offensive firepower on both sides, many fans and pundits expected a nonstop assault on the end zones. Not quite.

The rival quarterbacks each produced only 52 yards passing, and Army's dynamic duo of Davis and Blanchard mustered only 80 yards on 35 carries between them. Notre Dame gained 30 more yards overall but was plagued by fumbles and interceptions and penetrated Army territory just twice; the Irish scraped together just one first down in the final period.

The lack of scoring can be partly attributed to the leg injuries nagging at Lujack and Blanchard, to the conservative approach taken by both coaches ("I think Blaik and Leahy were more worried about losing than winning," a frustrated Blanchard said later), and to the era's macho mindset in which easy field goals were disdained as unmanly. (Notre Dame fullback Jim Mello later said, "If you couldn't ram it in, Leahy thought taking three points would be an insult.") Some observers questioned Leahy's unwillingness to trust his second unit, the squad that supposedly was going to wear Army down; even after Lujack got kicked in the head, Leahy refused to tinker, leaving backup quarterback George Ratterman on the bench, although some thought Ratterman a superior passer.

The reality was that despite Notre Dame's secrecy, both teams had done endless advance scouting, eliminating virtually all opportunities for the surprises that often create big yardage gains. And both of these rugged defenses were just superb, turning in one big play after another and stiffening up whenever the other team really threatened.

Early on, Army recovered a Notre Dame fumble on the Irish 24, but on 2nd-and-4 Blaik played it ultraconservative, hurling Blanchard up the middle on second, third, and even fourth down; each time Notre Dame's defense was equal to the challenge.

The biggest defensive plays, however, were made by the two offensive stars—in this era of the two-way player, Lujack and Tucker showed they could perform at either end. In the second quarter, Notre Dame's Jerry Cowhig took a lateral near midfield and exploded past the Army line, down to the 30 . . . the 20 . . . the 12 . . . but there

Tucker finally chased him down, saving a touchdown. Three plays later, the Irish, like their foe, eschewed "settling" for the field goal and went for it on 4th-and-1 from the 3. Lujack faked a run up the middle and tossed instead to Billy Gompers, who was trapped trying to get outside. Cowhig's breakaway yielded nothing.

Shortly before halftime, Lujack returned the favor when Tucker, having just picked off a pass, ran from scrimmage through left tackle, slithering for 30 yards to the Notre Dame 30, where Lujack finally slammed him down. Time ran out before Army could go any farther. The fans let their breath out and started their hearts again. Then it was time for the third quarter and another round of gut-wrenching thrills.

When Lujack tried playing hero by firing a third-down pass deep into the Army defense, Tucker snagged it at the Army 10 and burst up the sideline for 32 yards. (Afterwards, Leahy asked his star quarterback, "How did you happen to throw so many passes to Tucker?"—who finished with three pickoffs—and Lujack quipped, "He was the only man I could find open.") Army used misdirection, making it look like they were running the first play through Davis. Instead, Blanchard ran the opposite way and tore through a stunned Notre Dame line. Suddenly Mr. Inside was outside, momentarily free of the stifling Irish defense. He hurtled past Notre Dame's secondary, heading for glory. There was no one left but Lujack, racing to cut off the angle. Blanchard headed for the sideline, then tried deking the last defender by slowing down before one final acceleration, but Lujack didn't fall for it and lunged, smashing Blanchard to the ground at the Notre Dame 36. He had found a new destiny in the game's defining play.

Still, Army soon reached the Notre Dame 12. But the Cadets called for a halfback-option pass, and future Irish coach Terry Brennan intercepted to halt the threat. In the fourth, Army was stronger, yet Notre Dame continued its narrow escapes, stopping Army just inches from a first down on the Notre Dame 33, intercepting the ball on their own 10, and recovering one of their own fumbles on their 5. Near game's end, Army was again sweeping through Notre Dame territory when a sack and fumble rescued them. With 48 seconds left, Army's last chance died when Blanchard caught a pass at Notre Dame's 20 but his feet landed out of bounds.

Both teams trudged off after their terrible tangle still unbeaten. Although players on each team felt a curious blend of elation at having been a part of such a memorable game and despair at their inability to finish off their foe, it is clear that even a scoreless tie produced a decisive winner . . . or two.

Objectively, Army outplayed Notre Dame, with more drives and more real chances to score. Yet Blaik was the despondent one for failing to capitalize on opportunities while Leahy was happy to have averted disaster. Notre Dame was deemed the psychological victor for stopping the top-ranked team, avenging the two wartime routs, and ensuring that Army could not score off a Leahy-coached team. When both teams finished the season undefeated, Army, which also barely edged Navy, was perceived as less convincing than the Fighting Irish, which beat their opponents by a combined 271–24, so Notre Dame, on its way to 36 games without a loss and three national titles in four years, was crowned champion.

The game stands out even more because it turned out to be a farewell performance. At year's end, the schools released a statement saying that the rivalry, especially as it had played out on the Gotham stage, had spun out of control, growing too big and unwholesome for collegiate sports. The teams relocated their confrontation to South Bend, Indiana, the following year, then suspended it altogether. There was some speculation that Blaik simply couldn't abide the idea of losing to Leahy and Notre Dame anymore, and given that college football had been big business since their first game in New York back in 1923, the decision to end this grand tradition rings hollow and seems a shame.

But if it had to end, there was no better way to go out, with a scoreless game that scores high on the list of classics.

# 24. The Yankees and the Dodgers both win on the season's final day, October 2, 1949, Yankee Stadium and Shibe Park

The legacy of a decade in a single day. When it comes to the theater of baseball, that's pretty tough to match. Although no one knew it at the time, the fate of the most glorious era in New York City sports tilted most precariously on the fulcrum that was October 2, 1949.

The years 1947 to 1956 are hailed as the heyday of New York baseball: the New York Yankees appeared in eight World Series, the Brooklyn Dodgers in six, and the New York Giants in two; seven of the ten Fall Classics stayed entirely within reach of New York's subway system. (In that same era, boxing flourished here as well, the football Giants won their final championship, the Knicks were born and reached three NBA finals, and the Rangers made it to their last NHL final until 1972. Good ol' days indeed.)

But that perception rests on the success of the Yankees and the Dodgers on that October 2 as both teams won in heart-stopping fashion, barely holding a lead that would have haunted them had it slipped away. Had the Yankees and the Dodgers lost, 1949 would belong to the glory years of the St. Louis Cardinals and the Boston Red Sox, two teams whose fates were inextricably linked with New York's; one more pennant for each team and they'd have been able to stake claims as their league's best team of that era. Moreover, a Yankee loss might have seriously undermined rookie manager Casey Stengel, who would ultimately prove instrumental in the new Yankee dynasty, while an accompanying Dodger loss would have made boasts of a New York "era" ring hollow with non–New York teams winning the NL from 1948 to 1950.

The National League stretch run in 1949 culminated a long rivalry between the Dodgers and the Cardinals, the organization Branch Rickey had built up before taking over Brooklyn. (St. Louis was also the only club to beat the Yankees in a World Series after 1923—doing it in 1926 and 1942—and they were the Giants' archrivals in the 1930s.) Brooklyn had edged the Cards in 1941, then fallen just short to them the following year; St. Louis captured two more pennants during the war years while Brooklyn stumbled, and in 1946 St. Louis snatched the pennant from Brooklyn in baseball's first tiebreaker playoff. In 1947 Brooklyn reclaimed superiority. So it was fitting that the teams were still at it on the final day of this season as the Cardinals snapped a four-game losing streak to win their 96th game. The Dodgers started the day with 96 too—to avoid another playoff Brooklyn needed to win its 97th in Philadelphia. It would not be easy.

Staked to a 5–0 advantage, Dodger ace Don Newcombe lost his focus and was bounced in the fourth as the Phillies scored four times. The Dodgers retaliated with two in the fifth, but the Phillies inched back within one in the sixth, chasing reliever Rex Barney. Del Ennis greeted rookie

**Rookie manager Casey Stengel leads the Yankees in celebration after they beat Boston on the final day to clinch the pennant.**

sidearmer Jack Banta with a game-tying single, but Banta fanned Andy Seminick with the sacks full, then shut the Phillies out through the ninth. In the tenth, with dusk arriving and the score stuck at 7–7, Pee Wee Reese blooped a single to left, moved to second on a bunt, and scored when Duke Snider smoked a single; after Jackie Robinson walked, Snider scored on a single by Luis Olmo, making it 9–7. This lead held up, giving the Dodgers the pennant and the last laugh—the Cardinals had won one more pennant than Brooklyn in the 1940s but would stumble after this, finishing as high as second just once from 1950 to 1962, while Brooklyn earned three more pennants and its first World Series.

But back in New York the Dodgers, as usual, were the subhead to the Yankees' headlines as the Bronx Bombers defeated the Red Sox in even more dramatic fashion.

Boston had, of course, gone from champs to chumps after selling a certain Bambino to the Yankees. They'd recovered in the 1940s, however, to again challenge the Bombers, routing the competition in 1946 and tying for first in 1948 by beating the Yankees on the final two days before losing a one-game playoff to Cleveland. The Red Sox began 1949 as the AL favorites: they had the most potent offense and a younger, stronger team than New York. What's more, the Yankees, having run through four managers since 1946, were now in the hands of Casey Stengel, whose hiring was dismissed by many as a curious joke. He'd won in the minors but had never finished higher than fifth place managing the Boston Braves and Brooklyn Dodgers (admittedly two very bad clubs); he was good friends with general manager George Weiss and was best known during his playing days for hijinks like doffing his cap and having a bird fly out. When Stengel was hired, Dave Egan, a columnist in Boston, declared, "The Yankees have now been mathematically eliminated from the 1949 pennant race."

When Joe DiMaggio injured his right heel and missed the first 65 games, it seemed a safe bet that Boston would end the decade as the AL's best team, especially when the other Yankees followed DiMaggio's lead and one after another went down with injuries. But that actually freed Stengel to juggle his lineup, and everything he tried worked brilliantly, for the man was no clown . . . well, he *was* a clown, but that was merely a mask, a diversionary tactic that was part of his genius. His genius was enhanced by having a rotation headed by Vic Raschi, Eddie Lopat, and Allie Reynolds.

The Yankees started fast, going 25–12; after DiMaggio returned and single-handedly demolished the Red Sox with four homers and nine RBIs in a three-game sweep at Fenway Park, the Yankees built a 12-game lead by July 4. But Boston had two superb starters, Mel Parnell and Ellis Kinder (a combined 21–1 from August through late September), and an offense fueled by Ted Williams, who'd miss winning his third Triple Crown by just one hit, and outfielder Junior Stephens, who tied "the Splendid Splinter" in RBIs and finished second in homers. Given that Williams was DiMaggio's sole rival in skills and press attention, that Boston's center fielder was Joe's brother Dom, and that their manager was former Yankee skipper Joe McCarthy, the tension between these two clubs would be high even in meaningless games—and in the late 1940s there were no meaningless games.

Boston closed the gap to one and a half games by late August as those injuries ate the Yankees alive—budding young catcher Yogi Berra was sidelined with a wounded thumb; Johnny Mize, acquired to play first base and allow Tommy Henrich to return to the depleted outfield, pulled his arm out of its socket in his first week on the team; in that same game, Henrich crashed into the wall, fracturing several vertebrae. On September 18, the Yankees suffered "what looked like the death blow to their pennant dreams," as Bert Sugar wrote in *Baseball's 50 Greatest Games*: DiMaggio went down again, this time with viral pneumonia. On September 25, Boston beat the Yankees at Fenway to tie for first; the Bosox moved ahead in the Bronx the next day, winning 7–6 on an eighth-inning rally built around a hit by Dom DiMaggio that tore through the webbing of Phil Rizzuto's ancient glove and a controversial safe call on a squeeze play.

But neither team would surrender, and the race came down to the final weekend. Up one game, Boston needed just one win to clinch the pennant. The last two games would be at Yankee Stadium; the Sox, an astonishing 61–16 at home, had gone just 35–40 on the road. Still, they were confident enough that owner Tom Yawkey readied a train in Boston to whisk the players' wives to New York for a celebration. And when Boston, with Parnell on the mound, jumped out to a 4–0 lead, the conductor probably started shouting, "All aboard!"

But the Yankees derailed their plans. The weakened DiMaggio (who'd lost 18 pounds) rapped a double to spark a two-run rally in the fourth and added an infield hit in another two-run rally in the fifth that tied it. In the eighth, Stengel tried two lefty pinch-hitters but then decided against using a third (Charlie Keller), instead letting Johnny Lindell, who had two hits and a long out, bat. Lindell rewarded Stengel's hunch by blasting a home run for a 5–4 win.

That left one game for the pennant: Raschi versus Kinder, who had beaten the Yankees four times in his 23-win season.

In the first inning, Rizzuto spanked a ball into the left-field corner for what should have been a double, but Williams played it tentatively and Rizzuto raced to third. When bruised and battered Tommy Henrich poked a grounder to second, Rizzuto trotted home for a 1–0 lead.

It seemed that would be enough. Kinder was razor-sharp, allowing just three more hits through the seventh, but Raschi slashed through Boston's lineup like a machete, yielding only two hits through eight innings. When McCarthy pinch-hit for Kinder, the Yankees' eyes widened and their bats suddenly felt lighter.

McCarthy had no trusted reliever, so he went back to Parnell, a southpaw, to face the lefties Henrich and Berra. But Boston's lefty had nothing left—given the close race and Boston's shallow staff, he and Kinder started or relieved 17 times in Boston's final 19 games—and Henrich drilled a fastball into the right-field stands for a 2–0 lead. When Berra singled, McCarthy called on Tex Hughson, who got DiMaggio to hit into a double play before loading the bases.

Against Jerry Coleman, Hughson made the pitch he wanted, a fastball, high and tight, a tough pitch for anyone, but especially for a light-hitting little rookie. All Coleman could manage was a little light hit, but in the next day's box score it would resound as loudly as a line drive off the wall

—Coleman's dying, slicing blooper landed just beyond the outstretched glove of the right fielder, and with two outs all three runners scored. An alert Bobby Doerr threw out Coleman at third, but it was too late. The Yankees had a 5–0 lead with only three outs to go.

Getting those last three would be an arduous, painful task. With one out, Raschi walked Williams, a logical decision. But Stephens singled, and Doerr hit a long fly to deep center field. It was a ball most center fielders would have caught, and Sugar noted that DiMaggio once "would have flagged down such a drive with the style and grace that had made him famous." But now he was old, injured, sick, and weak; he struggled toward the ball "like he was swimming upstream." DiMaggio fell. The ball landed for a triple, making it 5–2. Worse, DiMaggio knew, in what must have been a painful and humiliating moment of clarity, that he was hurting the team. He removed himself from the game, trudging in to the fans' cheers. (He'd bat a mere .111 in the World Series, then play just two more seasons, diminishing steadily in effectiveness.)

Boston was alive. Raschi got one more out only to give up a single, making it 5–3 with batter Birdie Tebbetts representing the tying run. Henrich and Berra approached Raschi, but the surly pitcher chased them off with a growl: "Gimme the goddamn ball and get out of here."

Raschi was not about to relinquish the ball, the lead, or the game. Tebbetts lifted a high pop in foul territory behind first base. Henrich camped under it and caught it. The pennant belonged to New York.

Like the Cardinals, the Red Sox would not soon recover, finishing no higher than third until 1967, when they'd win the pennant but lose the World Series, fittingly, to the Cardinals.

But for New York it was fun city. The Dodgers and the Yankees were heading into another Subway Series, this time on equal footing, having each won 97 games and their respective pennants in unforgettable style. For the Yankees this game also marked the birth of a new dynasty. Babe Ruth and Lou Gehrig had ruled over the first golden age, Gehrig and DiMaggio over the second. DiMaggio would pass the bat to Mickey Mantle halfway through this run, but the face of the team in this most spectacular of dynasties—the only one to win five straight championships—would be the craggy visage of Casey Stengel. And the joke would be on everyone else in baseball. You could look it up.

# 25. The Marathon expands to all five boroughs, October 24, 1976

Stand on Fourth Avenue in Brooklyn or First Avenue in Manhattan on the first Sunday in November and you'll witness a miracle: the transformation of a city that never stops going. Instead of rushing around, people watch, cheer, and celebrate as others stream by. Some runners are certainly New Yorkers, but many come from across America and 100 other nations; some don serious running gear, others goofy wigs or costumes; most jog or run, but others keep on trucking even after they're reduced to a walk, while some zoom past in wheelchairs.

The New York City Marathon is most definitely a sporting event, but more than for any other athletic endeavor on this list, the emphasis is on "event." It attracts more than two million spectators, more than any other live sporting event in the world, and most don't know, or care, who will win. With bands playing and spectators urging on those brave or foolhardy marathoners, it is, *New York* magazine once declared, a pageant "that exalts not only those who participate, but those who observe."

In Ron Rubin's biography of Marathon impresario Fred Lebow, *Anything for a T-Shirt,* he calls the spectacle New York's "happiest, most unifying, most inspiring day of the year." That sounds simplistic, but anyone who has participated in or witnessed it understands the essential truth of that claim. The race touches every borough and countless ethnic enclaves. It provides Gothamites with something uniquely our own—a reminder of how special life can be in this often challenging metropolis. And unlike so many of New York's other wonderful attractions, it's free. The Marathon is truly our most glorious municipal holiday, a tribute to our city and ourselves.

Fittingly enough for something so quintessentially New York, this five-borough street festival of a race was cooked up in melting pot fashion by a Jewish immigrant from Transylvania working in the garment industry and a black transplant from Texas working in politics.

Fishl Lebowitz was forced into labor camps in Romania during World War II, then forced to flee when communism proved nearly as threatening as fascism. On his way to becoming Fred Lebow, Lebowitz bounced around Europe and then America, working as everything from a television salesman to a comedy club owner before settling in New York, where he eventually owned clothing companies that designed knockoffs.

In the mid-1960s, Lebow's only exercise was tennis, but he wasn't very good. Upon hearing that jogging would improve his fitness and thus his game, Lebow decided to race his tennis partner around the Central Park Reservoir. Lebow won easily. He also loved it so much that he dropped tennis. He joined the New York City Road Runners Club, and in the spring of 1970 he ran its annual Cherry Tree Marathon in the Bronx. Navigating through streets not closed to traffic, Lebow was struck by how uninviting and poorly organized the race was, so he and fellow runner Vince Chiappetta launched the New York City Marathon later that year.

The race looped around and around Central Park. Lebow drummed up some press and spent $1,000 of his own on soda and prizes (also dispensing leftover bowling trophies), but the race made little dent in the city's psyche and drew just 127 runners, with 55 finishers. (Local firefighter Gary Muhrcke won.) Most people didn't even realize a marathon was under way. *Sports Illustrated* said that most of the "spectators" were vendors yelling, "What's the big rush? Stop and buy a pretzel already."

Still, it was better than the Cherry Tree. Within three years, Lebow had ascended to the club's presidency, attracted over 400 entries to the race, and reeled in a few sponsors. But even as the club expanded the marathon's growth stalled, and it remained a small-time race for diehards who were considered eccentrics by outsiders. Its future was hardly assured.

Then one marathoner, Ted Corbitt, decided that New York could celebrate America's bicentennial by having teams from each borough race. Another marathoner, George Spitz, misunderstood this idea, thinking—in a stroke of inadvertent genius—that Corbitt had suggested a marathon traversing all five boroughs. Spitz took this promotional gambit to Lebow, who flatly rejected it. Though Lebow longed to create a "people's race," and though he'd eventually morph into the P. T. Barnum of running, he believed the concept was impractical and logistically impossible.

Undeterred, Spitz asked Manhattan borough president Percy Sutton for help. Sutton, a former Tuskegee airman, lawyer for Malcolm X, and black broadcasting pioneer, had greatly enjoyed himself shooting the starter's gun at the 1975 race. Now

**Bill Rodgers wins the race, but all New York comes out ahead as the city's marathon expands to all five boroughs, becoming a major civic event.**

he was contemplating a 1977 mayoral run, and in that "Ford to New York: Drop Dead" era of fiscal calamities and white flight, he loved this bold way to embrace the city and its ethnic groups. Rubin notes that when Lebow told Sutton there were too many factors — street closings, police for crowd control, sanitation workers to clean up, and so on — Sutton simply asked how much money Lebow would need. Lebow threw out $20,000, a number he thought would be a deterrent.

Sutton didn't flinch. He went to work, getting Mayor Abe Beame to give him authority to coordinate the involvement of city agencies, thus eliminating most of Lebow's obstacles — the highway department even painted blue lines through the streets so the runners wouldn't get lost. Sutton also persuaded real estate developers Lewis and Jack Rudin to donate $25,000 and turned his own office space and staff over to Lebow to help.

Now Lebow embraced his task, learning quickly and on the fly. No reporters showed for his first press conference in 1976, so he persuaded 1972 Olympic gold medalist Frank Shorter to sign up and flew him in for another press conference, at which Beame fired a starter's gun and Shorter briefly ran "against" four borough presidents. That got photos in the paper. Lebow then paid $2,000 out of his own pocket and under the table to land another big name: Bill Rodgers, winner of the prestigious Boston Marathon. (Four previous New York winners also returned.) Finally, he arranged for premarathon parties and a Club 21 luncheon, while frantically arranging volunteers in the outer boroughs to provide water to the marathoners.

On October 24, 1976, at 10:30 A.M., it was readily apparent that this was not the same old race but rather an event of, by, and for the people. There were 2,090 runners, ages 10 to 71, from 35 states and 12 other nations. Fifty-eight women ran (the most ever for a marathon), and the health craze among the educated was reflected in the presence among the runners of 317 doctors, lawyers, and scientists along with 300 students. And there was Dick Traum, who had lost a leg and wore a prosthetic. (Traum started early, at 6:49 A.M., and finished in 7 hours, 24 minutes; his inspiring story even inspired himself — he later started the Achilles Track Club for disabled runners.)

It was a brisk 40 degrees when Sutton fired the starter's gun. Finnish Olympian Pekka Paivarinta grabbed an early lead, while Shorter and Rodgers hung back. They passed through Brooklyn, leaving behind the utterly perplexed Hasidim of Williamsburg, and entered Queens, where Rodgers — wearing borrowed soccer shorts because he forgot to pack his own — took the lead. He never relinquished it.

Rodgers led virtually unchallenged the rest of the way, finishing in 2:10:10 — the fastest time in the world that year — while Miki Gorman won on the women's side in 2:39:11. They received Tiffany sterling silver trays, courtesy of the Rudins. Most noteworthy was the street turnout — about 500,000 spectators came to watch and party.

Rodgers recalled that he "fed off their energy," but it wasn't just the front-runners who were saluted. One runner, Melvin Marks, noted in a letter to the *New York Times* that supposedly jaded New Yorkers bubbled with enthusiasm and appreciation. "Children everywhere called out just to touch my hand," he wrote. "Pretty girls smiled at me and men as old or older than I urged me forward as if they were in this race too. . . . No one threw rocks or eggs — only love."

Lebow even made the one sour note sweet: Rodgers had unwittingly parked his car illegally, and it was towed during the race, but Lebow paid the fine.

After the supposed onetime success of 1976, there was no turning back . . . and not just for New York, but for the sport as a whole and the marathons that followed in London, Chicago, Paris, and Berlin. Pamela Cooper points out in *The American Marathon* that organizers used to close courses after four hours but Lebow's populist event altered that attitude. "New York changed things," Rodgers later said. "It was the role model for the urban marathon."

Today the New York City Marathon is the world's largest and is no longer reliant on big names. It's a week of parties followed by a race that's part folk festival, part street fair. It attracts 37,000 runners (including a highly competitive wheelchair division), 12,000 volunteers, 2 million spectators, dozens of bands, prize money, title sponsors, television coverage, special newspaper sections, and millions of dollars flowing into the local economy.

It was a long road from a concept pulled out of the rejection pile to serve as a singular bicentennial special, but the stunning success of 1976 prompted Lebow to push, prod, and promote the marathon into what Rodgers has called "maybe the most spectacular race in the world."

# 26. Arthur Ashe wins the first U.S. Open, September 9, 1968, West Side Tennis Club

It was a tumultuous year, inside and outside New York, inside and outside sports. It was the year of the King and Kennedy assassinations, the Tet Offensive, and the Soviet invasion of Czechoslovakia, of the student takeover at Columbia and the New York public school strike, of riots in the cities and black fists raised at the Olympics.

So it isn't surprising that it was in this year, 1968, that tennis finally opened its doors, albeit uneasily and awkwardly, nor that its stewards found everything turned upside down. In the first Grand Slam tournament in New York (and just the second overall) that allowed professional players to compete, an amateur won, and in a sport as white as its dress code, a black man won the U.S. crown for the first (and only) time ever.

Welcome to the Open era.

Tennis had started off as quite the snooty sport, a diversion for the British upper class. Even when it reached America, class lines remained sharply etched—it was an amateur sport played by those who could afford to. Although the middle class began following the sport after Bill Tilden won the U.S. Nationals and became a star in 1920, public courts remained scarce, participation was minimal, and the biggest tournaments were still held at private tennis clubs. (No Jews, blacks, or other outsiders allowed, thank you very much.)

Worse, the game suffered from the odd split personality that arose after Tilden helped develop the professional game. (Before he turned pro, the sanctioning body, the United States Lawn Tennis Association, had even tried banning him from accepting money for articles he wrote about tennis.) The International Lawn Tennis Association ensured that the most prestigious tournaments remained strictly and haughtily amateur. To keep the best players around to entertain their society crowds, amateur tournaments lured them with expenses and under-the-table money, giving rise to the phrase "shamateurism." Although some players made a decent living by subverting the rules and remaining subservient to the system, most, from Don Budge to Jack Kramer to Ken Rosewall and Rod Laver, still turned pro, traveling from city to city with another top player, playing the same foe nightly, toiling like carny performers.

Finally, in 1968, revolt arrived. Top pros like Rosewall and Laver were forming new circuits and grabbing the best amateurs, so the British Lawn Tennis Association and United States Lawn Tennis Association helped force change from within, transforming Wimbledon and the U.S. championship into "open" tournaments.

Thus, in late August, the world's top players descended on Forest Hills. Unsurprisingly, the pros (all Australian) were seeded highest: Rod Laver, Tony Roche, Ken Rosewall, and John Newcombe, who had reached the finals as an amateur the previous year. Arthur Ashe, winner of the recent U.S. Nationals amateur championship (which was held that year as a distinct event), was seeded fifth.

Ashe, who had grown up in segregated Richmond, Virginia, went to his first sanctioned tournament in his hometown when he was 12 in 1955. Although Althea Gibson had integrated Forest Hills five years earlier, Ashe was turned away because he was black. "I'll show them," he said. Ashe soon became the first black to play in the Maryland boys' championships. The skinny boy with the big power game proved good enough to earn a tennis scholarship to UCLA, winning both an individual and a team NCAA championship in 1965; in 1963 he also became the first black to represent the United States in Davis Cup play. (Radical blacks subsequently chastised Ashe for playing for "white America," but he preferred working within the system. Similarly, in 1968 he told black Olympians considering a boycott of the Games that he would not publicly support them—their subsequent participation and public display of strength had a far more lasting impact.) Ashe, 25, had been drafted into the Army, and because he was allowed to play in tournaments if he served on a national team, he remained an amateur so he would be eligible for Davis Cup play. (Under Army policy, playing the Open was considered Davis Cup preparation.)

Ashe played well early on at the Open, beating aging great Roy Emerson, but he was also extremely fortunate. The pros, after years on their insular and largely indoor tour, were both unaccustomed to playing outdoors—where the weather was variable and the surface was grass, which deteriorated over time—and unfamiliar with the new players, with their different styles; none reached the finals. (The pros had acclimated by the

**As professionals join the fray, amateur Arthur Ashe's all-around play enables him to make tennis history, winning the first U.S. Open and becoming the first black man to win a Grand Slam tournament.**

following year, when they reasserted their dominance—particularly Laver, who won the Grand Slam in 1969.) Cliff Drysdale, another pro, took care of Laver in the round of 16, and Ashe then disposed of Drysdale. He had an easier foe in the semis, besting Clark Graebner, while speedy Dutchman Tom Okker upset Rosewall, a once and future champion who also would have been tough for Ashe, in a five-set semifinal on the other side of the draw.

Rain and scheduling conflicts had pushed the first Open final back to Monday, September 9. Playing in front of just 7,100 fans, Ashe's powerful serve and aggressive volleying, along with the fast surface, overcame both his numerous errors and Okker's agility and court coverage. Ashe, in winning his 25th straight singles match, pounded 26 aces, including 15 in the 26-game, 64-minute, 14–12 first set. (After back-to-back aces from Ashe, Okker took his deep return position, then turned his back to his opponent, as if to joke that there was nothing he could do.)

"Always, when you played Arthur on a fast court, there were a lot of short rallies," Okker said. "A lot of aces. A lot of . . . not too much tennis."

But Ashe also surprised Okker with a deft touch on his lobs whenever Okker took the offensive. After Okker edged him in the second set 7–5, the two men traded 6–3 sets, bringing the final to a deciding fifth set.

"Nobody can imagine, unless they've been through it, what agony you face in a close, five-set match, especially in scorching weather," Ashe would later say. (He'd lose the 1972 Open finals to Ilie Nastase in five sets.) "Fifth sets of tennis matches separate the great from the good."

Down 0–1, Okker rushed the net at 30–30, only to watch a perfect lob float overhead and land just inside the baseline. Soon after Ashe hit a forehand winner. Ashe needed only to hold serve the rest of the way, and he did just that, facing only one break point at 4–2 and blasting one last ace in his final service game at 5–3, which he captured at love.

Okker took home $14,000 as runner-up, but the champion's strict amateur status meant he got nothing more than his free hotel room and $28 daily stipend. Ashe, who brought his father out of the stands and embraced him during an emotional trophy presentation, didn't mind. He had made history, not just as a black man but as an athlete. "There would be only one first U.S. Open," Ashe said years later.

The win also made him the first American men's tennis champion since 1955, which earned him cachet and gave him a platform for leadership both in and out of tennis. "If Ashe doesn't win, he doesn't become 'Arthur Ashe,'" said tennis writer Joel Drucker.

Ashe turned pro and helped force tournaments to dole out prize money properly; he later was a founding father of the Association of Tennis Players and in 1973 was among the leaders of a Wimbledon boycott that gained more rights and money for the athletes. Acutely aware that the obstacles he'd overcome still awaited future generations, he also cofounded a program to teach tennis to economically disadvantaged youth. And he devoted considerable time and capital to calling attention to the injustice of apartheid in South Africa. (When Nelson Mandela was finally released from prison, the first American he wanted to meet was Ashe.) After his playing days, Ashe also was involved with the United Negro College Fund and created the Safe Passage Foundation, which oversaw an inner-city tennis program and another program that worked to boost the graduation rates of minority athletes. After a heart attack forced his retirement, he became national campaign chairman of the American Heart Association, and in 1992, when he publicly acknowledged that he had AIDS, he launched a foundation to help raise money and remove the stigma that haunted the disease.

That 1968 tournament wasn't just a new beginning for Ashe — it had an instantaneous and monumental impact on the U.S. Open and on tennis overall. Advance sales for the 1969 Open tripled, and the sport's upscale audience drew more television coverage and dollars, which fueled viewership and participation. The number of people playing tennis tripled between 1970 and 1974, when Chris Evert and Jimmy Connors, representing a truly "Open" generation, would generate a whole new wave of excitement, virtually reinventing the sport. The growth would push the sport from the private club at Forest Hills to the very public National Tennis Center. And when the sport outgrew Louis Armstrong Stadium shortly after Ashe's tragic death in 1993, the U.S. Tennis Association built a new stadium alongside it. It was named for a man who was not the greatest tennis player of all time but who achieved greatness as a human being, who symbolized the potential in everyone, and who did it all in large part because of what he had achieved at the very first U.S. Open final: Arthur Ashe.

# 27. The Yankees win a fifth straight World Series, October 5, 1953, Yankee Stadium

Five World Series titles in a row.

Babe Ruth never reached the World Series more than three straight times.

George Steinbrenner—for whom appearing in but losing the Series is meaningless—has never won more than three straight.

Even Joe DiMaggio, Joe McCarthy, and the 1936 to 1939 Yankees managed "only" four straight titles and five in six years.

Look back through the prism of the Yankee Century as created by Ruth and reimagined by Steinbrenner and you have to marvel at the unique achievement of October 5, 1953, when Billy Martin drove home Hank Bauer with the winning run in the ninth inning of Game 6, crowning the Yankees champion for the fifth straight year.

The earlier dynasties had been built around superstars and stability. From 1926 to 1928, Ruth, Lou Gehrig, Tony Lazzeri, and Bob Meusel routinely ranked among the league leaders, and the Yankees fielded the same regulars at every position but catcher. The 1936 to 1939 squad had six hitters together—including Gehrig, DiMaggio, and Bill Dickey—until 1939, when Gehrig fell ill.

The 1949 to 1953 Yankees were different. Although their staff was anchored by three strong starters—Allie Reynolds, Vic Raschi, and Eddie Lopat—they rarely had the league's best pitching or the best offense. This team—which won so often that it became boring and supposedly was so monotonous and metronomic in its ruthless efficiency that cheering them on was likened during the 1953 Series to rooting for U.S. Steel—was unbeatable because manager Casey Stengel brilliantly fit all the necessary pieces together, creating a team that was greater than the sum of its parts. His was a modern approach that shaped and foreshadowed the changes in the way champions were built.

New York had Yogi Berra at catcher and Phil Rizzuto at shortstop throughout this run, but everything else was mix-and-match Stengel style—96 different Yankees in five years, 14 starting pitchers in 1952 alone. First base might have Tommy Henrich or Johnny Mize or Joe Collins. At second, Snuffy Stirnweiss gave way to Jerry Coleman, who was replaced by Billy Martin. Bobby Brown, Billy Johnson, and Gil McDougald all held down third base. (McDougald also filled in at second and later moved to shortstop.) The crowded outfield corners included Cliff Mapes, Johnny Lindell, Hank Bauer, Gene Woodling, and Irv Noren; in center, an aging DiMaggio gave way to a still maturing Mickey Mantle. Berra was really the only consistent threat through those years.

In hunting down their record fifth championship in 1953, the Yankees won more frequently and impressively than ever before. Raschi, Reynolds, and Lopat were nearing the end but weren't there yet, and they had help from veteran Johnny Sain and youngster Whitey Ford. Mantle set the tone in the fourth game when he hit his famous 565-foot home run in Washington. New York won

**Phil Rizzuto shows Billy Martin some love after Martin's Series-record 12th hit drove home the winning run for the Yankees' record fifth straight title.**

99 games—the most during this 1949 to 1953 stretch—and finished eight and a half games ahead of Cleveland, easily their widest margin; for the first time since 1947, the Yankees led the league in scoring, and for the second time they allowed the fewest runs.

Baseball's 50th World Series featured a rematch against Brooklyn, their fifth meeting in 13 years. This Dodger team was confident. They had been through the crucible—losing the Series in five in 1949, the pennant on the last day in 1950, the devastating playoff in 1951, and the Series in seven in 1952—but their core was intact, and they'd won 105 games thanks to their most overpowering offense ever. They'd hit 208 homers (to the Yankees' 139) and led the league in offense for the fifth straight year with 955 runs (to the Yankees' 801). Eight players hit at least 10 homers, and three—Gil Hodges (31, 122 RBIs), Roy Campanella (41, 142 RBIs), and Duke Snider (42, 126 RBIs)—were among the league's most dangerous hitters. Carl Furillo won the batting crown, and Brooklyn even led the league in stolen bases. (In the Series, the Dodgers would set a six-game record with 103 total bases and finished with a .300 average, the highest ever for a losing team.)

But the protagonist would be a Yankee, and fittingly, it would be a less famous name, a second baseman in just his second full season, the only time he'd ever bat 500 times: Billy Martin.

Stengel had nurtured Martin in the minors in Oakland and in New York; as Dan Daniel wrote in *The Sporting News,* he "had to hold Martin down, polish him up and, for a while, make some of the others like the boy from the Oakland slums." Weighing in at 155 pounds, Martin remained a roiling, turbulent middleweight of a second baseman who was constantly getting into scraps with foes. Yankees general manager George Weiss tried trading him, but Stengel talked him out of it; he saw Martin as a player who always found a way to contribute—in his rookie year in 1952 he batted .217 in the Series but made a running, lunging catch to save the Yankees in the seventh game. In 1953 Martin enjoyed what would be his best year offensively, with 151 hits, 24 doubles, 6 triples, 15 homers, and 75 RBIs.

In the Series, the bantam would rule the roost, banging out 12 hits to propel the Yankees. Although that record (since tied for a six-game Series and broken in a seven-game Series) lacks the dramatic heft of three-homer games by Babe Ruth in 1928 or Reggie Jackson in 1977, and although this Series lacked the tension and quality of the seven-game epic Yankee-Dodger confrontations of 1952, 1955, and 1956, the clincher in 1953 was a taut thriller that gave the Yankees a record no other baseball team is likely ever to match, much less surpass.

Martin's impact was immediate and profound. His bases-loaded triple in the first inning kick-started Game 1. With the Yankees clinging to a 6–5 lead in the eighth, Martin slapped Brooklyn down by singling for his third hit of the day, then stealing second to spark a three-run rally. In Game 2, Brooklyn led 2–1 until the seventh, when Martin smacked a home run (his second hit of the day); Mantle's two-run blast in the eighth won it.

The Yankees scored first in Game 3 when Martin singled to start a rally in the fifth; it was his only hit of the day, but he also avoided striking out as Carl Erskine fanned what was then a Series-record 14 in besting New York 3–2. Brooklyn won the next game too, the one low moment for Martin. Moved up to sixth in the order, Martin tripled and scored on McDougald's fifth-inning homer and singled in the ninth with New York down 7–2. His hit advanced Woodling to second, but after Woodling scored, Martin made the game's final out by foolishly coming home on Mantle's single to left fielder Don Thompson, who'd just been inserted for defensive purposes. Thompson threw Martin out by a mile, and when Martin tried plowing into the catcher, Campanella brushed him off like a gnat. But in Game 5, Martin responded with a single and a homer to break in five games Ruth's record 19 total bases in a six-game Series; Mantle hit a grand slam, and McDougald homered too, as the Yankees coasted 11–7. They were one game from the coveted crown.

At Yankee Stadium on October 5, the action began in predictable fashion: for the fifth time in six games, the Yankees drew first blood and—big surprise—Martin brought home one of the two runs, albeit on an error. Against Erskine, pitching his third Series start on just two days' rest, Woodling walked, Bauer singled with one out, and Berra doubled home a run. Inexplicably, Erskine walked Mantle intentionally to face Martin, who drilled a sharp grounder off second baseman Junior Gilliam's shoes, a shot many thought should have been scored a hit.

Erskine would be gone after four, although the Yankees lost a chance to break the game open in the second when Ford failed to tag from third on a fly ball, tried to go back, and got doubled off. Still, Ford, who'd had plenty of rest after a first-inning departure in Game 4, struck out seven and scattered six hits through seven innings. Jackie Robinson single-handedly created Brooklyn's run in the sixth—he doubled, stole third when Ford was holding the ball but not paying attention, then scored on a groundout.

When pinch-hitter Bobby Morgan blasted a ball to the right-field wall for the final out of the seventh, Stengel decided he wanted a fresh pitcher and a righty against Brooklyn's mostly righty lineup. The move was logical considering that the teams had already smashed 16 homers, tying the Series mark the two teams had set the previous year (needing seven games then). He called on Reynolds, who was effective in the eighth, but the Yankees failed to boost their 3–1 lead when Rizzuto was thrown out at the plate trying to score on a grounder. When Furillo smashed yet another homer—a two-out, two-run blast—off Reynolds in the ninth, he knotted the game at 3–3, and the Dodgers had momentum.

The Yankees' earlier failures seemed potentially disastrous, but they were ultimately the more solid fundamental ball club—their pitchers issued just 14 walks and the defense tied a record with just one error, while the Dodgers provided 24 free passes and made seven defensive blunders. Brooklyn continued its giveaway days in the last of the ninth when Clem Labine committed baseball's original sin and walked leadoff hitter Hank Bauer. With one out, Mantle hit a weak dribbler that no one could get to.

The winning run was on second base, and the one hitter the Dodgers didn't want to see was coming up: Billy Martin. He'd already doubled, and one more safety would give him a record-setting 12th hit and most likely a record-tying eighth RBI.

Labine knew he had to pitch carefully, but he also couldn't walk Martin with just one out. He had to stop him. Except, of course, he couldn't. On a 1–1 count, Martin smacked the ball back up the middle. Bauer scored as Snider didn't even throw home. The Yankees, World Series champions in 1949, 1950, 1951, and 1952, were World Series champions in 1953.

Red Smith urged consecration and appreciation of this surpassing performance, writing, "Never again, perhaps, will it be possible to look on a baseball team that has just won the championship of the world for a fifth consecutive year. It never was possible before, never in any age."

With Martin gone in the military service the next year, the Yankees would win 103 but finish second to Cleveland. The Yankee dynasty would go on and on, of course—they'd win eight of the next nine pennants—but it would never be the same, as they'd lose four of those Series. It was this 1953 team that would be the champion of champions.

# 28. Giants win 1-0 to finish the first "Subway Series," October 13, 1921, Polo Grounds

John McGraw versus Babe Ruth, Round 1.

The 1921 World Series is remembered today, if at all, primarily as the New York Yankees' first Fall Classic and the first between two New York teams. But at the time it boiled down to a simple, epochal clash: "the Little Napoleon" versus "the Sultan of Swat," old-time small ball versus the new swing-from-the-heels game. And in the ninth inning of Game 8, on October 13, 1921, the Series concluded with an inning laden with symbolism and featuring one final dramatic confrontation and the most exciting fielding play ever to end a season.

In 1921 Babe Ruth was baseball. Ruth, once among the game's premier pitchers, had astonished the baseball world in 1920 by smashing 54 home runs. No one had ever hit 30 before, and no American League team managed more than 50 that year. But that season was rife with distractions—the deadly beaning of Cleveland's Ray Chapman, the unspooling of the "Black Sox" scandal, and the appointment of Judge Kenesaw Mountain Landis as commissioner. In 1921 all eyes were on the Sultan of Swat as he broke his own record, lofting an awe-inspiring 59 home runs while upping his doubles to 44 from 36, his triples to 16 from 9, his runs scored to 177 from 158, and his RBIs to 171 from 137, all while hitting .378. (He even stole 17 bases.) Ruth transformed a longtime second-rate team into American League champions, brought new fans to the ballpark, and forever altered the game.

All the glory rained upon the big brute irked the tempestuous McGraw to no end. Baseball's reigning symbol, McGraw had helped spark the Baltimore Orioles to three straight NL flags as a player; as a manager, he'd led his team to seven NL pennants (along with seven second-place finishes) since 1904. He was the undisputed master of inside baseball, playing smart, aggressively, and often dirty to piece together enough offense to back strong pitching.

The Giants had allowed the lowly Yankees to sublease the Polo Grounds, but suddenly the Yankees, or one damned Yankee in particular, was the center of attention there, not just in New York but throughout baseball. Worse, Ruth had done it playing long ball, which McGraw disdained.

Now Ruth and McGraw would face off . . . and the Giants would have to act as the visiting team in half the games in their home ballpark. This was technically not a "Subway Series," since it took place in one park, but it was a crucial marker. Although 1905 marked New York's ascension in the baseball world and 1947 to 1956 is commonly celebrated as the city's baseball heyday, 1921 truly was the year New York became the sport's capital: it began a stretch of 44 World Series that featured 45 New York clubs, including 13 Series that resided entirely in Gotham. (Brooklyn had reached the Series in 1920, but given their proximity to the cellar for most of the next 20 years, that seemed less a new beginning than a fluke.)

The American League had won nine of the previous ten World Series (not counting 1919), and Ruth's looming presence had led most to believe the Yankees would stomp out McGraw's mighty mites. However, sportswriter Fred Lieb cautioned in his syndicated column that the Yanks were an "erratic and inconsistent" club that feasted on bad pitching but was unable to "nose out an adversary" in a well-pitched, tight game.

The stereotypes were a bit simplistic. The Giants led the National League in scoring—they led everyone in steals, but they had some pop too. George Kelly's 23 homers led the NL, his 42 doubles were second, Frankie Frisch pounded 17 triples, and McGraw's innovative platoon at catcher produced 17 homers there. The Yankees, meanwhile, led the AL in earned run average, thanks to Carl Mays and Waite Hoyt, both of whom outshone any Giant hurler.

Yankee pitching dominated the first two games, shutting out the Giants 3–0 both times. Although the experimental best-of-nine format gave the Giants more time to recover, no team had ever lost the first two games but won the Series. "The Giants are tamed," Yankee manager Miller Huggins unwisely boasted. "It is just a question of playing off the rest of the games."

The Yankees broke open a scoreless Game 3 with four third-inning runs sparked by Ruth's two-run single, but rather than slink away toward certain defeat, McGraw's men turned the tables, retaliating with four of their own and pounding out an eight-run seventh in a 13–5 rout. Worse, Ruth was forced to leave the game. In Game 2 he had cut his elbow sliding in the rocky dirt when, frustrated at being walked three times, he stole both second and third; now he'd irritated the wound in another slide. The infection that set in essentially cost the Yankees the Series.

Ruth surprised everyone by playing Game 4 despite his heavily bandaged arm, and he thrilled everyone with a ninth-inning roundtripper. But it came too late, since Mays yielded three runs in the eighth. (Rumors circulated that Mays may have thrown this game: defying Huggins's orders, he threw a lackluster curve at a crucial moment and fell while fielding a bunt. This pattern repeated itself in Game 7.)

In Game 5 Ruth again stole the show in a way that must have driven McGraw mad. Playing with a tube draining pus from his arm, baseball's home run king shocked the Giants by bunting for a hit; then he scored what would be the winning run, giving the Yanks a 3–2 lead in games. But Ruth also struck out feebly three times and was too hurt to go on. The Yankees' morale sagged, and their lineup was exposed; forced to play on the Giants' terms, they were stymied in Games 6 and 7. In the latter, they had five hits in the first three innings but, lacking the big blow, scored just once; the Giants manufactured one run on a steal and a bloop single, the second on an error and a double.

Looking to close out the Series in Game 8, McGraw turned to Art Nehf, his diminutive 20-game winner, while the Yankees, with no margin for

**Dave Bancroft scores on an error in the first, and that's enough as the Giants eke out a 1–0 victory over the Yankees to capture the first-ever World Series between two New York squads.**

error, sent out Hoyt, who'd already beaten Nehf in two tight games. But again the Yankees couldn't play inside ball as well as the Giants.

In the first, with two out but two on via walks, George Kelly's grounder rolled through the legs of reliable Roger Peckinpaugh, allowing Dave Bancroft to scamper home.

No other Giants reached third after that, but Hoyt watched his teammates struggle in vain to score: they left two in the bottom of the first and the bases loaded in the fourth.

In the bottom of the ninth, with the World Series on the line, Huggins was desperate. He pulled Wally Pipp and sent Ruth, the real-life Mighty Casey, to the bat.

But there was no long ball and no joy in Yankeedom that day as the debilitated slugger grounded to first. Then Nehf, pitching on two days' rest, walked Aaron Ward, bringing up another threat, Frank Baker, who had earned the moniker "Home Run" when he devastated the Giants with two crucial blasts in the 1911 Series.

Baker slammed a sharp grounder toward right field that looked as if it would put the tying run 90 feet from home with just one out. Instead, the Giants turned the greatest defensive play ever to end a World Series. Second baseman Johnny Rawlings, knowing the lefty Baker would try to use the hole created by the runner being held on first, had shrewdly inched over before the pitch and was thus able to make a diving grab of the ball. From the ground, he threw Baker out at first. Having foolishly assumed the ball got through, Ward obliviously but confidently rounded second. At first base, the alert Kelly (the Keith Hernandez of his day) fired a bullet to third, where Frisch welcomed Ward's hard slide with an uppercut of a tag to the jaw. The Yankees were through.

If Ruth hadn't been hurt, the Series and that ninth inning in particular would have been the ultimate vindication for McGraw. Even so, it was his first championship since 1905, and it brought him a handsome raise the following year—only Ruth made more money in baseball. That year, 1922, the Series would again pit McGraw against Ruth. McGraw's staff, following orders to feed the beast nothing but curves in the dirt, would humiliate Ruth, holding him to a .118 average as the Giants swept the Yankees. (Nehf again won the decider.) Looking back at those two Series, McGraw later said that shutting down Ruth and his heretical style was "possibly the most satisfying thing" in his life.

These triumphs marked the end of American League dominance—from 1921 on, the two leagues split the next 14 World Series. But for the Giant-Yankee rivalry and inside baseball, this was merely a last hurrah. Fans, players, and owners dug the long ball; in 1923 the Yankees would have their own stadium, and in a rematch against McGraw's Giants, Ruth would lead the Yankees to victory, becoming the first man to hit three homers in a Series. The Yankee century had begun.

Back in 1921, Nehf's Series-winning gem didn't seem unusual—there'd already been six complete-game shutouts in World Series clinchers—but with the offensive explosion that followed, there'd be just two in the next 33 years. There would be only one more 1–0 game in a Series over the next quarter-century, and no 1–0 clinchers again until 1962. So it was not just for Giant fans but for baseball purists—the lover of the pitcher's duel and the small-ball aficionado—that Game 8 achieved such bittersweet poignancy. It was McGraw's triumphant return to the top, but the beginning of the end of his civilization.

# 29. The Subway Series rides again, October 21, 2000, Yankee Stadium

New York, New York. How sweet it sounds. After a 44-year wait, New York baseball fans rejoiced when the Subway Series roared back into the station on October 21, 2000 . . . and they would not be disappointed. The opener was a dynamite game, the first Subway Series confrontation to extend to 12 innings, and the turning point in the Series.

From 1921 through 1956, the Yankees faced the Giants six times and the Dodgers seven times in the Fall Classic; with seven clashes from 1947 through 1956, the Subway Series seemed like a ritual of autumn sandwiched in between the first day of school and Thanksgiving.

Then the Giants and Dodgers betrayed New York and moved to California; the Mets replaced them, but another hometown showdown seemed an impossible dream.

The teams reached nine total World Series from 1962 through 1986 but were never competitive at the same time. It wasn't until the late 1990s that both teams played well enough to foster fantasies of an October confrontation. Even then the Mets fell short of the 1998 and 1999 Series, both of which the Yankees won.

In 2000 everything finally came together. The Yankees were no longer at the peak of their powers but were still the Yankees, while the Mets had new ace Mike Hampton, young outfielders Jay Payton and Benny Agbayani, and, of course, Mike Piazza, who hit 38 homers, drove in 113 runs, and batted .324 in 2000. When Roger Clemens beaned him in the head during interleague play and didn't have the class to apologize, it stoked this naturally flammable rivalry.

The Yankees almost didn't make it, losing 16 of 19 near season's end to barely beat out Boston; they then struggled to get past Oakland and Seattle in the playoffs. The Mets appeared stronger—although only a wild card, their 94–68 record was seven games better than the Yankees, and they seemed stronger in the playoffs.

The arrival of the Subway Series dominated hometown papers and local conversation and even became national news, with Derek Jeter and Piazza gracing the cover of *Newsweek* and reporters exploring the rooting preferences of senatorial candidates Hillary Clinton and Rick Lazio.

The Yankees may have seemed fragile, but they had a poise and a steely confidence built on their vast experience, their superior grasp of baseball's fundamentals, and, of course, their unparalleled bullpen, headed by closer-demigod Mariano Rivera. They played with a cool efficiency that reflected manager Joe Torre's persona, while the Mets' bubbly, almost hyper style flowed from manager Bobby Valentine, who'd taken 10 seasons as a player and 13 as a manager to reach the World Series. The Mets showed up at Yankee Stadium with camcorders to capture the carnival atmosphere, something the Yankees regarded as just part of another day at work.

But Game 1 would be more extraordinary than ordinary. Don Larsen, the hero of the last Subway Series (back when tokens cost 15 cents, not $1.50), tossed out the first ball to former batterymate Yogi Berra, and Billy Joel sang the national anthem as a bald eagle was released in center field. Then, after all the media hype and all the pomp and circumstance, it was time to play ball.

The suspense was high from the first pitch as both teams strived for first blood against Andy Pettitte and Al Leiter, tough lefties who thrived under pressure. Both teams left runners on, and Yankee Chuck Knoblauch was picked off in the third, but the Mets displayed their inexperience and nerves with one critical mistake after another. In the fourth, Piazza was picked off first, then Todd Zeile hit a grounder that started foul but rolled fair—he didn't run and was thrown out. In the fifth, after Agbayani doubled, Payton hit a grounder and started arguing that it was foul, but the umpires called it fair and he was thrown out.

But these guys were kids compared to the bighorned goats of the sixth inning. With two outs and the Mets' late-season sparkplug Timo Perez on first, Todd Zeile smashed the ball to deep left. Both he and Perez trotted as if the ball was a certain home run. Zeile had his arm ready to pump in celebration when the ball hit the padded wall and bounced back into play. Embarrassed, Perez accelerated to try to score anyway. David Justice, whom the Yankees had picked up for his powerful bat, fielded the carom perfectly and fired home. When his throw tailed, he was rescued by Jeter, who previewed his more famous postseason relay of 2001 by sprinting across the foul line, catching the ball, jumping, spinning, and throwing home to nail Perez at the plate. It was a crushing blow for the Mets and a reaffirmation for the Yankees that their old pros—the guys like Jeter, Pettitte, Paul O'Neill, and Rivera, who had won eight straight World Series games—would lift them up when the game was on the line.

The Yankees seized control with two runs in their half of the sixth, but the Mets demonstrated their resilience with a rally of their own—they tied the score off Pettite on a pinch-hit two-run single by Bubba Trammell, and Edgardo Alfonzo's infield single off reliever Jeff Nelson gave the Mets a 3–2 lead.

That made the ninth inning a battle of the closers. As everybody knew, few teams ever won such a clash against the Yankees. With his placid outward demeanor and his darting cutter, Mariano Rivera was not only the best closer but the best clutch closer in history. Since 1996, he'd pitched 385 regular-season innings, allowing 401 base runners and 91 runs—and since blowing a save in the 1997 divisional playoffs against Cleve-

**New Yorkers get caught up in the excitement as the Subway Series returns for the first time in 44 years.**

land in his first year as a closer, Rivera had allowed 24 base runners and one—that's right, just one—single, solitary run in $35^{1}/_{3}$ innings against baseball's best teams.

Mets closer Armando Benitez was the opposite in temperament, a big man with a tough glare and an explosive fastball who was easily rattled and had a disquieting tendency to melt down in the tightest situations. While in Baltimore, Benitez had a 7.71 ERA against the Yankees in the 1996 ALCS, and he had triggered a brawl with an unnecessary bean ball in 1998; with the Mets, Benitez blew a save in the 1999 NLDS clincher, an extra-inning lead in the NLCS to kill their comeback against Atlanta, and a save in the 2000 NLDS.

So when Paul O'Neill misplayed Kurt Abbott's line drive into a double, giving the Mets second and third with one out, Rivera remained calm, got Perez on a grounder to second, and fanned Alfonzo. Benitez's lack of composure became evident when O'Neill came up seeking redemption. The 37-year-old's bat speed had slowed considerably in 2000, and he was overmatched by Benitez's blistering heat, but he never gave in, fouling off pitch after pitch with defensive swings until Benitez finally lost the strike zone, walking O'Neill on the 10th delivery. That was it. Against much weaker hitters, Benitez let up: pinch-hitter Luis Polonia and ex-Met Jose Vizcaino, who'd had only two at-bats in the first two playoff rounds, both singled, and Knoblauch tied the game on a sacrifice fly.

To put Benitez's blown save in perspective, the Yankees had not come back from a ninth-inning deficit in the World Series since Dodger Mickey Owen famously failed to catch the third strike of the third out way back in 1941. Although "what if" is a foolish and ultimately futile exercise, it is one Met fans (like Dodger fans before them) find themselves playing all too often. What if they hadn't traded Nolan Ryan or Tom Seaver? Or Doc and Darryl hadn't succumbed to temptation? Or Mike Scioscia hadn't hit that ninth-inning homer in the 1988 NLCS? This one—what if Benitez hadn't blown Game 1?—ranks right up there in this painful memory game, for the Series probably would have played out quite differently.

But back in the real world, where Yankee fans never needed to daydream, Rivera and Stanton retired 11 straight Mets through the 12th inning. Meanwhile, the Yankees poked and prodded for vulnerable spots. In the 10th, they drew two walks off Dennis Cook; Glendon Rusch came on and wild-pitched them over a base, but the Mets drew the infield and outfield in and slipped the noose. In the 11th, after two walks and another Rusch wild pitch, Turk Wendell came on, and the Mets again escaped the gallows. But the Yankees were much closer to victory than the Mets, and both sides knew it.

The game was one of just a dozen in Series history to last a dozen innings, and just the second since the 1977 Yankees-Dodgers matchup. (Only two 14-inning marathons, one in 1914 and one in 2005, have ever gone longer.) In the Yankee 12th, Tino Martinez singled and Jorge Posada doubled. The Mets were at the end of their rope. Wendell walked O'Neill intentionally and Luis Sojo popped up, but on the game's 396th pitch, Vizcaino—whom Torre had nearly pinch-hit for several times only to show shrewd restraint—picked up his fourth single to win the game.

The Yankees had an edge, and in typical Yankee fashion they would not surrender it. The Series contained plenty of other memorable moments: Clemens hurling a broken bat at Piazza and the Mets nearly overcoming a six-run ninth-inning deficit in Game 2; Orlando Hernandez fanning 12 but the Mets keeping hope alive with a comeback 4–2 win in Game 3; Jeter demonstrating both his skill and leadership yet again by homering to lead off Game 4, suffocating those Met hopes; and Leiter's brilliant, gutty effort in Game 5 before he lost the game and the Series by yielding singles on his 141st and 142nd pitches of the night. But the first game remained the most exciting and pivotal, the one that delineated the differences between the two teams.

When it was all over, even the Yankees acknowledged that this had been something special, that there was something to that viewpoint offered in the famous *New Yorker* cartoon showing the local perspective on the city versus the rest of the world.

Bernie Williams admitted that being king of the hill in the battle for New York mattered more than just being top of the heap in an ordinary season: "It really made us feel like we were playing for something other than the World Series."

# 30. The Jets avenge their "Heidi" loss and win the AFL title, December 27, 1968, Shea Stadium

The New York Jets' improvement in the Joe Namath era went from incremental to exponential and finally, with one classic fourth-quarter bomb, accelerated up to explosive. The brash young quarterback from Alabama had been Rookie of the Year in 1965, giving the team some rare highlights; he led the Jets to their first .500 season in 1966, their first winning season in 1967, and finally to an

**Joe Namath steers the Jets to the AFL title over Ben Davidson and the hated Raiders.**

11–3 record and first place in the East in 1968.

They were nearly at the promised land, one step away from the Super Bowl. However, that one step would have to be a giant leap. Their opponents in the American Football League Championship game would be the 12–2 Oakland Raiders, the defending AFL champs who'd won the West by slaughtering Kansas City in a divisional tiebreaker the previous week, scoring 41 points against the league's best defense.

The swaggering, sinister Raiders never hesitated to sneak in cheap or late shots, and their target was always the same: Namath. Cut out the heart and kill the team.

They'd shoved his face in the mud until he choked, fractured his cheekbone, and punched him in the balls when the refs weren't looking . . . and they'd beaten New York six times in seven tries during Namath's career. Just that year, in the infamous "Heidi" game, NBC had cut away from an apparent Jets 32–29 victory with 65 seconds left, only to have the Raiders storm back for a 43–32 triumph.

The Raiders came in with the AFL's second-best defense and the best offense, a seemingly deadly combination. But the Jets were fourth in defense (Johnny Sample and Jim Hudson were both among the AFL leaders in interceptions) and second in offense. (George Sauer finished second with 68 catches; Don Maynard finished second in yards and averaged 22.7 per catch; Matt Snell and Emerson Boozer were fourth in rushing among backfield tandems; and Jim Turner was the most prolific scorer among kickers.) Plus, in Namath, they had an all-time great in his prime and ready to lead.

December 29, 1968, was a bad day to play football's roughest, toughest team. "Nature was in the meanest of moods," wrote Mark Kriegel in *Namath: A Biography:* temperatures were near freezing, and winds were gusting up to 50 miles an hour. The field was a wreck, churned up but with no give.

# Honorable Mention: The Jets Fly High

**1. Richard Todd comes of age, November 22, 1981, Shea Stadium**

New Yorkers had been waiting for Richard Todd, their latest Alabama-trained quarterback savior, to produce. He'd racked up major yardage, but Jets fans, raised on Broadway Joe, wanted toughness, they wanted courage, they wanted a winner. Against favored Miami in the most crucial game of his career, and in excruciating pain, Todd finally came through.

After a discouraging 0–3 start, Todd reduced his interceptions and led a 6–1–1 streak. But the Dolphins remained a game ahead in first place, and the wild-card race was tight, making this Shea Stadium game a must-win for the resurgent young team.

With 3:10 left, Miami was five yards away from a 10-point lead when the Jet defense forced them to settle for a field goal and a 15–9 lead.

The Jets started 77 yards from the end zone, with Todd hindered not only by his lackluster reputation—in years past he'd lost his job and was booed mercilessly—but also by a cracked rib, which had kept him out of practice all week and stung every time he shouted signals, and by a freshly sprained, badly swollen ankle, which prevented him from rolling out or passing well to his left. As Todd trotted out in his plastic-support elastic corset and protective flak jacket, Miami coach Don Shula sarcastically shouted that the Jets' "hero" was coming to the rescue.

"We've got three minutes," Todd told his teammates. "We're going to go in there and get a touchdown." Then he fired seven completions to six different receivers in 10 tries. The last was an 11-yard bullet to Jerome Barkum in the end zone with 16 seconds left. Todd danced off the field as Mark Gastineau led the fans in cheering. When Pat Leahy kicked the extra point, the Jets won 16–15.

The Jets didn't just win a game—they arrived as a team. With Todd at the helm, they reached the playoffs for the first time since 1969, and the following season he guided them within one game of the Super Bowl. It was their final run at glory in New York.

**2. The Jets win, the Giants win, everybody's happy, December 20, 1981, Shea Stadium**

The 1970s had been a disaster, a vast wasteland. No, this is not an anti-disco tirade, it's a simple summation of football in New York. The Giants had provided some moments from the 1920s through the 1960s until their 1964 collapse, when the Jets began their ascent toward the Super Bowl. But in the '70s, the Giants (who fled to New Jersey) and Jets were not just bad—they were awful. Make that laughingstocks. (Two words: Pisarcik, fumble.)

But five days before Christmas in 1981, the Jets, after beginning 0–3, had a chance for a holiday miracle: a win over Green Bay in the season's final game would lift them into the playoffs for the first time in 12 years while nudging the Giants past the Packers into the postseason for their first trip since 1963.

Green Bay had scored 101 points in its three previous games, but on a blustery, frigid day, the Jets' fearsome "Sack Exchange" turned in its most devastating performance. They introduced Green Bay quarterback Lynn Dickey to the frozen Shea turf nine—count 'em, nine—times: Joe Klecko had two and a half sacks, and Mark Gastineau had two. Meanwhile, Richard Todd, who'd led a 10–2–1 resurgence, had injury-prone receivers Wesley Walker and Johnny "Lam" Jones together for a full game for the first time all season, and despite the wind he fired a 47-yard TD pass to Jones and a 38-yard TD pass to Walker.

The Jets annihilated the Packers, 28–3. The Jets and Giants, who had never managed simultaneous winning seasons, had now done that and more. Although this year's playoff runs would end too soon, the 1980s suddenly looked a whole lot brighter.

**3. Broadway Joe returns, November 28, 1971, Shea Stadium**

Forget the "L" in the standings—this was a magical comeback.

Joe Namath long played on the gimpiest of knees without missing a game, but a wrist injury wiped out his last nine games in 1970, and then in a 1971 exhibition game he tore ligaments and cartilage in his left knee, requiring his fourth surgery and most traumatic rehabilitation. Namath's leg was briefly paralyzed, he endured constant, excruciating pain, and he lost 30 pounds. He no longer looked like a football player, much less a leader. As he slowly healed the Jets stumbled. When he was ready, the team was 4–6 and done for the year. Many believed Namath should recuperate until the following season. He disagreed.

Before the first play, Dave Herman made a request. Coach Weeb Ewbank had benched mistake-prone rookie Sam Walton, shifting Herman from guard to right tackle. Nervous about playing out of position, Herman asked Namath to run the first play through him as a show of confidence. On that play, Herman "hit big Ike Lassiter harder than I had ever hit anyone in my life." Lassiter was so infuriated that he focused on destroying Herman instead of doing his job. Namath, meanwhile, coolly engineered a four-play, 56-yard drive, finishing with a 14-yard touchdown pass to Maynard.

The Jets built their lead to 10–0 on a Turner field goal, but Fred Biletnikoff burned Sample for a 29-yard touchdown. Namath's bruised coccyx and sore right thumb got banged up again, and his left ring finger got dislocated. Then Oakland's Ben Davidson drove a knee into the quarterback's head, giving him a concussion; after a Lassiter body slam on the half's penultimate play, Namath was so disoriented that he didn't know where he was at halftime. The Jets' 13–10 lead seemed extremely tenuous.

In the third, Oakland quarterback Daryle Lamonica completed passes of 37 and 40 yards for 1st-and-goal from the Jets' 6. But Hudson led the Jets off the ropes, making three straight tackles, and Oakland had to settle for a game-tying field goal. A revived Namath helmed a 14-play drive to recapture the lead, 20–13. The Super Bowl seemed within reach. Biletnikoff beat Sample again for 57 yards to New York's 11 to open the fourth, but the Jets forced Oakland to settle for a field goal. The Jets led by four, and the clock was ticking.

Then came one of those plays that always seemed to spin these Jets-Raiders wars in Oakland's favor. Namath compounded a risky decision with a bad pass that George Atkinson intercepted at New York's 37 and ran back to the Jets' 5. The Raiders scored on the next play for a 23–20 advantage. The crowd was stunned, silent. The Raiders had done it again. . . . They must just have been better or tougher or something than the Jets.

But Namath was too great to be the goat, and he responded with his finest Shea Stadium moment.

On first down at his own 32, Namath saw Oakland's secondary playing prevent defense to avoid getting beat deep. By firing a quick 10-yard out pattern to Sauer, Namath reminded Oakland that he had time for a sustained drive. Now he had them set up perfectly. He cautioned his team to be ready for an audible. At the line, he saw what he'd hoped for: both Raider cornerbacks, afraid to

## The Jets Fly High (CONTINUED)

When the San Francisco 49ers knocked out Jets quarterback Bob Davis in the second quarter, on came Namath, the old gunslinger riding into town, striking fear in the hearts of foes and lifting the downtrodden. The crowd roared "as if he were a Messiah," the *New York Times* reported. But his mystical intangibles were no match for the hard realities of yearlong rust and the league's best defense. Overeager, Namath hurried several awful passes, including an interception that set up a San Francisco field goal. He turned conservative, finding his footing by handing off repeatedly to John Riggins.

In the second half, with the 49ers up 17–0, Namath rediscovered his boldness and with it his touch, firing three touchdown passes of at least 20 yards, including a 57-yarder to Rich Caster and a 22-yarder to Eddie Bell, while withstanding a shot to the jaw by 49er Cedrick "Nasty" Hardman.

Trailing 24–21, Namath got one last shot on his 28 with 1:41 left. Crisp passes and an audible trap play put them at San Francisco's 19 with time for three plays. Passing up a game-tying field goal to go for the win, Namath came up just short, with two incompletions and an interception on the final play.

No one cared. The hard-hitting Hardman told Namath, "You're still my idol," while the crowd cheered and cheered and cheered. Fifteen minutes later, they were still at it, pouring out love and appreciation for the return of Broadway Joe.

let Namath peck away with short passes, had crept up to the line to guard their man. Keeping both running backs blocking for extra protection, Namath sent Maynard, Sauer, and Pete Lammons deep. Then he faded nearly 10 yards and shifted toward the left hash mark, buying time, before lofting the ball deep and wide, across to the right sideline, where Maynard sprinted past Atkinson.

Maynard looked over his left shoulder, to where the pass should have been, but the wind carried it past, over his right. Maynard swirled around and made a spectacular catch before being shoved out of bounds at Oakland's 6.

Namath then drew inspiration from the oddest of places. According to Kriegel's bio, the quarterback recalled a short dumpy guy named Petey the Cabdriver who drank regularly at Namath's bar, Bachelors III, and always complained that the Jets were too risk-averse down near the goal, always running, never passing. So Namath called a play-action pass. Bill Mathis, Sauer, and Lammons were all covered, but perfect protection gave Namath time to find Maynard, the fourth option, free in the end zone. Sidearm, Namath zipped the ball hard past three defenders. It was low, but Maynard snared it. In three plays, Namath took the team 68 yards, right back into the lead, 27–23.

Namath had struck so quickly, however, that Oakland had 7:47 to try for another comeback. They reached New York's 26 before stalling out, then got down to the 12 on their final drive. Lamonica called for a short pass in the flat to Charley Smith, a play the Raiders had practiced all week and saved for this sort of opportunity. But the Jet defense, led by Verlon Biggs, pressured Lamonica, and the pass went awry; Jet Ralph Baker saw that Smith was behind Lamonica, meaning the play was considered a lateral, and scooped up the loose ball.

The Jets had finished Oakland off with the kind of dramatic and unpredictable play that the Raiders were accustomed to pulling off. Still, even though the Jets were now AFL champions, what had seemed unthinkable was no longer enough: in January they'd face the NFL's Baltimore Colts in the Super Bowl. The Colts, the media, and wise men like Jimmy the Greek would write them off, but the Jets now knew how good they really were. Namath, in fact, was ready to guarantee victory.

# 31. Notre Dame wins one for the Gipper, November 10, 1928, Yankee Stadium

Johnny O'Brien spent the entire game on the sidelines. With dusk settling late in the fourth quarter, he was wrapped in a blanket to ward off November's chill. This sophomore on the struggling Notre Dame team certainly didn't expect to see action in the big game against Army at Yankee Stadium.

With two minutes remaining, his team started an impressive drive, threatening to pull off a startling upset against the undefeated Cadets. Then, at Army's 16, everything crumbled: the snap from center went awry, and the ball bounded through the backfield. Star running back Jack Chevigny dove and recovered it but was injured, knocked out of the game, leaving the team facing 3rd-and-26 on Army's 32.

This was a different game than football today: substitutions in mid-drive were rare—usually made only for an injury—and subs could not speak to teammates on the first play, preventing coaches from sending in plays. Coach Knute Rockne sent Bill Dew in for the wounded Chevigny, but also slipped in O'Brien for John Colrick. O'Brien, who would letter in track, was willowy, fast, and well rested. He ran deep, slipping past Army's tiring All-American Chris Cagle. Johnny Niemic faded to the 43 to buy time, then looped a soft pass to O'Brien crossing the middle. O'Brien bobbled the throw briefly, then entered the end zone, giving the underdogs a 12–6 lead.

Notre Dame's fans, players, and coach were electrified. Rockne wrapped the kid—forever to be known as "One Play O'Brien"—in a hug, supposedly the only time Rockne ever embraced a player on the sidelines. And yet this dramatic sequence and the rest of the on-field action would eventually be overlooked as the 1928 Army–Notre Dame matchup became the greatest football game no one really remembers.

The sole image people conjure of the game is a sepia-toned reminiscence of Rockne's touching "Win One for the Gipper" speech. The saga of the speech—which won the big game, launched a movie, and catapulted an actor into the presidency—is pure Hollywood hokum, a story that evolved away from the truth while leaping from tabloid newspaper to national magazine to silver screen and into the nation's lifeblood. But the biggest problem is that the shadows of this tall tale obscure one of the most genuinely thrilling sporting events New York ever witnessed.

By 1928 the Army–Notre Dame rivalry had 15 years of tradition and was the preeminent regular-season game. It had graduated from West Point to Ebbets Field, to the Polo Grounds, and finally to the grandeur of Yankee Stadium. This game was in such demand that the teams gave away rights for both NBC and CBS to broadcast it on radio; traffic and subway overcrowding left the stands half-empty at game time, but the stands eventually filled, and 5,000 diehards peered in from roofs, fire escapes, and el platforms.

Notre Dame, after dominating for years, had been embarrassed by Army routs of 27–0 in 1925 and 18–0 in 1927. Laid low by injuries and inexperience, Rockne's team came in this time with only a 4–2 season record. Talk was simmering that it might be time for Rockne to move on. It was a rough period for Catholics given Al Smith's recent loss in the presidential election amid anti-Catholic sentiment. Another trouncing by the establishment (Army) would compound matters, and even Rockne had sounded down, calling his players "Minute Men" and quipping, "They'll be in the game one minute and the other team will score."

That afternoon, however, Rockne's boys resembled the original Minutemen, gamely sticking it to the more powerful British Army. Notre Dame battled Army to a scoreless standstill in the first half, and while Notre Dame failed to score from the Army 5 in the second quarter, the team must have felt ecstatic at halftime—they'd outplayed the favored foe, keeping West Point from even reaching midfield.

After the break, however, Army asserted itself, courtesy of Chris Cagle, who ran for 19 yards, then passed for 39 to set up the game's first touchdown. But Notre Dame didn't fold as Fred Collins and Chevigny pounded the ball on the ground until they finally scored to tie the score at 6–6.

The taut back-and-forth of the third quarter set the stage for the unforgettable final minutes. Notre Dame, buoyed by the confidence born from hanging tough against a better team, marched to Army's 37. Although Frank Carideo missed a 55-yard field goal, Notre Dame had Army reeling and trying to avert a gloomy fate. On their next possession, Notre Dame started on their own 47, and Carideo, Chevigny, Collins, and Johnny Niemic pounded their way down to Army's 16. That was when a bad snap and Chevigny's injury paved the way for O'Brien's startling touchdown catch.

But any chicken-counters underestimated Cagle's determination and skills. On the kickoff he busted loose for 55 yards, and one play later he broke free again, running to near the 10-yard line. But just as Notre Dame lost Chevigny at a crucial moment, Army faced its climactic finish without its star. Cagle had been involved in virtually every offensive and defensive play; now near collapse, he was helped off the field, according to many reports.

Just as O'Brien came through, so did Cagle's replacement, Dick Hutchinson. With time running down, Hutchinson fired a third-down pass through traffic to Charlie Allen on the 4, then called a keeper and came within inches of the end zone. But as Army set for one final play, the ref blew the whistle, ending the game and preserving Notre Dame's 12–6 upset. Some claimed Army had earned another first down—and thus another play according to the rules—but their protests were in vain.

Notre Dame would lose its next two games, but it had salvaged its season with this win, the only college game people would remember from 1928. Actually, what they recalled was not the game but the mythological halftime pep talk that put the fight in the Irish. Like so many great legends, however, this one is largely contradicted by the facts.

George Gipp, who had been spotted by Rockne throwing a football around campus, played for the team in 1919 and 1920. He was a great runner, passer, and receiver, but hardly a source of inspiration. He was aloof and selfish, a drinker and gambler. He ran routs on the knife's edge and was always in trouble and on the verge of being expelled. When he died of pneumonia and strep throat in 1920 (some rumors hint at venereal disease), his image was closer to that of today's soiled, surly athlete than the wholesome gentleman deified in the popular imagination ever since the whitewash of a movie *Knute Rockne, All-American.*

Rockne, by contrast, was an impressive, multifaceted man. He worked through college as a janitor and then a chemistry research assistant; besides playing football, he played flute in the orchestra, starred in student plays, and graduated magna cum laude. As a coach, he was a gifted teacher, an acute talent assessor, and a brilliant tactician. He designed equipment and uniforms that were less bulky and wind-resistant but provided more protection. His teams produced five unbeaten seasons and an unmatched 105–12–5 record.

Yet Rockne grew into an icon because he was also an impresario, a masterful performer who deftly manipulated school officials, players, and the media. He transformed Notre Dame into a national team by traveling the country, challenging the toughest competition. And boy, could he talk. He was shrewd enough to dole his motivational speeches out sparingly, and he was talented enough to move reporters and other bystanders to tears. But to score points with his listeners, Rockne was quick to stiff-arm the truth—he once tried inspiring his team to win against Georgia Tech by telling them a fib about his own perfectly healthy son Billy being hospitalized. In his book on coaching, Rockne wrote, "The history or traditions of the school are a great thing to recite to your team. . . . Exaggerate these as much as you can."

He did just that with Gipp, who was never called "the Gipper" by anyone, especially himself. Leading up to the 1928 game, some columnists wrote fondly of Gipp and Notre Dame's glory days but glossed over Gipp's tumultuous life. Perhaps this inspired Rockne, who knew his young squad was impressionable. From there, everything gets murky. Some say Rockne, who probably was never really alone with Gipp for a deathbed scene, passed on Gipp's request before the game, when boxer Jack Dempsey also offered encouragement. Others, in the belief that Rockne wouldn't compete with a heavyweight champ, place the speech at halftime. Still others say he didn't talk about Gipp at all. (Years later sportswriter Grantland Rice attempted to insinuate himself into the scene—he testified to the speech's veracity by claiming that the night before Rockne told him and another man he might ask the team to "pull one out for Gipp." But Murray Sperber's *Shaking Down the Thunder* reveals that Rice was in Atlanta and the third man, Hunk Anderson, was in St. Louis.)

The story first appeared two days after the game in a *Daily News* article headlined "Gipp's Ghost Beats Army" and written by Notre Dame

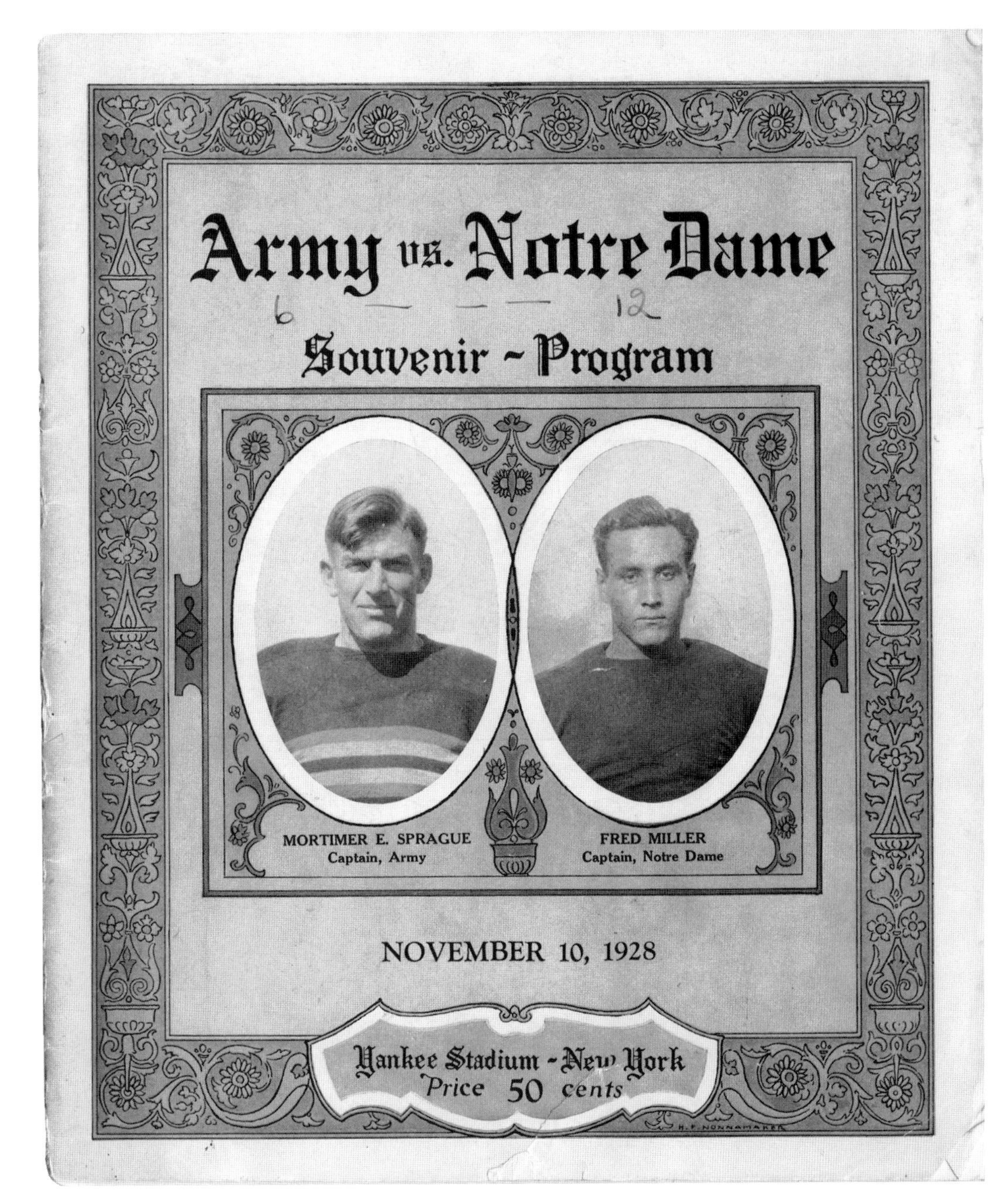


**Although Army is heavily favored, Notre Dame wins this game, whether it's for the Gipper or not.**

alum Francis Wallace. His story made it sound like a pregame speech in which Rockne said straightforwardly, "On his deathbed George Gipp told me that some day, when the time came, he wanted me to ask a Notre Dame team to beat the Army for him."

The tabloid's tale was forgotten until 1930, when Rockne "recounted" it in *Collier's*. The ghost-written version sounded unnatural, with Rockne uttering awkward phrases like "His eyes brightened in a frame of pallor" and mistakenly declaring that Chevigny shouted, "That's one for the Gipper," after scoring the *winning* touchdown.

That article embellished the speech into a tearjerker: "Some time, Rock, when the team's up against it; when things are wrong and the breaks are beating the boys—tell them to go in there with all they've got and win just one for the Gipper. I don't know where I'll be then, Rock. But I'll know about it, and I'll be happy." But it also placed the speech at halftime, when it made little sense since the boys weren't up against it or suffering bad breaks—they were surprisingly holding their own against a better team.

After Rockne died, this version resurfaced in his posthumous autobiography and in 1941 in *Knute Rockne, All-American,* starring Pat O'Brien as Rockne and Ronald Reagan as Gipp. And in the rewriting and retelling, the story's sentiment resonated. It might not have mattered during the Roaring Twenties, but this triumph over adversity was a perfect tale for a nation subsumed in the Great Depression, for a nation on the verge of war, and, in 1980, for a politician speaking of a bright new future during hard times. It's fitting that Reagan, who further distorted and dramatized the story to suit his purposes, inherited the story's success since he shared both Rockne's ability to inspire and his loose grasp of truth and reality.

It's hard to fathom, but had Army scored on that last play, the Gipper might never have surfaced, since nobody recounts inspirational speeches after losses. Perhaps Reagan would not have become president. (Sperber points out that many Reagan Democrats were Catholics responding to his "Win one for the Gipper" approach.) But maybe it's time to bench the Gipper anyway. Sure, dispelling the myth strips away the connection to Hollywood and the White House, diminishing the game's importance for some, but whatever Gipp did or didn't do and whatever Rockne did or didn't say, the truth is that Notre Dame's play in the second half was inspiring enough and both Army and the Fighting Irish gave New York a football game to remember.

# 32. The sky falls on Grady Little and Aaron Boone sinks the Sox, October 16, 2003, Yankee Stadium

Aaron Boone's middle name is John.

Russell "Bucky" Dent's middle name is Earl.

Yet if you pronounce both middle names with a Boston accent, they sound exactly the same: Bleeping.

Boone's 11th-inning blast into the night at Yankee Stadium on October 16, 2003, drove the stake through the heart of the Boston Red Sox, slamming down the exclamation point on a titanic seven-game battle. By then a Yankee win seemed inevitable, after an explosive eighth inning when Boston manager Grady Little incited in Red Sox Nation a winter's worth of expletives as his inaction gave easy runs to the Yankees in the annual Boston clearance sale on World Series dreams.

The Yankees had, of course, lorded their superiority over Boston for decades—from the acquisition of Babe Ruth through the pennant-clinching win over Boston in 1949's final game, through Dent's homer and the Yankees' 1978 tiebreaker playoff win, through New York's six straight first-place finishes from 1998 to 2003, during which period the Sox continually finished second.

In the off-season before 2003, agitated Boston president Larry Lucchino had dubbed big-spending New York "the Evil Empire," which only heightened the bad feelings. The Yankees, however, remained imperturbable. Although they hadn't won the World Series since 2000 and had lost key players, they had an unassailable core with Derek Jeter, Bernie Williams, Jorge Posada, and Mariano Rivera. The Yankees won 101 games and then flicked away Minnesota in the ALDS.

Boston, the wild-card winner, was waiting in the ALCS, believing they finally had the team to topple the big bad bullies, especially with a bullpen tandem (Alan Embree, Mike Timlin, and Scott Williamson) that had flourished down the stretch.

In Game 1, Tim Wakefield pitched brilliantly, but when he walked two batters in the seventh, Little "didn't mess around," immediately calling on Embree, Timlin, and then Williamson to preserve the lead. But the Red Sox blew their chance to put the Yankees deep in the hole when they failed to knock out Andy Pettitte during his early-inning struggles in Game 2, and New York evened the series.

Game 3 added a touch of WWF melodrama to an already tense series. Ex-Boston ace Roger Clemens faced Boston's new ace, Pedro Martinez, who gave up four early runs to New York, then stirred tension by zipping a fastball that grazed the head of Yankee right fielder Karim Garcia. Soon after, both teams started jawing, and Martinez appeared to threaten Posada. The next inning Manny Ramirez overreacted to a high (but not dangerously tight) fastball from Clemens, heading toward the mound with his bat, which brought out both benches, led by the Yankees' 72-year-old bench coach Don Zimmer, who foolishly attacked Martinez; forced to defend himself, the pitcher slammed the old-timer to the ground. Later Garcia and reliever Jeff Nelson got into a fight with a Boston groundskeeper. The Yankees eked out a 4–3 win, although Boston fluttered back on Wakefield's knuckler. The teams then split the next two games, with five Boston relievers holding New York to one run in $5^1/_3$ innings in Game 6.

The best sports dramas are built on stories and relationships, and the stage for Game 7 was set for an epic of Shakespearean dimensions. It was America's greatest rivalry at the cathedral of baseball, and it again pitted Clemens against Martinez, two often surly but always compelling future Hall of Famers who had won all five AL Cy Young Awards from 1997 to 2001.

In this game, however, Clemens lacked championship-caliber stuff. Trot Nixon and Kevin Millar homered early, knocking Clemens out in the fourth—a fitting way for the Red Sox to reverse the curse, or so it seemed with Martinez pitching like the Pedro of old, retiring 16 of 18 at one point and revving his velocity from 88 to 94, faster than he had thrown in weeks. Up in Boston that afternoon, the Fenway Park grounds crew had painted the 2003 World Series logo onto the field, a bit of hubris or optimism that was beginning to seem justified.

With the Sox up 4–1, it might have seemed logical for Little to call on the bullpen after six: Martinez's statistics grew markedly worse as his pitch count built, while Timlin, Embree, and Williamson had allowed just one run in their previous $16^1/_3$ innings, fanning 24. Additionally, the Yankees' over-the-top stretching of the seventh-inning stretch left Martinez cooling off for an extra seven minutes. When Jason Giambi ripped his second solo homer and the Yankees' number eight and nine hitters, the distinctly unthreatening Enrique Wilson and Garcia, both singled, Little certainly should have recognized the warning signs. He didn't. When Martinez struck out Alfonso Soriano with a 94-mph heater, Little misinterpreted it as a sign of strength, not a tired hurler finding one last big pitch.

Martinez himself thought he was through, pointing to the heavens and hugging his teammates in the dugout. When David Ortiz's homer built the lead back to 5–2, Red Sox fans finally let themselves relax, but then Little defied rational thinking.

Martinez had pitched into the eighth only four times all year. The Yankees hadn't hit him well all

**Aaron Boone floats toward first after burying Boston with his 11th-inning homer in Game 7 of the ALCS.**

day, but they'd remained poised and made him work for each out because they knew he'd fade. In 2003 the batting average against him on pitches 85 to 100 was .230; after that it was .370 until pitch 120, when it got even uglier. As he began the eighth, he had thrown exactly 100 pitches.

Nick Johnson popped out, but only after wringing seven pitches out of Martinez's arm. The Red Sox were five outs away from the World Series (just as the similarly jinxed Chicago Cubs had been in the NLCS before their collapse).

Jeter, playing despite a ruptured ligament in his thumb, slammed a double to right.

Little stayed put. The baseball gods had sent the Yankees another gift, and they capitalized. On pitch 115, Williams roped a single to left, making it 5–3.

Little trotted out to the mound but left his authority in the dugout. "Take him out," the entire New England region yelled at their television sets. Martinez said he could get the lefty Hideki Matsui. Even though Matsui had already doubled off Martinez twice in the series, and even though the southpaw Embree was ready to go, Little bowed before his ace and left. Later he'd say that several players had confessed to him they were afraid of becoming the next Bill Buckner, but at that moment Little took that burden on himself.

With two strikes, Matsui was able to pull Martinez's failing fastball down the right-field line for a ground-rule double. The tying runs were in scoring position, and Martinez had thrown 118 pitches. Worse, the story line now favored New York, with Posada, seeking revenge for the Game 3 tiff, wielding the bat.

Still Little failed to do the obvious thing.

Posada worked the count to 2–2 and Martinez

above the 120-pitch mark. On the next pitch he blooped a ball over second. Williams and Matsui raced home.

While Little earned his fair share of the blame, the Yankees don't get enough credit for their clutch hitting—even a .370 hitter makes out more than six in ten times, but in Martinez's final nine batters, New York produced three singles, three doubles, and a home run.

Posada's hit merely tied it at 5–5, but the Yankees (and Red Sox) knew immediately they would win. It was just a matter of time. Little finally called on Embree, who got Giambi on a fly-out, then Timlin walked two men to load the bases before escaping. Mariano Rivera limited the Red Sox to one hit in the ninth and one in the tenth. He hadn't pitched three innings in a game in seven years, but he strode out to the mound for the 11th and retired the side in order, fanning two. After Timlin got through the ninth, Wakefield, who had carried the Red Sox to two wins as a starter, pitched a 1–2–3 tenth.

Leading off the Yankee 11th was Aaron Boone; a pinch runner in the eighth, he was taking his first at-bat. Boone had been acquired midseason from Cincinnati but slumped in New York; going just 5-for-31 in the postseason, he'd been benched for Enrique Wilson. In a rut like that, a dancing knuckleball is the last pitch a hitter wants to see. But Wakefield's first pitch didn't knuckle, didn't flutter, didn't do much of anything . . . until Boone cracked it hard, launching it into the history books. "Derek Jeter told me that if we just waited the ghosts would show up," Boone said.

With eight straight division titles, six American League pennants, and four World Series crowns since 1996, the Yankees tended to be relatively low-key in their clinching celebrations. Not this time. Rivera ran to the mound and lay down while everyone jubilantly greeted Boone at the plate. "To beat our rival like we did, it couldn't be more satisfying," manager Joe Torre said. "This has to be the sweetest taste of all for me."

The Yankees lost the World Series that year. But their fans, like Giant fans in 1951, rocked comfortably by baseball's hot stove that winter, content at least with the shot heard breaking hearts 'round New England.

# 33. Patrick Ewing lifts the Knicks into the NBA Finals, June 5, 1994, Madison Square Garden

Patrick Ewing, triumphant at long last.

With 24 points, 22 rebounds, 7 assists, and 5 blocks to his credit, with the game-defining play fresh in everyone's memory—a thunderous dunk off a rebound to recover the lead with just 26.9 seconds left—Ewing celebrated the New York Knicks' long-awaited return to the NBA Finals by leaping onto the courtside press table, throwing out

**Patrick Ewing soaks it all up after finally leading the Knicks to the NBA Finals.**

his arms, and bellowing a marvelous, unabashed roar of elation as the crowd's unrestrained gratitude washed over him.

For nine years the reticent Jamaican had shouldered the expectations of New York Knick fans. It is never an easy task in this tabloid town, but Ewing had arrived at a particularly cruel juncture —sports radio, in the form of WFAN, was taking root, and the city, accustomed to and even demanding of championships, was hitting a rare dry patch. After the Mets' 1986 World Series victory and the suburban Giants' 1987 Super Bowl win, the 1980s ended with a whimper right as the city's real-life troubles exploded with crack, crime, and racial strife. In the early 1990s, the Giants won once more, but the city's teams kept falling short. Ewing, unable to overcome his on-court weaknesses, his off-court shyness, front-office mismanagement, and, of course, Chicago's Michael Jordan, often bore the brunt of the fans' frustrations. Yes, everyone knew he was one of the game's top centers, but why couldn't this team win it all or at least reach the Finals? The Knicks hadn't accomplished either goal since 1973.

With Jordan having abandoned hoops for baseball in 1993–94, Pat Riley's Knicks sensed their opportunity. To the beat of their customized song (and video) "Go New York Go," the team maintained a drive, capturing the division with 57 wins, then parading through the playoffs to the Eastern Conference Finals against Indiana. They took the first two at home from the upstart Pacers in games that were pugnacious, low-scoring, and occasionally ugly on both sides. Then New York went to Market Square Arena and collapsed. After 60 points in two games, Ewing went 0–10 from the field and 1–4 from the stripe in Game 3. That's right, one point in an 88–68 trouncing. Then Indiana's Reggie Miller shook free for 31 points in Game 4. Still, the Knicks had home court advantage and a comfortable 70–58 lead in Game 5 . . . until Miller took over. After scoring 25 points in the fourth quarter—including five three-pointers—and taunting New York's most famous heckler, Spike Lee, he became an instant villain. Irate fans and the back pages of New York's tabloids turned on the Knicks, with headlines blaring, "Chokers," and "Gag City."

Ewing remained defiantly confident. When the Knicks headed back to Indiana, he told the New York media just one thing: "See you Sunday." True to his word, this gritty, resilient squad won 98–91, forcing a return to New York for Game 7.

On Sunday, June 5, the Knicks demonstrated one more time that the selection of Billy Joel's "All About Soul" as a theme song was more than just marketing. Five Knicks scored in double figures, and they beat Indiana off the boards 59–38, hustling for 28 offensive rebounds, all of them seemingly crucial. They dug in for a thrilling third-quarter comeback, then Ewing topped things off with his clutch play in the final seconds.

With 4:39 left in the third, Indiana led 65–53. Ewing picked up his fourth foul, but Riley couldn't afford to remove his leading scorer, his leading rebounder, his entire game plan, so he took a chance and left him in. Ewing, Anthony Mason, and Derek Harper fueled a 14–4 run to pull within 69–67, and with 8:26 to go in the game, Ewing played Joe Namath, launching a long touchdown pass to Harper, who put the Knicks ahead 76–74. With 4:52 left, Ewing was whistled for his fifth foul; again Riley risked it all, and again his decision paid dividends. Seconds later, Ewing zipped a crisp one to Mason, who gave New York an 85–80 lead.

Then Miller silenced the crowd, burying a three-pointer that sparked a 10–4 run. After Ewing deftly swished a 21-foot turnaround jumper from the right corner, Miller hit his own jumper, and Dale Davis dunked with 34 seconds left: 90–89 Indiana. Suddenly the Knicks were back at the precipice, looking into the abyss.

During their timeout, Ewing urged Riley to forget the outside shots and pound the ball inside to him one last time. "If we lose, I'm going to take the blame anyway," he said afterwards.

Riley called a pick-and-roll with John Starks handling the ball, ideally to find a passing lane down into the Big Fella. It didn't work. Starks went right but had no place to pass. He did see an opening, however, and as the shot clock ticked he burst in and flipped up a lay-up. No good. The ball clunked off the backboard, then clanged off the front rim. Indiana's Dale Davis, Antonio Davis, and Derrick McKey were all underneath—if any of them grabbed the ball, the game was over. Instead, Ewing leapt up and over all three, capturing the rock and smashing home a resounding dunk with both hands: 91–90 New York.

There was still time for one last Miller miracle, but when the Knick-killer shook Starks off on a screen, Charles Oakley hurled himself into the fray, throwing up a hand that prompted Miller to throw up an air ball. Miller's subsequent foul on Starks was called flagrant, which crucially gave the Knicks two shots and possession. It was a bad call, but it didn't undo how the Knicks had outplayed the Pacers. The 94–90 final was indisputable. New York was going to the Finals, and Patrick Ewing had put them there.

So erase the asterisk of Jordan's absence (and Chicago's dominance upon his return). Forget what would happen in the Finals when Hakeem Olajuwon blocked Starks's championship-winning shot in Game 6 and when Riley allowed Starks to shoot the Knicks into oblivion in Game 7. Block out how extra sweet a title would have been in the same month the Rangers ended their 54-year championship drought. Instead, look back at what an accomplishment reaching the Finals really was—after all, the Knicks have done it just four times since 1953. And savor the memory of Ewing's dunk and his subsequent celebration. It was a roar for the ages.

# 34. Cookie Lavagetto ruins Floyd Bevens's no-hitter, October 3, 1947, Ebbets Field

There's an old baseball cliché that World Series games are won and lost by the little guys, when a Sandy Amoros or Al Weis, suddenly becoming Walter Mitty, is a hero among heroes. Like most clichés, there's a kernel of truth in this absurd simplification (Babe Ruth and Reggie Jackson were Series heroes too), and no game pumps up the little guy theory more than Game 4 of the 1947 World Series between the New York Yankees and Brooklyn Dodgers.

It was a historic season: Jackie Robinson smashed the color barrier, and the World Series was televised for the first time. It was also the year New York reasserted its place as capital of the sports world, surpassing even its 1920s heyday. For the next decade, the Yankees, Dodgers, and Giants would dominate baseball, in television's spotlight boxing would flourish at Yankee Stadium and Madison Square Garden, the football Giants would come into their own as champions and Madison Avenue's darlings, the Knicks would emerge as an annual contender in the fledgling NBA, and CCNY would reach the apex of college basketball before being felled by scandal.

Game 1 of the World Series attracted a former president, five governors, the secretary of state, and Hall of Famers Babe Ruth, Tris Speaker, Ty Cobb, Bill Terry, Rogers Hornsby, and even ancient Cy Young. But it is the fourth game, on October 3 at Ebbets Field, that lingers longest in our collective sports memory, and it was two quintessential forgotten men who produced one of the most memorable ninth-inning confrontations ever.

On that day, Floyd "Bill" Bevens made his final major league start. The 6'3", 215-pound pitcher had emerged from seven years' toil in the Yankee farm system to pitch impressively from 1944 through 1946, going 33–23 and finishing among the ERA leaders his third year. But arm problems in 1947 had led to a dismal 7–13 season.

On that day, Cookie Lavagetto banged out his final base hit in the major leagues. Lavagetto had been a solid but unremarkable infielder before the war, spending five years in Brooklyn's starting lineup. But at age 35, he had become a bit player, earning only 69 at-bats in 1947.

The brief moment when Bevens's and Lavagetto's lives intersected was so dramatic that it guaranteed both men lasting fame, even as it marked their baseball demise. The Yankees led the Series 2–1, so Brooklyn needed the win. Yet the Dodgers' pitching was so thin that manager Burt Shotton started rookie Harry Taylor; even though Taylor was nursing a torn elbow tendon, Shotton hoped that, against the underwhelming Bevens, he might be passable. Taylor lasted 11 pitches, getting yanked after walking Joe DiMaggio with the bases loaded. Hal Gregg pitched well in relief, but the Yankees added a second run in the fourth.

Bevens, meanwhile, was unhittable, despite several close calls: Stuffy Stirnweiss robbed Pee Wee Reese of a single on a grounder up the middle in the first, and Johnny Lindell made a diving outfield catch in the third. But Bevens created his

**Floyd Bevens forces a smile, but Cookie Lavagetto is ear-to-ear grin as they shake hands in the aftermath of Lavagetto's shocking hit to break up Bevens's no-hitter and beat him at the same time.**

own trouble. He walked four in the first three innings, inspiring Shotton to order his players to work the count. In the fifth, Bevens walked two more, and one, Spider Jorgensen, scored on a groundout, making it 2–1 New York.

Still, he plowed on. With each out, the Ebbets Field fans grew louder, more frantic with both hope and dismay—the television engineer shut the crowd microphone off because the shouting was drowning out Red Barber's broadcast. Chicago Cub Ed Reulbach had made it to the seventh inning of a World Series game with a no-hitter in 1906, and two Yankees had recently lasted until the eighth, Monte Pearson in 1939 and Red Ruffing in 1942. But no one ever completed the task.

In the eighth, Brooklyn's Gene Hermanski launched a long fly toward the wall in right, where Tommy Henrich leaped and, as Red Smith wrote, "stayed aloft so long he looked like an empty uniform hanging in its locker." Henrich came down with the ball. For just the second time, Bevens retired the Dodgers in order.

Three outs from history.

In the ninth, the Yankees threatened to break open the game, but Henrich bounced into a bases-loaded double play. Bevens returned to the hill. Bruce Edwards smashed the ball to left, but Johnny Lindell grabbed it near the fence. Two more outs.

Bevens was tired now, and if not for the no-hitter might well have been lifted, but he stayed on, even after tying a World Series record by issuing his ninth walk, to Carl Furillo. Jorgenson fouled out. Twenty-six down, one more to go.

But then came a close call, a questionable strategic maneuver, a managerial hunch, so many small decisions accumulating so rapidly that it could make skeptics believe in fate and destiny.

Shotton belatedly sent the speedy Al Gionfriddo to run for Furillo. Then he looked down the bench for a pinch hitter for the pitcher. Pete Reiser had been suffering dizzy spells from a horrific crash into an outfield wall that summer, and in Game 3 he broke his ankle stealing a base. The doctor ordered him to sit out, but Reiser had built his legend violating such orders. Shotton growled, "Aren't you going to volunteer to hit?" Reiser knew the question was a demand. He could barely hobble to the plate, but the Yankees didn't know how bad his injury was and saw only a dangerous lefty. The crowd raised the decibel reading to unimaginable levels.

With the count 2–1 on Reiser, Bevens threw twice to first. Gionfriddo still took off on the next pitch. He stumbled, but the throw was high, and while shortstop Phil Rizzuto was convinced he'd nailed Gionfriddo to seal the no-hitter, umpire Bill McGowan called the runner safe.

The tying run was in scoring position. Yankee manager Bucky Harris, known for breaking baseball's unwritten rules, ordered Bevens to walk Reiser intentionally even though it would put the winning run on base. He would be second-guessed for eternity. But Harris was no fool. With the count 3–1 and the World Series walk record looming, Bevens might have grooved a strike to Reiser, a more potent hitter than anyone the Dodgers had left. There was no clear answer.

Reiser limped to first, where Eddie Miksis replaced him. Shotton suddenly called back the next hitter, Eddie Stanky, in favor of Harry "Cookie" Lavagetto. Lavagetto, whose wife gave birth to their first child that day, was as shocked as Stanky, but the suddenness of the decision was one reason he felt no pressure.

Bevens fired a fastball. Lavagetto swung hard but missed. After 136 pitches, the no-hitter was still alive.

Bevens threw another fastball, up and away. Lavagetto went with it, driving the ball hard to right, where Henrich faced an impossible dilemma: go for a near-impossible catch to preserve the no-hitter or play conservatively and field the ball off the wall to stop the winning run from scoring.

Henrich went for the catch . . . but missed . . . by several feet. The ball clanged off the wall just above an ad for the new Danny Kaye movie, *The Secret Life of Walter Mitty*. Henrich couldn't recover, and the ball rebounded away.

Bevens was banished from the record books — the no-hitter was gone.

Gionfriddo scored easily — the lead was gone too.

Miksis raced home ahead of Henrich's off-balance throw — the game was gone as well.

Bevens was no longer the little-guy-turned-unlikely-hero. Instead, Lavagetto was at the center of Bedlam off Bedford.

Broadcaster Red Barber was so startled that he exclaimed over the air, "I'll be a suck-egg mule."

"The Dodgers pummeled Lavagetto," Smith wrote. "Gionfriddo and Miksis pummeled each other. Cops pummeled Lavagetto. Ushers pummeled Lavagetto. Ushers pummeled one another."

For the Dodgers and Lavagetto, the jubilation proved short-lived. In Game 5, with the Dodgers again trailing 2–1 with two outs in the ninth, Lavagetto again pinch-hit with the tying run on second. This time he felt nervous, knowing that everyone expected him to do it again. He became overanxious and whiffed. After pinch-hitting a game-tying sacrifice fly in Game 6, he failed again in Game 7, a game in which Bevens largely redeemed himself, giving up just one run-scoring double in nearly three innings of clutch relief, which helped the Yankees win both the game and the World Series.

The Bevens-Lavagetto game ultimately provided an ideal bookend with Don Larsen's 1956 perfect game — one marked the first year of the great rivalry between the Yankees, Dodgers, and Giants, while the other ended that era. The games are apt symbols as well. Larsen's game was neat and tidy, perfection leading to yet another championship for the U.S. Steel of baseball. This win, like the one that followed in Game 6 — which was highlighted by Al Gionfriddo's astonishing catch of Joe DiMaggio's long blast — fit the Dodgers: it was dramatic and unpredictable, ending with a burst of elation that set up the heartbreak that followed. But if you're going to lose in the end anyway, well, what a way to go.

# 35. Every match goes the distance on Super Saturday, September 8, 1984, National Tennis Center

When you shell out big bucks for U.S. Open tickets, especially for the final weekend's glamour days, you hope to get your money's worth with either a tense five-setter, elite rivals going at each other, or history being made. One of those three is exciting, two a lifetime memory, but to go three for three, well, you had to be at Louis Armstrong Stadium on September 8, 1984.

Super Saturday starred the game's greatest players, facing off in epochal rivalries: Chris Evert Lloyd versus Martina Navratilova and Jimmy Connors versus John McEnroe; with two other matches also going the distance, the cumulative impact was indeed historic.

Evert and Connors had detonated a tennis boom in 1974, infusing an explosion of excitement about the sport; McEnroe's 1980 Wimbledon and U.S. Open matches with Connors and Bjorn Borg marked the era's apex. Super Saturday was the last, great high, 979 points across 165 games in the morning, afternoon, evening, and nighttime, a signature event representing tennis at its emotional, dramatic, and exhausting best—an only-in-New-York kind of day. "New Yorkers love it when you spill your guts out there. You spill your guts at Wimbledon, they make you stop and clean it up," Connors said beforehand.

The day started with the men's 35s semifinal between former Open champions Stan Smith and John Newcombe, a match added to maximize CBS's telecast. Smith lost the first set 6–4 but won the second, 7–5, forcing a deciding set, which he won 6–2. No one knew that a template had been established: every match pushed to the limit, each more dramatic than the one before. After the old-timers came a riveting semifinal contest between Ivan Lendl and Pat Cash in which Lendl started shedding his "choker" reputation; a tense women's final in which Evert Lloyd nearly upset the indomitable Navratilova; and a classic semifinal joust between Connors and McEnroe, the only two men to have won the Open since it moved to Flushing Meadows in 1978 from Forest Hills (where Connors had won twice).

Lendl, a taciturn 24-year-old Czech, had come from two sets down to beat McEnroe at the French Open, but New Yorkers remembered him falling apart in the two previous Open finals against Connors. No one seemed disappointed when the second seed looked uprooted, dropping his first service game, 10 straight points, and the first set 6–3. The fans cheered Cash, a roguish Australian teen whose strong serve and frenetic net play had catapulted him into the Wimbledon semis. But Lendl bounced back, capturing the next two sets, 6–3, 6–4, by exploiting Cash's weak first volleys with stinging passing shots. After that first break, Lendl held 19 straight times, but with Cash up 6–5 in the fourth, the crowd implored the brash youngster to force a fifth set. Cash earned

**Martina Navratilova extends herself for a shot on Super Saturday, a day when all the players extended themselves, and their opponents, as far as possible.**

three break points and fed off the crowd, but the stoic Lendl refused to crumble, coming back to force a tiebreaker. Then Lendl let up, and Cash won it 7–5.

Lendl started the fifth set with another misstep — double-faulting on break point — but recovered immediately, scorching a backhand passing shot down the line to break Cash back. Cash, down 4–5, saved one match point, but Lendl, down 6–5, did the same. With the howling fans hoping he'd unravel, Lendl steeled himself instead, lifting a magnificent running topspin lob. When he broke to force another tiebreaker, he actually emoted, pumping his fist, Connors-style. A frustrated Cash pointed at him and shouted something. But Lendl was not intimidated — he pointed back, retorting, "Don't you yell at me."

In the tiebreaker, Lendl trailed 3–2 but played aggressively to win back the mini-break, whipped in two service winners for a 5–4 lead, and moved to match point on a running backhand passing shot. After 3 hours and 39 minutes, Cash misplayed his serve and volley and Lendl won. (Cash hurled his racket high into the stands, earning a $2,000 fine.) *Washington Post* columnist Thomas Boswell speculated that future historians might see this match as a turning point, "when a tin man found his heart": while Lendl lost the 1984 final, he'd win the next three Opens.

But from the fans' perspective, Saturday was just getting going. With the preliminaries out of the way, two epics remained: Chrissie versus Martina and Jimbo against Junior.

Evert Lloyd and Navratilova had shared a bagel and watched the men's semi together. Evert Lloyd and Navratilova were so dominant that their finals meeting seemed preordained — it was the tenth straight year one of the two had been there. But the results were starting to feel predetermined too: Evert Lloyd had reigned supreme beginning in 1974, but Navratilova had decisively taken over since the 1981 Australian Open, capturing nine of eleven Grand Slams since then, including her first Open in 1983. She'd lost only once in 1983 and once in 1984. Evert Lloyd had been the Ice Maiden, the iron-willed baseliner whom no one could crack. But Navratilova, once plagued by a reputation for blowing big matches, was in the midst of a 74-match winning streak and seemed like Superwoman: her unsurpassed athleticism and quick thinking allowed her to attack the net with both abandon and precision. Evert Lloyd felt intimidated, Johnette Howard wrote in her telling of their saga, *The Rivals,* and had begun working out with weights, yet she'd still lost to Navratilova 12 straight times, evening their rivalry at 30 wins apiece. With Navratilova cloaked in an aura of invincibility, this easily could have been a quickie.

Another rout here would have been devastating for Evert Lloyd, so she came out charging, keeping Navratilova on her heels. Swinging early, Evert Lloyd hit her crosscourt backhands with impunity, scoring numerous winners.

After Navratilova broke Evert Lloyd for a 4–3 lead, Evert Lloyd broke back at love with a backhand service return winner and a forehand into her opponent's body. With an ecstatic New York crowd urging her on—"I thought Chris was a blood relative of the Mets," Navratilova quipped after—she went up 5–4, then drove backhand and forehand winners to earn two set points. On the second, Evert Lloyd lobbed off Navratilova's approach, then crushed a crosscourt forehand and surprised everyone by racing to net, where she finished the set with a forehand volley.

Her opponent's shift in tactics and a crowd openly against her might once have rattled Navratilova, but she remained calm and adapted, working her way gradually to net instead of simply rushing in. It was Evert Lloyd whose nerves melted. When Navratilova served for the set at 5–4, Evert Lloyd pummeled three forehand winners, but with two break points, she turned "indecisive," failing to attack Navratilova's serve. Navratilova escaped to win 6–4.

In the third set, Navratilova broke at love, coming in four straight times off her service return. When she dug out a low forehand volley to finish the deciding set 6–4, she ended one of the best-played matches in their long and storied history.

Connors and McEnroe didn't start until nearly 7:30, but despite their wait, they also produced one of their finest Open battles, second to their 1980 semifinal. Connors, 32, had won two straight Opens but lost seven straight to McEnroe, six years his junior, including a thrashing at Wimbledon. It was widely (and accurately) presumed that this match would produce the tournament's champion.

Connors set the bar high on the first point with a backhand winner down the line. Both men met the challenge—McEnroe nailed 70 percent of his dangerous first serves and delivered 19 aces, yet Connors, the best returner ever, broke him seven times.

They traded 6–4 sets. In the third set, McEnroe, the game's best volleyer, switched up and rallied from the baseline. With Connors serving at deuce, 3–4 in games, the two foes launched their heaviest firepower, trading blows in a memorable 31-shot point. McEnroe won, and Newcombe—now in the broadcast booth—said, "You could teach a whole lesson out of that rally." McEnroe broke for 5–3, Connors clawed back to 5–5, then McEnroe won the set 7–5, coming from behind in the last game and winning on a crosscourt backhand volley placed perfectly onto the line.

In the fourth set, McEnroe tired, dumping volleys into the net, and Connors broke in the first and seventh games for a 5–2 lead. Then came the hidden turning point, according to Joel Drucker, author of the biography-memoir *Jimmy Connors Saved My Life.* McEnroe broke Connors and held, grinding down the elder statesman of tennis. Although Connors held off another break point to win the set 6–4, his momentum and much of his energy evaporated.

McEnroe leaped to a 3–0 fifth set lead, winning 12 of 13 points. Yet Connors never surrendered, charging to the net where he and McEnroe batted the ball at each other with startling ferocity. Down 4–2, Connors — who would finish with 45 winners to McEnroe's 20 — whistled a crosscourt service return past a charging McEnroe to earn one last break point. But he couldn't even things up, and McEnroe clinched at love for a 6–3 final set.

After 3 hours, 45 minutes, this match was over; after more than 12 hours, Super Saturday was finally complete, with every food concessionaire long since sold out. "It was," said longtime *Tennis* magazine writer Peter Bodo, "the greatest single day in tennis."

# 36. The Giants win the NFL Championship in the "Sneaker Game," December 9, 1934, Polo Grounds

Abe Cohen was five feet tall and 140 pounds. He never played a down of pro football, spending his life instead as a tailor. Yet Cohen was undoubtedly the MVP of the 8–5 New York Giants upset of the 13–0 Chicago Bears in the 1934 title game . . . if MVP stands for Most Valuable Procurer. Cohen made his contribution by running the best route of the day . . . to the Manhattan College supply room to hunt down sneakers.

The 1934 championship was a milestone for the NFL: just the league's second title game, the New York–Chicago confrontation would take place at the Polo Grounds, where the New York and national press would be able to see a big game and perhaps deem it as exciting and worthy of their attention as the biggest college games. A blowout by heavily favored Chicago — which had outscored its foes 286–86 — might have dampened the media's enthusiasm, but they got an instant classic, a hard-fought game that turned on a behind-the-scenes twist, one the writers used to mythologize the day, making this the first NFL game for the ages: "the Sneaker Game."

On December 9, a cold spell had just taken a turn for the worse, and the temperature was barely in double digits when team president Jack Mara inspected the Polo Grounds field that morning; he saw that the field was a block of ice and the tarpaulin was frozen to it.

Mara called coach Steve Owen, who informed some key players about the disastrous conditions awaiting them. "Why don't we wear sneakers?" asked captain Ray Flaherty, who had done that in a game at Gonzaga University in 1925 with great success. (With no soft grass to plunge into, regular cleats would provide even less traction than sneakers.)

Great idea, but where do you find sneakers on a Sunday morning? Before today's nonstop shopping culture, this was a true challenge. Owen, Flaherty, and tackle Bill Morgan hit the phones, but every sporting goods store was closed. Owen also called running back Ken Strong at home in Queens, since Strong had an off-season job with a sporting goods firm — no luck.

Dejected, Owen and his men headed to the Polo

The Giants' halftime shift to sneakers enables them to navigate this icy field and slide past the Chicago Bears.

Grounds. There in the locker room was Cohen, who loved football so much that in addition to tailoring Manhattan College's uniforms he volunteered on game days to help the Giants' trainers. When Owen learned that Cohen had a key to Manhattan College's supply room, he realized he'd found his hero. He called Cohen's play, sending the little man off in search of a taxi to the school.

Unfortunately, getting to Manhattan College at 242nd Street takes time even on days when the streets aren't slick with ice. On this day, Cohen was gone a while. The Giants got an early field goal, but the Bears, with their bigger, stronger line, shoved the Giants around — Strong was knocked out of the game by 246-pound Link Lyman — and Chicago headed into halftime with a 10–3 lead, leaving the Giants mentally and physically worn down.

But then into the Giants' locker room strode Abe Cohen, mission accomplished. He'd scrounged up nine pairs of sneakers. (According to Wellington Mara, Cohen may not have had the key and may have broken in to get the crucial footwear.)

Both teams had worn their cleats down practically to nubs on the hard surface, but not all the Giants players embraced the new equipment immediately. However, once they saw Ken Strong moving around well, they were convinced. When Chicago coach George Halas learned of the switch, he urged his men, "Step on their feet." But you can't step on what you can't catch up to.

"We were helpless," Bears star Bronco Nagurski recalled. "We had to mince about. We were down more than we were up."

Trailing 13–3, the Giants found their footing near the end of the third quarter. Ed Danowski stayed upright long enough to complete four passes — that long drive ended with an interception on Chicago's 4, but the Giants were encouraged. They were unstoppable in the fourth, making sharp cuts that left the Bears slipping and sliding. Strong tore off a 15-yard punt return that set up one touchdown, executed an off-tackle run for a 42-yard touchdown, and pulled off another touchdown on a reverse—a call that would have been unthinkable had the team still been in cleats. The score was 23–13, and the game was essentially over, but Danowski scored a final touchdown on two explosive runs. Call that some icing on the cake.

The fans were ecstatic; reacting like a college crowd, they flooded the field and tore down a goal post. They thought they were simply celebrating the tremendous effort turned in by their hard-charging Giants, but they would later learn that it was the most diminutive man in the locker room who'd made this a day to remember. Lewis Burton of the *New York American* wrote in celebration, "To the heroes of antiquity, to the Greek who raced across the Marathon plain, and to Paul Revere, add now the name of Abe Cohen."

# 37. The Brooklyn Atlantics hand the Cincinnati Red Stockings their first defeat, June 14, 1870, Capitoline Grounds

When the visitors in the red socks snatch a two-run lead in extra innings, all seems lost for the hometown team. Yet thanks to clutch hitting, a wild pitch, and an untimely error, the local boys prevail. The visitors seem haunted in the aftermath of this stunning turnaround.

This narrative sounds wonderfully familiar to those New Yorkers who rejoiced in 1986, "Mookie" and "Buckner" bubbling from their lips like a magical incantation. But this is in fact the long-forgotten tale of the Brooklyn Atlantics versus the Cincinnati Red Stockings, a tale of civic celebration given lasting importance as a symbol of baseball at the intersection of sport and business. The fact that it's the prologue of a ghost story is just the cherry on top.

In the 1860s Brooklyn was the center of baseball; among its native sons were James Creighton, who invented the fastball and was probably the first paid professional (albeit under the table); Dicky Pearce, credited as the first to define the shortstop position and inventor of the bunt; Candy Cummings, inventor of the curve; and Bob "Death to Flying Things" Ferguson, who appropriated one of baseball's greatest nicknames from teammate Jack Chapman and was the game's first switch hitter. Although variations on "base ball" —which had evolved through centuries—existed elsewhere, it was this "New York game" that had caught on, spread by soldiers during the Civil War.

It spread, among other places, to Cincinnati, whose power brokers hired former New York Knickerbocker Harry Wright to bring glory to the Queen City. Wright was a skilled ballplayer and a savvy entrepreneur. He assembled baseball's first fully professional team, the Red Stockings, by importing from New York players like his brother George (one of the game's greatest talents) and

Asa Brainard (a pitcher whose name supposedly begat the pitching term "ace"). The only Cincinnati native was first baseman Charlie Gould, whose reliable fielding earned him the moniker "Bushel Basket."

This pro team began playing in 1869 and proved unbeatable: their 1869–70 winning streak has been tallied at numbers ranging from 84 to 130 games, although Wright discounted exhibitions and put the official streak at 56 games. In June 1869, these Wright brothers brought their high-flying club east and beat three establishment powerhouses, the New York Mutuals, the Atlantics, and the Brooklyn Eckfords, giving Cincinnati the credibility it needed to propel its amazing road trip—the team traveled 11,877 miles by train and boat, journeying as far as California. The Red Stockings brought baseball to hundreds of thousands, making the game a national pastime.

By June 1870, when Cincinnati returned to New York, they were thought invincible. On the 13th, they lived up to the hype, walloping the Mutuals, 16–3. Next came the rematch against the Atlantics at the Capitoline Grounds in Bedford-Stuyvesant. (It ran from Halsey Street to Putnam Avenue between Marcy and Nostrand Avenues.)

The Red Stockings' roster was filled with former New Yorkers, but the Atlantics were playing for hometown pride, to show who was best at the New York game. With thousands shelling out 50 cents to stand the whole time and plenty more watching from holes in fences or the tops of nearby buildings, this game was played amid a heady excitement equal to any of the great World Series games that followed.

Cincinnati jumped out front 3–0, but Brooklyn was not intimidated, clawing back with two in the fourth and two more in the sixth. In the seventh, George Wright drove home two for a 5–4 lead. It was short-lived, however: the Atlantics tied it in the next inning when the Red Stocking catcher dropped the throw on a play at the plate.

The game remained 5–5 after nine innings. In those days ties often were simply called a draw. The Atlantics, thrilled to have held their own against the great Red Stockings, headed off to celebrate—even this tie "seemed the very acme of fame," wrote the *New York Daily Tribune*.

But Wright didn't want this stain on the Red Stockings' record, so he went over to the stands and appealed to *Brooklyn Daily Eagle* journalist Henry Chadwick, the godfather of baseball rules. Chadwick decreed that extra innings were in order—setting a precedent that would make this custom more the norm than the exception afterwards—and Bob Ferguson had to fetch the Atlantics from the clubhouse.

After this delay, Cincinnati went quickly in the 10th, but Brooklyn put two on before George Wright purposely let a harmless pop fall to trap the runners and turn one of his patented double plays. (The infield fly rule would later be introduced to prevent this tactic.)

In the 11th, Cincinnati reasserted itself on RBIs from Cal McVey and George Wright. Their 7–5 lead seemed insurmountable, just as Boston's 5–3 lead would seem in extra innings in Game 6 of the 1986 World Series.

But after allowing a single, Brainard—channeling the Red Sox's Bob Stanley—uncorked a wild pitch, sending the runner to third. Then a fly ball landed for a triple only because, legend has it, a Brooklyn fan jumped onto McVey's back. McVey later dismissed the impact, saying he shrugged off the interference attempt. (A policeman apparently then subdued the intruder with his club.) Now it was 7–6 with a runner on third.

One out later, the right-handed-hitting Ferguson came up . . . and turned around to bat lefty. Ferguson simply wanted to keep the ball away from George Wright at shortstop, but he simultaneously rattled Brainard and made history as the first recorded switch hitter. When he pulled a single to right, the Atlantics came, improbably enough, from two runs down in extra innings to tie it. Brooklyn fans were as wild with excitement as Met fans would be when Kevin Mitchell scored in 1986. And the tenuous link between these two historic but seemingly unique events was about to be strengthened.

Contemporary accounts of the final plays are murky and somewhat contradictory, but Brook-

**Cincinnati hadn't lost a game since forming the first pro team. Then they came to Brooklyn.**

lyn's George "the Charmer" Zettlein hit what the *New York World* called a "hummer" toward first base and the usually sure-handed Charlie Gould. Most sources say the ball was either hit too hard for Gould to reach or proved "too hot" for him to handle. What seems likely is that Gould knocked the ball down and, having no chance of getting back to first, hurried a throw to second for a force; that throw got past Charlie Sweasy, allowing Ferguson to dash all the way around, à la Ray Knight, with the winning run. Other sources, however, say Ferguson stopped at second and danced home instead on the next play, when Sweasy muffed either a grounder or a toss from George Wright.

Either way, there was joy that day in Brooklyn.

This game birthed a new era critical to professional baseball's development by demonstrating its commercial possibilities. The National Association would debut the following year, an evolutionary step toward the start of the National League in 1876. Teams would become businesses, paying players to draw fans so that higher admission could be charged and so on until the day finally arrived when television contracts would be negotiated in the hundreds of millions of dollars.

Meanwhile, the strange links to 1986 didn't end on that fateful day. After this defeat, Cincinnati's fans abandoned the team. With attendance plunging, investors backed off and the Red Stockings disbanded. Harry Wright took his best players and moved to a city he thought would support professional baseball more avidly: Boston. When the National League formed in 1876, Boston was a founding member; later it would change its nickname to the Beaneaters, then the Braves. Three decades later, when John Taylor, owner of the upstart American League's Boston Pilgrims, wanted a new name for his team, he reached back to the city's proud link to professional baseball's early days and named his team after the Red Stockings—though he used the more modern "Red Sox"—inadvertently bonding the past to the future.

Finally, in 1917 Charlie Gould, a lifelong Ohioan, died at age 69—a pivotal number in Mets history—while visiting his son in New York . . . not just anywhere in New York but in Queens . . . and not just anywhere in Queens but in Flushing . . . the future home of Shea Stadium. So even if his gaffe—if indeed, he made one—was less damaging than Sweasy's, it is easy to imagine that his ghost lingered till the moment he stopped Bill Buckner's glove from getting all the way down, bringing joy back to the locals while haunting the spirits of red-socked players and their fans.

# 38. Man o' War comes back to beat Grier at the Dwyer Stakes, July 10, 1920, Aqueduct Race Course

Man o' War was not undefeated, but he seemed invincible. Sure he'd lost once to a horse named Upset, but no one expected the great horse to lose again, especially not with his reputation on the line. So in the homestretch at Aqueduct, when John P. Grier pushed his nose out in front, a huge cry swept up from the stands. Was the Dwyer Stakes to be the end of the great horse's legend, or could Man o' War find something inside to reverse the momentum?

When that great age of sports heroes dawned in the 1920s, Man o' War broke out first, ahead of Babe Ruth, Jack Dempsey, and Red Grange. As a two-year-old in 1919, he'd won his debut by six lengths and captured nine of his ten races. In that lone upset, there were three false starts, and Man o' War was not even facing front when the race actually began. In 1920 "Big Red," as his trainer called him, was so dominant in the Preakness that only two horses challenged him in his next race, and only one showed at the Belmont Stakes, where he set a speed record. (He hadn't run the Kentucky Derby, which was just beginning to gain prestige, because owner Sam Riddle didn't like "western" races and believed three-year-olds shouldn't run long races early in the year.)

Harry Payne Whitney's John P. Grier was considered one of only two quality horses left to beat. (Riddle famously ducked any race with Exterminator, the other viable threat.) At the Dwyer Stakes on a steamy July 10, John P. Grier was the only horse game enough to take on the champion, turning this into a match race; Man o' War was so heavily favored that he had to carry 18 extra pounds as a handicap.

But in what the *New York Times* called a "whirlwind battle of speed and stamina," the great horse was not such a sure thing. John P. Grier's jockey, Eddie Ambrose, tried desperately to get out first, but Clarence Kummer pushed Man o' War too, and they shot out evenly. The two horses were virtually inseparable through the first turn and were still together as they passed the mile mark, beating the 1:36 record time that Man o' War had set at Belmont.

Other horses had stayed with Man o' War early, but always faded quickly. Not John P. Grier, who earned his place in history during what the *Times* called "the great struggle in the stretch."

That was when Grier's nose poked ahead. He had done it. He was winning. The surprised crowd let loose its yell—some urging the challenger on, others coaxing the champion to finish strong. Racing announcer Clem McCarthy burst out, "For one flashing moment—Grier's nose in front. He's got h——"

But McCarthy never got to finish the word "him." Kummer, who rarely whipped his great horse, did so, and within three strides his horse was a half-length ahead. Normality was restored.

Or was it? Responding like a champion, Grier suddenly drew even again with Man o' War. Kum-

**Man o' War needs everything he has to turn back John P. Grier at Aqueduct.**

mer resorted to the whip twice more, and Man o' War flew ever faster over the last 50 yards, a half-length in front, then a full length, then finally two lengths, finishing in 1:49 1/5, a new world record.

Afterwards, everyone marveled at John P. Grier's fortitude, though Kummer dismissed the hubbub, saying he never doubted his horse: "The moment I went after him in earnest the race was over."

Man o' War continued ending races at will, romping through six more victories that season—once officials had to plead for an opponent—before Riddle, incensed by the dangerously heavy weights his overwhelming favorite was burdened with, retired the horse. Today most of Man o' War's wins are remembered only as a blur in which the champion far outclassed his competition. But thanks to John P. Grier's great effort and Man o' War's resounding response, people at Aqueduct still point to the Man o' War Pole, where the great horse made his unforgettable stand while on the dead run.

# 39. The Yankees win their first World Series, October 15, 1923, Polo Grounds

You never forget your first.

For the New York Yankees, long second-class citizens both in New York and in the baseball world, their first great season seemed at hand in 1920 when Babe Ruth arrived. But the Yankees finished third, even though Ruth wowed everyone with his record-setting 54 homers. It seemed within reach again in 1921 when Ruth hit 59 homers and led the team to its first AL pennant, and again in 1922 when they duplicated the feat, but both times they were embarrassed in the World Series by the New York Giants, a team with a storied and successful past that the Yankees could only dream about.

But 1923 was the year of the Yankees, a turning point in baseball history. Evicted from the Polo Grounds by the Giants' John McGraw, the Yankees had opened a spectacular palace in the Bronx, which helped them win 98 games; having squeaked by in their first two pennants, they posted their highest winning percentage ever and annihilated the AL, besting second-place Detroit by 16 games. It was still Ruth's team, but the attack was much better balanced — four players drove in at least 80 runs, the Yankees led the AL in ERA, and five starters won at least 16 games.

The Giants, however, had an even more potent offense, having led the NL in batting average, slugging average, and runs scored. They had the mystique and aura that derived from the legendary McGraw — as well as from beating the Yankees in two straight Series in which they'd won seven games in a row (not counting a tie in 1922).

Their third confrontation produced an exceptionally dramatic Series. The first three games were monumental classics, revolving around the heroics of two of the most iconic figures in New York and baseball history, but it was the thrilling conclusion of the final game, on October 15 at the Polo Grounds, that marked the beginning of the Yankee century.

In Game 1, Ruth scored the first World Series run in Yankee Stadium when he singled and hustled home on Bob Meusel's double. Ruth also made a running catch, tripled (although he was thrown out at home on the next play), and nearly drove home the winning run in the eighth when he smashed the ball down the first-base line; George Kelly's superb fielding play and throw home, however, preserved the 4–4 tie. Instead of Ruth, the deliverer of the late-game long ball was another player who would one day hit 60 regular-season home runs, although it would take 14 seasons for Casey Stengel to amass that total. At 33, Stengel, a former Brooklyn Dodger and future manager of both the Yankees and the Mets, was nearing the end of his playing career and had hit .339 as a part-timer for McGraw. In the ninth, Stengel laced a liner into Yankee Stadium's "Death Valley" in left-center. As the Yankees chased it down and fired two relays toward home, Stengel chugged and churned around the bases, wobbling for the last 180 feet as the rubber pad in his shoe shifted, making him worry it was about to come off. Stengel slid into home just ahead of the tag, making him, for one day anyway, a bigger hero than Ruth, who was depicted as a great folkloric character by the likes of Damon Runyon and Grantland Rice.

More significantly, the game stirred up the notion that the Yankees, who'd frittered away a 3–0 lead, could not beat the Giants. Then came Game 2. In both the fourth and fifth innings, Ruth launched shots that could only be called Ruthian, leading the Yankees to their first World Series win since 1921 and inspiring *New York Morning World* columnist Heywood Broun to pen one of sportswriting's most famous lines, "The Ruth is mighty and shall prevail."

The Giants pitched around Ruth in Game 3, and it was again Stengel who rose to the occasion, homering for the game's only run in the seventh; to the delight of the crowd, he thumbed his nose and blew kisses at the Yankee bench as he rounded the bases. But the old hierarchy was about to topple once and for all. A paucity of hittable pitches limited Ruth to two hits and three walks in the next two games, but the entire Yankee offense exploded, tearing apart three pitchers in a six-run second in Game 4 and piling on seven runs in the first two innings in Game 5.

Desperate, McGraw sent Art Nehf, who'd shut out the Yankees in Game 3, back out on two days' rest. There'd be no shutout in Game 6. In the first inning, Nehf left a 3–2 pitch within reach, and Ruth detonated it into the upper deck, setting a new record with three homers in one Series. The Giant southpaw neutered the Yankees for six innings after that, allowing only one ball out of the infield while McGraw's men pecked away at Herb Pennock, playing classic Giant small ball. They tied it in the first on three singles; took the lead

# Honorable Mention: Ruthian Days

**1. Ruth leads the Yankees to their first pennant, September 26, 1921, Polo Grounds**

Once upon a time, the New York Yankees were upstarts, a team with little history, and what they had was ignoble: in their only crucial game from 1903 to 1919, they lost the pennant to rival Boston on the final day of 1904 when Jack Chesbro wild-pitched home the winning run.

Then Babe Ruth arrived, forever altering baseball and legitimizing the Yankees. In 1920 they still finished third behind Cleveland and Chicago, despite Ruth's 54 homers, but in 1921 Bob Meusel provided protection for Ruth, who'd finish with even gaudier statistics: 59 homers, 171 RBIs, and a .378 average. The Yankees kept pace with the Indians, and in September the defending champions arrived at the Polo Grounds for what the press dubbed "the little World Series." Excitement in New York was heightened because the Polo Grounds' real home team, the NL-leading Giants, were the likely opponents in the real World Series.

After splitting the first two games, the Yankees took a one-game lead by humiliating Cleveland 21–7. The series finale was crucial. One more win would essentially wrap up the title with just five games to play, but if the Indians rebounded, it would make for a nervous last week.

When Cleveland battered young Waite Hoyt for three first-inning runs, the outlook looked bleak for the New York nine. But the mighty Ruth brought joy to the Bronx that day, smashing a solo homer in the first, a long third-inning double that fueled a three-run rally, and a fifth-inning two-run homer—his 58th of the year—for a 6–3 lead.

It took a diving, skidding catch by Elmer Miller and relief help from ace Carly Mays, who had started the previous day, but the Yankees, propelled by Ruth's three long hits, won 8–7. They were on their way, transformed from feisty underdogs into a team headed for the World Series.

**2. Babe Ruth makes one final appearance, June 13, 1948, Yankee Stadium**

For baseball's seminal figure, one farewell would not be enough. Babe Ruth had two celebrated final trips to home plate at Yankee Stadium, one in 1947 and one just two months before his death in 1948.

On April 27, 1947, baseball held Babe Ruth Day at ballparks around the country, so fans sitting in Ebbets Field that day also heard the raspy whisper of the cancer-riddled Bambino as he told the Yankee Stadium crowd: "The only real game, I think, is baseball."

Ruth's last appearance, on June 13, 1948, was even more touching. The event was a 25th-anniversary celebration of Yankee Stadium, reuniting the team that won the franchise's first World Series. But as Dan Daniel wrote in *The Sporting News*, ballparks were steel and stone brought to life by those who inhabited them, and this was "the House That Ruth Built." So June 13 was all about Ruth.

Old-timers like Bob Meusel, Joe Dugan, Sam Jones, Bob Shawkey, and Wally Pipp were once again reduced to revolving around Ruth's orbit—in fact, after politely keeping their distance while his nurse helped him change into his old uniform, many former stars asked Ruth for his autograph.

It was a damp day, and Ruth sat in the dugout wearing his coat as the other old-timers were introduced, which only made his entrance more dramatic. When the time came, Ruth shucked his coat, took a bat as a cane, and walked onto the field one last time. All the previous cheers were whispers compared to the lengthy standing ovation that greeted Ruth, a noise that W. C. Heinz called "the cauldron of sound he must have known better than any man."

Ruth could not match Lou Gehrig's eloquence of nine years earlier, but it didn't matter, for he was the Babe. When he said, in his badly diminished voice, "I am proud that I hit the first home run in this stadium," many in the crowd were moved to tears.

"In 1947 you had the impression that he was not doing so well, but nobody knew how long that might mean for Ruth," says New York sports historian Bill Shannon. "But in 1948 he looked like he was going to die and people realized, 'We may never see him again.'"

The Yankees retired Ruth's number, a moment given extra poignancy by the most famous photo of that day: Nat Fein's image from behind of the shrunken Ruth leaning on his bat, the number 3 on his pinstriped back all that identifies him as the game's greatest player.

Ruth was too ill to stay for the Old-in the fourth when Frank Frisch bunted for his second hit, then scored on a two-out single; and added runs in the fifth and sixth, the latter coming when Frisch tripled and Irish Meusel (Bob's brother) singled through the drawn-in infield.

Heading into the eighth with a 4–1 lead, the Giants were supremely confident that they'd forced a seventh and deciding game. In the final innings of the final game between the year's two best teams—often with the two best pitching staffs—it's extraordinarily difficult to mount a large-scale comeback. Box scores for the deciding game of every World Series reveal strings of zeroes and ones in the eighth and ninth innings, with only the occasional outburst of two runs. The 1986 Mets would score eight runs to erase a 3–0 deficit in Game 7, but their comeback began in the sixth; only the 1960 Pittsburgh Pirates, who scored six times in the last two innings (to the Yankees' four), would erupt for a truly explosive last-ditch comeback. No other team has ever overcome a three-run deficit that late. Additionally, the Yankees had consistently done their damage early, scoring 18 of their 25 total Series runs in the first two innings—they had not scored at all in the eighth or ninth frames. That fit the Yankees' reputation—many old-school baseball men, including some in the press, believed "Murderers' Row" was a bunch of bullies who bashed homers against weak pitching but lacked the guts to carve a rally in a tight game.

But with one out in the eighth, catcher Wally Schang, trying to evade a high and tight heater, poked it for a single. It was a bad break for Nehf, who was finally wearing down. Everett Scott singled to right on the next pitch. After a four-pitch walk, Yankee manager Miller Huggins sent righty Joe Bush, a good-hitting pitcher, to bat for lefty center fielder Whitey Witt. Nehf's command was shot, and he walked Bush on four pitches too, forcing home a run.

## Ruthian Days (CONTINUED)

timers' Game. In the clubhouse afterwards, when Dugan poured him a beer and asked how he was, Ruth replied, "Joe, I'm gone."

Two months later, he was.

### 3. Babe Ruth returns to the mound, October 1, 1933, Yankee Stadium

It had been 20 seasons since Babe Ruth's major league debut, and baseball's greatest player was talking openly about retiring after 1933. But the 39-year-old Ruth was also baseball's greatest showman, so he wanted to go out with a bang—one last day of splendor.

Ruth went to Joe McCarthy, the old-school manager with whom he'd often clashed, and asked a favor: he wanted to pitch the season finale against the Boston Red Sox. Ruth had not only broken in with the Red Sox but established himself as the game's premier lefty hurler while pitching in Boston.

Ruth had pitched just four times for a total of 22 innings since arriving in New York in 1920; though he'd won all four of those starts, only one—in 1930—had come since 1921. By 1933 Ruth was badly overweight and, at season's end, worn down, his skills clearly eroded. Still, he was a vain, confident man with a knack for the dramatic gesture—that summer he'd hit the first home run in the very first All-Star Game, and he even made a fantastic catch.

McCarthy acceded to Ruth's request, which drew 25,000 people for a meaningless game. Ruth had worked his arm into shape for the occasion and shut the Red Sox out for the first five innings. In the home fifth, he capped the day with his 34th homer of the season for a 6–0 lead. In the sixth, he either began coasting or felt the onset of fatigue, and Boston rallied for four runs. Still, it was all singles and walks as Ruth refused to yield the big blow. Then he bore down and allowed just one run over the final three innings.

Ruth should have made this game his grand finale—he had little glory left in 1934 or in a brief stint with the Boston Braves in 1935. Regardless, thousands of fans, sensing they'd seen a special effort, waited for him outside the Stadium. As Robert Creamer wrote in *Babe*, they didn't shout and cheer but gave him steady applause as he walked to his car. Ruth tipped his hat with his right hand; his left arm hung by his side, aching and utterly spent. But Ruth was happy. He had done it . . . again.

**Old-school Giant John McGraw and long-ball revolutionary Babe Ruth faced off in three straight World Series, with the Bambino finally blasting the Yankees to their first crown in 1923.**

McGraw finally replaced Nehf with Rosy Ryan, who had smothered the Yankees twice already, but he proved as tentative as Nehf, walking Joe Dugan to make it 4–3. That brought up Ruth. There was nowhere to put the Sultan of Swat this time. Oh, what a delicious script this seemed for Yankee fans. But McGraw reached back for his playbook from 1922, when Ruth had gone 2-for-17, flailing at curves out of the strike zone. He had Ryan spin in two curves for strikes, then another for a ball. Then Ryan fired his 1–2 pitch, again low and away. Ruth ripped, but he was looking curve and was far too late to catch up with Ryan's fastball. Strike three.

Before McGraw could savor his last laugh, however, the Yankees proved again that they had more than Ruth's firepower going for them. Bob Meusel seemed to live in a permanent anticlimax batting behind Ruth, but frequently he benefited as pitchers let up a bit. This time he got just enough bat on the ball to bounce a single up the middle, scoring the tying and go-ahead runs, and an errant throw brought home an extra run for a 6–4 lead.

The Giants brought the tying run to the plate with two outs in the eighth, and McGraw sent Stengel up to pinch-hit. But Stengel had no heroics left and fouled out. Sam Jones cruised through the ninth, and the Yankees were, for the first time, World Series champions.

All this excitement did wonders for baseball's popularity—the interest fueled by Ruth's feats combined with a new technology made this the first Series carried nationwide on radio, while at the gate it became the first "Million Dollar Series," thanks to the record 301,430 paying fans. As memorable as the games themselves were, the *New York Times* declared the Series "probably most remarkable of all for the great interest it stirred in fandom. Large new grounds, just completed and built with an eye to the future proved inadequate to accommodate the thousands" flocking to the ballparks.

This Series also forever changed the Yankees' big game reputation—they had finally come into their own as a franchise, fulfilling their destiny as baseball's defining force. *The Sporting News* declared that the eighth-inning rally put the "stamp of gameness" on them. It also put the stamp of greatness on them . . . in indelible ink. The Yankees were mighty and would prevail.

# 40. Reed goes down, but the Knicks come back to win in Game 5, May 4, 1970, Madison Square Garden

Willis Reed was the Most Valuable Player of the 1969–70 NBA season.

Willis Reed was the player around whom the Knicks were built, their offensive core and their defensive anchor.

Playing on battered knees, Willis Reed led the Knicks through the first four games of the 1970 Finals against Los Angeles, averaging 32 points and 15 rebounds while guarding larger-than-life legend Wilt Chamberlain.

So when Reed slipped while driving to the hoop, then crumpled to the Madison Square Garden floor in Game 5 on May 4, grabbing his hip and covering his face to hide the pain, the Knicks' championship aspirations seemed to deflate instantly. With Reed gone, Chamberlain would likely erupt, scoring at will; with Reed gone, the Knicks offense would lose its go-to guy; with Reed gone. . . . It was impossible to imagine winning with Reed gone. But the Knicks, already trailing by 10, stunned everyone with a win for the ages, a perfect representation of the team's intelligence, fortitude, discipline, and teamwork.

The day before Game 5, *New York Times* writer

Wilt Chamberlain looms large as Willis Reed crumples to the floor, yet the Knicks rally for a shocking victory.

Leonard Koppett wrote that despite the possibility of three games in five nights, "there is no question Reed will play, and probably play well, until and unless he actually collapses."

Now, with under four minutes left in the first, he had done just that. Down 25–15, Knick coach Red Holzman tried backup center Nate Bowman, but in seven minutes Chamberlain scored seven points and the Lakers' lead grew to 37–24. Holzman next turned to little-used Bill Hosket, but the Knicks failed to gain traction—eventually the Laker lead would reach 16—so after another four minutes Holzman made an unusual but shrewd move. He shifted Dave DeBusschere in the low post. At 6'6", DeBusschere gave away at least seven inches against Chamberlain, but he was perhaps the game's best defensive forward, and in the half's final four and a half minutes the Laker superstar did not score.

At halftime, when it was obvious that Reed, on the trainer's table and unable to move, would not return, Holzman gave what he called "my best Gipper treatment" and asked the players to win for their fallen leader.

In the second half, Holzman stuck with DeBusschere—and when he picked up his fifth foul early in the fourth quarter, 6'7" Dave Stallworth—in the pivot. Both men did their best to front Chamberlain and deny him the ball. They had help, of course: Holzman's Knicks always played a well-rounded team defense, and this game represented the pinnacle of those efforts. Walt Frazier and Dick Barnett, who seemed to have read the Laker playbook at intermission, anticipated every move. The Knicks allowed Los Angeles just 22 shots in the second half and had 10 steals or interceptions in the last 16 minutes. They wreaked havoc by double-teaming Jerry West, Mr. Outside to Chamberlain's Mr. Inside, which prevented West from getting off good shots or dumping the ball in to Chamberlain. The frustrated Lakers committed 19 turnovers in the second half (compared to New York's 2), while Chamberlain and West managed just 5 of their team's 26 shots, scoring a grand total of 8 points.

Some observers, like Koppett, felt the Lakers were "robbed, pure and simple," as officials let the undersized home team mug the big, bad visitors. Still, there's little doubt that Chamberlain let up and that the Knicks' aggressive, rotating defense and screaming fans unnerved the Lakers, who lost their poise when their most obvious game plan faltered. Elgin Baylor, their sole hot hand in the second half (scoring 15 of his 21 then), hit only three field goals in the fourth quarter, passing up open looks in desperate but failed attempts to get the ball to Chamberlain. Unlike the Knicks, the Lakers lacked the temperament for improvisation; by alternately playing too passively and too frantically, they let their tremendous advantage evaporate.

Under normal circumstances, Chamberlain's mere presence in the middle on the other end of the court might have been enough to stave off a Knick comeback. But at halftime, Bill Bradley, the thoughtful Rhodes Scholar from Princeton, presented Holzman with a solution to the quandary of what the *Daily News* called a "donut" offense (a reference to the missing center). At Bradley's suggestion, the Knicks went to a 1–3–1 offense, in which Frazier played up high, Bradley hovered around the top of the key, Barnett and Cazzie Russell spread to the wings near the free throw line, and DeBusschere roved down deep. Because all the Knicks could handle the ball and hit from outside, they were able to stretch the court, either drawing Chamberlain out (enabling them to use their speed to drive around him) or minimizing his impact in the lane.

"It was like having five guards on the court at the same time," Frazier said afterwards. (Zone offenses, like zone defenses, were technically illegal, but L.A.'s complaints were ignored, perhaps because Chamberlain was hovering in the middle, in an illegal defensive zone.)

The Knicks chipped away in the third, outscoring Los Angeles 35–29, but they still trailed 82–75 as the fourth began. Early in the last quarter, however, the Knicks went on a 12–5 spurt, which featured Stallworth hitting from outside as Chamberlain scrambled out after him and culminated with 7:43 left on a long shot by Bradley to tie the game at 87. At 91–91 with 5:19 to go, Bradley again drained one from downtown to give New York its first lead. The Lakers were so rattled that they couldn't even get the ball in-bounds, and Stallworth hit a running one-hander for a 95–91 edge. The Lakers would not get another shot at tying it up as Russell caught fire, scoring six points to give the Knicks a 101–94 cushion. Stallworth drove the final nail in the coffin when he exploited his earlier success from outside and blew past Chamberlain with a head fake, went under the basket, and laid in a short reverse hook for a 103–96 lead with under two minutes remaining.

That clinched it, and the Knicks finished L.A. off 107–100; Frazier had 21 points (and 12 assists), but there was not one star—the team finished with six players in double figures and five with at least six rebounds.

The win was overshadowed by the news of the day (May 4 was the day of the Kent State shootings) and by the unforgettable Game 7 that followed. But had the Knicks failed to pull together in Game 5, they would have headed to L.A. facing elimination, and without Reed for Game 6, there probably would not have been a Game 7. Reed—who listened in the locker room to public address announcer John Condon's calls via a special hookup—believed this game "was really the most significant game of that series."

# 41. The Mets come back once more to win Game 7, October 27, 1986, Shea Stadium

It almost felt cruel to force the Boston Red Sox to play a Game 7.

It wasn't because they'd faced three Game 7s since 1918 and lost all three. No, this was about Game 6 of 1986. The New York Mets' Mookifizing comeback in the 10th inning doused the Sox with defeat—they positively reeked of it. Boston legend Carl Yastrzemski confessed afterwards, "After they lost the sixth game, you just knew somehow they wouldn't win the seventh game."

The Mets, by contrast, felt invincible, certain that having returned from the dead, they would not lose their grip on their destiny.

Sure, a day of rain worked to Boston's advantage, allowing them to start the tough lefty Bruce Hurst instead of mediocre loudmouth "Oil Can" Boyd.

Yes, Ron Darling looked awful yielding back-to-back homers to Dwight Evans and Rich Gedman as Boston jumped out to a 3–0 lead, while Hurst twirled a one-hitter through five.

Still, the Mets and their fans at Shea Stadium on October 27 were not worried. A comeback was on the way. The Mets had faced tougher spots against the Houston Astros in the playoffs, and they'd rebounded after losing the first two games at home in this Series. This game, this championship, had been locked up with their resurrection—it may have come the moment Mookie Wilson jacknifed away from Bob Stanley's pitch, or perhaps when he tumbled that ball through Bill Buckner's legs.

Just look at Sid Fernandez's relief job to keep the Mets in Game 7 after Darling faltered. The portly El Sid had grumbled about being bumped from the rotation in the Series but made the most of his moment, retiring seven straight with four strikeouts. "The necessary hero," Keith Hernandez called him afterwards.

For inspiration, the video scoreboard replayed Bill Buckner's infamous error just before the home sixth. That wasn't playing nice, but it certainly seemed to work.

The Mets loaded the bases with one out. Working on three days' rest, Hurst was wearing down, but Boston's bullpen could by that point charitably be described as unreliable; doomed was more appropriate.

So Hurst stayed in, lefty against lefty, facing Keith Hernandez. The Mets' leader was only 5-for-24 in the Series, but he'd hit the ball hard and was one of his generation's fiercest clutch hitters. (The short-lived "game-winning RBI" stat seemed to have been invented to show off his prowess under pressure.) As Roger Angell wrote in *The New Yorker,* knowledgeable fans "understood that this was the arrangement—this particular batter and this precise set of circumstances—that the Mets wanted most and the Red Sox least at the end of their long adventures."

Hurst froze the Met first baseman with a curve, but when he left a fastball up over the plate, Hernandez smoked it into the gap in left-center, scor-

After one more comeback, Gary Carter and the Mets celebrate.

ing two. It was a one-run game, but the Mets knew they were not done. Gary Carter had a terrible cut and lifted a pathetic pop to right. On this day, for this team, that was enough. Playing deep, Dwight Evans barely got there—he dived and smothered the ball, recovering quickly enough to force Hernandez at second base . . . but the tying run was already home.

Roger Clemens was in the bullpen, but for the seventh Boston manager John McNamara inexplicably turned back to Game 6 loser Calvin Schiraldi, who'd said beforehand, "I don't deserve another chance."

Met fans let out a collective "Wheeeee!!!" If Schiraldi couldn't handle the tension of preserving a lead in Game 6, how well would he fare with his back to the wall in Game 7? Schiraldi quickly bid farewell to the ball, the game, and the season as the first hitter, Ray Knight, blasted a meaty 2–1 fastball over that wall and off the bleachers in left-center field.

Schiraldi only got worse. With taunts of "Caaaalll-viiiin" in his ears, he yielded a single, heaved the ball to the backstop on a pitchout, then allowed another run home on another single. McNamara tried another former Met, Joe Sambito, who walked two hitters and then yielded another run on a sacrifice fly.

The Red Sox valiantly staged their own rally but fell short, not because of "the Curse of the Bambino" but because the better team, with the better manager and better bullpen, won out in the end. When Buckner and Jim Rice singled and scored on Evans's double to make it 6–5, Mets manager Davey Johnson replaced Roger McDowell with Jesse Orosco, who set down Gedman, Dave Henderson, and pinch hitter Don Baylor. Crisis over.

Then the Mets added not one but two finishing touches, showing off their multifaceted ball club one last time. McNamara shoved Al Nipper, who had a 5.38 ERA and had pitched once in three weeks, onto the hill in this tight spot instead of the Cy Young–winning Clemens. Darryl Strawberry greeted him by launching a moonshot. Then, with two men on base, Johnson had Orosco fake a bunt and swing away; the Met reliever, who was 0-for-3 in all of 1986, punched a single through the drawn-in infield, scoring another run.

In 1969 Jerry Koosman was on the mound when the Mets won their first World Series. In 1978 the Mets traded Koosman to Minnesota for two young pitchers, one of whom was Jesse Orosco. In 1986 Orosco was on the mound as the Mets won their second World Series. At 11:26 P.M., Orosco struck out Marty Barrett on a high 2–2 fastball, leaped into the air, threw his glove even higher, and dropped to his knees, where he was buried beneath a pile of Mets crazed with triumph.

This comeback, with its air of inevitability, may not have the notoriety of Game 6, but the game was still filled with drama, which was only enhanced by it being the end of the line.

A New York team has played in only two other seventh games in the last 40 years, and they lost both — the Mets lost in Oakland in 1973, and the Yankees lost in Arizona in 2001.

This was the only Game 7 held in New York since 1957, and the only time ever that the home team won a grand finale in New York against an out-of-town team. (The Yankees won Game 7 in 1958 on the road in Milwaukee, but the other four local Series that went the distance pitted the Yankees against the Dodgers; those triumphs were bittersweet since half the city's fans suffered in the end.)

Additionally, while no other expansion club had yet won a World Series, the Mets had now won their second. In a city without any championship in any sport in eight years, this win, capping the unforgettable year of 108 wins, four brawls, three NLCS thrillers, and the miracle of Game 6, was particularly satisfying.

Even low-key Mookie Wilson got swept up in the glory of it all. "Now," he said, "we can be as cocky as we want to be."

# 42. Billy Martin saves the Yankees, October 7, 1952, Ebbets Field

Call it fate, call it fortune, or call it the baseball gods. Whatever your term, these forces always seemed to beam munificently on the Yankees. Well, perhaps it would be more accurate to say the Yankees had signed them to a lucrative, long-term contract no other team could afford. But in Game 7 of the 1952 World Series against the Brooklyn Dodgers, those otherworldly powers suddenly rebelled and took an active role against the Bombers — using Ebbets Field's low sun and high wind to put the Yankees' dynastic aspirations in peril.

Then Billy Martin stepped in. Martin never liked leaving a ball game in the hands of anyone else — rival players, meddling owners, muddling teammates, or fate. This feisty fireball wanted, even needed, to mix 'em up, to thrust himself into

the action. And on October 7, 1952, the Yankee second baseman made one of the most sensational infield plays in World Series history.

The Cleveland Indians, with three sluggers and three 20-game winners, had seemed on paper like the best team in the American League in 1952, but the Yankees had replaced Joe DiMaggio with a kid named Mickey Mantle in center field, and manager Casey Stengel again proved he was unparalleled in getting the most out of all his players. When Jerry Coleman was drafted, he moved Gil McDougald from third to second base. When Bobby Brown was also conscripted, Stengel stuck one of his pet projects, Billy Martin, at second and shifted McDougald back to third. The Yankees held off the Indians to win the pennant by two games.

The Dodgers, meanwhile, rode their overwhelming offense to a 60–22 start before their shallow pitching staff nearly blew a 10-game lead to the New York Giants. With his weak rotation exposed, Brooklyn manager Charlie Dressen made his lord of the bullpen, Joe Black, a starter for the Series.

Black, the Rookie of the Year, boasted, "There's nothing in that lineup to be scared of," and backed his words up in three strong starts. But with the Yankees trailing 2–1 in games, Stengel outmaneuvered Dressen. During the regular season, Yankee first baseman Joe Collins had batted .280 with 18 homers in 428 at-bats; his Brooklyn counterpart, Gil Hodges, had batted .254 with 32 homers in 508 at-bats. But in the Series, both men went hitless through three games. Dressen lacked the bench depth and the nerve to bench his first baseman, but Stengel called on Johnny Mize, who was nearly 40 and had served almost exclusively as a pinch hitter that year; a Hall of Fame slugger four years removed from his last big season, Mize had managed just four homers in 137 at-bats. But after he blasted a pinch-hit homer in Game 3, Stengel handed him the starting job for Game 4, and he homered again to help the Yankees even the Series. (Hodges finished the seven games 0-for-21.) Mize hit a three-run blast in Game 5, but Brooklyn won Game 5, 6–5, behind Duke Snider's two-run four-bagger and his 11th-inning single.

Back home, Brooklyn needed just one win in two games. But while balls continued jumping the fence—there'd be six more homers for a total of 16—the Series turned on two balls that never left the infield.

In a tense Game 6, Snider homered off Yankee Vic Raschi in the sixth for a 1–0 lead. But Yogi Berra led off the seventh with his own homer off Brooklyn rookie Billy Loes. Then, with Gene Woodling on first, Loes dropped the ball while on the mound, and a balk was called. Raschi hit a grounder right back to Loes, which should have helped him out of the jam, but the ball ricocheted off his leg, and Woodling scored to give the Yankees a 2–1 lead. When the Yankees won 3–2, Loes was widely mocked for saying he lost the grounder in the sun, but given how low the sun was in the sky, he might have been unable to pick up the ball after his pitch. Still, that sort of thing only happened to Dem Bums, never the Bombers.

Meanwhile, Stengel had bypassed his bullpen and got a save out of ace Allie Reynolds, his scheduled Game 7 starter. That meant he needed a new plan for the deciding game. Just hours before game time, Stengel announced that Eddie Lopat, who'd struggled with injuries in 1952 but pitched respectably in Game 3, would start. Lopat was a lefty pitching against a heavy-hitting and almost entirely right-handed lineup, one that feasted on lefties in tiny Ebbets Field. But Stengel coaxed three shutout innings out of Lopat; staked to a 1–0 lead on Mize's RBI single, Lopat faltered in the fourth, but when Brooklyn loaded the bases, Stengel called once again on Reynolds—who'd started Game 1 and Game 4 on three days' rest, then relieved in Game 6 on one day's rest—to give whatever he had left. Hodges mustered his lone Series RBI by flying out, but Reynolds then struck out George Shuba and got Carl Furillo on a grounder.

The score was tied at 2–2 after five, but Joe Black was tiring, as was only to be expected with a rookie reliever asked to start for the third time in six days. Dressen no longer had anyone in the bullpen to bail him out, however, so he sent Black back for the sixth.

**Billy Martin runs down this breeze-blown pop-up and saves the Yankees' 4–2 lead over Brooklyn with the bases loaded in the seventh inning of Game 7.**

Mickey Mantle greeted the exhausted pitcher by launching a home run over the top of the scoreboard. After Mize singled again, Preacher Roe came on and foiled that rally but yielded another run in the seventh. The Yankees led 4–2.

The 37-year-old Reynolds let Stengel know that his arm was shot, so Stengel, in addition to replacing Mize with Collins for defensive purposes, brought Raschi in for the seventh. But Raschi pitched well only when rested, and he'd gone nearly eight innings the previous day on top of a complete game four days prior. With shadows cutting across the infield, the tension mounted and the Brooklyn faithful grew louder and louder as Raschi went 3–2 on every batter—Furillo walked, and with one out Billy Cox singled and Pee Wee Reese walked, loading the bases.

All year long the Dodgers had had a feast-or-famine offense: Hodges would hit four homers and they'd win 19–3, but then they'd lose a game when they failed to get a runner home from third with less than two outs. Hoping to make sure this famine didn't become a feast, Stengel called on reliever Bob Kuzava, a dangerous choice with the sacks full because he hadn't pitched at all in the Series and had control problems. But Stengel wanted a lefty against the red-hot Snider, who had tied Babe Ruth and Lou Gehrig with four homers in a Series and set a new record with 24 total bases. Kuzava fell behind 3–2 but, with no margin for error, got Snider to pop up on a tailing fastball. Two outs.

With the right-handed Jackie Robinson up, Stengel came out of the dugout to make another pitching change. Then he abruptly turned back, as if he'd just had a hunch—after all, Kuzava loved busting righties inside with that same fastball (the equivalent of today's cutter), and Stengel had brought him in with the bases loaded in the ninth inning of Game 6 in 1951 and he'd gotten three straight righties out.

Robinson stayed alive with a 2–2 count by fouling back several pitches—one was a long, hard foul into the left-field stands that brought Stengel back out for a peek. When Robinson pulled the next pitch for a hard foul grounder, Berra went halfway to the mound to remind Kuzava not to leave the ball out over the plate.

The next pitch was in on Robinson's hands, and he lifted a meek infield pop that should have quashed the Dodger threat. On the left side of the infield, Gil McDougald and Phil Rizzuto took a few steps in, then realized the wind would keep it on the other side of the diamond. Kuzava stood on the mound. It was clearly the first baseman's ball. But Collins, looking directly into the low sun cutting across the grandstand roof, could not see a thing. As Dodgers circled the bases with great haste, the baseball gods seemed to have finally thrown their lot in with the underdogs.

"For what seemed a full week, nobody moved," Red Smith wrote. If the ball fell safely, the game would be tied but the momentum would belong to Brooklyn. Then second baseman Billy Martin noticed just how clueless Collins looked.

Stengel's protégé, like Stengel and his mentor, John McGraw, saw everything on a ball field. In Game 4, Martin had saved a crucial run by spotting Dressen clutching his left shoulder; recognizing the suicide squeeze sign from 1949 when Dressen coached on Martin's minor league team in Oakland, Martin had called out to Allie Reynolds; the Yankees nailed the runner at the plate.

With Collins frozen, Martin started moving toward the ball, but the capricious wind blew the sphere back toward home plate, closer to Kuzava and Berra. As the ball hurtled toward earth Martin shifted gears and raced full speed across the infield, his hat flying off, and lunged on the dead run, grabbing the ball perhaps two feet from a total fiasco.

Noisy Ebbets Field fell silent. There were two more innings, but the Dodgers were dead. Even fate and fortune couldn't beat the New York Yankees. As Charles Einstein wrote in his syndicated story, they could have skipped the entire Fall Classic—memorable though it was—if they'd read the record books carefully, "down in the small print where it says the Dodgers don't win World Series and the Yankees do."

## 43. Stephane Matteau scores in double overtime in Game 7 of the Eastern Conference Finals, May 27, 1994, Madison Square Garden

Tick. Tock. Tick. Tock. The Eastern Conference Finals never should have lasted this long. In their winter of great expectations, the 1993–94 New York Rangers had zipped through 82 regular-season games with the league's best record, then raced through blowouts of the New York Islanders and Washington Capitals in the early rounds of the playoffs. And the conference finals foe was the New Jersey Devils, a team that had not beaten the Rangers once that year.

Tick. Tock. Tick. Tock. The Devils gained their first win against New York in Game 1, tying the game with just 43 seconds left and triumphing in double overtime. The Devils, after four straight years of falling in the semis, suddenly seemed ready for the big time. Soon time appeared to be running out on the Rangers as the Devils took a 3–2 lead in games home to New Jersey, hoping to finish the Rangers off. But Mark Messier hauled New York back from the abyss: he guaranteed victory in Game 6, then delivered with a hat trick to force a Game 7 at Madison Square Garden on May 27.

Tick. Tock. Tick. Tock. Still, the Rangers could

# Honorable Mention: Blueshirt Building Blocks

## 1. Rangers rout the Islanders, April 17, 1994, Madison Square Garden

!

Grammarians will be horrified; you don't start a story with an exclamation point. But that was precisely how the New York Rangers began the story of their march through the 1994 playoffs to the coveted, elusive Stanley Cup. They started by pumping out an emphatic victory, humiliating their ultimate rivals, the New York Islanders, 6–0.

The Islanders, born in 1972, had won four championships in the 1980s, while the Rangers hadn't won it all in, oh, approximately, forever. (Not in 54 years, if anyone was counting.)

Though by 1994 the Islanders were no longer a powerhouse and barely made the playoffs, they'd beaten the Rangers five times in seven playoff matchups, and everyone expected a hard-fought series. The Rangers quickly dispelled that notion.

The strafing started just 3:32 into the game when Brian Leetch scored on a power play. Steve Larmer added another goal 12 minutes later. About halfway through the second period came the deluge—Mark Messier (at 9:13), Adam Graves (at 12:19), Aleksei Kovalev (14:05), and Sergei Zubov (17:38) pounded Islander goalie Ron Hextall for four goals in eight minutes, sending him to an early shower, accompanied by the singsong taunts of riled-up Ranger fans.

This was the worst playoff loss in Islander history, and it proved the Rangers had the firepower, defense, and killer instinct to win it all. For good measure, the Rangers won again, 6–0, in Game 2, then outscored the Islanders 10–3 over two games to finish off this most devastating of sweeps.

!

## 2. New York shuts out Boston, March 26, 1940, Madison Square Garden

In 1940 the second-place New York Rangers owned the tightest defense, but the first-place Boston Bruins were the league's most explosive offense. New York's Dave Kerr, the NHL's top goalie, made their memorable playoff clash a historic one.

Kerr had posted a Game 1 shutout at home before New York got smacked around for eight goals in two losses in Boston. Back at Madison Square Garden for Game 4, New York faced a must-win situation, knowing two of the three final games would be in Boston.

Kerr was spotless in the first period, but the Rangers couldn't score.

Aided by his sparkling work from his defensemen, Kerr was flawless in the second, but again the Rangers came up empty.

Halfway through the third, Ranger Muzz Patrick fired in a 40-footer for a 1–0 lead. Boston stepped up its attacks, but to no avail. Once three Bruins fired a shot in a five-second span at the isolated goalie, yet Kerr rejected all three.

Two days later in Boston, Kerr repeated the feat, again stifling the Bruins 1–0. The Rangers won the Stanley Cup that year. Ranger fans then waited 54 years for another set of back-to-back playoff shutouts—in the opening 1994 series, Mike Richter led two 6–0 blankings of the New York Islanders. That postseason also yielded another happy result that Ranger fans hadn't experienced since 1940.

## 3. The Rangers edge Detroit in a goal game, March 30, 1933, Madison Square Garden

The 1933 New York Rangers hoped to become the first third-place team to win the Stanley Cup. They blew out the Montreal Canadiens in the first game of the opening round and won easily. Next up were the Detroit Red Wings, a much tougher team.

Those early rounds lasted just two games, home-and-home, with the team amassing the most total goals declared the winner. Winning the first game, especially by more than one goal, was crucial, since it would enable the team to work the clock in the second game.

Game 1 was a battle of the goalies—Detroit's net-minder, ex-Ranger John Ross Roach, came up with 27 saves, while New York's rookie, Andy Aitkenhead, made 28. The difference was the two shots Roach couldn't stop.

At 17:46 in the first, crowd favorite Ching Johnson intercepted a pass deep in his own territory, skated the length of the ice down the right alley, and zipped past lunging Red Wings before lifting the puck over Roach's shoulder into the net. At 13:48 in the third, Murray Murdoch found Cecil Dillon open, and he drove home the score. That 2–0 win freed the Rangers to play more conservatively in Game 2; their 4–3 victory sent them on to the finals, where they won their second Stanley Cup.

**Stephane Matteau finally finishes off the New Jersey Devils in the second overtime of Game 7 of the Eastern Conference Finals.**

not vanquish the Devils. In the first period, Ranger veteran goalie Mike Richter was flawless, but the Devils' outstanding rookie, Martin Brodeur, matched him.

Halfway through the second, the Rangers finally grabbed the lead when Messier won a face-off, Adam Graves pushed the puck toward the blue line, and Messier sprung Brian Leetch free with a pick. Leetch raced down the ice, spun around, then powered home a goal.

Tick. Tock. Tick. Tock. In the game's final minute, the Devils pulled Brodeur for an extra attacker, and loyal Ranger fans counted down the seconds until their first Finals since 1979. But the clock started and stopped in maddening fits.

With 48 seconds to go, the Rangers were called for icing.

With 24 seconds left, another icing call.

With a mere 16.4 seconds remaining, the whistle blew again. Yup, icing.

This time the Devils argued that 2.2 seconds should be put back, and the officials agreed.

Tick. Tock. Tick. Tock. Back to 18.6 seconds.

New Jersey's Bernie Nicholls, whom Ranger fans had been heckling with tremendous venom for his rough play, won the face-off, and the puck headed to the boards near the Rangers' goal. Claude Lemieux got a shot off, but Richter deflected it off his pads. Just 7.7 seconds left.

Richter looked like the hero—a remarkable turnaround for a goalie who'd taken the blame for the 1992 playoff loss to Pittsburgh, lost his confidence, and been shipped out to the minors. Stellar throughout the regular season, Richter knew he had to prove himself in the playoffs, in the clutch, and he had, with four shutouts already to his credit. With 23 Devil shots already stopped in Game 7, Richter was just a tick and a tock away from his fifth.

But with the fans cheering his name, the puck rebounded to Valeri Zelpukin, who thrust it into the net. The shutout, the lead, the role of hero, the end of the series—all gone: 1–1.

They headed to overtime with the Rangers reeling. Silence enveloped the locker room during the break, and the smell of defeat began creeping in until Messier, the man with five Stanley Cups to his credit, took control, urging his teammates to be aggressive and stay positive.

"We'll win this game," he told them. "We'll play all night if we have to."

Tick. Tock. Tick. Tock. Perhaps it would take all night. Another overtime period elapsed, and Richter and Brodeur were again unassailable, with Brodeur turning away 15 shots. (By game's end, the Rangers would take 48 shots to the Devils' 32.)

As the teams headed to the third double overtime of the series, officials moved the Prince of Wales Trophy into position between the two locker rooms for its postgame presentation. Left wing Stephane Matteau, a midseason acquisition who had scored the winning goal in Game 3's second OT, had stayed behind to repair his skate. As he belatedly headed to the ice he noticed the trophy and touched it for luck.

Richter redeemed himself by stopping five difficult shots; nearly four minutes into the period he dove across the length of the crease to flick away a loose puck. This was getting scary.

Less than a half-minute later, Matteau zipped around the net and took his first shot of the game. He banked a wraparound off Brodeur's stick and into the goal. At 4:24 of the period, the Rangers were Eastern Conference champions. Brodeur stood, unmoving, weeping, as the Rangers leaped into a wild pile of celebrating teammates.

The Garden fans were ecstatic, but they also knew that this could not be the end of the 1994 season. "We want the Cup," they chanted. "We want the Cup."

One Cup was coming right up.

# 44. Tommie Agee saves the day . . . then does it again, October 14, 1969, Shea Stadium

New York Met left fielder Cleon Jones is forever frozen in time for fans, catching the final out of the 1969 World Series in Game 5. Right fielder Ron Swoboda will always be remembered for his diving catch in Game 4. Tommie Agee didn't make a single defining catch—he made two, both spectacularly memorable, and both in the same game, the game that marked the turning point of the Series.

The Baltimore Orioles had brusquely dismissed Tom Seaver and the Mets in Game 1, raising the question of whether the Mets really were as great and powerful as their 100-win season and playoff sweep of Atlanta seemed, or whether the man behind the curtain was about to be exposed. Jerry Koosman's masterful pitching and a flurry of clutch two-out hits in Game 2 had shown that New York was for real, but it remained to be seen whether they could outplay the masterful O's over an entire series.

So Game 3 at Shea Stadium was pivotal. It would be the Mets' first (and, it turned out, only) effort without one of their two aces on the hill,

**Tommie Agee makes a seemingly impossible catch for the second time in one World Series game.**

and that matchup favored Baltimore. Jim Palmer was both talented (16–4, 2.34 ERA) and experienced (he'd outpitched Sandy Koufax in the 1966 World Series); the Mets' countered with Gary Gentry, whose rookie season 13–12 record and 3.43 ERA represented promise and potential. Game 3 was also a historic event: New York's first chance to root for a National League team in the Series since 1956, and the first Series appearance for the Mets at Shea Stadium before their loyal fans. Among those fans were Governor Nelson Rockefeller, Mayor John Lindsay, Aristotle and Jackie Onassis (with Caroline and John Jr. in tow), Joe DiMaggio, Casey Stengel, and Roy Campanella, who threw out the first pitch.

But Agee, 28, made it clear from the beginning that this was his day. The Mets had spiraled through 27 center fielders in just six seasons before acquiring Agee from the White Sox. He'd slumped badly with the White Sox in 1967 and fared even worse in his first year in New York, but after another slow start in 1969, Agee came on strong, hitting .271 with 26 homers, 97 runs scored, and 76 RBIs. He'd bashed two homers in the playoffs before descending into an 0-for-8 funk in the Series. In the bottom of the first, Agee slammed a liner over the center-field fence. He was just getting started.

In the second, the Mets put two men on to bring up Gentry, an .081 hitter. But that season the Mets' mantra should have been "Why not?" The pitcher doubled deep in the gap, and New York led 3–0.

After three hitless innings, the Orioles began rumbling. Frank Robinson smoked a ball to left that Jones charged and caught in midtumble, only to have it ruled a trap. The next batter, Boog Powell, singled to right. With two outs and two on, lefty pull hitter Elrod Hendricks lined a ball the other way to deep left-center. Agee "ran for several minutes," Roger Angell wrote in *The New Yorker.* It was actually about 40 yards on the dead run, but the Mets of 1969 did seem to demolish such basic principles of life as the space-time continuum.

Just before the wall, Agee reached up and made a dazzling backhand grab. The ball — a sure triple — nearly snuck through the webbing, but Agee held on with a vintage snowcone catch. He had saved two runs.

The Mets made it 4–0 in the sixth when Ken Boswell, one of four lefties manager Gil Hodges had inserted into the lineup against the righty Palmer, singled and scored on Grote's double. Moments later Baltimore nearly made it a one-run game, but Agee again raced to the rescue, making his second spectacular catch.

With two outs, Gentry had abruptly lost it, walking three straight batters. Hodges had seen enough and lifted Gentry for 22-year-old Nolan Ryan, who possessed a dangerous fastball but not much control. Paul Blair wasn't intimidated and slashed a ball into the gap in right-center. Running in the opposite direction from his earlier catch, Agee again covered the Great Plains of Shea in a heartbeat. And when the wind made the ball dip at the last minute, he dove, then skidded across the ground, stretching out to make a one-handed catch at the warning track.

Agee had single-handedly saved five runs — or six, since the speedy Blair claimed he'd have have had an inside-the-park homer if Agee had missed.

In the eighth, lefty Ed Kranepool, another of Hodges's Irregulars, made the manager look smart yet again, giving the Mets an extra cushion with a home run that made it a 5–0 game. With two outs in the ninth, Ryan, like Gentry, went wild, and the Orioles loaded the bases with an infield hit and two walks. Blair was next. This time Agee was not needed — with two strikes, Ryan buckled Blair's knees with a curve to end the game.

The Mets had proven themselves twice and led 2–1, but many experts still considered Baltimore slight favorites. In Game 4, the Mets would quickly force them to revise that notion.

# 45. John McEnroe gets revenge against Bjorn Borg, September 7, 1980, National Tennis Center

Revenge is a match best served hot . . . and sweaty and exhausted and filled with shouts and grunts, served after five sets in the unfriendly confines at the National Tennis Center, and served in the trademark style — the impossibly wide leg spread, the short back swing, and the deadly uncoiling at awkward angles — unique to the ultimate bad boy of tennis, New York's own John McEnroe.

On September 7, 1980, McEnroe indeed attained glorious and grand (slam) revenge at Louis Armstrong Stadium in five exhilarating and draining sets against his polar opposite and favorite dueling partner, the stoic Swede Bjorn Borg.

The two had staged the tennis equivalent of Ali-Frazier I at Wimbledon that summer, with Borg prevailing 1–6, 7–5, 6–3, 6–7, 8–6. McEnroe had staved off seven match points in a mesmerizing, 34-point fourth-set tiebreaker that was the zenith of the heyday of tennis. Although the U.S. Open rematch is often overlooked, it was the rivals' Thrilla in Manila.

Borg, 24, was the dominant force in tennis, winning three straight French Opens and three straight Wimbledons. He had lost only once in 1980 and was reaping $3 million a year in endorsements. But he had yet to solve the U.S. Open, having lost two finals to Jimmy Connors and been upset by ace Roscoe Tanner under the lights in 1979. After his Wimbledon epic, however, Borg publicly declared himself ready to conquer New York, stating his aim of a complete Grand Slam. At Flushing Meadows, Borg overcame Tanner in five sets in the quarterfinals, then dropped two sets to Johan Kriek in the semifinals before whipping him 6–1, 6–1, 6–1. McEnroe, the defending champion, was all that stood in his way.

McEnroe, 21, had beat up-and-comer Ivan Lendl in four sets in the quarterfinals on Thursday, went five sets in the men's doubles final Friday, and on Saturday outlasted his other archrival, the hard-punching, menacing Jimmy Connors in the role of George Foreman. Mac had mouthed off and rope-a-doped through Connors's pounding in the middle sets to emerge the victor after 4 hours, 16 minutes, with a hard-fought fifth-set tiebreaker.

Lefties like McEnroe had won the previous six Opens, but Borg seemed unbeatable. The U.S. Open had hard courts, McEnroe's favorite surface and Borg's least favorite, but Borg had defeated McEnroe in four of their five previous meetings —on grass, carpet, and even hard courts twice. The New York environment—noisy fans, noisy planes, the glare of the lights—favored the hometown kid, but the crowd preferred the polite foreigner to the bratty native. (Oddly, McEnroe's fiery tenacity had won over the snooty British crowd at Wimbledon, but at the Open, where the equally voluble Jimmy Connors had become a New York hero with his blue-collar charm, McEnroe remained the enemy.) Somehow this seemed both the top-ranked Borg's best shot at capturing the elusive crown and the second-ranked McEnroe's best hope at breaking Borg's hold on tennis.

The first set was suitably close, despite Borg's cautious play, atypical sloppiness (he'd finish with 95 unforced errors, nearly two per game), and poor serving. Borg broke McEnroe for a 5–4 lead, but then made just three of six first serves, and Mac broke back. Borg returned the favor, although he lost his focus standing around while McEnroe yelled at the linesman and umpire over a call, then lost his serve at love. In the tiebreaker, Borg got a bad break when McEnroe's apparent double fault was called in for a second-serve ace. McEnroe often used anger and frustration to rally himself (when he didn't become totally unhinged), but Borg, after shooting a dirty look at the linesman (a Swedish outburst), became dispirited, rolling over and losing the last two points as McEnroe finished him with winners at the net.

Borg's confidence was shaken, and McEnroe's was booming. Zeroed in, McEnroe was among the most talented players ever, with quick feet and an uncanny ability to read shots. Employing a dazzling arsenal of weapons from the baseline and particularly the net, he had a magical sense of timing, touch, and restraint (although this marvelous self-discipline in shot-making often did not extend to the emotional and mental side of the game). In the second set, McEnroe trampled a diffident Borg into submission, winning 13 straight points. Borg missed 14 of 22 first serves, botched easy baseline shots, and blew an overhead smash. He seemed to be running the white flag up the pole of surrender.

Down a game and 0–30 in the third set, Borg recovered his equilibrium, pitting his inimitable passing shots against McEnroe's unsurpassed net game and his aggressive service return against McEnroe's array of serves. McEnroe remained in fine fettle: when Borg served for the set up 5–4, McEnroe broke easily, and when Borg served to stay in the match down 5–6, McEnroe dragged him through four deuces before Borg's passing shot down the line and sharply angled crosscourt backhand beat him. The seemingly inevitable tiebreaker began with Borg's backhand winner down the line. At 3–3, McEnroe yelled at chair umpire Ken Slye, "You just made the worst call I've seen in the biggest match of all time." But it

**John McEnroe cuts loose as he finally vanquishes Bjorn Borg in the U.S. Open final.**

was Borg who was the real obstacle as he fired home five winners to pull the tiebreak out 7–5.

The fourth set was nearly as close, with both players holding before Borg, switching his backhand from down the line back to crosscourt, broke McEnroe after four deuces to win the set 7–5.

After three and a half hours, it was time for another fifth set. "Ice Borg" had been unsinkable, winning 13 straight five-setters since 1976. He won with talent, conditioning, and an unruffled mystique. McEnroe was more than fatigued—he was psyched out. "I started to think I was never going to beat the guy," he confessed after. Although there was no change of sides, McEnroe shrewdly took advantage of the crowd's lengthy ovation to walk off and sip some water. "I wanted to take a minute to get my head back together."

As the heat of the day gave way to the cool of the evening the momentum shifted from the hotheaded New Yorker to the cold-blooded Swede. Even though the final set would be played under the lights, and even though McEnroe would nail 70 percent of his first serves in the final set to Borg's 49 percent, it was Borg who held easily in the first three tries while McEnroe twice struggled past deuce. Eventually, it seemed McEnroe would have to give.

But at 3–3, when McEnroe's return of Borg's serve appeared deep by an inch, Borg didn't play it, and the linesman never called it out. Love-15. The normally placid Borg angrily blurted out his disagreement and briefly lost his composure—at 15–15 he double-faulted, and at 30–30 he did it again. He passed McEnroe once on break point, but McEnroe chipped and approached again, and Borg missed. McEnroe converted this break with a crosscourt backhand Borg couldn't handle.

McEnroe fired three service winners for a 5–3 lead. Borg responded in kind, holding at love. Connors had broken McEnroe the previous day at 4–5 to force the eventual tiebreaker, but this time McEnroe would not relinquish his hard-earned lead. At 15-all, he pounded a deep service winner. Then he resumed his relentless attack, slashing to the net and finishing with a forehand volley. At match point, he again rushed the net and, after 4 hours and 11 minutes and an unimaginable 55 games, finally put Borg away once and for all. (No other final since 1970 has required so many games.) "I thought my body was going to fall off," McEnroe said.

McEnroe lounged in the locker room long after this sweetest of triumphs. Borg left as quickly as possible. He said all the right things before departing, but his flat tone betrayed his devastation. Like Frazier after Manila, Borg was never the same—the following year McEnroe became number one, beating Borg in four sets both at Wimbledon and at the Open, chasing the Swede into early retirement. For McEnroe, this triumph did more than just avenge Wimbledon. Although his Wimbledon loss remains more famous, this triumph—which made him the first man to win two straight U.S. Opens—had a more lasting impact, marking his ascendancy to the top of the tennis world. It helped make the Brat into the Greatest.

# 46. Tony Zale drops Rocky Graziano, September 27, 1946, Yankee Stadium

Whom do you root for?

Here's the 33-year-old middleweight champ, a hard, precise hitter who zeros in on his opponent's body; he's a shy, mild-mannered family man from the steel mill towns of middle America, reduced to the underdog because of four years of rust that accumulated on his body and his crown while he was serving his country in World War II.

Here's the betting favorite, the 24-year-old hometown boy, a scattershot windmill of a slugger; up from the streets of New York, the challenger is a rambunctious character with a penchant for fighting dirty and getting into trouble outside the ring—while the champ was protecting America, this former juvenile delinquent was punching a captain, going AWOL, getting sent to Leavenworth, and then being dishonorably discharged.

Tony Zale versus Rocky Graziano. Yankee Stadium. September 27, 1946. Even before the punching began, this was a saga packed with drama.

Anthony Zaleski was born in Gary, Indiana, and worked in the mills, but by the time he volunteered for the Navy in 1942 he was better known not only as Tony Zale but as the Man of Steel, middleweight champ. His punches to the body inspired fear and awe: "When he hit you in the belly, it was like a hot poker hit you and it stayed there," opponent Billy Soose once said.

Thomas Rocco Barbella was born on the Lower East Side and spent his youth prowling those streets or getting packed off to reform school. He was kicked out of the Army for running away to box, which he did using a friend's name, Rocky Graziano. A popular up-and-comer, he was still known more for his prison record than his boxing record. Where Zale once said, "If my mother had ever caught me stealing, she'd have broken my neck," this Dead End Kid joked that he'd steal "anything beginning with an 'a': a car, a piece of jewelry, a purse . . ."

There were others equally deserving of a shot at the title, says historian Herb Goldman, but Zale, after knocking everyone out in a half-dozen warm-up bouts, wanted Graziano for his first defense because Graziano's roguish charm meant more tickets sold and a bigger payday. As the *New York Herald-Tribune* said, "Graziano is a puncher of demoniac fighting fury who has always created excitement, win lose or draw."

Graziano made sure Zale paid for the privilege. Indeed, this was more than just a cute story line about opposites attracting—this was an all-out, knockdown brawl of epic proportions. W. C. Heinz once referred to the two men as "two prehistoric

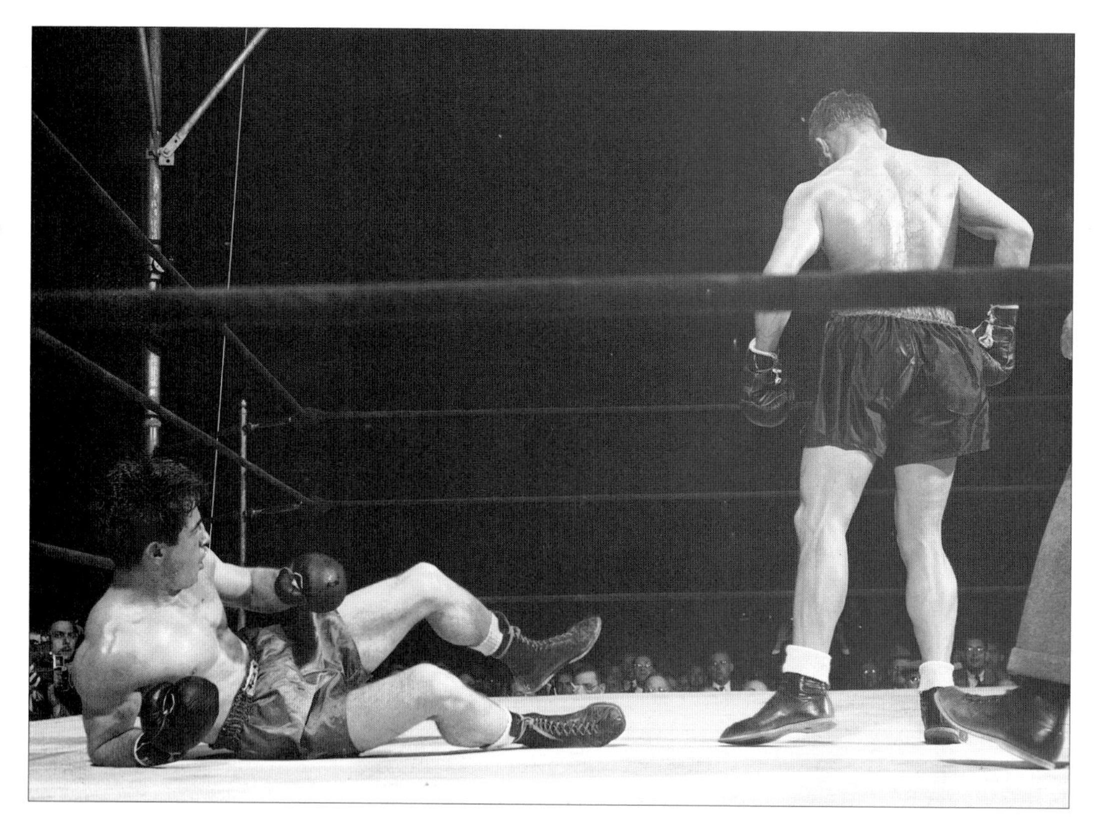

**Tony Zale walks off, his work done: Rocky Graziano is down for the count after six fast and furious rounds.**

monsters, knee-deep in the primeval ooze, ready to fight to the death and with the jungle all around them echoing to the noise and horror of it."

The New York crowd rooted for Rocky, hoping he could bombard the champ early—Zale was the better boxer, but he had a rep as a slow starter and had also just recovered from pneumonia (which had delayed the bout two months).

Zale dispelled such thinking almost immediately by exploiting Graziano's tendency to keep his hands low, his left hook to the jaw sending Graziano to the floor for a four count early in the first. But Graziano recovered and then some, pounding Zale's head hard by round's end and bouncing him off the ropes.

In the second round, Graziano became "a human volcano," the *New York Times* wrote. He seemed on the verge of victory, ruthlessly beating Zale, splitting his lip, and, with four big rights to the head, sending him down. Zale was saved by the bell, which rang while the ref was at three.

The violence was, in the manner unique to boxing, simultaneously excruciating and exhilarating. And it only increased: Zale was revived, only to take another beating in Round 3. "Zale presented a pitiful spectacle, his face a mask of gore as Rocky punched him, heeled him with his gloves and pounded him around the ring at will," sportswriter Shirley Povich later wrote of this round.

Somehow, Zale looked rejuvenated in Round 4 and returned to basics, backing Graziano off and pounding the challenger's body, despite having badly injured his right hand. In the fifth, Zale whaled Graziano's body, but Graziano absorbed it all in order to stand in and rifle shots into Zale's head. Zale was so disoriented that he headed for the wrong corner afterwards, fueling calls for referee Rudy Goldstein to stop the fight.

Still, despite the damage Graziano had wrought, Zale was entering uncharted waters: he had built his record knocking out ambitious welterweights who couldn't handle a heavier foe. Zale was a genuine middleweight and a true champion.

In Round 6, Graziano turned desperate, or perhaps just more aggressive and uninhibited. He went for the kill, but staying in and punching left him vulnerable. Zale—knowing his body blows had a cumulative effect—waded in with a blast just under Graziano's heart, a devastating hot poker. Zale capitalized with a left hook to the jaw that sent Graziano crashing to the canvas.

Graziano, who'd gone the distance in every previous fight, pulled himself up . . . but only after Goldstein counted to 10 and signaled that Zale had won at 1:43 in the sixth. Graziano raged that he wanted more and was ready to punch; he had to be led away by his handlers. Had he recovered a few seconds sooner, he might very well have won because Zale was so battered he could barely stand. But despite Graziano's protests, he was, in reality, a beaten man. "I was out on my feet," he'd later admit. (He also urinated blood for weeks afterwards.) "I didn't even know where I was."

The hand-to-hand combat was over . . . temporarily. This rivalry was just beginning. Graziano soon landed in more trouble—he was banned from fighting in New York for failing to report a bribe attempt—but in 1947 he and Zale would go to Chicago and stage another classic in the annals of mutually assured destruction. There Graziano knocked Zale out in the sixth to claim the middleweight title, but the following year Zale would exact revenge in Newark, shredding Graziano in three rounds.

Of the three fights, the first stands out and is consistently ranked as one of the greatest of all time. But all told their battles, though lasting just 15 rounds combined, earned the two men their hyphenated legend, alongside Dempsey-Tunney, Pep-Saddler, Ali-Frazier, Hagler-Hearns, and Robinson-LaMotta. "For sustained fury, Zale vs. Graziano surpassed them all," Povich wrote.

It was not the modest Man of Steel but the gregarious Graziano (eventually every bit the family man as Zale) who—despite losing on his home turf and losing the rubber match—captured the public's imagination and became a media star. But even then, Graziano's fame was always linked to Zale and his powerful knockout punches.

In 1956 Graziano's autobiography, *Somebody Up There Likes Me,* was made into a movie starring a young buck named Paul Newman. Zale worked with Newman in the ring off-screen, but while his training was helpful, it was also dangerous. According to Hollywood lore, Zale proved congenitally unable to pull his punches, and again and again he'd knock Newman out, proving once and for all that art imitates life.

# 47. Carl Lewis lifts off at the Millrose Games, January 27, 1984, Madison Square Garden

For one blissful moment, nothing mattered, neither the too-short runway behind him nor the too-hard landing pit awaiting him—Carl Lewis was flying. He soared through the air at Madison Square Garden like no one had ever done before, like no one may ever do again. He was a bird, a plane, Superman, no, he was King Carl, the most dominant performer the track world has ever known, in his greatest moment yet.

At 22, Lewis was already track's biggest star, annually the top-ranked track athlete, winner the previous year of three gold medals in the world championships and the Sullivan Trophy as America's outstanding amateur athlete. Expectations were tremendous, and he liked it that way. Lewis would never be a fan favorite: he was booed for

**Carl Lewis leaps into the record books with a 28′10¼″ jump on his final try at the Millrose Games.**

jumping far enough to win and then, to conserve energy for his races, passing on subsequent attempts; he was also dogged by rumors in the media, often spread by competitors, about his sexuality and about performance-enhancing drugs. But Lewis blocked everything out and usually met those expectations. On January 27, 1984, at the Millrose Games, the prestigious indoor track meet, he'd exceed them.

It didn't come easily. The short Garden runway was problematic for Lewis, who utilized a longer-than-usual approach, and on his first try a loose board further threw off his rhythm. The 6'2", 175-pound New Jersey native, who had also been battling a bad cold, leaped nearly two feet too soon, jumping a startlingly low 22'2½". In the second round, he mustered a 26'11¼"—below his usual standards but good enough for first place. After failing to improve in the third round, he passed on the fourth, thinking he'd end with an unsatisfying feeling but a victory nonetheless that would sustain his 33-match winning streak.

But as Lewis put on his sweats, Larry Myricks—the last person to beat him, way back in 1981—jumped 27'3¼", forcing Lewis back into action. Lewis's 27'2¾" fell short, and then Myricks upped the ante, matching his best-ever indoor jump at 27'6".

Lewis's streak rode on his last leap. Losing to Myricks, an archrival who often badmouthed him (and whom Lewis later dismissed as a choke artist in his autobiography), would be extra painful. Lewis's coach Tom Tellez weighed in with a tip: start running a foot farther back. Lewis's sister Carol, the women's long jump record-holder, sat trackside steadying that annoying loose board.

Lewis did much more than pass Myricks. Rising to the occasion, he ran hard and came as close to the line as possible without fouling. Then he was up, up, and away.

Once airborne, Lewis knew he had nailed it, beating Myricks and even setting a new world indoor mark. But he didn't realize how far he'd taken that magic carpet ride. He landed and wheeled in triumph, thrusting both arms in the air. He waved to the gasping crowd. Lewis had done more than break a record: his feat boggled the mind of track experts everywhere. The final number was awe-inspiring—in another sport it would be called Ruthian. Lewis had jumped 28'10¼", shattering the previous indoor mark (which he held) by more than nine inches.

Put the book down for a minute and measure 28'10¼". It is hard for the normal person to fathom jumping anywhere close to that far, but given the circumstances, it was hard even for track stars to imagine such an achievement, especially in those circumstances.

Lewis had jumped that far the previous June... outside with an ideal track and a slight aiding wind. The only person who had ever jumped farther anywhere was Bob Beamon in the 1968 Olympics. Not to diminish Beamon's 29'2½" leap, but it was in Mexico City's high altitude, with an aiding wind of two meters per second. *Track & Field News* calculates that conditions boosted Beamon's jump by 6 to 12 inches, whereas Lewis was hindered by his surroundings. It's likely his jump would have traveled from 29'6" to 30' outdoors in Mexico City.

When the result was announced, Lewis took a celebratory victory lap around the inside part of the track during the 800-meter race. That race was part of a memorable night—it ended in a photo finish, and meet records were set or tied in the pole vault, the 600-yard race, and the men's and women's relays. But just like Michael Jordan during his prime, Lewis overshadowed everyone else.

Lewis, of course, was just getting started. He'd win four Olympic gold medals that summer and nine all told; he'd win 65 straight long jump competitions and break the 29' mark outdoors; he'd briefly hold the 100-meter dash record as well. But impressive as all those accomplishments were, his majestic flight in 1984 stands apart. Mike Powell broke Beamon's outdoor record in 1991, but Lewis's indoor record survives unchallenged more than two decades later. Veteran track and field writer Peter Gambaccini calls it "maybe the most amazing thing he ever did."

# Honorable Mention: Jumping Jewels

**1. Franklin Jacobs makes an outsized jump, January 27, 1978, Madison Square Garden**

For a world-class high-jumper, Franklin Jacobs stood small at 5'8". But at the 1978 Millrose Games, the 20-year-old Farleigh Dickinson University student certainly jumped tall, outleaping three Olympic medalists and setting a world record at 7'7¼".

Jacobs began high-jumping in high school when his basketball coach noted his dunking ability. As a relative latecomer, he lacked polish — coaches and competitors sneered at his inelegant sloping flop — but he produced results. Still, the Millrose favorites were 1976 gold medalist Jacek Wszola, silver medalist Greg Joy, and bronze medalist Dwight Stone, king of the American high jump.

It was Stone who suggested raising the bar to world-record height. The star could not attain his dream, but the little guy did. When Jacobs cleared the bar, the crowd gasped.

Although the 7'7¼" mark has been broken numerous times since that day, no other jumper has truly equaled Jacobs's feat — he remains the only person ever to jump 23¼ inches above his own height.

**2. John Thomas soars into the record books . . . again, January 31, 1959, Madison Square Garden**

John Thomas became a record-setting machine in January 1959. The 6'5" Boston University freshman became the first high-jumper to clear 6'11" indoors, then the first to clear 6'11¾". At the Millrose Games, he outdid himself one more time.

First, Thomas and USC's Charley Dumas — the first to break seven feet outside — set a Millrose record, 6'9". Then they both set a Madison Square Garden record, clearing 6'10".

The bar moved to seven feet.

Thomas missed once.

Dumas missed too.

Thomas stood, head bowed, focusing, for a full minute. The crowd watched silently.

He ran his seven steps, planted his left foot. . . .

Then he was up, straddle style, right leg over the bar, then left. . . .

And over.

Thomas was flat on his back in the pit, but the crowd was up, thundering for 10 seconds. Thomas had left Dumas behind, skying to his own spot in the record book.

By the time he retired, Thomas had won the Millrose high jump six times — so often they named the event after him.

**3. Carl Lewis leaps past Mike Powell, June 15, 1991, Downing Stadium**

Carl Lewis's 10-year-long jump win streak belongs alongside Joe DiMaggio's hitting streak and Cal Ripken's games-played streak. Among Lewis's most memorable wins was the last one, at the 1991 national championships on Randall's Island.

The event was poorly attended and terribly run, but saved by memorable performances — Dan O'Brien nearly set a decathlon world record, and Leroy Burrell edged Lewis in setting a 100-meter sprint world record. But nothing matched the long-jump drama. Lewis, track's biggest superstar, had 64 straight long-jump wins, including 14 over rival Mike Powell, and knew he was the favorite.

He confidently nailed 27'2½".

Unintimidated, Powell responded with a dazzling 28'1¾".

Lewis fired back with 28'2¼".

Powell was ready for "can you top this," blasting off to 28'3¾".

That mark stood for three rounds as the 91-degree heat seemed to take its toll on Lewis, possibly ending the fabled streak. But in the sixth and final round, Lewis dipped into his near-superhuman reserves and let loose a titanic effort — 28'4¼", a half-inch farther than Powell. It was Lewis's closest margin of victory since 1981.

The streak ended the next time out, at the Tokyo World Championships, despite Lewis's best day ever. He finally shattered the 29-foot mark not once but three times, but Powell went one better, setting a new record at 29'4½". (Lewis did beat Burrell with a new record in the 100-meter.) The defeat, however, made this final triumph seem sweeter and loom larger, the final win in a streak that may never be topped.

# 48. Bill Tilden becomes the first tennis superstar with his revenge win over Bill Johnston, September 6, 1920, West Side Tennis Club

You know it when you see it, and you can't help but get excited—your opponent is taller than you and stronger too, he has a booming serve and a big forehand, but . . . there it is, plain as day as you warm up . . . he has no backhand. This guy's a chump. He can't beat you.

In 1919 Bill Tilden was that chump.

Soon to be hailed as the world's greatest player, Tilden had been knocked out of the U.S. National Championship (forerunner to the U.S. Open) in the first round in 1916. Two years later he reached the finals, but R. Lindley Murray bounced him in straight sets. In the 1919 finals at Forest Hills, Bill Johnston endlessly exploited Tilden's lackluster slice backhand, aggressively attacking it and coming to the net. He too ran Tilden off in straight sets.

Tilden, 26, realized his shot at greatness was slipping away, and he could no longer afford his 97-pound weakling of a backhand. He wintered in Providence, Rhode Island, where a wealthy patron gave him access to one of the Northeast's few indoor courts. Day after day he retrained himself, shaking free of his slice, forcing himself to learn a new grip and fire flat backhands back across the net. In 1920 he was ready to conquer.

His timing was perfect. Although the sport was still the domain of elitist private clubs, the national tennis championship had recently moved from tony Newport to Forest Hills in Queens, helping get the attention of both press and public. And as the Roaring Twenties dawned and prosperous America was going mad for sports, sportswriters gushed and fawned over new gods for a new era. New York was the center of it all. In April 1920, Babe Ruth began hitting home runs for the New York Yankees. In July, Man o' War turned back John P. Grier in the home stretch at Aqueduct.

That summer Tilden unleashed his hard-earned creation and became the first American to win at Wimbledon—Johnston had been favored but was upset early. At Forest Hills on September 6, Tilden avenged himself against his old rival, capturing the U.S. championship and becoming the first tennis superstar.

Most of the 10,000 crammed into the undersized grandstand for the finals that cloudy Monday believed that Tilden's England win was a fluke and were confident Johnston would retain his U.S. crown.

Johnston, who was under 5'8" and would ultimately become "Little Bill" to the 6'1½" "Big Bill" Tilden, had a big forehand and attacked the net three times as often as Tilden. But this time Tilden had the strokes from both sides at the baseline . . . in addition to an unstoppable serve that yielded a service winner on the match's first point plus 20 aces. (Johnston had none.) Aided by what the *New York Times* called his "marvel of a backhand drive," Tilden overpowered Johnston 6–1 in the first set, reaching, the *Times* wrote, "a pinnacle of supremacy, overwhelming in its magnificence . . . that permitted no resistance and thought of nothing but its own perfection."

But after a letdown in the second, when Johnston broke him twice, Tilden purposely tanked the rest of the set. Then an unexpected drama interrupted the match at the start of the third set. A Navy airplane carrying a photographer was circling Forest Hills when the engine cut out and the plane plunged to earth, just missing the stands. Tilden felt the ground shake. Much of the crowd rushed off to the tragedy; the umpire, to prevent a stampede, urged the men to play on.

At 3–3 in the third, Tilden kicked off with an ace, but Johnston's crisp volleying produced a crucial break. With Johnston a point from 5–3, Tilden drilled a hard running forehand off the net cord and subsequently broke back. At 5–5, he fired three aces, then broke his rival for the set with a blistering crosscourt passing shot.

Tilden fell behind 3–1 in the fourth, then roared back for a 5–4 lead. He even had match point but netted a volley; Johnston then saved his serve with two passing shots. Rain began coming down in earnest, and just as Tilden served, people began flooding the exits. Tilden saw the umpire raise his hand for time and stopped playing. But the tournament referee overruled the umpire and deemed Johnston's return worthy of a point.

At 30–30, the rain finally forced a halt, and when play resumed, Tilden had lost his rhythm, double-faulting three times. But the men were so evenly matched that the game still required 20 points before Johnston prevailed on a deep forehand Tilden couldn't handle. Johnston held for a 7–5 win, forcing a fifth set.

Johnston was exhausted, so Tilden switched tactics, laying back, forcing Johnston to play the aggressor to shorten the points. While his serve had carried him through four sets, Tilden's crisp passing shots won him the match; down a break, he reeled off four games for a 6–1, 1–6, 7–5, 5–7, 6–3 triumph. The valiant Johnston fought hard till the end—down 5–3, he thrice extended Tilden to deuce before the big man finally ended it with his 20th ace. (When critics carped that he'd won merely because of a bigger serve, he promised to beat Johnston the next year just with ground strokes and did so, winning without an ace.)

No Open final had ever produced such high-caliber and adventurous play or a five-setter that finished with three sets as close as this one. The match was breathlessly pronounced the greatest in the sport's history, and the press gave it prominent play: both the *Herald* and the *Tribune* (which hadn't even put the previous year's Tilden-Johnston match on the front of its sports section) put it on the front page. Tilden was a star, and when he helped America win the Davis Cup—then the most prestigious triumph in tennis—he became a national hero. He would not lose a major tournament match again until 1926, beating Johnston in the finals in Queens five more times. Along the way he created the modern foundation for spins, shot selection, strategy, and court psychology through his on-court performance and his writings.

He was also a consummate showman, believing, "The player owes the gallery as much as an actor owes an audience." He'd seem to tank early in matches to create dramatic finishes, or purposely blow points, games, or even sets to offset a bad call in his favor; when calls went against him, he'd look to the heavens and ask, "Is there no justice?" or bully the offending linesman with an imperious glare. (He was so intimidating, Frank Deford reports in *Big Bill Tilden,* that the U.S. Lawn Tennis Association briefly weighed a "no-glare rule," but he pressured officials into backing down.)

Despite his blue-blood background and patrician air, Tilden's arrogance, showboating, and constant challenging of the established order made him an outsider. He pushed for everything from

**Bill Tilden establishes himself as the first tennis superstar with his big wins at Forest Hills.**

hard courts to open tennis, where pros and amateurs could compete, and he flagrantly broke absurd amateur rules by accepting money for instructional films and writing tennis articles. He was the original Jimmy Connors. And like Connors, his hard-hitting, hard-charging, break-your-opponent style earned jeers but helped tennis take a crucial step toward shedding its sissy image. After his 1920 win, interest surged so high that the West Side club quickly replaced its temporary grandstand with a 14,000-seat stadium (which lasted until Connors's popularity forced the move to still larger quarters).

After winning Forest Hills one final time in 1929 and Wimbledon in 1930 at age 37, Tilden turned pro, creating the Tilden Tennis Tour, which ultimately attracted top amateurs, giving the pro game credibility and laying the groundwork for the Open era.

"It was not just that he could not be beaten, it was nearly as if he had invented the sport he conquered," Frank Deford wrote in *Big Bill Tilden.* "Babe Ruth, Jack Dempsey, Red Grange . . . stood at the head of more popular games, but Tilden simply was tennis in the public mind."

The chump was the ultimate champ.

# 49. Summerall kicks a field goal in the snow, December 14, 1958, Yankee Stadium

Under the best of circumstances, Pat Summerall would probably not make a field goal from near midfield. In the fourth quarter at Yankee Stadium on December 14, 1958, circumstances were definitely not the best: the thermometer read 25 degrees, wet, large snowflakes tumbled from the sky, the wind blew in his face, the field was a mess . . . and the New York Giants' season was on the line.

"I could barely see the goal post," Summerall recalled later.

Puzzled, owner Wellington Mara peered down from the press box, barely able to make out Summerall in the descending gloom. "He can't kick it that far," Mara speculated aloud. "What are we doing?"

Offensive coach Vince Lombardi was furious. Sure, Charlie Conerly had failed to complete a pass on first, second, and third downs, but Lombardi would rather try once more than accept what he thought was the inevitability of a failed kick. Normally, head coach Jim Lee Howell deferred on strategy to both Lombardi and defensive coach Tom Landry. Not this time.

The Giants were not actually losing—the score against Cleveland was 10–10—but the Browns were one game ahead in the standings on the season's final day, so a tie would give Cleveland the Eastern Division title, sending them to the NFL Championship and leaving New York out in the cold.

Paul Brown's Cleveland squads were accustomed to winning big games. The Browns won all four titles in the upstart All-American Football Conference, and when the league folded into the NFL, they were undeterred by the stronger competition: in 1950 the Browns edged the Giants in a tiebreaking playoff game to go to the championship, then topped the Giants and the rest of the East to return to the championship game in six of the next seven years. The only year the Browns stumbled was 1956, when the Giants won it all, but Brown drafted running back Jim Brown and in 1957 topped New York once more. The Browns' margin was their two triumphs over the Giants.

The 1958 season seemed like more of the same—as the Giants struggled to a 2–2 start the Browns began undefeated. But Big Blue reeled off three straight, including a win in Cleveland and six of seven. The Giants entered this final game 8–3, the Browns at 9–2.

At first it hardly seemed like a game that would come down to the final moments. On the Browns' first play from scrimmage, quarterback Milt Plum faked a pitchout, then handed off to Jim Brown, who'd set a new NFL record that year with 1,527 rushing yards. Brown burst through the middle and raced 65 yards virtually untouched for a touchdown.

In the swirling snow, Cleveland's Lou "The Toe" Groza missed two field goals from under 40 yards while Summerall missed a 45-yarder, but both men made one, giving the Browns a 10–3 halftime lead. In the third quarter, Cleveland marched to the Giants' 12, but the drive stalled, and Paul

**On a day far snowier than the one pictured here, Pat Summerall used his foot in that shoe to kick that ball through the uprights and send the Giants on to a special divisional tie-breaker against Cleveland.**

Brown opted for trickery, faking the field goal and having Bobby Freeman try to run it in. He failed, and the Giants remained within a touchdown. Many Browns were furious at their coach's folly and had trouble recovering their focus.

After being shoved around, the Giants finally came alive in the fourth, mounting two solid drives. On the first, Bob Schnelker's seven-yard touchdown catch tied the game. Then, with just under five minutes left, they reached the 33-yard line and sent Summerall in to kick a field goal that would give the Giants the lead.

The Giants had traded for Summerall that season despite his 45 percent average with Chicago; after all, he could also play tight end and defense and even return kicks. He was awful early in 1958, missing seven of his first ten attempts along with two extra points. He'd settled down, hitting seven of his next eleven field goal attempts, but the previous week he'd injured his leg and had been unable to practice all week, nearly missing this game. He told Landry he could not kick off but maybe could hit extra points or a short field goal. But 33 yards proved too long, and Summerall missed.

With the score tied, the Giants were really still losing. They stopped Cleveland and had time for one last drive. On second down near midfield, Conerly fired a short pass to Frank Gifford, who appeared to catch it and take a few steps before being hit by a Cleveland linebacker, causing him to drop the ball. Cleveland's Walt Michaels scooped it up, racing the length of the field toward a game-clinching touchdown . . . or not. Head linesman Charley Berry ruled the pass incomplete. Paul Brown argued vociferously, but there was no such thing as instant replay then and no way to change Berry's mind. (Michaels later said that Brown used his clout to make sure Berry never officiated another Browns game.)

The Giants' situation remained bleak, but they still had the ball and, with just over two minutes left, one final chance. But that third-down play fizzled when Alex Webster, free down near the goal line, lost the pass coming out of the snow and dropped it. Over the vehement argument of Lombardi, Howell turned once more to Summerall.

When Summerall was born, his right foot faced completely backwards; when he was six months old, the doctor broke the bones and turned the foot around. He'll walk, the doctor told his mother, but don't expect him to run or play on it. The doctor was wrong.

In 1956, when Summerall was with Chicago, he kicked three field goals to beat Cleveland 9–7. Afterwards, Paul Brown sneered in his direction, "Enjoy it. It'll never happen again." Here was a chance to prove Brown wrong too.

With snow covering the field, no one knows exactly how long the kick really was — the record books marked it at 49 yards, but estimates by players and reporters ranged from 45 to 55. No matter what, it was a daunting prospect. When Summerall arrived in the huddle, Conerly was shocked, barking, "What the fuck are you doing here?" So much for a vote of confidence.

As Summerall got set Browns defensive back Kenny Konz screamed and shouted to distract him. The snap was perfect, and Summerall let fly. He knew instinctively he had the distance, but as the ball weaved toward the side he wasn't sure it would remain on line. The ball disappeared into the snowy night, and when Summerall heard the cheering and the celebrating, he knew he'd made it. The Giants led 13–10.

An ecstatic Summerall floated back to the sideline, where Lombardi greeted him, not in joy, but in disbelief that he had been wrong too, saying, "You know, you son of a bitch, you can't kick it that far."

But he could, and he did.

The kick's impact lasted long after the ball cleared the goal post. It gave Summerall a celebrity's shine, which earned him his first radio job after the season. And it discouraged the Browns, who lacked their usual fire in a tiebreaking game the next week. The Giants' defense shut Cleveland down, 10–0, sending New York into the championship game against Johnny Unitas and Baltimore. There the Giants would lose one of the closest and most important championship games ever, but they'd be elevated to immortals in the process.

## 50. Chris Chambliss homers the Yankees back into the World Series, October 14 1976, Yankee Stadium

Chris Chambliss was not alone. The bases were full as he made his triumphant circuit — not with fellow Yankees, since Chambliss had led off the bottom of the ninth inning, but with Yankee fans.

This was no metaphorical "with him in spirit" kind of thing. This crowd was too spirited for that . . . if you take "crowd" to mean mob and "spirited" to mean exuberantly rambunctious in a frightening, 1970s, city-on-the-brink-of-chaos way. For the first generation of Yankee fans in over half a century who grew up with a second-rate club, this moment was too stimulating to be witnessed passively from their seats. The fans wanted in on this celebration. So they joined Chambliss on the base paths. Well, "joined" is perhaps an understatement. They stampeded him and his teammates, making his journey as memorable as the game-winning, playoff-clinching home run itself.

It made sense that the highlight of '76 would be a home run and that it would be tumultuous. The homer was fitting, since the Yankees had returned that year to a renovated House That Ruth Built after a dismal two-year exile to Shea Stadium. And since 1976 marked Billy Martin's first full season as manager and George Steinbrenner's return after a suspension caused by felonious contributions to Richard Nixon's 1972 presidential campaign, turmoil, be it feuds with the players' union and commissioner over player transactions or on-field brawls, was a Bronx staple. This stormy team was a perfect fit for a city barely holding it together amid financial ruin, demographic shifts, and societal upheaval; attendance climbed by 57 percent (nearly 750,000) as the 97-win Yankees captured their division by 10½ games.

For Martin and Steinbrenner, reaching the playoffs was exciting but not satisfying. When the Yankees had last finished on top, in 1964, first place meant an American League pennant and a trip back to the World Series. But after 12 dismal years in the wilderness—including un-Yankee-like years in sixth, tenth, and ninth place—a mere divisional title would not suffice. They wanted the Series.

In the best-of-five ALCS against Kansas City, the Yankees split the first four games, aided by Chambliss's two-run homer in Game 3's comeback win. The stakes were high enough for Game 5 on October 14 at Yankee Stadium that Baltimore Oriole–turned–free agent Reggie Jackson, moonlighting as a television color commentator, declared, "Everything is magnified tonight. You hit a home run, it'll be, for sure, heard 'round the country."

The first home run was a two-run shot in the opening inning by John Mayberry off Ed Figueroa. But the Yankees struck back immediately, tying the score on hits by Mickey Rivers, Roy White, and Thurman Munson (which knocked out Dennis Leonard) and a sacrifice fly by Chambliss.

Those top four hitters would finish with all 11 of the team's hits, plus two walks and two steals. The Royals snuck ahead 3–2 in the second, but in the fourth the fab four produced another two-run rally for a 4–3 lead as Chambliss added his second RBI on a groundout.

In the sixth, the fearsome foursome sacked the Royals staff again. Rivers bunted for a hit, advanced on White's sacrifice, and scored on Munson's single. Munson was thrown out trying to stretch his hit, but Chambliss singled and—despite having just one steal all year—swiped second, allowing him to score on an error.

Up 6–3 in the eighth, Figueroa needed just six more outs. He didn't get any. When Al Cowens singled, Martin went to the bullpen but bypassed closer (and AL save leader) Sparky Lyle for veteran lefty Grant Jackson, who had allowed an eighth-inning run the previous day. Jackson was touched for a single by pinch hitter Jim Wohlford.

That brought up George Brett, whose .333 average had led the AL. Jackson had allowed just one homer in $58^2/_3$ innings since the Yankees acquired him over the summer, while Brett had hit just seven homers in over 600 at-bats.

Boom. Brett launched an 0–1 pitch just fair into the short porch in right.

Whoosh. All at once the air was sucked out of Yankee Stadium. It was 6–6.

With two outs in the ninth, the Royals threatened again when Buck Martinez singled and Cowens walked, bringing up Wohlford, with Brett and his eight ALCS hits on deck. With the runners in motion, Tidrow induced a chopper to Graig Nettles, who barely nipped Cowens at second base.

Heading into the bottom of the ninth, the Yankees were excited and jittery, but the fans were rabid. Bottles and beer cans, toilet paper and firecrackers, appeared out of the night, littering the field and disrupting play before Chambliss could step in.

**Chris Chambliss makes a mad dash around the bases as Yankee fans overrun the field in the aftermath of his ALCS-clinching ninth-inning homer.**

Did it disrupt Mark Littell, the Royal closer who had retired five in a row? Perhaps. But Chambliss was the perfect man for this moment. He had smashed 17 homers in 1976 (more than in the previous two years combined) and driven in 96 runs (up from 72 in 1975). In the ALCS, he had been the Man, already setting a new record with 10 hits (in 20 at-bats) while tying Hank Aaron's 1969 mark of seven RBIs.

Littell knew that if he could get past Chambliss, the bottom of the Yankee lineup had been hitless that night. And the Royals had Brett and Mayberry due up in the 10th. But Littell couldn't even get one pitch past the Yankee first baseman. Chambliss ripped the reliever's fastball toward right-center. He stood and watched, not quite believing what he had done. But when right fielder Hal McRae went up wishing and came down despairing, Chambliss leaped into the air, delighted, exultant. The Yankees were back. They had made it to the World Series . . . if, that is, they could get out alive.

Before Chambliss was even halfway around the bases, the fans had breached the playing field and were rampaging toward their new hero. Between second and third, Chambliss momentarily disappeared, tripped up by one fan as another tried swiping his helmet. His unruly entourage expanding exponentially, Chambliss tucked his headgear under his arm and headed toward third. Well, not to third exactly, since someone had made off with the base. Chambliss went wide around the thickening crowd and skated the edge till he got near the Yankee dugout, where he lowered his shoulder and knocked another maniac aside, escaping into the safety of the dugout and the clubhouse.

Amid the celebration, Nettles asked Chambliss if he'd touched home to make the run official. There had been no way to get there and no plate left if he had, but Nettles sent him back out . . . where umpire Art Frantz was waiting. Wearing a jacket to disguise his superhero identity, Chambliss was escorted by two cops and picked his way through the remaining crowd to touch the area where home plate should have been.

That sufficed. Not that the Yankees would have brooked any dispute. With the humor and menace that symbolized those 1970s Bronx Bombers, Thurman Munson declared afterwards that no official could have deemed Chambliss a modern Fred Merkle. "I saw about 50,000 people touch home plate—he could have been one of them," Munson said. "I want to see them take it back."

# 51. The Rangers beat the Islanders to reach the Stanley Cup finals, May 8, 1979, Madison Square Garden

Finally, a moment of absolute glory.

The New York Rangers' 2–1 triumph over the New York Islanders on May 8, 1979, did not win a Stanley Cup, but it gave the long-suffering club an upset of epic proportions against the one team the Rangers most wanted to beat.

To truly appreciate the triumph, steep yourself in the sorrows of Rangerdom, decade after disastrous decade of losing dumped on the team's loyal Garden rooters.

The 1940s: after winning their third Stanley Cup in just 14 years in 1939–40, the club did not win another playoff series for the rest of the decade and failed to make the postseason at all for five straight years.

The 1950s: the briefest hint of happiness in 1950 when a sub-.500 club snuck into the playoffs, beat the Montreal Canadiens, and then extended Detroit to seven games in the finals. Then came five more seasons without playoffs. It wasn't until 1955–56 that they even topped .500 for the first time in 14 seasons. That year they won just one game in their playoff loss to Montreal.

The 1960s: with a streak begun in 1958–59, the Rangers put together eight straight sub-.500 years, making the playoffs just once. In the decade's second half, their regular-season record improved dramatically—beginning an impressive run of nine straight playoff appearances—but they lost 16 of 20 playoff games through the 1969–70 season.

The 1970s: this was to be the turnaround decade. In 1971 the team won a playoff series and took the Chicago Blackhawks to seven games with a huge triple-overtime win in Game 6 of the second round; in 1972 the Rangers won 48 games and reached the Stanley Cup finals for the first time in 22 years. Although they lost to the Boston Bruins, life was sweet and the future seemed bright.

Then the unimaginable happened. It wasn't just that the Rangers began backsliding. It was that they did it while an expansion team—a suburban club that encroached on their fan base amid the "white flight" of the 1970s—passed them with surprising ease on its way up. In 1972–73 the Rangers had won 47 and beat Boston in the playoffs while the fledgling New York Islanders managed just 12 victories. The next year the Rangers won seven fewer while their weak cousin added seven wins. In 1974–75 disaster arrived. The Rangers edged their new rival 37–33 in regular-season wins but lost to the upstarts in a stunning three-game playoff series. In the next three seasons, while the Islanders challenged the Philadelphia Flyers and eventually gained supremacy atop the division, the Rangers languished in the cellar, missing two playoffs and winning just one postseason game in 1978.

The Rangers of 1978–79 were no match for the 51–15–14 Islanders, but their 40–29–11 marked an 18-point improvement over the previous year and landed them in third place. At age 37, Phil Esposito scored 42 goals and gave the club some glamour and leadership, newcomers Anders Hedberg and Ulf Nilsson added speed and skills, while John Davidson was the team's rock in goal.

The Rangers rolled through Los Angeles and Philadelphia in the playoffs' first two rounds and were one step away from the Stanley Cup finals for just the third time since 1940. Standing in their way were the big, bad Islanders, a team expected to win its first Cup.

Hockey rarely captured the headlines in New York, in part because of the Rangers' perennial struggles and in part because hockey simply couldn't compete with baseball, football, and bas-

## Honorable Mention: Nice on Ice

**1. The Americans beat the Rangers, March 27, 1938, Madison Square Garden**

It's an age-old story: the native Americans' good life is ruined when newcomers take their land and eventually wipe them out. It happened in hockey too.

The New York Americans were the first local NHL franchise, joining the young league in 1925 and renting ice time in the newly built, second Madison Square Garden. But Garden boss Tex Rickard decided he'd make more money owning a team of his own, which the press soon dubbed "Tex's Rangers."

The Americans-Rangers rivalry fueled the Garden's success, but the Americans quickly became second-class tenants, bumped to the Canadian Division and always struggling to compete because they lacked the financial resources of their affluent brethren.

Then, in 1937–38, the Americans finished second to reach the playoffs, where they exacted revenge on their archrivals, who had finished second in their division.

All Rangers-Americans matchups were events, "like a civil war," Ranger Muzz Patrick once said. "The landlords against the tenants. The aristocrats against the people's choice." The Americans won the opener 2–1 in double-overtime, but the Rangers won Game 2, 4–3. For the deciding Game 3, people lined up at dawn for tickets.

The Rangers grabbed a 2–0 lead, but the Americans struck back in the third to tie it. The game was tense, tight, and scoreless . . . through the end of regulation . . . through one overtime . . . through two overtimes . . . through three. The longest game on Garden ice had stretched well past midnight. At 1:30 A.M., 40 seconds into the fourth overtime, Lorne Carr came through with his second goal of the night, and the Americans had vanquished the bullies of Broadway.

The game made the *New York Times* front page, a hockey first. But the Americans' joy was short-lived. They failed to win the Stanley Cup, and four years later they folded.

**2. Wayne Gretzky pulls out one last hat trick, April 23, 1997, Madison Square Garden**

"The Great One" at his greatest—was it so much to ask for? On April 23, 1997, New York Ranger fans got just that.

Wayne Gretzky came to the Rangers at age 36, joining former Edmonton teammate Mark Messier and fueling fantasies of one last Stanley Cup. But despite Gretzky's 97-point season, the aging team mustered only a 38–34–10 record. After dropping the first playoff game to the defending conference champion Florida Panthers, the

ketball. But in May 1979, the Rangers-Islanders series was *the* story in town. Scalpers reaped $250 for $22 tickets, and with the games televised only for the small number of cable subscribers back then, thousands of fans paid to watch on closed circuit at the Felt Forum and at Roosevelt Raceway.

The team's personas fit their geography—many Rangers were single and enjoyed the Manhattan nightlife, while more Islanders were married and settled down. The rivalry had become venomous near season's end when a rough—Ranger fans think dirty—check by Islander Dennis Potvin broke center Ulf Nilsson's ankle. The play would echo through the years with thousands of "Potvin sucks" cheers.

In this series, the Rangers seeking a tactical edge more than revenge hounded Potvin, an all-star defenseman, with hard forechecking to cramp his style. The surprisingly tough Rangers also got in the faces of the immensely talented front line of Brian Trottier, Mike Bossy, and Clark Gillies. Throughout the series, the Rangers' execution was disciplined, but with nothing to lose, their mood was loose and light; the Islanders seemed tight, fretting about falling to an inferior team, while the media's constant pronouncements on the subject only exacerbated the difference in moods. Islander goalie Chico Resch called this "Newton's Law of Tightivity."

The teams split the first four games, but both

## Nice on Ice (CONTINUED)

Rangers were written off, with Gretzky and Messier receiving the brunt of the blame.

Gretzky scored the winning goal in Game 2, but skeptics doubted he'd hold up, especially when a scheduling conflict put Games 3 and 4 on back-to-back nights at the Garden against their younger foes. Messier and Gretzky came through with assists on the last-minute goal that forced overtime in New York's Game 3 win, but Game 4 was even more remarkable.

The Rangers trailed 1–0 in the second when Gretzky—legs as fresh as ever—took over as only he could, completing his first New York hat trick (and his first in four years) in just 6:23. He scored from near the crease on a power play to tie it; finished a give-and-go with Luc Robitalle to give New York a lead less than four minutes later; and took a pass, faked Ed Jovanovski out of his skates, then circled back and found the perfect angle to slap home his last goal, which provided the margin of victory in the 3–2 win. Unable to contain his glee, the reserved Gretzky even did a small celebration dance.

Inspired, Messier scored two goals in Game 5 in Miami to finish the Panthers, and the Rangers streaked to the conference finals. Messier's messy departure from New York that summer started the club's descent into years of disaster, so Gretzky's glorious trick remains the last high point of a golden era.

### 3. The Smurfs stomp the bullies, April 9, 1983, Madison Square Garden

The Philadelphia Flyers were big shots until coach Bob McCammon opened his big mouth about how small the New York Rangers were. After dismissing their diminutive front line as "Smurfs," McCammon was forced to backtrack until he was blue in the face when the Rangers swept their 1983 playoff series.

The Smurfs—Rob McClanahan, Mark Pavelich, and Anders Hedberg, who averaged just 5'9½" and 175 pounds—got the ultimate revenge in Game 3.

The Flyers, who had bullied a superior Ranger team into submission back in 1974, resorted to rough stuff again—Darryl Sittler slammed Pavelich face-first onto the ice at the opening face-off, then provoked a brawl less than a minute later. But the Rangers mostly ducked their heads and zoomed past their bigger, slower foes.

McClanahan scored New York's first goal. Ron Greschner made it 2–0 after another Flyer penalty. The slaughter had begun. Barry Beck added a goal, McClanahan came up with his second, and Hedberg his first. When the Flyers cut New York's lead to 5–3 in the third, the Rangers poured in three goals in just 4:11, humiliating Flyer goalie Pelle Lindbergh. The rout finished 9–3, and the Smurf line had four of those scores. Up in the blue seats, the most rabid of Ranger fans waved a huge, inflated Smurf, turning the Flyers' taunt into a salute to the Rangers' grit and determination.

**Reaching the Stanley Cup finals is thrilling enough, but beating the Islanders to get there is really a cause for celebration.**

Islander wins were narrow escapes in overtime. When Hedberg scored the winning goal in a well-played Game 5, the Rangers had two shots at the Finals. But the Rangers didn't want to relinquish their edge, and they also wanted to win at Madison Square Garden instead of playing a perilous Game 7 in enemy territory on Long Island.

In Game 6, the Islanders snatched an early lead on a power play at 8:56 when the righty Bossy, switching on the go, shot lefty and flipped in a rebound off a Trottier shot. It was the team's first power play goal in 21 tries, and the first score from the Islanders' famed triumvirate since the first goal of Game 1. Was this a signal that the dike was about to burst? The Islanders played their best hockey of the series in the opening period, but they could not score again as Walt Tkaczuk and company again throttled the Trio Grande.

At 5:03 of the second, Ranger Mario Marois bounced a shot off Resch's pads and into Don Murdoch's skates, nearly tripping him. Murdoch recovered, spun, and wristed the puck into the net. The Rangers were back on an even rink. Less than four minutes later, the Rangers converted on a power play of their own — Esposito blocked Resch's view while Don Maloney fed Ron Greschner near the blue line, and he banged home a slap shot for the go-ahead goal. (The goal was originally credited to Esposito because the ref thought he tipped it in, but Espo insisted to the official scorers that Greschner get the score.)

The momentum had turned, and the Rangers never let the Islanders recover, swarming the puck at every opportunity — they allowed only three shots in the final 20 minutes, and Davidson, who had been stellar throughout, turned away each. The clock wound down, and the raucous fans screamed and cheered, counted down and threw confetti, and celebrated like there was no tomorrow.

There was a tomorrow, of course, and it wasn't

nearly as wonderful: as John Davidson struggled with an injured knee, and after coach Fred Shero failed to rein in his bachelors partying in Montreal, the Rangers lost to the Canadiens in the Stanley Cup finals. In subsequent seasons, the Rangers mounted their longest sustained run of quality hockey—reaching at least .500 in four of five seasons while winning five playoff series—but the Islanders handily trumped them, winning four straight Stanley Cup trophies and beating the Rangers in the playoffs four straight years.

But on May 8, 1979, all that was in the future. The Rangers finally had a win no one could ever take away.

# 52. Sugar Ray Robinson melts against Joey Maxim, June 25, 1952, Yankee Stadium

The bell rang for the 14th round. The favorite of the press and public, the man clearly leading on points, sat on his stool, unmoving. He may have been the greatest fighter ever, he may have been a better boxer than his opponent, but Sugar Ray Robinson had finally confronted a force even more unstoppable than himself: Mother Nature.

A third weight-class title—the light-heavyweight championship—had seemed so tantalizingly close all night. But Robinson could not grasp it, not now, not ever as oppressive heat and humidity conspired with the dark side of that informal "pound for pound" title to sap him of his strength and his fierce will.

Born Walker Smith in 1921, Robinson spent his early years in Detroit before moving to Harlem. There the kid with the fancy footwork earned pocket change dancing outside of theaters but found his future boxing in amateur fights. To take part in an American Amateur Union fight for which he was too young, the 15-year-old was snuck the card of another fighter, Ray Robinson. Later a sportswriter wrote that his style was sweet as sugar. Sugar Ray was born.

As a welterweight in the 1940s, Robinson was indestructible, losing only once in over 120 pro fights. In 1951 he moved up and easily captured the middleweight title, butchering rival Jake La-Motta in the process. He was a masterful strategist who possessed an unheard-of combination of skills—he punched with the best but was fast and graceful on defense; he had style and elegance yet could explode in what Jimmy Cannon called "a controlled competitive fury."

The flamboyant and confident Robinson, with his flashy pink Cadillac and stretch of Harlem businesses, was also a symbol of postwar prosperity and opportunity for blacks, someone on whom they could hang their hopes and aspirations. He inspired Muhammad Ali, but his presence was most powerful in New York's black community, which often saw Robinson up close. Robinson had some of his greatest triumphs in Chicago and

**Joey Maxim looks down on an overheated Sugar Ray Robinson, who has floored himself with a wild, lunging miss in Round 13.**

some of his most brutal defeats in New York, but this was home turf, and his fights here, for better or worse, had an extra glow.

And it was in New York, at Yankee Stadium on June 25, 1952, that Robinson faced Joey Maxim for the light-heavyweight crown. It may not have been Robinson's most exciting New York fight—his bashfest with Carmen Basilio five years later would earn that accolade—but his struggle to become only the second three-division champion in the 20th century after Henry Armstrong was the most memorable as circumstances conspired to lift it into fight lore.

The fight had been postponed from Monday, June 23, because of rain, a change that undermined Robinson when Wednesday proved a scorcher. When the fight started at 10:00 P.M., it was still 90 degrees, and the stadium lights and densely packed crowd made it 104 degrees inside the ring.

Robinson was a better fighter than Maxim, no one doubted that. But his reach advantage as a welterweight and middleweight evaporated against this bigger man, and he also faced a weight disadvantage at 157½ to Maxim's 173. Blows that would damage a lighter man inflicted far less damage on Maxim, who for years fought above his class against heavyweights and who could take a punch even if he wasn't the most electrifying hitter. Maxim, whom the *New York Herald-Tribune* called "the plodding, dull defender," fought a stolid, cautious fight, staying in the center of the ring, conserving energy and forcing Robinson to come after him.

The crowd was disappointed, with people

clapping and stamping their feet to urge more action. Maxim's muddling seemed a recipe for defeat but on this night ultimately proved shrewd as Robinson spent 13 rounds stalking his own self-destruction.

In the first seven rounds, Robinson was "the master of versatility, the virtuoso," Jesse Abramson wrote in the *Herald-Tribune*. "He played on Maxim as though he were a violin. He played up and down his body with left leads, he stormed into volleys and barrages and fusillades."

Robinson was ahead on points, but Maxim absorbed everything he threw — jabs, body blows in the clinch, even a crunching shot to the jaw in the seventh.

Imagine the tortoise and the hare of fable fame in a ring instead of a race. In this epic war of attrition, the hare should slow down and pace himself. *New York Times* columnist Arthur Daley noted that Robinson performed with an artistry that was "positively breathtaking" but perhaps "became too enamored by his own magnificence."

By the ninth, Robinson felt groggy. Maxim hit him clean on the jaw, and Robinson would have no memory of anything that came after. But the first participant to melt away was the third man in the ring, referee Ruby Goldstein, who was so exhausted after the 10th round that he had to step down, the first ref ever to leave a championship bout. Replacement Ray Miller was handed a scorecard with notations blurred with sweat. Coming in fresh, Miller pushed the pace, breaking up the increasingly frequent clinches with more alacrity, which harmed the tiring challenger. (Robinson complained later that his handlers should have protested when Goldstein left, ending the fight then.)

In the 11th, two vivid danger signs emerged for Robinson when he mustered all he could into a looping right that landed squarely on Maxim's jaw — it was the shot that had floored middleweight Randy Turpin nine months earlier — but the heavier Maxim staggered without going down. Meanwhile, Robinson, the man famed for his savage ability to finish off foes, was meandering around the ring, unable to summon the energy to capitalize on the opening. Shuffling to his corner at the bell, Robinson looked far weaker than Maxim.

Winning individual rounds was irrelevant now — if Robinson remained on his feet, he'd win the fight. But in the 12th, Maxim snapped the smaller man's head back twice with lefts, and Robinson needed smelling salts to return for Round 13. He was virtually out on his feet, walking "as if he had the gout in both feet and dreaded putting them down," wrote A. J. Liebling in *The New Yorker*. His infrequent punches were "as late, and as wild, as an amateur," and his arms hung limp by his sides in between each draining effort.

Maxim, by contrast, seemed relatively fresh, throwing crisp punches. Even his glancing blows wobbled Robinson, and a combination sent the weakened man reeling. Desperate, Robinson countered with a huge right, which became the lowest moment in his glorious career. His flailing blow missed Maxim completely; Robinson lost his balance, falling hard on his face. Sugar Ray Robinson had knocked himself down.

The trip to the canvas was humiliating — Maxim stepped casually over him and walked away — but also excruciatingly painful. Somehow Robinson pulled himself up, but he offered little resistance as Maxim battered him along the ropes. When the bell saved him, he was unable to make it back to his corner, staggering senseless and bent over before his handlers rushed out to fetch him. They went at Robinson with ice packs and smelling salts. Doctor Alexander Schiff entered the ring to examine the fighter, but when the bell rang to commence Round 14, Robinson, leading handily on all three cards, was unable to rise and could barely shake his head to indicate he was through. *No mas.*

Back in his dressing room, Robinson, who had melted off 16 pounds in the previous hour, was delirious. His wife Edna Mae and the doctor decided that the vain Robinson would be happier at home than in a hospital. His blood was so hot that his body was covered with fever blisters. He couldn't keep food or liquid down for two days and remained irrational most of that time, although he came to his senses long enough to ask pridefully, "He didn't knock me out, did he?"

For a long time it seemed the Maxim bout might be Robinson's last. He did not recover fully for six months. Having conquered the welterweight and middleweight worlds, and with a bitter taste of the light-heavyweight world, he announced his retirement. Over the next two years Robinson made his living as a cabaret performer, tap dancing without worrying about getting hit. But his appeal diminished, and when bad news from his Harlem businesses and the IRS slugged him, he was forced to return to the ring. He reclaimed his middleweight title in 1955 and held it on and off until the age of 39 in 1960. But Robinson, whose genius for strategy and determination enabled him to defeat in a rematch anyone who managed to defeat him — Jake LaMotta, Randy Turpin, Gene Fullmer, Carmen Basilio — never sought to avenge his loss to Maxim, nor did he again venture into the ring as a light-heavyweight. That was a once-in-a-lifetime fight.

# 53. Fred Lebow and Grete Waitz run side by side, November 1, 1992, New York City Marathon

Each Marathon morning, Fred Lebow was awakened by a 2:30 A.M. phone call to the Manhattan hotel where he stayed with his staff and the top runners. From there, he'd start readying everything before leading the race, his baby, in his pace car. But 1992 was different. Lebow was sleeping in Staten Island just yards from the starting line. And he approached the line not as leader of the pack but as a runner himself.

Lebow's run was two years in the making, born from the most trying circumstances. In early 1990 doctors had found a large brain tumor in this energetic marathon man and given him six months to live. Facing his fate, the founder of the New York City Marathon suddenly realized that while he'd run 68 marathons around the world, he had been too busy to run his own race since the first year back in 1970, when the race was confined to circling Central Park. So the Romanian immigrant who had endured World War II work camps and escaped communism decided he would defy expectations and survive . . . not just survive but run, in celebration of hope, through the streets of his adopted city.

"It is the most dramatic way I know to fight my illness," he said later. He did it, making the 1992 New York City Marathon a testimony to determination and resilience, one of the most moving human stories in New York City sports history.

Lebow's training began in hospital hallways where he calculated how many laps equaled a mile. He dragged his body, slowly at first, while encouraging other patients to join him. That fall the doctors declared him in remission, crediting both his remarkable attitude and his physical relentlessness, although he remained woefully frail even after his release. Even in 1992, handling a marathon still seemed a stretch. He ran some mid-length races, but some days he was too weak to run even two miles.

But Lebow persisted, and a plan fell into place. Grete Waitz, who had won New York nine times before retiring, volunteered to run alongside him

**Marathon founder Fred Lebow overcomes the destruction wreaked by his brain tumor to run the five-borough race for the first time, crossing the finish line with old friend Grete Waitz.**

for support, although she privately fretted that her friend was pushing himself too hard. Meanwhile, Lebow's deputy, Allan Steinfeld, formed an entourage that included a local fireman and policeman and television meteorologists Storm Field and Irv "Mr. G" Gurofsky, as a buffer from distractions like spectators looking for a handshake or photo.

Lebow devoted most of his energy that final week to promoting and managing (make that micromanaging) the marathon. Although the staff moved him to Staten Island so that he'd relax and sleep, he awoke November 1 at 5:30, five hours before the race, checking over everything with his usual gusto.

At race time, Lebow, wearing number 60 for his age, supposedly became just one of 26,000 runners hoping to finish. (His personal best was 3 hours and 30 minutes, but now he was aiming for five hours.) But some second-tier runners pushed forward a minute too soon and triggered a false start that couldn't be undone. Lebow was distracted, angry, and unhappy about yielding control, yelling, "I don't want to run. I shouldn't have run this race." Waitz calmed him, however, and off they went.

A motorcycle policeman and television camera truck rode alongside while two million people lining the streets rooted in numerous languages for the marathon's biggest celebrity. But Lebow, though buoyed by the heartfelt outpouring, rarely waved or responded, and within the entourage he spoke almost exclusively to Waitz while keeping his own counsel. Waitz asked him to rest at the three-mile mark, but he blew right through, instead slowing to a walk several times after Mile 10.

On the Queensboro Bridge, Lebow appeared drained, stopping to stretch and buy time, but the crowds along First Avenue roaring in anticipation of his arrival — loudspeakers announced his progress — spurred him on. At the 17-mile mark, he made an exception and stopped to wave and hug some of the spectators — cancer patients and their doctors at Memorial Sloan-Kettering Cancer Center, where he'd been treated. (Lebow had also added a charity component to the Marathon and would raise $1.2 million for the center.)

Soon Lebow wilted. He seemed uncertain, tilting toward the right, guided gently back by his entourage. At 92nd Street, the tired old man bent over, clutching his stomach. This was the end, everyone thought. Tenacity could take you only so far. There would be no happy ending. But when Waitz came to comfort her friend, Lebow lifted

## Honorable Mention: Women Run for Glory

**1. Grete Waitz surprises herself, and everyone else, October 22, 1978**

In 1978, Grete Waitz was retiring from running. The 25-year-old Norwegian schoolteacher held records in several middle-distance categories and had seemingly done it all. But before hanging up her sneakers, she wondered — even though she'd never run more than 12 miles, spoke little English, and had never been to America, why not inquire about the famous New York City Marathon?

She called New York, but a secretary hung up on her after Waitz confessed she'd never run 26 miles. But marathon director Fred Lebow saw her name jotted down and called her back, thinking Waitz would make a fine pacesetter. He even paid for her flight over. Knowing no one expected her to finish, Waitz treated the trip as a second honeymoon with her husband Jack. The night before the race they celebrated with a four-course meal, from shrimp cocktail to ice cream. "I didn't think about the marathon, had no idea how to prepare for one," she recalled.

Then came the race. The pigtailed blonde did her duty and started fast. She hit the proverbial wall at Mile 19 and, compounding matters, was unable to convert miles to meters and was too embarrassed to ask how much was left. Her quads cramped, and she spilled most of the water she tried to drink. Still, she kept going. "Every time I saw a patch of trees, I thought, *Oh, this must be Central Park*, but no," she said. "To keep motivated, I started swearing at my husband for getting me into this mess in the first place."

She finally reached the finish line far ahead of any other woman — any woman ever, with a world record 2:32:29.

Afterwards, Waitz swore she'd never run again, but Lebow changed her mind. Waitz ran again and won again . . . and again and again, nine times in all, until the woman who ran on a lark became the face of the New York City Marathon.

**2. Paula Radcliffe resurrects herself, November 7, 2004**

Two hours into the 2004 New York City Marathon, Paula Radcliffe's career hung in the balance.

Seventy-seven days earlier, the Englishwoman, owner of the two fastest women's marathons ever, had been favored to win the Athens Olympics' gold medal. But brutal heat and side effects

his head and in his heavy accent chortled, "Fooled you, fooled you," and bolted ahead, rejuvenated.

The homestretch, however, was a genuine struggle. At 135th Street, pain shot through Lebow's knee. A spectator produced a chair, and Lebow sat, donning a knee brace he'd carried just in case. After Mile 20, Lebow's stride became wobbly, and he repeatedly slowed to a walk. At times he was unaware of his surroundings and unable to recognize people he knew.

Spectators passionately, desperately urged him on, and Lebow lurched onward. "I was very much in doubt he could make it," Waitz said. "But when we came into the park and saw all the people waiting for him, he got extra energy."

When 80-year-old Joe Kleinerman, Lebow's close friend and mentor, stepped out and kissed Lebow, Waitz was so moved that she began crying. Lebow asked if she was hurt, since she'd never run that slowly before, but when she explained, he welled up too. For the last two miles, Lebow and Waitz cried and held hands . . . and kept going.

It wasn't just street crowds rooting for Lebow. ABC's regular coverage had long since ended—highlighted by the historic triumph of Willie Mtolo, the first South African allowed to run in the United States after sanctions were lifted with apartheid's demise. But the network regularly cut into subsequent programming to update Lebow's progress. Across the nation, viewers waited and hoped.

Finally, Waitz and Lebow neared the finish line, where "New York, New York" played on the sound system. Waitz briefly stepped ahead, and she windmilled her arm to wave Lebow home, as

## *Women Run for Glory* (CONTINUED)

from medication for a leg injury left her nauseated and near collapse; she quit several miles early, sobbing by the side of the road. British tabloids lacerated her with headlines like "Shame on You, Paula" and "It's Not British to Quit."

Radcliffe requested permission for a late entry in New York, knowing she needed to redeem herself. If she finished strong, she'd restore her luster. If not . . .

Radcliffe started fast and took the lead in Mile 11. By Mile 13, it was just Radcliffe and three Kenyan-born runners, including her friend Susan Chepkemei. By Mile 20, it was just Chepkemei spurting uphill and Radcliffe tagging along behind.

This was the real test. For the final five miles, the two women raced head to head. During Mile 24, Radcliffe, suffering after-effects from a bad pre-marathon dinner, got sick to her stomach. But this time she pressed on. When Chepkemei challenged her with another burst, Radcliffe pulled even.

In the final few yards, Radcliffe found one last reserve of energy. She finished in 2:23:10, squeaking past Chepkemei by four seconds in the closest women's finish in a New York Marathon. Wrapped in a Union Jack afterwards, Radcliffe radiated joy that was testament to her determination and resilience.

### 3. Margaret Okayo outruns her fellow Kenyans, November 2, 2003

In 2003, Kenyan native Lornah Kiplagat broke the New York City Marathon's course record for women, finishing in 2:23:43. Unfortunately for Kiplagat, she finished third.

World champ and fellow Kenyan Catherine Ndereba also tasted bittersweet success, breaking the record at 2:23:04. But that was good enough only for second.

True happiness belonged to another Kenyan, the remarkable Margaret Okayo, who annihilated by nearly two minutes the record she had set in 2001, crossing the line in 2:22:31.

Not quite five feet tall and under 100 pounds, Okayo started running at 13, intrigued by watching her father chase giraffes. Racing through New York's concrete jungle, she glided uphill on Mile 17 in 5:05, then increased her lead with a 5:02 Mile 21. Even as Kiplagat and Ndereba maintained their record pace, Okayo expanded her lead, pulling off an impressive "negative split"—running faster in the race's second half.

One year earlier, Marathon organizers had altered the race's start, sending elite women ahead of the pack to bask in the spotlight on their own. On this day, Kiplagat, Ndereba, and Okayo made the decision look like a stroke of genius.

he had done for thousands of others. Then she held out her hand and together they crossed the tape—held by Mtolo and Mayor David Dinkins—and embraced. It had required 5 hours, 32 minutes, and 34 seconds, but Lebow made it.

He hugged friends, coworkers, and family, then bent to kiss the finish line. He needed help getting up, but when he did, he was the same old Fred, ready to charm the media. "I never realized that a marathon can be this long," he said. "Grete was hurting, she was running so slow. I was hurting from running, period."

The 1992 marathon was Lebow's final moment of glory. The illness soon returned, and he died on October 9, 1994. About 4,000 people, including Waitz, paid tribute to Lebow at a memorial service in Central Park, where a statue of him now stands. "I know Fred wanted me to win ten, and I got only nine," Waitz recalled. "But crossing that finish line with Fred in 1992 made up for it."

# 54. Joe Louis comes back to KO Billy Conn, June 18, 1941, Polo Grounds

Oh so close to beating the indomitable Joe Louis and pulling off the most astonishing upset in boxing, perhaps in all sports, Billy Conn never even considered running, much less hiding. "I'd tasted some of Joe's best blows, and I was still standing," Conn said later about sipping at the goblet of greatness at the Polo Grounds on June 18, 1941. "I wasn't surprised, but now I was sure. I felt I could win if I went to work."

Confidence is a wonderful thing, but in the wrong place and at the wrong time it spells doom. Trapped in a square ring with Louis, one of the strongest punchers ever, especially when he was desperate for a knockout, definitely counts as just such a situation.

Conn was hardly alone in getting pounded by the heavyweight champ. After gaining the crown by pummeling Max Schmeling to avenge his sole loss and steamrollering everyone in sight, Louis and his team stirred up interest by stepping up the pace of his conquests to unparalleled levels. In December 1940, after averaging four title defenses a year, he began drawing crowds with his "Bum of the Month Club" campaign, taking on all comers, one per month.

Billy Conn, the Pittsburgh Kid, was number seven on the list. He was no bum, but he was no heavyweight either—he was giving away 25 pounds to Louis, prompting nearly every gambler and writer to dismiss his chances. Still, he was a quality fighter—the light-heavyweight champ, with 19 straight wins—and he generated excitement by boasting that his quickness would be Louis's undoing: "I'm going to knock him out, win his title, and hold it for 20 years." That cockiness helped draw the largest crowd since the Louis-Schmeling bout, and it carried Conn further than anyone expected, making this fight second only to the Schmeling bout as the most dramatic of Louis's record 25 successful title defenses. But

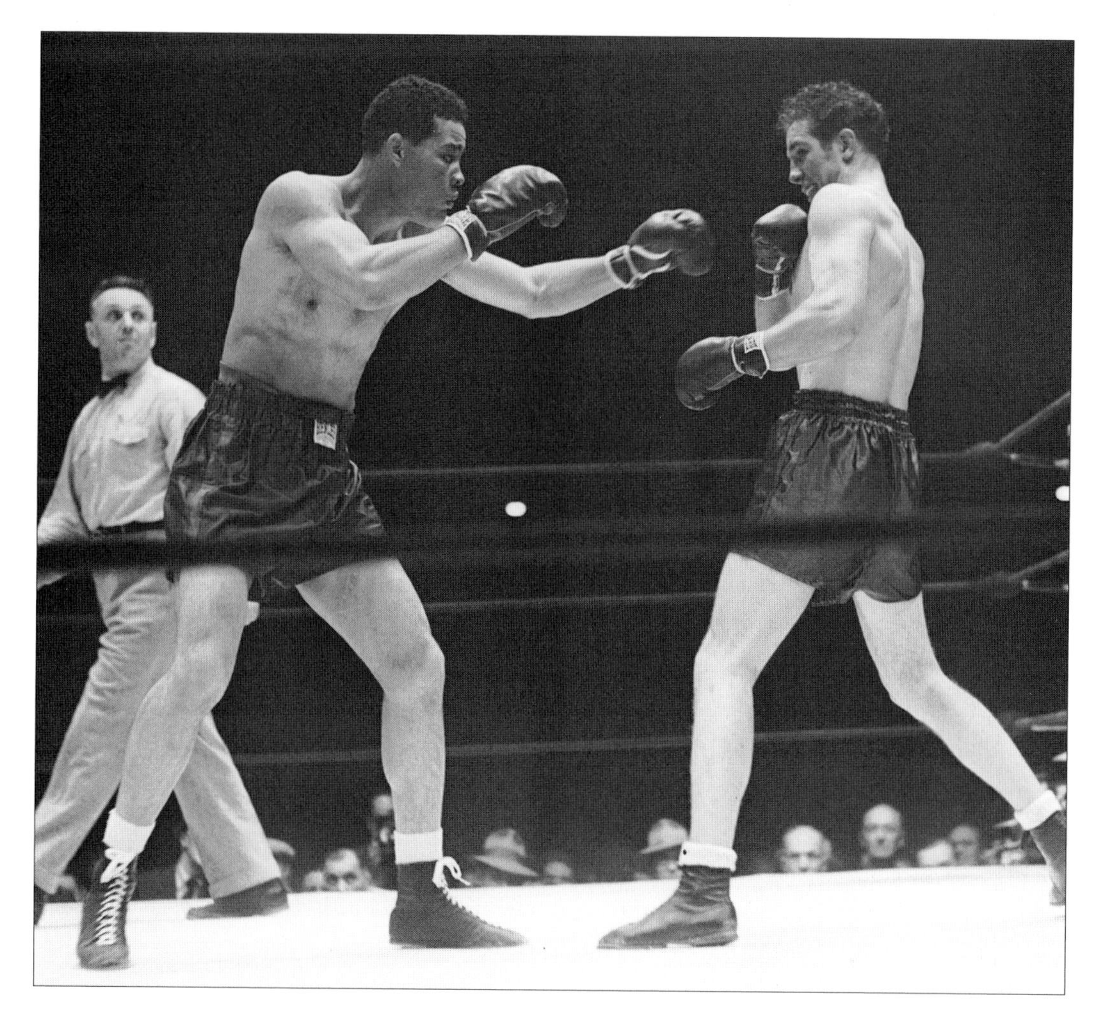

**Joe Louis stalks Billy Conn, who'll eventually forget to run and to hide and will be KO'd by the champ.**

it would ultimately prove Conn's own undoing.

Conn spent the early rounds in fleet retreat, although he came off the ropes at the end of Round 3 to stun Louis with a stinging combo and left hook. Encouraged, Conn attacked more frequently in the fourth and came in closer still in the fifth. Louis, of course, thrived inside—although Conn hurt him, Louis did far more damage. Conn needed smelling salts before Round 6, and then Louis made him wish he'd stayed on his stool, delivering harsh punishment, including a shot to the body that buckled Conn and blows to the face that opened cuts by his nose and right eye. With Louis ahead in rounds, the fight seemed headed for the dustbin of predictable history.

But in the seventh, Louis hurt his right wrist, muffling his chief weapon. The pain wouldn't subside until the 10th, and by then Conn had stopped fleeing and started blocking Louis's punches, enabling him to counterattack. A flurry of blows to Louis's head in the eighth jangled Louis, and at the end of the ninth, Conn hurled a potent right to the body that badly hurt the champ. Conn was even mouthing off, saying things like, "You're in for a tough fight tonight."

This was a whole new fight. Even as Louis's wrist improved, he could do little more than trade blows and tie Conn up, hoping to slow him down. In Round 11, Louis rocked Conn's head, but Conn fired back with a left hook; Louis chased him to a corner, but Conn slithered away and threw a barrage of punches that forced Louis onto the defensive and into the clinches. In Round 12, Louis opened a cut over Conn's other eye, but the challenger smashed the champ back onto his heels with a left hook to the jaw. Again, it seemed, Conn was close to finishing Louis off, but Louis managed to clinch and stay erect. Unfortunately for Conn, those two rounds planted a seed in his mind, a bad seed.

Conn was up 7–4–1 on one card and 7–5 on another, while the third was 6–6. If he won just one more round, the championship would be his. Although he could not know that for sure, everyone smelled an upset. "Chappie, you got to knock him out," trainer Jack Blackburn urged the champ.

Although completely exhausted, Louis knew he had to make Conn "lose his head and gamble, or I could see myself saying, 'Bye, bye, title.'" Conn had fought shrewdly, but Louis had spotted a flaw — Conn left himself vulnerable whenever he unfurled his long left hook — and decided to risk it all to exploit that weakness.

In Round 13, Louis willingly absorbed a left hook to the face for the opportunity to detonate his rights. His first two landed too high, however, barely harming Conn. But they did give Conn false confidence.

He ripped off a flood of unanswered punches, backing up his opponent. Thinking he had Louis in trouble, Conn decided not to ride out a decision but to go for the KO. As he reached back for the big blow he dropped his left . . . and Louis stepped into the opening, zapping a chopping right to the head. This one was right on target, stopping Conn cold.

Louis seized control, bombarding Conn with a volley of heavy artillery that sent him down for good at 2:58 of Round 13, just six minutes and two seconds from victory.

After both men served in World War II (with Louis fighting exhibitions and donating over $100,000 to the war effort), the two fought a rematch in New York in 1946. When Louis was questioned about Conn's elusiveness, he responded famously, "He can run, but he can't hide." Then he KO'd the challenger in the eighth round.

But in 1941, Conn had run and hid and hit too. If only he'd been satisfied with winning by decision and spent the final rounds dancing away instead of conning himself into believing he could trade punches with and knock out the legendary Louis. But that hubris stopped Conn from ascending to the heavyweight throne, although this salt-of-the-earth fighter would probably have scoffed at using words from Greek tragedy. He was too proud of his own heritage for that. "I lost my head. You can't trade punches with that man," he said afterwards. And with a rueful grin, he took a jab at himself: "What's the use of being Irish if you can't do something stupid once in a while?"

# 55. The U.S. Open crowns two unique but very different champions, September 9, 1974, West Side Tennis Club

With the disgraced Richard Nixon resigning and the Vietnam War finally winding down, 1974 marked the end of the countercultural '60s, in spirit if not numerical terms. So it was only appropriate that September 9, 1974, was a day for antiestablishment heroes at Forest Hills. And with the '60s giving ground to the "Me Decade" '70s, it's also fitting that the rebel without a cause grabbed the spotlight from the athlete most committed to the common good.

When 31-year-old Billie Jean King took the court for her U.S. Open finals against Evonne Goolagong, her place in the history books was already secure, and not just because she'd won three U.S. Open crowns, five Wimbledon titles, an Australian, and a French title. This daughter of a fireman and of public tennis courts had fought for the rights of outsiders, underdogs, and especially women in sports. She was cofounder of the Virginia Slims Circuit and the Women's Tennis Association, founder of the Women's Sports Foundation and *Women's Sports* magazine, and a vocal advocate for Title IX. She had also beaten self-proclaimed male chauvinist Bobby Riggs in the nationally televised "Battle of the Sexes," which she called the "culmination" of her career. "Tennis has always been reserved for the rich, the white, the males—and I've always been pledged to change all that," she said.

Against the 22-year-old Goolagong, King dropped the first set 6–3 but bounced back to win the second, 6–3. She trailed 3–0 in the third, but again she dug in, breaking for a 6–5 lead and holding to win what would be her final Open singles crown, a capstone on her career there. (She'd win one last Wimbledon title the next summer.)

King's triumph, however, was relegated to the shadows and soon forgotten because of a player whose sheer personal force would noisily revolutionize the sport, for better and worse. Barbarian Jimmy Connors had smashed down the gate and set the sedate world of tennis ablaze, capping his year with a brutal ass-kicking the likes of which the sport had rarely witnessed. The physicality of the word "Slam" was a perfect fit for Connors, and nothing symbolized the tennis year of 1974 more than the 22-year-old's third and final Grand Slam win: his U.S. Open obliteration of 39-year-old Ken Rosewall, who had conquered Forest Hills as an amateur and a pro in a world that, as Connors emphatically proved, no longer existed.

Throughout its amateur era, tennis was a country club sport and often denigrated as elitist and effete. When the welcome professionalism of the Open era arrived in 1968, the sport—despite internal convulsions and political strife—attracted more top athletes and higher television ratings; in addition, more courts were built, and more people began playing the game. But most champions—Rod Laver, Ken Rosewall, even Arthur Ashe—were decidedly old-school in persona—elegant, cool, and contained. They played by the rules. Not Connors.

"Connors was for tennis like Dylan at the Newport Folk Festival, plugging in and going electric," says Joel Drucker, author of the biography-memoir *Jimmy Connors Saved My Life*.

If ever there was a modern incarnation of Bill Tilden's dictum that a great player must disrupt his opponent's game, get inside his head, and try to destroy him, Connors was it, with his relentless intensity, loud grunts, squeaky sneakers of superior footwork, unequaled return of serve, extra bounces of the ball before serving, brilliantly nervy shot selection, smart-ass bow after a winner, mooning or verbal reaming of linesmen, and unorthodox Wilson T-2000 racket with which he mashed an unorthodox, flat, two-handed backhand. "What Connors brought to the game in 1974 could be found right there in the phrase two-fisted backhand: pugilism and contempt," Alexander Wolff reflected decades later in *Sports Illustrated*.

Connors had been trained that way by his mother Gloria, who taught him the strokes but also the attitude, the tennis-as-combat, you-against-the-world, anti-authority, rules-are-for-breaking mindset. If Oakland Raider owner Al Davis had been a tennis mom, he would have been Gloria Connors. "People don't understand," Connors once said, "that it's a goddamned war out there." Just win, baby, indeed.

Connors emerged as a genuine threat in 1973, but critics raked him for hiding on the lesser circuit organized by his Barnum-esque manager Bill Riordan, who'd promised, "I'll make you the best-known tennis player in the world." (By contrast, Lamar Hunt's World Championship Tennis featured Laver, Rosewall, Ashe, John Newcombe, and Stan Smith.) Connors served notice at a tournament in Boston when he beat both Smith and Ashe, then began his assault on the game in earnest on New Year's Day 1974, when he won the Australian Open. He was banned from the French Open for participating in the upstart new World

**Jimmy Connors takes the tennis world by storm, kicking butt everywhere he goes and capping his year by winning at Forest Hills.**

Team Tennis league, which the international federations deemed a threat to the old order—but he won the U.S. clay championships by beating French Open champ Bjorn Borg.

Connors also sued French Open officials and the Association of Tennis Players, the union he had refused to join. Although much of this combative grandstanding was Riordan exploiting his young star for his own ends, the posturing was certainly true to Connors's persona. By Wimbledon, everyone wanted to see him lose, but he refused, stomping Rosewall in 94 minutes in the final, 6–1, 6–1, 6–4.

"Everybody is saying that I might be the most unpopular champion in the history of Wimbledon. And I might be," Connors smirked. "But what do I care? Because I *am* the champion."

Thanks to Connors and his equally talented girlfriend and fellow Wimbledon champ, Chris Evert, tennis jumped from the back to the front of the sports pages and then into lifestyle and feature sections. A phenomenon was under way, and it was crossing the ocean to New York.

At the Open, Connors wanted, even expected, to slam an exclamation point (or three) on his year to end all years. The crowds wanted to see him, the television audiences too. His coup de grâce was the finals rematch against Rosewall. Connors's harshest critics had made excuses at Wimbledon because Rosewall was tired after tough matches against Newcombe and Smith. He'd be fresher at Forest Hills, which he'd won twice. Yeah, right, like any of that mattered one bit to the tornado sports fans were calling Jimbo.

Connors made the Wimbledon match look like a war of attrition—this time he disposed of Rosewall 6–1, 6–0, 6–1, in just 68 minutes, and for a lot of that time Rosewall stared "at his opponent as if he were a wizard," the *New York Times* wrote. It was the worst humiliation ever seen in a Grand Slam final, and the worst of Rosewall's career. Rosewall managed just 12 points in each of the first two sets, and Connors, who had the best service return in tennis history, yielded just 19 points in Rosewall's 10 games serving, occasionally knocking the racket from Rosewall's hands with his blasts. Connors was the youngest champion since Rosewall had first won in 1956, and he did it with the greatest one-sided display of tennis ever.

He never let up, not for a second, and he had an answer for everything. When someone in the stands jeered, "You're a bum," Connors retorted, "I agree." And when Connors met the press afterwards, he had, thanks to Riordan, a line ready for them: "Get me Laver," Connors sneered, referring to the legend who had skipped the Open.

Although Connors never wanted a cause, by the time he was through at Forest Hills he had one. Despite what the stuffed shirts, old-timers, and journalists thought, he popularized tennis like no one else could, bringing in middle-class and working-class sports fans who had previously been turned off by the prim and insular game.

"Somehow he made tennis a contact sport," says commentator Mary Carillo. "He changed what a match could look like and feel like and sound like. He demanded that the fans give a rip."

Love Connors or hate him, everyone was riveted. Suddenly, everyone was comparing him to Muhammad Ali and Joe Namath. After Connors won 95 of 99 matches in 1974, Riordan declared him the "heavyweight champion of tennis"; in the Open's afterglow, Riordan arranged televised bouts in Las Vegas the following year against Laver, Newcombe, and Ilie Nastase, matches that would replicate the Open final's charged atmosphere (and its winning results).

Thanks to Connors's mass appeal, the tennis boom would explode like a fireball. One poll showed that the number of Americans following tennis jumped from 17 percent to 26 percent during 1974. By 1976 tennis balls were being bought at three times the rate of purchase in 1970, the number of courts being built annually had jumped from under 5,000 to 11,000, and tennis had 13 percent of the three networks' sports coverage, up from just 2 percent. A generation of kids would grow up insisting on learning a two-handed backhand. "Fans walk away from a Connors match feeling that they have carried away a piece of him, after becoming engaged with him in an almost personal way," tennis writer Peter Bodo once wrote.

At decade's end, 15 of the 16 matches with the highest TV ratings ever featured Connors. It was his popularity that hurled the game beyond the sanctity of the private tennis club to the more public National Tennis Center. "All Jimmy Connors did was show up at the sport and blow open its doors, blow down its sides, blow off its roof," Carillo wrote in her introduction to Drucker's book. "He changed the way the game was played by the pros, perceived by the fans and produced by the television networks. He made it bigger, more exciting, more vulgar, and in all those ways, I suppose he made it more American. He made tennis matter."

# 56. At the All-Star Game, Carl Hubbell strikes out Babe Ruth, Lou Gehrig, Jimmie Foxx, Al Simmons, and Joe Cronin . . . in a row, July 10, 1934, the Polo Grounds

When the stands are packed, the pressure is on, and the first two guys get on base, you may think you're in trouble. But when you look at the next few hitters and the easiest out, the

# Honorable Mention: Strike One, Strike Two, Strike Three

## 1. Tom is terrific . . . and unhittable, April 22, 1970, Shea Stadium

After nearly six innings, Tom Seaver had fanned nine San Diego Padres. Not bad, but not unexpected for a power pitcher. What Seaver did over the final three and a third innings, however, was not only unexpected but unimaginable and unmatchable: the final 10 batters failed to put a single ball in play as Seaver struck out every single one.

Al Ferrara: caught looking to finish the sixth.

Nate Colbert: down swinging to start the seventh. Dave Campbell and Jerry Morales go down looking.

Bob Barton led off the eighth, but soon sat right back down. Ray Webster flailed futilely. The scoreboard congratulated Seaver on tying Nolan Ryan's new club record of 15 Ks. Seaver hadn't known how many he had, but then he consciously tried for number 16 and pinch hitter Ivan Murrell complied.

Van Kelly swung and missed to start the ninth-inning parade. Cito Gaston went down looking. Once more, Seaver decided to go for the strikeout, forgoing his usual waste pitch on 0–2 for one final burst of heat. Ferrara, having learned from his past mistake, went out in a (relative) blaze of glory, swinging and missing at that last fastball.

Ten strikeouts in a row. The previous mark was eight, held by four pitchers, including former Brooklyn Dodger Johnny Podres, who was in the stands that day as a Padres minor league pitching instructor.

Seaver had a two-hit victory but had also tied Steve Carlton's major league mark of 19 Ks in one game; although Roger Clemens and Kerry Wood have since broken the 20-strikeout barrier, Seaver—the very definition of unhittable—still has the unfathomable mark of 10 straight Ks.

## 2. Doctor K fans 16, September 12, 1984, Shea Stadium

Dwight Gooden was just 19 and had only one year in the minors—at A ball no less. Sure, he'd fanned 300 batters in 191 innings, but those were kids, and this was the big time. Could he make the leap?

Early in 1984, the Mets' decision to promote Gooden had seemed rushed; in mid-May his ERA was above 4.00. But beginning in August, Doctor K—then a respectable 9–8 with a 3.42 ERA—sent all doubters back to the bench, eyes wide with awe, jaws scraping along the ground. With his exploding high fastball and vicious Lord Charles curve, Gooden—in the middle of a pennant race for the revived Mets—showed he wasn't future promise but present payoff.

In his final nine starts, the teenager went 8–1, pitching 76 innings and allowing just 9 runs and 56 base runners while striking out 95. Reread those numbers slowly to appreciate how implausible they sound.

The high point came September 12 against Pittsburgh. Fresh off a one-hitter against first-place Chicago, Gooden fanned at least two Pirates per inning from the second through the eighth, which was his second inning with three Ks.

Gooden's 10th strikeout broke Tom Seaver's single-season Met record of 13 games with at least 10 whiffs. His 15th smashed Nolan Ryan's club rookie record of 14 Ks in a game. Pretty heady company.

Sandwiched between the two came his 11th strikeout, which brought his season total to 246, breaking Herb Score's major league rookie record set in 1945. Between innings, Score, a Cleveland broadcaster, appeared on the video scoreboard to offer congratulations.

Gooden scattered five hits among 16 strikeouts in his second straight shutout. He'd fan 16 again in his next start and end the year with 276. Of course, Score or Brooklyn Dodger phenom Karl Spooner—who had once made history by striking out 27 in his first two games (both shutouts) back in 1954 before injuring his arm and quickly fading away—could have told Gooden that from the top of the world there's no place to go but down. Gooden shone brighter and longer than Score, and especially Spooner, yet that only made his self-inflicted burnout from drug abuse more tragic.

Met fans, however, like their Dodger fan ancestors (but unlike Yankee fans, for whom glory and success are a presumed birthright), must sometimes dispense with the "what ifs" and "who knows" and simply celebrate "what happened": in September 1984, Dwight Gooden became Doctor K, finding a home in the record books

supposed weak link, is Babe Freakin' Ruth, you know you're in trouble. That's where Carl Hubbell found himself in the 1934 All-Star Game on July 10 at the Polo Grounds. This was just the second such midsummer affair, and the rivalry between the American and National Leagues then was genuine and heated. But expectations for the screwballer were particularly high that day — the game was being played in front of Hubbell's hometown fans, and prior to the first inning he'd been honored with the Most Valuable Player Award he'd earned the previous year pitching the New York Giants to their World Series crown.

Hubbell hadn't invented the screwball, although he threw it so often that his arm actually turned inward. The pitch, which a southpaw like him could make break away from righties (the reverse of a curveball), was a variation on the renowned "fadeaway" that had made his Giant predecessor Christy Mathewson a legend. "Hub" threw it better than anyone in a generation, however, hurling a record 46⅓ straight scoreless innings in 1933 and 20 more innings without an earned run in the World Series; he'd won 24 straight over two years, a new record.

But Hubbell looked less than imposing yielding a leadoff single to Charlie Gehringer on a pitch meant to be out of the strike zone and walking Heinie Manush. With the crowd hollering more disparagement than encouragement, it seemed that Hubbell didn't have his best stuff. The infielders converged to give comfort and advice, but what could they really say given what was awaiting Hubbell?

Babe Ruth: Sure, the aging Bambino would finish his last season as a Yankee with just 22 homers

## Strike One, Strike Two, Strike Three (CONTINUED)

as he electrified the baseball world and New York City.

**3. Louisiana Lightning strikes in the Bronx, June 17, 1978, Yankee Stadium**

It was hot and muggy, and Ron Guidry felt sluggish as he took the mound against the California Angels. Guidry, the quiet anchor in a crazy clubhouse, was 10–0 in 1978, and the only thing keeping the struggling Yankees from oblivion. He had to hope his torpor would dissipate, and soon.

After yielding a leadoff double, Guidry fanned two as the Angels chased his high heat. Then the humidity broke, the Yankees grabbed an early 4–0 lead, and Guidry relaxed, finding his rhythm.

That's when the 5'11", 160-pound "Louisiana Lightning" really struck — in the fourth, fifth, and sixth, the Angels managed just one groundout amid eight whiffs. As Guidry blazed the fans also found their rhythm and started a practice that lasts to this day: clapping and stamping each time the southpaw reached two strikes.

With the major league record of 19 strikeouts in sight, the fans booed every time the Angels hit the ball. Soon his teammates were urging him on too, specifically catcher Thurman Munson, who reportedly threatened bodily harm if Guidry didn't go for strikeouts. Guidry agreed but said the win was more important, so if anybody got on base he would reset his focus.

Guidry set a Yankee record with 16 strikeouts after eight and snagged the AL record for lefties when he started the ninth by whiffing Dave Chalk and Joe Rudi. But after giving up a single, Guidry, true to his goals, concentrated just on getting the final out. When Ron Jackson bounced to third, the crowd briefly sagged in disappointment but rallied to give Guidry a tremendous ovation.

In 1978, two years after he nearly quit baseball because he hadn't been given a real shot in the majors and one year after George Steinbrenner nearly traded him to the White Sox, Guidry finished 25–3, with a 1.74 ERA and nine shutouts. In the greatest year a Yankee pitcher ever put together, this was his greatest start.

**Carl Hubbell, 1930s Giants ace, shows off the stuff he uses to strike out Babe Ruth, Lou Gehrig, Jimmie Foxx, Al Simmons, and Joe Cronin in succession in the All-Star Game.**

and a .288 average, but no one equaled the Sultan of Swat's flair for drama—he'd already crashed the first All-Star Game home run the previous year.

Lou Gehrig: The Iron Horse was on his way to capturing the Triple Crown, with 49 homers, 165 RBIs, and a .363 batting average. He'd also be tops in total bases and finish second in hits and walks and fourth in runs scored, striking out only 31 times.

Jimmie Foxx: The Philadelphia muscleman was the only one of the bunch who'd finish 1934 among the strikeout leaders, ending with 75, but his 44 homers, 130 RBIs, and .334 average made him nearly as dangerous as Gehrig.

Al Simmons: Foxx's teammate would, like Gehrig and Foxx, finish with more than 100 runs and 100 RBIs, while his .344 average would be fourth in the league.

Joe Cronin: Washington's future Hall of Famer was far less intimidating, but he too would drive in over 100 runs in 1934. And he was the toughest of all to strike out, fanning just 28 times that season.

Going over the lineup before the game, Hubbell had realized that "we couldn't discuss weaknesses . . . they didn't have any." The goal was to keep the curve and fastball out of the strike zone and throw only the famed screwball for strikes. Of course, that hadn't worked against Gehringer and Manush.

Hubbell was never a great strikeout pitcher. To get out of this jam he wanted a grounder from Ruth, who'd be easy to double up. Looking for a pitch he could launch, Ruth watched a fastball go by for a ball, then was frozen by three consecutive low screwballs. Strike one, strike two, strike three.

Gehrig too was confounded by the scrooge—he took a big rip at the last one but wasn't particularly close. Even though the two runners pulled off a double steal on that pitch, the crowd was back on Hubbell's side, and the pitcher was breathing easier. On his way back to the dugout, Gehrig whispered to Foxx, "You might as well cut, the ball won't get any higher."

With Foxx up, Hubbell went for the K. Producing nothing but screwballs, he sent Foxx down swinging. After his rocky start, the southpaw had fanned Ruth, Gehrig, and Foxx on 12 pitches.

Hubbell wasn't done. After the National League took a 1–0 lead, he returned to the mound for the second inning to face Simmons, Cronin, and Bill Dickey. Simmons and Cronin met the same fate as the others, going down swinging, victimized by screwballs they couldn't quite fathom.

"It was as big a surprise to me . . . as it probably was to them," Hubbell said of his five-strikeout run.

Then, perhaps because weak-hitting pitcher Lefty Gomez, with his .104 lifetime batting average, was on deck, Hubbell let up briefly, and Dickey managed a single. Whiffing Gomez was a cinch. (One of baseball's great quipsters, Gomez complained afterwards that if only Dickey had fanned, Hub's streak would have been seven and Gomez would have been forever lumped in with baseball's greatest sluggers.)

Hubbell hurled another scoreless inning and left with a 4–0 lead. The AL stormed back with a six-run fifth to win 9–7, with Foxx, Simmons, and Cronin combining for seven hits, five runs, and four RBIs. It barely registered. All anyone talked about was Hubbell slaying one dragon after another.

After such palpable excitement, *The Sporting News* reported that baseball officials had declared themselves "strongly in favor of continuing the event."

"It was no accident the second game had been in New York—they wanted to give it stature," says New York sports historian Bill Shannon. "But had it been a ho-hum affair there might not have been another All-Star Game. Hubbell's feat elevated the All-Star Game to a level of importance for the next 50 years. This became huge in baseball lore."

# 57. Seabiscuit wins the Brooklyn in a photo finish, June 26, 1937, Aqueduct Race Course

Looking back at the sweeping narrative of Seabiscuit's marvelous saga, especially in the Hollywood movie made from Laura Hillenbrand's compelling book, it's easy to see his destiny as inevitable, given his talent and the country's desperate need for heroes during the Depression. And maybe, once owner Charles Howard, trainer Tom Smith, and riders Red Pollard and George Wolff climbed aboard, success could not be denied. But in 1937 it certainly didn't seem that way.

When Seabiscuit began winning and building a following in California, skeptics abounded back east. That's the West, writers sneered; let's see this horse prove his speed and toughness here, where

**It's down to the wire, but it'll be Seabiscuit by a nose over Aneroid.**

it counts. Among the crucial building blocks in the legend of Seabiscuit, and the first step in earning the pivotal match race against Triple Crown winner War Admiral in 1938, was the Brooklyn Handicap at Aqueduct Race Course on June 26, 1937.

Seabiscuit was less than imposing physically; he was described as "dung-colored," and his gait was far from fluid. A loser as a two-year-old, he'd been bought by a relatively novice owner whose greatest skill was his ability to charm the press, resurrected by a laconic and enigmatic trainer, and coaxed toward greatness by an afterthought of a jockey. Life was still far from perfect as Seabiscuit blew a lead and narrowly lost the $100,000 Santa Anita Handicap. Hillenbrand says Pollard was blind in one eye—something he couldn't admit without being banned—and hadn't seen eventual winner Rosemont closing the gap until it was too late. But that painful loss only made ordinary citizens toughing out the Depression love the horse even more.

At Aqueduct, Aneroid—whom Hillenbrand describes as the "rawhide-tough king of the eastern handicap ranks"—was just the slight favorite in odds, but as the local product was "very much the public's horse" in attracting bettors and thus vocal rooters, according to the *New York Times*. The race drew a record crowd of 20,000, and Hillenbrand notes that the cagy Smith calmed his horse by using stablemate Pumpkin as a buffer between Seabiscuit and the raucous New York fans.

Still, once at the post Seabiscuit was among the worst-behaved horses, delaying the race's start. Aneroid broke quickly on the outside, but then let Seabiscuit, who was on the rail, jump to the front, where he tore off. Aneroid and Rosemont seemed content to let lightly regarded Bulwark, carrying only 101 pounds to Seabiscuit's 122, challenge the front-runner and wear him down.

At the far turn of the mile-and-an-eighth race, Rosemont made his move, briefly catching Seabiscuit and sending shivers through those who had witnessed the Santa Anita stunner. But Rosemont soon faded (finishing seventh), and it was Aneroid blasting through, pulling within a half-length with about three furlongs left.

There were no gaps the rest of the way in what the *Brooklyn Daily Eagle* described as a "heart-throbbing, nerve jumping finish." Aneroid briefly passed Seabiscuit with a quarter-mile left, but Pollard, who rarely used the whip, didn't hesitate this time, driving his horse forward and lunging toward the finish line.

"It was anybody's guess as to the winner," the *Times* noted of the "most thrilling" race in the Brooklyn's 49 years. Shouts of "dead heat" rose from the stands, but the photo finish revealed one slight but clear winner: Seabiscuit.

Now Seabiscuit was more than just a fan favorite. Although still the outsider, as the *Eagle*'s "Aneroid Beaten by Seabiscuit" perspective revealed, he'd displayed the tenacity for which he would become renowned and was suddenly a force to be reckoned with. From the Brooklyn he traversed the Eastern Seaboard, winning races and pushing Sam Riddle, who owned War Admiral, to agree to a match race. When Seabiscuit won that race in 1938, it was a triumph not just for the beloved horse but for western racing as well. Later Seabiscuit topped his legend off by winning the elusive Santa Anita Handicap in 1940 well past an age when anyone thought he'd even be running.

The growth of radio and the thirst for escapist entertainment during the Depression transformed Seabiscuit from racehorse into celebrity—he inspired sales of everything from a Seabiscuit hat to Seabiscuit board games. But it might never have happened if he hadn't held off Aneroid to win the Brooklyn Handicap.

# 58. Columbia ends Army's winning streak, October 25, 1947, Baker Field

Just seconds before the first half ended at Baker Field on October 25, 1947, Army kicker Jack Mackmull missed an extra point, low and to the left.

A minor issue, no big deal, right? What was one measly point to the powerful Black Knights? Before this game against Columbia, West Point had racked up 93 points over four games in 1947 without yielding a single point. In fact, Army had not lost in 32 straight games, dating back to 1943. By contrast, the 2–2 Lions were coming off bad losses to Yale and Penn. But this game would turn the football world upside down.

Army drove 54 yards for a touchdown with seeming ease on their first try, then added another TD to start the second quarter as cadets in the stands shook white handkerchiefs at Columbia's fans, telling them to surrender. Columbia did manage to break West Point's scoreless streak on defense, but the Army invaders cheered again when Rip Rowan ran off left tackle and cut back into a huge hole, galloping 84 yards for the touchdown that preceded Jack Mackmull's failed kick. On their way to 302 yards rushing, and armed with a comfortable 20–7 lead, the content Cadets cruised into the locker room.

"They were very cocky," Columbia left guard Joe Karas recalled later. "They thought they were going to run over us. They were very mouthy, making wise cracks on the line."

There were hints that Mackmull's lonely little point might matter. From the Lions' perspective, the game could easily have been 14–14. Quarterback Gene Rossides and receiver Bill Swiacki found a groove on the Lions' 69-yard scoring drive, teaming for completions of 14 and 32 yards. (Swiacki caught the latter one-handed on Army's 5.) Then the Morningside men recovered a fumble on the Cadets' 4, but when star running back Lou Kusserow reached the 1-yard line on first down, the play was called back because an official was on the sideline talking to Army's coach. The Black Knights' defense tightened, and Columbia's Ventan Yablonski missed a field goal. It was then that Rowan broke loose to make it 20–7.

Yet the Lions were not dispirited. They were furious with the ref's mistake, and with themselves for not scoring and then letting up for that one moment. But they were also inspired, finally believing they could stick it to Army. "We had been playing well enough to convince ourselves we could win," line coach John Bateman said later.

Coach Lou Little had ripped his players the previous week for lying down against Penn, but at halftime of the Army game, when Little saw his players screaming and shouting and revving each other up, he quietly stepped aside; for the first time ever, he neither gave a speech nor drew a single play on the blackboard to prepare for the second half.

Little and his men wanted this game for reasons beyond their won-loss record. For the Lions, pride was at stake. The previous year Army had humiliated them 48–14, a loss particularly galling for the militaristic Little, an infantry captain in World War I, and for the 29 Ivy Leaguers who had just served as enlisted men in World War II under West Point–trained officers. Among the most motivated was tackle Hank O'Shaughnessy, who had landed at Normandy, fought at the Battle of the Bulge, and earned a Bronze Star, Silver Star, and Purple Heart. After the 1946 blowout, O'Shaughnessy, who wore a brace on his knee because of a shrapnel wound, ran into a lieutenant colonel he knew, and the officer had verbally run down O'Shaughnessy and his team.

In the third quarter, nothing on the scoreboard raised doubts about the Black Knights' supremacy, but as the teams shoved back and forth the Lions felt they were wearing down the Cadets and controlling the game's tone.

The *New York Post* had written beforehand that this was an "unpredictable Columbia team that has flashed some brilliant football in spasmodic surges." Yet the paper still favored the Cadets by 13½ points. When the final 15 minutes began, the Lions flashed just enough brilliance to make history.

Rossides fired to Bill Olson for a 16-yard gain to Army's 44, then found Olson again one play later on the 32. After advancing to the 28, Rossides called another deep pass, going back to Swiacki, who came up with a catch more mind-boggling than his first one-hander: with defender John Shelley seemingly attached to him in the end zone, Swiacki lunged for Rossides's low pass, stretching out and scooping the ball up just before it hit the ground. (Coach Earl Blaik and Shelley forever insisted that Swiacki trapped it.) Suddenly the Lions were within six.

Army confidently marched right back to the Columbia 28, but the Lions' defense held and Army botched its snap on fourth down, giving Columbia decent field position. Seeing an opportunity, the Lions pounced. Yablonski gained 12 yards on a trap. Then Rossides weaved and dodged on a bootleg for 22 yards. From the Army 29, Rossides again called Swiacki's number, sending him down and out. Forced to scramble toward the opposite sideline, Rossides floated the ball diagonally back across, leading Swiacki, who dove and came up with the pass at the Army 3.

Everyone was stunned. Swiacki "leaped and plunged like a dervish and brought off the greatest line of impossible catches of the twentieth century," wrote the *Herald-Tribune* of his eight receptions for 138 yards.

Two plays later, Kusserow scored. It was 20–20. Just one more thing to take care of: Yablonski's

**Columbia's Bill Swiacki catches the ball at the Army 3 in the fourth quarter, setting the stage for one of college football's great upsets.**

kick was deflected by a Cadet, but the ball still cleared the upright. That gave the Lions the extra point . . . literally. They led 21–20.

There was still 6:38 to go, but it was abundantly clear that the Lions were now the predator and the Cadets their prey. "They were beaten emotionally," Yablonski said later. "They were swearing and calling us bastards and SOBs, everything under the sun." (Blaik acknowledged afterwards that Army had been overconfident, "not ready to meet as good a team as Columbia was.")

Kusserow intercepted an errant Army pass at midfield, and as the clock counted down the final minutes Columbia students waved white hankies back at their former tormenters, some of whom were reduced to tears.

Red Smith called the comeback "an orgy of melodrama that paralyzed reason and ruptured credulity." Indeed, reason evaporated as the fans erupted, storming the field and tearing down the goal posts in celebration—the sole policeman guarding one end zone not only gave up but joined the festivities.

Knowing how much the game meant to O'Shaughnessy, the Lions awarded the former soldier the game ball. Then he proudly headed off to see his wife, who had given birth to their daughter days earlier. Standing on the subway platform, he saw the same lieutenant colonel he'd encountered in 1946. Triumphant, O'Shaughnessy asked, "How do you like Columbia now?"

# 59. Ingemar Johansson's "Toonder and Lightning" strikes Floyd Patterson, June 26, 1959, Yankee Stadium

Floyd Patterson was perplexed. Things had been going his way in his heavyweight title defense against Ingemar Johansson, but suddenly his whole world seemed jumbled. He went to a neutral corner thinking he'd knocked down his foe only to find out, courtesy of yet another second hard blow to his head, that his brain had just been scrambled and he was really the one who'd been floored moments earlier. And soon he found himself falling . . . again and again and again.

Once more he noticed something unusual: "I was looking straight across the ring at John Wayne sitting ringside, and I couldn't understand why Wayne's head was at such a weird angle," Patterson said later about locking eyes with America's symbol of manly strength. "Then I realized it was caused by me looking at him as I lay on the floor."

Floyd Patterson's brain, meet Ingemar Johansson's right hand.

The Johansson-Patterson fight was not the defining upset in heavyweight history, with a dominating champion suddenly deflated (think of Buster Douglas astounding the world by ending undefeated Mike Tyson's reign of terror) or a new force seizing center stage and transforming history (think of a loudmouth nobody from Louisville, name of Cassius Clay, flooring the supposedly indomitable Sonny Liston).

No, Floyd Patterson was a suspect champion at best, and Johansson would prove even less well suited to wearing the crown. Yet in New York's long, storied prizefighting history, there was never an upset as electrifying as Johansson's 1959 hammering of Patterson. For all the drama in the other heavyweight slugfests on this list, there were few surprises. The winners — Louis, Frazier, Dempsey, Jeffries, Marciano — all had impeccable and intimidating credentials. Of New York's other notable stunners, James Braddock's besting of Max Baer was a bore, and Max Schmeling's surprising win over Joe Louis in 1936 was a nontitle fight.

Indeed, outside of Tyson-Douglas and Liston-Clay, Patterson-Johansson ranks with the other contenders for the all-time greatest upset in heavyweight title fights — Gene Tunney over Jack Dempsey, Braddock over Baer, and Leon Spinks over Muhammad Ali included.

Additionally, this first Johansson-Patterson fight set the stage for two more title tilts, producing a spectacular overall tally of 13 knockdowns in just 14 rounds of fighting and a wild unpredictability that made virtually every moment utterly enthralling.

Picture Johansson, undefeated as a pro but best known for the shame he brought upon himself and Sweden after being disqualified for not trying hard enough in the 1952 Olympics. (Johansson said he planned to fight defensively for two rounds, then cut loose in the third; the Patterson fight certainly lends credence to this claim.)

Picture a big Swede whose most impressive win, his first-round knockout of top contender Eddie Machen, happened in Sweden and thus was seen by few and dismissed as a fluke.

Picture this happy-go-lucky guy taking breaks from training to dance late at night with a blond girlfriend, making it deliciously and flagrantly clear that he was violating the traditional "no sex before a fight" rule.

Picture a challenger promising reporters that his big straight right, upon which he had lovingly bestowed the nickname "Toonder and Lightning," would win it for him. "When I throw my right, it moves so fast that no one can see it," he swore. "When I hit any man, he cannot stand up." Yet the press and public never saw this vicious right throughout training, and skeptics (meaning everyone) remained convinced that such a fabulous punch existed only in Johansson's imagination.

Picture the press hyping the fight by playing up the wonderful color of this man, especially since Patterson was reserved and dull. Patterson, an Olympic champion and at 21 the youngest heavyweight crown-holder ever, had been criticized because in a weak division his handlers set him up against patsies. His first four defenses were against unknowns like Roy Harris and Pete Rademacher, who was fighting his first professional bout. Given Patterson's penchant for pushovers, few took Johansson all that seriously either.

Now picture the Yankee Stadium crowd on June 26, looking for the Brooklyn-born Patterson to beat the eccentric foreigner. Folks at ringside paid $100 a ticket for the first time since Joe Louis fought Billy Conn in 1946. The first two rounds conformed to the prediction of an unexciting, methodical title defense. The unusually quiet crowd waited for something worth shouting about. Johansson moved better than expected but offered little more than looping lefts—the nothing jabs that got him kicked out of the Olympics—while Patterson, the 7–1 favorite, bobbed underneath and slammed lefts into the body in the first and the face in the second. The champ was cautious and defensive but seemed in control.

Now erase all those pictures. Round 3 is framed on an entirely different canvas. Patterson, really a bulked-up light-heavyweight, was a fighter of grace and speed, someone who had to outthink and outmaneuver bigger and stronger men like Johansson, who had a 14-pound advantage. But believing the "Toonder" was indeed mere myth, Patterson grew impatient: he stopped ducking under his foe's jabs, instead intercepting them with his own glove, which left him erect and vulnerable.

He also stepped up his attack, throwing two straight lefts; this aggressiveness, however, came at a steep price. Even if Johansson offered little in style and strategy (and perhaps he deserved more tactical credit than he's given), what he did bring was easy to define: one big weapon. It turned out he'd thrown the big right often during training but purposely kept it under wraps during public sessions to develop his mystique. When Patterson threw his second left, he dropped his defenses and Johansson hurled the long-awaited right.

As promised, Patterson never saw it coming. He was flat on his back for an eight count before rising, the *Herald-Tribune* wrote, "glazed of eye, bereft of senses." So disoriented that he thought he knocked down Johansson, Patterson headed toward the neutral corner, arms down, back to his foe. Johansson rushed him, drilling a left to the back of the head. After a nine count, Patterson was up on his feet, more or less, when Johansson thundered another right. Patterson went down, this time for six. At this point, Patterson's wife began pleading with referee Ruby Goldstein to stop the fight.

Goldstein stood aside through knockdowns four (the right uppercut that left Patterson staring at John Wayne), five (another "toonder" right), six (a right-left-right combo), and seven (two big rights) before declaring what everyone already knew: after that 90-second barrage, Patterson was humiliated, and Johansson was Europe's first heavyweight champion in a quarter-century.

Johansson lived large afterwards, relishing the limelight—he was *Sports Illustrated*'s Sportsman of the Year, made a movie and a record, and appeared regularly on TV—and helping to revive interest in a heavyweight division that had been

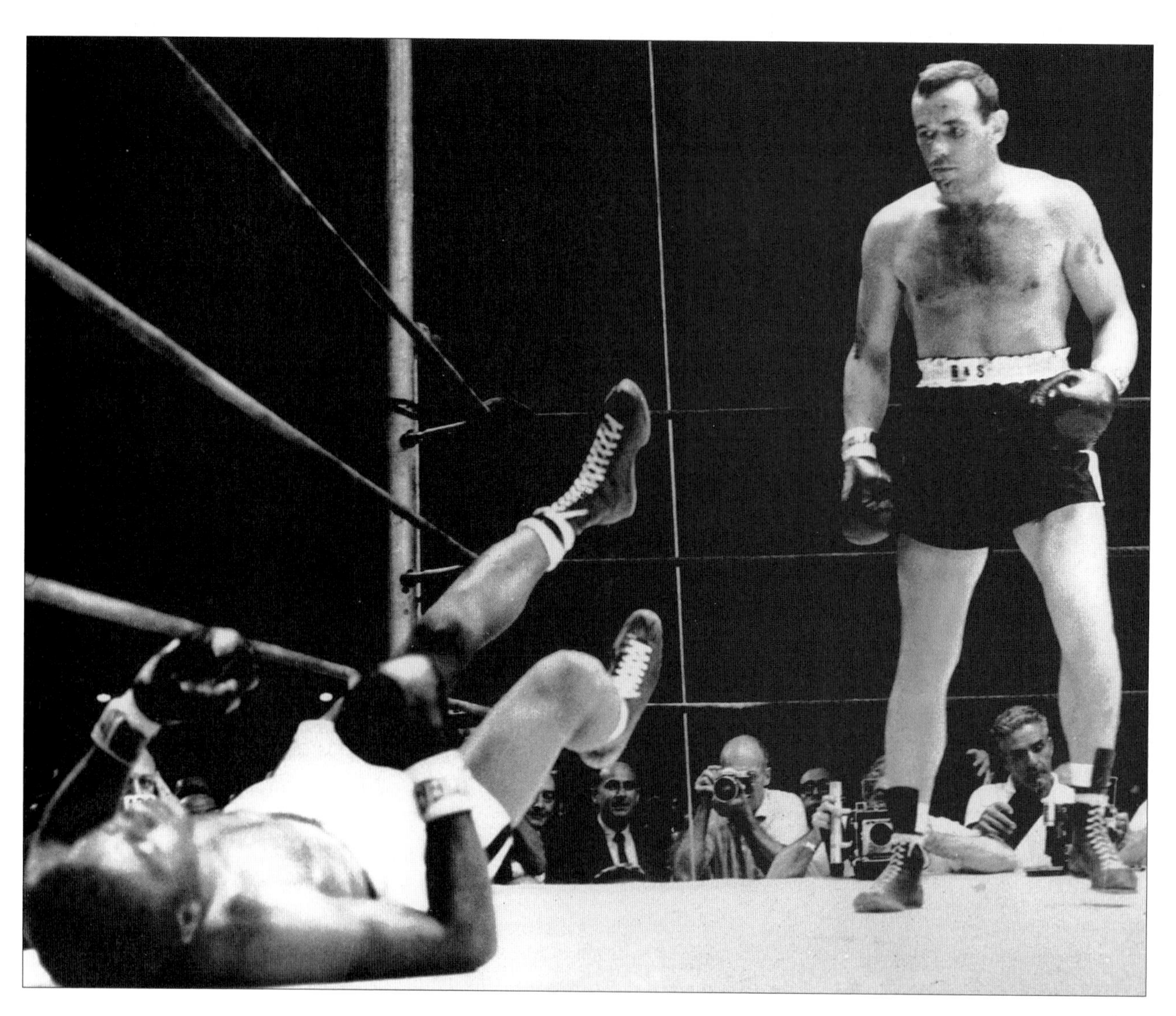

**Ingemar Johansson looks down at Floyd Patterson after flattening him with his "toonder and lightning."**

in decline since the retirement of popular champion Rocky Marciano. Patterson, always plagued by his lack of self-confidence and killer instinct, slunk away from Yankee Stadium that night in disguise before sinking into a lengthy and profound depression. It seemed that he might be finished, yet instead he briefly resurrected his career and reached a new zenith. On June 20, 1960, at the Polo Grounds, an aggressive Patterson became the first heavyweight to regain his title, dropping Johansson twice in the fifth and treating New Yorkers to a fight that would have been on this top 100 list were it not for the initial upset. (Distraught when Johansson lay on the canvas, leg twitching, blood leaking from his mouth and nose, Patterson went to check on his fallen opponent rather than revel immediately in his comeback.) In a wild rubber match in Miami in 1961, Johansson knocked Patterson down twice but was knocked down once himself in a breathtaking first round; Patterson knocked Johansson out in the sixth.

Patterson's second reign soon ended—he'd find again and again that he couldn't take the big hits of boxing's biggest men, getting knocked out by Sonny Liston, who took the championship away in one round, and Muhammad Ali, who finished off Patterson's career. But even those all-time greats didn't have the "toonder" that Johansson packed. Looking back on his first time with his great rival, Patterson would later admit: "I was never in my life ever hit as hard as that."

# 60. Larry Johnson shocks the Pacers with his four-pointer, June 5, 1999, Madison Square Garden

Larry Johnson grabbed the loose ball. It was a good hustle play, but with a man in his face and time running out, it was most likely in vain. Although the Knicks had won Game 1 of their 1999 Eastern Conference Final against Indiana, they'd lost Game 2 and, more significantly, lost Patrick Ewing for the duration as his damaged Achilles tendon finally gave way. When Johnson captured the ball with under a dozen seconds remaining in Game 3 at Madison Square Garden, they trailed 91–88. Without their star center to bail them out, a home loss might well seal their fate, leaving no room for error.

The play started when Johnson got open for an in-bounds pass, only to have Indiana's Jalen Rose tip it away. Johnson beat Antonio Davis to the ball, then faced up his Indiana counterpart. He head-faked Davis, dribbled to his left, and, with 5.7 seconds left, went up for a long-range three-pointer.

The Knicks and Pacers had engaged in countless thrillers over the years, filled with violence (John Starks head-butting Reggie Miller), animosity (Miller flashing the choke sign at Spike Lee and all of New York), and endgame heroics (Ewing's series-clinching dunk in 1994; Miller's eight-point outburst in 1995). Still, this finish was unique.

The 6'7", 235-pound Johnson had once been an explosive player, a force to build an offense around, but by 1999 that was long ago and far away. Back surgery had robbed him of his leaping ability, and while the onetime Charlotte All-Star had remade himself as an inside player, he'd been reduced by injuries and team priorities to second or even third fiddle on Ewing's Knicks, on Allan Houston's Knicks, on Latrell Sprewell's Knicks. With Ewing out, the Knicks had asked LJ to be their guy in the low post, not the sharpshooter with a miracle from downtown.

It had been a strange game in a strange season for the Knicks. The season had lasted just 50 games because of a labor lockout, and incorporating Sprewell, the flashy and controversial newcomer, had taken time. (Johnson assumed a crucial role as clubhouse leader.) The club snuck into the playoffs as the eighth seed, yet it outlasted top-seeded Miami and swept Atlanta to reach the conference final. Johnson had had little impact against Indiana during the regular season, averaging just under 11 points per game, but he'd fired in 22 points in Game 2, and heading into the final seconds of Game 3, he had matched that total while pulling down eight boards. His performance offset Ewing's absence and the disappointing play of Sprewell and Houston, who shot just 12 of 36, a disaster that would normally have been enough to undo the Knicks. Johnson had been aided by inconsistent young jumping bean Marcus Camby, who'd scored 21 points and grabbed 11 rebounds.

Ewing was missed, however, as Pacer center Rik Smits delivered 25 points, leading an 18–6 fourth-quarter run for an 89–81 lead. Still, tenacious defense remained New York's trademark, and beginning at the 3:21 mark, they locked up the Pacer offense. Sparked by Chris Childs's three-pointer, they crawled to 89–88 with 13.8 seconds left. But Mark Jackson's two free throws gave Indiana what seemed like an insurmountable 91–88 edge.

The Knicks planned for Houston to drive for a quick two—perhaps he'd get fouled, or perhaps he'd kick it out. If he only got two, they'd press or foul to get the ball back. Their best hope was for a tie, and that possibility was slim and dissolving rapidly toward none when Houston was covered and Rose deflected the inbound pass.

When Johnson grabbed the ball in front of the Pacer bench, he had already flung home a 30-footer at the first-quarter buzzer and an ugly-but-effective bank shot from behind the line. Those would make most highlight reels, but he'd also missed four other tries. Could he defy the odds again and hit from 26 feet to tie the game?

His shot swished through the net, and at the same instant something even more startling occurred—ref Jess Kersey called a continuation foul on Davis, who had made minor contact before Johnson left the ground. Johnson raced toward center court, roaring with glee. Only when Childs hugged Johnson, reminding him that he still had to sink the free throw, did he calm down.

Johnson guided the winning point home from the stripe, and New York vanquished Indiana 92–91. On another day, Reggie Miller might have fired up another heartbreaker, but this day was Johnson's. After Jackson clanged one final shot, Johnson made his "Big L" symbol with his arms and danced among the fans on the sideline as the crowd chanted his name and Spike Lee jumped into his arms. Three games later, the Knicks finished off the Pacers to return to the finals for just the second time in 26 years. Although Tim Duncan sent the Ewing-less Knicks home without a trophy, this was a season for the scrapbooks, and Johnson's shot was the brightest moment on their home court.

**New York's Larry Johnson hits from downtown and gets fouled on a four-point play in the fourth quarter that sends Indiana reeling.**

# Honorable Mention: Cardiac Comebacks

**1. The Knicks score 19 straight points to beat the Bucks, November 18, 1972, Madison Square Garden**

The Knicks were an aging team. After winning their first championship in 1970, they'd lost on a blocked buzzer-beater in the 1971 playoffs and were dominated in the 1972 Finals. By the 1972–73 season, these veterans seemed destined to be onetime champs.

And this game, against the young Buck of Milwaukee, perennial MVP Kareem Abdul-Jabbar, seemed to prove it: with less than half of the fourth quarter to go, the Bucks were trouncing the sloppy Knicks 86–68, making the home team look like a team of the past.

Then Red Holzman went to the man-to-man press and the Bucks stopped scoring. The Garden crowd got louder. Earl Monroe took over the offense, scoring 11 points. The crowd got louder still. Abdul-Jabbar missed shot after shot.

The noise reached epic proportions. The Bucks couldn't hear themselves in the huddle, couldn't think straight—Bob Dandridge fired away after an offensive rebound instead of killing time, and with the Knicks within one, Lucius Allen bricked two foul shots. When Monroe hit a jumper with 36 seconds left, the Knicks had a shocking 87–86 lead on 19 unanswered points. After the Knicks committed a foolish 24-second violation trying to run out the clock, Abdul-Jabbar missed one last time, and the Knicks walked off exhausted but refreshed, their sense of mission restored, a championship run in the making.

**2. The Knicks win on the "one-second play," December 25, 1969, Madison Square Garden**

They couldn't lose to those loudmouths from Detroit, they just couldn't, especially on Christmas at the Garden.

The lackluster Pistons had recently ended the Knicks' then–NBA record 18-game winning streak and had boasted that they'd beat New York again. The Knicks, who had stumbled through some injuries and four straight losses against mediocre teams after the streak ended, needed to show their fans that this team was the real deal.

But at the very end of a seesaw game, ex-Knick Howard Komives passed to ex-Knick Walt Bellamy for a lay-up and a 111–110 lead. The clock contained just one more tick.

Red Holzman called his "one-second play" knowing full well that it rarely worked—even in practice Walt Frazier often lobbed the pass over the backboard by mistake. But after Dick Barnett set a screen to free up Willis Reed, Frazier hurled a bomb that would have made Joe Namath proud. Reed took two steps and soared, laying the ball in at the buzzer. 112–111, New York. A Merry Christmas and Happy Championship Year to all.

**3. Santa Ewing brings cheer to the Garden, December 25, 1985, Madison Square Garden**

The lowly Knicks were no match for Larry Bird's Boston Celtics. But Christmas at the Garden often produced strange magic, from 1969's buzzer-beater win to 1984's 60-point outburst by Bernard King in a losing cause.

So even after New York missed 10 straight shots while the future champs commandeered a 58–33 third-quarter lead, maybe it shouldn't have been a surprise that the Knicks started chipping away. Guard Rory Sparrow spoke up, saying, "Let's make the next two minutes a personal thing. Don't let your man score for the next two minutes."

But it was the fourth quarter that provided a glimpse of things to come: while the Knicks' frenetic defense forced a wave of turnovers, rookie center Patrick Ewing finally demonstrated to a national television audience what the hype had been about, pouring in 18 points over nine minutes, including 12 straight. The Knicks forced one overtime, and then, on a Ewing hook and a Trent Tucker three-pointer, a second. There Ewing, who'd finish with 32 points and 11 rebounds, put the Knicks up for good on a bank shot, sealing a 113–104 win that gave hope to Knick fans who could see a future beyond that lost season.

# 61. In a match for the aged, Pete Sampras beats Andre Agassi one last time, September 8, 2002, Arthur Ashe Stadium

Thirty-three straight winless tournaments over 26 months. That's quite the dreary oh-fer.

Winning matches is one thing, tournaments another. When you're perhaps the greatest ever, all that matters is taking home the trophy.

Mired in the slump of his life at the U.S. Open in September 2002, Pete Sampras needed what he'd later call "a little destiny."

By 1999 Sampras had fallen from his inestimable peak, but because he won Wimbledon that year and the next, garnering accolades for his record 13th Grand Slam crown in 2000, no one wrote him off. As Lisa Dillman later wrote in the *Los Angeles Times,* however, "his journey from zero to 13 was nothing compared to the march from 13 to 14."

In his next eight Slams, Sampras reached just two finals—the 2000 and 2001 Opens, where he was raked by confident young guns Marat Safin and Lleyton Hewitt. Worse, he wasn't even reaching the quarters in the other majors and lost four first-round matches in early 2002. Tasting fear and failure, Sampras became Steinbrennerian, whipping through three coaches. Mutterings and murmurings burbled in the press and on the tour: Sampras should retire before he embarrassed himself. Though stung, Sampras responded with more humiliating losses, and after losing in Wimbledon's second round in 2002 to some nobody named George Bastl, on a side court no less, he wondered if maybe he really was washed up.

Sampras knew history would treat him well: he'd ranked number one in the world six years running, won seven Wimbledons in eight years, and four U.S. Opens in seven. But Sampras wanted respect in his own time and to go out on his own terms. He wanted his peers, the press, and the fans to remember him as a winner who was at his best when it counted most. To do that, Sampras, 31, would have to prove himself one last time.

Sampras was seeded just 17th at the Open but looked like the 1990s version of himself in beating Greg Rusedski, Tommy Hass, and a young Andy Roddick. His semifinal foe was someone named Sjeng Schalken, who, it turned out, was no George Bastl.

Sampras was back in the final. Now destiny played its card, dealing him an ace in the hole. On the other side of the net was sixth-seeded Andre Agassi.

After an early career marred by frivolous distractions, Agassi, 32, had become a genuine champion in his own right, winning seven Slams, including four between 1999 and 2001; unlike Sampras, who'd never conquered the clay courts of the French Open, Agassi had won all four majors. He also burnished his off-court reputation in ways Sampras the loner never could, helping

**Once again, Pete Sampras is the champion and Andre Agassi is stuck in his shadow.**

younger players while committing more to Davis Cup play and philanthropic work.

Yet for all that, Agassi seemed too keenly aware that in their inextricably linked careers, Sampras's legend burned brighter. Agassi won their first match, when he was ten and Sampras nine, and their first pro match in Italy in 1989 in front of perhaps 100 people. But when the stakes were highest, Sampras would go from great to unfathomable, finding a way to win. He'd done it in their 1990 and 1995 Open finals, the 1999 Wimbledon final, and the fourth-set tiebreaker of their classic all-tiebreak 2001 Open quarterfinals.

It was their on-court differences that had made this rivalry shimmer. Sampras had an overpowering serve, but Agassi was his generation's premier returner; Sampras's sharp volleys and leaping overheads countered Agassi's passing shots and lobs; Sampras swung aggressively with long, fluid strokes, while Agassi had a compressed game—superior reaction time, a compact swing, and great speed through the zone—that gave him the edge in baseline rallies. Agassi was emotionally vulnerable and played from a sense of insecurity, yet was remarkably fit (he ran sprints up the mountains in Nevada); Sampras played from confidence and a sense of belonging to history, yet was often lax in his conditioning, counting on superior ability to pull him through in close scraps. Even watching these two friendly rivals practice on adjacent side courts in their prime was a study in contrasts. Agassi played to the crowd, acknowledging their cheers and hitting fancy shots, going between his legs to return a lob. Sampras just worked. Agassi approached Sampras and suggested they hit together, put on a show for some lucky fans. He coaxed, he charmed, he goaded . . . no luck. Sampras simply wanted to hone his game.

"He's made me a better player," Sampras would say after their 2002 final. "I've needed Andre over the course of my career. He's pushed me, forced me to add things to my game. He's the only guy that was able to do that. He's the best I've played."

After Agassi's arduous semifinal against the top-seeded Hewitt, he was asked about the roaring crowd. "Wait till tomorrow," he responded.

He was right, of course. For the fans and the press, Sunday was a guaranteed winner, promising tension and emotion at a level rarely matched on the court. The Open era had never seen two players in their thirties reach the finals, nor two finals opponents who owned 20 Grand Slam titles; this would be Sampras's and Agassi's 34th and final meeting, equaling the Jimmy Connors–John McEnroe rivalry. (Sampras held a 19–14 edge.)

"They may represent the one exception to the winner-take-all notion of sports . . . what is remembered is not the outcome of their various matches, but the quality of their rivalry," Peter de Jonge had written in the *New York Times Magazine* at the height of their rivalry in 1995. "If both players can each hold up his end of the bargain long enough, no one has to go down in history alone."

On one level, this match was that payoff, but in a truer sense, Sampras had always flown solo, chasing and surpassing Rod Laver and Roy Emerson on what S. L. Price in *Sports Illustrated* called his "cool and lonely march to greatness." For Sampras, this was his last chance to declare emphatically, I am Pete Sampras. I am the greatest.

On that Sunday the crowd was wracked with emotion even before the first point—September 8, 2002, was the first men's final since 9/11, so a pregame ceremony honored the attack's victims and featured Queens native Art Garfunkel singing a heartbreaking version of "Bridge over Troubled Water."

Agassi was usually the crowd favorite, but Sampras was the underdog for the first time ever, and fans backed him from the start. He didn't play like an underdog—he played like the winner of four Opens. With Agassi looking hung over from his arduous semifinal, Sampras blasted 16 aces (reaching 132 mph) and 36 winners in winning the first two sets, 6–3, 6–4. When Agassi earned a break point down 5–3 in the first, Sampras unleashed a 109-mph second-serve ace. In the second set, he held at love four times, ending the set with another ace.

Then Agassi found his legs while Sampras's started to wobble. In the sixth game, Agassi produced a stunning crosscourt passing shot on the run and earned three break points. Sampras came up with two aces and escaped, but the crowd, wanting more tennis, switched sides, cheering even when Sampras missed a serve. Up 6–5, Agassi dragged Sampras through deuce after deuce, finally earning a break point and sizzling a backhand return that Sampras volleyed meekly into the net. The crowd gave Agassi a standing ovation.

Sampras shrewdly took a bathroom break to build some reserves. He'd need them desperately. The fourth set would be the deciding one—if Sampras couldn't finish Agassi, it was unlikely he'd stand a chance in the fifth.

It was a taut set, filled with potential turning points. With Agassi up 2–1, the fourth game took everyone's breath away. Sampras, slow to the net and struggling with his serve, found himself looking into the abyss. Agassi punched backhands into the corners, snapping hungrily for a break. Sampras twice faced break points. On the first, Mike Lupica wrote, "he reached down—maybe all the way back to his prime—and somehow begged a backhand half-volley off the tops of his sneakers and over the net." On the second, a fatigued Sampras resorted to a drop shot to short-circuit the rally; from off the court Agassi tried flicking it around the side, but it ricocheted off the net post. On the 20th point of the game, Sampras put away a forehand volley, pulling back from the precipice, winning the fans back with his tenacity.

At 4–4, Agassi, the terrier who wouldn't let go, fought for another break point, then got it when Sampras double-faulted. But Agassi botched his backhand return, and Sampras revived the great champion within, the one who seized on the smallest of openings and cracked them wide. He finished that game with an ace, then cracked big ground strokes for 0–30 in the next game; after earning the break, he raced out to 40–0, thanks to his 33rd ace of the day. Agassi staved off elimination once with a crosscourt forehand, earning a final ovation, but nearly three hours after they began, Sampras finished Agassi off with his 84th winner of the day, a crisp backhand volley.

Sampras had rewritten the record book, which confirmed his place at the top of the tennis pantheon, but he'd also polished his legacy, touching everyone with his determination and resilience in a triumph that John Powers of the *Boston Globe* called "one of the most lovely and fulfilling moments in tennis history."

That sentiment echoed loudly as Sampras hugged Agassi at the net, then climbed into the seats to embrace Bridgette Wilson, his pregnant wife and steadfast supporter. "This [title] might mean more than any of them," Sampras said. Having done what no one thought he could, he walked away from tennis, satisfied.

# 62. Jim Corbett has his finest hour in a loss against Jim Jeffries, May 11, 1900, Greater New York Athletic Club, Coney Island

Jim Corbett sat in the corner after the 22nd round and let himself daydream, just for a moment: "I was actually deciding what size type I would use on the big posters that would proclaim me Champion of the World again."

On May 11, 1900, at Coney Island's Greater New York Athletic Club, Corbett indeed seemed poised for a stunning upset over heavyweight champion Jim Jeffries.

No one expected Corbett to be in such a position. At age 33, Corbett had been considered washed up—or worse, tainted. He had become the first heavyweight champion under the Marquis of Queensbury rules by upsetting legendary brawler John L. Sullivan back in 1892. For winning under rules that specified three-minute rounds and quality gloves while forbidding kicking and grappling, and for doing it with footwork and strategy as opposed to pure brawn, Corbett had earned the (somewhat inaccurate) moniker "Gentleman Jim," lending the sport a much-needed air of respectability. Jeffries was polished and sophisticated, acquitting himself creditably on Broadway; he was also a skilled athlete who played minor league baseball between bouts. But in 1897 Bob Fitzsimmons snatched the heavyweight title away with one perfect punch to the solar plexus, and Corbett became despondent. He fought only one exhibition in the next 16 months, and in the next three years he would have only one real fight, which he lost under suspicious circumstances when his second jumped into the ring, causing a disqualification. Rumors of a fix also preceded this fight, but Corbett had instead surprised everyone, turning in the fight of his life against the finest competitor he'd ever faced.

In the opposite corner sat Jeffries being bombarded with advice from his handlers. Jeffries had eagerly awaited this matchup—he had served as Corbett's sparring partner back in Corbett's hey-

## Honorable Mention: No Mas

**1. Benny Leonard bloodies Ritchie Mitchell, January 14, 1921, Madison Square Garden**

Lightweight champ Benny Leonard entered the ring and saw challenger Ritchie Mitchell. Referring to the new rule that fighters had to go to a neutral corner after knockdowns, Leonard loudly inquired, "Which corner do I go to after I knock him down?"

Mitchell was rattled, and Leonard was ready to pounce.

Leonard, "the Ghetto Wizard," was the quintessential up-from-the-streets fighter—a Jewish kid from Eighth Street and Avenue C on the Lower East Side who learned to fight against bullying Irish and Italian kids. At 5'6" and 130 pounds, and with a Star of David on his trunks, he was an inspirational superhero to struggling Jewish immigrants. Born Benjamin Leiner, he "proved the advantage of brain over brawn, fighting the united efforts of the goyim establishment to keep [Jews] in their ghettos," wrote noted author Budd Schulberg.

Leonard turned pro at 15 and, except for one disqualification, was unbeaten during his reign from 1917 until he retired in 1925. Among boxing's greatest fighters pound for pound, Leonard punched hard, moved fast, thought even faster, and loved talking trash.

Leonard and Mitchell banged out a wild first round. Leonard attacked savagely, knocking Mitchell to the canvas three times in the opening minutes. But with total control comes total confidence, and Leonard let down his guard. Mitchell walloped him with a left hook to the jaw. Barely roused by 10, a dazed and bleeding Leonard covered up like a wounded animal to survive.

By the fourth, Leonard was still retreating, but just as Ali would later do, he was retreating strategically, sneering, "Is that the best you can do?" as if his nickname were the Lower East Side Lip. Enraged, Mitchell swung wildly, missing the target as his opportunity vanished. By the fifth, Leonard was pressing his case, sending Mitchell to his knees.

Round 6 was all Leonard—lefts and rights to the face, cutting both of Mitchell's eyes, drawing blood from the nose. Mitchell went down twice, unable to see. His corner man reached in and wiped his face. The crowd screamed for the fight to be stopped, and even Leonard looked reluctant, but the ref wasn't listening. So Leonard plowed back in. Finally, Mitchell's handlers could stand no more and threw in the white towel of surrender, drenched in blood.

**2. "Yankee" Sullivan demolishes William Bell, August 29, 1842, Hart Island**

One of the first big bouts in what is now New York City took place in one of its most obscure and out-of-the-way locations, a spot that even today most New Yorkers know nothing about: Hart Island. Back then, obscurity had its selling points.

In the 19th century, police regularly raided bare-knuckled bouts, charging anyone they could grab with everything from drunkenness to gambling to criminal intent to foul language, all the way down to

day, and Corbett had used his fancy footwork to slice and dice the big, raw country boy. Jeffries had sworn revenge, and tonight he'd expected to have it. At 6'2" and 218 pounds, he was quite large for those times and had 2 inches and 30 pounds over his rival. Paul Bunyan–esque stories were told of this strongman once carrying a deer he had shot nine miles without stopping back to his campsite; he could also high-jump over six feet and was one of the only athletes ever to beat Corbett in a footrace. He reportedly ran the 100-yard dash in under 11 seconds, just off that era's world record. (Jeffries also once allegedly treated a cold by drinking a gallon of whiskey.) In the ring, veteran promoter Tex Rickard said years later, Jeffries "was the hardest hitter I ever saw and that includes Jack Dempsey."

Jeffries was among the first heavyweights to use the crouch—a style he adopted to dethrone Fitzsimmons—yet he continued to be labeled an unrefined lug overly reliant on his deadly left hook. Like Rocky Marciano, another crude fighter, Jeffries also had tremendous stamina that enabled him to take a terrible licking, then finish his foe

## No Mas (CONTINUED)

littering. So remote Hart Island, a sliver of land in Long Island Sound that would later become the city's potter's field, became popular for fisticuffs since police could not sneak up without being noticed.

On August 29, 1842, thousands of New Yorkers traveled there by boat. "Yankee" Sullivan, an Irishman who had battered foes in Australia and England, was one of the first boxers to become a celebrity, his controversial life fodder for writers across the decades. He was facing Englishman William Bell, best known for teaching Brooklynites the art of self-defense. At stake was a $300 purse.

Rounds ended when someone went down; fighters got a half-minute break sitting on the knee of one of their seconds. In the August heat, Sullivan rang Bell relentlessly over 24 rounds in 38 minutes before the Englishman finally tossed in the towel. Sullivan was the winner, but so was the city—with all the hoodlums and hooligans on Hart Island watching the fight, New York's crime rate plunged that day.

### 3. John L. Sullivan brings boxing to the Garden, May 14, 1883, Madison Square Garden

Madison Square Garden's promoters declare it "the world's most famous arena." In the earliest days of the first Garden—the one in Madison Square—John L. Sullivan laid the first cornerstone of that claim.

"The Boston Strong Boy" became America's first superstar of sport in 1882 when he beat Paddy Ryan down south, becoming world champion at the end of the bare-knuckle era. Boxing was largely an outlaw sport and would remain so after Sullivan's day, but this hard-drinking bully's mass appeal helped legitimize the fight game.

Five months after topping Ryan, Sullivan beat Tug Wilson before 5,000 people at the newly built Garden. That bout incited interest for his next fight, against Englishman Charley Mitchell.

That fight attracted 10,000—with 10,000 more reportedly turned away—including local and national politicians and members of high society, whose interest spurred greater and more serious coverage of boxing.

To avoid arrests, the event was staged as an "exhibition" (nudge, nudge, wink, wink). But Sullivan was intent enough on winning that he stayed sober the entire day before the bout.

With an eye to the future, the men wore soft gloves. In the opening round, Mitchell stunned Sullivan and the crowd by ducking the champ's attack and counterpunching with a quick left that floored Sullivan. The crowd roared; Sullivan was enraged.

Sullivan, who had a 40-pound advantage, pummeled Mitchell, smashing him to the ropes in Round 2 and knocking him down several times in Round 3, once falling atop his foe—Mitchell was badly dazed when the police staged their customary "break it up." Sullivan, whose lack of artistry had been exposed, wanted to dole out more punishment, but this was "just short of murder," according to the captain.

From the 1930s through the 1960s, the Garden would seal its place in sports history in part by averaging 30 fights a year, a glorious period that owes much of its success to the arena's first major attraction.

**Diligent training nearly allows Jim Corbett to upset Jim Jeffries in their memorable heavyweight title fight.**

with one punch. That was what Jeffries, who was not prepared for such heightened competition, needed to save this fight.

Corbett had seemed as fast as ever, using a hit-and-run approach to score points and shake up Jeffries without exposing himself to danger. His footwork was still too much for Jeffries. In the sixth, Corbett had landed seven straight jabs to the nose. In the ninth, he'd switched to the hook and slammed two into the champion's jaw, staggering him. In Round 10, he bloodied Jeffries' nose and mouth. By then, the crowd was pulling loudly for the underdog, who'd won virtually every round.

Had the fight been a 15-rounder, Corbett would have been champion; however, back then fights went 25 rounds, and Corbett's age, his nonstop tactics, and the withering heat of the primitive lights used to film this indoor fight all took their toll. Corbett's feet slowed down, leaving him vulnerable. In the 15th, he was jolted by a big right. By the 18th, his corner men were urging him to be careful, to just stay away, while Jeffries' pressed him to stalk the challenger. Jeffries was winning the later rounds now, but Corbett was so far ahead on points that only a knockdown would beat him. The challenger made it through rounds 20, 21, and 22, although blows to the shoulder and ribs jangled him at the end of Round 22.

Only nine minutes of fighting remained as Corbett sat fantasizing about his coronation. But this reverie proved disastrous — he started thinking it would be "quite dramatic" if instead of simply outlasting Jeffries he knocked him out. Big mistake.

Just as Billy Conn would famously learn against Joe Louis 41 years later, attacking a wounded champion is a dangerous business. Corbett came out aggressively, but Jeffries was lying in wait. The champ's left hook to the body slammed Corbett into the ropes. Jeffries followed with a straight left to the face, then faked a right. This feint brought Corbett forward off the ropes and — *bam.* The heralded left hook to the jaw. The champion had done just what he intended.

"He fell to the floor solidly, like a sack of grain," Jeffries wrote with evident satisfaction. He hit Corbett so hard that the challenger didn't ever remember the final attack.

A decade later, the two men found themselves on the same side . . . the wrong one. Jeffries had KO'd Corbett in a rematch and won three other title defenses before retiring undefeated, an exalted status later attained only by Marciano. But he foolishly returned to the ring at age 35 after six years away. Like much of white America, Jeffries was galled by the fact that a black man, Jack Johnson, had emerged as champion; Johnson's audacious personality only made it worse. In Jeffries's corner was "Gentleman Jim," who verbally sniped at Johnson only to have Johnson mock him, inviting him into the ring for a beating of his own. Johnson shredded Jeffries, leaving an ugly stain on Jeffries' otherwise admirable career.

But the fight in Coney Island back in 1900 had the opposite effect — both men came out better than they began. Jeffries proved himself unbeatable, while Corbett won the admiration and respect of everyone who followed the fight game, restoring his reputation and his legacy.

# 63. Steffi Graf, struggling with her father's arrest, battles Monica Seles, struggling to overcome her stabbing injury, September 9, 1995, National Tennis Center

Call it Soap Opera Saturday. September 9, 1995, was, after Super Saturday 1984, the most dramatic all-day affair in U.S. Open history. This episode of *As the Tennis World Turns* starred six current or former number ones with 43 Grand Slam titles to their combined credit.

In the men's semis, *All Nick Bollettieri's Children,* the top two seeds — friendly rivals since childhood, winners of the two previous Opens, and costars in an attention-getting new Nike ad — fulfilled virtually everyone's hopes and expectations by winning hard-fought matches, setting the stage for a dynamic final. Yet these tense showdowns were overshadowed by the *Young and Anguished* melodrama of the women's final in which two haunted victims — both ranked number one together — somehow managed to emerge triumphant even though only one walked off the winner.

First, two-time champion Pete Sampras talked by phone with cancer-stricken coach Tim Gullickson before facing off against Jim Courier, once the sparring partner who'd pushed Sampras to attain the conditioning necessary for greatness. (Both had done time at Bollettieri's famed Florida tennis academy.) It was vintage Sampras — a tight match in which his numbers weren't great (50 percent first serves in), but he capitalized on opportunities and slammed the door on Courier's chances. Sampras saved two break points at 4–4 in the first set. At two-all in the third set, he responded to triple break point with five straight points. When Courier, down 5–4 in the third, thought he'd snatched a 40–30 lead by whizzing a forehand into the corner, Sampras ran it down and ripped a crosscourt winner. Eventually, and seemingly inevitably, Sampras emerged on top, 7–5, 4–6, 6–4, 7–5.

The other men's semifinal, defending champion Andre Agassi versus Boris Becker, was even closer and certainly tenser. At Wimbledon that summer, Becker had upset Agassi, then badmouthed Nike and Agassi, claiming the corporate sponsor got its star preferential treatment. Tensions were heightened because Becker was working with Bollettieri, Agassi's former coach with whom he was feuding.

At the Open, Becker boomed in 25 aces, but Agassi returned well enough to force Becker to engage from the baseline, which proved crucial when each of the first two sets went to a tiebreaker — both times Agassi won big points on Becker's serve to go up 7–6 (7–4), 7–6 (7–2). Racing to a 4–1 lead in the third, he seemed on the verge of a sweep when Becker dashed off five straight games. Becker then had two break points at 2–2 in the fourth, but Agassi, who'd pound out 23 winners in the final set, rallied to stay on serve. At 4–4, he finished his foe with eight straight points, including three huge, untouchable forehand serve returns to annihilate Becker in the final game.

Afterwards, Agassi offered a brief, lukewarm handshake, then criticized Becker's Wimbledon comments before refocusing by looking into the camera and declaring, "Pete, I'm coming." (Soon enough, he was going, as Sampras won the men's final on Sunday.)

But on this day — when ratings were up about 50 percent from the previous year — even Sampras and Agassi seemed secondary. The women's final was more than eagerly awaited, it felt absolutely necessary, a much-needed shot at closure on one of the most horrifying chapters in sports.

In the late 1980s, levelheaded Steffi Graf was briefly the Babe Ruth of women's tennis, her powerful forehand lifting her above everyone. In 1988 she won the Grand Slam, and the next year she captured three of the four majors. But in 1990 a new, more powerful force burst onto the scene. Wielding her racket with two hands from both sides and grunting with the ferocity of a feral animal, Monica Seles bested Graf in the finals of the French Open. She was just getting started. She won three of four Grand Slams both in 1991 and 1992.

After winning the 1993 Australian, it seemed she was playing for the record books with eight Slams by the age of 19. Unlike other teen prodigies such as Jennifer Capriati, Seles seemed immune to burnout.

But on April 30, 1993, tragedy struck.

During a changeover at a tournament in Hamburg, a deranged man brutally stabbed Seles in the back. Worse, he proclaimed himself a diehard Graf fan who had committed the heinous act because he wanted his favorite restored to number one.

Seles would be out of action for more than two years, recovering physically relatively quickly but battling the psychic wounds for far longer. For Graf too, this period felt endless, her career stuck in purgatory. She won 65 of her next 67 matches, including the next four Grand Slam tournaments, but the whispers and articles repeated endlessly, "Would she have won if not for the stabbing?" (At home, Seles cried when watching those tournaments.)

Battling injuries and unable to maintain her drive with Seles's spectral presence looming, Graf began disintegrating: she failed to win any of the next four Slams. Then things got really strange. Seles began preparing to return, and Graf, despite back problems, promptly won the 1995 French Open and Wimbledon. But with Seles finally back in action at the U.S. Open (after just one warm-up tournament), trouble again found Graf.

Just before the Open, her father, Peter Graf, was arrested at home in Germany on tax evasion charges; compounding the issue was Peter's role as manager of Steffi's multimillion-dollar business empire. Although she wasn't implicated in any wrongdoing, she was ensnared in the net that

**Steffi Graf wins the U.S. Open, but the crowd saves its loudest ovations for Monica Seles upon her return to the tennis center stage more than two years after her stabbing.**

trapped him, and not even allowed to speak to him because German authorities didn't want them coordinating stories. The German media hungrily devoured this tabloid tale, trailing Graf everywhere, even in a supermarket. Overwhelmed by the trauma, she decided to hide in broad daylight on the courts, although she was convinced she'd be too drained to win. But Graf had a warrior's concentration and determination and blocked out not only the swirl of chaos surrounding the fiasco with her father but also the chronic bone spur in her back and a new one in her left foot.

She was cheered by Seles's gleeful parade through the other half of the draw — the return of Seles's smile and smashes let one ghost lift off from Graf. Seles not only reached the finals without losing a set but took the time to enjoy the sights and sounds like she never had while racing to victory. She bought hats at Barney's, caught Broadway shows, served as a presenter at the MTV Video Awards at Radio City, and hung out on the sidelines of a Dallas–New York *Monday Night Football* game at the Meadowlands.

Although she still had to fight back occasional flashbacks of the stabbing on the court, every interview seemed peppered with happy words like "fun." Once shunned by Open crowds for her thrashing of local favorites and offhanded arrogance, she was now embraced and even adored, held up as testimony to human resilience and bravery and credited with reviving women's tennis. It was, Stefan Edberg said, the "Seles Open."

Finally, the face-off at Louis Armstrong Stadium everyone was waiting for arrived. In an unprecedented maneuver, Graf, 26, and Seles, 21, had been ranked as co-number ones to acknowledge the unfortunate incident that bound them together. Between the two men's semis, their final began the process of eradicating some of the echoes of the previous 28 months.

In a taut first set, both women were on target and remained on serve, forcing a tiebreaker. Seles finally had the tiniest opening, a mini-break for a 6–5 tiebreak lead and set point, but then the layoff took its toll in the most unlikely of ways. Seles blasted a set-ending ace and trotted happily toward her chair. But wait, it was called wide. (Replays supported the call.) Graf had new life. The original Seles incarnation was so tough, so willful, she'd have put the unpleasantness behind her and plowed ahead. Having lost the habits of a lifetime, she couldn't shake off the reversal and lost three straight points and the set.

After the changeover, Seles reasserted herself while Graf began thinking ahead too much, thinking about what this victory would mean . . . and before she knew it victory seemed very far away. Seles drove her from one corner to the other, shocking Graf by winning the second set at love.

But the shock awoke Graf. The two women were even until two-all in the third, when Graf pulled off her first — and only — service break of the match for a 3–2 lead. If she could hold serve three times, she'd be champion. With each game she inched closer, until at 5–4 she finally had double match point at 40–15. "There is absolute stillness in the air," *Sports Illustrated* noted, as if the entire crowd, no, the entire city, was holding its collective breath.

Graf missed her first serve, and on the second Seles mashed an untouchable crosscourt backhand. The crowd cheered and screamed and wondered. Could Seles cap her comeback with the ultimate comeback? But Graf wanted this badly too, and on her second match point she nailed a stronger serve. When Seles misfired a forehand, it was over . . . not just the match but the waiting. The women hugged and kissed, grateful and relieved.

"I want to thank you," Seles told the fans afterward. "This is one of the reasons I wanted to come back, to feel the electricity. Thank you, for all of you."

Although the soap opera was far from over for Graf — in her postmatch press conference questions about her father prompted her to flee to a bathroom to cry in private — she had proved herself where it mattered most to her: on the court, against Seles.

"This is the biggest win I have ever achieved," Graf said. "There is nothing that even comes close to this one."

# 64. Tony Lazzeri, Joe DiMaggio, and the Yankees make a statement against the Giants and start a new Yankee dynasty, October 2, 1936, Polo Grounds

Babe Ruth had retired.

The Yankees had finished second for three straight years and won only one World Series in the last seven.

Manager Joe McCarthy was dismissively called "Second Place Joe."

Perhaps their days as the feared powerhouse were done . . . or perhaps this skinny new Italian kid from San Francisco who had shredded the Pacific Coast League could make a difference in 1936.

Then the kid, 21-year-old Joe DiMaggio, missed the start of the season after he burned his foot on a machine because he was too shy to ask why it felt so hot.

But when the rookie debuted in May, everything changed. He had three hits in his first game, then batted .323 with 206 hits, 29 homers, and 125 RBIs in 138 games. He graced the cover of *Time* magazine. Teaming with Lou Gehrig and Bill Dickey, he helped the Yankees win the pennant by 19½ games. A marvelous rookie campaign showing signs of true greatness, to be sure, but there was still the proving ground of the World Series. Not just any World Series but a Subway Series, the first since 1923.

The Bombers had won it all in 1932, but the New York Giants were champions the year after; the Yankees had eight pennants to their credit, but the Giants had twelve. Both had won four championships, and 1936 was the battle for supremacy in New York.

The Series did not begin auspiciously for the Yankees—Giant ace Carl Hubbell shut them down, and the Giants exploded with a four-run eighth in a 6–1 win. The Yankees needed to make a statement in Game 2 at the Polo Grounds on October 2 or lose control of the Series—no team had won a best-of-seven after losing the first two games.

The Yankees did more than make a statement—they issued a manifesto, declaring that while Ruth was exceptional, his era would not be an exception. A new dynasty—one that some historians deem the most impressive of all Yankee reigns—had taken hold, built on an awesome blend of slugging, pitching, and defense. Game 2 linked the glory of the old and the new, highlighting Tony Lazzeri, a holdover from the Murderers' Row lineup of the 1920s, and DiMaggio, who finished with a personal flourish that made it clear these were his Yankees.

With two on in the first, DiMaggio surprised everyone by dropping a bunt for a single, filling the sacks for Gehrig, who'd hit more regular-season grand slams than anyone. There had only been one slam in Series history, by Cleveland's Elmer Smith against Brooklyn in 1920. Gehrig lifted a fly

**Rookie Joe DiMaggio sits with mentors Tony Lazzeri and Frankie Crosetti. They will establish a new Yankee dynasty in the 1936 World Series.**

to right, but it was catchable. Still, one run scored and another soon followed. The Yankees led 2–0.

The Giants got a run back in the second, but in the third the Yankees expanded their lead to 5–1 and had loaded the bases again when Dick Coffman, the Giants' third pitcher, faced Lazzeri.

Nearing the end of his career, Lazzeri, a fellow Italian American from San Francisco, had (with shortstop Frankie Crosetti) been a valuable mentor to the young DiMaggio. He'd also driven in 109 runs. Still, he was remembered for a different World Series appearance with the bases loaded—in 1926 Grover Cleveland Alexander had fanned him in Game 7 to help St. Louis sneak past New York. But Dick Coffman was no Grover Cleveland Alexander, and Lazzeri smashed just the second World Series grand slam to punctuate the seven-run outburst.

The Giants managed three in the fourth, perhaps because the Yankees' famously flaky Lefty Gomez was growing bored—he even stopped pitching to watch a plane fly overhead. But the Yankees padded their lead with one in the sixth and two in the seventh.

A 12–4 rout is not particularly noteworthy, but in the ninth the Yankees performed with enough panache at bat and in the field to make this a game for the record and history books. Jake Powell singled, stole second, and went to third on a fly-out. Yes, with an eight-run lead in the ninth, the Bombers played small ball. Gomez—one of the game's worst-hitting pitchers—singled him home, then Crosetti, Red Rolfe, and DiMaggio singled in succession. One out later, Dickey cracked a homer to make it 18–4. That gave Dickey five RBIs, tying a single-game Series record . . . set by Lazzeri earlier that afternoon. (Yankee Bobby Richardson broke it in 1960.) Every Yankee had at least one hit and one run. They broke or tied 12 records in all. No other team has scored 18 in a Series game before or since. It remains the most lopsided rout in Series history, and a clear sign of what the Yankees had in store for opponents in years to come.

One more sign soon emerged showing that the Yankees had a new superstar who belonged in elite company. Before the ninth inning, there'd been an announcement asking everyone to remain seated afterwards until President Franklin Roosevelt departed in a car driven specially through the center-field gate. In the Giants' last chance, DiMaggio corralled two easy flies. Then, with a runner on second, Hank Leiber blasted the ball some 475 feet from home plate—a home run in many other ballparks, but in Yankee Stadium's Death Valley merely an excuse for DiMaggio to display his long, graceful strides and knack for making even the most difficult plays look easy. He caught the ball on the dead run and took two steps up the stairs in center field toward the clubhouse. Suddenly, he remembered the president.

The immigrant's son from Fisherman's Wharf stopped short and stood at attention, waiting. The president's car rolled by, and Roosevelt, the young outfielder later told writers, gave DiMaggio a wink and a wave or the V for Victory sign.

In the years to come DiMaggio would ensure that Yankee pinstripes continued to symbolize victory just as surely as Roosevelt's V sign; the club would capture 16 of the next 18 World Series games played in capturing four straight titles. "I've always heard that one player could make the difference between a losing team and winner, and I never believed it," Giant manager Bill Terry said about DiMaggio after that 1936 Series. "Now I know it's true."

# 65. The Giants hold off the Packers for the NFL Championship, December 11, 1938, Polo Grounds

In the brutal 1938 championship game between New York and Green Bay, the fearsome Packers amassed 378 yards to the Giants' 212, had twice as many first downs in the second half, and pulled off their patented big plays, including a 40-yard touchdown pass, a 66-yard breakaway off a screen, and a 34-yard run. Yet the defending champions and owners of the NFL's leading offense could not fend off the Giants, who proved their greatness by displaying a vigilant opportunism, swooping in at crucial junctures to alter the game's dynamic.

The game on December 11 at the Polo Grounds was a pitched battle, with intermittent fisticuffs and numerous injuries from the hard-fought plays. Giant Johnny Dell Isola left on a stretcher with a spinal concussion that was nearly a frac-

**Despite Green Bay's vaunted offense, the Giants hold on to win the NFL Championship.**

tured vertebra, Ward Cuff departed with his sternum possibly fractured but returned, and Leland Shaffer stayed in with a broken bone in his leg. Even the biggest names weren't exempt: NFL MVP and Giant leader Mel Hein was temporarily knocked out with a concussion, while Green Bay suffered a tough injury too when their big play threat, unstoppable wideout Don Huston, missed much of the second half with an injured knee.

Much of the Packers' yardage was given up willingly by the Giants, in a game plan designed by Hein, who knew that the gravest danger was not grinding drives but Green Bay's lightning strikes; he'd ordered his unit to grudgingly give inch after inch to prevent explosive outbursts. The Giants couldn't completely contain Green Bay, but the defense produced some stunners of their own.

On Green Bay's second possession, future Giant coach Jim Lee Howell blocked a punt, giving New York the ball on the Packer 7 and setting up a field goal. On the next possession, after another blocked punt, Howell recovered the loose ball on Green Bay's 28. Four plays later, Tuffy Leemans, the league's second-leading rusher, scored a touchdown for a 9–0 Giant lead. In the second quarter, Green Bay closed within 9–7, but soon after Hein recovered a fumble near midfield, and the Giants drove for a quick score, with the quarterback Ed Danowski hurling a 20-yard touchdown pass. Again Green Bay struck back, when Wayland Becker caught a short pass — the sort of

# Honorable Mention: Stay Out of Our End Zone

**1. The Giants hold Jim Brown to eight yards, December 21, 1958, Yankee Stadium**

Jim Brown had nearly done in the Giants' playoff aspirations on December 14, 1958, romping 65 yards for a touchdown on the game's first play and bulling for 148 yards overall. But Pat Summerall's field goal in the snow had given New York a 13–10 win over Cleveland and forced a tiebreaking playoff game on December 21 . . . against Cleveland and Jim Brown again.

It often seemed like Brown was unstoppable, but for one day middle linebacker Sam Huff and the Giants' defense stifled the game's greatest back. Brown carried just seven times and managed just eight yards. In other words, he went nowhere. "I don't know that anyone ever hit me harder than Sam Huff," Brown said. "Especially in that playoff game, he had my number on a couple of plays."

On the frozen field, the Giants eked out 10 points, just enough against a team still reeling from the previous defeat. Huff became a star, and the Giants moved on to the championship game with the Baltimore Colts and their date with destiny.

**2. The Giants' goal-line stand holds off the Bears, November 27, 1927, Polo Grounds**

When the ball is on your five-yard line, there's little room for error. When the league championship is at stake, there's even less. When the other team has first down, it may seem hopeless. It isn't.

That's where the New York Giants found themselves against the Chicago Bears back when the fledgling NFL had no championship game and the team with the best record won the crown. With three games left, the 8–1–1 Giants had to stop second-place Chicago, 7–2–1.

Football then was built on running and defense, and no one did Big D like Big Blue, on its way to notching 10 shutouts while yielding just 20 points over 13 games. No lockdown was more important than this one. The Giants had not allowed a first-half score all year, and a first-quarter touchdown by Chicago would bode ill.

On first down, the defense yielded just one yard. Second down, one more. Third down, and the Giants grudgingly allowed three more feet. On fourth down from the 2, Chicago's Roy White took the snap and dove straight ahead, but guard Al Nesser—playing bareheaded and without shoulder pads—lunged underneath the Bears' blockers to drag White down on the 1.

The Giants stopped several more drives, finishing with an interception on their own 10 with two minutes left to seal the 13–7 victory. When they clinched the title at 13–1–1, they looked back proudly and pointed to the ultimate goal-line stand as their proving ground.

**3. The Giants stomp the Redskins to reach the championship, December 4, 1938, Polo Grounds**

The turnover. There's nothing quite like it: taking the ball away has a greater impact than a goal-line stand and is more devastating than a sack. With the season on the line and a shot at the title within their grasp, the 1938 New York Giants made one big play after another, treating the ball like it was their own, even during the Washington Redskins' possessions.

After beginning the season 1–2, New York had climbed out of the cellar with a comeback win in Washington. They'd reached the finale at 7–2–1 and in first place, but Washington was 6–2–2, and a win would slip them into the championship game. The previous year Washington had routed New York 49–14 to win the East. Not this time.

Before the second-largest crowd in NFL history, New York's defense stripped the 'Skins almost immediately. Under four minutes in, Ward Cuff intercepted a pass and ran it back 37 yards; after Hank Soar scored on a 43-yard run, New York recovered a fumble to set up another touchdown.

Up 17–0 in the third, the Giants faced their first threat of the day when Washington drove deep. But Cuff picked off another ball on New York's 4 and raced 96 yards for a touchdown. By game's end, the Giants had six interceptions, four fumble recoveries . . . and a 36–0 stomping. A week later, they were NFL champions.

play Hein was content to allow—but broke free for 66 yards to set up a touchdown. At the half, New York was clinging to a 16–14 lead.

In the third quarter, the Packers finally seized the lead, 17–16, on a field goal, meaning that for the first time all day the Giants' offense needed to mount a sustained drive. They did. Or rather, Hank Soar did. Soar, later the first-base umpire in Don Larsen's perfect game, carried the team by carrying the ball five times and catching one pass to move the ball 39 yards to the Packer 23. Then Ed Danowski lofted a ball downfield. Two Packer defenders were there, but Soar hauled it in at the 6. Then, with Clark Hinkle trying to drag him down, Soar shoved his way into the end zone.

New York had a 23–17 lead, but there was a full quarter to play. Green Bay mounted two last marches, but both times the Giant defense cut them down with two big plays, an interception inside New York's 30 and a fumble recovery. The Giants held on for a 23–17 win, making them, not Green Bay, the first NFL team to win two championship games and, with their fourth appearance in the title game in six years of existence, the Giants could unofficially but proudly claim the crown as the NFL's first modern dynasty.

# 66. Graig Nettles flashes his leather and saves the World Series, October 13, 1978, Yankee Stadium

Graig Nettles was an old-school player who got his uniform dirty and cracked plenty of sarcastic quotes, but kept his ego neatly stored in his locker (his license plate read "E5"). Naturally, he garnered far fewer headlines than Bronx Zoo denizens like Reggie Jackson, Thurman Munson, Billy Martin, George Steinbrenner, Mickey Rivers, Catfish Hunter, Sparky Lyle, Goose Gossage, and Ron Guidry. But in the 1978 World Series, Nettles, who'd won his second straight Gold Glove while tying with Jackson for the team lead in homers with 27 and finishing second in RBIs with 93, commandeered the spotlight in Game 3 with one of the most dazzling postseason defensive performances ever, single-handedly turning around the Yankees' battle with the Dodgers. His handiwork ensured that this New York squad would earn the right to call themselves a dynasty.

The Yankees had made history that season by storming from 14 games back to tie the Boston Red Sox before beating them in a historic one-game playoff at Fenway Park. They easily handled Kansas City in the playoffs, but in the Series they immediately dropped the first two games to Los Angeles, whom they'd beaten the previous year. Only twice in the previous 20 years had a team managed to come back from such a deficit, and the Yankees' losses were particularly disheartening: in Game 1, L.A. knocked out Ed Figueroa in the second inning and shredded the bullpen, scoring 11 runs on 15 hits; in Game 2, rookie fastballer Bob

**Time and again, Graig Nettles flashes his leather to bring the Yankees back from the abyss in Game 3 of the 1978 World Series.**

Welch entered a one-run game in the ninth and blew away Reggie "Mr. October" Jackson to end it.

For Game 3 on October 13 back at Yankee Stadium, the Yankees did have an ace—not in the hole but on the mound—in Ron Guidry, whose 25–3 record and 1.74 ERA was the best performance by any Yankee pitcher in history. But Guidry couldn't find the groove—he'd go the full nine, but L.A. would snipe at him constantly, generating eight hits and seven walks and hitting the ball hard throughout. It was up to Nettles to keep most of those runners from scoring.

Nettles was an innovator: he played deeper and farther to his left than most other third basemen, figuring he saved more runs in the long haul (while allowing his shortstop to cheat toward the middle); he could make this shift because of his extraordinary range, a super-quick first two steps, and an uncanny ability to bounce back up after a dive. He'd need all that and more in this game to protect the Yankees' lead.

In the third, the Dodgers cut the Yankees' 2–0 edge in half and nearly tied it up when, with a runner on first, Reggie Smith doubled down the line... well, he would have doubled down the line, except that Nettles, who'd already handled one hard liner that inning, made an awesome, lunging backhanded stop, pulled himself up, and threw Smith out at first, quashing the threat.

In the fifth, Smith again ripped a ball ticketed for the left-field corner, this time with two runners on base. But nothing got past Nettles—he got to the ball, keeping it in the infield; although he had no play at first, he'd saved another two runs. With

## Honorable Mention: The Yankees in the Clutch

**1. Yankees come back on a ninth-inning homer... again, November 1, 2001, Yankee Stadium**

They say lightning doesn't strike twice in the same place. Tell that to Byung Hyun Kim.

Flash! On October 31, 2001, Kim, Arizona's closer, endured the most horrifying Halloween imaginable in Game 4 of the World Series when he yielded Tino Martinez's two-out, two-run, game-tying homer. The Yankees won in the next inning on Derek Jeter's home run, evening the Series at two apiece. That comeback might have warranted honorable mention entry were it not for the next night.

Flash! On November 1, Kim again stood on the same mound in the ninth inning with another two-run lead.

The Yankees had had five men on base from the sixth through the eighth, but the big blow proved elusive. The biggest cheers had come in the top of the ninth when fans serenaded right fielder Paul O'Neill, knowing it was his last game at the Stadium. Scott Brosius would change all that.

With two outs and Jorge Posada on base, Brosius did his best Tino Martinez impression, smashing a game-tying homer, the first time in Series history a team had pulled off this ninth-inning feat twice in a row.

Arizona didn't crumble: they loaded the bases off closer Mariano Rivera in the 11th with one out. Even a broken-bat bloop single would have sufficed, but Rivera escaped, and in the 12th Alfonso Soriano singled home Chuck Knoblauch to cap the most exciting pair of comebacks Yankee Stadium had ever hosted.

**2. Tommy Henrich comes through again, October 5, 1949, Yankee Stadium**

Tommy Henrich homered in the first game of the 1949 season. Henrich also homered in the final game, with the pennant at stake. So don't expect an O. Henry twist in a story about how he ended Game 1 of the 1949 World Series.

Starters Allie Reynolds and Don Newcombe dominated the game: Reynolds fanned nine Dodgers and allowed just two hits; he even picked up two of the four hits Newcombe scattered as the big Dodger rookie struck out 11 through eight.

Then came the bottom of the ninth and Henrich. A scoreless game. A 2–0 count. Newcombe had to come over—he couldn't walk the leadoff hitter—and Henrich was among the game's best fastball hitters. Newcombe

the bases now loaded, Steve Garvey smacked a screamer down the line. But Nettles inhaled that too, forcing Smith at second.

After five innings, Nettles had saved at least four runs. But Guidry wasn't done getting into trouble, and Nettles wasn't done bailing him out. With two outs in the sixth, the Dodgers loaded the bases again for Davey Lopes, who'd hit two homers in Game 1 and angered the Yankees with his cocky behavior during and after that rout. Lopes smacked Guidry's offering hard but made the same mistake his teammates had — pulling the inside slider hard down the line. Another bullet. Another stunner of a stop by Nettles. Another force at second. Another rally killed.

There was no doubt who made the headlines this time around as Yankee fans drew two tips of the cap from Nettles in their lengthy ovation. Nettles had saved at least six runs and possibly more. Inspired, the Yankees opened up a 5–1 lead in the seventh, and Guidry had his best inning in the ninth when he got two of the last three outs with strikeouts. The only man to make contact in that inning was Lopes, who grounded to third. Nettles, not surprisingly, threw him out easily.

"We felt we were going to take that game," Dodger catcher Joe Ferguson said about Game 3. The Dodgers sagged afterwards, and the Yankees became the first team ever to win four straight games after losing the first two.

Bucky Dent hit .417 and was named Series MVP. Nettles, by contrast, hit only .160. But he set a Series record with 20 assists and in the space of four innings in Game 3 made this his World Series.

## The Yankees in the Clutch (CONTINUED)

snapped off a curve. Henrich ripped it over right fielder Carl Furillo's head. They didn't have the phrase "walk-off homer" back then, but Newcombe knew instantly what had happened and walked off so quickly that he was in the dugout before Henrich rounded the bases. When Henrich reached home plate, the Yankees were en route to another World Series crown. There was a reason they called this guy "Ol' Reliable."

### 3. Phil Rizzuto lays down a beauty, September 17, 1951, Yankee Stadium

The year 1951 featured one of baseball's great pennant races, with fortunes turning rapidly on one pitch in the bottom of the ninth inning of the big game . . . on a bunt.

The season is best remembered for a different ninth-inning hit — Bobby Thomson's famous playoff-ending homer — but the Dodgers-Giants pennant race didn't heat up until mid-September. And while the Yankees' pennant may seem inevitable in retrospect (they won nearly every year from 1947 to 1964), that year they had to battle Chicago, then Cleveland and Boston, every step of the way.

The Yankees had lost four of five and were staggering when Cleveland arrived on September 16, one game up, for a critical two-game set. Of the Yankees' 12 subsequent games, 11 were with third-place Boston and fourth-place Chicago; most of Cleveland's eight games were with sub-.500 Detroit.

Allie Reynolds outpitched Bob Feller, while manager Casey Stengel's revamped lineup produced five runs for just the second time in a week. The teams were deadlocked. The next day Eddie Lopat went for his 20th win against Cleveland's Bob Lemon. With the game tied 1–1 in the ninth inning, the Yankees loaded the bases with one out. Phil Rizzuto was up. He'd finish the year hitting just .254 — a drop of 70 points from his 1950 MVP season — and with just 43 RBIs, but this was the one that they needed most of all.

Rizzuto was among the best bunters in baseball history. He didn't show bunt on the first pitch but on the second, and Joe DiMaggio broke for home . . . a suicide squeeze. Lemon saw the movement and fired a fastball high and tight at Rizzuto's head. It was an impossible pitch to bunt, but Rizzuto not only got it down, he placed it perfectly. By the time Lemon fielded the ball, DiMaggio had scored. No one yelled, "The Yankees win the pennant, the Yankees win the pennant," but nobody had to: Lemon hurled his glove into the stands. Everyone knew the race was as good as over.

# 67. Ned Irish launches college basketball with the first double-header, December 29, 1934, Madison Square Garden

When Ned Irish was a young sportswriter, he went to cover a college basketball game at Manhattan College in 1933 only to find it sold out and the doors shut. Irish crawled through a small athletic department window, ripping his best suit pants in the process, but not only did he get to see the game, he had an epiphany that changed basketball and the city: if basketball's appeal had outgrown this tiny gym, maybe it could fill Madison Square Garden. And so, on December 29, 1934, Ned Irish brought hoops to the Garden.

That's how the legend goes.

In reality, in 1931 Irish and other sportswriters staged a triple-header basketball benefit for Mayor Jimmy Walker's Unemployment Relief Fund; in the depths of the Depression, the event sold out. It packed the house in 1932 and 1933 too. Irish, a 29-year-old Brooklyn native, was not only a sportswriter for the *New York World-Telegram* but also publicity man for the football Giants (such conflicts of interest were acceptable then), and he sensed the sport's potential. So, on December 29, 1934, Ned Irish officially brought hoops to the Garden.

By today's fast-paced standards, the game that night was boring—with no shot clock and jump balls after every basket, the final tallies were so low they resembled football scores. But on this long-ago winter's night, the games between St. John's and Westminster College and between NYU and Notre Dame thrilled the appreciative crowd of 16,188 and, most importantly, left them wanting more.

The story of these games was not the specifics of Westminster's 37–33 win over St. John's or the main attraction, NYU's 25–18 triumph over Notre Dame—for tense championship play, you'd choose undefeated NYU beating undefeated CCNY 24–18 the previous March. But that game was played before 5,000 people in the 102nd Engineers Armory and had no impact on the sport or the city. This twin bill was the start of something new, something big, something very New York—it was the beginning of college basketball's elevation to major sports status and the turning point for the Garden, which thereafter became a mecca for college basketball and for sports in general.

The Garden had faced troubled times since its main force, Tex Rickard, died in 1929 just months before the Depression hit. Million-dollar profits shrank to $130,000 in 1931, and by 1933 the Garden was losing money. (Hockey was the main sports attraction, since boxing was between the Jack Dempsey and Joe Louis eras.) Although it may be too strong to say that this double-header saved the Garden, it did propel the arena toward the future by delivering Irish as a basketball director—he would build college hoops and help launch the National Invitation Tournament (NIT), the Basketball Association of America (which

**Ned Irish establishes Madison Square Garden as the basketball mecca when he launches the college double-header in 1934.**

evolved into the NBA), and the New York Knicks, for whom he served as president until 1974.

Showing savvy and foresight, Irish worked out a sweet deal, getting the rights to host six double-headers without laying out a penny. "The Garden was dark a lot of nights," he once explained. "The only guarantee the Garden wanted was that its percentage of the gate would average the cost of renting the building, which at the time was $4,000 a night. If I didn't meet it, my option would not be renewed."

Irish understood not just business but basketball. According to Dennis D'Agostino, author of *Garden Glory,* a book about the Knicks, many teams still played on courts drawn in chalk on hard surfaces and in "cages" (the netting that surrounded the court, keeping the ball constantly in play). For the charity series, the Garden had stretched a canvas over the composition stone floor, which tripped players and disrupted dribbling. For this first double-header, Irish brought in a real wood basketball floor and installed glass backboards so that patrons sitting behind them could see the action. He also fed this information to his press-box colleagues, who effusively previewed the event. "Metropolitan college basketball will step out of its cramped gymnasiums and gloomy armories tonight into the bright lights and spaciousness of Madison Square Garden," trumpeted the *New York Herald-Tribune.*

Irish hoped to draw at least 10,000; he needn't have worried. In addition to the 16,188 who made it in, thousands more were turned away; it was the largest crowd ever to see official basketball games in the East. In the first game, St. John's led 16–12 early in the second half but couldn't finish off the "big" Westminster squad (with many 6'4" giants)—they tied the game at 16, 18, 19, and 21 before grabbing the lead themselves. In the second game, NYU extended its two-year winning streak to 20 games: trailing 14–10 early in the second half, the squad seized control with a 10–0 run.

Irish added two more dates to his schedule, featuring strong local teams like City College and

# Honorable Mention: The Nation's Mecca for College Hoops

**1. Jimmy V makes a national splash, February 21, 1980, Madison Square Garden**

From this upset, Jimmy V was born.

Jim Valvano spent several years stocking tiny Iona of New Rochelle with Long Island stars. He'd scout 'em all, then persuade them to come play for him with the promise that some day they'd beat a top-ranked team on prime-time TV in Madison Square Garden and bask in the spotlight. Although Valvano's scruples and honesty would later be called into question, this was the whole and absolute truth.

Led by star center Jeff Ruland, Iona faced second-ranked Louisville at 9:00 P.M. on network television. The Gaels—unranked and dismissed as a "pipsqueak" by *Sports Illustrated*—walked on 17-point underdogs. After Ruland dominated with 30 points and 21 rebounds, Iona walked off 17-point victors, 77–60.

Iona later lost in the second round of the NCAA, while Louisville never lost again en route to the title, but that only added luster to this shocker. It established the Gaels as a force—they earned five more NCAA invites in the following decade—and sent other top coaches scurrying to Long Island. But it also cost Iona its coach—after the 29–5 season, Valvano earned his spot with the big boys and was wooed down to North Carolina State. Three years later, he won an NCAA championship of his own.

**2. Bill Bradley and Cazzie Russell shoot it out on the Garden floor, December 30, 1964, Madison Square Garden**

No one gave Princeton a chance against bigger, stronger Michigan, the nation's top-ranked team. Yet the hoops world was still abuzz about this semifinal matchup in the 1964 Holiday Classic: people couldn't wait to see budding superstars Bill Bradley and Cazzie Russell—each of whom had poured in 36 points in opening-round wins—hit the Garden floor at the same time.

"Whaddaya say we just play them one on one," Princeton coach Bill Van Breda Kolff joked to Michigan assistant Jim Skala at a press conference. Everyone salivated at the notion.

The hype was worth it. Princeton's Bradley dazzled the crowd and nearly pulled off a miracle—he scored 41 points, grabbed nine boards, held his man to one point, and brought up the ball to break Michigan's press, staking Princeton to a 76–63 lead. But he was going it alone—no other Tiger reached double digits—and paid the price, committing tired fouls that sent him to the bench for good with 4:37 to go. The crowd cheered for two minutes, roaring so loudly that play was briefly halted.

Afterwards, Princeton was overmatched and repeatedly turned over the ball as Michigan went on a 17–2 run, led by Russell, who created magic down the stretch to win the game. He scored 19 of his 27 points in the second half (he also had nine boards). With three seconds left, Russell buried a 15-foot jumper from the left side, clinching the 80–78 win.

Later the Knicks found that having Russell and Bradley together in the Garden would often create more conflict than magic, but on this night both players staked their claim in the hearts of New York sports fans.

**3. The Big O comes to the Big Apple, January 9, 1958, Madison Square Garden**

Before he was the Big O, Oscar Robertson was just another kid from middle America in awe of the Big Apple. After his first day in New York, however, all Gotham was agape at the slick sophomore scorer.

That one day was January 9, 1958, when Robertson's Cincinnati squad played Seton Hall. "I was dumbstruck by the majestic chaos of New York City," he wrote in *The Big O*. But on the court, the boy who'd been born frail and sickly in a Tennessee farmhouse, then raised in Indianapolis, felt right at home.

After missing his first shot, the 6'5" scoring machine used his height and bulk, backing down his defender and spinning past for a lay-up. He buried jumpers, running hooks, and more lay-ups. "I didn't know how many points I had, how many baskets I'd made, how many I'd missed," Robertson recalled. Everyone else did: he outscored the entire Seton Hall team.

Robertson had 56 points—a new Garden record—when he was pulled with just under three minutes left, his team en route to a 118–54 rout. A special night anywhere but in New York, it made him a star as everyone from coaching legend Joe Lapchick to sportswriter Jimmy Cannon sang his praises. Cincinnati sold out the rest of its games that season—at home and on the road. The Big O had arrived.

Fordham and out-of-town contenders like Pitt, Purdue, and Kentucky. Thanks to his relentless promotion, the eight double-headers drew 99,528 people. In addition to putting college basketball and the Garden on the map at the same time in the same place, the Garden double-headers improved the game itself by encouraging standardized rules and officiating.

Soon more top teams wanted in as the New York press made schools famous, players celebrities, and hoops a major spectator sport. By 1938 basketball was so big that the Garden debuted the NIT. From 1942 to 1949, more than 500,000 fans a year came to see college basketball at Madison Square Garden; the NCAA joined the NIT there, while nationally the sport became a phenomenon, giving birth to new professional leagues that would develop into the NBA. By the time the point-shaving scandal chased many of college's biggest games away in 1951, the Knicks were ready to step in as a new basketball attraction. And when the Big East tournament was born in the 1980s, its roots traced back to Irish's inspiration. On some level, all college basketball, down to March Madness's nationally televised Final Four, owes a debt to a couple of low-scoring games on a cold December night in New York and to the man who brought it to life.

# 68. New York gets its first glimpse of a sports-mad future, May 27, 1823, Union Course

Long before Major League Baseball, the National Football League, and the National Basketball Association ruled the world of sports, long before there even was baseball, football, and basketball, much less a world of sports, there was a horse race. Not just any horse race, mind you, but a match race so intense, so relentlessly hyped, and so closely followed that it may well have marked the birth of our sports-mad society. When American Eclipse barreled down the track against Sir Henry at the Union Course in 1823, it seemed that everyone, not just in the city but in this young nation, went along for the ride.

American Eclipse, descended from the great English horse Eclipse, was an unbeaten nine-year-old champion born in Queens and owned by New Yorker Cornelius Van Ranst. Sir Henry was an unknown from North Carolina, while his owner, William Ransom Johnson, "the Napoleon of the Turf," was a Virginian.

This match race had more than just money at stake.

After the War of 1812 against Great Britain, people had soured on the idea of importing English horses, so this race, one of the first major showdowns between two American-born steeds, offered breeders of native horses a chance to prove their worth and affirm our national identity. More significantly, this race was the latest in a slew of races that attracted attention by pitting North against South, sharpening a deeply felt identity split heightened by the recent Missouri Compromise.

With Samuel Purdy aboard, American Eclipse wins the final two races to defeat Sir Henry in the famous match race at Union Course.

But what made this bigger than any previous North-South showdown was Johnson's formidable reputation in the racing world and the shocking amount of gambling that quickly piled up. Backers for Van Ranst and his partner, John Cox Stevens, and Johnson put up more than $20,000 as stakes, and then the men bet on top of that. Bankers grew nervous as folks bet all their cash holdings—one southerner put up five years' worth of tobacco crop. A local paper called *The Statesman* estimated that $150,000 to $200,000 was in play.

One publication proclaimed this the biggest national event since Thomas Jefferson and Aaron Burr's battle for the presidency had to be decided by the House of Representatives. (Burr, along with presidential candidate Andrew Jackson and Vice President Daniel Tompkins, attended the race.) The excitement was so great that *The Statesman* headlined one story "The Races," because "who will this week look at a newspaper paragraph which is not headed 'The Races'?"

The spectacular affair of May 27, 1823, transformed the Union Course in the town of Jamaica (now the Richmond Hill–Woodhaven area) into the country's most prominent racecourse. The race supposedly attracted 50,000 spectators, though that is probably an exaggeration. Regardless of the actual number, it was the largest sporting event to date. The New York Stock Exchange closed, and people across the nation were riveted. All local hotels were full (one-third of the crowd journeyed from the South), and *The Statesman* noted that "whoever is on this [Manhattan] side of the East River today may enjoy the benefits and pleasures of solitude to the highest degree. . . . The streets are silent as midnight."

In a tactical maneuver aimed at confounding his foe, Johnson had brought five horses north and did not publicly announce Sir Henry as his horse until a half-hour before post time. Then overflow from the stands poured onto the track, delaying the race's start. Victory required winning two of three races, each lasting four miles, nearly four times the length of today's Triple Crown races. Eclipse carried 126 pounds, nearly 20 pounds more than his young rival, but his owners ensured he was well rested, while Johnson was racing his horses hard to find the perfect foe. So the northerners were stunned when Henry aggressively took control, passing Eclipse early in the opening race. Henry turned back Eclipse's late charge, winning by a half-length and setting a new record time of 7 minutes, 37 seconds. With Henry's speed mark, America asserted its independence from England. (The Union Course's newfangled dirt track, as opposed to the traditional turf, also suddenly took hold as a part of racing's future.) Messengers rushed back to Manhattan with the news, and several investment houses closed for the day, fearing panic by Eclipse's heavy bettors.

In *The Great Match Race,* John Eisenberg blames the loss on a tactical error by Van Ranst; to everyone's surprise, the owner had ditched legendary jockey Samuel Purdy at the last minute, replacing him with the younger, more agile Billy Craft.

But Craft was also far less experienced, and Van Ranst blamed his lack of artistry—Eisenberg writes that he was inconsistent and indecisive; he also used the whip too much on Eclipse and may have cut the great stallion's testicle—for the horse's loss. Upon learning that Purdy was in the stands that day, Van Ranst sent Stevens to grovel and ask if he'd come back into the fold. But even after the 49-year-old Purdy agreed, Henry remained the three-to-one favorite for the second race. He sprinted out, hoping to wear down the older horse, but after trailing for nearly three miles, Purdy stunned the crowd when he pushed Eclipse inside and past Henry, beating him by 30 feet, in 7 minutes, 49 seconds, the second-fastest winning time on record.

This time Johnson switched jockeys, dumping a rider named John Walden for veteran trainer Arthur Taylor. But it was no use. Eclipse demonstrated a champion's stamina, leading the third race almost the entire way, even battling through a herd of fans who had spilled onto the track. Although he "was compelled to strain every nerve to secure the victory," according to the *Statesman,* he staved off one desperate rally by Henry in the third mile and won by three lengths, in 8 minutes, 24 seconds.

Although subsequent North-South match races further fed regional tensions, the distinctions between horses began blurring in the 1830s when Johnson became part-owner of Eclipse and brought him to stud down south. (Henry was bought by Stevens's brother and was moved north.) Thoroughbred racing endured up-and-down periods, but sports in general would not relinquish its hold on the public's imagination. And after this race, newspapers not only supported the idea of spectator sports as good for society but also touted big races as a way of attracting tourist dollars to their city, paving the way not only for the Triple Crown races but for the modern events, from the Super Bowl to the X Games, that define the business of the sports world.

# 69. St. John's revs up the Big East, March 12, 1983, Madison Square Garden

It had been three decades since the Garden was the center of the college basketball universe. It felt like centuries.

College hoops had been huge once—Nat Holman's CCNY teams, Clair Bee's LIU squads, and Joe Lapchik's St. John's were fan favorites in the 1930s and '40s. But after the infamous 1951 point-shaving scandal, college hoops at the Garden largely died, sending up only occasional

**Billy Goodwin of St. John's is sky-high after his team wins the Big East final over Boston College.**

flares as a smallish sideshow between Knick and Ranger games.

The mythology of the city game still held, but most talk was about kids who had left the city and made their name elsewhere: Lew Alcindor and Dean Meminger, Bernard King and Ernie Grunfeld, Billy Cunningham and Charlie Scott. Or they'd talk about those who didn't get out, the legends of the playgrounds, the Goat and the Destroyer and the Helicopter, wraiths whom only a privileged few in Harlem ever saw.

But in 1983 a tribal drumbeat rose out of the glorious past, a huge noise that boomed tradition yet set a cadence for a shout to the future:

*We are . . .*
*St. John's!*
*We are . . .*
*St. John's!*

The Big East Tournament, just four years old, was making its Madison Square Garden debut, with St. John's facing off in the final against Boston College. The old-timers were saying: This is how college basketball used to be. This is how college basketball oughta be.

Indeed, this was how college basketball would be for the next decade — bigger than ever thanks to a convergence of television, money, and opportunity. Big East commissioner Dave Gavitt had successfully designed a made-for-TV league featuring popular schools in the major East Coast media markets of New York, Washington, Boston, and Philly that played in front of an estimated 30 percent of the nation's TV homes and copied the successful Atlantic Coast Conference tournament. He'd auditioned his tourney off-Broadway in Hartford, Providence, and Syracuse for three years, but with the emergence of star players who'd write chapters in NCAA history (Patrick Ewing, Chris Mullin, and Ed Pinckney) and bigger-than-life coaches (Thompson and Boeheim and Carnesecca and Massimino), Gavitt was ready for the big town.

All year people had hoped that Looie Carnesecca's St. John's club could make a run here. Nine of the 11 kids were from the city or Long Island, so this was a home team in front of its home crowd. This kid Mullin from Brooklyn was the most estimable underestimated player you ever saw. The well-told secret was that he could shoot, he could handle, he had great body control, and at 6'6", he was too long for guards to cover and too quick for forwards. His story was a city version of midwestern corn: gym rat begs for the keys to the gym at his parish and hones his game on the green tile floor of Monsignor King Hall. In the semifinals the kid answered the call, erupting for 25 points in the second half, his lefty jumper burying Villanova.

The final was less a thriller than a coronation as the Redmen thwarted overachieving Boston College, led by 5'9" dynamo Michael Adams. St. John's played nearly flawless basketball, backing off the quicker Adams to take away his penetration, making him miss jumpers (he shot just 1–13). On offense, St. John's, burned by BC's press in two regular-season losses, sent Mullin and Bronx boy Billy Goodwin downcourt and hit them, wide receiver–style, with deep passes for easy lay-ups. The two also lit the Eagles up outside, launching rain-

## Honorable Mention: We Are St. John's

**1. St. John's edges Syracuse to win the Big East, March 8, 1986, Madison Square Garden**

The mid-'80s marked the zenith of the Big East—an era of star-filled, action-packed games—and the 1986 tournament final between St. John's and Syracuse on March 8 was the highest point of all at the Garden.

Syracuse built a 13-point lead, after shooting 73 percent from the floor, before St. John's Willie Glass finally shut down hot hand Rafael Addison and St. John's clawed back. Unheralded freshman Marco Baldi from Italy hit six straight points for the Redmen, and with 32 seconds left, Glass buried two free throws, trimming the lead to 69–68.

With star shooter Chris Mullin having graduated the previous year, the Redmen learned to share the spotlight, so when they got the ball back with 19 seconds left, coach Lou Carnesecca said that anyone with a good shot should take it. It wasn't Glass (who had 19 points), or John Wooden Award winner Walter Berry (16 points), or floor leader Mark Jackson (4–7 in the half). No, with eight seconds left, Ron Rowan, who had struggled against Syracuse's trapping defense, found himself in midair, firing a hanging, leaning jumper.

Rowan hit. It was the first time St. John's had led: 70–69. Still, eight seconds was plenty of time for Dwayne "Pearl" Washington, even though the Orangemen had no timeouts to set up a play.

Just two city kids: Washington from Brooklyn versus Berry from the Bronx. Washington, with 20 points and 14 assists, swerved and spun downcourt, eyes on the prize. Berry raced over from the opposite side of the lane. "He *always* makes you think he's going right and then goes left," Berry said.

Washington started up for the game-winner, but before he could launch it, Berry, perfectly positioned, smothered the ball. The game, the Big East, and the memories belonged to St. John's.

bows from 20 feet and more. Mullin, the tournament MVP, finished with 23 points, Goodwin with 20. St. John's was also helped by its size in the pivot — after BC pulled within 40–39, 6'11" center Bill Wennington scored seven points, building St. John's back to 47–41, a lead that wasn't truly threatened again.

St. John's 85–77 victory gave them a school record of 27 victories. The triumph not only ended the tournament but also marked a beginning. This '83 tournament marked the return to the national stage of New York hoops and was the harbinger of a run of Big East dominance as the tournament helped convince a generation of top talent like Alonzo Mourning, Pearl Washington, and Mark Jackson that the Big East was the place to be. Two years later, Georgetown, St. John's, and Villanova reached the Final Four together — with 'Nova beating the Hoyas in one of the most memorable games ever — and by decade's end conference stepchild Seton Hall would take a nucleus of New York natives to the NCAA final.

But there was a flip side to success. The attention and intensity created a boiling cauldron that included a penchant for fisticuffs and creeping commercialism, which became noticeable when Georgetown's Ewing helped pioneer the wearing of the Nike logo. The big bucks that lifted the Big East to unimaginable heights would ultimately tear it apart as college sports became an even bigger business in the Bowl Championship Series (BCS) era.

But that was all in the future. On this one day, as the Big East announced itself loud and clear with this first salvo in the Garden, the Garden crowd grew louder and louder, the drumbeat ever steadier:

*We are . . .*
*St. John's!*
*We are . . .*
*St. John's!*

## We Are St. John's (CONTINUED)

**2. A team effort and one big play bring St. John's the NIT, March 20, 1959, Madison Square Garden**

In 1958, St. John's, trying to win their first NIT since 1944, had fallen in the semifinal. In 1959 they made it to the finals but ran into top-seeded Bradley. It took everything the team had to pull it off — both a well-balanced performance and one big play at the end.

Four players finished in double digits: Al Seiden, with 22; tournament MVP Tony Jackson, with 21 (and 27 rebounds); Lou Roethel, with 12; and Gus Alfieri, who'd finish with 15 and who saved the game in overtime.

St. John's overcame a first-half deficit for a 63–61 lead before Bradley's Al Saunders tied the game in the final minute. Then, with less than 90 seconds left in OT, Saunders intercepted a pass to help whittle the latest St. John's lead back to two. But with 30 seconds to go, Alfieri drove to the lane and hit his shot even while being hacked. He calmly nailed the free throw to finish off Bradley. St. John's won 76–71, becoming the first team to capture three NIT championships.

**3. Joe Lapchick is unconscious in St. John's NIT win, March 24, 1944, Madison Square Garden**

Joe Lapchick was an excitable man. He was always pacing, leaping, clutching, shouting. But in the 1944 NIT finals, Lapchick inadvertently added an unusual move to his repertoire.

St. John's was the defending NIT champ, but the loss of key players to World War II had many experts doubting that they'd even reach the final. Yet there they were, staying close against the favored DePaul Blue Demons and formidable George Mikan. Then, in the first half, the tightly wound Lapchick suddenly fainted and lay unconscious for at least a minute. With their coach kayoed, the Redmen spurt, grabbing the lead from DePaul. "I dealt strategy a helluva blow," Lapchick quipped after coming to and seeing what had transpired.

St. John's held on — up 26–24 at the half and 35–31 six minutes into the second — until Mikan fouled out and the Blue Demons crumbled. St. John's coasted to a 47–39 victory, and when it was finally over, even Lapchick relaxed.

# 70. The "Four Horsemen of Notre Dame" triumph over Army, October 18, 1924, Polo Grounds

One fateful fall afternoon, George Strickler stepped into the fray and wiped clean the slate of sports journalism, unleashing rivers of purple prose that flowed on black ink across this great nation, lifting along with them a university, a genre of journalism, and indeed an entire sport.

That's an approximation of how Grantland Rice, the *New York Herald-Tribune*'s master of breathless extravagance, might have started this book's recounting of the 1924 Notre Dame–Army game at the Polo Grounds. It's both more poetic and less descriptive than the simpler but more accurate modern style that has forsaken him.

George Strickler helped produce one of the biggest scores in college football history without playing a single down. With a stray pop culture reference, a goofy photo op, and a large assist from legendarily hyperbolic sportswriter Grantland Rice, Strickler begat the iconic "Four Horsemen of Notre Dame." In one great rush, this accident of history forever enhanced the stature of the school, its backfield, sportswriting, and all of college football.

Either approach certainly tackles a long-standing myth—that it was Rice alone who remade the sports landscape with his account of the game that famously began, "Outlined against a blue-gray October sky, the Four Horsemen rode again. . . ." Without Strickler, that image might not have found its way into print, and history might not have granted this game its status as symbol of an era.

Notre Dame and Army had made headlines beginning with their first game at West Point in 1913 when the Ramblers upset undefeated Army 35–13. The forward pass had been legal for less than a decade, the ball's circumference had been reduced the previous year to make passing easier, and this Notre Dame squad—led by quarterback Gus Dorias and an end by the name of Knute Rockne—was the first to feature a real aerial attack. Rockne became coach in 1918 and transformed Notre Dame into football's great powerhouse; his team became so popular that games with no admission charge at West Point gave way to the big game in the big city, where in 1923 the rivals debuted at Ebbets Field and had to turn 15,000 people away. College football was coming of age. And thanks to the unlikely combo of Strickler and Rice, October 18, 1924, at the Polo Grounds would be its coming-out party.

Although New York was only an hour south of West Point, it felt like a hometown crowd for Notre Dame thanks to thousands of what would become known as "the Subway Alumni." They'd come to see the backfield of Harry Stuhldreher, Jim Crowley, Don Miller, and Elmer Layden, and in the second quarter this group gave the fans their money's worth while giving birth to their own legend. Crowley slithered for 15 yards on a reverse. Layden ate up 6 or 7 more through left tackle. Miller pushed through for almost another 10, Stuhldreher

**Inspired by Grantland Rice's line in his column, Notre Dame student press assistant George Strickler assembles his team's celebrated backfield for what will become an iconic photo.**

connected with Crowley for 12 yards, and Crowley rushed for 5 more. Then Miller rampaged around the right side for 20 yards. Crowley drove within yards of the goal line, and Layden scored the touchdown. Soon after, the offense again slammed its way to the Army 10 before an intercepted pass ended the drive. Though only up 6–0 at halftime, Notre Dame dominated the second quarter, racking up eight first downs while yielding none.

It was at halftime that the game headed for the history books. Strickler, a lowly student press assistant for Notre Dame, commented to several sportswriters that Notre Dame's backfield reminded him of a Rudolph Valentino movie, *The Four Horsemen of the Apocalypse,* which he and the players had watched a few days earlier back in South Bend. He was just making conversation, that's all. Except that Rice, the fabulist par excellence whose presence had already lent the game an air of importance, overheard the comment and soon translated the observation into a memorable piece of American sports mythology.

The third quarter was all Notre Dame. After Layden intercepted a pass, the backfield plowed 22 yards in three plays; Crowley then ditched two would-be tacklers, stiff-armed another, and raced 21 yards into the corner of the end zone. 13–0. Notre Dame nearly scored twice more, stopped once by an Army interception and once by Army's tough four-down stand on their own 9. (Army's lone score came near the end when punts and penalties started the Cadets inside Notre Dame's 20-yard line.)

The 13–7 win was hardly overwhelming for a team that had lost only once each in 1922 and 1923 and was en route to a 10–0 season capped by a trouncing of undefeated Stanford in the Rose Bowl. The *World* credited Notre Dame for having a "soundly coached team," and the *Times,* though praising the "speed, power and precision" of Rockne's "football machine"—especially the "poetry of motion" in the backfield—also had kind words for "Army's brave stand and gallant counterattack." It seemed like just another W in a long string of impressive Ws, not an all-time classic.

But Rice was someone who once said, "When a sportswriter stops making heroes out of athletes, it's time to get out of the business." Inspired by Strickler's halftime snippet, he showed, in his signature style, why he would be in the business for decades to come.

> Outlined against a blue-gray October sky, the Four Horsemen rode again. In dramatic lore they are known as Famine, Pestilence, Destruction and Death. These are only aliases. Their real names are Stuhldreher, Miller, Crowley and Layden. They formed the crest of the South Bend cyclone before which another fighting Army football team was swept over the precipice. . . .
>
> A cyclone can't be snared. It may be surrounded, but somewhere it breaks through to keep on going. When the cyclone starts from South Bend, where the candle lights still gleam through the Indiana sycamores, those in the way must take to storm cellars at top speed.

There are several problems beyond the florid style, which inspired a generation of imitators (and some stats that Rice got wrong). As Red Smith later pointed out, only someone lying on the field would have seen the players outlined against the sky. Moreover, for all their skills, this foursome, topping out at 162 pounds, were hardly physically imposing; Army was not swept away (they kept it closer than any other 1924 foe); and if this team was a cyclone that couldn't be snared, then why had it lost in '22 and '23 to Nebraska, the one top team with a significant size advantage on the Four Horsemen?

Also, how and why does one "surround" a cyclone?

The article ran on the *Herald-Tribune*'s front page and was syndicated in 100 newspapers, but the story still could easily have died the death of so many daily reports. Rice largely ditched the Horsemen concept after the first paragraph, playing up his cyclone imagery and throwing around references to tigers, antelopes, tanks, and motorcycles as well. (He'd still be recycling his "South Bend cyclone" phrase five years later to describe the 1929 Notre Dame offense.) Later in the week he moved on completely, not even bothering to preview Notre Dame's next game.

The savvy Strickler, however, called his dad back in South Bend and had him rent four horses from a corral next to his saloon. Upon the team's return home, Strickler posed the four athletes on the steeds, clutching footballs and looking a bit uncomfortable. He sent the photo to wire services and newspapers around the country, and they rode the ploy for all it was worth. By the following weekend, every columnist was referring to the newfound celebrities as "the Four Horsemen," and Rice, the 1920s Roaring Hypester, was touting them further as a way of praising his own acumen.

Notre Dame would play better games and have better backfields, but this confluence of events made these men and this game symbols of the Golden Age. It was an era when sportswriters polished history to a gleam and swung for the fences to create larger-than-life sports legends. And in this postwar boom, the Jazz Age public was ready to think big.

Sport was moving front and center in America—this game was the first one broadcast to radio, airing on two New York stations, WJZ and WEAF, and their affiliates. By the following year, newspaper coverage was double that of 1915. Although much of this new interest stemmed from genuine public demand, sportswriters like Rice certainly stirred the pot. From 1921 to 1930, attendance at college football games doubled and receipts tripled while universities devoted financial resources to the sport, building huge new stadiums. A skeptical minority complained about the business of sports usurping academics and sportsmanship, but cheering fans drowned out those voices.

As countless publications echoed Strickler's photo echoing Rice's article echoing the original game itself, the reality faded — the four players, Notre Dame, college football, and the sportswriter and his "Gee Whiz" approach to sportswriting all got caught up in the cyclone of glory.

# 71. Chris Evert becomes the "It Girl" with her comeback win, September 4, 1971, West Side Tennis Club

She turned heads because she was a pretty, young thing, but she captivated everyone because of her gutsy play and icy determination. Chris Evert was not the first teen prodigy, but in an era filled with veterans like Billie Jean King and Margaret Court, along with one-handed backhands, serve-and-volley tactics, and uncertainty about the viability of the women's tour, Evert revolutionized the women's game.

On September 4, 1971, in her first Open at Forest Hills, this 16-year-old perky blonde with a 12-tournament, 44-match winning streak landed on the stadium court for her second-round match against fourth-seeded Mary Ann Eisel.

She was not yet the Ice Maiden. "I was petrified," Evert said afterwards of being thrust center stage. Her wins had largely been against lesser lights or on clay, which favored her relentless baseline game. But on the grass against one of the surface's top players, she was unable to simply grind down her opponent. And so, on the same day that collegiate champ Jim Connors got bumped in the second round of the men's draw, Evert — an amateur who had taken two weeks off from high school in Fort Lauderdale for this tournament — seemed headed for home.

She lost a close first set 6–4 and trailed 6–5 in the second when Eisel stockpiled three match points. As television announcers Bud Collins and Jack Kramer gave her a warm, "nice try, kid," send-off, Evert suddenly showed Forest Hills and a national television audience that she had the makings of a champion.

On Eisel's first effort, Evert set the tone, whistling a big backhand service return down the line. Then, on a second serve, Evert mashed a crosscourt forehand winner. The crowd erupted, shaking Eisel, who'd been mixing shots brilliantly. As Eisel focused (unsuccessfully) on steadying herself, Evert continued playing predator, even as she fended off four more match points before breaking serve on a sizzling crosscourt forehand passing shot.

Evert easily captured the tiebreaker 5–1, then crushed her demoralized foe 6–1 in the third set.

**In her first U.S. Open, Chris Evert pulls off a stunning comeback against Mary Ann Eisel.**

King, who'd come over to watch the rookie, was impressed by how she handled the pressure, saying later: "A star was born in my eyes that match."

This tournament had seemed a bit dreary: Wimbledon champ Evonne Goolagong had stayed home, defending Open champion Margaret Court was pregnant, and top contender Virginia Wade was injured; in addition, many top men—including the past two champs, Rod Laver and Ken Rosewall—were boycotting the tournament over a dispute between their pro circuit and the International Lawn Tennis Federation. So this win made Evert an instant sensation. The *New York Times* dubbed her "Cinderella in Sneakers," and all her matches were moved to stadium court to meet public demand.

"She was the It Girl," says tennis writer Joel Drucker. "King laid the template for women's ten-

# Honorable Mention: Never Say Never

**1. Agassi and Blake play their hearts out, September 7, 2005, National Tennis Center**

There were two great stories at the U.S. Open in 2005, and when they collided in the quarterfinals, they stirred up one of the most memorable matches in Open history.

James Blake had captured the public's imagination, upsetting the 2nd and 19th seeds to reach his first quarterfinals just one year after enduring the most horrifying stretch imaginable—losing his father to cancer, breaking his neck in a practice mishap, and having his face paralyzed by shingles. It was a feel-good story enhanced by his own boisterous rooting section, which showed up daily from Connecticut.

But Andre Agassi was the fan favorite, the image-conscious rebel turned family man and philanthropist, the squanderer of talent turned symbol of diligence and perseverance. Plagued by a creaky back, the 35-year-old was thought to be winding down before he charged his way through the early rounds.

Each man lavished extravagant praise on the other. But only one could win. From the start it appeared that would be Blake, 25, whose explosive shots and aggressive tactics made Agassi look old. At one point, Blake reeled off 12 of 13 points, and he captured the first two sets, 6–3, 6–3.

When Blake broke Agassi for a 3–2 lead in the third, a few fans started filing out. But Agassi turned the tide with a break of his own, then found the strength to outlast his younger foe. He zipped through four straight games to take the third set and captured the fourth, 6–3, as well.

Blake regained his stride, however, and in the fifth set even served for the match at 5–4. But after an ace, Agassi showed yet again that he was the best returner of his generation (which by 2005 was really a second generation). Agassi pummeled three straight returns that Blake couldn't handle and then broke him.

The two went to a tiebreaker—the first fifth-set tiebreaker in Agassi's 20 years at the Open—and again Blake surged ahead only to have Agassi patiently work his way back. Blake took a 3–0 lead and had two serves at 5–4. But Agassi ripped a winner on the return, and then Blake's big swing led to another unforced error. Blake saved one match point, but when Agassi got a second shot, he nailed one last winner off the service return for an 8–6 triumph. "It couldn't have been more fun to lose," Blake said to him at the net.

Agassi, the oldest man in the semis since Jimmy Connors in 1991, managed to turn back another young American, Robby Ginepri, to become the oldest man in the finals since Ken Rosewall in 1974. There he actually split the first two sets against unbeatable Roger Federer and even went up a break in the third at 4–2. Although Federer chopped down the fairy-tale finish to win another Grand Slam title, the story of the tournament was Andre Agassi, and the match everyone would remember was his comeback against James Blake.

**2. Jennifer Capriati's comeback is undone by Justine Henin-Hardenne's, September 5, 2003, National Tennis Center**

Jennifer Capriati was a feel-good comeback story; she'd turned around a troubled life and resurrected an off-the-rails career with back-to-back Australian Open titles. She was at it again in the 2003 U.S. Open semifinals when she stormed back from a 4–1 deficit to seize a decisive 6–4, 5–3, advantage over French Open champ Justine Henin-Hardenne. With the crowd behind her and with the Williams sisters—winners of the four previous Opens—sidelined, the 27-year-old Capriati, pumping fists and shouting aloud, had the confidence of a winner. Then she ran into a better comeback, pulled off by the undersized Henin-Hardenne, a high-strung player who suddenly displayed the cool fearlessness of Chris Evert or Tracy Austin.

Two points from victory, Capriati sizzled a crosscourt forehand, but the 5′5″, 126-pound Belgian tore in, intercepted it, and dropped a volley just over the net. In the next game, Henin-Hardenne broke serve by retrieving a superb lob and responding with a better one. Capriati's exuberance dampened, and she let the set slip away, but she recovered to grab a 5–2 third-set lead. But again Henin-Hardenne persevered, holding and then breaking serve even as she broke down physically—dehydration was causing cramping in her left thigh. Capriati again came within two points, but Henin-Hardenne cranked up her play or Capriati choked each time. In the tiebreaker, Henin-Hardenne remained indomitable even

nis, but Chrissie changed how people thought about the sport. It was the beginning of the princess era of tennis."

By the time she deposed veterans Françoise Durr and Lesley Hunt in two more come-from-behind three-setters, "the only player, male or female, that anyone talked about was Chris Evert," Herbert Warren Wind wrote in *The New Yorker.* With New York's crowd roaring for the youngster, Durr and Hunt both left the court in tears; Hunt sobbed, "I can beat Chris Evert, but not twelve thousand people."

Most pros snubbed Evert during the tournament; thinking her shyness was aloofness, they resented an amateur reducing their earnings and seducing the crowd while coolly dissecting their games. Finally King, the tour's leading force and a forceful women's rights advocate, called a meeting. She told the players that Evert was the next big star and essential to their future, so they should stop the pettiness and start accepting her. Still, King—the draw's sole superstar—was privately panicked: if this amateur beat her too, it could undermine the credibility of the pro tour.

In the first of her 17 Open semifinals, Evert's winning streak finally ended when King beat her in straight sets. Still, tennis fans had a new favorite. In her book on Evert and Martina Navratilova, *The Rivals,* Johnette Howard notes that when Evert returned home, she received a congratulatory telegram from King and roses from Fort Lauderdale's mayor, while *Life* magazine sent a reporter and photographer to follow her around at school.

"It was big for the Open, but it was a seminal moment for women's sports," says tennis commentator Mary Carillo, who as a teen player herself was inspired by Evert's performance. "The women's tour was new and needed to show how good the players were as athletes, but they also needed to show they had a marketable product. Chris was the whole package."

## Never Say Never (CONTINUED)

while doubled over. She kept the first three rallies going until Capriati blew three backhands, and after 183 minutes, Henin-Hardenne held on for a 7–4 win.

Conquest complete, she collapsed, then limped off the court, unable to even carry her rackets. While Capriati felt like her "heart was being ripped out," Henin-Hardenne had an IV stuck in her. She finally left at 3:00 A.M., uncertain whether she'd play the next day's final. She did, beating fellow Belgian and rival Kim Clijsters, but the semifinal remained the tournament's biggest thrill. "This match has just become part of the USA Network rain delay library," said commentator John McEnroe. "We will be watching this for years to come."

**3. Manuel Orantes digs the deepest hole, then climbs out, September 6, 1975, West Side Tennis Club**

You can't bury yourself much deeper than this: Manuel Orantes lost the first two sets of his U.S. Open semifinals match against Guillermo Vilas. After winning the third set, his game collapsed completely, and he fell behind 5–0.

That's right, 5–0.

Then Orantes fell behind on his own serve. Three match points for Vilas. Three times Orantes escaped. He'd avoided the schneid, but no one expected anything more.

5–1.

Vilas earned two match points on his serve. Twice more Orantes escaped. It was nice to see him make Vilas work.

5–2.

Orantes held serve. Well, that was nothing extraordinary.

5–3.

The turning point. Vilas turned cautious, and Orantes didn't miss. He broke Vilas's serve en route to a stunning 7–5 comeback. In the final set, Orantes broke once more at 4–4 and walked off after 3 hours and 44 minutes with a fantastical five-set comeback.

Orantes's day was not over. After dealing with the press, he made it back to his hotel room at 2:00 A.M. and found his bathroom flooded. For this mess, he had to call a plumber.

The next day, Orantes faced defending champion Jimmy Connors. Orantes lobbed Connors into oblivion in straight sets, the only time in history someone found playing Connors in a final to be the most relaxing part of his weekend.

# 72. Robin Ventura hits a grand-slam single, October 17, 1999, Shea Stadium

A roller coaster balanced on a giant spinning top riding up and down on an oversized yo-yo.

This vertiginous image is the best possible metaphor for the 1999 New York Mets' season. Even by the Mets' wild and wacky standards, this was a madcap ride, one that required a winter's worth of deep breaths. The game that best summed it up was their final win, a 15-inning, rain-drenched marathon that produced the most bizarre ending to an important game since "Merkle's Boner" in 1908: the Walk-off Grand-Slam Single.

It was a long, strange trip to that point, however, and not just through the first 14 innings of that fifth National League Champion Series game at Shea Stadium.

In late April, the Mets had fashioned a six-game winning streak, then lost six of seven; by June 5, they had stalled at 27–28. Coaches Bob Apodaca, Tom Robson, and Randy Niemann were fired, and manager Bobby Valentine presumably had his head on the chopping block. The Mets responded by capturing 15 of 18. Consistency, it seemed, might prove elusive.

By August 6, they'd soared from third to first place and were 67–43, one and a half games ahead of their nemesis, the Atlanta Braves. It didn't last, of course, but September 19 found them with a stellar 92–58 record and a four-game wild-card edge over Cincinnati. Mike Piazza was banging his way to 40 home runs, the pitching staff looked solid, and the infield was too good to be believed — John Olerud, Edgardo Alfonzo, Rey Ordonez, and Robin Ventura had been hailed by *Sports Illustrated* as perhaps the greatest defensive quartet ever.

*Crash.*

The yo-yo's string got tangled, the top went off its axis, and the roller coaster derailed as the Mets lost eight of nine, ending with an 11-inning heartbreaker against Atlanta that seemed to signal not just the end of the season but the end of the line for a team that had choked away its wild-card spot the previous year by losing its final five games. Another loss would mean elimination, a heavy blow for a franchise that hoped to end what had been a depressing, ugly decade on a high note. As the choker label tightened it seemed the end for the tightly wound Valentine, who was convinced (often justifiably) that he knew more about baseball than anyone else but who had managed more than 1,700 games without reaching the postseason.

After tumbling to the depths of the abyss, however, the Mets bounded out, seemingly unruffled. They won two straight, and then on Sunday, October 3 — the anniversary of Bobby Thomson's celebrated home run — Bobby Valentine's father-in-law Ralph Branca watched the Mets win a finale thriller in the bottom of the ninth: rookie Melvin Mora got just his fifth hit of the year and scored the winning run when Pittsburgh reliever Brad Clontz (Mora's former teammate in the Mets system) wild-pitched him home.

The Miracle Mets were back.

The Reds won their game at 12:30 A.M., tying New York at 96–66. To reach the postseason for the first time since 1988 the Mets needed to win the kind of tiebreaker playoff that Branca had helped make famous. In Cincinnati on October 4 for their fourth straight do-or-die gem, Al Leiter pitched a two-hit shutout. That sent the Mets to Arizona and the NLDS on October 5. The Mets smacked Cy Young winner Randy Johnson and won on Alfonzo's ninth-inning grand slam before finally clinching the series back in New York on backup catcher Todd Pratt's 10th-inning homer in Game 4. With the Yankees romping through the AL playoffs, a Subway Series suddenly seemed feasible.

Except, of course, for the Atlanta Braves.

Since the Braves, baseball's best regular-season team since 1991, had moved into the East in 1995, they'd repeatedly dashed the Mets' hopes. The Braves' eighth straight NLCS would be no different. Articles stirred up bad blood by insinuating that the Braves did not respect the Mets and quoting Atlanta slugger Chipper Jones and closer John Rocker about their low opinions of Met fans as well.

Then Atlanta shut New York up on the field. In the first three games, Atlanta's heralded rotation of Greg Maddux, Kevin Millwood, and Tom Glavine shut the Mets down 4–2, 4–3, and 1–0. In Game 4, Rick Reed blew a 1–0 lead at Shea Stadium on eighth-inning homers by Brian Jordan and Ryan Klesko. It was bad enough losing to Atlanta, but going down meekly in front of the home crowd would be particularly humiliating. Instead, the Mets roused themselves for a frantic finish that few would ever forget. Rallying in their half of the eighth, Roger Cedeno and Mora executed a double steal against Rocker, then scored on Olerud's single. Still, that was just one game, a face-saver. To make the Braves take notice the Mets needed to send the series back to Atlanta. They did it in memorable fashion in Game 5.

Facing extinction for the sixth time in 17 days, the Mets asserted themselves immediately when Olerud reached Maddux for a two-run homer in the opening frame. In the fourth, Atlanta chased starter Masato Yoshii with three hits and a walk, but Orel Hershiser retired the side, keeping the score tied at 2–2.

**Todd Pratt inadvertently invents the grand-slam single when he interrupts Robin Ventura's trip around the bases to celebrate the Mets' 15th-inning win over Atlanta in the NLCS.**

That was it for scoring for a long, long time. But all through the damp night both teams ratcheted up the tension, parking runners on base in nearly every inning, threatening without following through—each team escaped a bases-loaded jam in the sixth via a double play. The Braves, who'd set a postseason record by leaving 19 men on base, loaded the bases again in the seventh, on two walks and a hit batter, but having jumped into the frying pan, the Mets, who cycled through four pitchers that inning (with lefty Dennis Cook inserted for two pitches solely to get Bobby Cox to remove the lefty Klesko), jumped right back out.

The Mets continued watching their season pass before their eyes as Atlanta left five men on from the 8th through the 11th. In the 13th, they nearly ended the Mets' year with two outs when light-hitting Keith Lockhart singled off newly arrived Octavio Dotel and Chipper Jones doubled to right. But Lockhart briefly slowed down, unsure of the ball's location, and Mora's great peg and Alfonzo's crisp relay caught him at home.

The 14th was relatively quiet—except when the fans were treated to a "14th-inning stretch" and a second shot at "Take Me Out to the Ball Game," whose line "I don't care if I never get back" was sounding frighteningly realistic. With the rain a steady nuisance, the field, players, and fans were pretty much soaked, and any run across the outfield grass was an adventure. In the 15th, the Braves capitalized on the sloppy conditions to send the hopes of Met fans plummeting. Walt Weiss singled and stole second. With two out, Lockhart hit a ball to deep center. On a normal field, any decent center fielder would probably have run it down. But the field was a pond, and the Mets had a bench player in center, and a shortstop at that. Shawon Dunston could not find traction, and the ball landed for a triple as the Braves finally seized a 3–2 lead.

The veteran Dunston, a Brooklyn native, felt awful. Approaching home plate to lead off the Mets' last chance, he expected to be roundly booed. Instead, the fans, trying to will one more fantastic finish, cheered him long and hard. Inspired, Dunston fought Brave rookie Kevin McGlinchy, fouling off six pitches with a full count before singling to center on the 12th pitch. There was life yet.

McGlinchy was rattled, and Dunston cranked the cheers from desperate to hopeful by stealing second. Braves manager Bobby Cox could have brought in Game 6 starter Kevin Millwood or Game 7 starter Tom Glavine, but he was unwilling to disrupt his schedule. Pinch hitter Matt Franco, showing superb discipline for someone who'd sat waiting for more than five hours to swing the bat, walked on a full count. Edgardo Alfonzo bunted the runners along, and Olerud was given a free pass. After four intentional balls, McGlinchy misplaced the strike zone and walked Todd Pratt to send home Dunston with the tying run.

That brought up the 126th batter of the night, Robin Ventura. The Met third baseman had provided Gold Glove defense, 32 homers, 120 RBIs, and a .301 average. But a torn cartilage in his left knee had derailed his swing, leaving him hitting on one leg. Facing McGlinchy, Ventura had just one hit in 18 at-bats; back in the seventh, some boos had even surfaced when he hit into an inning-ending double play.

Ventura, however, loved hitting with the bases loaded (he'd finish with 18 career grand slams, tied for third all-time), and this assignment felt particularly easy: McGlinchy absolutely had to throw strikes, particularly after falling behind 2–1, and Ventura knew that even a medium-deep fly ball would win the game with speedy Roger Cedeno pinch-running at third.

McGlinchy's pitch was right out over the plate, and Ventura turned on it. Nearly five hours after Olerud had homered for the Mets' first two runs, Ventura's liner through the raindrops cleared the fence in right for a grand slam . . . kind of.

Having waited a new record of 5 hours, 46 minutes, the Mets started celebrating as soon as the ball rocketed off Ventura's bat: knowing it was deep enough to score Cedeno, Bobby Valentine didn't even see the ball clear the fence and didn't learn that it had until much later. No one was more enthusiastic than Pratt, who stopped before second and turned back, intercepting Ventura with a tremendous hug befitting the muscular catcher's nickname of "Tank." Cedeno had scored and the game was over, and once Pratt lifted Ventura into the air, the hero's home run trot was over too.

And thus, the Grand-Slam Single was born. Instead of a 7–3 final and a homer and four RBIs credited to Ventura, the Mets eked out a 4–3 win, and Ventura had the longest single known to man. It was a perfect fit for this team and this season.

No team had ever come back from 3–0 in

games, but the Mets had forced the series back to Atlanta. In Game 6 there, they battled back from a 5–0 first-inning deficit, again dragging the Braves into extra innings before finally coming up short. But unlike other lost postseason series—the 1973 World Series, the 1988 NLCS, the 2000 World Series—this one had Met fans putting aside their "It could've been . . ." moans to remember how happy they were again singing and dancing in the rain.

# 73. John Starks dunks over Michael Jordan in the Eastern Conference Finals, May 25, 1993, Madison Square Garden

Teaming with Patrick Ewing, John Starks burst off a pick-and-roll, finally ditching Chicago's B. J. Armstrong, who had overplayed the whole game to prevent just such a play. With two quick dribbles, Starks surged toward the basket along the right baseline before he saw his opening filled by 6'10" shot-blocker Horace Grant. Never a master planner, the 6'3" Starks leaped toward the bucket, leaving from farther out than he intended. Suddenly, in midair, with a playoff game on the line against archrival Chicago, Starks discovered that he'd run into not only Grant but, coming in from the lane, His Airness himself, Michael Jordan.

Look, be honest. During the Michael Jordan era, the Chicago Bulls were just plain better than the Knicks. The Knicks were gritty and gutty and colorful, and the Bulls provided plenty to root against, but New York had no answer to the world champions. There was Scottie Pippen and Phil Jackson and the Triangle Offense, but especially Jordan, who'd torched the Knicks for 40 or more three times in the 1989 playoffs, for 42 more in Game 7 in 1992, and who would retaliate after this Game 2 of the 1993 Eastern Conference Finals with a 54-pointer and then a triple-double.

But in this indelible moment, none of that mattered. The Knicks had won Game 1 behind Starks's four three-pointers down the stretch. Starks had also contained Jordan, prompting the game's greatest player—who had spoken dismissively of Starks in 1992—to concede, "Starks is totally confident, a 100 percent better player than a year ago, a threat at both ends of the court."

Starks was a fan favorite and finally a starter after emerging as a sixth man the previous year, but he remained mercurial. He was a streaky shooter who'd lift the team one game then drag it down the next, and a rugged, emotional defender who charged up the Garden crowd but committed unnecessary fouls and boneheaded transgressions. (He'd thrown water at former teammate Mark Jackson, leading to a benching by coach Pat Riley, and in the playoffs he'd head-butted Indiana's Reggie Miller, prompting a public scolding from Patrick Ewing.) His passion for hard work, almost lovable intensity, maddening inconsis-

**John Starks dunks . . . over 6'10" Horace Grant . . . and over His Airness, Michael Jordan.**

tency, and so-close-to-greatness-but-never-quite-there performance made Starks, as much as Charles Oakley, a symbol of Riley's Knicks. And Starks was a quintessential New Yorker — like so many classic success stories, he'd overcome hardship elsewhere in order to make it to the capital of the world.

Starks grew up in Oklahoma. Fatherless among six siblings, he often went hungry or shoplifted food to get by. When he was kicked off the high school basketball team, he began stealing cars. He dropped out of college both for financial and disciplinary reasons and bagged groceries in a late-night shift. He landed at a junior college, where his play finally earned him another shot at college and later a spot with the Golden State Warriors. Almost immediately bounced down to the Continental Basketball Association, Starks kept scrapping until he finally caught the Knicks' attention.

In 1993 the Knicks had 60 regular-season wins, the league's best defense, and — after beating Charlotte and Indiana — home court advantage against Chicago in the Eastern Conference Finals. When they built a 14-point second-half lead in Game 2 while shutting down Jordan, it appeared they might dethrone the Bulls.

Chicago responded with a run that pulled the Bulls within 91–88 with 47 seconds left.

Then Starks made his move, soaring up and over Grant . . . and over Jordan too, audaciously switching the ball into his left hand and slamming down a thunderous dunk.

Let's repeat: John Starks dunked over Michael Jordan to ice the game. Starks didn't even realize at the time what had happened or how significant it would be to New Yorkers. For perhaps the first time in his magnificent career, Jordan, as David Aldridge wrote in the next day's *Washington Post,* had been "postered." Indeed, the photo of "The Dunk"—as it was immediately called in New York—became a hot item. (The stark contrast of this shot and Starks's notorious 2–18 fiasco in Game 7 of the 1994 Finals perfectly encapsulates his up-and-down career.) No other moment for this Knick team and its fans would be so wondrous, so hopeful.

Sure, after sparking this 96–91 win Starks went 2–7 with seven turnovers in Game 3 before being ejected for slapping at Jordan's royal hands, and yes, the Knicks lost four straight and the series, and we all know they never beat Jordan's Bulls when it counted. But for one moment on May 25, 1993, when Starks headed skyward with Madison Square Garden rocking with roars of approval and disbelief, New Yorkers felt they actually had the better of them.

## 74. Bernard King scores 44 in Game 6 to keep the Knicks alive against the Celtics, May 11, 1984, Madison Square Garden

Here's what Bernard King had done: playing with two dislocated fingers and pain so severe that he had to learn new ways to catch and shoot the ball, the New York Knick forward *averaged* more than 42 points per game in the five-game playoff win over Detroit.

Here's what Boston Celtic Cedric Maxwell said prior to guarding King in the Eastern Conference Semifinal: "He ain't getting forty on us. We're going to stop the bitch."

Here's what King did after being held to 21 points per game in the first three games against Boston: he averaged 39 points over the next three, twice breaking the magic 40 mark to shock the heavily favored Celtics and force a seventh game. The most significant performance—the biggest thrill the Madison Square Garden crowd experienced in the 1980s—came on May 11 in Game 6: with the Knicks facing elimination and Boston knowing exactly who'd be doing all the shooting, King rained in a series-high 44 points in a huge win.

New York had been constantly shamed by Boston during the Bill Russell era, and after a close rivalry during the early 1970s, Boston had soared high above again during the early years of the Larry Bird era. In that period the Knicks won just one playoff series while the Celtics won a championship and also reached the conference finals. During the 1984–85 regular season, the 47–35 Knicks managed to split six games with the vastly superior 62–20 Boston squad, amid verbal snip-

For much of the playoff series against Boston, Bernard King's shooting single-handedly keeps his team in the running against Larry Bird's superior squad.

ing and general animosity. So it was no surprise when this series became intensely physical, featuring ten technicals, three ejections, and one brawl. But it defied all expectations by reaching Game 6, especially after New York lost the first two games. "They're in the grave, and we've got the shovel in our hands," Boston forward Kevin McHale boasted at that point, before King took over and did some burying of his own, dropping down bucket after bucket.

Still, after Boston's 121–99 thrashing in Game 5—which included a bench-clearing rhubarb starring Darrell Walker and Danny Ainge—the Knicks seemed spent.

Not so, King insisted. The 6'7" Brooklyn native dunked to start warm-ups, then vocally revved his teammates and the crowd. He hoisted the team up on his jumper as he poured in 14 of New York's first 21 points. Although Boston hit nearly 65 percent of its first-quarter shots, King kept New York in front 30–28. Shooting 11–13 in the first half, King swept New York to a 59–51 advantage at intermission. When Boston concentrated on the star in the third, the King-ettes foiled the Celtic plan by picking up the slack, finishing the quarter up 82–75.

But the game still rested in King's hands. (The Knicks' next highest scorers were Bill Cartwright and Ray Williams, who'd both finish with 14.) Those wounded appendages came through time and again in the fourth, firing in 10 more points. His classic fallaway jumper with 3:31 left gave the Knicks a 104–91 lead, which the team clung to desperately as Boston mounted a furious comeback, led by Larry Bird, who'd finish with 35 points. Boston finally pulled within two at 106–104, but Bird missed a short shot with six seconds left. Maxwell's final heave was also off, and the buzzer sounded. The Knicks had climbed out of their grave to force a deciding game back in Boston.

The raucous fans refused to leave, buzzing in the stands long after the game ended. Although the Knicks' magical ride would end in Game 7, King had given New York's fans a royal treat.

# 75. Mike Piazza picks up New York with his post-9/11 game-winning homer, September 21, 2001, Shea Stadium

It is all too easy to summon up—or perhaps all too impossible to completely bury—the visceral reactions we felt on the surface and in our souls on September 11, 2001: disbelief, sorrow, outrage, fear, nausea.

What has dissipated more with time are the emotions that spun us this way and that in the aftermath: the perpetual shakiness, the despair over innocence lost, the sense not just that our future was forever altered but that there might not be a future. Out of all those emotions in those first few weeks there soon emerged a desperation for some

# Honorable Mention: Mets Magic in the Regular Season

## 1. Meet the Mets, April 12, 1962, lower Broadway

On April 10, 1962, the first game in New York Mets history was rained out; most of the team instead spent some of that day in St. Louis stuck in a hotel elevator.

On April 11, the Mets committed two errors and a balk in their major league debut while being routed 11–4.

Then the Mets came home for the first time—their New York premiere was scheduled for Friday the thirteenth.

The script could not be more obvious: the Mets were going to be losers, an odd amalgam of misfits, outcasts, has-beens, and never-weres. This was the one team in baseball capable of falling nine and a half games out of first in their first nine games, the one lineup with the ability (or lack thereof) to lose 120 games with mind-bogglingly diverse ineptitude—and then repeat the pattern for years to come.

But the one day missing in that sequence, April 12, revealed something equally vital: they were going to be loved.

The Mets couldn't replace the Brooklyn Dodgers, with their intimate connection to their home borough, or the New York Giants, with their storied history from John McGraw to Carl Hubbell to Willie Mays. But they were bringing National League baseball back to New York, and that was enough, especially since they'd adopted Dodger blue and Giant orange as their colors and acquired former Dodgers like Gil Hodges, Clem Labine, Don Zimmer, and Roger Craig.

On that Thursday, 40,000 New Yorkers turned out for a 14-car ticker-tape parade for a team that had not yet won a game. The hapless Mets were feted, as the *New York Times* noted, "in the style reserved for national heroes and heads of state." The Yankees, fresh off their eighth World Series championship in 13 years, had never been accorded such an honor.

As the motorcade drove down lower Broadway, the Mets tossed to the throngs 10,000 plastic baseballs, adorned with the words MEET THE METS and the signature of manager Casey Stengel. Many fans batted the balls back with umbrellas. (No report on how many the Mets misplayed.)

Stengel, who'd been unceremoniously dumped by the Yankees, would be the most beloved Met of all, and he rallied the throngs by declaring, "We hope to build this Met team better than the Yankees—and put that down in your hat."

Attorney Bill Shea, who spearheaded the negotiations to bring NL baseball back to New York, was more candid . . . perhaps too candid. Surrounded by Mets, he told the crowd, "Be patient with us until we can bring some real ballplayers in here."

Undeterred, the Mets went up to the Polo Grounds for a workout, to show off for the press. They found that their opponents, the Pirates, had canceled their drill because the visiting clubhouse was under construction, and that their own spikes had not arrived with the other equipment from their hotel. Their first home practice was delayed by an hour.

Patience would definitely be necessary.

## 2. The Mets win in a miracle finish in the 13th inning, September 20, 1973, Shea Stadium

You gotta believe.

If ever a team earned its slogans, it was the 1973 New York Mets, a team that provided joy, hope, and inspiration with their unlikely journey from the cellar to the World Series.

If one day made people believe, it was September 20, when the Mets, emotionally drained from Willie Mays's retirement announcement that afternoon, won by a half-inch in 13 innings, delivering a body blow to the defending division champion Pittsburgh Pirates.

Early that season, the Mets had nearly been buried by a lack of offensive firepower and depth when a seemingly contagious rash of injuries took down John Milner, Jerry Grote, Cleon Jones, Buddy Harrelson, and Jon Matlack. Stopper Tug McGraw was injury-free but flat-out awful, blowing save after save.

# Mets Magic in the Regular Season (CONTINUED)

The Mets sank to last place, but the rest of the division was so thoroughly mediocre that when president M. Donald Grant gave a desultory speech in mid-August urging them to keep plugging, it wasn't ludicrous. Then the 0–5 McGraw, who had just taken up self-actualization, playfully mocked his boss, shouting his new personal mantra, "You gotta believe." The Mets had a war cry, and soon they had an unhittable closer. In 19 appearances down the stretch, McGraw pitched 41 innings with an ERA of 0.88 and 38 strikeouts, garnering 5 wins and 12 saves while always bounding off the mound at inning's end, banging his glove on his leg and whooping it up.

By September 20, the Mets were 75–77 and tied for third. Three times in that game first-place Pittsburgh took a one-run lead, but each time the Mets rallied, finally forcing extra innings on ninth-inning pinch-hits by Ken Boswell and Duffy Dyer.

Then, with the score tied at 3–3 in the 13th, Pittsburgh's Richie Zisk singled, and with two outs Dave Augustine smashed the ball to deep left field. The ball was way back. It was going . . . going . . . but the Shea fence was perhaps a half-inch too high, and the ball stayed in the park. Still, Zisk, running with two outs, would certainly score . . . except the ball ricocheted on a straight line to the one spot it had to go, right into Cleon Jones's glove. Jones was surprised but not flustered; he whirled and fired to third baseman Wayne Garrett, who spun and relayed the ball home to the rookie catcher Ron Hodges, who blocked the plate and put the tag on a stunned Zisk.

Fittingly, in the bottom of the 13th, Hodges singled home the winning run. This improbable victory pushed New York into second, just a half-game behind the devastated Pirates; the next night Tom Seaver pitched the Mets into first.

There were other big wins, but none better summed up this season, affirming not just McGraw's slogan but another one coined that September by their sagacious manager, Yogi Berra: "It ain't over till it's over."

### 3. The Mets avenge three years of suffering in one amazing inning, June 30, 2000, Shea Stadium

In 1998 the Atlanta Braves won nine of twelve and knocked the Mets from the playoffs with a season-ending sweep. In 1999 Atlanta again took nine of twelve, nearly ruined the Mets' wild-card chances by capturing five of six down the stretch, then finished them off in the heart-stopping, heartbreaking NLCS.

When the Braves showed up in 2000, the focus was not on wins and losses but on Atlanta's big-mouthed, small-brained closer, John Rocker, who had made inflammatory racist and homophobic comments about New Yorkers in the off-season. Fearing violent retaliation, the Mets had constructed a canopy over the Braves' bullpen and provided police protection, but Met fans limited themselves to jeering and heckling Rocker, who dominated as usual to help snap New York's seven-game win streak.

But the next night, New York staged one of the most Mets-merizing comebacks in baseball history, one that changed the tone and gave the club the confidence they needed to reach their first World Series since 1986.

Trailing 8–1 in the eighth, Derek Bell singled. One out later, Mike Piazza did too. An error and groundout made it 8–2, but there were two down.

Todd Zeile and Jay Payton singled. 8–3.

Reliever Don Wengert was done. The fans called for Rocker, hoping for a shot at revenge. But Rocker, nursing a blistered thumb, stayed hidden; Kerry Ligtenberg came on instead. Ligtenberg walked Benny Agbayani, then Mark Johnson. 8–4. Fans, suddenly hopeful, screamed themselves hoarse.

Ligtenberg walked Melvin Mora. 8–5. The frenzied crowd smelled blood.

On came veteran Terry Mulholland to restore order. He walked Bell. 8–6.

Mulholland threw strikes to the next two batters . . . with disastrous results. Edgardo Alfonzo singled into left. 8–8. The Mets had done the improbable and tied it.

Up came Piazza again. He'd been carrying the club in the midst of a torrid stretch that would conclude with RBIs in 15 straight games. On the first pitch, he ripped a cut fastball, a laser that cleared the left-field fence in a nano-second. A three-run homer. 11–8. As the fans went berserk even the quiet Met catcher punched the air and roared exuberantly.

The Mets had embarrassed the Braves and turned the tables. Counting June 30, the Mets split their final 12 with Atlanta. The spell was broken.

**Mike Piazza responds to the crowd's cathartic cheering after his game-winning homer in the first game at Shea after 9/11.**

semblance of normalcy, for a diversion, something to pump life into our hearts. If ever sports seemed frivolous and unnecessary it was in mid-September 2001, but it was precisely those traits that made those games so vital.

There was no baseball for six days. Everything was just too raw, too confusing, too chaotic. During the break, many Mets and Yankees pitched in by carrying supplies to rescue workers, making morale-boosting visits, and doing anything else asked of them. Shea Stadium's parking lot was used as a staging area for supplies and a rest area for Ground Zero cleanup workers, so when play resumed, the Mets' home games were shifted to Pittsburgh.

In Pittsburgh the Mets replaced their regular caps with NYPD, FDNY, and other emergency services caps in tribute to the rescue workers and their fallen brethren. They won three straight, starting with a tiebreaking, three-run, ninth-inning rally (fittingly, native New Yorker John Franco got the win) and following the next night with four runs in the last two innings.

Across the nation it seemed that everyone was suddenly pulling for the Mets, who had played dismally in 2001 before going on a 17–5 tear that was interrupted by the tragedy. The Yankees were playing again as well, but New York City was wearing the persona of the downtrodden and the underdog in need of support, an image that fit the Mets far better than the Bronx Bombers, winners of three straight World Series and cruising along in first place again.

On September 21, the Mets returned to Shea Stadium. It was more than a ball game. As the first large-scale event since 9/11, it was a national news story, and it provided a catharsis, a much-needed communal experience, and a chance to pay tribute to those who had died and those who were still working heroically.

Long lines caused by strict new security measures delayed the start time, but New Yorkers, the most impatient people in the world, did not complain. The Mets darkened the lights of the Twin Towers in their scoreboard skyline, wrapping those missing icons in red, white, and blue ribbon; they also replaced the large Budweiser ad in the outfield with the American flag. The lengthy pregame program moved many of the fans and athletes, including Met superstar Mike Piazza, to tears. There was a joint color guard from the various agencies that lost personnel in the Towers (NYPD, FDNY, EMS, the Port Authority Police, and the State Court Officers Association), the NYPD bagpipe troupe, a Marine Corps 21-gun salute,

Diana Ross singing "God Bless America," and Marc Anthony singing the national anthem. Mayor Rudy Giuliani, a Yankee fan who anytime in the weeks preceding September 11 would have been booed by many New Yorkers, especially Met fans, was cheered heartily. Then the Mets and Atlanta Braves, bitter rivals for years, shook hands and hugged each other in a touching display.

After the solemn processions, it was time to play—to acknowledge that for the living life must go on. It was hardly a marquee matchup—Bruce Chen versus Jason Marquis—but it was a close contest. The Braves snagged a 1–0 lead in the fourth, but the Mets responded immediately with a double by Piazza, a single by Robin Ventura, and a sacrifice fly by Tsuyoshi Shinjo to tie it at 1–1.

But the Mets left two on, did it again in the fifth, and hit into a double play in the sixth. In the eighth, closer Armando Benitez yielded an RBI double, and suddenly the Mets were in a 2–1 hole.

Recent events had redefined everyone's perspective, yet it still was hard not to feel glum about the idea of this special night ending in typical fashion, with Benitez blowing another important game.

In the Mets' eighth, Edgardo Alfonzo walked, and up came Piazza as the go-ahead run. Not since Darryl Strawberry had a Met hit home runs with such complete authority, and that was what Piazza did now, his bat whipping through the strike zone and finishing on his shoulder as the ball launched high and deep into the night. New Yorkers finally had cause, no matter how inconsequential, to be briefly, blissfully happy. "A small miracle," manager Bobby Valentine called the blast.

In the long run, it was nothing to get excited about: the Mets would improve to 79–74 and close within three games of perennial leader Atlanta before fading in the final week to 82–80. But on that night the victory wasn't about the National League East standings. Many of the players lingered on the field afterwards, and many fans did the same in the stands, knowing New York would never experience anything quite like this again—all the anguish, joy, and relief commingling in the community of baseball.

## 76. Brooklyn goes bonkers for its "Bums," September 29, 1941, Brooklyn

In the first 40 years of the 20th century, the New York Giants won 12 National League pennants and 4 World Series championships, but no one in the city threw them a parade. The New York Yankees won 11 AL pennants and brought home the ultimate baseball glory 8 times—no parade for them either.

The Brooklyn Dodgers, well, they always were a little different: "Dem Bums" reached the Series only in 1916 and 1920, losing both times, before spiraling down into a second-rate club. So when the team edged the St. Louis Cardinals in 1941 and prepared to face the Yankees in their first World Series in a generation, Brooklynites could not curb their enthusiasm. On

September 25, when the Dodgers clinched in Boston, they arrived at Grand Central Terminal after 11:00 p.m. to find 10,000 giddy fans cheering and hoisting signs proclaiming THE BUMS DONE IT AND MOIDER DUH YANKS.

But even that wasn't enough. The day after the regular season—before the Dodgers had won or even played a single World Series game—the borough hosted one of New York's wildest lovefests ever. The *New York Times* called it "an extraordinary hysterical victory parade," adding that it was "a parade, carnival and Mardi Gras rolled up in one, unmatched in Brooklyn's history for sheer spontaneous madness."

Police estimated that over a million people—nearly half the borough's population—packed the streets on September 29. It sounds like an exaggeration until you see the pictures and read the descriptions of mobbed sidewalks and people watching from fire escapes, stuck trolleys, and treetops. When a teenager dislocated his knee in the surging crowd down by Borough Hall, no doctor could reach him, so he had to be passed overhead to the reviewing stand.

The staggering turnout served as a reminder that while the Yankees and Giants were competent (and in the Yankees' case seemingly cold-blooded) professionals, the Dodgers were, to use the Brooklyn-accented nickname they'd bestowed on popular right fielder Dixie Walker, "the People's Cherce."

## Honorable Mention: Regular-Season Heroics

**1. The Dodgers get revenge against the Giants, September 29, 1934, Polo Grounds**

"Is Brooklyn still in the league?" New York Giant player-manager Bill Terry sneered when asked his predictions for 1934. Given the Dodgers' perennial second-division status, Terry thought his answer, like a big lead, was safe. Baseball's reigning champions found out otherwise.

The Giants had blown their seven-game Labor Day lead over St. Louis to wind up tied for first with two games left. The baseball gods arranged it perfectly: to win, Terry's Giants had to vanquish the sixth-place Dodgers, whose rookie manager, Casey Stengel, resurrected Terry's attack: "It's nonsense to say that we have nothing to gain by knocking the Giants out of the race. . . . I think I know our fans. If the Cardinals win . . . because we beat the Giants, they'll be cheering about it all winter."

Most fans at the Polo Grounds on that drizzly day hailed from Brooklyn, banging cowbells and carrying homemade signs. While Paul Dean won in St. Louis, Brooklyn's erratic Van Lingle Mungo allowed only five hits while scoring the game's first run in the fifth and driving in the second in the sixth. When Terry's failure to field a ball led to another run, Stengel yelled, "Tough luck, Bill. . . . They're gonna say you kicked away the pennant."

Up 5–1 in the ninth, Mungo put two on, then struck out the side. The Cardinals had first to themselves. The Dodgers won again the next day in a comeback, extra-inning affair, but it was anticlimactic—St. Louis had clinched by winning themselves. Stengel and Terry nearly came to blows afterwards, then Stengel rode the subway for hours, celebrating with giddy Brooklyn fans.

The "Section M Rooters" of Ebbets Field gave Stengel a suitcase, and section N gave him a pen-and-pencil set. Mungo likened the thrill to winning the World Series. The *Brooklyn Times-Union* got the ultimate revenge with a front-page headline: "Yes, Indeed, Mr. Terry, Brooklyn Is Still in the League."

**2. The Brooklyn Bombers score and score and score, May 21, 1952, Ebbets Field**

The "Boys of Summer" deserved a more fearsome moniker . . . like "Murderers' Row" or "the Brooklyn Bombers." From 1949 to 1955, they topped the majors in homers; from 1949 to 1953, and again in 1955, they led the NL in runs scored and steals.

Ebbets Field hosted plenty of outbursts—such as the 19–3 win in 1950 when Gil Hodges became just the second modern slugger to launch four homers in a nine-inning game—but May 21, 1952, was special.

Politicians sensed this, of course, and the parade drew Mayor Fiorello La Guardia, a senator, the district attorney, and the city council president; even President Franklin Delano Roosevelt wrote to say he was sorry he couldn't make it. Bronx borough president James Lyons stayed away but snidely reminded his Brooklyn counterpart John Cashmore via telegram that "the winning of pennants and World Series is so commonplace in the Bronx that our people view the situation with cool heads and calmness." Actually, the Yankees and Giants, by virtue of their NY logos, had weaker associations with their home boroughs. By contrast, the parade was another symbol of the kinship that Brooklyn—still smarting from losing its independence in the consolidation of 1898—felt with its Dodgers.

The Dodgers rode in open cars through the arch at Grand Army Plaza down to Borough Hall. The official parade featured veterans groups and 50 civic organizations, including the Knot Hole Gang, the British War Relief Society, the Bay Ridge Civic League, the Cypress Hills Board of Trade, and the Taxpayers Association.

"All that was needed to remind Brooklynites of the historic triumphal processions of ancient Rome were laurel wreaths on the heads of their smiling heroes," the *Brooklyn Daily Eagle* wrote.

There were no laurel wreaths, but everything else was on display—after the team and the civic

## Regular-Season Heroics (CONTINUED)

Cincinnati's righty sidearmer Ewell "the Whip" Blackwell typically gave the Dodgers fits. But this day was different from all other days. Even with Roy Campanella and Carl Furillo resting, the Dodgers were unstoppable.

In the first inning, Blackwell got one out. Then came the deluge: over the next hour, the Dodgers ripped Blackwell and three more pitchers for 10 hits; seven more batters walked, and two were hit. Before three outs were made, every Dodger had scored and driven home at least one run. The score was 15–0.

The win was notable for pushing Brooklyn into first place for good, but it's that single-inning scoring record that has withstood the test of time.

### 3. Brooklyn upstages New York in a pitching duel for the ages, April 15, 1909, Polo Grounds

On Opening Day 1909, fans flocked into the Polo Grounds to see their Giants rebound from a heartbreaking finish in 1908 and reassert themselves with a fast start against lowly Brooklyn. But the weather was cold, so the teams' marquee pitchers—New York's legendary Christy Mathewson and Brooklyn ace Nap Rucker—were held back. Reliable Red Ames of the Giants and woeful Irvin "Kaiser" Wilhelm of the Dodgers were suddenly thrust onto the stage. They would exceed anything even their more famous counterparts might have been expected to produce. Ames responded with a mighty effort, but like the 1908 pennant race, it ended badly when Wilhelm, sporting a woeful 39–71 career record, pitched the game of his life.

For inning after inning, both men pitched not just shutouts but no-hitters. Wilhelm walked two in the eighth, then lost his no-hitter, but Art Devlin was thrown out at the plate to keep the game scoreless.

So Ames had to keep going. He pitched nine no-hit innings, but it wasn't enough. In the 10th, he yielded his first hit. Still, he matched Wilhelm, posting zeros through the 10th, 11th, and finally 12th innings. But in the 13th, Brooklyn's Harry Lumley tripled, sparking a three-run rally to finally give Brooklyn and Wilhelm a surprising victory.

The Giants never got back on track and would finish third. Ames would continue his hard luck, earning the nickname "Kalamity" (his middle initial was K): on Opening Day 1910, he had a no-hitter for seven innings, but the Giants lost in 11; on Opening Day 1912, he pitched six no-hit innings but lost on two ninth-inning runs.

Meanwhile, in 1909, Wilhelm won only twice more in Brooklyn's dismal 55–98 season. But back when the season was young, he and Ames provided an astonishing Opening Day duel that has never been matched.

groups, 60,000 fans took it upon themselves to join in, marching behind their heroes. The two-hour improvised parade featured Brooklynites dressed as Uncle Sam, bums, Arabs, Indians, pirates, Mother Hubbard, and even a lion, which badly spooked several police horses. (The "lion," a.k.a. Hughie Curry of 55 Pineapple Street, bore a sign reading LEO THE KING, a tribute to the Dodgers' ferocious Durocher.) There was confetti, Yankees in effigy, and a coffin float filled with Yankee remains.

Downtown the celebratory sirens, honking

**Brooklyn fans pack the streets to cheer on the pennant-winning Bums of 1941.**

horns, and shouting fans were so loud that Borough Hall "seemed to shake with the uproar," the *Times* claimed, and no one heard the speeches, which ended early to avoid further trampling.

Unfortunately, there'd be no more parades that year: the Dodgers lost Game 3 when pitcher Freddie Fitzsimmons got his kneecap shattered by a batted ball and Game 4 when Mickey Owen dropped the third strike in the ninth, allowing the Yankees to rally for the win. But while losing the Series to the Yankees hurt, Brooklynites showed that when it came to their Dodgers, they'd be back for more.

# 77. Baseball returns to Brooklyn, June 25, 2001, Keyspan Park

For 43 long, long years there had been an aching baseball void in Brooklyn. Sure, the Mets gave New York an anti-Yankee, National League team, but Brooklyn yearned to regain a sports identity that would distinguish it from the other boroughs. Finally it happened, in Coney Island at 7:19 P.M. on June 25, 2001, to the shouts and screams of an eager crowd when pitcher Matt Peterson fired in ball one in the very first home game for the Brooklyn Cyclones.

This being New York, nothing had come easy. The Cyclones were a Single A team, which angered some, like borough president Howard Golden, who'd argued for a Double or Triple A team—Brooklyn could certainly support longer seasons and larger stadiums, but the Mets and Yankees would never have permitted such serious competition. Residents in other boroughs grumbled that the city spent $39 million on a stadium for Brooklyn (and more millions on another one in Staten Island for the Yankees' Single A club), while some locals were peeved that Mayor Rudy Giuliani, in typical no-compromise fashion, had shoved aside a proposed nonprofit, multipurpose Sportsplex—which would have provided year-round jobs and athletic facilities for underserved Coney Island—in favor of a short-season stadium handed over to Fred Wilpon, the wealthy Mets owner.

On Opening Day, however, the political power plays were set aside. Sure, Single A ballplayers in the New York–Penn League are just 18 or 19 years old, usually stay just one season, and are unlikely to reach the majors, but no one minded. The intimacy of minor league ball was a throwback to when Dodgers lived in the neighborhood, and Brooklyn was glad to become a small town again. By June 25, more than 80 percent of all available seats for *the entire season* were sold, the Cyclones Internet fan club was the busiest site in minor league baseball, and Cyclones caps were on back order.

Fans arrived four hours before game time, well before even the pregame festivities that started with a parade up Surf Avenue. The event attracted more than 300 reporters from around the world, and 7,500 fans jammed into sparkling Keyspan Park, built on the site of the legendary amusement park Steeplechase Park. The biggest cheers poured out for former Dodger Ralph Branca, Gil Hodges's widow Joan, the surviving members of the Dodgers Sym-Phony Band, and Cyclones coaches Howard Johnson and Bobby Ojeda, stars of the

**Baseball finally returns to Brooklyn, in a beautiful new ballpark by the sea.**

Mets' last World Series winner, who added an extra layer of nostalgia. The stadium itself brimmed with atmosphere, from the Garage Clothing HIT SIGN WIN SUIT ad — a tribute to Abe Stark's Ebbets Field original — to the hull of the old Parachute Jump ride (lovingly dubbed "the Eiffel Tower of Brooklyn") looming over right field, to the glittering views of the sun over the Atlantic Ocean and the lights coming up on the Wonder Wheel and, of course, the world-famous roller coaster for which the team had been named.

The Cyclones (already 3–3 on an opening road trip) and Mahoning Valley Scrappers played a surprisingly crisp game. In the ninth inning, the Cyclones trailed 2–0 and were down to their final strike when Edgar Rodriguez unleashed a dramatic two-run homer over the scoreboard in left field, setting off fireworks, both from real explosives and from jubilant fans.

In the 10th, the Cyclones loaded the bases for Mike Jacobs, who'd had little to celebrate, striking out four times in front of his new home crowd. But this time Jacobs lofted a fly ball to left field that was catchable but deep enough to score the runner from third base. (Jacobs would become one of the first Cyclones to have an impact in the majors when he hit 11 homers in a late-season outburst for the Mets in 2005 before being traded to Florida for Carlos Delgado.) With the game over, the crowd flowed back out into Brooklyn, thrilled to experience again the roller-coaster emotions so familiar to those old enough to have watched the Dodgers. But this time they were cheering a larger victory, a triumph over time and the changes it brings.

This was the beginning of a magical season. The team drew nearly 290,000 fans, a league record. Inspired by the boisterous crowds—who roared for great plays and between innings when contestants were announced by name and Brooklyn neighborhood—the Cyclones finished an astonishing 30–8 at home, with a league-best 52–24 record. Then they defeated the Staten Island Yankees in the playoffs—oh, the joy in that triumph—before tragedy interrupted their dream season.

The Cyclones had beaten the Williamsport Crosscutters in Game 1 of the championship on September 10, 2001, and Game 2 was scheduled at home for September 12. But after the September 11 attack, the league canceled the remaining games, declaring the teams co-champions.

Even the incomplete championship and the failures to win in subsequent seasons did not dim the ardor of Brooklynites, a passion they made so evident on July 25, 2001, when baseball was reborn in Brooklyn for that night, that season, and every "next year" to follow.

# 78. Dykstra rolls a homer in NLCS Game 3, October 11, 1986, Shea Stadium

In Game 3 of the 1986 National League playoffs, Lenny Dykstra rolled the dice and came up big.

The unproven Dykstra had gotten an opportunity to prove himself in 1986 when fan favorite Mookie Wilson suffered a freak spring training accident—a ball shattered his sunglasses, injuring his eye. The feisty Dykstra took over in center field and in the leadoff spot, winning over the Mets and their fans with his hard-charging, hardheaded intensity. He and number-two hitter Wally Backman were a dangerous and distracting pair of table-setters.

But just as Wilson (who eventually came back and played mostly in left) was a less than ideal leadoff hitter because he swung at virtually every offering, Dykstra had his own serious flaw. He had hit a home run in his first major league game in 1985, but none in his next 233 at-bats. In '86, he stopped choking up, to "hold the bat like a man," and mustered eight home runs; as a result, he often fancied himself a big man and swung from his heels when a ground ball single the other way should have been his goal. Manager Davey Johnson lectured Dykstra, to no avail.

The Mets cruised into the NLCS against Houston, but Astro ace Mike Scott slapped New York's face with a 1–0 whitewash in the opener. New York jumped on Nolan Ryan for five runs in Game 2, and Dykstra demonstrated his toughness and ability to hit in the clutch when he fueled a crucial three-run rally with a single that came right after Ryan knocked him down with a fastball near his head and then froze him with a curve.

In Game 3, Houston started Bob Knepper, a tricky lefty who had beaten New York three times that season. Houston pumped out four runs in the first two innings, and with both Dykstra and Backman benched against the southpaw, Knepper smothered New York's league-leading offense until the sixth.

# Honorable Mention: Mets Miracles in the Postseason

**1. The Kid finally comes through, October 14, 1986, Shea Stadium**

In 1986, Gary Carter finished third in the National League with 105 RBIs, helping lead the New York Mets to the postseason for the first time in a generation. In the playoffs, however, Carter was awful. No, beyond awful—he was truly pathetic: with one hit in 21 at-bats, he was a cleanup hitter the Houston Astros could taunt without fear of reprisal.

In Game 2, Houston twice intentionally walked Keith Hernandez to pitch to Carter. In Game 3, rambunctious reliever Charlie Kerfeld—who had made snide comments about Carter's penchant for camera-hogging—snatched Carter's comebacker behind his back, then waved the ball mockingly toward home plate.

With the playoffs tied at two games apiece, Carter got his shot at redemption.

It began as a Wild West showdown: Houston's old flamethrower Nolan Ryan versus young gun Dwight Gooden. Ryan had been rocked by the team of his youth in Game 2, but on October 14—17 years to the day after his brilliant relief performance in the 1969 World Series—he sent the first 13 Mets back to the bench. Pitching with a hairline fracture in his left ankle, Ryan threw 134 pitches in nine innings—almost exclusively heaters—fanning 12 and allowing one walk and two hits. But one was a Darryl Strawberry home run in the second. Gooden allowed 11 base runners while posting just four Ks, yet he escaped each jam and pitched 10 innings for the first time.

The game reached the 12th, tied 1–1. If the Mets lost, they'd have to beat Mike Scott—unhittable in Games 1 and 4—to reach the World Series. As the Mets' bench donned their rally caps, Wally Backman banged a one-out single, then advanced to second on Kerfeld's errant pickoff attempt. Kerfeld gave Hernandez a free pass to bring up Carter, who had begun hearing boos and "1-for-21" chants from the crowd.

The 6'6", 250-pound pitcher fell behind 3–1. Carter fouled off three pitches before getting a fat fastball he could handle. He smacked it right past Kerfeld and into center field. As Backman scored the winning run and the fans cheered "2-for-22," Carter raised his arms and screamed in triumph.

**2. Bobby Jones nearly pulls a Don Larsen, October 8, 2000, Shea Stadium**

Don Larsen's postseason perfection has never been matched, and few have even come close. But amazingly enough, with a Subway Series on the horizon during the 2000 playoffs, Met Bobby Jones and Yankee Roger Clemens threw just the third and fourth one-hit, complete-game shutouts in postseason history.

Though Clemens's outing in Seattle was perhaps more impressive (it was in the championship, not the divisional, round, and he had 15 strikeouts), it was Jones's showing in the NLDS against San Francisco that evoked more of a sense of delight and wonder in baseball fans.

His entertainingly unpredictable performance before the hometown crowd clinched an entertainingly unpredictable series, making the 30-year-old a perfect symbol of an entertainingly unpredictable wild-card team striving for their first World Series since 1986.

After the Mets lost Game 1, they eked out a 10-inning, 6–5 win in Game 2 and won Game 3 on Benny Agbayani's 13th-inning homer. Manager Bobby Valentine considered yanking Jones from the rotation and starting ace Mike Hampton on three days' rest in Game 4 to avoid having to fly cross-country for a decisive fifth game. Although Jones had attended the same high school as Tom Seaver and been an All-Star in 1997, he'd slumped in that season's second half, then struggled with inconsistency and injuries; Valentine had even left Jones off his 1999 postseason roster. By 2000, Jones's career was in jeopardy—he was shipped to the minors during the season, and when the Mets added a reliever with the same name, he even lost his basic identity when he was distinguished in the papers as Bobby J. Jones. But at least those articles finally turned positive as Jones finished 7–2.

Fortunately, on October 8, the anniversary of Larsen's famous game, he made sure New York remembered the real Bobby Jones. Unlike Clemens,

Then two singles and an error got the Mets on the board without a hard-hit ball. Up came Darryl Strawberry, a moody slugger who'd had trouble hitting at Shea that year, trouble hitting in the playoffs, trouble hitting most lefties, and trouble hitting Knepper . . . he was 2–20 lifetime against him. But Strawberry received some simple encouragement from Dysktra before approaching the plate. "We need a fucking homer," Dykstra said. Strawberry drove Knepper's first pitch into the mezzanine in right field, a three-run blast that tied the game at 4–4.

The Mets' momentum dissipated quickly. In the seventh, Ray Knight bobbled a sacrifice bunt, then threw the ball away, allowing Houston to score the go-ahead run without a hit. And Charlie Kerfeld blew the Mets away in relief, even taunting catcher Gary Carter after retiring him.

Things looked particularly grim because Scott would pitch Game 4, after which, if they lost this

## Mets Miracles in the Postseason (CONTINUED)

Jones didn't clock 90 mph, much less 96. But staked to a 2–0 lead, Jones deftly hit his spots with his mid-80s "heater" and kept the increasingly anxious Giants lunging at his below-70 curves and changeups.

Jones retired the first 12 before ex-Met Jeff Kent led off the fifth with a liner off the tip of Robin Ventura's outstretched glove that landed for a double. After two walks and two outs, Jones got a gift from Giant manager Dusty Baker. Believing Jones was eminently hittable, Baker preserved his depleted bullpen by letting pitcher Mark Gardner bat with the bases full. He popped out. The Mets scored two more off him in their next at-bat.

Jones easily set down the final 12 Giants, ending the series by getting Barry Bonds to fly out. For a team without any no-hitters at any time of year, this October one-hitter was a gem worth preserving.

### 3. Todd Pratt becomes Mike Piazza for the day, October 9, 1999, Shea Stadium

From the crack of the bat and the ball's trajectory, you could just tell that this one was deep and might not be playable.

Taking your eyes off the ball to check the outfielder and realizing it was Steve Finley, you groaned. Arizona's center fielder had a flair for gracefully racing to the wall, perfectly timing his leap, then calmly robbing a hitter of a home run. Even New York Met catcher Todd Pratt, who blasted this ball toward the 410-foot mark, was unwilling to celebrate what would be his biggest hit—he stopped running and warily watched the Gold Glover track the ball toward the fence.

It was surprising enough to see Pratt at the plate in the NLDS. Just three years earlier, he'd been managing a Domino's Pizza franchise, before returning to the game as the Mets' second-stringer. And only a thumb injury to slugger Mike Piazza in Game 2 had thrust Pratt onto center stage.

But in the late innings of Game 4, the spotlight naturally gravitated again and again toward the Mets' catcher position, where it found Pratt each time.

In the sixth, Pratt came up with runners on second and third, hoping to build upon a 2–1 lead. Alas, he grounded to third.

In the eighth, closer Armando Benitez (mis)handled the pressure by yielding two runs but was saved from further damage when Pratt snatched an off-target throw home by Melvin Mora and tagged out Jay Bell.

In the bottom of that inning, the Mets tied the game, but Pratt blew a chance to take back the lead, grounding out with men on first and third.

In the 10th, Pratt finally connected with that big, long swing. The ball went back, back, back; Finley went back, back, back. Finley leaped and stretched. The ball hit the glove. Finley came down and looked. Pratt was stopped in his tracks, expecting the worst. But when Finley sagged against the wall, Pratt knew that the glove was empty and it was his turn to leap—in celebration.

The Mets earned their first postseason series win since 1986 on just the fourth walk-off, series-ending homer in postseason history. The previous three had been hit by All-Stars with consistent power—Joe Carter hit 33 homers in 1993, Chris Chambliss had 17 in 1976, and even Bill Mazeroski came up with 11 in 1960. Pratt, by contrast, had just 3 homers in only 140 at-bats in 1999. The Mets, however, do things their own way, so it's fitting that their entry was the pizza man, a guy lucky to be in the lineup.

**Lenny Dykstra swings for the fences . . . and reaches them, giving the Mets a surprising ninth-inning comeback win over Houston in Game 3 of the NLCS.**

game, the Mets would probably be at a 3–1 disadvantage. Still, even though the Mets' 108-win march through the season had given them a reputation as arrogant showboats, they'd won because they were cutthroat competitors who never stopped coming; they'd tied Houston with 39 comeback wins and had won in every way imaginable—and some that were utterly unfathomable. Once, they'd rallied to tie the score after Cincinnati's Dave Parker dropped an easy fly ball with two outs; an extra-inning brawl led to so many ejections that the Mets had to use Carter at third while relievers Jesse Orosco and Roger McDowell took turns pitching and playing outfield. But the Mets had prevailed.

True to form, they caught a break in this game when Astro manager Hal Lanier ditched Kerfeld for Dave Smith in the ninth. Sure, Smith was the closer and had 33 saves, but he also had a 15.00 ERA against New York.

So maybe a ninth-inning rally was not a huge surprise, but the final swing certainly was a stunner. Wally Backman pinch-hit and bunted for a hit, evading Glenn Davis as he dived into first base. Three yards and a cloud of dust. Houston argued that Backman left the baseline, but to no avail. When a passed ball advanced him to second, a "small ball" comeback seemed within reach. Danny Heep flew out, but that brought up the pesky Dykstra, whom skipper Davey Johnson had used as a pinch hitter in the seventh to get him into the flow of the game so he'd be ready to face the Astros' righty relievers.

In July, Dykstra had doubled off the wall against Smith on a fastball, yet Smith still viewed him as a singles hitter and chanced a first-pitch heater. Dykstra took a huge rip but fouled it off. On the bench, Johnson got heartburn watching that swing; on second Backman urged Dykstra to cut down and just try tying the game with a single.

But Dykstra was a gambler. After that good rip, he figured Smith would switch up, so he looked forkball. Bat straight up, body almost leaning forward, bursting with eagerness, the hyper, twitchy little guy got the pitch he wanted and swung for the fences. As the ball zoomed into the stands in right field, Backman threw his arms in the air and danced toward third, Dykstra pumped his fist, Shea Stadium exploded with noise, and what had seemed like a tight, well-played series was suddenly on track for an Emmy Award for Best Drama. The 6–5 win would be just the first of three over-the-top Met finishes in this classic NLCS.

"The last time I hit a home run in the ninth inning to win a game I was playing Strat-O-Matic with my brother," Dykstra said. "The game with the dice."

# 79. The Mets sing the praises of their unsung heroes, October 15, 1969, Shea Stadium

Baseball is a team game that, more than any other sport, relies on individual performances. One special feature of the 1969 New York Mets was that everybody on the team contributed — they were the first World Series team with only two players who'd had more than 400 at-bats for the season — and often in the most surprising ways. Ron Swoboda hit .400 in the World Series against Baltimore but is remembered for one defensive play. J. C. Martin batted .000, with zero official at-bats, yet was immortalized by his single trip to the plate.

The Mets' moments in the sun only arose, however, because of a masterful performance by the one Met who always stood out: Tom Seaver. Beginning with his Rookie of the Year season in 1967, he'd given the Mets instant confidence as well as credibility in the eyes of opponents and the press. In July 1969, he made teammates and foes alike realize the Mets were a legitimate threat when he pitched his famous "Imperfect Game" against the first-place Cubs, setting down 25 straight hitters before giving up a ninth-inning single to Jimmy Qualls.

Seaver had gone on to a 25–7 record with a 2.21 ERA, but the Cy Young Award winner-to-be had pitched through a calf injury near the end of the season, and he'd been roughed up in the playoffs and in the first game of the Series. Game 4 was on October 15, declared Moratorium Day by Vietnam War protesters, and Seaver faced an added distraction when, against his wishes, activists tried to capitalize on his fame by publicizing his antiwar quotes. In addition to protesters in the Shea Stadium parking lot, there was an indirect scuffle that day between New York City mayor John Lindsay, who ordered flags on all city buildings (like Shea) flown at half-mast in mourning to honor the peace movement, and baseball commissioner Bowie Kuhn, who asked the Mets to raise the flags to avoid a boycott by the military color guard on hand for the pregame ceremony. (The flags were raised but the decision was made too late, and the military band refused to provide musical accompaniment for the national anthem.)

However, Seaver, whom Baltimore had beaten in Game 1, brooked no diversions or opposition that day. He escaped a two-on, no-out jam in the third and retired 19 of 20 Orioles to take a 1–0 lead into the ninth.

Then, with one out, Frank Robinson and Boog Powell singled, putting runners on the corners. When Brooks Robinson nailed a sinking low liner to right, the rally suddenly looked dangerous—more so because of the always adventurous and occasionally reckless outfielder the ball was heading toward.

## Honorable Mention: World Series Catches

### 1. Al Gionfriddo robs Joe DiMaggio, who actually shows emotion, October 5, 1947, Yankee Stadium

With a record 38 players banging out 14 runs and 27 hits, Game 6 of the 1947 World Series was all about offense. But what made the game stand out was one defensive play by one small player. Days earlier, the fleet Al Gionfriddo had made his biggest contribution to Brooklyn by helping disrupt Floyd Bevens's potential no-hitter, but in this game his speed would earn him lasting fame.

Down 3–2 in games, the Dodgers scored four runs early. The Yankees retaliated with five. Brooklyn bounced back with four more in the sixth. But in the home sixth, perennial hero Joe DiMaggio lashed what appeared to be a game-tying, three-run homer.

Gionfriddo, recently inserted in left field, raced to the wall and then reached beyond it, snatching the shot that seemed destined for the left-field bullpen 415 feet from home plate. The play gained extra cachet when the stoic Yankee Clipper kicked the infield dirt in frustration. As the next inning started he was, the *New York Times* recorded, "still walking inconsolably in circles doubtless wondering whether he could believe his senses."

Few people had heard of Gionfriddo before the Series, Red Smith wrote, but "now he has two legs on a pedestal at Cooperstown."

The Yankees loaded the bases in the seventh and the ninth but couldn't pull closer than 8–6. The Series went to Game 7. Had the Dodgers won that, Al Gionfriddo, not Sandy Amoros, would have landed in the top 10 for the most important catch in Brooklyn history. Still, Gionfriddo, who never again appeared in the majors, made his mark. Just ask Joe DiMaggio.

### 2. Bill Cunningham robs Babe Ruth, October 7, 1922, Polo Grounds

Babe Ruth had slumped in the first three games of the 1922 World Series as John McGraw's Giants threw curve after curve in the dirt. The mighty Yankee eked out just one single and one double, while the Giants—who'd bested their rival the previous year—took a 2–0 lead. (One game was called a tie for darkness.)

But with two men on in the first inning, Ruth finally connected. As his monstrous moon shot journeyed through space, Bill Cunningham, subbing for center fielder Casey Stengel, took off. If ESPN and Chris Berman had been around, he'd have shouted, "Back, back, back, back, back," so many times that he'd have hyperventilated. More than 460 feet from home, Cunningham finally swerved past the monument to Eddie Grant (a Giant killed during World War I), caught the ball near the wooden bleachers, and tumbled to the ground.

Ruth didn't manage another hit, and

Ron Swoboda had arrived in 1965, making him among the longest-tenured Mets. On those early losing teams, his constant effort and flashes of power had made his inconsistency at the plate and in the field tolerable. But in 1969, with a stronger, more competitive team, he'd gotten less playing time. Although he'd hit well in the Series, Swoboda was never surefooted defensively; in Game 1 his poor footwork and timing had allowed Don Buford's blast to go over his glove for a homer.

This time he was no more graceful but far more effective. Swoboda never thought about playing it safe and letting the ball fall as a single. Instead, he charged hard, then took to the air. If he merely knocked the ball down there'd be trouble, if the ball got past him there'd be absolute disaster, and either way the game would probably get away, tying the Series at two apiece. "If there's even one chance in a thousand to catch it, I'm going to try," he said afterwards.

The 1969 Mets always seemed to just barely make the play they needed, and Swoboda made this one, hurtling and rolling his way to a backhanded grab that many, including *New Yorker* writer Roger Angell, called "the finest World Series catch of all time." Robinson did tag and score anyway, tying the game, but with the second out in hand and Powell unable to advance, the threat was

## World Series Catches (CONTINUED)

the Giants won that game and the next. Had Cunningham made the catch on television some 30 years later, today it might be the one referred to as "the Catch."

### 3. Hank Bauer saves Bob Kuzava, Casey Stengel, and the Yankees, October 10, 1951, Yankee Stadium

It was the ninth inning, and the 1951 Giants, down 4–1, were facing a long winter. Sound familiar? They chipped away at the lead, and Bobby Thomson, with a chance to pull out a miracle and win it all, blasted the ball into left field. Sound familiar?

And then Gene Woodling made a running catch. Say what?

The forgotten World Series of 1951 climaxed with a taut Game 6 that demonstrated the difference—by the narrowest of margins—between the New York Yankees and their cross-town rivals in Brooklyn and Manhattan.

Hank Bauer's sixth-inning, bases-loaded triple had been the key hit, but in the ninth, three Giant singles loaded the bases. Yankee skipper Casey Stengel knew aging starter Johnny Sain could not wrap things up, so he brought in . . . Bob Kuzava?

This midseason pickup was seemingly as odd a choice for the Yankees as Ralph Branca had been for Brooklyn in their similar situation: Kuzava was plagued by control problems; he had not pitched since the season ended; and he was a lefty facing the Giants' two most dangerous righties, RBI leader Monte Irvin and home run leader Bobby Thomson.

Stengel was counting on Kuzava's hard, sinking fastball to flummox them. It didn't work out that way, but outfield defense made Stengel look like a genius.

Irvin smashed a ball to deep left-center. In most ballparks, it would have been a three-run homer, but in Death Valley, Woodling had room for a fine running grab. Eddie Stanky tagged and scored, making it 4–2 for Thomson . . . just like October 3.

First base was open, but like Brooklyn's Charlie Dressen, Stengel thought his pitcher could get Thomson out. Thomson smashed this ball farther than his "Shot Heard 'Round the World," but it too died in Woodling's glove deep in the Alley. Another run scored, however, making it 4–3.

Down to his final out, Giant manager Leo Durocher called Sal Yvars in from the bullpen to pinch-hit. Yvars had only 41 at-bats all season and had not batted in the Series, yet he swung at the first pitch. Like his two predecessors, Yvars crushed the ball, smoking a hard, sinking liner to right field. Bauer made a spectacular circus catch that made Ron Swoboda's 1969 grab look graceful.

Playing shallow in order to have a play at the plate on a single, Bauer charged hard but lost sight of the ball in the afternoon shadows and then lost his footing. Slipping and sliding, he stuck his glove where he thought the ball should be. As the tying run reached home plate, Bauer grabbed the ball for the final out, the most exciting catch ever to end a World Series.

**Ron Swoboda's diving catch keeps the Mets alive in the ninth inning of Game 4 of the World Series.**

quashed. Swoboda ran down Elrod Hendricks's deep fly to retire the side.

The Mets stranded two in the ninth, but the Orioles did the same in the 10th. Still, after 150 pitches Seaver had run out of steam. He needed his offense to pick him up. Once again the Mets came through, and once again they did it in a most unusual fashion.

In the 10th, Jerry Grote blooped a ball to left, where Buford lost it in the glare and took a step back before charging too late. Hustling hard, Grote made it to second. Red-hot Al Weis was walked intentionally. Manager Gil Hodges sent lefty J. C. Martin to pinch-hit, so Baltimore countered with lefty Pete Richert.

Martin was a weak-hitting, seldom-used backup catcher. His job in this situation was to bunt the runners over. In his lone Series at-bat, Martin laid down a beauty that rolled to a stop about 10 feet up the first-base line. It was a tough chance for the defense. Catcher Elrod Hendricks shouted that it was his play—he had the better angle—but before he scooped up the ball, Richert, who hadn't heard him, snatched it, pivoted, and fired.

His throw ricocheted off Martin's left wrist and bounded away in what shortstop Mark Belanger called "a Met bounce," allowing pinch runner Rod Gaspar to race home with the winning run. Martin should have been called out for interference, since replays show him illegally running in fair territory, blocking the ball's route to first. But Baltimore manager Earl Weaver, who probably would have lodged a vociferous protest, had been ejected back in the third, and the play went unchallenged. The umpires later said they believed that Martin's foot was on the line and his actions accidental.

The Mets, it seemed, could do no wrong. The underdogs were invincible.

# 80. Dave DeBusschere saves the NBA Finals, May 8, 1973, Madison Square Garden

With the New York Knicks' shot at history slipping through their fingers, Dave DeBusschere grabbed hold of the ball and propelled his team to a crucial victory that all but finished off the Los Angeles Lakers in the 1972–73 NBA Finals.

When the Finals started that year, the Knicks had one championship to their credit, their stirring triumph over the Lakers in 1970. The Lakers also had won just one championship since leaving Minneapolis, a dismissal of the Knicks in five games in 1972 (although the Knicks felt they might have prevailed in that series if there hadn't been so many Knicks, particularly DeBusschere, who were hurt).

As the two oldest teams around, both squads sensed that this was winner-take-all, one final Final confrontation to decide which team had assumed the mantle from Bill Russell's domineering Boston Celtics as ruler of the early 1970s.

Drained by a tough seven-game Eastern Final series against Boston, the Knicks lost Game 1 in Los Angeles 115–112 after a late spurt fell short. They bounced back to take the next two games—but even with Jerry West suffering two pulled hamstrings and 36-year-old Wilt Chamberlain vanishing at crucial moments, the Knicks managed margins of just 99–95 and 87–83 and fretted that their luck might not hold.

Game 4 was at Madison Square Garden on May 8, the anniversary of 1970's memorable finale. This time May 8 wouldn't be the last game, but it would prove decisive. No team had ever come back from a 3–1 deficit, so a win would virtually clinch the championship. But a loss would even the series with two of the final three games to be played in Los Angeles.

The Knicks nearly blew the Lakers out of the Garden, outscoring them 29–16 in the first and building up a 21-point lead in the second. The charge was led by DeBusschere, who'd finish with his finest playoff showing ever—team highs of 33 points on 13–21 shooting and 14 rebounds along with 7 assists; he also held counterpart Jim McMillian to 6–20 shooting.

The first three games had proven, however, that nothing would ever be easy. New York, which had the NBA's top defense, would hold the Lakers below 100 points again, but for the fourth straight game a potential laugher—the Knicks entered the fourth quarter coasting 82–69—turned exceedingly tight.

With seven minutes left, DeBusschere's right knee got banged up, and he went to the bench. The Knick fans confidently chanted, "Good-bye, Lakers," but the Knicks, typically the NBA's most poised team, lost their equilibrium, missing seven straight shots while committing turnovers and bad fouls, including Walt Frazier's sixth, as the Lakers spun off eight unanswered points. L.A. pulled within 94–92 at the 1:16 mark on West's jumper.

DeBusschere had returned, but with Frazier gone, the Knicks' offense stagnated, and with the shot clock winding down, Bill Bradley was forced to take an uncomfortable 15-footer. With 48 sec-

**Dave DeBusschere comes up big time in the 1973 Finals as the Knicks avenge their 1972 loss to L.A.**

onds left, the shot bounced out, and Chamberlain battled Willis Reed for the rebound, hoping to grab the ball and give L.A. a chance to tie. Reed tipped the ball upward, and Chamberlain got his fingers on it, but neither man could control it. Suddenly, in swooped DeBusschere. He saved the wilting Knicks by grabbing the ball and emerging from the tangle of bodies to nail his follow-up shot and draw a foul from Chamberlain. After he drained the free throw, New York's lead was back up to 97–92.

Still, that merely provided breathing room. The Lakers kept on coming, and after West scored his 22nd and 23rd points to make it 99–96, L.A. forced a jump ball on the Knick inbound pass. L.A. got the ball and went to Chamberlain, who missed. Again, it was DeBusschere who stepped forward, gathering in the rebound and, in the waning seconds, hitting four more free throws to seal the 103–98 victory and the Lakers' fate. Back in Los Angeles, an energized Knick squad outplayed a defeated Laker team in Game 5 to win the championship, firming up their stature as one of the greatest teams in NBA history.

# 81. St. John's gives Joe Lapchick a going-away championship, March 20, 1965, Madison Square Garden

In the world of New York City basketball, Joe Lapchick had done it all.

As a player with the Original Celtics beginning in the 1920s, he'd helped build the first significant professional team into the sport's first dynasty. He'd also taken a stand against racism: when his team became the first white team to play the all-black Harlem Rens, Lapchick often embraced his counterpart beforehand on the court.

After retiring as a player, Lapchick took over as St. John's coach and won the National Invitational Tournament championships in 1943 and 1944, back when the NIT was *the* tournament. After the NBA was born (as the Basketball Association of America), he took a crack there too, coaching the fledgling Knicks for eight years—he produced winning records in each season, guiding the team to three NBA Finals and helping integrate the league by making Nat "Sweetwater" Clifton the first black given an NBA contract.

Then Lapchick returned to St. John's and won another NIT title in 1959. In 1965, facing mandatory retirement at age 65, Lapchick attained his fifth 20-win season and reached one last NIT final. Although the NIT had lost much of its clout after the 1951 point-shaving scandal and the NCAA had moved out of New York, the latter was not yet the behemoth it is today, and the NIT retained a certain aura in the college basketball world. No team had ever won four NIT titles, and this was Lapchick's final chance.

At the Garden on March 20, 1965, the 6'5" Lapchick did not look ready to go quietly into the

# Honorable Mention: NIT Classics

**1. Walt Frazier catches the Knicks' eye, March 18, 1967, Madison Square Garden**

Southern Illinois was nobody, a small school new to Division I with no chance of winning the 1967 NIT with Al McGuire's Marquette in the field. But they had this guard, a quiet guy who wore penny loafers and button-down shirts, a guy who would make a name for himself at the Garden, earning his ticket to the big city for good. His name was Walt Frazier, and his NIT run was his first step en route to becoming "Clyde."

In the tourney's four games, Frazier swished and dished for 88 points and 19 assists; he even hauled in 19 rebounds. In the finals against Marquette, Frazier was the difference. Marquette held a 34–23 halftime lead, but Frazier, who'd finish with 21 points, sparked an offensive charge and headed a smothering defense as Southern Illinois outscored their foe by 26 in the second half for a slick steal of a win, 71–56.

Frazier's dazzling play caught the eye of Knick scout Red Holzman. The team made him the sixth pick overall in the NBA draft, and Frazier went on to make sure the NIT crown wasn't his last championship at the Garden.

**2. The original Big Man posts some big numbers, March 21, 1945, Madison Square Garden**

Basketball has long loved the Big Man. Before Shaq, before Hakeem, before Kareem, and even before Wilt, there was the original Big Man, George Mikan. At 6'9", Mikan loomed large over his college and pro career competition, and for one night at the NIT in 1945 he was virtually unstoppable.

Leading his DePaul Blue Demons against the Rhode Island State Rams in the semifinal, Mikan poured in 21 points in the opening half as DePaul built a comfy 42–25 lead. Had this been a fight, the referee would have stopped it in the second half when Mikan tallied 17 more points in the first 10 minutes to break the NIT record of 37. He added another 15 in the next eight minutes, reaching 53 points before checking out with two minutes left. The team scored 97, a Madison Square Garden record, while Rhode Island managed only 53—same as the Big Man. In the finals, Mikan led his team to an easy 71–54 win, even though he scored "only" 34 points.

**3. A little guy makes a big heave, March 14, 1946, Madison Square Garden**

With 5'11", 145-pound Ernie Calverley at center, Rhode Island State supposedly had no hope against Bowling Green and 6'11½" Don Otten in the NIT's opening round. Otten scored 31, which was no shock, but the big surprise as the clock ticked down was how close Rhode Island kept it—the score was tied 13 times, and Bowling Green led just 74–72 with three seconds left.

Then everything changed. Rhode Island couldn't get the ball inbounds, so Calverley—who played with a heart condition and collapsed after being hit earlier in the game—raced to the backcourt to get free. He grabbed the pass and as time expired heaved a 55-foot prayer . . . swish . . . overtime.

Calverley didn't score again—his 16 points were just third on the Rams—but when Rhode Island pulled out an 82–79 upset, Calverley's bomb became the most famous shot in NIT history.

night. He retained the nervous energy that had driven him for decades. (He suffered two heart attacks while coaching, endured hypertension with the Knicks, and joked about "getting ulcers on my ulcers.") Lapchick hadn't slept much for several days before this last go-round against top-seeded Villanova, and he'd spent hours beforehand pacing the locker room. Fifteen seconds into the game he was jumping around, exhorting his players and the refs, shaking his fists, falling to his knees.

Led by Ken McIntyre, who would finish with 18 points, the Redmen played impeccably in the first half, building a lead as high as 14 until Villanova—the eighth-ranked team in the nation and victors over St. John's during the regular season—switched from a zone to a man-to-man defense. Lapchick fretted as the Redmen frittered, their 10-point second-half lead dwindling to 53–51

**Joe Lapchick cheers on his St. John's squad one last time in the NIT finals, as does assistant and heir apparent Lou Carnesecca.**

with four minutes left. St. John's went into a freeze offense, hoping to run down the clock while looking for an easy shot, but Lapchick nearly convulsed in agony as his boys twice turned the ball over, then twice missed the front end of one-and-one foul shots. But Villanova missed from the field and then was called for traveling with 20 seconds left. Finally, with just three seconds to go, St. John's Jerry Houston clinched it with two foul shots for a 55–51 final and Lapchick's 335th triumph.

The fans chanted, "We want Joe," cheerleaders kissed the coach, and players hoisted him on their shoulders; when Lapchick was presented with the team trophy, the Garden din grew greater than it had been during the game's tense waning moments. Finally, Lapchick returned one last time to the locker room, where he couldn't stop yelling, "What a way to go, hey, what a way to go."

# 82. NYU topples Fordham's "Seven Blocks of Granite," November 26, 1936, Yankee Stadium

The Fordham Rams were heading for bigger and better things. They were sure of it.

Al Babartsky, John Druze, and Leo Paquin had NFL careers in their future, as did All-Americans Ed Franco and Alex Wojciechowicz; the latter would reach both the collegiate and pro football Halls of Fame. Vince Lombardi was on his way to, well, becoming Vince Lombardi. Along with Nat Pierce, they formed the defensive line known as "the Seven Blocks of Granite," and before Thanksgiving 1936 they just knew they were on their way to Fordham's first Rose Bowl. All they had to do was tromp on the Violets of New York University.

Coming off a 6–1–2, five-shutout season in 1935, this 1936 squad was touted in the press as among the best Rams teams ever. It wasn't just the players. Head coach Jim Crowley, who'd switched Lombardi from the backfield to that line, had worn one of sport's greatest appellations himself as one of Notre Dame's famous "Four Horsemen." He sported a 58–13–7 record in his nine years at Fordham, third best in the nation. The line coach responsible for the formidable seven was Frank Leahy, who not only influenced Lombardi's career but would soon nearly match Knute Rockne's success as head coach of Notre Dame.

Meanwhile, Tim Cohane, Fordham's sports information director, had dug up the Granite nickname. "The Seven Samsons" had flopped the previous year, but he had subsequently discovered the "Granite" moniker. Attached to the 1929–30 Fordham lineup that went 15–1–2, it had faded from use after they graduated, but after Cohane revived the appellation, its use by writers like Grantland Rice and Damon Runyon carried weight. All season long powerful scribes like these had given Fordham plenty of ink, inspiring media hordes and huge crowds to turn out to see the team and its gaudy new uniforms.

By Thanksgiving the Rams were undefeated, with three shutouts, but with their second tie of the season the week prior, they needed this game at Yankee Stadium to garner a Rose Bowl invite. They eagerly eyed NYU, which had not won their annual matchup since 1928. This year's Violets had lost their first game 60–0 and then stumbled to a lackluster 3–3–1 record. But they had no plans to cooperate with Fordham's vision of Rose Bowl glory—in 1935 it was NYU that had been undefeated and looking for a Rose Bowl berth, but their dreams had been shattered by a 21–0 humiliation at the hands of Fordham's powerful line.

Snow flurries flickered down and the field became messy, but more important factors were NYU's defensive grit and punter Howard Dunney, who gave his school the edge in the battle for field position by averaging 48.6 yards in his dozen punts. (Later it also came out that several key Fordham members were playing hurt after get-

**The "Seven Blocks of Granite" look imposing, but NYU will break through to stop Fordham's march to the Rose Bowl.**

ting injured in an illicit semipro game the previous week.)

Dunney, who would win the Madow Trophy as the game's MVP, set up the game's first score in the second quarter by nailing Fordham at its 5-yard line. NYU began its next possession on the Rams' 35. Two running plays notched nine yards, and then fleet-footed George Savarese, "the Pelham Phantom" in his days at James Monroe High School in the Bronx, caught a short pass, shook off a tackler, and galloped to near the 11. Another running play gave NYU first down at the 1.

The "Seven Blocks" hardened, halting the Violets on first and second down. But on third down, NYU's Milt Miller took the snap and headed right end while several decoys rushed left. Then Miller pitched out to Savarese, who cut back through the middle and lugged a straining Lombardi into the end zone. This crack in the Granite was the only rushing touchdown the line allowed all season, and it earned the halfback a new nickname: "Stonecutter Savarese."

This shocking turn of events sparked the Rams. Trailing 7–0, they forced a fumble on NYU's next possession. Wojciechowicz gained 40 on a lateral, and George McKnight fired a 20-yard TD pass to make it 7–6. McKnight missed the extra point, but still, there was more than half a game to go.

At day's end, Fordham would finish with more yards than NYU, both on the ground (117–111) and in the air (50–20), but NYU refused to relinquish its lead. In the third, McKnight picked off a pass near midfield but almost immediately fumbled right back to NYU's Harry Shorten. When Druze later knocked loose a ball and recovered it in NYU territory, Shorten again saved the day by

# Honorable Mention: The Old College Try

## 1. Army humiliates Notre Dame, November 11, 1944, Yankee Stadium

For years, decades even, Army suffered as Notre Dame's most famous sparring partner. In 1944 they'd lost 22 of 30 to the Irish and hadn't even scored against them since 1937. They were weary of being punching bags, and with Notre Dame's older players and head coach serving in World War II and the Cadets boasting their strongest lineup ever, it was time for revenge.

Army, led by "Mr. Inside" Doc Blanchard and "Mr. Outside" Glenn Davis, dismantled Notre Dame. The swarming defense produced eight interceptions, while the offense romped at will. As Military Academy students cheered wildly, Army ran the score to 59–0. Afterwards, Notre Dame's fill-in coach, Ed McKeever, sent a telegram declaring, "Have just seen Superman in the flesh. He wears No. 35 on his Army jersey. His name is Felix 'Doc' Blanchard."

Army men around the world rejoiced. It's said that when German undercover agents tried infiltrating American units before the Battle of the Bulge, they were exposed because they didn't know who won the big game.

Army won not only in Europe but again at Yankee Stadium the following year, a 48–0 stomping. But in 1946 Notre Dame reclaimed its pride, battling Army to a 0–0 tie and derailing Army's run for a third national championship.

## 2. Columbia wins . . . finally, October 8, 1988, Wien Stadium

The Lions had lost all dignity. Ending Columbia's torturous 44-game losing streak in 1988 was merely a matter of staving off further humiliation. After all, this was a team whose own band played the *Mickey Mouse Club* theme when they took the field.

From 1979 through the streak's beginning in 1983, the team never won more than once per season. Embarrassments abounded in flat-out routs and games they should have won.

In Wien Stadium—in which they'd not yet won since its 1984 opening—everything initially seemed depressingly familiar as Princeton led 10–0 after three possessions. But Lion tailback Greg Abruzzese, who'd finish with 182 yards, helped cut the deficit to 10–9 by halftime. In the fourth quarter, the Lions—playing their first turnover-free game in 16 years—seized a 16–13 lead with 5:13 to go.

Most weeks this would simply set up a heartbreak. Princeton did push into Columbia territory, but the Tigers—coached by former Lion coach Jim Garrett and quarterbacked by former Lion quarterback Jason Garrett—wanted to win, not tie, so they went for broke on fourth down, and Lion Mark Zielinski sacked Garrett.

Princeton had one more chance. On the game's final play, the Lions' destiny fluttered through the air on Tiger Chris Lutz's 48-yard kick. It fell short. Columbia won. Finally.

The streak's burden wasn't truly lifted until the 1990s, when Prairie View, a Texas college, set a new Division I-AA record by losing 80 straight. But when this game ended, coach Larry McElreavy wept joyfully while students tore down goal posts and marched around the stadium. It was as if the Lions had accomplished something monumental . . . and in their own way, they had.

## 3. The big Thanksgiving game arrives, November 27, 1890, Eastern Park

The crowd at Eastern Park in Brooklyn on a raw Thanksgiving in 1890 was so vast that extra stands were imported from Philadelphia. After years of gradual growth, college football, born in 1869, was finally capturing the attention of fans and press.

The Princeton-Yale game was the centerpiece of a day's activities that had included a Fifth Avenue parade and pregame tailgating in Brooklyn, with local restaurants catering picnics and drinks. Inside the park, some of the 25,000 fans lacked seats and were shoved onto the sidelines. "The crowd became denser and denser until it lost its identity as a crowd and became a solid bank of material," the *Brooklyn Daily Eagle* wrote. Nearby telegraph pools and roofs were "black with humanity." The temporary bleachers briefly overshadowed the action when they collapsed.

The *New York Herald*'s coverage declared that the swarming crowd "overtaxed . . . the intellect of the Brooklyn police force, many of whose members behaved disgracefully." But it wasn't only the police getting wild—Yale and Princeton boys drinking from what the *Eagle* called "black or brown bottles of suspicious aspect" acted rambunctiously. (That night 500 Yale students marched up Broadway and went into theaters, heckling the entertainers.)

The game was completely one-sided, with Yale destroying Princeton, 32–0, but that was almost beside the point. Everyone from promoters to ministers took note of the throngs. The former bought into the notion that football could be a big-time sport, and by mid-decade Thanksgiving games were a major event all over the country. The clergy complained about being forced to start services earlier to accommodate the mad rush to the games. Football fever had arrived.

intercepting a deep pass. By the fourth, the Violet People Eaters seemed the stronger team as they prohibited an increasingly desperate Fordham squad from even entering NYU territory.

The 7–6 loss finished off the Rams' Rose Bowl aspirations and was the final game for three of the linesmen, including Lombardi. (Ironically, he was probably the least accomplished of the seven, yet the subsequent Lombardi legend is the main reason this team is remembered more than the 1929–30 team and the superior 1937 team.) Even though he would pace the sidelines for numerous big games as an offensive coordinator for the New York Giants and as head coach for the Green Bay Packers, he thought this was the most bitter and devastating loss he ever experienced. The 1937 Blocks of Granite would cement their place in history with an undefeated season, giving the Rams a three-year mark of 18–2–5 with 13 shutouts and the number-three spot in that year's rankings. But what their greatness really did was elevate the Violets, who would forever be remembered for pulling off one of the greatest upsets in the annals of New York City sports.

# 83. Althea Gibson wins the U.S. National Championships, September 8, 1957, West Side Tennis Club

A quick glimpse at her childhood suggested she would never fit into the prim and proper world of women's tennis in the 1940s and '50s. It wasn't just the lack of a privileged background and access to country club courts. No, she was a troublemaker —even beatings from her father couldn't halt the truancy, petty thievery, and fisticuffs with girls, with boys, with grown-ups. And don't forget, even after sports like baseball and football integrated, tennis remained lily-white. Althea Gibson was black.

But there was one thing: when Gibson, who would make tennis history at Forest Hills in 1950 and again in 1957, played hooky in Harlem's streets, she was usually doing it in the name of sports: basketball, softball, stickball, paddle tennis. She was a gifted and passionate athlete—her father even trained her as a boxer—and once refocused, her cockiness, stubbornness, and sense of daring would serve her well on the courts.

A man named Buddy Walker who worked for the Police Athletic League saw Gibson playing paddle tennis and recognized her innate talents. He introduced her to tennis and to opportunities that led to Dr. Walter Johnson, who would later nurture Arthur Ashe. Johnson, believing Gibson could be the Jackie Robinson of tennis, took her down south, where he got her an education in the classroom, in life, and on the courts. The black-run American Tennis Association had achieved minor victories, getting Reginald Weir into a lesser USLTA men's tournament in 1946, but no black player had yet gained entry into the U.S. National Championships at Forest Hills.

Gibson excelled in ATA tournaments and got

# Honorable Mention: History at the Open

## 1. Don Budge wins the first Grand Slam, September 24, 1938, West Side Tennis Club

Don Budge didn't just win the Grand Slam, he invented it.

After the 1937 season, the lanky redhead with the deadly backhand was about to turn pro but decided to give the amateur game one more year. Then he realized that no other player had ever won the four major championships, so he strived to be the first. He told no one but his doubles partner, Gene Mako, then went out and just did it.

Yet while Budge ranks among the all-time tennis greats, his 1938 U.S. Nationals championship, the capper on this signature accomplishment, failed to crack the top 100, for several reasons.

Few top players back then competed in all four tournaments—the boat trip to Australia alone took three weeks (Budge himself had skipped it in 1937)—leaving the pools extremely shallow.

The Nazis detained his chief rival, the German Baron Gottfried von Cramm, for speaking out against Adolf Hitler's policies, so the clay court master missed the French championship. (Budge was among those petitioning Germany to let Cramm play.)

The amateur ranks were thin in the late 1930s; leading men like Fred Perry and Ellsworth Vines had left for the pro tour. Budge won the finals of the first three championships in straight sets and in under an hour each time.

His Forest Hills finals also sorely lacked drama—he beat the unseeded Mako, 6–3, 6–8, 6–2, 6–1; he blew a 5–2 second-set lead, raising suspicions that he tanked to spare Mako total humiliation. (He also won the doubles and mixed doubles crowns, just as he had at Wimbledon.)

Still, Budge deserves credit for his skill and perseverance. By being the first to win the Grand Slam, he gave Maureen Connolly, Rod Laver, Margaret Court, Steffi Graf, and every Slam wannabe someone to measure themselves against.

## 2. The Williams sisters drag women's tennis into prime time, September 8, 2001, National Tennis Center

You gotta admit, Richard Williams was right.

For all his loudmouth trash talk, his daughters were indeed the best in women's tennis, and the best thing for women's tennis too.

They might not have made a lot of friends, but they were good . . . and compelling. Everybody wanted to see what they'd wear, what they'd do, and how they'd win.

Serena won the U.S. Open at 17 in 1999. Venus won it at 20 in 2000.

In 2001 they met in the finals—the first time two black players met in any major finals; the first time two sisters had met in a major final since the Watson gals (Maud and Lillian) at Wimbledon in 1884; and thanks to their riveting personalities and powerful playing, the first time women's tennis was deemed to have players ready for prime time. After years squeezed between the men's semis, the women's final got its own show under the stars.

And what a show. And what stars. The Harlem Gospel Choir performed, a Marine guard unfurled a court-sized flag, Grucci provided fireworks, and Diana Ross sang "God Bless America." There was enough celebrity glitter to recall Ali-Frazier: Joe Namath, Robert Redford, Carl Lewis, Robert Duvall, P. Diddy, and countless others, not to mention tennis pioneer Billie Jean King.

Then came the tennis, which, though historic, was mostly boring. The five prior intra-Williams matches had been pretty awful too. This match was better, but both sisters still played nervously, not because of the pomp and circumstance, which they both relished, but because facing each other meant one sister would go home as the loser. Venus was, if not more serene, less erratic, making 19 unforced errors to her younger sister's 36 in a humdrum 6–2, 6–4 win.

Before Hollywood, fashion, and injuries began distracting them, the Williams sisters staged an encore in 2002. That time Serena won. But both nights the big winner was women's tennis. It had indeed come a long way.

## 3. Edberg and Chang stage the longest match in Open history, September 12, 1992, National Tennis Center

At the 1992 U.S. Open, Stefan Edberg became the first back-to-back winner since 1987 while regaining the number-one ranking he'd frittered away with frustrating losses over the summer.

It wasn't easy.

Down a break in the fifth set of the fourth round, Edberg outlasted Richard

into secondary USLTA tournaments by 1949. But USLTA officials said she'd need a good showing in other invitational tournaments to play at Forest Hills, knowing she likely would not be invited to participate in those secondary tourneys. But public pressure mounted and four-time champion Alice Marble sealed segregation's fate with a scathing letter in *American Lawn Tennis* magazine in which she blasted USLTA officials for putting Gibson "over a very cunningly wrought barrel" and acting like "sanctimonious hypocrites."

Gibson got invited to the National Clay Court Championships in Chicago; her quarterfinal showing landed her at the Eastern Grass Court Tournament in South Orange, New Jersey. Gibson had never played on grass courts, which were exclusive to the private clubs that had long excluded her, and she lost in the second round. Still, the momentum could not be stopped, and Gibson was selected for the National Championships at the West Side Tennis Club at Forest Hills.

Although tennis never underwent the seismic shift that occurred in other sports after they were integrated, walking onto the court to play Barbara Knapp in the first round in 1950 was a major triumph for Gibson and America. She trounced Knapp, 6–2, 6–2, but then, against former champion Louise Brough, Gibson was winning the third set 7–6 when thunderstorms suspended play—the postponement gave the veteran rest and the rookie a case of nerves, and Brough eliminated Gibson, 9–7, the next day.

Having reached the promised land and become a local hero, Gibson faltered. She was thrilled to play Wimbledon in 1951 but reached only the third round; she would not return until 1956. By 1954 she was slipping in the rankings, and *Jet* magazine called her "the Biggest Disappointment in Tennis." Had she been a novelty act?

Gibson teamed with a new coach, Sydney Llewellyn, and rebuilt her game. In 1956 she won the French title and the doubles crown at Wimbledon, pairing with Angela Buxton, who, as one of the few top Jewish players, was another outsider. But the real jewels—even more so than today—were the singles titles at Wimbledon and Forest Hills.

In 1957, Gibson, 30, finally put it all together, winning the Wimbledon final in straight sets over Darlene Hard. She was welcomed back to New York with a ticker-tape parade and a party at the

## History at the Open (CONTINUED)

Krajicek in four hours; down a break in the fifth set of the quarters, he outlasted Ivan Lendl in the tiebreaker.

Then came Michael Chang, the most dogged, determined player around.

Chang, who won the French Open at 17 in 1989 by outlasting Edberg in a five-set final, had beaten Wayne Ferreira in five sets in his quarterfinal match. But nothing equaled this epic.

These indefatigable pros moved each other around for 404 points over 60 games. It was downright ragged at times—Edberg made 67 unforced errors and double-faulted 18 times, while Chang converted only 11 of 34 break points—but always wildly dramatic.

Chang blew a 5–2 lead in the opener and needed eight set points before squeaking by 7–6. Edberg nearly blew a 4–0 lead in the second before winning 7–5. Chang came back from down 5–2 in the third, only to lose 7–6. After blowing his own 5–2 lead in the fourth, he saved a break point at 5–5 and gutted out a 7–5 win.

Down 3–0 and facing another two break points in the fifth, Edberg fought back once more. He finished with four straight games, turning away two last break points to win at last, 6–4.

"This was Edberg's shining moment," said TV analyst Mary Carillo, and an especially impressive moment because the Open had historically proven difficult for Swedish players, who preferred Wimbledon's quiet to Flushing Meadows, "which is so frigging New York."

At 5 hours and 26 minutes, this marathon is believed to be the longest in U.S. championship history, and the longest Grand Slam match in the Open era. The next day Edberg came back once more to beat Pete Sampras in the finals. But it was his arduous journey past Michael Chang that defined the tournament.

**Althea Gibson accepts congratulations from Vice President Richard Nixon upon winning at Forest Hills.**

Waldorf-Astoria thrown by mayor Robert Wagner. All that remained was to win on her home turf.

Determined to capture this elusive but coveted crown, Gibson blocked everything else out. She checked into a Manhattan hotel and rode a USLTA courtesy car out to Queens by herself each day. She methodically crushed all opposition—from the second round through the semifinals, she yielded just twelve games in four matches. Waiting for her in the finals was Louise Brough.

This time around, Gibson was the calm veteran. On September 8, 1950, she coasted up to 125th Street to get her hair done, then went back to the hotel for breakfast with Llewellyn. Finally, she headed to Forest Hills, where she played a more relaxed game, letting Brough work hard and make the errors, en route to a 6–3, 6–2 rout. Near the end, Brough was reduced to tears of frustration.

For the New Yorker, this title was the ultimate prize. "Winning at Wimbledon was wonderful," Gibson told the crowd. "But there is nothing quite like winning the championship of your own country."

Gibson would win both Wimbledon and Forest Hills again in 1958 before turning pro, but 1957 meant more—it was when she went from being a pioneer to a true champion.

# 84. Carmen Basilio and Sugar Ray Robinson go to war, September 23, 1957, Yankee Stadium

Sugar Ray Robinson was a flashy fighter, a flamboyant showman, and a Harlem entrepreneur, admired by sports writers and adored by the public. Carmen Basilio loathed him.

"He was arrogant and selfish and greedy," Basilio once said. "I didn't like him, and neither did a lot of the people who had to deal with him."

Robinson's supporters saw a stylish slugger, a technical and tactical master, and a symbol of hope for both aspiring blacks and a new generation of athletes — his fierce sense of ownership in negotiating his fights paved the way for the likes of Curt Flood.

Basilio, a former onion farmer and proud ex-Marine, saw a haughty son of a bitch and a show-off who was as concerned with gouging opponents in business dealings as in the ring. Indeed, even their prefight negotiations were hard-hitting. When Basilio vacated his welterweight title in 1957 to challenge Robinson for the middleweight crown, the champ — who was still in the ring at age 36 only because the IRS had him on the ropes — demanded that Basilio accept a mere 10 percent of the purse, half the customary amount for a challenger. When Basilio balked, Robinson backed down, but the bad feelings lingered.

So when Basilio climbed into the Yankee Stadium ring on September 23, 1957, he was not only going after the title, he was going after Robinson. With the heavyweight division in between the Rocky Marciano and Muhammad Ali eras, this was the year's biggest fight — Joe Louis, Gene Tunney, Archie Moore, Willie Pep, Sandy Saddler, Ernest Hemingway, and Douglas MacArthur all showed up for 15 rounds of a toe-to-toe, nerve-wracking, smash-mouth festival of violence. Only Ali-Frazier would eventually surpass it in New York's fight annals.

The 30-year-old Basilio, with youth on his side, was the slight betting favorite, but at 5'6", 153½ pounds, he was giving away five inches and nearly seven pounds. Only one 20th-century welterweight champion had managed to dethrone a middleweight belt-holder before — Robinson himself, when he slaughtered Jake LaMotta in 1951.

Early on, the implacable Robinson was the predator, sticking and feinting, using his reach to keep a safe distance while landing jab after jab after jab after jab. Basilio lacked Robinson's defensive skills and cut easily: Robinson drew blood from Basilio's nose in the second and from his left eye in the fourth. In Round 6, Robinson drilled home six straight masterful jabs, making Basilio look momentarily defenseless. But Basilio had enormous capacity for taking punch after punch and for returning fire when hurt. While Robinson sometimes disdained everything about boxing except the fat checks, the aggressive Basilio relished the confrontations. "When people buy a fight ticket, they're paying to see blood and knockdowns," he said. "Every time I go into the ring, I expect to be busted up; it's as much a part of the business as the boxing gloves." Basilio contin-

# Honorable Mention: Harlem's Own Sugar Ray

### 1. Sugar Ray gets revenge against Randy Turpin, September 12, 1951, Polo Grounds

Sugar Ray Robinson wanted his title back. The middleweight champ had gone on a European vacation in 1951, and after making whoopee in old Paree, he'd arrived soft and overconfident in London, where he was dethroned by British contender Randy Turpin. In 125 professional fights, it was just Robinson's second loss, and his first in nearly a decade.

Back home at the Polo Grounds, Robinson prodded and probed Turpin for nine rounds, looking for an opening. Not the most exciting of fights, but Robinson's methodical approach earned him a slight lead.

Then Robinson was imperiled, and his greatness emerged. In the ninth, Turpin opened a nasty cut above Robinson's left eye. It bled so badly that ref Ruby Goldstein warned Robinson he would have to stop the fight. Robinson asked for one more round.

In the 10th, Turpin came out aggressively, but Robinson detonated a left to the body and a right to the jaw, blasting Turpin to the floor. Turpin got up at seven, and Robinson unleashed what Nat Fleischer, editor of *The Ring*, called "a savage, searing, deadly attack." The combination of speed and power was immediately etched into the memory of all who saw it. On the ropes, Turpin covered up as best he could, but Robinson was relentless. Goldstein did stop the fight, but to save Turpin. Robinson was, once again, middleweight champ.

### 2. A rivalry is born, October 2, 1942, Madison Square Garden

It wasn't a heavyweight bout. It wasn't a title fight. It didn't even feature the sport's biggest names. Yet fight night at the Garden on October 2, 1942, was a crucial night in boxing history.

The welterweight matchup that night pit Sugar Ray Robinson of Harlem and Jake LaMotta of the Bronx. It was the first chapter in a storied rivalry that would last nearly a decade and later ascend into American lore.

Robinson had won his first 35 pro fights, 27 by knockout, but at 145 pounds, he was nearly 13 pounds lighter than "the Raging Bull," the division's top contender.

LaMotta scored with body blows in a tough first round, but Robinson responded by peppering LaMotta with left jabs to the head, controlling the tempo and the spacing. After reducing the impact of LaMotta's strength by staying away and wearing him out, Robinson mixed in rights to the jaw that wobbled LaMotta. In Round 8, LaMotta finally trapped Robinson in a corner and pounded his torso, but Robinson endured, proving he was not only sweet but tough. He pulled out a unanimous decision.

The win vaulted Robinson to the top of the welterweight class but made him overconfident, and in a rematch four months later in Detroit, LaMotta knocked him down and ruined his perfect record. Three weeks later, Robinson avenged his sole welterweight loss. Robinson eventually gained the title and won twice more against LaMotta before the latter moved up to become middleweight champ.

Their history together climaxed with 1951's "St. Valentine's Day Massacre" in Chicago, when Robinson dethroned and destroyed LaMotta; the Bull wouldn't go down, but Robinson won on a TKO in 13. Nearly 30 years later, the two met in the ring again when Martin Scorsese made the elegantly brutal *Raging Bull*, a movie that redefined fight films with its mesmerizing depiction of this great rivalry.

### 3. Sugar Ray gets his belt, December 20, 1946, Madison Square Garden

The world champion. Finally.

For years Sugar Ray Robinson—with just one loss in 75 pro fights—was considered the best welterweight, beating everyone from Jake LaMotta to Henry Armstrong. He'd fought 15 times in 1946 alone. Yet, before 1946, he never got a shot at the title, in part because he'd been serving in the Army, but largely because boxing's power brokers didn't want such a dominant black champion. With public pressure on his side, however, and Marty Servo vacating the welterweight title, Robinson finally got his shot against underrated Tommy Bell.

Robinson, who had beaten Bell previously, was among those who underestimated his opponent. In the second round, Bell leveled him with a left hook to the jaw; after Robinson got up, Bell bombarded him with more shots to the head. The crowd sensed a potential shocker, but Robinson finally danced away. Stirred up, he responded magnificently, gradually taking control in the middle rounds

*(continued on page 288)*

**Carmen Basilio and champ Sugar Ray Robinson slug it out for the middleweight crown.**

ually charged inside to pound Robinson's body.

After the sixth, Robinson slowed and Basilio got his punches off quicker and with more snap. He lacked Robinson's knockout power, but he certainly could hit. In the famous 11th round—considered one of the most enthralling boxing rounds ever—Robinson briefly rallied with hard rights to the body before Basilio countered with three blazing rights to the jaw that sent Robinson sailing into the ropes; some reports estimated that Basilio landed 34 straight punches before the bell. But Robinson demonstrated his famous perseverance, coming back in the 12th and pummeling Basilio with several combos. Suddenly, Bert Sugar wrote later in *The Great Fights,* it was Basilio looking wobbly, "his balance that of a marionette with its strings cut . . . reeling around the ring looking for a place to fall down."

But like Robinson, Basilio demonstrated determination and resilience rarely seen even in the upper echelons of sport. Ahead in the scoring, he held on, even after Robinson sliced up his face with another eruption of left jabs in Round 13. Although he was running out of steam and launching wild punches, one perfectly precise right to the jaw rattled Robinson, shifting the momentum yet again. Robinson, having gone through his second, third, and fourth winds, had nothing left in reserve. In the last two rounds, Robinson landed some good punches, but Basilio set the pace and inflicted more damage.

The referee scored the fight to Robinson 9–6, but the two judges voted for Basilio, 9–5–1 and 8–6–1. A ringside poll of the press gave 19 votes to Basilio and 8 to Robinson, with 7 draws.

The new middleweight champion had taken such a beating that he locked himself in the dressing room out of embarrassment: "I didn't want anyone to see what a bloody mess I was," Basilio said.

Robinson too was a wreck, though he downplayed how much Basilio had hurt him (prompt-

## Harlem's Own Sugar Ray (CONTINUED)

and completely dominating the final five rounds. He floored Bell in the 11th and battered him mercilessly in the 12th and 13th. Although Bell withstood it all, Robinson won a unanimous decision.

Robinson fought 46 more times as a welterweight, including six title defenses. He never lost, only relinquishing the belt in 1951 when he moved up to middleweight. There he became champion yet again.

ing his foe to sneer, "Robinson wouldn't tell the truth to God"). Worse still, the IRS decked him with a right cross of a tax bill for $514,000 to snatch his earnings.

Although this fight lacked the near-mythological stature of Robinson's fight against Joey Maxim and the 104-degree heat for the light-heavyweight title, it was his most dramatic fight in his hometown. *Ring* magazine voted it the Fight of the Year.

And in an odd way, the loss helped secure Robinson's legacy. He was so savvy a fighter and so headstrong a man that no one could beat him twice—he always had the last word, avenging losses to Jake LaMotta, Randy Turpin, and Gene Fullmer in rematches. By losing the fight and the belt to Basilio, Robinson set himself up to do the unthinkable. And he pulled it off in his last great fight, when he and Basilio bashed each other for another 15 savage rounds in what would be *Ring* magazine's Fight of the Year for 1958. This time Robinson switched to more right-hand leads and uppercuts, decimated Basilio's eyes, and came out on top in the split decision, regaining the middleweight title for an unprecedented fifth time.

Basilio may not have liked Robinson any more after those fights, but he certainly respected him. "You have to give him credit," Basilio said. "He had guts, and he was a terrific fighter. You'd be crazy to deny that."

After what Basilio endured in the ring with Robinson, it's hard to imagine anyone better qualified to speak on the subject.

# 85. Rocky has to go the distance, July 17, 1954, Yankee Stadium

Rocky Marciano won. Sure, there were harder hitters, more graceful boxers, better strategists, but all of them—Jeffries, Dempsey, Louis, Ali, Frazier, Holmes, Tyson—lost sooner or later. Not the Rock. By the time he retired to the good life, he was 49–0, the only undefeated heavyweight champion in history.

Marciano fought some of the sport's biggest names—on the way up he KO'd

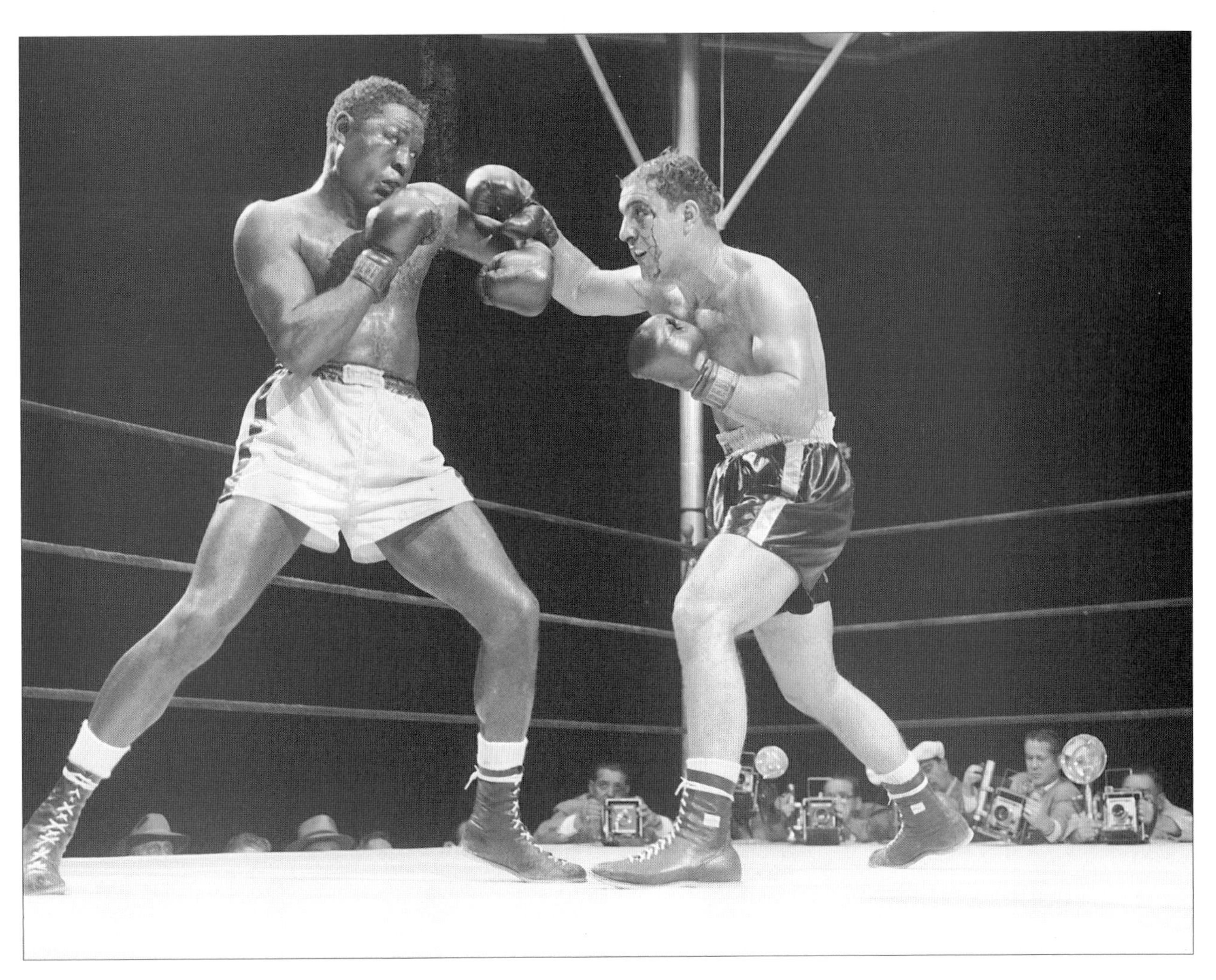

**Bloodied but not beaten, heavyweight champion Rocky Marciano attacks Ezzard Charles.**

Joe Louis, ending the former champ's comeback hopes, and in his final fight he finished off Archie Moore after suffering a shocking knockdown—but of all his bouts, his two Yankee Stadium fights against underrated Ezzard Charles were like Marciano himself: impossible to beat.

Born in Brockton, Massachusetts, Rocco Marchegiano nearly died of pneumonia at 18 months, dropped out of high school, bounced from one menial job to the next, and suffered claustrophobia and possibly depression before joining the Army during World War II. Then he took up boxing and started winning and winning and winning. He was small for a heavyweight—5'10" and 185 pounds—and looked awkward fighting out of his crouch, but he trained and fought relentlessly. "Marciano wore you down," says boxing historian Herb Goldman. "He kept coming at you."

Charles, a product of rural Georgia, had been a top light-heavyweight before winning the heavyweight crown by first beating Joe Walcott and then Louis. But after he lost the title back to Walcott, everyone wrote him off. When Marciano became champ, it was hard to imagine anyone in the division giving him a hard time.

Certainly, when Charles got his shot at Marciano on July 17, 1954, few expected him to put up much of a fight, much less go the distance. After all, Charles was almost 33, while Marciano already had 40 KOs in 45 wins. But in an exchange of heavy fire, Charles took everything Marciano had and gave plenty back—ref Ruby Goldstein separated them only twice, and Charles didn't touch the ropes until the final round.

Charles's superior speed made Marciano look

foolish, Charles's body blows stung the favorite, and a right cross cut Marciano's left eye. After five rounds, the champ was bleeding and the challenger was winning handily.

In the sixth, Marciano finally connected, jarring Charles with a left hook. Charles regained control over the next two rounds, however, and after eight an upset appeared quite possible. But in the eighth, Charles took a blow to the Adam's apple and began having trouble breathing. By the 10th, Charles's power was gone; he was still up on points, but his hopes were fading.

Marciano wrested control, but Charles refused to go down, enduring a brutal right in the 11th and everything else Marciano threw. Both men, faces battered and bruised, remained standing after 15 rounds. Marciano was the clear-cut winner, but Charles had won the respect of everyone in boxing.

"He not only outboxed me, but he mixed with me and I couldn't knock him out," Marciano said. "I couldn't even knock him down."

Three months later, Marciano did just that. In their rematch, Charles split the champ's left nostril wide open in the sixth, but Marciano, always dangerous when hurt, knew the doctors might stop the fight, so he stalked Charles with renewed fire. In the eighth, he sent Charles crashing to the ring, unable to rise.

Rocky Marciano won.

# 86. Rod Dixon surges past Geoff Smith in the Marathon, October 23, 1983, Central Park

The image has endured, in newspapers and magazines around the world, on posters tacked above the beds of aspiring marathoners, in a photo decorating the lobby of the New York Road Runners Club, and it's been reimagined as a Leroy Neiman picture in a shoe company's headquarters. Frozen in time is Rod Dixon standing in the rain, his arms raised in celebration and relief after his stunning come-from-behind New York City Marathon victory while Geoff Smith, who'd led for more than 10 miles until the final 385 yards, lies crumpled on the wet ground in excruciating physical and emotional pain.

"It is the single iconic image of the New York Marathon," says Peter Gambaccini, author of *The New York City Marathon: 25 Years.*

Marathon director Fred Lebow was not expecting such a classic when the race started on October 23. In fact, he was worried. In 1982 he'd had excitement aplenty with Alberto Salazar winning his third straight title in the closest run to date; Salazar literally emerged from a cloud of dust to edge Rodolfo Gomez by four seconds. But Salazar had skipped the 1983 race, and Chicago's marathon, with $135,000 in prize money, had seduced away four-time New York winner Bill Rodgers, 1983 Boston winner Greg Meyer, and others. With a seemingly weaker field and a drizzly, overcast day, could Lebow's race command the attention of spectators, television viewers, and the media?

**Rod Dixon raises his hands in triumph, while defeated Geoff Smith collapses behind him.**

Dixon and Smith knew that this would be the first year someone other than Rodgers and Salazar won the five-borough race, and each hoped to be that person. Dixon had only one marathon to his name and so he was not an obvious choice, but he was a talented miler who'd won the bronze in the 1972 Olympic 1,500 meters and was riding a 19-race winning streak (of mostly 10K races). A charismatic, 33-year-old New Zealander with a taste for the nightlife, Dixon had spent three months living ascetically and training rigorously in the forests of Reading, Pennsylvania.

The slight Smith, 29, was even more of an unknown than Dixon. A fireman in his native Liverpool before moving to America to attend Providence College, he'd made his reputation as a

# Honorable Mention: Memorable Men's Marathons

**1. Alberto Salazar backs up his prediction, October 26, 1980**

The New York City Marathon had never seen anything like Alberto Salazar. The brazen 21-year-old University of Oregon track star strode into this relatively genteel sport and threw down a dare—having never run a marathon, he promised to finish the 1980 race in under 2:10—which no first-timer had ever done—and to win.

The 6', 140-pound Salazar faced a strong field led by Bill Rodgers, winner of the first four citywide marathons. Both men settled into a pack of elite runners but let others set the pace. Around Mile 12, Rodgers was accidentally bumped to the ground and never fully recovered. At Mile 16, Salazar, Rodolfo Gomez, and two others began sharing the lead until Mile 20, "the wall," which wipes out many novices. "I heard all this stuff about the magic mark, where all your energy gets used up and you get double vision," Salazar said after cruising to victory 32 seconds ahead of Gomez. "But I really didn't hurt until the last half-mile, and it sure felt good to cross the finish line."

Salazar maintained a sub-five-minute pace the entire way to finish in 2:09:41. He was a man of his word.

Salazar secured his legend by winning the next two years—in 1982 by a mere four seconds over Gomez—before mysteriously losing his effectiveness to what eventually was revealed to be bronchitis-induced asthma. But the last American man to win New York is still saluted each year when the top American finishers take home the Alberto Salazar Award.

**2. German Silva wins despite taking a wrong turn, November 6, 1994**

Make one wrong turn in New York and you can find yourself in trouble. Just ask German Silva. But the fastest way into the history books is by overcoming adversity—even if it's of your own making. Just ask German Silva.

Less than half a mile remained in the 1994 marathon, and the Mexican runner, who had publicly predicted victory, was ahead of the pack, running side by side with countryman and training partner Benjamin Paredes.

Then, inexplicably, Silva turned, taking 12 wrong strides toward Central Park before spectators and police caught his attention. Suddenly he was 60 yards behind.

But Paredes failed to seize the opportunity, as though he believed Silva was destined to beat him. "It was as if he thinks, 'You mean I'm supposed to win?'" said marathon historian Peter Gambaccini.

Silva, a faster finisher than Paredes, erased his gaffe by closing strong. He edged Paredes 2:11:21 to 2:11:23, the closest finish ever. (That record was finally broken in 2005 when Paul Tergatof of Kenya beat Hendrick Ramaala of South Africa by less than one second.)

The next year organizers positioned motorcycle cops at Seventh Avenue and Central Park South to prevent another mishap. Silva, who had used his New York winnings and prestige to bring electricity to his tiny hometown of Tecomate, won again, but frankly, without the drama of a wrong turn, no one remembers it.

**3. John Kagwe wins in the closest three-way race, November 1, 1998**

John Kagwe could not break free.

Throughout the 1998 marathon, a cluster of runners hung close to the defending champion despite his efforts—at Miles 10, 12, and 16—to pull away. Gradually, by the 23-mile mark, he'd whittled the pack from about 15 to 9 men, but 1997 runner-up Joseph Chebet and Los Angeles winner Zebedayo Bayo did not fall away. Kagwe entered the homestretch with the two literally by his side. There they remained.

The Kenyan Kagwe, who had beaten his countryman Chebet easily the previous year, remained confident behind his dark sunglasses. Streaking down Central Park South before turning into the park, Kagwe let loose a grin. "I knew that I would outkick them," he said.

He did, but just barely. After an impressive 4:44 in Mile 25 and 4:51 in Mile 26, Kagwe screeched through the final 385 yards in a jaw-dropping 61 seconds. He pulled ahead of Chebet for good on the hill 200 yards from the finish, but his margin was almost too small to be believed. Kagwe's 2:08:45 was three seconds ahead of Chebet, and just six seconds better than Bayo. This was, by far, the closest three-man finish ever.

middle-distance runner and had never run a competitive marathon. Although recovering from minor injuries, he would spend much of the race seemingly destined to make history.

At the start, Smith hung close behind the Tanzanian Guidamis Shahanga, who moved ahead at seven miles. The front-runner faded past Mile 15, and Smith captured the lead on the Queensboro Bridge. Coming off onto First Avenue, he felt like he was floating, buoyed by the vast crowd hailing his world-record pace. "I was like a rocket down First Avenue, I felt so good," Smith said later. That pace would cost him dearly at the end. After a 4:43 mile up First Avenue, he boasted a 12-second lead; exuding confidence, he followed with a 4:44 mile, widening the gap to 40 seconds.

Dixon, meanwhile, struggled after slipping and overextending his right leg at the five-mile mark. But he stuck with his desired "splits" (planned times for each mile), written on his fingers, even as he fell far off the lead. After the bridge, he began what he'd call his "long, lonely haul" toward the pacesetters, fretting as he ran down First Avenue that there wouldn't be time enough to catch Smith. Still, he stayed with his set pace. Smith could not maintain his, slowing to 5:02, 5:08, and 5:15 miles, while Dixon nibbled away, cutting the lead to 35 seconds by the 20-mile mark and 18 seconds by the 23-mile mark.

In Central Park, Smith, who was battling leg spasms, strictly followed the blue line painted to guide the runners, "entranced" by it spooling out in front of him and too fatigued to think about strategy. Dixon, who was occasionally clutching his hamstring, knew he couldn't gain speed but still needed to gain ground. So he began "running the tangents"—legally cutting corners and taking each turn as sharply as possible, occasionally coming dangerously close to spectators. "Being that far down, well into the park, I had to use every trick in the book," Dixon said afterwards.

There's no precise measure of how much time Dixon saved, but the maneuver also added a psychological boost, especially as Smith's lead withered to 12 seconds at the 25-mile mark. Back in 1981 at a 10-K New Year's Eve midnight run in Central Park, Dixon had trailed Smith before passing him a mile from the finish. With his dedicated training and Smith's injury-shortened season, Dixon was about to make history repeat itself.

Dixon found a second wind while Smith lost his stride, then panicked and stumbled four times as the crowd yelled that Dixon was gaining. Now the tortoise could pass the hare with one final spurt. As Dixon told himself over and over, "A miler's kick will do the trick."

Right at the 26 Mile sign, indicating a mere 385 yards to go, Dixon surged by Smith, who cursed loudly but had nothing left to give. Dixon crossed the finish line in an impressive 2:08:59. He joyfully kissed the ground, then stood, exulting, throwing his arms to the sky. As he did—and as photographers snapped away—a despondent Smith crossed the line and crashed to the ground. His 2:09:08 was the fastest debut marathon ever run, but to no avail. He was nine tiny ticks of the clock too late.

Lebow's fears proved unfounded—the men's field proved exceptionally strong with 11 runners finishing under 2:12, and Grete Waitz wowed everyone with her fifth victory on the women's side. But it was the thrill of the chase that would long be remembered.

Smith was fairly philosophical, reasoning that had he been just another New York winner, he probably would have been long forgotten; instead, he—like Ralph Branca—achieved a sort of lasting fame. He taped the famous photo to his bed for inspiration and twice won the Boston Marathon (though without equaling his time that bittersweet fall morning in New York). Dixon, on the other hand, never earned another major victory, although he had the pleasure of returning to New York 10 years later with his girlfriend and, after a run in Central Park, posing for a photo that replicated his glorious moment.

But nothing can match the original, which captures the ultimate in athletic competition, according to Allan Steinfeld, then technical coordinator and later marathon director. "It truly represents the agony and the ecstasy."

# 87. Salvator and Tenny go down to the wire, June 25, 1890, Coney Island Jockey Club

As the 19th century headed into the homestretch, southern Brooklyn, from Coney Island to Sheepshead Bay, became America's most dazzling playground. From two-bit gamblers to high-society millionaires, everyone flocked there — for sun, surf, and sand; for the world's first roller coasters; for restaurants like Feltman's, where the hot dog was invented; for the wondrously elegant Manhattan Beach, Brighton Beach, and Oriental Hotels; and for the races. With three major tracks — Gravesend (where the Preakness was held for 15 years), Brighton, and Sheepshead Bay — this was the country's horse-racing capital.

The era's greatest race was the Coney Island Jockey Club's matchup at Sheepshead Bay on June 25, 1890, a meeting of two top horses, Salvator and Tenny, ridden by two legendary jockeys, Isaac Murphy and Edward "Snapper" Garrison. The result — thanks to an enterprising photographer — was racing's first "photo finish."

The *Brooklyn Daily Eagle* declared it "the grandest race ever witnessed in this country," and when it was over, the *New York Times* wrote, "men and women alike seemed crazy and hugged each other and shouted themselves hoarse and threw hats, umbrellas, parasols and handkerchiefs into the air."

Murphy was a towering figure in sports. In those days there had been a number of top black jockeys, but that era of tolerance was ending, and he was among the last greats. Riding upright in the traditional English style and using soft words to encourage his horses, he'd been the first to win the Kentucky Derby three times and to capture the American Derby, then the richest race, four times. He won more than one-third of his races, a feat as difficult as batting .400 today. Considered the master of pace, he was perhaps the highest-paid athlete and the highest-paid black in America.

Garrison, who was white, was nearly as successful despite a different approach: he used the newer "high crouch" technique, bending over the horse and whipping his rides hard and often. Even more than Murphy, Garrison was a grandstander who created drama at the wire — "Garrison finish" is still in dictionaries, defined as a close, come-from-behind win.

This race was born out of frustration. Salvator, the 1889 Horse of the Year, had beaten Tenny by a neck in the mile-and-a-quarter Suburban Handicap earlier that June, but D. T. Pulsifer, Tenny's owner, felt that his horse had been interfered with and challenged Salvator to a rematch.

In this eagerly anticipated showdown, the horses sprinted out together before Murphy and Salvator grabbed the rail and set off at a record pace, twice opening leads that seemed impossible to overcome. But twice Garrison and Tenny fought back. Salvator maintained a two-length lead heading into the homestretch, but the last quarter-mile was "a battle royal," the *Times* wrote, with Garrison whipping his horse furiously, riding the renowned sprinter "like a very demon."

Hearing the onslaught of the challenger, Murphy coaxed every last bit of speed from his ride.

**Neck and neck, nose to nose, Salvator and Tenny race to their photo finish.**

But Tenny kept closing, within one length, then up to Salvator's shoulders, then his neck, then . . .

As they galloped across the finish line all that was certain was that both horses had beaten Salvator's Suburban time and every time for that distance, setting a new record at 2:05.

But who won? Another 10 yards and there would have been another clear-cut Garrison finish, but he and his horse ran out of room. This was too close to call. Fortunately for race fans, it turned out that Jockey Club photographer John Hemment had snapped a photo at the finish and captured the moment precisely. His picture told a story all right—Salvator, in the midst of a 16-race winning streak, had held on to win.

Salvator beat Tenny one more time and was named Horse of the Year again. As for the jockeys, Garrison raced for years and lived until 1930; Murphy died at age 35 in 1896 after his career disintegrated amid several controversial performances in which he was either—depending on the source—drunk, drugged by someone else, or dizzy from dieting to make his weight. But long after their deaths, the two men would be celebrated together going in side by side in the first class of the National Museum of Racing's Hall of Fame in 1955.

By then the racetracks and hotels and the glitz and glamour had disappeared from the Brooklyn shoreline, but that one brilliant day in 1890 left behind a classic story of two very different men guiding their horses to one of racing's most thrilling finishes ever.

# 88. The Knicks beat the Celtics in double overtime in the Eastern Conference Finals, April 22, 1973, Madison Square Garden

In the fourth quarter of Game 4 of the 1973 Eastern Conference Finals, the New York Knicks trailed the division champion Boston Celtics by 16, and the restless Madison Square Garden crowd was booing. Victory seemed like a distant notion.

Still later, with the game on the line, the Knicks were reduced to a lineup that included a third-string center, a rookie guard, and a backup forward. It was a far cry from coach Red Holzman's original game plan.

In their championship era, two Knick hallmarks were their ability to come back and to get critical production out of virtually everyone on the floor. On April 22, 1973—Easter Sunday—these traits produced one of the most memorable wins in the run to their second crown.

New York had taken two of the first three games in the Eastern Conference Finals against the heavily favored Celtics, who'd romped through the season with a 68–14 record. (New York won 57 games.) But now the Knicks faced Game 4 without an injured Earl Monroe; although the Celtics had lost their leading scorer, John Havlicek, the Knicks bogged down without Monroe's ability to slither and slide, especially as Boston's defensive specialist, Don Chaney, clamped down on Walt Frazier. The Knicks didn't move well with or without the ball, and they didn't hit the open man or the open shot—in the second and third quarters, they shot a woeful 11-for-33. With less than 10 minutes remaining, they lagged behind 76–60. The fans let the home team know exactly what they thought of this uninspired effort.

Then Frazier, who'd managed only 12 points, hit a jumper . . . and another . . . and when he got the ball back, Chaney committed his sixth foul. With his oppressor gone, Frazier shook off his shackles and took over, transforming the game almost instantly—after inducing snores, it switched to heart attacks.

Third-string center John Gianelli (playing because of foul trouble to Willis Reed and Jerry Lucas) added two buckets to Frazier's nine points in a 13–0 run that nearly caught Boston. The Celtics stabilized and built the lead back to 85–77, but Boston center (and league MVP) Dave Cowens and offensive catalyst JoJo White, who'd finish with 34 points, were both playing with five fouls and thus had to forsake some aggressiveness. The Knicks launched another tear, for 10 points and the lead.

The Celtics moved back on top 89–87, but Frazier tied it on a fallaway jumper with 17 seconds left. Boston coach Tom Heinsohn yelled for a time-out, and his team complied, forgetting a new rule

**Phil Jackson played a crucial role in the Knicks' double-overtime win over the Celtics in the 1973 playoffs, and with New York having finally finished off Boston, his exuberance cannot be held in check.**

that required a team to first push the ball past center court. Then the Knicks and the Celtics each blew one last opportunity to win in regulation.

In overtime, the Knicks nearly undid all that effort as Reed and then Dean Meminger, who'd started in place of Monroe, both fouled out. Boston led 101–97, with 40 seconds left, when Frazier saved his team again, putting back his own miss and then grabbing a rebound of White's miss at the other end. Backup forward Phil Jackson hit two foul shots to force a second overtime.

The depleted Knicks had to send out Gianelli, Jackson, and rookie point guard Henry Bibby alongside Frazier (who'd finish with 37) and Dave DeBusschere (who'd finish with 22 points and 10 rebounds). But the Knicks' bench players were more than just scrimmage partners: Gianelli and Jackson combined for 11 points in the overtimes; Jackson started the second OT by stealing the ball from White and driving all the way for a lay-up; and Gianelli drew two crucial fouls down low and blocked shots by Cowens and White to help clinch the game.

The Knicks ended the game with an 11–4 spurt, to finish with a 117–110 win and a 3–1 lead in the series. They'd falter in Games 5 and 6 before defying the odds by beating the Celtics in Game 7 at Boston Garden. That triumph overshadowed the rest of the series, but this Easter resurrection remains a signature win of the Knicks' defining era.

# Honorable Mention: Peaking in the Playoffs

**1. The Knicks turn back Earl the Pearl, March 26, 1970, Madison Square Garden**

The 1969–70 Knicks believed they were a championship team, and they didn't expect the Baltimore Bullets—a team they'd toppled in the previous year's playoffs and beaten in nine of the last ten regular-season matchups—to stand in their way.

But in Game 1, Baltimore's scouting had the Bullet defense perfectly positioned, while Earl Monroe's dazzling moves and surprising willingness to pass shredded the Knicks, preventing gambles, helps, and rotations. The Bullets shot out 12–2 and led 52–46 at halftime.

The Knicks scrambled back, with Dave DeBusschere scoring 13 and swiping six boards in the third. When Monroe missed with two seconds left, they headed to overtime at 102-all. Twice Walt Frazier swiped the ball from Monroe to force a second OT, where the Knicks finally pulled away. When the Bullets scraped back again, Willis Reed, named league MVP that day, finished them off with a dunk to break a 117–117 tie.

Fans expecting the start of a triumphant procession instead witnessed a harbinger of a seven-game thriller. This win proved that when tested the Knicks could fight and find a way to win, which became the true story of their memorable championship season.

**2. The Knicks tear through Miami, 32–2, May 12, 1999, Madison Square Garden**

It was only Game 3 of a first-round playoff series, but every meeting between the Knicks and the Miami Heat felt like a heavyweight title bout. With Patrick Ewing nursing a sore Achilles tendon, the Knicks were packing less punch than usual, and this Knick roster, with mainstays Charles Oakley and John Starks gone, was considered vulnerable to an early knockout.

Maybe it was Starks's presence in the stands—he drew the night's largest ovation—but something inspired a tenacious tear. Down 37–33 with 4:41 left in the first half, the Knicks totally shut down the Heat, outscoring Miami 32–2 on a run that lasted well into the third period. The Knicks got points from eight players, while Miami endured one seven-minute stretch with no points from anyone. As the Garden resounded with "Riley Sucks"—chants aimed at the former Knick maestro turned Heat coach—the Knicks coasted to a 97–73 rout in a crucial step toward their improbable run to the 1999 Finals.

**3. The Knicks turn things around in a hurry, April 4, 1951, 69th Regiment Armory**

If New York was looking for a feel-good basketball story in the wake of the 1951 CCNY point-shaving scandals, it didn't look like they were going to get one on April 4. In the deciding game of their playoff series with the Syracuse Nationals, the Knicks blew an eight-point second-quarter lead, trailed 64–57 after three, and, after getting beaten repeatedly on the board, fell behind 70–58 with just 10 minutes to go.

The situation at the 69th Regiment Armory looked bleak. (Pro basketball was so low in the Madison Square Garden lineup that the Knicks didn't play a full home schedule there until 1960. Instead, the team often lugged 5,000 portable seats that Yankee Stadium had for boxing down from the Bronx to the Armory at Lexington Avenue and 26th Street, then broke it all down afterwards so the National Guard could run its drills.)

But suddenly everything started clicking. Max Zaslofsky, playing with five fouls, and Ernie Vandeweghe each made two interceptions as the Knicks ran off an 18–5 spurt to regain the lead, 76–75. The Nats struck back immediately, but Zaslofsky, who scored 11 points in the last eight minutes, fueled one last seven-point run as New York pulled out a stunning 83–81 win. For the first time, New York was going to the NBA Finals.

# 89. Willie Pep gets revenge against Sandy Saddler, February 11, 1949, Madison Square Garden

After 15 rounds of being peppered by Sandy Saddler's fists, Willie Pep's features were distorted and bloated, his eyes virtually sealed. He was a mess. But Pep had survived, and he'd done even more—at Madison Square Garden on February 11, 1949, Pep had won the most memorable fight of what was on its way to becoming one of boxing's most compelling and brutal rivalries between two legendary champions. Along the way, Pep had also made history, becoming the first featherweight to regain a lost crown.

Pep, 26, had learned the hard way that Saddler, 22, was a superior puncher. In October 1948, Pep had been the featherweight champ and proud owner of a 135–1 record. Though acclaimed as one of boxing's most graceful movers and shrewd tacticians, he was also overconfident and mistakenly decided to go toe to toe with his little-known challenger. Saddler, a Harlemite of West Indian descent, was 5'8½"; unusually tall for a featherweight, his height gave him tremendous reach. He owned a fearsome right and a vicious left that operated as jab, hook, and uppercut, and he'd eventually set the featherweight record for most career KOs. By the fourth round, Pep was horizontal, counted out.

In this rematch, the master craftsman was now the underdog. More than a quarter of the sellout crowd came from Pep's home state of Connecticut to root him on, but Pep, who trained diligently this time, knew the danger: Saddler was the real deal, taller, stronger, and immensely talented. To regain his title, Pep, quicker with his hands and feet, had to control the pace and make the brawler fight on his terms. So Pep came out moving, sticking and jabbing with his left, absorbing some blows but escaping each time. Sometimes he even moved so fast that he dished it out without having to take it: he landed 37 unanswered jabs at one point in the first round. Though many were mere taps, aimed more at scoring points than doing damage, Pep was a blur, and Saddler's blows were glancing at best. Pep won seven of the first eight rounds, while Saddler, despite blasting a left to the face in Round 4 and opening a cut near Pep's eye in the fifth, often looked "baffled and bewildered," James F. Dawson wrote in the *Times*.

Still, it was a dangerous and exhausting strategy. When Pep slowed in the ninth, Saddler, realizing he needed another knockout, caught Pep with a right and a combo. In the 10th, Saddler staggered Pep with a right cross, then ripped a barrage of rights and lefts before Pep finally clinched.

But going for broke exposed Saddler to more of Pep's pesky assault. In the next two rounds, a rejuvenated Pep hit with more authority than he had all night, landing a hard one-two to the champ's head. As a desperate Saddler grew anxious Pep pummeled him mercilessly, throwing jabs to get Saddler to open up, then attacking the jaw and the body. Saddler tired and began to look as though he might go down.

But Saddler dug in and seemed rejuvenated by Round 14, when he slammed Pep with two head-rattling shots to the jaw. Cuts near both eyes left Pep barely able to see, and by the final round

**Willie Pep launches a two-fisted barrage to regain his featherweight title from Sandy Saddler.**

Saddler was clearly stronger, nearly doubling over Pep, who relied increasingly on tying up the champ. The bell tolled not a minute too soon for Pep. He looked far worse than Saddler, but by winning 10 rounds on the ref's card and 9 on each of the judges', he recaptured the title, pulling off what the *New York Times* called "one of the most startling upsets in boxing annals."

Pep defended his title three times before meeting Saddler again in 1950, this time at Yankee Stadium, to accommodate crowds eager for a rubber match. Saddler forced his mauling style on Pep, who retired in the eighth round with a dislocated shoulder and Saddler's shouts of "quitter" ringing in his ear. The following year they scrapped once more in the Polo Grounds, but the animosity worked in Saddler's favor—this was more brawl than sweet science, filled with wrestling, shoving, and tripping. Often labeled the dirtiest fight of all time, it was won again by Saddler on a TKO after nine rounds owing to a wound over Pep's right eye allegedly caused by Saddler's thumb.

Saddler came away the undisputed champion but ended up bitter about being overshadowed by his opponent—he'd bested Pep in three of the four fights, but Pep was better remembered because he won the best one of all.

# 90. Eamonn Coghlan breaks Glenn Cunningham's record by winning his seventh Wanamaker Mile, January 30, 1987, Madison Square Garden

As the final lap of the prestigious Wanamaker Mile began, six-time winner Eamonn Coghlan was on the verge of becoming an also-ran. Fellow Irishman and defending champion Marcus O'Sullivan was gliding into his shoes as heir apparent, the new king of the indoor mile.

Coghlan, the first man to run a sub-3:50 mile indoors, had dominated the sport for over a decade, particularly the 11-lap Wanamaker Mile, the centerpiece of the Millrose Games. (The race was named for the founding family of the entire event, the oldest indoor track and field contest.) "The Chairman of the Boards" won more than 70 percent of his indoor-mile and 1,500-meter efforts over 13 years, including 15 straight miles through the end of 1985. He'd won the Wanamaker in 1977, three times from 1979 to 1981, then again in 1983 and 1985.

In 1986 Coghlan tried a faddish diet, but it depleted his strength, and he lost every race. Then he was attacked by a dog and hospitalized for three weeks. He'd resurrected himself in the past, notably after missing 1982 with injuries, but there was speculation that the 34-year-old was on his last lap. Yet Coghlan, the wild kid from Dublin who ran away from school till he discovered running on the track, had been feeling his quick acceleration returning to his final kicks. And on January 30 at the Garden, he was clearly the crowd favorite—the fans roared the moment he stepped onto the track.

Content to let others set the pace, Coghlan settled back comfortably in fourth place, conserving energy for his trademark fiery sprint. Coghlan remembered that three years earlier the legendary Glenn Cunningham—who shared the record with six Wanamaker wins—had emphasized to him the value of experience. Now Coghlan was counting on it against overeager younger runners like O'Sullivan and another contender, Jose Abascal.

When Coghlan dropped to sixth of eight after a half-mile, however, two questions bubbled up: Was he really lying in wait, or was he simply struggling? And even if he turned it on, would he be able to fight past so many skilled runners?

The pace was relatively unimpressive: 58.7 seconds for the first quarter, a full minute for the second, and just over a minute for the third. In the final three laps, however, a sense of urgency and a new look arrived: both O'Sullivan and Coghlan stepped up, closing in on the front-runners. With a lap and a half remaining, O'Sullivan—who had won nine straight indoor races in 1986—swung wide and shot for the lead. He thrust past Abascal with a lap left, but Coghlan was now stalking him, dusting the rest of the field

# Honorable Mention: Run to Glory

## 1. Glenn Cunningham becomes king of the mile, February 4, 1933, Madison Square Garden

Glenn Cunningham's greatness was born from tragedy. At age seven, his legs were burned so badly in a schoolhouse fire that the doctor suggested amputation and told the young Kansan he might never walk again. Cunningham relearned walking by holding on to cow and horse tails. Then he forced himself to run, run, run, run.

By 12, Cunningham — taunted as "Scarlegs" — was winning races. By high school, he held the prep mile record. By 1933, Cunningham was one of America's top milers. But Gene Venzke remained "King of the Indoor Milers," undefeated since 1931 . . . until the 1933 Wanamaker Mile at the Millrose Games.

Cunningham hung back in fourth place before making his move with one lap left, breezing past Venzke. The crowd awaited Venzke's reply, but he had nothing left. Within a half-lap, Cunningham led by two yards, and by the end he'd padded his lead by another six, finishing in 4:13.

"The Kansas Comet" was the new king. He remained unbeaten in the mile for 1933, winning the Sullivan Award as America's top amateur athlete. With five more Wanamaker wins from 1934 to 1939, he was the champ until Eamonn Coghlan came along.

## 2. American track stars give notice, July 11, 1936, Randall's Island Stadium

The 1936 Olympic trials could have ranked among New York's all-time great moments. Yet it started off as what the *Daily News* called "the most poorly-conducted major meet in the history of American track." Only wondrous athletic feats by American track stars, who provided a taste of what was to come in Berlin, redeemed the event.

Robert Moses had thought his new Randall's Island Stadium could make New York a major track-and-field venue, especially with the trials scheduled there to inaugurate it. But Moses got greedy: on July 11, he simultaneously opened the stadium and the Triborough Bridge; the bridge attracted President Franklin Delano Roosevelt, the media, and 200,000 cars; the result was the worst traffic jam since the car's invention. The new stadium, rendered inaccessible, sat half-empty, forgotten.

Worse still, it wasn't ready: locker rooms leaked, and the public address system broke — athletes didn't know when to report, and fans and reporters didn't know what they were watching. They did see Jesse Owens win the broad jump and 100 meters and John Woodruff's come-from-behind victory in the 800 meters, but it was a dismal day for New York track. "Out-of-town writers wrote reams of ridicule of the big city's small town efforts," the *News* complained, while the *Post* wrote that officials had "clinched the world's egg-laying championship."

Day 2 atoned for much of the first day's disarray. The PA system functioned, the stadium was mostly full, and the American stars shone brightly at midday, putting the Germans on notice by breaking two world records, two area records, and three Olympic records. Both Cornelius Johnson and Dave Albritton broke the world high-jump mark. Most impressive was Owens, who finished his meet with a record-setting 21-second performance in the 200 meters.

Randall's Island never became a track-and-field mecca, but the second day of the 1936 Olympic trials stands out as the one time it all came together, offering promise for the future and a harbinger of the historic 1936 Olympic games.

## 3. Nielsen wins the wildest Wanamaker of all, February 5, 1955, Madison Square Garden

Here's what the crowd watched:

Two angry runners wrapping each other up like "inebriated waltzers," as the *New York Times* said of the memorable 1955 Wanamaker Mile.

Here's what the crowd missed:

A third runner's explosive sprint toward the week-old indoor-mile record.

Here's how it happened:

Record-holder Wes Santee set a brisk pace, but Gunnar Nielsen and Fred Dwyer charged hard with two laps to go. The tiring Santee swung out to try blocking Nielsen on the final turn, but Nielsen blew past too quickly.

Dwyer then pushed toward the inside gap, so Santee slid back inside. He inadvertently bumped Dwyer onto the infield. Dwyer was technically eliminated but didn't know it and forced his way back, only to have Santee bump him off again. When it happened again, the frustrated Dwyer stiff-armed Santee, who retaliated in kind. Dwyer spun sideways, facing Santee; their arms tangled as they duked it out for the final 20 yards. Afterwards, they sheepishly shook hands and posed for photos.

By that time, of course, Nielsen had finished, virtually unnoticed. Ahead of the fray, he set a new record, 4:03, although it's one that's memorable mostly for the literal fight for second.

With a flying finish, Eamonn Coghlan wins his record seventh Wanamaker Mile.

and moving into third, just two yards off the lead.

The crowd was on its feet, cheering for the champion-turned-challenger, and both he and his protégé knew it. The younger runner—who would eventually win five Wanamakers—lacked Coghlan's grit and determination. Both seemed to know that too. With about 80 yards left, Coghlan zoomed outside and flew past Abascal and O'Sullivan. He won going away, five yards ahead, both fists raised in triumph. His time was 3:55:91, but most impressive was his final quarter-mile of 55.4 seconds.

Even O'Sullivan seemed thrilled with the new all-time Wanamaker record-holder. "I couldn't help but smile as I crossed the line," he said. "I had given everything I had, and I was just so happy for him. It's good to see the old fella back again."

On an exciting night when Pitt junior Lee McRae upset Carl Lewis in the 60-yard dash and Greg Foster barely turned back archrival Renaldo Nehemiah (just returned after four years in pro football) in the 60-yard hurdles, the "old fella" stole the show. He jogged a victory lap, grabbed his trophy, then lingered, signing autographs and savoring the win long after he had said he had to get back to his wife and kids.

"This comeback gives me more satisfaction than any of the others because everyone thought I was done—except me," he said. "Maybe," he quipped, "they should call this the Coghlan Mile." On that night, no one was about to dispute him.

# 91. Rod Laver wins the Grand Slam . . . again, September 8, 1969, West Side Tennis Club

Rod Laver grew up sickly and scrawny out in the Australian bush, but by the time "the Rocket" reached his prime, he was a notable physical specimen. Or rather, his powerful left arm was. Bud Collins once wrote that Laver's body "seemed to dangle from a massive left arm that belonged to a gorilla." Measurably larger than his right, the left arm featured a wrist bigger than Floyd Patterson's right and a forearm as big as Rocky Marciano's right. Laver scored knockouts on the court with his power, his topspin drives, and his hard slice backhand that enabled him to commandeer the net. Like most power players, he was erratic—if his timing was off, he'd make plenty of mistakes—but in 1962 and again in 1969, he stayed in a year-long groove. The second time around Laver made history.

Don Budge and Maureen Connolly each won a Grand Slam before Laver, in the amateur era; Margaret Court and Steffi Graf have each done it since, in the professional era. Yet each was relegated to this list's honorable mention. Laver achieved something even those four never managed: he mastered the Grand Slam twice—first as an amateur in 1962 (when he also took home the national championships of Italy, Germany, Norway, Ireland, and Switzerland), and then seven years later once those prestigious events had finally been opened to professionals. It was Laver's U.S. Open finals win over Tony Roche on September 8, 1969, to finish off his second victory lap around the globe that sealed his reputation as one of the best tennis players ever.

He did it at age 31, despite declines in speed and agility and an increase in vulnerability to injury, and he won it all even though he often seemed on the verge of blowing it. At the Australian Open, Laver had tough matches against three Australians—fellow legend Roy Emerson, Fred Stolle, and Roche—before he swept Andres Gimeno in the finals. His semifinal against Roche was the most brutal: a four-hour five-setter in searing 105-degree heat that featured a 7–5 set, an 11–9 set, and a two-hour, 22–20 set. Laver put wet cabbage leaves under his hat in a desperate attempt to cool down.

The French Open featured more close calls before another finals sweep (of another Aussie, defending champion Ken Rosewall). Laver dropped the first two sets against yet one more fellow Aussie, Dick Crealy, in the second round before overpowering him; then he lost the first set of his quarters and semis matches before prevailing.

At Wimbledon, nagged by persistent elbow pain, Laver again dropped the first two sets in the second round, this time against Premjit Lall. He also needed five sets against Stan Smith, dropped the first set to Arthur Ashe in the semi, and in a brilliant but tight 6–4, 5–7, 6–4, 6–4 final edged another Australian, John Newcombe, who had won the tournament in 1967.

By U.S. Open time, Laver was the focal point. He had an easy early draw, losing only 28 games against three unknowns. Then obstacles started

# Honorable Mention: The Feminine Side of the Grand Slam

**1. Little Mo reigns supreme, September 7, 1953, West Side Tennis Club**

Maureen Connolly streaked across the tennis sky more brightly but flamed out more quickly and tragically than anyone before or since. "Little Mo" won her first Grand Slam title at 16 and her ninth and final one at 19. In between, she won every Slam she entered, losing just four matches in three years. And in 1953 this teen became the first woman and youngest tennis player to complete the Grand Slam.

Since Connolly, Margaret Court and Steffi Graf have also won Slams, but Little Mo's clincher at the U.S. Nationals is more notable not only because she was the first and the youngest but also because her foe was far more accomplished. Neither Court's nor Graf's foe (Rosie Casals and Gabriela Sabatini) had won a Slam singles title (Sabatini later won one), but Connolly's opponent, Doris Hart, had already won the Australian, French (twice), and Wimbledon crowns, and she would subsequently win Forest Hills.

In Italy, Hart had handed Connolly one of her only two 1953 losses, but this match more closely resembled the rivals' French and Wimbledon finals, in which Connolly prevailed. The youngster hadn't lost a set the entire Forest Hills tournament, and nothing the versatile Hart tried—lobs, spins, changes of pace—could change that. Connolly blew her out, 6–2, 6–4, in just 43 minutes.

After winning the French and Wimbledon again in 1954, Connolly was horseback riding at home in San Diego when a cement mixer scared the horse, which reared and slammed into the truck, breaking the teenager's right leg and severing her calf muscles. Her career was over. Sadder still, in 1969 she died of cancer at 34. But unlike so many of the teen phenoms whose names blur together, Connolly attained immortality at Forest Hills.

**2. Margaret Smith Court has it all, September 14, 1970, West Side Tennis Club**

In the middle of the women's liberation movement, Margaret Smith Court proved that women could indeed have it all.

The tall, powerful Court, nicknamed "the Arm" for her astonishing reach, was the top singles player in the early 1960s, winning 13 singles Slam crowns as well as roomfuls of doubles and mixed-doubles Slam trophies. Then she decided to retire. But after getting married, Court changed her mind and came back with the extraordinary goal of completing the Grand Slam. In 1969 she won three Opens but lost Wimbledon. Impressive, but incomplete.

In 1970 Court won the first two legs, then at Wimbledon hobbled on a bad ankle through an exhausting 14–12, 11–9 classic over Billie Jean King. In the U.S. Open finals, Court romped through the first set, 6–2, over doubles specialist Rosie Casals. But if Court had any weakness, it was her nerves—she tended to think herself into trouble. She did just that in the second set, falling 2–6. But Court reasserted herself in the third, routing her overmatched opponent 6–1. She even took home the Triple Crown, winning the women's doubles and mixed-doubles tournaments. Then, for good measure, she retired again to have children but came back in 1973 and won three of the four Slams, including the U.S. Open.

**3. Steffi wins the Gold Slam, September 10, 1988, National Tennis Center**

In 1988 at the U.S. Open, Steffi Graf's strongest opponent was the burden of history.

Winning a major tournament is never easy, but relatively speaking, the 1988 U.S. Open was a cinch. Graf had dominated the Australian Open, the French, and Wimbledon, and in Queens she clearly outclassed the field—the recurring comment was that "only a broken leg" would keep her from completing the first Grand Slam since 1970. All the toughest players except Chris Evert landed in the draw's other half, and a virus prompted Evert to default their semifinal match.

Graf cruised through the first set against Gabriela Sabatini in the final, 6–3, before the expectations finally got her. She tensed up and allowed Sabatini to pull off her own 6–3 victory. But Graf reverted to form and steamrollered Sabatini 6–1 in the final set. The Slam was hers. Weeks later, Graf became the first person to win a Gold Grand Slam by taking the gold in the '88 Olympics . . . just in case anyone was wondering if she was truly unbeatable.

**Rod Laver returns a backhand en route to beating Tony Roche to complete his second Grand Slam.**

piling up and tension mounted. Laver faced off against U.S. Davis Cup coach Dennis Ralston, who had won three Forest Hills doubles titles but was not a top singles star; then Emerson, who owned a then-record 12 Slam titles, including more than one at each event; followed by Ashe, the defending champion; and finally 24-year-old Roche, the only player with a winning record against Laver in 1969 (he'd beat Laver in five of seven matches).

Meanwhile, rain — nearly six inches in 24 hours at one point — ruined the grass surface and disrupted the schedule. By the time the delayed finals arrived, Laver's wife Mary was three days past her due date with the couple's first child.

The weakest of the bunch, Ralston, gave Laver fits, going up two sets to one before fading. Beating Emerson required 58 games over four sets. Then Laver caught a break. His semifinal against Ashe was at 12–12 in the third set when a downpour ended play. The next day Laver quickly finished the set 14–12, while Roche endured a five-setter against Newcombe.

Only 3,700 fans made it to the final, which had been pushed back from Sunday to Tuesday. Morning rain forced a 90-minute delay, which featured a low-hovering helicopter drying the court with its propeller.

Roche came back from deficits of 4–1 and 5–3 to win the first set 9–7, but after his challenging semifinal, this drained him. Also, near the end of the set Laver switched to spiked shoes, which gave him much better traction on the damp grass. Roche never changed footwear.

When Roche, drilling big backhands, grabbed a break point on Laver's serve in the first game of the second set, the Slam seemed to be slipping away once and for all. A break could spiral into an insurmountable deficit. But Laver found his form and bashed three booming first serves to win the game. He would not lose another in the set.

Only a third-set rain delay could slow Laver's march to history at that point. Roche was overwhelmed as Laver took the last two sets, 6–3, 6–2, not even allowing Roche to reach deuce on his serve.

Laver was the first repeat Grand Slam winner and the first person to win $100,000 in a year from tennis, soon after he became a father. His achievement was overshadowed in New York, which was witnessing its greatest sports year ever in 1969 — the Jets, Mets, and Knicks were all playing championship ball — but in the tennis world everyone knew they'd just seen something special.

The new Open era, Roy Blount Jr. wrote in *Sports Illustrated,* "will have to be opened considerably wider, to include angels, highly trained kangaroos or something as yet unenvisaged, before anyone else will be in Laver's league."

Unlike the three amateur Slams, this one was completed against the toughest possible competition and deepest draw. And the fact that Laver did it at 31, seven years after his first Slam, was truly astounding. Given the current tour's demands — with night tennis and hard courts having been added to grass and clay — it's extraordinarily difficult for anyone to win a Grand Slam. To win two as Laver did is absurdly unlikely. To break his record and win three seems utterly impossible. Thus, Laver's 1969 win at Forest Hills remains a tennis landmark for the ages.

# 92. Jack Elder leads Notre Dame to victory with a 98-yard interception return, November 30, 1929, Yankee Stadium

In the last game of 1929, on a slippery tundra at Yankee Stadium, Notre Dame's unbeaten season and presumed national championship were in jeopardy. Facing 14-degree weather, 30-mile-per-hour winds, and frostbite, the potent Irish backfield — one both Knute Rockne and Grantland Rice rated the best ever — was unable to score. They were being held to just one yard in the second quarter when Army threatened to seize control of the game.

This game on November 30 is the forgotten Notre Dame–Army classic, the one with no "Four Horsemen" nicknames, no "Win one for the Gipper" speech, no "Battle of the Century" hype. But it was filled with nearly as much drama as its more famous brethren, including a decisive knockout blow that ranks among the most exciting plays ever in New York City.

The annual showdown came just after the stock market crash, but fans shelled out as much as $300 for box seats, the equivalent of a year's rent. Among the 83,000 attending were Babe Ruth, Al Smith, Samuel Goldwyn, Vincent Astor,

**Jack Elder navigates the icy turf and outmaneuvers Army's defenders, traversing nearly the entire field for the game's lone touchdown.**

and 40 coaches, including Pop Warner. Noticeably absent was Knute Rockne. The legendary coach spent most of the season home in South Bend recuperating from phlebitis while his team played nine straight road games. (Recent success, particularly in these Army battles, had made Notre Dame so popular that the school was building a vast new stadium.) Rockne did give a pregame speech to the players by phone with a loudspeaker attached—a primitive speakerphone.

Army, 6–2–1, played inspired football, knowing it was the last game for senior stars Chris Cagle and Hertz Murrell as well as for departing coach Biff Jones. Army used just 11 men playing both ways the whole game and still stopped the offense of favored Notre Dame cold, outgaining them 137 to 108 yards rushing and outplaying them overall.

Cagle pulled off some phenomenal plays that on another day might have set up scores, but the wind and cold were so brutal that neither team completed a pass. While Notre Dame went 0–4, Army's 0–7 included three interceptions. The most devastating incompletion for Army came in the fourth after Cagle ran a punt back nearly 40 yards to the Notre Dame 35, only to have the subsequent drive die when his pass to Dick Hutchinson behind the Irish defenders near the goal line escaped Hutchinson's frozen digits when he dove face first into the icy field.

Great teams like Notre Dame almost always find a way to win, and this game turned on just one play, the lone score of the afternoon. It came in that second quarter when all seemed lost. After an Army drive pinned Notre Dame deep, cadet Jack Price blocked a punt, setting Army up at Notre Dame's 13.

Cagle fired a pass toward the Irish end zone. Notre Dame had practiced defending this very play the previous day, when Jack Elder had spaced out and failed to pick up his man, drawing a blistering critique from an assistant coach. Elder, who'd scored six touchdowns on the season (the same amount the Irish defense allowed), was a senior playing his final game. As Army's Carl Carlmark cut sharply left, Elder saw his chance at redemption. "It clicked in my mind, 'This is it. This is yesterday,'" he said later.

Cagle had waited an extra beat for his men to run their routes on the tricky surface, and the wind held up the ball just a bit. Elder stayed close, leaped, and intercepted the pass near the goal line. (Some sources placed him at the end zone and others at the 2, but most say the 4.)

Elder bobbled the pass, then struggled to maintain his balance on the ice near the sideline. Then All-American Jack Cannon—the last man to play football without a helmet—threw a crucial block to open up the field, and Elder, a track star who ran a 9.8 100-yard dash, zoomed off. He outraced everyone the entire length of the field to score the touchdown, win the game, clinch the championship, and earn a place in the history books with his dash to glory.

# 93. Monica Seles and Jennifer Capriati introduce power to women's tennis while Martina does her best Jimbo, September 6, 1991, National Tennis Center

Dominated by one or two stars at a time, women's tennis long stood accused of lacking depth and diversity of playing styles. On September 6, 1991, in the midst of a U.S. Open focused on Jimmy Connors's miraculous resurrection, the sport shushed the naysayers with a volley of female grunts and squeals. One semifinal match pitted perhaps the greatest woman of all time against her successor, while the other served up the game's newest queen against its next heralded princess. Between them, they featured a little of everything: aging veteran and teen prodigy, net-rusher and baseliner, poise and breathless emotion, classic forehand and an unorthodox two-handed version.

When it was over, Martina Navratilova and Steffi Graf, with 28 singles Grand Slams between them, had thrilled the crowd with their remarkable precision in a back-and-forth tussle that produced three times as many winners as unforced errors, while youngsters Monica Seles and Jennifer Capriati had wowed the crowd with their raw, unharnessed power.

**Monica Seles grunts and blasts her way to victory over Jennifer Capriati in a wild, free-swinging semifinal.**

Navratilova, the best women's player of the 1980s, was seeded just sixth but doing her best Connors impression at age 34: she'd survived several three-setters to reach the semifinals. The top-ranked Graf, who had replaced Navratilova as the game's dominant player, had battled a shoulder injury after winning Wimbledon, but the 22-year-old still coasted to the semis. Their rivalry was even at 7–7, but Navratilova hadn't won since the 1987 Open final.

The match pitted the game's best attacker (Navratilova) against the owner of the most powerful baseline forehand (Graf). The margin of victory would be impossibly thin. To impose her will at the net Navratilova bullied Graf's second serve and backhand. At 5–5, the normally willful Graf altered her game to approach the net twice, but both times she was burned and Navratilova broke serve. Navratilova briefly unraveled after a bad call and lost her own serve before recovering to win the tiebreaker 7–2.

Navratilova had Graf pinned in the second set too, but she wriggled free. Down 5–3, Graf earned four break points before finally converting, en route to forcing another tiebreaker too. After Graf grabbed a 6–2 lead and Navratilova ran off four points to even things up, Graf not only rebounded to win the tiebreaker, 8–6, but did it on her first winner at the net, a beautifully angled backhand.

In the final set, however, another early lead for Navratilova would prove insurmountable. Pumping her fist, Navratilova broke twice for a 3–0 lead. Graf charged back to pull within 4–3 and even had a love-30 lead on Navratilova's serve. But Navratilova produced two inspired volley winners and eventually held. When Navratilova served for the set at 5–4, Graf earned two more break points, but Navratilova responded to the first with an ace, and to the second with a service winner. Graf's resistance broke down. Navratilova won, 7–6, 6–7, 6–4. She'd play the final against someone half her age . . . or younger.

Seles, just 17, had risen to number one after winning the 1991 Australian and French Opens with her overwhelming two-handed shots from both sides. Although she'd alienated purists and lost her top ranking by skipping Wimbledon, she'd crushed all opposition at the Open. A win would get her the top ranking back. Capriati, 15, had been reaping millions in endorsements even before she played her first pro match at 14; having beaten defending champion Gabriela Sabatini three days earlier, she was bidding to become the youngest player ever in the Open final.

Navratilova had transformed women's tennis with her superb athleticism and her attacking style, but her unique skill set allowed very few imitators. These two girls were both baseliners, but you'd never mistake Seles or Capriati for Chris Evert or Tracy Austin — instead, they brought

Navratilova-style oomph to the back of the court. This match, which Robin Finn in the *New York Times* called "a slugfest conducted by a pair of teenagers whose strokes defied age, gender and the legal speed limit," emphatically introduced a new power game to women's tennis and set the stage for an era ruled more by Seles, Lindsay Davenport, and the Williams sisters than smaller, cagier champs like Martina Hingis or Justine Henin-Hardenne.

This was tennis as hand-to-hand combat, with little subtlety and no stinting on either recklessness or bravery, depending on your viewpoint. Although Seles mixed in some lobs and drop shots, every point featured heavy artillery fired within inches of the lines. Although Capriati would say later that she should have been even more aggressive, the two players were remarkably free-swinging, going for broke at the slightest opportunity.

At first, it seemed there'd be no third set as Seles bombarded the crowd favorite to win nine of the first eleven games for a 6–3, 3–1 lead. But Capriati pounded back, reeling off five straight games for the second set.

The third set was topsy-turvy, roiling and turbulent, perfect for a couple of adolescents: more than half the 84 total unforced errors came in this set, and neither player held serve through the last seven games. Capriati broke at 1–1, then fought off a break point for a 3–1 lead. But she couldn't drive the stake through Seles's powerful heart. At 5–4 and at 6–5, Capriati served for the match, but Seles hit harder, deeper, and with more aggression. Capriati even missed entirely on some swings. Finally, they went to a tiebreaker. Capriati led 3–2, but blew a short backhand at 3–3; Seles produced a service winner, demolished a backhand down the line, then blasted a forehand into the corner to win 7–3.

Capriati left in tears and tumbled away from the cusp of greatness. For Seles, the match marked her 11th final in 11 tournaments for 1991. Two days later, winning her sixth crown of the year would establish her as the future of the game.

# 94. Henry Armstrong collects another title as Barney Ross hangs on, May 31, 1938, Madison Square Garden Bowl

Henry Armstrong and Barney Ross have been largely forgotten, especially compared to the other boxers populating this top 100: Joe Louis, Muhammad Ali, Joe Frazier, Jack Dempsey, Rocky Marciano, Sugar Ray Robinson. And the Madison Square Garden Bowl (also known as the Long Island Bowl) has faded completely into obscurity in a city that glorifies the homes of its biggest fights—Madison Square Garden, Yankee Stadium, and even the long-gone Polo Grounds.

These names lacked the staying power to go the distance, historically speaking, but during a bear market for heavyweights in the years before the second Louis-Schmeling fight, these lighter-weight boxers captivated the public. Along with Tony Canzoneri and Jimmy McLarnin, who engaged in a series of scintillating slam-fests, mostly in New York, this quartet was an urban promoter's dream—with a Jew, a black, an Italian American, and an Irishman, everyone's roots could be tugged to create rooting interests. On May 31, 1938, Ross and Armstrong treated New Yorkers to the most rousing ruckus of all.

Ross was the last of the great Jewish fighters (yes, there was such a thing). Born Beryl Rosofsky in Chicago in 1909, he was to be a Talmudic scholar, but at 14 his plans and his world were shattered. His father, an immigrant rabbi who also owned a grocery store, was killed in a holdup; afterwards, his mother had a nervous breakdown, and Ross and his four siblings were split up. Ross turned his back on his faith and set about earning the money to reunite his family by any means necessary. He boxed as an amateur, then pawned off the medals. He tried petty thievery, numbers running, racketeering. According to lore, Al Capone thought a rabbi's son deserved better, gave him money, and banned him from the streets.

Ross won the 1929 featherweight Golden Gloves, then turned pro. He had small hands and a slight build but was a deft counter-puncher with indefatigable resilience. In 1933 he earned enough to reunite his family, then edged Canzoneri in Chicago to win the lightweight and junior welterweight titles simultaneously. To dispel rumors about hometown favoritism, he came to Canzoneri's territory and bested him at the Polo Grounds. In 1934 Ross outgrew the lightweight division and survived his first knockdown, capturing the welterweight title in a back-and-forth 15-rounder with McLarnin. Ross lost the rematch in a controversial split decision but persevered the following year in the rubber match despite breaking his thumb in the sixth round.

At that point, few had heard of Henry Armstrong. Born Henry Jackson in 1912, he was the 11th of 15 children of an Irish-black father and a black-Cherokee mother in Jackson, Mississippi. They lived in a three-room shack under the sharecropper system until they moved to St. Louis when Henry was four. After graduating from high school as class poet laureate, he was laying railroad track for a $1.50 a day when, he later told reporters, a newspaper blew into his leg—upon reading that a boxer named Kid Chocolate had earned $75,000 for one fight, he hoboed to California and began fighting.

The 5'5½" Armstrong (as he called himself) had a thick, muscular upper body, skinny legs, and remarkable stamina—credited alternately to an abnormally slow heart rate and an atypically large heart. The heart of his popularity with fight fans and the secret of his extraordinary success was his hyperaggressive frenzy of an attack. It was capped off by his "blackout punch," a short, high, fast right that was not quite hook, not quite jab, but caught the chin square and hard. Often penalized for infractions because he fought in almost delirious agitation, he was nicknamed "Hurricane Henry" for the torrent of punches he rained on opponents.

Al Jolson and George Raft bought Armstrong's contract and arranged a title fight with featherweight champion Petey Sarron at Madison Square Garden in 1937; Armstrong dropped him in six, on his way to fashioning 26 KOs in his 27 wins and earning $90,000 that year. Jolson told Armstrong that he'd become the first 20th-century fighter to earn titles in three pure weight classes. Perhaps seeking attention, they scheduled Armstrong to jump two weight classes and go for Ross's welterweight title, with plans to drop back down and capture the lightweight crown afterwards.

To make the mandated weight, Armstrong ate steak, potatoes, and candy and drank beer every day, beefing up from 124 to 139 pounds; having officially made the weight, he was able to shed six pounds of bloat when bad weather delayed the fight. Ross, who weighed 142, figured his weight and experience would counter Armstrong's relative youth and the burden of history: the Madison Square Garden Bowl, a large wooden stadium in Long Island City, Queens, was nicknamed "the Jinx Bowl" because every champion fighting there lost—including McLarnin to Ross himself.

Ross, the favorite, looked like he might break

**Henry Armstrong pummels Barney Ross with his storm of punches.**

the pattern—light on his feet, he set the pace, landing just enough right uppercuts to sting his foe while keeping the hurricane at bay. He won the first two rounds.

Then reality set in.

"Barney Ross stood on the railroad track . . . and as usual the locomotive won," the *New York Herald-Tribune* wrote.

Ross was past his prime, and Armstrong was just reaching his, so trying to score against Armstrong while evading him wore Ross out. Armstrong chipped away at Ross's reserves while slicing and dicing his face. Ross won the seventh round only because Armstrong was penalized for a low blow. Ross's right eye was closed, his mouth was cut, and his nose was bleeding. He was utterly fatigued. And then Armstrong stepped up the tempo. There were no more misses, just a gale force of punches by the dozens, all connecting.

Yet Ross, who had never been knocked out, gamely held on. By Round 11, referee Arthur Donovan thought Ross was through. Ross said no. After Round 12, with fans pleading for Donovan to end it, the ref asked Ross's corner men to toss in the towel. Ross said something like, "You do that and I'll never talk to you again. I want to go out like a champion." That meant nothing less than going the distance.

Ross wobbled around, keeping his body half-turned away, simply covering up to avoid blows. Donovan warned that he'd end it if Ross couldn't fight back. Valiantly, Ross mustered some erratic, feeble punches. Armstrong later said that he carried Ross the final three rounds. Asked how he felt in the 13th, Ross replied, "I'm dead," so Armstrong supposedly counseled, "Just shoot your left, but if you shoot your right, you're [really] dead," allowing Ross to leave the ring standing.

Armstrong looked fresh enough for another 15 rounds, but the crowd's ovation was as much for Ross's bravery and courage (foolhardy though it may have been) as it was for Armstrong's accomplishment.

Ross spent a week in the hospital, then retired, finding nobler ways to demonstrate courage. During World War II, he enlisted in the Marines, rejected official suggestions that he teach boxing, and instead went to the front line. Pinned down in a foxhole on Guadalcanal, he killed Japanese snipers while several of his comrades died; later Ross was given the Silver Star — as well as plenty of morphine to cope with the shrapnel and malaria in his body. Soon he was a full-blown junkie, ruining his marriage and blowing perhaps a half-million dollars. After he went cold turkey, he wrote an autobiography and spent the last years of his life lecturing against drug addiction.

Meanwhile, Armstrong, the first simultaneous featherweight and welterweight champion, beat Lou Ambers in 15 rounds at Madison Square Garden that August to ascend to the lightweight throne. He was then the only 20th-century fighter to hold three belts, and the only one ever to do it simultaneously. (A rule later forced fighters to relinquish belts before moving up, and the import of attaining multiple crowns would also diminish with the explosion of weight divisions and officiating bodies.)

Armstrong gave up the featherweight crown when he could no longer slim down to 126 pounds, and he later lost the lightweight back to Ambers, but in 1940 he nearly beat middleweight champion Ceferino Garcia in a much-debated decision for what would have been his fourth crown. After retiring, Armstrong had ups (becoming a minister and helping run a boys club in St. Louis) and downs (battling alcoholism in the 1940s and dying penniless in the 1980s), but he would have one more shining moment. In 1953 the Boxing Hall of Fame inducted its first three men: two world-renowned heavyweights — Joe Louis and Jack Dempsey — and Henry Armstrong. That singular honor was reserved for a man who achieved glory in triplicate.

## 95. Harry Greb bests Mickey Walker amid a cavalcade of fists, July 2, 1925, Polo Grounds

Here's Harry Greb: he was two weight classes and perhaps 30 pounds lighter than Jack Dempsey, yet he embarrassed the heavyweight great so badly during a 1920 sparring session that the Manassa Mauler's manager never again let Greb publicly spar with him, much less fight him. The middleweight champ had also been the only man to defeat Gene Tunney, from whom he'd briefly captured the light-heavyweight title. And he did it all while blind in one eye.

Here's Mickey Walker: the 5'7" "Toy Bulldog" had spent three and a half years as welterweight champion and would go on to another four and a half years defeating bigger men as middleweight champion before challenging heavyweights, including champions Jack Sharkey and Max Schmeling.

On July 2, 1925, these two men—among the best fighters of their generation, but also the dirtiest and hardest-living—capped off a festival of fisticuffs at the Polo Grounds with 15 rounds of astonishing ferocity.

Some boxing historians argue that Greb's 1922 win over Tunney—a vicious 15-rounder in which Tunney suffered a fractured nose and cuts around both eyes that reportedly caused him to lose two pints of blood—has historical heft and should be Greb's entry to this list. But while Tunney's singular loss is statistically notable in retrospect, back then Greb was not yet a champion and Tunney was not yet a figure of national renown, so it was just another fight at the Garden, not a major event.

By contrast, the Greb-Walker brawl was one of the era's most anticipated spectacles, pitting two colorful champions in what would prove to be a highlight of both careers. The event, a charity fund-raiser, reaped nearly $100,000 for local hospitals and attracted a heavyweight crowd that included a who's who of New York politicians, a coterie of movie and theater stars, and baseball legends like John McGraw and Babe Ruth.

Even before the main event, fists were flying. On the under-card, welterweight Dave Shade upset favored Jimmy Slattery in just three rounds (earning Shade a welterweight title shot, which he'd lose to Walker), and Harry Willis, a leading heavyweight, slew Charlie Weinert in the second round.

Then it was time for Greb and Walker.

Greb, the middleweight champ, could handle a shot to the jaw or even a thumb in the eye like few others—in 1921 a foe's thumb had detached his retina, blinding him in that eye, but he kept it secret so he could keep fighting. (Live by the thumb, go blind by the thumb—this illegal gouging was one of Greb's personal favorites.)

He was also remarkably quick on his feet. Dempsey called him "the fastest fighter I ever saw." But most of all, Greb, "the Human Windmill," was known for fast, relentless punching.

"It was like fighting an octopus," Gene Tunney said.

"I thought somebody had opened up the ceiling and dumped a carload of boxing gloves on me," opponent Pat Walsh recalled.

"He threw so many punches that the breeze from his misses gave opponents pneumonia," opined veteran fight manager Dan Morgan.

At 32, Greb was seven years older than Walker and starting to thicken; he'd been unusually disciplined during training, yet strained to shed 18 pounds in order to meet weight specifications. He'd run two laps around the Central Park Reservoir the morning of the weigh-in to reach 159 pounds; he hoped that being seven pounds heavier than his younger foe would give him an edge that might offset the age difference.

Yet Greb defended his crown as the underdog thanks to a devious ploy. Just before the showdown, Greb, who often bet his entire purse on himself, took two showgirls to Lindy's, a gamblers' hangout, and staggered around "drunk." It was an act, and a successful one: by fight night the odds were stacked against Greb.

Walker, the welterweight champ, shared Greb's aggressive, anything-goes style but punched even harder. (He'd later beat heavyweight contenders like King Levinsky and extend Sharkey to 15 rounds despite tremendous weight differentials.) Also like Greb, Walker preferred whiskey and women to roadwork and seemed best suited to barroom brawls, although out of the ring he was a skilled golfer and painter whose works would later hang in respected galleries.

Once in the ring, the two men fought savagely. Even the clinches bristled with mauling and wrestling. Once, Greb worked his way behind Walker and then punched; twice the ref was knocked to the floor trying to separate them. (Greb is said to have done it on purpose.)

Greb adopted a rope-a-dope variation in the early rounds, hoping to tire out the superbly conditioned Walker. Greb himself, however, seemed destined for disaster. By fighting in close, he absorbed blow after blow to the stomach, ribs, and heart. The newspapers' round-by-round accounts are rife with repetition—"Walker hooked another left to the body. . . . Walker hooked a terrific left

# Honorable Mention: I'm Gonna Go the Distance

## 1. Jim Jeffries beats Tom Sharkey under the movie lights, November 3, 1899, Coney Island

Sometimes it's not the humidity, it really is the heat. In 1899 Jim Jeffries and Tom Sharkey slugged through perhaps the most savage heavyweight title fight ever, yet the horrific physical punishment they received from on high was far worse—not divine intervention but man's primitive invention, which baked and boiled them under klieg lights that raised the ring temperature to 115 degrees.

This bout at the Greater New York Athletic Club was the first sporting event successfully filmed with artificial lights. An outdoor fight had been recorded in 1897, but film of the previous Coney Island title fight, between Jeffries and Bob Fitzsimmons, came out completely blank. So this was a momentous occasion, starting the world unwittingly toward Howard Cosell, instant replay, and *SportsCenter*.

It was pure torture for the boxers. Hundreds of arc lamps, providing 80,000 candlepower, along with what the *Brooklyn Daily Eagle* called "bright sheet tin reflectors," hung just above on a tremendous overhead framework, low enough for the 6'2" Jeffries to touch. The lights slowly roasted the men, who sat beneath umbrellas between rounds, and nearly blinded them as well. Yet for 25 rounds they assailed each other with every weapon they possessed.

Jeffries, the champion, had an advantage of 5 inches and 30 pounds, enabling him to sting Sharkey with his left but also manhandle him inside, literally shoving him into the ropes. Sharkey was knocked down and had his ear split, his eye lacerated, and two ribs broken. But Sharkey drew blood from Jeffries' mouth and ear, bludgeoned his face, and then broke his nose with a head butt.

In the final round, Sharkey trapped Jeffries' hand under his arm. Jeffries hurled Sharkey down head over heels, tearing the glove off. Even as the referee was putting the glove back on, Sharkey launched another attack; he also kept swinging after the final bell. Jeffries won the decision because his punches were clean and crisp, while Sharkey countered with low blows, chokeholds, late hits, head butts, and forearms.

Fourteen miles of footage were filmed, but several things went terribly awry:

- Both men were well-done: fried to a crisp by the lights, they both suffered burns and had the hair literally cooked off their heads. Sharkey was hospitalized because of the heat.
- A fight nearly erupted in the stands between the Biograph Company—started by a former employee of Thomas Edison—which had the film contract, and Albert Smith of the Vitagraph Company, who'd capitalized on the blazing lights by secretly filming with a camera hidden by a pile of umbrellas. Smith reportedly resorted to piracy because of fiscal woes and pressure from Edison, who viewed Biograph as a rival.
- Vitagraph captured the entire fight, but Biograph's cameras malfunctioned in the final round, so the producers persuaded Jeffries and Sharkey to return to the ring for reshooting after they recovered. Continuity was deemed irrelevant: the producers got a substitute ref and trotted out the two fighters—now bald—to refight the 25th round again . . . and again . . . and again . . . and again, four times before the filmmakers called it a wrap.

Even then, the fight just wouldn't go away. More than 20 years later, Jeffries and Sharkey teamed up for a vaudeville tour replicating the original action nightly in an exhibition bout. That time they made do with just spotlights.

## 2. Beau Jack and Bob Montgomery slug it out for a good cause, August 4, 1944, Madison Square Garden

Beau Jack and Bob Montgomery had fought three times for the lightweight title; each battle was bloody and brutal, and each went the distance. Their fourth fight had no belt on the line, but this time the stakes were much larger—a fund-raising effort for truly bloody battlers—and the result was one of boxing's finest hours.

In 1943 Montgomery had wrested the lightweight crown away from Beau Jack; he lost it back six months later, then regained it from his rival four months after that. Madison Square Garden hosted each fight, and all went the full 15 rounds. Soon after, both men joined the Army. Less than two months after D-Day, they came once more to the Garden. But they fought this 10-rounder for free, and everyone in attento the body. . . . Walker hooked a hard left to the body"—that convey the terrible beating he received from the stronger man.

By the fifth, fans were calling for the ref to stop the fight, but Greb's savvy was paying dividends: Walker would have been far more dangerous throwing long punches, and his inside game was further neutralized by Greb's weight advantage and constant clinching. So, although Walker was way ahead on the scorecards, the damage was minimized and he was growing weary.

In the fifth round, after Greb backed Walker into the ropes with a barrage of blows, Walker finally moved upstairs, smashing Greb's face with his best punch. Greb was unfazed: he spit out a few teeth, then continued fighting. That was when Walker's window of opportunity closed; from the sixth round on, it was almost all Greb.

Greb lacked a knockout blow, however, and Walker possessed a tenacious spirit, so the two men just kept swinging, exchanging blows toe to toe, sneaking inside to smash each other's kidneys, grab each other's arms, and use their thumbs to unseemly advantage. Greb was more expert at such tricks. Walker's lip got bloodied and split, his nose bloodied and battered, his right eye bloodied and puffed. But still he kept coming. And while Greb flashed fists at a lightning pace, Walker occasionally snatched a round, lending hope that he might snatch a decision. In the ninth, after taking right after right on the chin, Walker retaliated so hard to his opponent's body that the press could hear Greb grunt in agony; Walker won the round.

What made this fight remarkable was that the

## *I'm Gonna Go the Distance* (CONTINUED)

dance bought a war bond to get in, except for the servicemen who received donated tickets.

Jack won the first four rounds easily, but Montgomery found his footing and evened the score. In the late rounds, Jack recovered and eked out a decision. The two men had each won twice, but with the event raising an astonishing $35.8 million, the big winner was America.

**3. Jim Braddock becomes "the Cinderella Man," June 14, 1935, Madison Square Garden Bowl**

Great story, lousy fight.

If Prince Charming was as much of a boor and a tease as Max Baer, Cinderella would have left the ball early, hailing a cab instead of awaiting her pumpkin. So give Jim Braddock, dubbed "the Cinderella Man," credit for sticking it out as he stuck it to the heavily favored Baer while the heavyweight champ pranced and clowned his title away at the outdoor Madison Square Garden Bowl in Long Island City.

A book and Hollywood movie have recently raised Braddock's profile, and his Depression-era saga—middleweight and light-heavyweight up-and-comer, injured has-been working the docks and collecting relief, heavyweight champ—has undeniable appeal. He was a human version of Seabiscuit, albeit a less accomplished one.

But given Baer's propensity for goofing around, Braddock's win may not have been the great upset the press proclaimed; one prefight poll of fighters, managers, and promoters in fact tilted heavily toward the challenger. Even acknowledging it as one of the dozen greatest upsets in heavyweight history only partly compensates for the action, or lack thereof. The crowd booed Baer's lackluster performance, while the ref penalized him in three rounds for backhanding. Combine Baer's seeming disinterest and Braddock's plodding style and the fight was a snore. On the front page, the *New York Times* hailed the result as "stunningly amazing," but called the fighting "utterly lacking in competitive appeal . . . one of the worst heavyweight championship contests in all the long history of the ring."

"The only news was that Braddock won and it was more that Baer lost," says boxing expert Bert Sugar. "It was a terrible fight. Baer didn't give a shit, he was more interested in winking at women in the crowd. Give it 'Horrible Mention.'"

Braddock didn't last long as champ. One bout later, there was a new heavyweight champ, one with not only a good story but plenty of great fights in him. His name was Joe Louis.

**In the 1920s middleweight champ Harry Greb ranks among the boxing elite, and his battle royal with Mickey Walker fills the Polo Grounds.**

momentum seemed to change in every round. Greb won the 10th, using his weight to shove Walker around and his windmill delivery to slash Walker's face and body. But in Round 11, after Greb pushed and prodded and did who-knows-what-else inside, Walker escaped with a left to the jaw that sent Greb reeling, clinching desperately until the bell.

It wasn't until Greb won the 13th round that the math took its toll—any decision would go to Greb, so only a knockout could save the challenger. When Greb caught him flush on the jaw in Round 14, however, Walker seemed to be the one more likely to go down. "For one full minute Mickey was a broken blossom, dazed and beaten," wrote Grantland Rice. "For that one minute he took everything Greb had, a gory, helpless figure unable to raise a glove, but he had enough heart to stand up before the leather salvo."

The overeager Greb moved so quickly that he inadvertently trapped Walker against the ropes, leaving the sagging body nowhere to fall. Walker, essentially out on his feet, somehow still managed one last fistic flurry before the bell. And amazingly, in Round 15 both men fired shot after shot, trading blows even as the final bell rang.

The fight was so astonishing that it lingered long after the last punch—a little embellishing here, a sordid detail added there, until it sounded like something out of the Roman Coliseum. Stories abound about Greb twirling Walker around to make him dizzy, about Greb biting his foe, about Walker becoming so disoriented that he started crying. The cherry atop the swirling sundae of myth is the woolly tale about Walker and Greb running into each other at a Manhattan bar that night and coming to blows on the street, though many historians, including boxing writer Bert Sugar, dismiss the tale as outright malarkey.

The real story was that both boxers' fortunes changed dramatically soon after. Greb's hold on the title did not last long. Losing sight in his good eye and weakened by again shedding the necessary weight, he lost the next year to Tiger Flowers, then lost the rematch on a decision everyone from the referee to Gene Tunney to the New York Athletic Commission thought unjust. Greb bitterly said that Flowers was no champ and would lose his next title defense. It would not come against Greb, who was injured in a car crash; unable to breathe properly, he underwent surgery but died on the operating table. Two months later, Flowers did indeed lose the middleweight crown, dethroned by none other than Mickey Walker.

# 96. Pete Sampras shows his guts against Alex Corretja, September 5, 1996, National Tennis Center

Every great champion has his defining moment, the triumph that provides full measure not just of his ability but of his heart, his guts.

For Pete Sampras—a far less emotive player than the U.S. Open era's first two great champions, Jimmy Connors and John McEnroe—that moment found him doubled over in agony, vomiting and helpless before the crowd and television audience. Strange, but it was just what Sampras needed.

In 1990 Sampras had become the youngest man to win the U.S. Open, but while he'd eventually win more major singles titles then anyone, including five Opens in eight finals, at first he felt burdened by his crown, and by 1992 he was struggling badly. It was a new coach, Tim Gullickson, who revived him, convincing Sampras to become somewhat less reliant on serves and winners and to play a more disciplined game. The new Sampras nabbed Wimbledon and the Open in 1993, Wimbledon and the Australian Open the following year, then Wimbledon and the Open again in 1995.

Yet few people rooted for him; fans preferred colorful players like Boris Becker and Andre Agassi or underdogs like Michael Chang. Sampras's overpowering serve and excruciatingly bland personality made even the even-keeled Stefan Edberg seem thrilling. "He was so completely unfascinating that much of the blame for the lack of magnetism in men's tennis was laid right at his feet," Michael Wilbon wrote in the *Washington Post.*

In 1995 Sampras at last began revealing his human side, sobbing during an Australian Open match on the day he learned that Gullickson had a brain tumor and later playing through cramps and dehydration in a Davis Cup match. Playing tennis with Agassi on the city's streets in Nike's charming commercial helped too. Still, when Sampras beat Becker in the 1995 Wimbledon final, the crowd showered the defeated man with adulation while granting Sampras polite applause.

In 1996 Sampras would finally win over the public by facing genuine adversity with courage and class. Gullickson, who was both coach and friend to the somewhat isolated champion, died in May. Sampras became determined to keep alive his streak of winning at least one Slam a year so that he could dedicate a title to his departed friend, but that explicit desire was a heavy burden for a player already drained, distracted, and distraught. When Sampras reached the French Open semis against Yevgeny Kafelnikov, he abruptly lost his momentum and will, trudging aimlessly through the final two sets, 0–6, 2–6. He lost at Wimbledon in the quarters, then strained his Achilles tendon, an injury that forced him out of the Olympics. The pressure was grinding him down. "He's got to get to the point where he's play-

# Honorable Mention: Tennis at Its Most Tense: The Tiebreaker

**1. Pete and Andre play to perfection, September 5, 2001, National Tennis Center**

Pete Sampras and Andre Agassi had had a friendly rivalry since childhood. But Sampras's consistency made it a rather one-sided affair: from 1990 to 1999, Sampras won 17 of their 28 matches, including two U.S. Open finals. But then Sampras slowed while Agassi showed surprising tenacity; the latter took three straight matchups. At the 2001 U.S. Open, Agassi was seeded second while the slumping Sampras was just 10th, but in the quarterfinals Sampras revived his game while Agassi maintained his.

They played with pace and precision in what was a stunning performance even by their own lofty standards, and as close to perfection as possible in one of the greatest Open showdowns ever: of 338 points, there were 178 winners and only 59 unforced errors. Neither player gave an inch.

First set: Hold, hold, hold, until 6–6. Even the tiebreaker was close, with Agassi squeaking by 9–7.

Second set: Hold, hold, hold . . . the buzz started. Something was going on. This time Sampras won the tiebreaker, 7–2.

Third set: Hold, hold, holy smoke, these guys were unbelievable, pounding the ball with terrifying force yet remarkable crispness. Both played aggressively, without a hint of tentativeness. Sampras captured the tiebreaker, 7–2.

Fourth set: Hold, hold, hold everything. More than an epic duel, this was history. 'Round midnight, at 6–6 again, after nearly three and a half hours and 48 games, there had not been a single service break. In fact, Sampras had faced only three break points (he poured in 25 aces against the game's best returner), while Agassi confronted just six (and came up with 18 aces of his own). This was an Open first.

The crowd of 23,033 showered both men with a heartfelt standing ovation. Agassi was moved. "It was chilling. I've never experienced that."

Sampras, realizing he would probably not keep up with his fitter foe in a fifth set, raced to a 6–3 lead in the tiebreaker. Agassi saved two match points before coming up just short once more. The final line was unlike any other in Grand Slam history: 6–7, 7–6, 7–6, 7–6.

"I can't believe I never lost serve—and lost," Agassi said.

Were it not for their 2002 reunion—Sampras's emotional last moment of glory—this instant classic would have made the top 100. But that 2002 final gained the slightest edge, beating this match in, well, call it a tiebreaker.

**2. Austin wins the match, and Navratilova wins the fans, September 12, 1981, National Tennis Center**

Only in New York. The rules are different here, the pace faster. At Wimbledon and the French and Australian Opens, there can be no final-set tiebreaker, but at the U.S. Open it's do-or-die. And in 1981 Tracy Austin and Martina Navratilova squared off in the first final-set tiebreaker, and one of only two ever.

Austin had won the Open at 16 in 1979, but in 1981 she'd been sidelined by sciatic nerve injuries. Navratilova had won Wimbledon twice and the Australian in '81 but was still an erratic, emotionally vulnerable player. She'd become an American citizen that summer, endured tabloid stories about her sexuality, finally subdued rival and top seed Chris Evert Lloyd in the semis, and was desperately eager to win. Navratilova seemed to have the trophy in her grip after grabbing the first set 6–1. But Austin, noted for her steely determination and concentration, began grinding away. Navratilova's aggressiveness and gambling proved her undoing as she blew several break points with unforced errors—she'd make 43 to Austin's 17 by day's end. Austin snuck off with the second set, 7–6, 7–4, in the tiebreaker.

The third set was equally tight. Down 6–5, Navratilova committed eight unforced errors and double-faulted twice, but saved three match points to force another tiebreak. Then Austin showed her greatness, switching suddenly from hitting short to Navratilova's backhand to slamming balls deep to her fierce forehand. This bold move rattled Navratilova, who fell behind 6–1, then double-faulted on her final point.

It was Austin's final moment of glory before back injuries derailed her

ing for himself," Tim Gullickson's twin Tom said. "It's an emotional roller coaster playing for other people."

Sampras's ride turned particularly hairy in the quarterfinals at the Open, his last shot at a 1996 major. The 31st-ranked Alex Corretja hardly seemed an imposing obstacle, but he played the match of his life, serving at Sampras's level and driving deep topspin forehands from all angles. Sampras battled not only the man across the court but first his own inconsistency and then his physical depletion. In five sets, Corretja and Sampras each blasted 25 aces, but Corretja would make only 30 unforced errors to the defending champion's 68.

Sampras seemed low-energy from the start: head down, shoulders hunched, he was unable to rev up in the heat baking the Louis Armstrong Stadium court. Still, his superior skills carried him a long way on his off days—he saved two set points in the opener, then won a tiebreaker. But Corretja took the second set 7–5 and then duplicated his feat in the third. Sampras seemed unable to fully exert himself; reverting to his pre-Gullickson form, he went for broke and slammed shots he could reach rather than engage in rallies, fight off topspin, and create opportunities.

In the fourth set, he finally awoke to the task at hand, breaking his young foe for a 2–1 edge, then serving masterfully, finishing the 6–4 set with a 124-mph ace. But he was leaning heavily on his serve and was clearly not fully operational. Early in the set, he gulped Pepsi for energy, and after the fifth game he called for the trainer and took a pill.

By the fifth set, Sampras was shuffling around, giving up on shots he'd normally chase. He lacked the wherewithal to break Corretja, propelling the match toward a tiebreaker—the 60th game—which finished the match and nearly finished off Sampras.

After four hours, Corretja was bright-eyed and

## Tennis at Its Most Tense: The Tiebreaker (CONTINUED)

career, but she had to share the spotlight with Navratilova. When Navratilova received her runner-up award, the crowd gave the vanquished player a lengthy and emotional ovation for her efforts on the court and for becoming an American; the outspoken Navratilova was speechless, crying tears of joy. Only in New York.

### 3. Steffi Graf comes of age against Pam Shriver, September 4, 1985, National Tennis Center

From the tiebreaker's introduction in 1970 through 1985, no match had gone the maximum 39 games; only two had lasted 38. But in a grandstand match in the 1985 quarterfinals, an up-and-comer named Steffi Graf took Pam Shriver the distance.

Graf was just 16 and the 11th seed, and she had lost to Shriver at Wimbledon. After blowing a 6–5 lead in the first, she fell behind 0–3 in the tiebreaker before running off seven of eight points. Shriver had been the young prodigy once, stunning Martina Navratilova to reach the 1978 final, and she was not easily discouraged. The world's third-ranked player was the one rallying in the second-set tiebreaker—down 3–1, Shriver won six of seven.

Shriver's momentum carried over for a 4–1 third-set lead, but Graf gave a glimpse of the superstar within, the one who would reach 31 Grand Slam singles finals. Pounding balls from the baseline, she wore down her veteran opponent physically and psychologically.

Shriver held a 4–3 lead in the final tiebreaker but was too fatigued and frustrated to finish Graf off. Graf won both points off Shriver's serve, then slammed a service winner. On the final point, Graf induced one more miss, a backhand that sailed long.

After 2 hours, 46 minutes, 39 games, and 3 tiebreakers, Graf had won. Shriver, a doubles legend who'd always been stuck behind Chris Evert and Martina Navratilova in singles, was devastated to realize she would never achieve singles greatness. By contrast, Graf, headed to her first Slam semifinals, was on her way.

**Pete Sampras leaves his all on the court in the fifth set against Alex Corretja.**

bushy-tailed compared to the ailing, stoop-shouldered gentleman across the way. On the second point, Sampras weakly floated a ball in, and Corretja smashed it down. Then Sampras was unable to serve. He wandered from the baseline, doubled over and threw up. As the ballboy cleaned up, the chair umpire called a code violation for delay of serve. The crowd sided with Sampras, heckling the call, but Sampras dragged himself to the line and—with vomit still on his face—served a ball Corretja couldn't handle.

Sampras could barely hold himself together—between points he bent over in agony, leaning on his racket, or he simply rested, head down, hands on knees. Occasionally he'd look to the sky as if asking Gullickson for support. (Some, including Jim Courier, thought Sampras was acting a bit to psych out Corretja, which Sampras vehemently denied. It was subsequently revealed that Sampras suffers from thalassemia minor, a genetic form of anemia that reduces stamina, but he blamed his suffering on poor conditioning and drinking that soda.)

With energy for one, perhaps two shots per point, he missed a forehand service return but hit the next one for a winner and a 3–2 edge before serving and missing a volley. During the changeover, the crowd rewarded both players with a tremendous ovation, but it was clear that Sampras had touched them with his game effort.

After that brief respite, Sampras blazed in a

122-mph ace. Eventually, he staggered his way to match point at 6–5. But he faded again—he missed one shot, then failed to run down a crisp Corretja forehand. The underdog had match point, 7–6. The crowd, on its feet after every point, urged both men on, but especially Sampras.

The next two points clinched Sampras's reputation as the ultimate money player. It had seemed for the entire set that Sampras might have to withdraw from the match. Yet he never stopped coming. Facing match point, he weakly floated a 79-mph first serve but attacked the net anyway, desperate for short points. Corretja hit a brilliant, all-out, crosscourt, forehand passing shot. Surely this was the end.

Not quite. Sampras thrust his body and arm toward the ball and staved off defeat with a forehand volley winner. "I didn't believe it," Corretja said later.

At 7–7, Sampras's first serve sank to 76 mph. This one missed. Yet again, he stunned Corretja—who had snuck inside the baseline. His jaw-droppingly perfect 90-mph second serve angled into the corner and beyond Corretja's reach for his 25th ace. Those two points undid Corretja. Down 7–8, he double-faulted, and the match finally belonged to Sampras.

Sampras virtually collapsed and needed two liters of intravenous fluids. Then he recovered to win both the semifinals and the final—beating Chang in the latter on what would have been Gullickson's 45th birthday—for the Grand Slam he wanted and needed. But the most enduring—and in its odd way endearing—win was the war of attrition against Corretja. After that exhausting win, all Sampras could say was, "This was for Tim. He got me through that one."

# 97. Secretariat shows his stuff, April 7, 1973, Aqueduct Race Course

If you can make it here, you can make it anywhere, including Lexington, Baltimore, and Elmhurst. Secretariat became the world's most celebrated horse for his 1973 Triple Crown run at the Kentucky Derby, Preakness, and Belmont Stakes, but first, on April 7, he captured everyone's attention at the Aqueduct Race Course.

Secretariat had come into his own at Aqueduct. In his debut the previous July 4, the big red colt was bumped right out of the gate and blocked behind other rookie horses, but he closed in a hurry to finish fourth. Less than two weeks later, Secretariat won by four lengths here, starting down the track to becoming the first two-year-old unanimously voted Horse of the Year.

Some thought he represented the best shot in a generation to win the Triple Crown, something no horse had captured since Citation a quarter-century before. Others, however, remained unconvinced that Secretariat could win those longer races, since his sire, Bold Ruler, had lacked stamina (as did Bold Ruler's other offspring).

And in January 1973, Secretariat's development was hindered when owner Christopher Chenery died, leaving a massive estate tax burden; the horse's training was curtailed while the situation was resolved. The family's eventual sale of Secretariat to a syndicate for a record $6.08 million only heightened expectations for the horse and increased the pressure on trainer Lucien Laurin and jockey Ron Turcotte. "I never thought that $6 million would feel so heavy," Turcotte said later.

Secretariat kicked off his 1973 back at Aqueduct, routing the field in the $25,000 Bay Shore Stakes, a short-distance tune-up. Turcotte kept the horse running after the wire to get him ready for the $50,000 Gotham Stakes, the one-mile race that would be the first of two big tests on the road to the Kentucky Derby.

A field of seven with three legitimate challengers lined up for the Gotham, but the crowd of 41,998 came to see just one horse. Carrying a whopping 126 pounds, the heavily favored Secretariat hit the stall's side coming out of the gate, wobbling a bit, yet still ran aggressively from the start, as if unconcerned by the longer distance. He stayed closer to the leaders and closer to the rail

# Honorable Mention: A Day at the Races

**1. Kelso and Gun Bow race to the wire, October 3, 1964, Aqueduct Race Course**

It was one of the tightest, most thrilling races in history, and for one brief moment, by the tiniest of margins, it seemed America's great and beloved champion had been dethroned.

Kelso, grandson of Triple Crown winner Count Fleet, never ran a Triple Crown race, but after a late start he became known as one of the all-time greats, winning 53 races, including five straight Jockey Club Gold Cups (no other horse has ever won five straight in any major stakes race); racing historian David Alexander rated him tops, and *Blood Horse* magazine ranked him fourth, behind Man O' War, Secretariat, and Citation. By 1964, when the seven-year-old superstar charged after his fifth straight Horse of the Year title, the question was no longer how long can this horse keep going, but is there a horse out there who can challenge him.

But that year a rival emerged. Gun Bow, grandson of Triple Crown winner War Admiral, had won six races as a three-year-old the previous year and started strong in 1964. In their first matchup in July, at the Brooklyn Handicap at Aqueduct, Kelso banged his head on the gate, knocking himself dizzy, and he failed even to place. Gun Bow wowed everyone with a track record for 10 furlongs, winning by 12 lengths.

On Labor Day the two squared off again, before 64,000 fans at Aqueduct, in the Aqueduct Stakes. Gun Bow had a three-race winning streak, and Kelso had rebounded with a win at Saratoga. The crowd put more money on the young challenger, the first time that had happened to Kelso since 1960. Gun Bow snatched an early five-length lead, but Kelso, a great stretch runner, pushed himself early, catching Gun Bow to win by three-quarters of a length as the fans cheered his name in what Alexander called "the greatest ovation ever given any horse."

It seemed the season might be on the line when they faced off again at Aqueduct in the 1¼-mile Woodward Stakes on October 3. Kelso was seeking a fourth straight Woodward title, which would wrap up his Horse of the Year honors and give him the career record for money earned. Five horses entered, but for all intents and purposes, the *New York Times* wrote, it was "a match race."

This time the fans put their money on Kelso. Gun Bow, ridden by Brooklyn native and future Hall of Famer Walter Blum, rushed out to an early one-length lead and held it for the first seven furlongs. Kelso's jockey, Ismael Valenzuela, urged his horse on, and in the last quarter-mile he pulled even . . . Blum went to the whip once, pushing Gun Bow back up, but at the eighth pole Kelso grabbed a slight lead . . . at the 16th pole Gun Bow inched ahead . . . then it was Kelso . . . then it was the finish line . . . and . . . who won?

No one could tell. As the minutes dragged on, fans started yelling, "Dead heat!" Finally the photo finish was posted on screens around the track. People gasped, then cheered. The difference was 1/16 inch—not a nose, the *Times* wrote, but "a beetle's nose." And the winner . . . Gun Bow.

than usual, pulling in front by the half-mile pole. Could the sprinter maintain his pace and hold off late chargers? Champagne Charlie issued a firm challenge, but Turcotte, who had merely been giving his great horse a breather, tapped Secretariat twice with his whip, and the horse blasted to the finish three lengths ahead, tying a track record with a sensational 1:33:40. The horse "made difficult tasks seem easy" in this "dramatically impressive" win, gushed the *New York Times.*

Once again, Turcotte showed that his eyes were on bigger prizes: he kept Secretariat going for an extra quarter-mile to equal the Kentucky Derby distance, the length a son of Bold Ruler supposedly couldn't handle. Although it was unofficial, the clockers timed this young horse at 1:59:40, slightly faster than the Derby record.

To insiders, the performance was a marvel. People openly talked about Secretariat as a once-in-a-lifetime horse, a Man o' War, a Seabiscuit, a Citation. But equally important was that suddenly it wasn't just insiders paying attention. Secre-

## A Day at the Races (CONTINUED)

Had the story ended there, this heart-stopping race would have cracked the top 100. But in November the horses found themselves head to head again; had this grand finale been in New York, it might have made the top 100. But it was Laurel, Maryland, on grass, a surface on which Kelso had never won. Kelso established his greatness once and for all by churning out a win in 2:23.4, the fastest 1½ miles ever (better even than Secretariat's much-lauded Belmont Stakes run). With that win, Kelso set a career earnings mark that would last 15 years, and edged Gun Bow to capture his fifth straight Horse of the Year title. But the showdown at the Woodward Stakes was the race of the year and one of the greatest in New York of all time.

### 2. Three horses win . . . in one race, June 10, 1944, Aqueduct Race Course

You know a race is close when it needs a photo finish. You know a race is impossibly close when even the picture can't separate the front-runners. But you know you've made history when it's three horses reaching the finish line together.

Of racing's rare triple dead heats, only one was in a stakes race: Brownie, Bossuet, and Wait A Bit all hit the wire together at Aqueduct's Carter Handicap. Photo-finish cameras had only recently become standard; previously, judges had usually chosen a winner.

On a sloppy track, Brownie got out front early and was on the rail with a slight lead in the final eighth when Bossuet, carrying the most weight, came up through the middle and Wait A Bit made up for a sluggish start with a strong finish on the outside. They all finished the seven-eighths of a mile at exactly 1:23⅖. With the race—four days after D-Day—raising money for the War Relief Fund, the tie gave new meaning to the phrase "Everyone's a winner."

### 3. Fashion and Peytona draw a crowd, May 13, 1845, Union Course

Wall Street stood empty; the railroad station, by contrast, was packed beyond capacity. When people realized there weren't enough trains, 1,000 ticket-holders "wrecked the railroad station in vengeance and rolled several cars off the tracks," according to diarist Philip Hone.

Where was all New York hurrying off to? Union Course, of course, for what would be the last of the great North-South match races that had begun more than two decades earlier. This one—which drew more spectators than any previous American sporting event—pitted young challenger Peytona against aging local hero Fashion, who'd earned the moniker "Queen of the Turf" in 1842 by defeating an old southern horse named Boston.

In horse terms, the whole North-South conflict had become blurred—though she trained up north and her jockey was northern, Peytona was born down south and owned by southerners—but with American society increasingly pulled apart, the race still bore the burden of regional conflict.

The rambunctious spillover crowd delayed the start by an hour and badly spooked Fashion. Peytona won the first race by a length, then repeated in the second race. The South had won, this time. Though Fashion would gain revenge in a rematch at Camden and the North would rise again when the real battles arrived, this day belonged to Peytona.

**Secretariat barrels to victory at the Gotham, a major step on the path to the Triple Crown.**

tariat's fame spilled beyond the track's borders. Sports fans who wouldn't have known Bold Ruler from Northern Dancer were champing at the bit, eagerly awaiting the Triple Crown races.

Before the Triple Crown came one more Aqueduct tune-up, the $1^1/_8$-mile Wood Memorial, now presumed to be a cakewalk. Had Secretariat triumphed, that race would be the one celebrated here and probably would be higher up on the list. But Secretariat's prerace workout was interrupted by a riderless horse, and on the day of the race he suffered from a painful abscess in his mouth. Laurin knew but kept his mouth shut because he wanted the horse to run in preparation for the Derby. When Secretariat finished third, the press speculated again about faulty genes. William Nack recalled later in *Sports Illustrated,* "In the most important race of his career, Secretariat had come up as hollow as a gourd. I couldn't help but suspect that Secretariat was another Bold Ruler, who ran into walls beyond a mile."

But look back at the Gotham: Secretariat had shown speed, he'd shown guts in holding off the late challenge, and he'd shown stamina in his post-wire run. That was the real Secretariat and that Secretariat was for real. When the Triple Crown series arrived, he proved it, destroying the competition, especially in his astonishing Belmont Stakes performance: the unstoppable colt won by an unimaginable 31 lengths.

Even before that last race, Secretariat had made the covers of *Time, Newsweek,* and *Sports Illustrated,* becoming, as Nack observed, "a cultural phenomenon, a sort of undeclared national holiday from the tortures of Watergate and the Vietnam War."

Indeed, there was a wonderful giddiness to the coverage. "Secretariat generates a crackling tension and excitement wherever he goes," Pete Axthelm wrote in *Newsweek*. "Even in the kind of gray weather that shrouds lesser animals in anonymity, Secretariat's muscular build identifies him immediately; his glowing reddish coat is a banner of health and rippling power."

Although horse racing still recedes into the shadows of the sports pages for much of the year, the story of Secretariat made the Triple Crown races a bigger annual story, so that horses from Seattle Slew to Smarty Jones would streak briefly across the athletic firmament. And while that legacy was passed down only because Secretariat "made it" elsewhere, he had to make it here first, dazzling the racing world and becoming a media star by capturing the Gotham in record time.

# 98. The Giants Beat Knute Rockne's Notre Dame All-Stars, December 14, 1930, Polo Grounds

As a star on Knute Rockne's 1930 team—winner of Notre Dame's second straight national championship and undefeated over two seasons—Johnny Law was used to feeling invincible. But at the Polo Grounds on December 14, 1930, Law took one look at the opposing defense and felt something completely different: fear.

"Can you tell me," he asked referee Tom Thorp only half in jest before the game's first play, "how much time is there left to play?"

The opposing team was not some pushover college squad: it was the 13–4 New York Giants, the NFL's second-best team, and, as the 170-pound halfback noticed, a team whose line averaged 230 pounds per man.

Although Red Grange had helped popularize and stabilize the NFL in 1925, it was still considered a dull cousin to the college game. The glamour, press coverage, and ticket sales remained with men like Rockne and his charges. So when the Giants proposed an exhibition game to benefit the mayor's Depression-era New York Unemployment Fund, Rockne agreed, proposing to bring not his 1930 team but an All-Star squad of Fighting Irish past and present.

Sure, this team was thrown together and had practiced for just one week, and yes, some of his former stars were no longer in top-flight game condition, but this was Rockne and Notre Dame and still an impressive lineup: "the Four Horsemen" of 1924 (Harry Stuhldreher, Jim Crowley, Elmer Layden, and Don Miller); five of that team's "Seven Mules," including Adam Walsh; 1928 leading man Jack Chevigny; numerous 1929 stars, including John Cannon and Jack Elder; and from the current

# Honorable Mention: Big Blue Breaks Loose

### 1. Y. A. Tittle throws for seven TDs, October 28, 1962, Yankee Stadium

Y. A. Tittle hurt. The 35-year-old had suffered a huge contusion the previous Sunday and had not thrown until the day before this game against undefeated, first-place Washington; he'd looked terrible in that practice.

He also looked terrible in the game, which he began by tossing seven straight incomplete passes. Tittle had more than just pain to worry about. His pride, his job, and the Giants' hopes for retaining the Eastern crown were now all on the line.

Tittle finally managed one completion, then another. At the end of the first quarter, he zipped a 22-yard touchdown pass. In the second, he ran his completion streak to 12 straight and added two more short TD passes for a 21–13 lead.

Washington's Norm Snead would finish with four TD passes and a touchdown running, so Tittle actually needed to step up the pace in the second half. In the third quarter, he lofted a 32-yard touchdown pass to Del Shofner, who'd finish with 11 catches for 269 yards, and launched a 63-yard TD bomb to Frank Gifford.

In the fourth, Tittle returned to Shofner for a 50-yarder. "Tittle and Shofner seemed oblivious to the Redskins," the *New York Times* wrote, "as if warming up for a big game at some later date."

Tittle finally put the game away with his record-tying seventh touchdown pass. The Redskins were finished for the game and the season as the Giants waltzed to their second straight Eastern Conference title.

Tittle, who'd finish 27–39 with 505 yards, had plenty of time to shoot for an eighth TD but demurred, following tradition and grinding out the clock on the ground in the 49–34 rout. "It would have been in bad taste," he said.

### 2. The Giants score twice at the end to win Eastern Division championship, 1941, Polo Grounds

Some offensive outbursts, like Y. A. Tittle's seven-touchdown game, are daylong affairs. Some find their soul in their brevity.

In the 1941 Eastern Division playoff game, the New York Giants watched their 10–0 fourth-quarter lead over Washington evaporate as the Redskins' Sammy Baugh slung for two quick scores and a 13–10 lead. With the field a mud pit and under five minutes left, both the momentum and the game seemingly belonged to Washington, the defending Eastern champs.

But one great comeback deserved another, and the Giants exploded with the most lethal 1–2 knockout combo that side of Joe Louis. Facing 3rd-and-4 on their own 26, Ward Cuff burst through the line for a first down, fueling a 51-yard drive that culminated in Cuff's 38-yard field goal. On Washington's next play, Jim Poole intercepted Baugh's pass near the Redskin 30 and raced to the 7. Giant rookie George Franck churned through the slop to score on a reverse. In mere minutes, the Giants transformed a 13–10 deficit into a 20–13 lead. The lead would not change hands again.

### 3. Benny Friedman hurls four TDs in one game, 1929, Polo Grounds

Imagine pumping the pigskin up until it's stubby on the ends and so fat around the middle you can barely hold it one-handed — the "old balloon," as Red Grange called it. That's what Benny Friedman held when he pioneered the modern passing game in an era when the ball and the rules discouraged passing. (There were no roughing-the-passer penalties, and two consecutive incompletions earned a five-yard penalty.)

When the NFL's Detroit Wolverines folded after 1928, Giants owner Tim Mara bought the whole roster just to get Friedman, whom he paid $10,000, the highest salary in the league. It was well worth it: after Grange, Friedman was football's biggest draw, but playing in New York, he really made his mark. In 1929 Friedman hurled 20 touchdown passes — the next three most prolific passers threw for just 22 TDs *combined.*

Friedman's greatest show came in a must-win for the Giants to have a shot at the de facto championship. (They ultimately finished second to the Green Bay Packers, who won the league by having the best record.)

Friedman went 12–23 in a 34–0 rout of Chicago, firing an unheard-of four touchdown passes, including a 55-yarder. On his final pass, Friedman escaped a near-sack before zinging a 28-yard completion to Hap Moran in the end zone. With the game in hand, Friedman actually spent much of the last quarter resting, while Moran threw the team's fifth touchdown pass.

"Benny revolutionized football," the Bears' George Halas said later. "He forced defenses out of the dark ages."

**When the NFL's Giants faced off against Notre Dame in a charity fund-raiser, the out-of-town college squad was the bigger draw, even earning an invitation to City Hall to publicize the event.**

team, Law, Bucky O'Connor, and Frank Carideo.

The game loomed so large that Giants coach Leroy Andrews succumbed to the pressure in the final weeks of the regular season, getting distracted from his team's championship aspirations. He berated his players with such ferocity that stars Benny Friedman and Steve Owen led a mutiny, prompting owner Tim Mara to fire Andrews and put the rebels in charge. (The next year Owen became head coach, a position he would hold for more than two decades.)

Meanwhile, it was not the Giants but Rockne and his players who were interviewed on national radio to promote the game. Notre Dame's household names had the desired impact, raising over $100,000 in ticket sales. The Giants didn't even get a home field edge—the majority of the 55,000 New Yorkers on hand were rooting for the Fighting Irish, as they had done since before the Giants existed.

In the locker room, Rockne warned his players about the Giants' size advantage but remained confident about his squad's ability to exploit it: "These Giants are heavy but slow," he said. "Go out there, score two or three touchdowns on passes in the first quarter, and then defend."

Rockne, who would die in a plane crash before the next season, was noted for inspiring his players with pep talks, but this one had little motivational or strategic impact. The Giants were too big, too strong, and too good. They were about to show once and for all that the pro game was not only here to stay but an exciting and superior brand of football.

In the opening minutes, Bill Owen sacked Stuhldreher in the end zone for a safety. Notre Dame finished the first quarter with negative 12 yards of offense and Crowley sidelined by injury.

Friedman, who revolutionized the pro game with his passing, scored two touchdowns rushing in the second quarter. The second was notable for his smarts and execution. Lining up on 3rd-and-7 from the Notre Dame 22, Friedman knew Hunk Anderson would drop back to protect against the pass, as he had done on every third down. So Friedman faked a pass in that direction, then burst through the spot Anderson vacated; 22 yards later the Giants had a 15–0 lead.

To avoid completely humiliating Notre Dame the Giants pulled their regulars in the second half but were still too big, too strong, and too good. On one "drive," the Irish started on their own 37, lost four yards on first down, nine on second, and thirteen on third. On 4th-and-36 from the 11, they punted the ball back to the 42. The Giants won 22–0, but the gap between pro and college was really wider — New York had outgained Notre Dame 232 yards to 34, and Notre Dame never once got past midfield.

In the *New York Times,* Allison Danzig decreed that this game sacked the notion that "the professional brand of football is of the laissez-faire variety and that the paid player does not throw himself into the game with the spirit and inspiration of the college player."

This easy victory was crucial in giving the NFL credibility with the press and the public. The fallacy about "the old college try" giving the amateur version of the sport greater urgency and nobility had been wiped out like the fabled Notre Dame offense.

# 99. Marathon mania reaches its peak, April 3, 1909, Polo Grounds

Look at them awaiting the starting gun. Such a motley collection from around the globe, a surreal lineup for the quaintly named "Marathon Derby." The roster reads like something conjured up by T. Coraghessan Boyle or maybe the Marx Brothers: an Italian candymaker who earned lasting fame for collapsing in front of the Queen of England; an Irish-American who brought as much glory to his employer, Bloomingdale's, as he did to his homeland; an Onondaga Indian from Canada stained by doping controversy and so caught up in the marathon craze that he was running himself into the ground; an Englishman who held countless records at shorter distances but was unable to complete a marathon; an Irishman from Yonkers whose recent world record was disregarded because the distance was considered considerably off; and a waiter from France about whom no one knew anything . . . yet.

But this wasn't satire, and it wasn't slapstick. This was the climax of the first modern marathon era. "It is a craze such as athletic America has not known for years," the *New York Herald* wrote in 1909. "This was the greatest professional athletic event ever held in America. . . . If the Man from Mars had only been there wouldn't he have had a

**Henri St. Yves bursts out of obscurity to top a field of well-known runners in the Marathon Derby.**

tale to tell of the 'crazy Americans' and the 'Marathon Derby.'"

The passion began with the birth of the Olympics in 1896 and the first American marathon (from Connecticut to New York City) and the Boston Marathon, both the following year. But the fuse for the explosion of events leading to the Marathon Derby was the 1908 Olympics.

The International Olympic Committee had standardized the race's length at 26 miles, but England's Queen Alexandra wanted the runners, who departed from Windsor Castle, to finish right in front of her Olympic Stadium royal box, so she had insisted that the course run 26 miles and 385 yards to her preferred spot. England, meanwhile, had angered the Irish and American delegations, in the latter case by failing to raise an American flag; the Americans retaliated by refusing to dip their flag while passing before King Edward.

On a day of searing heat, the front-runner, the Italian Pietri Dorando, entered the stadium but was so disoriented — from the weather or, some alleged, from gobbling strychnine as a performance enhancer — that he headed the wrong way. Then he collapsed. Officials helped him to his feet, and the crowd, knowing Irish-American Johnny Hayes was closing in, urged him on. Dorando collapsed three more times, and each time he was lifted and carried forward by sympathetic Brits. Although Dorando reached the finish line first, a lengthy American protest earned the deserving Hayes the gold. But Dorando, given his own gold trophy by the Queen as consolation, emerged as the popular hero in Europe.

Hayes — the Bloomingdale's employee who, some speculated, was paid not for working there but to train because of the publicity he brought to the store — agreed to a rematch with Dorando on his home turf at Madison Square Garden on November 25. The Amateur Athletic Union had begun staging marathons locally the previous year, and the Millrose Games had debuted in 1908, so New York sports fans were primed for a track spectacle — especially a grudge match (as professionals this time) between an Irish-American and an Italian whom immigrants from both countries could rally around.

Lines snaked around the block for tickets, and scalpers had a field day. Dorando, struggling not through heat this time but through the clouds of cigar smoke, grabbed an early lead and turned back each Hayes charge. He shook free with a spurt in the last three laps to win by 60 yards as Italian supporters, overwhelming police and officials, rushed the track. Marathon madness had begun: in the four months after the rematch, nine major marathons were run in the New York area alone, including another Dorando-Hayes rematch and match races between Dorando and Onondaga Indian Tom Longboat and between Longboat and Englishman Alfred Shrubbs, both of whom would run in the Derby. (Dorando ran six marathons during that stretch, along with eleven shorter races.)

Finally, promoters thought to move beyond match races to stage a splashy major event. The $10,000 Marathon Derby on April 3, 1909, at the Polo Grounds would crown the greatest marathoner once and for all. With bands playing, flags from the runners' native countries adorning the track, and 30,000 fans screaming and chanting despite persistently damp weather, the six men lined up: Hayes, with his gold medal but subsequent string of defeats; Dorando, with his international acclaim and desire for revenge against Hayes; Longboat, who had faltered in the Olympics under strychnine accusations but had since bested Dorando and Shrubbs and emerged as the betting favorite; Shrubbs, who was the greatest middle-distance runner of his time but faded over the long haul; Matt Maloney, fresh off his disputed marathon record run from Rye to New York; and Henri St. Yves, a chubby, diminutive 20-year-old Parisian who worked in a restaurant in London and had won a marathon in Edinburgh, but went off here at 10-to-1 odds and was so unknown that he was "looked upon as a rank outsider and practically despised in the betting," according to the *New York Times.*

New York was riveted — people crammed Times Square to watch the updates posted in the Times Building windows. The *Times* would make it the lead story the following day, the *Herald* would spread four photos and three columns of coverage across its front page, and the *Tribune* would feature a huge three-column photo and a lengthy story.

Dorando, the crowd favorite, raced out front, but St. Yves, barely five feet tall, stayed at his shoulder, passed him at the one-mile mark, and was soon two-thirds of a mile ahead. In contrast to the long, graceful strides of Shrubbs, Dorando, and especially Longboat, the Frenchman's short, choppy gait looked awkward, yet on the soggy track its concision proved helpful. Many questioned his judgment in setting such a furious pace — "the majority of the spectators laughed in derision," the *Times* reported — but St. Yves burst forth at each challenge.

At Mile 11, Shrubbs overtook him, and the critics smiled smugly. But St. Yves remained dogged in pursuit. At the 19th mile, Shrubbs finally wilted and St. Yves regained his lead, maintaining his brisk pace the last seven miles. Shrubbs eventually dropped out near collapse, and Longboat, running through excruciating foot pain caused by his heavy schedule, quit too. Dorando was in second four laps behind, while Hayes, closing in a rush, had waited far too long and was unable to even catch Dorando. (Maloney finished a distant fourth.)

St. Yves was unstoppable, finishing in a record 2:40:50. "He came down the final stretch like a quarter miler," the *Herald* sang. His performance was so remarkable that all the nationalism faded away, and as a band played the French national anthem, the *Tribune* observed, "a veritable wall of humanity rose as one man to welcome a new idol."

St. Yves won a follow-up race against nine men at the Polo Grounds in May on a day that also witnessed amateur marathons in Brooklyn and the Bronx. Although the boom soon faded, the marathon was now established as a significant sport, and Henri St. Yves had earned a place in history as its first undisputed champion.

# 100. Charles Miller rides (and rides and rides) into the record books, December 10, 1898, Madison Square Garden

On December 10, 1898, Charles Miller got married at Madison Square Garden . . . during the middle of a bicycle race . . . which had been going on for six days . . . which he was winning.

This was the last of the original six-day bike races, an endeavor that, in its outrageous demands on the human mind and body, puts today's extreme sports to shame. Bicycles had become a fad, and bike racing had become a full-fledged mania, with everything from short sprints to the "Century," a 100-mile ride. But the six-day event was more than a race—it was a combination endurance test, torture, and freak show.

Riders navigated smoke-filled indoor ovals thousands of times for hundreds of miles each day, usually eating meals from pots while biking and enduring crashes, aching muscles, exhaustion, delirium, and often fistfights with managers who pushed them past their breaking point. (Prominent racers were given rooms to rest in during breaks, but lesser lights were shunted off into tiny tents.) Meanwhile, competing bands and pickpockets worked the crowds, which occasionally disintegrated into hooliganism.

A *New York Times* editorial called the six-days a "Brutal Exhibition" and wrote of cyclists' "faces that become hideous with the tortures that rack

# Honorable Mention: Going the Distance

**1. Gil Anderson drives like a New Yorker, October 9, 1915, Sheepshead Bay Speedway Racetrack**

Once upon a time, you could drive 100 miles an hour in Brooklyn without getting a speeding ticket. Instead, you'd take home a prize and your fair share of glory. This was back in the automobile's infancy when the Sheepshead Bay Speedway opened in high fashion, with a new world record set before a huge crowd, many of whom were decked out in fancy furs and jewels.

After reformers closed Brooklyn's famous horse tracks in the early 1900s, the Speedway was built on the Coney Island Jockey Club's Sheepshead Bay Racetrack. It featured two-by-fours of Georgia pine laid around the high-banked, two-mile racing oval. Nicknamed "the Shrine of Speed," it became one of the world's fastest tracks.

Millionaire Vincent Astor laid out the money for the Speedway's debut race. Among the 60,000 attending the Astor Cup race were society members from as far away as Chicago and Montreal. "Socially, the contest was a national one," noted the *New York Times*.

"The exhibition of costly furs far eclipsed any display of recent years." (The top fur coat was valued at $35,000, more than the $20,000 racing prize.)

Twenty drivers entered the 350-mile race, a test for American-made cars. Foreign cars, especially Peugeot and Mercedes, had ruled racing's early years, but homegrown Stutz hoped to make a splash.

Only eight drivers finished, and the competition was largely between four men: Gil Anderson and Tom Rooney in Stutzes and Bob Burman and Johnny Aitken in Peugeots. Aitken led until his valve broke at the 240-mile mark. Anderson, Burman, and Rooney raced virtually side by side until Burman was sidelined by transmission problems.

It was a grand day for Stutz as Anderson finished in 3:24:22, 47 seconds ahead of Rooney. Anderson averaged a stunning 102.9 miles an hour, shattering all existing records.

The Speedway lived a fast, short life, closing after its owner died in the 1919 influenza epidemic. But unless and until NASCAR builds its proposed Staten Island track, Gil Anderson's performance at the Astor Cup remains the best day anyone has ever had driving in New York.

**2. Racing moves from quadrupeds to bipeds, April 24, 1835, Union Course**

The first championship race on two legs in America was born out of a wager, one wealthy man telling another that no one could run 10 miles in an hour. Back in 1835, John Stevens told Samuel Gouverneur, "It's a bet," though he had no intention of exerting himself.

Stevens laid out $1,300 in prize money and rounded up nine men from as far away as Ireland and Prussia for "the Great Footrace" at the famed Union Course track in what is now Queens.

A gusting wind tempted Stevens to cancel, but the huge turnout changed his mind. Irishman Patrick Mahoney grabbed an early lead, and the pack thinned rapidly—after five miles, five men were done. Long Islander Isaac Davis (whom the *New York Evening Post* called "decidedly the handsomest runner") was first for three miles before hurting his foot and dropping out in Mile 8.

Henry Stannard, a 6'1", 165-pound Connecticut farmer fortified by the brandy and water Stevens provided at Mile 6, seized the lead. With Stevens exhorting him on horseback inside the track, Stannard ran the last two miles in under six minutes each, finishing in 59 minutes, 48 seconds, to win the bet for Stevens.

The Great Footrace sparked a new craze. By the 1840s, "pedestrian races" were the second-most popular sport in the country behind harness racing.

**3. Runners defy Horace Greeley and go east to seek fame and fortune, May 26, 1928, Madison Square Garden**

People have always made long, perilous journeys to reach New York seeking fame and fortune, but the 1928 "Bunion Derby" took that concept to ludicrous extremes. The city was on competitors' minds and in their dreams throughout a 3,422-mile, 84-day trek from Los Angeles.

Formally called "the Transcontinental Foot Race," the event was conjured to market the new Route 66, one of the first designated U.S. high-

them." The League of American Wheelmen, cycling's governing body, loathed these races and fined all who participated in the 1898 race. It would be the last of its kind in New York anyway, because a new state law would prohibit cyclists from riding more than 12 hours a day.

The solo six-day's swan song was a memorable affair. Thirty-one cyclists hailing from as far away as Australia and Sweden set out, but seven dropped out the first day. Canadian racer Burns Pierce traveled more than 400 miles around the Garden's wooden velodrome on Day 1, a record pace. On Day 3, two riders were ordered out by medical staff; Pierce remained in record form, but defending champ Miller and feisty George Waller hung close, with Miller grabbing the lead when Pierce took breaks.

Pierce faded on Day 4 (he'd finish third), while Miller and Waller stayed within shouting distance of each other after 1,400 miles. Day 5 decided matters. Waller led by four miles that morning when both men started sprinting; they crashed into each other, and though neither was hurt, Waller soon came undone, losing control of his bike and veering off the track. Then, at 8:30 A.M., while half-asleep, he slammed into a railing. While Waller was out for nearly three hours, Miller maintained his steady pace, building a 30-mile lead.

By Saturday, Miller had clinched the victory, and all that remained was to break the record of 1,983 miles that he'd set the previous year—and to marry his fiancée, Genevieve Hanson, who was watching from a box. Promoters promised an extra $200 if they wed in front of the crowds, and Hanson, whose mother had made a last-minute trip from Chicago to give her away, agreed, though she hoped Miller would at least wear a suit.

Miller left the track at 3:00 P.M. At 4:40, a band played "The Wedding March" for the cheering, standing-room-only crowd. Miller emerged decked out in an outrageous racing suit, pants with one white leg and one pink, and a shirt with the colors reversed and an embroidered eagle on the back. A silk American flag was wrapped around his waist.

## Going the Distance (CONTINUED)

ways and the longest link in a network of roads finally connecting the coasts. One of America's first sports agents, C. C. Pyle, took on the task of pulling the event off.

On March 4, before 500,000 spectators, 275 runners, ages 16 to 63 and hailing from around the world, began their quest for the $25,000 first prize. Millions watched them pass through Flagstaff, Arizona; Amarillo, Texas; St. Louis; Chicago; and Indianapolis. (Pyle, nicknamed "Cash & Carry," sought revenue through selling programs, foot ointments, and other merchandise and set the route based on towns' willingness to pay promotional fees.)

A dozen runners dropped out the second day, and another dozen were hit by cars, motorcycles, and a bike. The men slept on cots in tents and were called on to perform nightly with the vaudeville acts for small-town crowds.

Andy Payne, a 21-year-old Oklahoma farm boy (and part Cherokee), raced through six pairs of shoes, as well as through freezing rain and the fever and tonsillitis that followed; he also raced with a police escort in New Jersey after rumors circulated that he'd be shot so that Passaic native John Salo could win. He raced and raced for 573 hours, 4 minutes, and 34 seconds (an average of 41 miles per day), finishing on May 26 by racing from the Hudson River to Madison Square Garden, where he and the others ran 20 final miles while Pyle client Red Grange emceed the saga's end. Only 55 men finished, and Payne completed the task 15 hours ahead of second-place Salo.

Although the event was a financial bust, Pyle, heavily in debt, resurrected the idea in 1929, reversing the course; once again, financial success eluded him. (Others would revive it in the 1990s, and again early in this century.) Payne paid off the mortgage on his family's farm and became a hero for his determination and perseverance. The Bunion Derby, the *Herald-Tribune* wrote, was "one of the most heroic, if one of the most absurd athletic contests ever held."

**In the year of the consolidation of what are now the five boroughs into Greater New York, Madison Square Garden remained the center of the sports and entertainment worlds and home to major events like the final solo six-day bicycle race.**

After marrying and kissing the bride, Miller biked around for a few minutes, lapping up the applause. After a brief break, he returned and in one last push completed his new record, finishing with 2,007 miles over 142 hours. During that time, he was off the track for merely fifteen hours, sleeping only nine and a half. After a victory lap with the other eleven survivors, Miller and his bride had their wedding dinner at the Waldorf-Astoria.

The next year a new six-day race, with two-man teams and a point system based on laps, sprang up to replace the solo one. It remained popular through the Depression, and the style became known internationally as "the Madison," after its Madison Square Garden birthplace. But those riders never knew the bliss Miller achieved on his wedding day, when he set a record that would never be broken.

# Honorable Mention #100. Pele gets people to watch soccer, June 15, 1975, Downing Stadium

Edson Arantes do Nascimento faced a straightforward yet daunting task: to make New York and America embrace soccer. Better known by his nickname—Pele—the Brazilian superstar did briefly attain that seemingly impossible goal.

The North American Soccer League was struggling so much that *Newsweek* quipped it was "operating in virtual secrecy" when Pele, who had scored 1,220 goals in 1,253 games over 18 seasons in Brazil, signed a multimillion-dollar deal to come out of retirement and play for the New York Cosmos in 1975.

The move startled the soccer world and woke up America's sports fans, prompting the *Daily News* to declare breathlessly: "Move over Tom Seaver . . . and Walt Frazier and Earl the Pearl Monroe. . . ."

Nearly 2,000 people came to Randall's Island simply to watch Pele's first practice session, but that was nothing compared to the June 15 exhibition game against the Dallas Tornado. Fans lined up at 10:00 A.M., and scalpers commanded three times the ticket price; 21,278 people would show up, well more than double the club's typical crowd, along with 300 media members from 22 countries. The game was televised nationally and in 13 other countries.

Still working himself back into shape, Pele had said he'd play one half and expected to play at just 70 percent. He proved himself doubly wrong. Riding the fans' enthusiasm and his own adrenaline, Pele played the whole game, and at a speed that had him several steps—physically and mentally—ahead of his inexperienced teammates. The Cosmos looked nervous in the first half and fell behind 2–0. Pele missed a header off the crossbar but asserted himself as the commander, teaching his young charges where and when to move.

Twelve minutes into the second half, Pele passed, got the ball back, dribbled, then set up Mordechai Schpigler for the team's first goal. About nine minutes later, Pele leaped for a pass from Schpigler and headed it in, tying the score at 2–2. Pele jumped again, pumping his fist before teammates, fans, and even photographers mobbed him in celebration. The game ended in a tie.

As long as Pele played, soccer succeeded: he drew 22,500 for his first official game and 5,000 cars were turned away. The traffic backups prompted the Cosmos to move to Yankee Stadium and in 1977 to the Meadowlands. Although many Americans agreed with columnist Phil Pepe, who declared the televised version a "crashing bore," the stands remained packed, drawing as many as 77,000 for a game.

But when Pele retired and the NASL greedily expanded from 18 to 24 teams, attendance fell and financial problems arose. By the mid-1980s, the league was gone and soccer had receded from the American consciousness. It made a fleeting return when the U.S. women's team won the World Cup in the 1990s, but nothing could recapture the days when Pele strode into New York and soccer briefly commanded everyone's attention.

# On the Road: The Top 25

## 1. Broadway Joe makes good on his guarantee, January 12, 1969, Orange Bowl, Miami

Joe Namath never posted the greatest numbers. It just doesn't matter.

Joe Namath won only two postseason games. It just doesn't matter.

On statistics alone, Super Bowl III was far from Joe Namath's greatest day. It just doesn't matter.

The unsung defense, not the quarterback, was the real key to football's biggest upset, the New York Jets' 16–7 win over the Baltimore Colts. It just doesn't matter.

It just doesn't matter because in football's greatest underdog story it was Joe Namath who was the superhero. In Miami on January 12, 1969, it was Joe Namath who led and inspired the Jets, it was Joe Namath who saved the Super Bowl and legitimized the AFL-NFL merger, and it was Joe Namath who transformed football as it headed into a new decade and a new era.

Well, not Joe Namath . . . Broadway Joe. This larger-than-life persona, the brash talker with the hard-eyed confidence and ferocious desire to win, that's who won Super Bowl III and created the lasting image—wagging his finger to symbolize that he and his team were indeed number one—that's who stunned the sports world and became an American idol.

The Jets and the AFL had come a long way since their fiscally unstable days in the early 1960s. New York's turnaround began when Sonny Werblin took over and hired coach Weeb Ewbank, who had masterminded the Baltimore Colts to two NFL Championships over the New York Giants. A move into Shea Stadium, which boosted attendance, and a league rights deal with NBC provided spending money, which Werblin used to splurge on Namath. In 1965 the NFL's St. Louis Cardinals offered the University of Alabama star $200,000 and a Lincoln Continental. The Jets, understanding the publicity bonanza a talented, personable quarterback might reap in New York, doubled the offer. This ignited more outrageous spending, which prompted the NFL to offer the AFL a merger in 1966. Although the leagues wouldn't combine until 1970, they began sharing a draft and squaring off in a championship game, which became the Super Bowl.

But the championship showdown merely reinforced the notion that the AFL was bush league as Vince Lombardi's Green Bay Packers annihilated the Kansas City Chiefs 35–10 in 1967 and the Oakland Raiders 33–14 in 1968.

Meanwhile, guided by Namath, the Jets gradually improved until 1968, when they bested the hated Raiders for the AFL Championship. They were still the outsiders in the big city, and their fans a distinct minority outside Long Island, but with the Mets being lovable losers and the Yankees, Knicks, Rangers, and Giants total losers, this scrappy bunch was attracting a following in a city looking for sports heroes.

To most experts, it just didn't matter. The NFL champion Baltimore Colts seemed stronger than the Packers had been: even after Johnny Unitas was injured in the preseason, Earl Morrall guided the club to a 13–1 record, and in the playoff the Colts avenged their sole loss by humiliating Cleveland 34–0. The Jets were a bunch of nobodies led by a long-haired loudmouth with a white mink coat and a llama rug and zebra pillows in his apartment. (The hair issue sounds overblown today, but back then the NCAA was threatening to revoke scholarships for athletes whose hair was deemed too long.)

Oddsmakers put the spread so wide—between 17 and 19 points—that it hardly seemed worth playing the game; Jimmy the Greek specifically tacked on three extra points "for the NFL mystique and Don Shula's coaching." Of 55 writers polled, 49 picked the Colts, with *Sports Illustrated*'s Tex Maule projecting a 43–0 rout.

***Previous page*: Why is this man smiling? Because he guaranteed victory, then produced it.**

Pete Rozelle was so alarmed that he held a press conference in which he promised to consider rejiggering the championship — just formally named the Super Bowl — so as to allow two superior (read NFL) teams to meet for the title. "Rozelle Indicates Tomorrow's Super Bowl Contest Could Be Next to Last," the *New York Times* declared.

But Rozelle's comments attracted far less attention than Namath, who lived beneath a floating spotlight in Miami in what the *New York Post*'s Larry Merchant called "Joe Namath Week."

Namath was the starkest possible contrast to crew-cut guys like Morrall, Unitas, and Colts coach Don Shula. When Ewbank thanked the players' wives for their support, Namath thanked "all the broads in New York." He particularly infuriated Shula by declaring Morrall — the NFL Player of the Year — inferior not only to himself but to all the "top young quarterbacks in the AFL." This remark implied that AFL quarterbacks were real men because they threw deep, unlike the NFL's pansy-ass conservatives. Though the implication was certainly unfair to Morrall (whose receiver Jimmy Orr averaged 25.6 yards per catch), Namath did represent a new league and a new era, a risk-taking, wide-open game that reflected the swinging '60s, while the NFL largely retained its 1950s mindset. Still, Namath knew these fighting words might provoke Morrall, and he also wanted the Colts defense to focus on Don Maynard, who was hiding an injured left hamstring and unsure if he'd even be able to play.

Then came "the Guarantee."

Just days before the game, Namath was at the Miami Touchdown Club giving his acceptance speech as the first AFL player selected as Player of the Year. When a Colts supporter heckled him, Namath, drinking Johnnie Walker, broke from his semiprepared rambling to audible a bold declaration:

"The Jets will win Sunday. I guarantee it."

Namath wasn't just mouthing off — he'd studied the Colts and been genuinely unimpressed by their traditional zones. (The Jets defense was similarly shocked by how static Baltimore's offense seemed.) The Colts had keyed on and thus shut down most NFL running games because older NFL quarterbacks couldn't handle their pass pressure, but Namath saw that those QBs lacked his fast feet, deep backpedal, and astonishingly rapid release. He'd spread the defense on quick outs. Given the Jets' relative youth, he also figured they'd hold up better in Miami's heat.

The media made only passing mention of Namath's comment, but it did get both teams' attention. Shula commented curtly, "He's given our players more incentive." Then, at the start of the broadcast, announcer Curt Gowdy relayed Namath's boast to the entire nation.

All Namath's sizzle — broads, booze, and controversies — obscured his true self: the ultimate gamer, a tough guy who played through unimaginable pain and spurred his men to greatness. And while he was a gambler who won big but frequently lost because of his interceptions, he was smart and ambitious enough to subvert his personal style and adapt for the biggest game of his life. In Super Bowl III, he quarterbacked like a stereotypical NFL quarterback, with restraint and precision, while the Colts, reacting to Namath's declarations, played a riskier, sloppier game.

The game was held in the Orange Bowl, but so many people had bet the Colts and were dying to see Namath torn to shreds — tickets scalped at 10 times face value — that the Roman Coliseum might have been more appropriate.

The Jets came out loose. Ewbank, who had pieced together much of that Colt team before being fired and replaced by his protégé Shula, confidently told his troops, "When we win, don't carry me off the field. I have a bad hip. I don't want to get hurt."

The Colts were on edge, feeling the pressure that the media and Namath had heaped on them. "If we blow it, we destroy the whole season," Shula said.

The first quarter was a scoreless affair but not a meaningless one. The Jets made two strong statements, while the flustered Colts frittered away two huge opportunities. The game's first drive delivered what Jet offensive lineman Randy Rasmussen called "the tone-setter." Running back

Matt Snell took a handoff and plowed head-first into safety Rich Volk, forcing him temporarily from the game with a concussion. The Jets were not going to be intimidated. (Volk returned but was hospitalized after the game with convulsions; Namath sent him flowers.)

The Colts sped down to New York's 19. Uh-oh. NFL superiority flexing its muscles. The Colts wanted that first touchdown badly . . . so badly they played tight and blew it. Willie Richardson dropped one pass, Morrall overthrew another, and the third play collapsed as linebacker Al Atkinson hurled Morrall down at the line. After a missed field goal, the Jets escaped.

Namath, who audibled frequently in the first half, went short for two first downs. He had the Colts primed: knowing from the film that the secondary never helped on deep plays, he sent Maynard flying down the right side. Bad leg and all, Maynard blew past everyone. Although he was a step or two slower than usual and the 55-yard bomb grazed his fingertips, this play — along with a similar one in the next quarter — had the same impact as Johnny Unitas's successful bomb to Lenny Moore early in the 1958 Colts-Giants game. "It changed the geometry of the field," Mark Kriegel wrote in *Namath.* When the Colts rotated toward the strong side and frequently doubled the injured Maynard — who caught no passes all day — it opened up the weak side.

Then the Jets fumbled deep in their own territory. As Larry Fox noted in *Broadway Joe and the Super Jets,* it was precisely this sort of mistake that had spelled doom for AFL teams in previous Super Bowls. But on third down from the Jet 6, Morrall, wanting to shut Namath up, played like an overeager rookie. He fired hard into traffic, where Atkinson deflected the pass into the hands of diving cornerback Randy Beverly.

Soon after, Namath, assuming the Unitas role, asserted his team's superiority by patiently captaining a 12-play, 80-yard touchdown drive. Four straight handoffs to Snell for 26 yards and three passes — two to George Sauer — moved the Jets to Baltimore's 23. Snell caught a 12-yard pass and ran it twice more to give New York a 7–0 lead.

Meanwhile, Morrall continued to gamble and lose. A pass from New York's 16 was intercepted at the 2 by former Colt Johnny Sample, and just before the half he failed to see Orr wide open down the sideline on a flea flicker; his pass over the middle was picked off by safety Jim Hudson.

At halftime, Shula decided to give Morrall just one more chance before calling on Unitas. But Baltimore fumbled on the first play, and after New York chewed up the clock and kicked a field goal, Shula gave his starter one more series. Morrall promptly lost two yards on three plays. Then the Jets added another field goal for a 13–0 advantage, which meant Unitas would not have time to mix in a ground game and would thus be easier to defend.

Still, when the legendary quarterback trotted onto the field, Jet offensive lineman Dave Herman's "heart stopped for about ten seconds." Snell too feared the Unitas mystique, until he saw how little velocity the injured veteran could muster. Three and out, it was back to New York. In the third quarter, the Jets yielded 10 yards on seven plays.

Namath, who had briefly left the game because of a jammed right thumb, fired two crisp passes to Sauer totaling 50 yards. As the fourth quarter began he let Snell and Bill Mathis pound the line, settling for a field goal that bolstered the lead to 16–0 with 13:26 left. Baltimore was crumbling now — Beverly intercepted Unitas in the end zone, and Colt Tom Matte lost his cool and attacked Sample, who ducked his charge and flipped him away.

But Jet fans did start squirming after kicker Jim Turner missed a field goal and Unitas, facing a 4th-and-10 at his own 20, dug into that old bag of magic. He nailed Orr for 17 yards and John Mackey for 11, starting an 80-yard march to pull within 16–7 with 3:19 left.

They writhed more nervously after Baltimore recovered their onside kick in Jet territory and Unitas moved 25 yards to New York's 19. But on 4th-and-5, Larry Grantham deflected Unitas's final pass. It was essentially over.

In all, Snell had carried 30 times for 121 yards,

Sauer had caught eight passes for 133 yards, and Beverly had made two crucial interceptions. Namath's numbers — 17–28 for 206 yards, no fourth-quarter passes — seemed dinky by his standards, but as he ran off, wagging his index finger high, there was no question about the MVP. Namath's teammates also gave him the game ball, but Namath said he'd donate it to the AFL as a symbol of the league's vindication. Afterwards, when Jet management planned to give the players watches, Namath berated them, forcing them to come up with diamond-encrusted rings, just like those received by Lombardi's Packers.

Many Jets failed to grasp their conquest's historical magnitude — eradicating the demon Raiders had been more emotional and their subsequent preseason triumph over the New York Giants seemed to count as much toward their credibility as the Super Bowl. They even left their Super Bowl trophy behind the front desk in the hotel (an unfortunate indicator, along with the watch incident, of the cheap, sloppy mismanagement to come).

But the impact was tremendous. In a country reeling from the horrors of 1968 — the deaths of Martin Luther King Jr. and Robert Kennedy, the riots, the atrocities in Vietnam and the growing protests, the school strike and white flight from the city — everyone zeroed in on this feel-good story. Tom Wicker wrote a column in the *New York Times* cautioning incoming president Richard Nixon to learn the Super Bowl's lessons of unpredictability; Johnny Carson wrote the introduction to Fox's *Broadway Joe*; and even lesser stars like defensive lineman Gerry Philbin got endorsement deals. For New York, the Jets had also kicked off an astonishing run: the Mets would win their first World Series that fall, and the Knicks capture their first NBA championship the following spring.

Namath was an iconoclastic icon, the heroic antihero on whom the NFL and television could piggyback for as long as his knees could bear it. Emboldened AFL owners went into realignment meetings with the NFL and successfully insisted on staying together in the format. (Baltimore was one of three teams forced to shift into the new AFC.) Thanks to Namath, the game opened up — quarterbacks like Dan Fouts took to the air, and receivers like Lynn Swann and John Stallworth became Super Bowl legends. This new, more exciting and colorful game was ready for prime time. *Monday Night Football* rode in on the wake of Super Bowl III.

Most of all, the championship became a major event, growing from 20 million viewers in 1969 to 102 million by 1978. By living up to its new name in 1969, the Super Bowl took a giant leap toward the national holiday stature it has since attained. And it was all because Joe Namath was truly super.

## 2. Bucky Dent tops the Green Monster, October 2, 1978, Fenway Park, Boston

Bucky Dent waited at home plate. Mike Torrez checked the runners. He rocked and delivered. Dent swung and . . . the bat shattered, and Rick Burleson gathered in the infield pop for the third out, ending New York's fifth-inning threat. The Boston Red Sox held on to win this special tie-breaker and the 1978 AL East.

It didn't happen that way, but if not for the professional vigilance of Mickey Rivers, that alternative history might have become a reality. On October 2, 1978, with two out and two on in the fifth inning of the most significant non–World Series game since the Giants-Dodgers playoff of 1951, Rivers noticed his teammate was swinging a cracked bat and gave him fresh lumber. On the next pitch, Dent broke his 0–13 streak, earned a new "bleeping" nickname, and made history with his game-changing three-run homer. (True Sox fans would admit that if Rivers hadn't seen the fissure, the flying piece of wood in the imagined scenario probably would have conked Burleson on the head as the ball fell safely behind him, allow-

**Bucky Dent feels right at home in Fenway Park after launching his seventh-inning fly over the Green Monster in left for a three-run homer.**

ing two runs to score. Some histories really can't be rewritten.)

Perhaps the most astonishing thing about this regular-season tiebreaker is the way Dent's homer has grown in baseball lore until it has obscured the remaining nine innings of spine-tingling baseball. Dent's shot over the Green Monster in Fenway Park's left field transformed a 2–0 deficit into a 3–2 lead, but in the 163rd game of the season these archrivals would wrestle each other down to the final out in the bottom of the ninth. The Yankees would require offensive fireworks from Reggie Jackson and crucial and clever defense by Lou Piniella in right field to finish their hardest-fought victory over Boston.

Back in the spring, it had seemed like the only tension in the AL East in 1978 would be the arguments spilling out of the fractured Yankee clubhouse. While Boston started 47–26, the Yankees battled injuries and each other. George Steinbrenner and Billy Martin fought constantly (a dynamic immortalized in a Miller Lite commercial), and Martin would rapidly disintegrate under the pressure of trying to win, appease Steinbrenner, cope with his zoo of a clubhouse, and keep a lid on his own inner demons, most notably his drinking and the nastiness it conjured up.

Only Ron Guidry's 13–0 start kept Boston within sight. "If Boston keeps playing like this, even Affirmed couldn't catch them," Jackson said, referring to that year's Triple Crown winner. "We'll need motorcycles."

On July 17, the Yankees were in fourth, 14 games behind Boston, when another conflagration between Reggie Jackson, Martin, and Steinbrenner finally cost Martin his job. Steinbrenner replaced him with Bob Lemon, who dispelled the sour atmosphere in the clubhouse and motivated his players by trusting their skills and staying out of their way. As injured players like Rivers and Catfish Hunter returned to action the Yankees started winning, and a local newspaper strike helped Lemon keep them focused on baseball. In Boston, meanwhile, manager Don Zimmer pushed his club too hard; key players like Dwight Evans, Butch Hobson, and Bill Campbell were banged up, while others, like Mike Torrez, began playing tight under pressure.

The Yankees had closed within four when they rode into Boston on September 7 (no motorcycles necessary). Four games later, they were tied for first, having pounded the scared and slumping Sox into submission, 15–3, 13–2, 7–0, and 7–4. A week after the Boston Massacre, Ron Guidry beat Boston 4–0 at Yankee Stadium, and Hunter edged Torrez. New York's three-and-a-half-game lead marked a turnaround that outdid the Giants' 1951 miracle run.

But the Yankees peaked too soon, and the Red Sox recovered, winning 12 of their last 14, including the final eight. The Yankees won six straight to maintain a one-game edge until the season's last day, when Cleveland routed them 9–2. With the regular season over, New York and Boston had each won 99 games. It would take 100 to resolve just the second tiebreaker playoff in American League history—back in 1948, Cleveland, with a 20-game winner named Bob Lemon on its staff, had beaten Boston.

Zimmer had needed Dennis Eckersley and Luis Tiant over the weekend to reach the playoff, so he had to turn to Torrez for the playoff. Torrez had won two games for the Yankees in the 1977 World Series, then signed with Boston. He'd won 16 games that year but during the heat of the race had dropped six straight, and his ERA was worst among Red Sox starters. The Yankees countered with Guidry, 24–3. They were so confident that they sent their bags on to Kansas City for the ALCS.

Guidry, who'd made two straight starts on three days' rest, did not have his Zeus-like lightning bolts, but he got by on his slider and his determination, allowing a homer by Carl Yastrzemski in the second, but just one other hit in the first

## Honorable Mention: Tiebreaker Playoffs

**The Mets beat Cincinnati to ward off the choke label, October 4, 1999, Riverfront Stadium**

In 1998 the Mets had been on the verge of reaching the postseason for the first time in a decade, but they choked away their wild-card spot. In 1999 they'd nearly done it again before rallying on the season's final weekend to tie Cincinnati with 96 wins.

So the Mets traveled to Cincinnati for a tiebreaker. Taking the mound was Al Leiter, who'd been awful in big games early in his career but came into his own with six strong innings for Florida in Game 7 of the 1997 World Series. When Leiter migrated to New York, he evolved into a superb clutch pitcher. According to Greg Prince, co-author of the "Fear and Faith in Flushing" blog, from 1998 to 2001 Leiter pitched 38 "money" starts—games against Atlanta or the Yankees and all games in September and October (including the postseason)—and produced a remarkable 3.07 ERA. In 1999 he had stopped a Met eight-game losing streak by beating Roger Clemens at Yankee Stadium and a seven-game skid by besting Greg Maddux on September 29.

This game was his finest showing, among baseball's great do-or-die starts. Backed by Edgardo Alfonzo's two-run homer and RBI-double, Leiter suffocated the Reds with his cut fastball, striking out seven and yielding just two hits. No Red even reached second base until the ninth inning; by then the Mets were close to finishing this 5–0 gem, which propelled them back to the playoffs for just the fourth time in club history.

five innings. Torrez was even better than Guidry, however, holding New York scoreless.

Before the sixth inning, Piniella checked with catcher Thurman Munson, who confirmed that Guidry's pitches lacked zip, meaning good hitters would pull him. Rick Burleson proved this by doubling into the left-field corner. He scored one out later on Jim Rice's single. The southpaw Guidry walked Carlton Fisk to face lefty Fred Lynn, who worked the count full, then ripped a shot into the right-field corner. On any other day or against any other outfielder, he'd have had a two-run double for a 4–0 Boston lead. But Piniella had just shifted 50 feet closer to the line and was perfectly positioned to corral the ball and snuff the rally. The Red Sox were shocked. Thomas Boswell wrote later in the *Washington Post* that 2–0 was the "quintessential Red Sox lead—just enough to merit euphoria, just enough to squander."

The squandering commenced immediately. After Torrez gave up two one-out singles, Lemon sent up pinch hitter Jim Spencer for Brian Doyle, who had been playing second only because Willie Randolph was injured. Had Randolph been playing, Lemon would probably have used Spencer to bat for the number-nine hitter, Bucky Dent.

Spencer flied out. Dent came up and fouled the second pitch hard off his foot. He hobbled away and trainer Gene Monahan numbed the foot with ethyl chloride. During this interlude, Rivers brought in the new bat—during batting practice, he'd noticed that the Roy White model bat he and Dent both used was chipped, so he asked clubhouse man Nick Priori for a duplicate and taped up the handle. But now, noticing that Dent was still using the cracked bat, Rivers switched him to the healthy lumber; Torrez, meanwhile, failed to request any warm-up pitches after the delay, which lasted several minutes and disrupted his concentration and rhythm.

As a result, Torrez's 0–2 pitch, meant as a waste pitch inside, sat out over the plate. Dent lifted a fly to left. In any other ballpark, it would have been the third out—Fisk, Torrez, and Zimmer thought that was the case in Boston too. But the Green Monster was 37 feet high and just 315 feet away; Dent and Yastrzemski, the left fielder, thought the ball would carom off the wall, scoring a run.

But the wind, which had kept Reggie Jackson's first-inning fly in the park, now was blowing out. To everyone's astonishment, Dent's fly carried into the netting above the wall for a three-run homer. Ernie Harwell's call expressed it perfectly: "It's a fly ball to left field. Oh, it's a home run."

The slumping .243 shortstop had given New York a 3–2 lead. "The silence was deafening," Randolph said. "It was the eeriest sound I've ever heard at a ball game."

Boston was devastated, and it would only get worse. Torrez walked Rivers, prompting Zimmer to call on Stanley to face Munson, whom Torrez had fanned three times. After Rivers stole second, Munson doubled him home for a 4–2 lead. In the seventh, Jackson blasted a leadoff homer 420 feet to center to make it 5–2.

But no matter how many different ways the Yankees smacked the Red Sox down, they dragged themselves up off the canvas to keep fighting. In the eighth, Goose Gossage yielded four hits for a two-run rally, and the Sox pulled within one.

Ninth inning. Last chance. Burleson walked with one out. Jerry Remy poked a ball to right. By this point, the sun was so blinding that even though Piniella knew where the ball was heading, he couldn't see it. Thinking fast, he decided to at least look like he was about to catch it, deking Burleson—who, watching Piniella instead of the third-base coach waving him on, froze between first and second.

"Winning is an ancient Yankee story, a heritage of talent mixed with an audacious self-confidence and an unnerving good fortune," Boswell wrote. "Losing is an old sadness for the Sox, a lineage of self-doubt and misfortune."

By the time Burleson realized Piniella was fortunate just to catch the ball on the bounce, it was too late and he had to stop at second—too far away to tag and score the tying run on Rice's out to deep right on the next play.

Two out. The tying run at third, the winning run at first. Gossage, a power pitcher, against Yastrzemski, a fastball hitter past his prime but still plenty dangerous, as his two hits and two RBIs that day indicated. With no reason to pace himself, Gossage threw his fastest pitch of the day and the season, Yaz swung late—way late—and lifted a harmless foul pop.

A day after there were supposed to be no tomorrows, the Yankees had finally prevailed, with the tying run just 90 feet away. Not much margin for error, but in the case of New York and Boston it was, as always, just enough.

## 3. Babe Ruth calls his home run, October 1, 1932, Wrigley Field, Chicago

Ladies and gentlemen of the jury, we will now hear closing arguments in the never-ending case of *The "Called" Home Run vs. It's Just a Myth.*

Well, no, actually, we won't. Babe Ruth's mammoth blast into the Wrigley Field bleachers on October 1, 1932, deserves its place as the World Series' most celebrated long ball, one of the final highlights for the man who essentially was baseball. Although it's impossible to definitively close debate on whether Ruth actually pointed to center field indicating where his hit would land, the point is moot, since Ruth certainly "called" his home run by taunting Chicago Cub pitcher Charlie Root and the entire Cub bench in a wondrous and unique flourish of showmanship that left little doubt about what his plans were. His dramatic flair was all the more remarkable given the late stage of his long, glorious career.

By 1932 Ruth was old—at 37, he was aging in a hurry, resting more frequently, and often leaving games during the late innings.

By 1932 Ruth was fat—he'd once been big but muscular; now the extra weight was clearly padding that slowed him down.

By 1932 Ruth had been dethroned as home run king—he swatted 41, but Phillie Jimmie Foxx's 58 four-baggers had made it the first time since 1918 that Ruth had at least 500 plate appearances but lost the crown.

But in 1932 Babe Ruth was still Babe Ruth, and his output—Foxx's superiority notwithstanding—was still prodigious, remaining, well, Ruthian. And the Yankees were back on top. From 1929 to 1931, the Philadelphia A's had been the American League's dynasty as the Yankees' pitching faltered and their secondary players struggled. But by 1932 Joe McCarthy had assembled a winning team. In addition to Ruth and Lou Gehrig, who led an offense that scored 1,002 runs, New York also led the league in ERA en route to winning 107 games, making this one of the strongest Yankee teams ever.

Still, all anyone remembers is Ruth's home run in Game 3 of the World Series against Chicago, the team that had fired McCarthy in 1930.

Ruth and his teammates found the extra incentive when the Cubs voted only a half World Series share for midseason pickup Mark Koenig, despite his .353 average—that stinginess rankled because Koenig had been the Yankees' shortstop in the 1920s. New York easily won the first two games at Yankee Stadium, 12–6 and 5–2, amid fierce bench jockeying from both sides. The Cubs directed much of their vitriol at the Yankees' biggest target, Ruth.

But New York was a love-in compared to Game 3, where the Cubs injected their insults with an extra dose of venom, particularly regarding Ruth's racial background. (The quickest way to get under Ruth's skin was to question the color of it—specious rumors had long floated about black ancestry.) The Chicago fans at intimate Wrigley joined in—Ruth and his wife Claire had been spat on by a woman at their hotel upon their arrival, and during outfield practice fans hurled lemons at Ruth every time a ball was hit toward him. Ruth picked them up and tossed them back. Then he and Gehrig awed the crowd by smashing 16 balls into the stands during batting practice.

When the jeering resumed in the first inning, Ruth provided a most impressive rejoinder,

**Did he call it? Did he point to center or the dugout? Impossible to prove, but Babe Ruth most definitely enjoys his trip around the bases after his fifth-inning homer.**

smashing a three-run homer into the right-field bleachers. Interestingly, Richards Vidmer wrote in the *New York Herald-Tribune* that Ruth pointed to the right-field bleachers just before he walloped the ball, although this bit of "calling" seems to have been almost entirely forgotten.

In the third, Ruth's shot to right-center was caught at the fence, but Gehrig hit the next one over. Then the Cubs struck back, tying it at 4–4 in the fourth after Ruth embarrassed himself by misplaying an attempted shoestring catch. As Cub fans heckled him, Ruth jauntily doffed his cap. But with the Cubs showing resilience, it suddenly seemed this Series might develop into a competitive matchup.

Then came the fateful fifth, which essentially decided the Series and gave Ruth his greatest story line. Another lemon was tossed at Ruth while he waited his turn. He stepped in and took strike one from Root. The din at Wrigley was tremendous as every fan and every Cub seemed to feel compelled to share their thoughts on Ruth's failings. Remaining jocular, Ruth turned to the Chicago dugout and raised one finger, saying, in effect, "That's just one strike, I've got two more."

Root missed inside and then outside, running the count to 2–1. Then Root pegged strike two, encouraging another outpouring of catcalls—Chicago's Guy Bush actually came a few steps out of the dugout to make sure Ruth could hear his contributions.

Ruth remained unperturbed. He shooed the Cubs back into their dugout and held up two fingers. What happened next is the stuff of myth.

Ruth certainly pointed his bat before the next pitch. Perhaps he did point toward center, though it seems unlikely, since not only was he a pull hitter, but the wind was gusting toward right. Perhaps he pointed his bat at Root—Gehrig said there was one final heated exchange between pitcher and hitter that Ruth finished with "I'm going to knock the next pitch right down your goddamned throat." Perhaps he pointed at his enemies in the Cubs' dugout, as stated by some recent analysis of two contemporary home movies. It's irrelevant where exactly he pointed.

Imagine standing before a hostile crowd, holding up two fingers, pointing your bat, and saying, as Chicago catcher Gabby Hartnett reported, "It only takes one to hit it." Not much room for mistake at that point. Anything short of a rocket off the fence would be a failure, and a strikeout would have doomed Ruth to public humiliation for at least the remainder of the Series. But Ruth was writing the script for the Hollywood version of his life, and he was the only one who could deliver such a perfect ending.

Root delivered an off-speed pitch low and away, a difficult pitch to lift out, but Ruth got the bat down and whacked the ball up, up, and away. It soared more than 430 feet to center, the longest home run ever hit in suddenly silent Wrigley. Well, it wasn't completely quiet, for while Ruth had shut up his antagonists, he himself was cackling and shouting at the fans and the Cubs as he rounded the bases, clasping his hands over his head like the champion he was.

Only Joe Williams in the *New York World-Telegram* specified that "Ruth pointed to center," but others made it abundantly clear that this was a "called" home run. Gehrig complained to Fred Lieb that night, "What do you think of the nerve of that big monkey, calling his shot and getting away with it?" while John Drebinger in the *New York Times* wrote that "in no mistaken motions Ruth notified the crowd that the nature of his retaliation would be a wallop right out the confines of the park."

Yes, other journalists looking to fill inches, sell papers, and glorify themselves ginned up accounts with revisionist histories that unnecessar-

## Honorable Mention: Legendary Launches

**Mickey Mantle hits the first "tape measure" home run, April 17, 1953, Griffith Stadium, Washington, D.C.**

Mickey Mantle forced the invention of the "tape measure" home run by hitting a ball farther than anyone not named Babe Ruth.

The Yankees had passed the mantle of greatness from Babe Ruth through Lou Gehrig to Joe DiMaggio, but by 1951 they needed another heir. The blond kid from Commerce, Oklahoma, struggled as a rookie but improved in 1952, and early in 1953 he showed he had the stuff of legend. With a man on and two outs in the fifth, the switch-hitting Mantle, batting righty against Washington Senator southpaw Chuck Stobbs, launched a ball over the fence in left-center, 391 feet from the plate. Aided by the wind, the ball hurtled toward the back wall, another 69 feet away. Atop that 50-foot wall was a scoreboard, which the ball glanced off of before disappearing into the afternoon.

Yankee publicist Red Patterson told reporters that a 10-year-old boy brought him to the backyard where he'd found the ball, and Patterson paced off the distance, measuring the blast at a whopping 565 feet.

A truly great shot and a great story. As for the truth, a boy had found the ball after it *rolled* into a backyard. Patterson approximated the distance. In other words, he made it up. Some historians believe the ball traveled 510 feet on the fly. But the shot had been astonishing and was an indication of what Mantle could and would do. It was also an indication of what a savvy PR guy could accomplish. The Washington long ball earned Mantle headlines, and soon he was posing for pictures with Patterson, holding up a giant tape measure. From then on, everyone's mammoth home runs would be part of the semifantastical "Tale of the Tape" that Mantle started with one swing of the bat.

ily embellished the moment. But Ruth had made his intentions clear. And the home run was not just climactic but timely, giving the Yankees a 5–4 lead. On the very next pitch, Gehrig smacked another home run—also his second of the day—to make it 6–4. The Yankees would win 7–5 and sweep the humbled Cubs with a 13–6 rout in Game 4. Gehrig led everyone with nine hits, three homers, eight RBIs, and a .529 average—no one had produced such tremendous World Series figures since Gehrig himself back in 1928.

But as always, even when Gehrig was the star, Ruth was the story. And in this case, the story was one of baseball's best, a case where you could print the legend but know it was indeed fact.

## 4. The Mets finally vanquish Houston in the 16th, October 15, 1986, Houston Astrodome

The famed Houston Astrodome roof blocked out the sun, but shadows—cutting forward and backward in time—still spread across one of the most thrilling baseball games ever played: Game 6 of the 1986 National League Championship Series.

Every pitch, every play, was made with the shadow of Houston ace and Game 7 starter Mike Scott looming over it. And 10 days later, it was covered by the shadows of another Game 6 when the Mets' World Series comeback became one of baseball's defining moments.

Still, this 7–6, 16-inning affair—then the longest postseason game ever—was an instant classic, hailed as one of the most exciting games in baseball history. Throughout the game the Mets demonstrated the tenacity that made them great, prevailing not because of one factor but because of many—pitching prowess, solid fundamentals, depth, resiliency, a knack for clutch hits, and a flair for capitalizing on an opponent's mistakes. Their triumph was a wild finish to a hold-your-breath, clutch-the-edge-of-your-seat, don't-even-leave-to-go-to-the-bathroom series in which five games were decided by one run and three Met wins came in their last at-bat.

The supremely talented and arrogant '86 Mets crushed opponents and intimidated them in the process. With their easy ride and cocky manner, they seemed set to coast into history . . . until they met the Astros in the playoffs. On paper, the weak-hitting Astros were no match for the mighty Mets, but occasionally one pitcher can carry a playoff. Mike Scott was that pitcher. After May 9, he'd gone 15–8 with a 1.87 ERA, clinching the NL West with a no-hitter against San Francisco and fanning 55 in his last five starts. Scott was a Mets castoff: he'd been dumped because of his lack of intensity and breaking stuff. Having developed the split-finger fastball that made him unhittable, he was accused by his ex-club of scuffing the ball. "It's the consensus around the league that Mike Scott cheats," Gary Carter said after Scott's no-hitter.

True or not, the Mets were psyched out. Scott won the first game 1–0, tying an NLCS record with 14 strikeouts, and he returned on three days' rest in Game 4 to retire 20 of the first 22 batters. Overall, Scott yielded just eight hits, one walk, and one run over two complete games.

When Scott wasn't pitching, the Mets were the better club, though not by much: they beat Nolan Ryan handily in Game 2, but needed Lenny Dykstra's ninth-inning, two-run homer in Game 3 and Carter's slump-breaking, 12th-inning single in Game 5. Heading to Houston with a 3–2 advantage, the Mets still felt that their backs were to the wall. A loss meant facing Scott, so Game 6 was for all practical purposes a Game 7.

"Mike Scott haunted us," Carter said later. "The man had a power over us, even when he was spending the game on the bench."

The Astrodome crowd got revved early that afternoon when Houston manufactured three first-inning runs off Bobby Ojeda. But they lost a chance to break open the game when Alan Ashby missed a suicide squeeze. The Mets, meanwhile, seemed focused on Scott's shadow rather than the ball. Lefty Bob Knepper, whose guile contrasted starkly with the power pitching of Scott and Ryan, clamped them down on two hits over eight innings. The Astros were bouncing around their dugout chanting, "Scotty tomorrow! Scotty tomorrow!"

The game was less than two hours old, the Astros led 3–0, and it felt nearly over. In reality, it was just getting started.

In the ninth, Mets manager Davey Johnson sent the left-handed Dykstra to pinch-hit against Knepper. With two strikes, center fielder Billy Hatcher figured an uncomfortable Dykstra would try for contact and edged toward left field. Knepper threw an outside slider, but Dykstra turned on it, driving it into the gap in right-center for a triple. Mookie Wilson blooped a soft liner that second baseman Bill Doran misjudged. The ball skimmed his glove and landed for an RBI single. Wilson scored on Keith Hernandez's one-out double, and Knepper, who'd blown a lead in Game 3, was done.

But closer Dave Smith, who'd yielded Dykstra's Game 3 homer, seemed rattled. He walked Carter on a full count and complained about the call. He walked Darryl Strawberry on a full count. The bases were loaded. Smith complained about another call with Ray Knight batting, as did manager Hal Lanier and Ashby, the catcher. When Knight—an ex-Astro—snapped at Ashby to "stop umpiring," Dickie Thon came in from shortstop to yell at Knight. Order was restored, but Smith pitched cautiously and left his next pitch over the plate. Knight drove it to right field for a sacrifice fly that tied the game.

**After six tough games and 16 wild innings, Jesse Orosco leaps skyward to celebrate the end of the NLCS.**

The Mets had the advantage, thanks to their stronger bullpen. Rick Aguilera had already posted three scoreless innings, and now Roger McDowell stepped in with five of his own. Johnson knew he was draining his bullpen, but, he explained later, "it felt like a seventh game."

The Mets offense disappeared as quickly as it had arrived, but by the 14th the Astros bullpen was depleted. They called on little-used 38-year-old Aurelio Lopez. He put two on, and with one out, Wally Backman singled to right. The Astros had already suffered Ashby's missed bunt, Hatcher's bad guess, Doran's mistimed leap, and Smith's lost temper; now right fielder Kevin Bass couldn't get the ball out of his glove quickly, and Darryl Strawberry scored from second for a 4–3 lead.

New York could smell victory. Closer Jesse Orosco struck out Doran. The Astros hadn't scored in 12 innings, but Billy Hatcher, with only six homers all season, swung for the fences. When he crushed a fastball high and deep into the left-field stands, the crowd stood and cheered until . . . at the last minute . . . it curved left of the foul pole. With the count full, Orosco tried another fastball, and Hatcher hit it to virtually the same place—but this time he conjured up enough Carlton Fisk to will the ball into the netting on the fair side of the pole. The game was tied again, 4–4. The Mets were shocked. Hatcher was shouting, "We're going to win it, we're going to win it."

Lopez and Orosco both survived the 15th. The 16th inning would be the first in postseason history, and it had enough dramatics for an entire game. Strawberry led off with a high, short fly to center. Hatcher, playing deep against a power hitter, couldn't get there, and the hang-time and Astroturf hop gave Strawberry a bloop double.

As they had all game—indeed, all season—the Mets capitalized on the small break. The hitless Knight asked Davey Johnson if he should bunt the runner to third. Johnson went for broke. "Get a ball you can drive to right field," he said. Knight roped an outside fastball down the right-field line to score Strawberry and seized an extra base on Bass's ill-advised throw to the plate.

Lanier was reduced to calling on Jeff Calhoun, who had pitched just 26 innings all season and none in the playoffs. Calhoun threw a wild pitch, advancing Knight to third. Then he uncorked another, and Knight scored. Backman walked and scored on a Dykstra single for a seemingly insurmountable 7–4 lead.

But Orosco had an unnerving habit of pitching himself into trouble. A walk and two singles with one out made it 7–5. But while Houston's defense had failed, the Mets made the big play when Denny Walling hit a sharp bouncer in the hole and Hernandez, perhaps the greatest defensive first baseman ever, robbed Walling of a hit and threw from one knee to second base for the force. Keeping the tying run out of scoring position proved critical when Glenn Davis singled home Doran, making it 7–6.

Hernandez, who was so tense during this dramatic classic that he smoked two and a half *packs* of cigarettes between innings, then stormed over to the mound. "If you throw another fastball, I'll kill you," he threatened Orosco. The reliever threw only sliders, down and in, to Kevin Bass. The first was out of the strike zone, but Bass swung and missed. He took strike two. Orosco missed, ball one, ball two, and—on an extremely close pitch—ball three.

The count was full.

The runners were going.

Mike Scott was lurking in the dugout.

Orosco threw one more slider.

Down and in, it was way out of the zone. But Bass chased it. Strike three.

After 4 hours and 42 minutes, Orosco threw his glove high in the air as the Mets simultaneously celebrated and sighed in relief.

Houston's fans applauded both teams, while back in New York the city went crazy. Thousands of New Yorkers had gone to the nearest bar right after work, unwilling to risk missing the ending; the result was a raucous celebration and a rush hour that arrived three hours late that day.

This instant classic made the Mets National League champs. Soon enough, the only Mets opponent being talked about was Bill Buckner, but the second Game 6 miracle might never have happened had it not been for the first one.

## 5. Columbia pulls off a stunning Rose Bowl upset, January 1, 1934, Pasadena

Some numbers lie. Others don't.

Look at some seemingly crucial stats from the 1934 Rose Bowl between Columbia and heavily favored Stanford.

First downs: Stanford 16, Columbia 6.

Total yardage: Stanford 272, Columbia 114.

Scoring threats: Stanford 6, Columbia 3.

Now here's the only number that counts—the final score:

Columbia 7, Stanford 0.

Columbia was lucky to even play in the Rose Bowl back when it was the sole New Year's Day event, much less to pull off a historic upset. At the time the best West Coast team picked its opponent. Stanford's first choice was undefeated Princeton, but the Tigers, who had trounced Columbia's Lions 20–0, refused the invite because of an agreement with Yale that restricted postseason games.

Other obvious choices included Army, Nebraska, Duke, Pitt, Michigan, and Minnesota. Stanford asked Columbia to the big dance. Some writers grumbled that Stanford was looking for an easy time — Lou Little's Columbia squad had some excellent players, but it was far from great and lacked depth. Columbia would be outweighed by about 17 pounds per man and, most thought, badly overmatched. (Making matters worse, cocaptain and leading lineman Joe Ferrara was declared ineligible after failing physics and French midterms.)

The Lions set out by train from New York on December 19, stopping to practice in St. Louis, Dallas, and Tucson. Finally, they arrived in sunny southern California to find the worst deluge of rain Los Angeles had ever experienced — 18 inches fell during the three days preceding the game. Mudslides, flooding, and the resulting car crashes would claim dozens of lives.

At the stadium, the players' benches floated along the sidelines, and the field was submerged. The game was nearly canceled, but after 25 fire engines and two electric pumps slurped water from the field for hours, it seemed dry enough to play on. The horrific weather and pregame spread favoring Stanford by 18 suppressed attendance — only 35,000 bothered showing up, the smallest Rose Bowl crowd ever. (Once Columbia proved its mettle, another 5,000 arrived at halftime.) The surface remained treacherous, and rain continued during the game. Some predicted that a mudfest would favor Stanford's heavier, sturdier backs, and Stanford did churn out plenty of yardage — Bobby Grayson's 152 yards was more than the entire Columbia team. Yet ultimately the muck proved a tremendous break for the Lions: it inhibited Stanford's superior offense just enough — they completed only 2 of 12 passes and fumbled the slippery ball away five times — that they always fell shy of the goal line.

## Honorable Mention: New York as a Big-Time College Town

**Ken Strong leads NYU past Carnegie Tech, November 24, 1928, Forbes Field, Pittsburgh**

Two undefeated teams arrived at Forbes Field on November 24, 1928. But only one had Ken Strong.

Carnegie Tech had home field advantage, a reputation as the East's best team, and an early 7–0 lead, but New York University triumphed, thanks to Strong, a 6', 205-pound, running, passing, and kicking machine on his way to leading the nation in scoring with 162 points. (He was also a fearsome slugger whose major league baseball career was derailed only by a broken wrist and a surgeon who removed the wrong bone.)

This game was Strong's finest hour: he threw a 17-yard touchdown pass, was in the middle of a double-lateral to set up the second touchdown pass, and ran amok from scrimmage, including four bursts of more than 20 yards and two TDs, one on a 40-yard jaunt. He also kicked three extra points and nailed punts as long as 60 yards. In other words, he was singularly responsible for NYU's 27–13 thrashing of Carnegie Tech.

Grantland Rice later deemed Strong second only to Jim Thorpe among all-around gridiron greats, but after Strong overpowered his team this day, Carnegie Tech's veteran coach Walter Steffen was even more effusive: "Ken Strong is easily the greatest football player I ever saw."

**Cliff Montgomery lets loose a punt on a rainy day in Pasadena, but it was his passing and play-calling that produced the lone score in Columbia's Rose Bowl upset of Stanford.**

Columbia reached the end zone only once—on a seemingly miraculous two-play drive in the second quarter—but that would prove enough. Starting at Stanford's 45, quarterback Cliff Montgomery made his sole completion (in just two tries), hitting Red Matal, who splashed to the 17.

All week the Lions had practiced trick plays to spring on their bigger, stronger opponents, hoping Ivy League brains could triumph over brawn. Now Montgomery decided to try one. Knowing Stanford expected a rushing play through the line, he called KF-79, a play Little had designed. K stood for Kicker (the quarterback was often called the kicker then), who handed the ball to F (the Fullback). The offensive line overloaded the right side, and the K, Montgomery, slammed in as if carrying the ball while the F, 23-year-old sophomore Al Barabas, glided the opposite way through the left side's 7 and 9 slots.

That was the plan. Amazingly, the execution worked to perfection. Montgomery had set the play up by faking handoffs to Barabas and halfback Ed Brominski early in the game. Now Montgomery "faked" a handoff to Barabas, but in reality stuck it to the runner's left hip, then, pretending he had the ball himself, Montgomery plunged into the right side. The entire defense fell for it, attacking the line while Barabas sauntered by untouched—no one from Stanford even saw him until he was at the 10. Just as he coasted into the end zone the sun suddenly burst out from behind the clouds.

Still, sun or rain (and there was plenty more rain), no one expected that to be the last score. With Little relying on only 17 players the entire game, the Lions tired in the second half. Time after time, Stanford "swept over all things Columbian as the stream in the Arroyo Seco swept over its embankments in this greatest of all California floods," Stanley Woodward wrote in the *Herald-Tribune.*

Yet each time Columbia dug in. Once Stanford had first down on Columbia's 3, but the Lions allowed only two yards on the next four plays, forcing a fumble on the final effort. When Stanford later had a second down on the 8, the Lions—armed with a rare wave of fresh substitutes—tossed the Cardinals back two yards on two plays. When a desperate Stanford squad took to the air, Columbia intercepted Grayson's pass. Columbia kept Stanford's slate blank, walking off with a shocking 7–0 victory.

When the Lions arrived back in New York, they were hailed as conquering heroes. Newly sworn-in mayor Fiorello La Guardia, who had promised not to waste time on trivial nonsense like official greetings, was at Pennsylvania Station to welcome the team home; the city celebrated with a parade from 34th Street uptown to the Columbia campus.

Even the Lions themselves remained forever amazed at what they accomplished. At a reunion 15 years later, Little showed filmed footage of the game. When the second half was about to begin, Barabas said, "Turn it off, Lou, don't show the second half. They might beat us."

## 6. This time around Ralph Terry finds success and happiness in the ninth inning of a Game 7, October 16, 1962, Candlestick Park, San Francisco

The quintessential sports moment, a finale so fraught with tension that it almost felt scripted: Game 7 of the World Series, the bottom of the ninth inning, the score 1–0, and the home team sending the top of the order to the plate. Every imaginable factor would come into play over the final three outs—the weather, managerial and coaching decisions, the right fielder's overlooked defensive skill, the imprecise positioning of the second baseman, a quest for redemption by an all-time World Series goat, and the menacing presence of three future Hall of Famers at the plate. The inning has been broken down and analyzed endlessly, but add it all back up and the final showdown of the 1962 World Series between the New York Yankees and the San Francisco Giants reveals nothing less than the magnificent and endless intrigue of baseball.

The World Series should have been a slugfest. The defending champion Yankees featured "the M&M Boys," Mickey Mantle and Roger Maris, who, one year after blasting 115 homers, combined for "just" 63, and three other players hit at least 20 dingers. While the Yankees led the AL in runs scored, the Giants led everyone, thanks to Willie Mays, Orlando Cepeda, Felipe Alou, and Willie McCovey, who combined for 129 home runs. But despite winning 101 games, the Giants had to mount a last-minute charge to tie their archrival, the Los Angeles Dodgers, forcing a replay of the 1951 playoff—the Giants even overcame a 4–2 ninth-inning deficit in the deciding game (the score when Bobby Thomson hit his famous home run).

Whitey Ford beat the exhausted Giants 6–2 in Game 1, but 24-game winner Jack Sanford evened things up with a 2–0 three-hitter over the Yankees' 23-game winner Ralph Terry. The teams split the next two games. Game 5 pitted Sanford and Terry again; it was 2–2 in the eighth before New York captured it 5–3. The teams returned to San Francisco, where Billy Pierce's three-hitter—postponed for three days by a deluge of rainstorms—forced a seventh game. Thanks to the extra days off, Game 7 would once more pit Sanford against Terry.

There had been only two other best-of-seven Series in which two pitchers faced each other three times—Detroit's Hal Newhouser versus Chicago's Hank Borowy in 1945 and Milwaukee's Warren Spahn versus New York's Whitey Ford in 1958—but neither showdown produced consistent duels. (Three such confrontations since 1962—Yankee Mel Stottlemyre versus Cardinal Bob Gibson in 1964, Dodger Sandy Koufax against

**Ralph Terry's strong outing in Game 5 at the Stadium set the stage for his Game 7, Series-winning 1-0 masterpiece in San Francisco.**

Twin Jim Kaat in 1965, and Met Jon Matlack against the A's Ken Holzman in 1973—also produced uneven results.)

But on October 16 at Candlestick Park, Sanford and Terry exceeded expectations. Sanford yielded seven hits and four walks but pitched out of nearly every jam he created: the Yankees got their lone run home in the fifth when Tony Kubek bounced into a bases-loaded double play.

The way Terry was pitching, that lone run loomed awfully large. He was perfect through five and two-thirds before allowing a harmless single to Sanford, of all people. The final three innings of this World Series were racked with tension. With two outs in the seventh, the Yankees ratcheted it up when Boyer and Terry singled, but Sanford got out of it. In the Giants' seventh, Mays was robbed of an extra-base hit by Tom Tresh; McCovey followed with a triple that would have tied the game. With the tying run 90 feet away, Terry fanned Cepeda. One last threat finally chased Sanford in the eighth, but reliever Billy O'Dell came on with the bases full and no outs and performed a Houdini-esque act of his own, escaping without allowing a run.

Terry took his two-hitter into the bottom of the ninth. The Yankees needed three more outs to earn back-to-back titles for the fourth time overall and for the first time since 1953.

Baseball had not had a 1–0 clincher since the Giants beat the Yankees back in 1921 and this one was soon in jeopardy. Catcher Elston Howard muffed Matty Alou's pop foul near the Giant dugout. (Terry later claimed that one of the Giants, possibly manager Alvin Dark, bumped Howard.) Given new life, Alou dragged a bunt for a hit. Trouble had begun.

Matty's brother Felipe had hit 25 homers and bunted just twice all year, but Dark turned conservative at the wrong time and called for a sacrifice. After one failed attempt, Dark changed his mind, but Alou, already in the hole, whiffed. Terry fanned Chuck Hiller too, but to finish the Giants he'd have to defeat perhaps the best ballplayer since Babe Ruth. Willie Mays led the league with 49 homers in 1962 and wanted one more. Terry, unfortunately, knew from Game 7 ninth-inning home runs—two years earlier, he'd surrendered one to Pittsburgh Pirate Bill Mazeroski.

Trying to avoid the goat tag for a second time, Terry pitched Mays away. Mays wisely went with the pitch and roped the ball into right. Had it not been for the excessive rain, the ball would have skittered into the corner, allowing Alou to score from first. But the wet field slowed everything down, and Maris, always underrated as a fielder, hustled over, cut the ball off, and made a perfect relay to second baseman Bobby Richardson. The play has long been a debate topic in San Francisco: most Giants agreed with third-base coach Whitey Lockman's decision to slam the brakes on the speedy Alou, because it's bad baseball to make the final out at the plate with two of your best hitters coming up. But Mays disagreed, saying Richardson's throw home was a bit off-line and might have been worse had he felt the pressure of a runner steaming home; he himself, Mays always maintained, would have run through Lockman's stop sign (and run over Yankee catcher Elston Howard if need be).

With Alou on third and Mays on second, Yankee manager Ralph Houk visited Terry to talk tactics. Up next was the lefty McCovey, who had homered off Terry in Game 2 and just tripled off him. The following batter was Orlando Cepeda, a more feared hitter then. (Cepeda hit 81 homers in 1961 and 1962; McCovey, who would break out in 1963, had just 38 over those years.) But Cepeda was, like Terry, a righty, and except for three Game 6 hits off the lefty Ford, he'd been hitless the entire Series. The choice seemed obvious, yet Houk inexplicably deferred to Terry's inexplicable decision to go after McCovey, albeit carefully.

Terry's idea of careful, however, conjured Mazeroski memories: he left the first pitch right out over the plate. McCovey, not expecting to see a strike, was so surprised that he overreacted and hit a long hard foul. The next pitch was a ball. On the 1–1 pitch, Terry tried coming inside on McCovey, but the slugger stepped back and took a vicious swing. He made contact. Well, he did more than that. He crushed the ball, smoking a liner toward the outfield in a spot that under normal circumstances would have resulted in a two-run hit. McCovey was such a dead pull hitter that most NL teams shifted their second baseman over in the hole against him and often pulled their shortstop on the other side of the bag. But Yankee second baseman Bobby Richardson, who wasn't as familiar with McCovey's tendencies, didn't play him as far toward right as he should have. By being out of position, Richardson was inadvertently perfectly positioned.

It was a moment McCovey would long relive in his dreams. Richardson took one step, read the topspin, and put his mitt out. For a fraction of a second as McCovey's bat met the ball, the Giants and their fans had begun leaping out of their seats—they were World Series champions. But before the jubilation could travel from their brains to their vocal cords, the ball smacked into Richardson's glove, choking off the cheers.

Terry, the goat of 1960, became the Most Valuable Player of 1962 as the Bombers won what would be their last championship for 15 years.

## 7. Mark Messier backs up his guarantee, May 25, 1994, Byrne Brendan Arena, East Rutherford, New Jersey

His team was on the brink, their dream season souring into yet another nightmare. It was a time that called for, no, demanded, something special, something spectacular. On May 25, 1994, Mark Messier came through with a dynamic display of both his remarkable skill and his immeasurable will, proving once and for all that he was the captain who could lead the New York Rangers to the promised land.

The Rangers and their fans had waited since 1940 for a championship. This was the season it was supposed to happen. Their fearsome, balanced lineup compiled the NHL's best record, then demolished the New York Islanders and Washington Capitols in the playoffs' early rounds. The New Jersey Devils should have been an easy mark in the conference finals — the Rangers had gone 6–0 against them in the regular season. But New York lost a late lead in the first game and dropped it in double-overtime, then fell behind 3–2 in games with surprisingly shoddy play in Games 4 and 5 at home. They'd almost melted down off the ice too, as coach Mike Keenan faced a near-mutiny for benching Brian Leetch and pulling goalie Mike Richter. Only Messier kept the team and the coach from imploding. Still, the 33-year-old Messier was skating with bruised ribs, and in the *New York Times* columnist George Vescey wrote that "poor Messier looks 62 years old."

But the foundation of Messier's game was his pride and determination; though he had talent to spare, it was his warrior demeanor that stood out. His hard-eyed stare could change physical properties, transforming solids to liquids and tough veterans to weak-kneed rookies. The 15-year veteran knew the Rangers looked to him, more than general manager Neil Smith or Keenan, as their leader and motivator. Although he generally avoided comments that might stir up opponents, as the Rangers headed for New Jersey he told every newspaper, "We're going to go in there and win Game Six." "Messier Vows," *Newsday* reported, while the *Bergen Record* linked Messier to Joe Namath, pasting the word "Guarantee" in big letters; the *New York Post* highlighted "Captain Courageous' Bold Prediction."

Here's the thing about brash statements, however. You gotta back 'em up. Muhammad Ali's rhyming boasts and Namath's cocky declaration before the 1969 Super Bowl made them into legends because they won. A guarantee sounds awfully lame when your team continues its slide, getting soundly beaten at both ends of the ice.

In Game 6 on May 25, the Devils controlled the tempo and grabbed an early lead on a play that seemed to signal that destiny did not consider the Rangers her darlings — on a pass across the crease from New Jersey's Scott Niedermayer to Jim Dowd, the puck hit Ranger forward Sergei Nemchinov's stick and ricocheted into the New York net for an accidental goal. Messier calmed the team between periods, but still the Rangers seemed lost early in the second.

Distressed, Keenan made a bold move that counted more than any pregame predictions. He called a timeout but said little, glaring out at the ice while the players gathered their thoughts. Then he shook up the lineup again, but this time, instead of dissension, he got results. Keenan paired Doug Lidster with Leetch, while moving the struggling Alexei Kovalev to right wing alongside Adam Graves and Messier.

The offense started opening up, but it was still only the inspired play of Richter, with 24 saves over the first two periods, that prevented an avalanche. When the Devils built their lead to 2–0 near the end of the second, fans wondered if the curse of 1940 was stronger than the guarantee of 1994.

But the 6'1", 205-pound Messier proved he could not only talk the talk but skate the skate. With 1:49 left in the second, he helped break the ice by setting up Kovalev with a drop pass; Kovalev, without a point in the series, responded with a long slap shot through a screen to put the Rangers on the board.

In the final period, Messier took over completely. Just 2:48 in, Messier, who'd had just one goal in the series, took a pass from Kovalev and slipped in a backhand from the bottom of the right circle, tying the game at 2–2. Less than 10 minutes later, he changed the tenor of the game for good: when Devil goaltender Martin Brodeur blocked another Kovalev shot, Messier stepped up and put home the rebound for a 3–2 lead.

For his finishing touch, Messier — who had never completed a playoff hat trick — scored his third goal in dramatic fashion. After a penalty

**The Rangers' Mark Messier puts the puck in the net past the Devils' goaltender Martin Brodeur—one of three third-period goals Messier scored to give the Rangers a 4-2 win that tied the Eastern Conference Finals at three games apiece.**

gave the Devils a 5-on-4 advantage with under two minutes left, coach Jacques Lemaire made it 6-on-4 by pulling Brodeur. But New York's number 11 got his stick on the puck and fired it about 160 feet down the ice into the empty net to guarantee, as it were, a Ranger victory.

Afterwards, Messier chose not to gloat but to lead. In the dressing room, before anyone could cut loose, he issued a stern reminder about the Game 7 awaiting them: "We haven't won anything yet."

But with Messier there, the team was pretty sure it finally would.

## 8. The Knicks finally beat Boston in Game 7, April 29, 1973, Boston Garden

The odds, and history, were firmly stacked against the New York Knicks on April 29, 1973.

They were facing the Boston Celtics, who had the best NBA record that season, an astonishing 68–14 mark.

They were facing the Celtics in Boston, on the fabled parquet floor, where only Red Auerbach's men knew the dead spots, where the home team had lost more than nine games in a season only thrice since 1950.

They were reeling, having blown two straight games to watch a 3–1 edge evaporate and force this decisive seventh game in the Eastern Conference Finals.

Their opponents, the team that defined NBA greatness, had never lost a seventh game in its history, boasting 10 straight wins in such confrontations.

But odds never mattered much to the comeback-happy Knicks of the 1969–73 era. This 1972–73 edition had made its statement in November, scoring 19 straight points to turn an 86–68 deficit against Milwaukee into an 87–86 win. And they'd already pulled out one improbable win earlier in the series, coming back from 16 points down to win in double-overtime. This time their defense—which led the NBA by allowing an average of just 98.2 points per game—came up big facing the ultimate pressure and harassed the Celtics for a dandy 94–78 win that returned them to the NBA Finals for the third time in four years.

The Knicks had known from the start of the season that this might be this squad's last shot at a second crown. The core of the 1969–70 championship team remained—future Hall of Famers Willis Reed, Walt Frazier, Bill Bradley, and Dave DeBusschere—with Earl Monroe and Jerry Lucas joining them. But the front line was old and vulnerable—Lucas and DeBusschere were 32, and Reed's knees seemed twice that age.

The Knicks finished second to Boston in the East with 57 wins, although they'd split the eight regular-season matchups. After vanquishing the Baltimore Bullets in the first playoff round, they went to Boston, where MVP Dave Cowens, along with John Havlicek, JoJo White, Paul Silas, and Don Chaney, routed them in Game 1.

New York retaliated back in Madison Square Garden, humiliating the Celtics 129–96 in Game 2, Boston's worst playoff loss ever. When the Knicks won Game 3 on the road and in that double-overtime win at home, the series seemed over, especially with Havlicek having banged up his shoulder. But Boston won Game 5 on a lucky shot and Game 6 too.

Coach Red Holzman shook things up for Game 7, and just enough of his moves paid off to reaffirm his genius reputation. He had Dave DeBusschere, more agile than Reed, cover Cowens, hoping to stop his outside shooting. It didn't work: Cowens poured in 15 first-half points. When the Celtics snatched a 22–19 lead after one, Holzman benched Monroe, who was hobbled by an ankle injury, in favor of defensive specialist Dean Meminger. "The Dream" forced JoJo White to shoot jumpers instead of driving, holding him to just two second-quarter points.

With the lightning-quick Meminger and the super-smooth Frazier together, the Knicks could

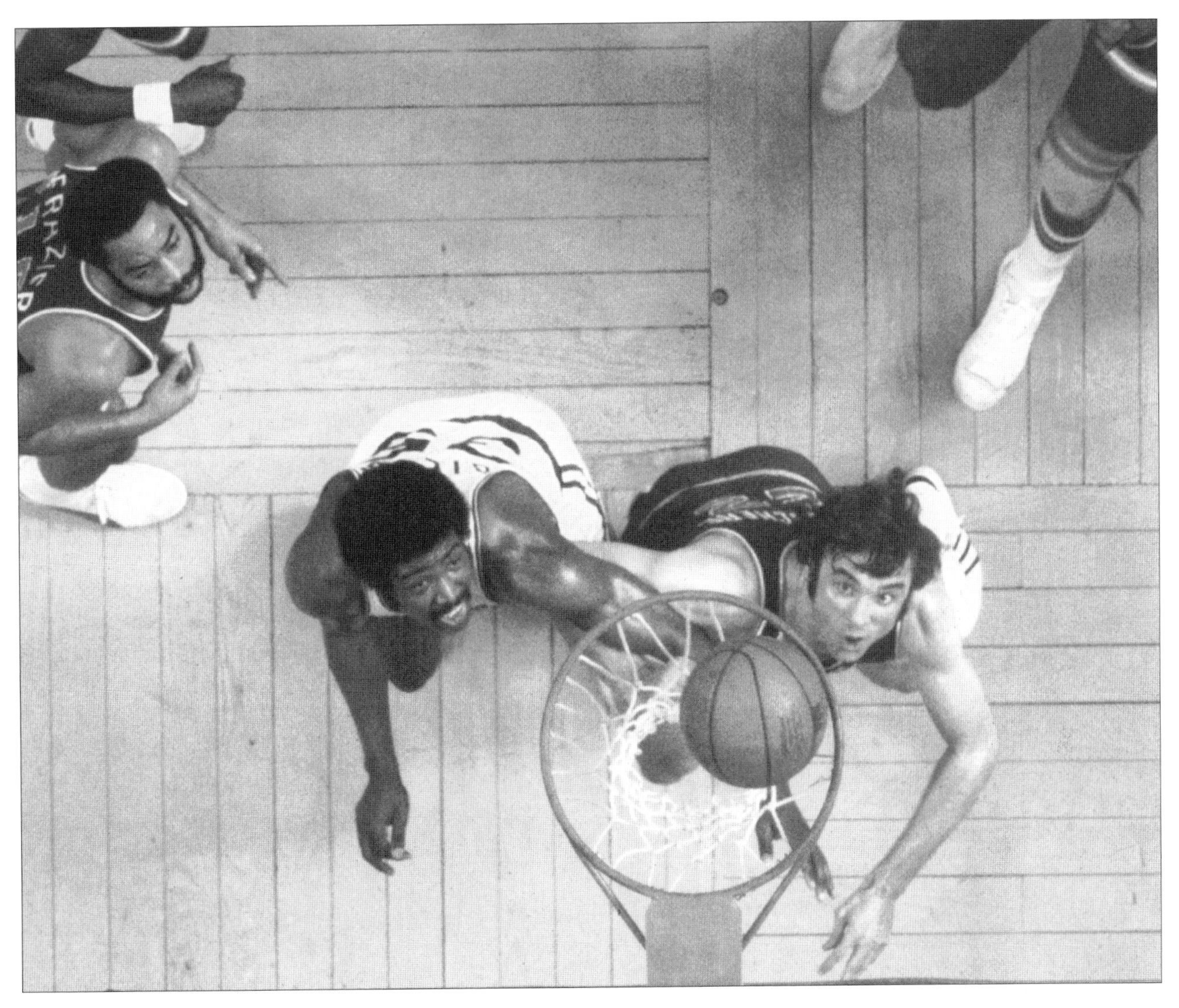

**In a hard-fought series, Boston usually had the advantage on their parquet floor, but the Knicks finally win in Beantown in 1973.**

press more; following Meminger's suggestion, Holzman also sent his forwards up into Boston's backcourt, chewing up the 24-second clock and rushing the Celtics out of their planned plays. Previously Meminger had hampered the Knicks at the offensive end, passing up open shots from outside; that allowed Boston to sag off him and clog the middle. At Holzman's urging, Meminger shot more and poured in nine second-quarter points as the Knicks came back to snatch a 45–40 halftime lead.

Frazier, who played 47 minutes, would lead all scorers with 25 points and 10 rebounds, but it was a vintage all-around team effort, with five players scoring in double figures and five hauling in at least six rebounds. When DeBusschere ran into foul trouble, Holzman reverted to putting his centers, first Lucas, then Reed, on Cowens — they held him to two points in the third quarter — and in the second and third quarters combined, the Knicks held Boston to just 35 points on a measly 12–39 shooting, building up a 68–53 lead they would not relinquish.

Holzman called this win "the most satisfying of my career."

But to become champions the Knicks still had to beat the 60–22 Lakers. No team had ever beaten two 60-win teams in the playoffs en route to becoming champion. It would give the Knicks one more chance to show what they thought of such history.

## 9. The Giants win but the Dodgers come from 6–1, 8–5 down on the final day against Philadelphia in 14 innings to force a playoff, September 30, 1951, Shibe Park, Philadelphia

The Brooklyn Dodgers were desperate for a hero.

It was the bottom of the 12th on September 30, the final day of the 1951 season, and the Bums were trapped in the most dire baseball scenario imaginable: they'd blown their 13½-game August lead over their archrivals, the New York Giants, and come into the final weekend of the season tied for first. And in the half-light of settling dusk at Philadelphia's Shibe Park, the Philadelphia Phillies had loaded the bases. A single run and the Dodgers—already selling World Series tickets—would go home for a long winter of reliving the ultimate collapse.

Ace Don Newcombe had already played jut-jawed leading man pitching on zero—yes, that's right, zero—days' rest. He'd come on as the sixth Dodger to man the hill and shut Philadelphia out on one hit after the eighth inning. He'd escaped several jams, most notably in the 11th when Andy Pafko robbed Andy Seminick of a possible game-winning double with a running catch down the left-field line.

But by the 12th, Newcombe was drained, out of heroics.

Every Dodger and Giant was exhausted from the long season and the tightening vise of the pennant race—the Dodgers had been watching their lead shrink slowly but steadily since mid-August, while the Giants had been playing with virtually no margin for error.

In the penultimate games on Saturday, September 29, both teams had known a loss could finish them off, so they'd sent their finest, toughest pitchers to the mound. But their foes, though long since eliminated, played as if they too had a pennant at stake. Giant Sal Maglie was pitted against Boston's Warren Spahn, while Newcombe squared off against Philadelphia's Robin Roberts. Against these 20-game winners the Barber and Newk had risen to the occasion, each pitching a shutout.

So it came down to September 30. If both teams won or lost, there'd be a special tiebreaking playoff for just the third time in baseball history, but if only one won, that team would face the Yankees in the World Series.

The Dodgers and Phillies had been meeting like this for three years, and each final game had been a wild one. In 1949 Brooklyn—needing to win to avoid a tiebreaker with St. Louis—blew a 5–0 lead yet won 9–7 in extra innings. In 1950 Philadelphia edged Brooklyn for the pennant on Dick Sisler's 10th-inning homer.

This time, Preacher Roe, pitching on two days' rest, was flattened in the second, and the Bums trailed 6–1 after three, but no one was foolish enough to make predictions about the final score. (No one except Brooklyn owner Walter O'Malley, who, lacking an appreciation for tradition, was already "going over the phrasing for the wire of congratulations" to the Giants.)

In the fifth, Jackie Robinson keyed a three-run rally, tripling in Duke Snider and scoring on Pafko's single. But the Phils responded with two runs, boosting the lead back to 8–5 as the Dodgers cycled through two more pitchers. In the sixth inning, the scoreboard announced the Giants' final score. The Giants had won 3–2 for their seventh in a row, and their 37th in the final 44, thanks to superior starting pitching by Larry Jansen and a homer by red-hot Bobby Thomson.

Robinson was the only Dodger who turned to acknowledge the crowd's reaction to this news, but every Dodger knew that New York had slammed their backs against the proverbial wall. In New York, the entire city remained riveted by this never-ending drama. At Yankee Stadium, thousands stayed after the Yankees beat the Red Sox 3–0 to listen to Mel Allen's play-by-play of the Brooklyn game over the public address system.

Brooklyn shoved back in the eighth when Rube

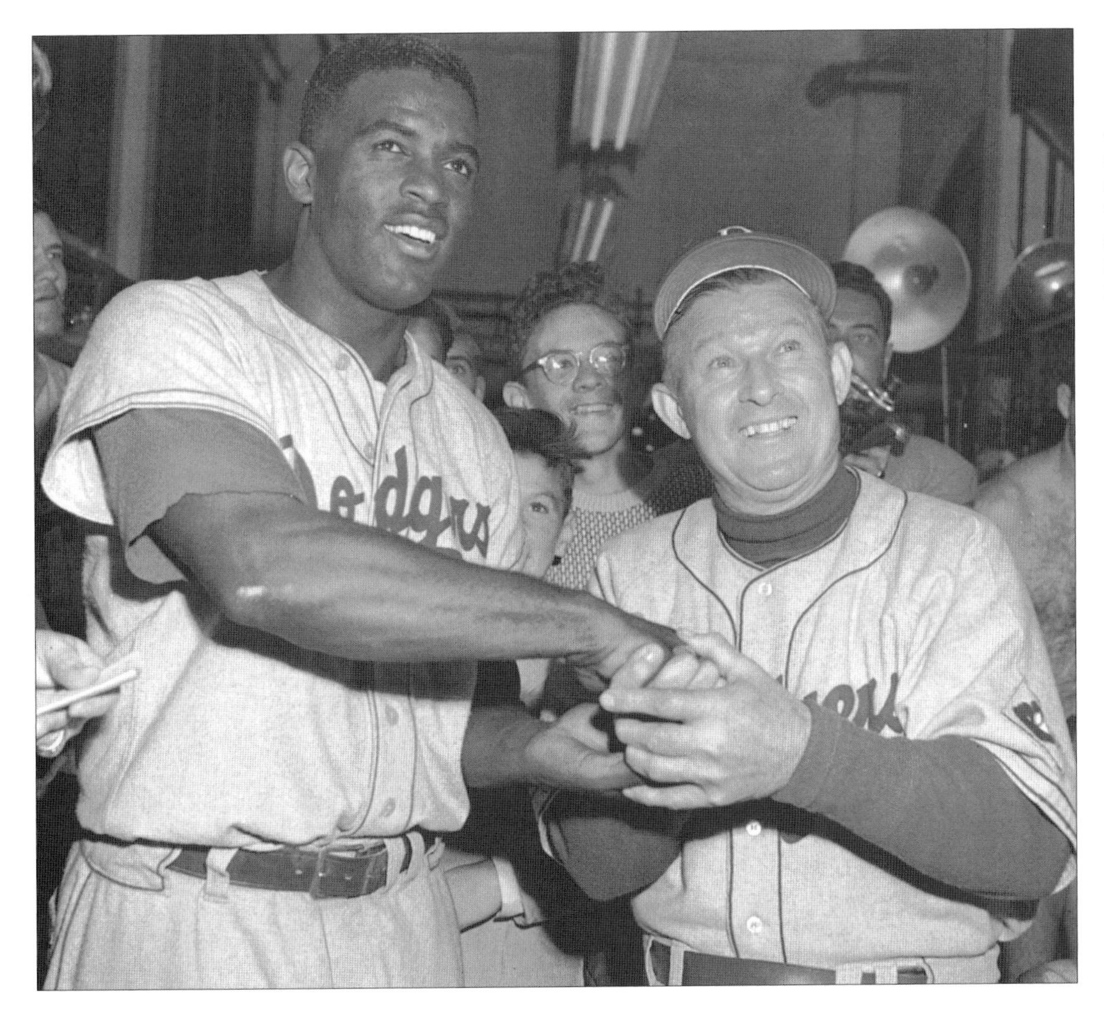


**Jackie Robinson savors the moment after his 12th-inning catch and 14th-inning homer save the Dodgers' season.**

Walker drove home two on a pinch-hit double. Roberts, who had pitched the previous day against Newcombe, came on and yielded a single to Carl Furillo. The Dodgers had finally caught up, 8–8. Newcombe matched Roberts until the 12th, when he dug his deepest hole yet and was too utterly exhausted to climb out. He created the mess by walking two and throwing away a ball on a bunt. The Dodger hurler tried dredging up some last bit of something, anything, but there was nothing left.

With the bases full and no one else ready to pitch, someone else was going to have to ride to Brooklyn's rescue. But that seemed unlikely when Eddie Waitkus drilled the ball hard, a low, nasty liner heading for center field. This ball was traveling so fast that it could not be caught. Even in that era of comic-book superheroes, it was hard to fathom a mere mortal saving the day.

But there was Jackie Robinson, the man with the strongest will in baseball, hurling himself through the air, lunging at just the right angle to snag the ball. It was, as Red Smith wrote, "the unconquerable doing the impossible."

The second baseman landed with a thud, jamming his elbow into his side, knocking the wind out of himself. He held onto the ball, then tossed it to the umpire. Then he lay still, unable to move for several minutes. A rumor flew through the stands that Robinson had suffered a heart attack. When he was finally helped to his feet and off the field, even the Phillies' fans cheered him. Robinson slumped in the dugout, spent. But he wasn't through.

In the 13th, Newcombe returned to the mound, but when the big righty walked two with two down, he told manager Charlie Dressen he was done, and Bud Pobelian got the third out. Still, it had been a magnificent showing: often maligned for not being a clutch pitcher, Newcombe had pitched back-to-back games on only two days' rest, compiling $14^2/_3$ scoreless innings.

As the 14th inning began the umpires, hoping to finish before darkness descended, hurried the Phils out to their positions. Roberts, still going strong, retired Pee Wee Reese and Snider to bring up the weary Robinson.

Donning the proverbial superhero cape yet again, Robinson found some untapped energy to smack a 1–1 fastball into the left-field stands for a 9–8 Brooklyn lead.

In the home 14th, Richie Ashburn reached scoring position with two outs to bring up Waitkus . . . again. But Waitkus had used up his magic and lofted a harmless fly to Pafko.

The Dodgers tied for the pennant. The Dodgers tied for the pennant. It lacked a certain ring, but Rachel Robinson later said that beating the Phils—the team hardest on her husband in his first year—in that game "always ranked as one of Jack's biggest thrills in baseball."

At the time, Jackie Robinson's heroics seemed like they'd be remembered forever. Then, of course, came Bobby Thomson's unfathomable feat, and history was rewritten.

# Honorable Mention: The Giants and the Dodgers Down to the Wire

**Willie Mays wins the batting title on the season's final day, September 26, 1954, Shibe Park, Philadelphia**

Willie Mays was leading the National League with 36 homers after 99 games in 1954 and threatening Babe Ruth's home run record when Giant manager Leo Durocher asked him to help the team by hitting for average instead of power. Although he was already hitting .326, Mays agreed, understanding he could do better.

By the season's final week, the Giants had won the pennant, and Mays, who'd hit only five homers since July but would bat .379 over those final 55 games, was atop one of the hottest batting races ever with teammate Don Mueller and cross-town rival Duke Snider of the Brooklyn Dodgers.

Durocher couldn't rest either Mays or Mueller without seeming to show favoritism, and friction already existed because right fielder Mueller resented Durocher's earlier orders for Mays to cover as much territory as he wanted from center field. On the penultimate day, going 0-for-4 dumped Mays to third, while Mueller's two hits shoved him to the top for the first time.

On the final day, September 26, Mueller was batting .3426, Snider .3425, and Mays .3422. Snider, who had often sat against tough lefties to preserve his average, played at home against Jake Thies, a Pittsburgh nobody with a 3–8 record. The righty Mays and lefty Mueller were in Philadelphia facing righty ace Robin Roberts.

Mueller singled his first time up, extending his lead. Mays matched him.

Mueller and Mays both made outs their second time up.

Mueller flied to left his next two times up. Mays tripled and doubled, apparently clinching the title as Snider went 0-for-3, falling to .341 and third place.

But Mays's triple keyed a two-run rally that forced extra innings, and in the 10th Mueller's double inched him closer . . . but left first base open. Roberts, caring only about winning, walked Mays. In the 11th, Mueller grounded into a force play that kept the winning rally alive but ended his season at .342.

Mays finished at .345 and back in New York landed on *The Ed Sullivan Show, The Colgate Comedy Hour, The Today Show,* and *The Tonight Show*—and in the front car of the Giants' ticker-tape parade to City Hall. He would soon be named Most Valuable Player, but after the World Series his seasonlong hitting exploits would be overshadowed forever by "the Catch."

Babe Ruth crosses the plate, something he makes a habit of with three homers in one World Series game.

## 10. Babe Ruth hits three homers to finish off St. Louis, October 8, 1928, Sportsman's Park

There was only one person who could put the perfect finishing touch on the first New York Yankee dynasty: Babe Ruth.

It was Ruth who'd led them to the promised land, who personified the Yankee image—the team that in 1928 reached its sixth and won its third World Series in eight years. In the first championship season of 1923, Ruth had hit three home runs in the Yanks' first Fall Classic triumph against the Giants; in the second, 1927, he'd walloped two more as Murderers' Row swept the Pittsburgh Pirates.

In 1928, after nearly blowing the pennant as they struggled through an injury-plagued season, the Yankees took the first three games from St. Louis, the team that had barely defeated them two years earlier. In that Series, Ruth had smashed three homers in one game but had become the goat when he was caught stealing for the final out of Game 7. This time around, Ruth, playing on an injured leg, was relatively quiet. He scored six runs on seven hits but had no homers and just one RBI, while Lou Gehrig, with two homers in Game 3, was the star.

Then came Game 4 on October 8 at Sportsman's Park, where the Yankees strived to become the first team to sweep back-to-back World Series. In the fourth, with the Yankees down 1–0, Ruth hit a curve from 21-game winner Willie Sherdel past the right-field bleachers.

In the seventh, with New York trailing 2–1, Ruth again faced the southpaw in a controversial and oft-forgotten at-bat. With two strikes, Ruth had his head turned and was ribbing Cardinal backstop Earl Smith when Sherdel hurriedly threw to the plate for what he thought was strike three. The quick pitch was a legal NL tactic, but both teams had been warned off it for the Series, so umpire Cy Pfirman declared it didn't count. A flock of Cardinals argued vociferously but in vain. When the Cards folded, Ruth gave them a round of mocking applause, then briefly taunted Sherdel. The crowd hurled programs and bottles at him. Sherdel wasted two pitches, evening the count. In *Babe,* author Robert Creamer quotes Ruth from a 1929 interview saying that he ended the next round of barbs with Sherdel by boasting, "Put one right here and I'll knock it out of the park for you."

Sherdel challenged Ruth, who indeed knocked another curve over the right-field bleachers, over the roof of the pavilion, and into the ether. Ruth trotted the base paths, laughing at and waving to the silenced crowd.

Ruth had rattled Sherdel, who grooved a pitch to Gehrig. The ball eventually landed in the right-field stands, making Gehrig the first person to drive in nine and the first other than Ruth to hit four homers in a Series. He also gave New York a 3–2 lead. Sherdel departed, but his replacement, Grover Cleveland Alexander, lacked the magic he had in shutting the Yankees down in 1926.

In the eighth, with the score 6–2, Ruth got one last turn. With one strike, Alexander tried his curve, and Ruth treated it as rudely as he did Sherdel's breaking stuff, lofting it far and gone to right. His display was so astonishing that to convey Ruth's awesome power *New York Times* writer James R. Harrison joked, "To show you how badly the Babe was slipping, this ball only hit on the roof of the pavilion."

## Honorable Mention: In a Long-Ball Groove

**Lou Gehrig becomes the first modern player to hit four homers in a game, June 3, 1932, Shibe Park, Philadelphia**

In the first inning on June 3, 1932, at Shibe Park, Lou Gehrig launched a two-run homer to left-center field off Philadelphia's George Earnshaw.

In the fourth, Gehrig blasted a ball to the stands in right.

In the fifth inning, after Earle Combs and Babe Ruth had homered, Gehrig lifted another ball to left-center, becoming the first player to achieve four three-homer games in his career. That marked the end of Earnshaw.

In this wild slugfest—the Yankees had five homers but trailed Philadelphia 8–7 thanks partly to a Gehrig error—Gehrig would clearly get at least one more shot. Although two 19th-century players had cracked four roundtrippers in a game, no modern player, not even Ruth, had done it.

Philadelphia owner-manager Connie Mack patronizingly said to Earnshaw, "Sit here for a few minutes, son. I want you to see how [Leroy] Mahaffey does it. You've been pitching entirely wrong to Gehrig."

With Philadelphia's fans rooting Gehrig on, the Yankee crushed Mahaffey's fastball to right. In four at-bats, he'd hit four homers. Earnshaw deadpanned, "I understand now, Mr. Mack. Mahaffey made Lou change his direction. Can I shower now?"

Gehrig grounded out in the eighth, but the Yankees—en route to a 20–13 triumph featuring a record 50 total bases—pounded out six more runs in the ninth, giving Gehrig one more shot, against Eddie Rommel. He smashed his hardest-hit ball of the day, but in the deepest corner of the park Al Simmons made a running, leaping catch near the wall to rob Gehrig of what might have been an inside-the-park homer.

Still, Gehrig's accomplishment was undeniable—eight decades later, only nine other men had achieved this feat in nine innings. Unfortunately, Gehrig, who spent his whole career overshadowed by Babe Ruth and Joe DiMaggio, suffered the same treatment at the hands of another New York icon. That afternoon Giant manager John McGraw announced his retirement after 31 years, grabbing the biggest headlines in the next day's papers.

Ruth had now hit three homers in one World Series game twice in three years. It would take nearly 50 years until someone else did it even once. The round-trippers gave him a record .625 Series batting average and 22 total bases, tying in four games a mark he himself had set in a seven-game series. Although Ruth's Yankees would not win their one last title for another four years, with this coup de grâce Ruth had reached the apex, Creamer wrote, "the happiest moment of three years of great accomplishment and relative serenity."

And he wasn't even done. With two outs in the ninth inning and the Yankees up 7–3, the Cards had a man on when Frankie Frisch lifted a foul fly down near the railing in left. As fans bombarded Ruth with newspapers and programs and reached out to swat him, Ruth sprinted in hard and caught the Series' final out on the dead run. Without stopping, he held it up to show he had finished off St. Louis and was, as Harrison wrote, "Ruth, indomitable, unconquerable, triumphant."

## 11. The Yankees resurrect themselves with a 10th-inning win, October 8, 1958, County Stadium, Milwaukee

The magic was gone. When Milwaukee's Warren Spahn blanked the New York Yankees 3–0 in Game 4 of the 1958 World Series, an era seemed over. Formerly omnipotent, the Bronx Bombers had failed to reach the World Series in 1954, lost to (gasp!) Brooklyn in 1955, and, after squeaking by the Dodgers in 1956, fallen in 1957 to Milwaukee . . . in a Game 7 at Yankee Stadium no less.

In 1958 New York won the American League but staggered to a 29–32 finish, so when they dropped three of the first four in the Series, the end seemed nigh—only once, back in 1925, had a team rebounded from such a deficit. After Game 2, Lew Burdette, who had accumulated his fourth Series win against the Yankees in two years (and even hit a three-run homer), sneered that the Yankees "would have trouble in our league," an echo of Spahn's harsh dismissal from 1957 that "the Yankees couldn't finish fifth in the National League."

Such boasting contained a kernel of truth—the NL had integrated far more rapidly than the AL and thus had more strong teams; the league had won three of the four previous Series and would win the following two. The Braves, who had moved to their new city from stodgy old Boston just six years earlier, represented the future, while the segregationist, tradition-bound Yankees—who won just 92 games that year (fewest of the franchise's World Series champions until 2000) beating up perennially underfinanced weaklings like the Athletics—looked like a relic. (Indeed, the same could be said of New York in general, which in 1958 lost its two NL franchises to westward relocation.)

The Yankees, however, weren't quite through yet. Goliath would get up off the floor and smite David but hard, winning three straight to capture the Series. If so many other great Yankee triumphs did not already dominate these lists, all three victories might merit a place on them. Forced to choose, beating Spahn in extra innings in Game 6 stands out as the Series' highlight.

The turnaround began in Game 5 when Bob Turley pitched a complete-game shutout. With the Yankees clinging to a 1–0 lead in the sixth, catcher-turned-outfielder Elston Howard made a diving catch on a sinking liner, bounced up, and pegged the ball to Gil McDougald, who relayed to first for a double play. Pumped up, the Yankees churned out six runs in their turn as Burdette finally wore down.

Still, the Yankees needed to take Game 6 to force yet another winner-take-all showdown. The years 1955 to 1958 mark baseball's only stretch of four straight seven-game Series, and while the two Dodger-Yankees battles are more renowned, the Braves-Yankees matchup proved every bit their equal for electrifying baseball.

For Game 6, Milwaukee manager Fred Haney

**On Elston Howard's strong throw, Yogi Berra tags Milwaukee's Andy Pafko at the plate to help New York escape from a potentially disastrous second inning in a crucial Game 6 in 1958.**

got greedy and started his ace Spahn on two days' rest (and on top of 10 innings in Game 1) instead of Bob Rush on three days' rest after six solid innings in Game 3. But Spahn wanted the assignment. Early in his career, a different Braves manager—none other than current Yankee skipper Casey Stengel—had questioned his courage when he refused to throw at Pee Wee Reese, and he wanted to avenge himself. (He had pitched poorly in the 1957 Series.)

Spahn, who'd been masterful in winning both Games 1 and 4, gave up a first-inning homer to Hank Bauer, but Milwaukee tied it in the first and knocked out starter Whitey Ford in the second with three singles and a walk for a 2–1 lead. The Yankees escaped only when Howard made another big defensive play, throwing Andy Pafko out at home.

The Yankees scratched out a run in the sixth on Yogi Berra's sacrifice fly to tie it at 2–2, so Stengel called on closer Ryne Duren, who had led the AL with 20 saves. Duren kept the Yankees alive by burying the Braves, fanning seven in four innings and allowing just one hit and one walk. But Spahn was equally magnificent, and the game went to the 10th inning.

Haney left Spahn in for his 29th inning in a week. It would be the Braves' downfall. Spahn gave up a leadoff homer to Gil McDougald, then two-out singles to Howard and Berra before Haney finally pulled him. Moose Skowron greeted reliever Don McMahon by singling home an insurance run, and the Yankees led 4–2.

But Duren, who'd averaged less than two innings per appearance all year, was also out of gas. With one out, he walked Johnny Logan, bringing up the Braves' big bats. Representing the tying run would be Eddie Mathews (averaging 38 homers annually over six seasons), Hank Aaron (averaging 32 in his first four full years), and Joe Adcock (who hit 19 in just 320 at-bats that year).

Duren found that proverbial something extra on his fastball to pick up his eighth and final strikeout on Mathews (with Logan taking second in the process). And he kept Aaron and Adcock in the yard . . . but he couldn't get them out. Aaron singled home Logan, making it 4–3. Then Adcock singled Aaron to third, putting the tying run 90 feet away and the winning run on first.

Stengel called on the one person besides Duren he'd seen dominate the Braves: Bob Turley.

Pinch hitter Frank Torre (then known for his .309 average, not for being Joe's older brother) lifted the ball toward right field, but it never got there: second baseman McDougald snared it for the final out. In the year of the movie *Damn Yankees,* those damn Yankees had forced a seventh game. The Yankees won that one too, beating Burdette again as Turley again saved the day with six and a third innings of one-run relief.

When it was over, Stengel, for whom this would be the final Series crown, had the last words: "Well, I guess we showed them we could play in the National League after all."

## 12. The Rangers win the Stanley Cup after a six-year void, April 13, 1940, Maple Leaf Gardens, Toronto

1940. As the years of futility rolled on for the New York Rangers, it became a haunting number, one that opposing fans used in a singsong mocking tone. But back in the day, 1940 symbolized only a glorious achievement, a crowning moment for "the Classiest Team in Hockey." And when they won it all on April 13 that year, they did it with a come-from-behind overtime gem equal in drama to the thrillers of 1994.

The Rangers had won Stanley Cups in 1928 and 1933, but many contemporaries considered the 1939–40 club the most talented and the deepest squad ever: "the Bread Line" of Neil and Mac Colville, along with Alex Shibicky, was backed by two potent lines: one featuring Phil Watson, Lynn Patrick, and high scorer Bryan Hextall, and the other the three lefties, Alf Pike, Clint Smith, and Dutch Hiller, perhaps the league's fastest skater. Equally impressive were the two punishing and intense defensive units, one featuring captain Art Coulter and Muzz Patrick, the other Babe Pratt and Ott Heller, the last holdover from the 1933 squad. In the net, veteran Dave Kerr played every minute, posted eight shutouts, and was the league's top goalie.

Legendary coach Lester Patrick (father of Lynn and Muzz) had moved up to the general manager's office and been replaced rinkside by Frank Boucher, who'd scored the Cup-clinching goal back in 1928. Boucher implemented new techniques, most notably when the team played shorthanded—he'd either go to a protective "box defense" in front of the goalie or take the opposite tack and send all four skaters to the other end in a forechecking frenzy.

The Rangers had torn off a 19–1–3 run from late November to late January, including a team-record 19-game unbeaten streak that still stands, and they finished second to the defending champion Boston Bruins. Though the Bruins owned the most potent offense, the Rangers scored the second-most goals and had, by far, the stingiest defense, yielding just 77 goals in 48 games against a league average of 127. They vanquished Boston in the playoffs and faced off against third-place Toronto in New York's sixth Stanley Cup final.

The Rangers won the first two games at home, 2–1 and 6–2, before facing their annual eviction from Madison Square Garden to make way for the circus. Homeless, they faced trouble when Toronto reasserted itself at Maple Leaf Gardens with 2–1 and 3–0 victories. In the critical fifth game, the

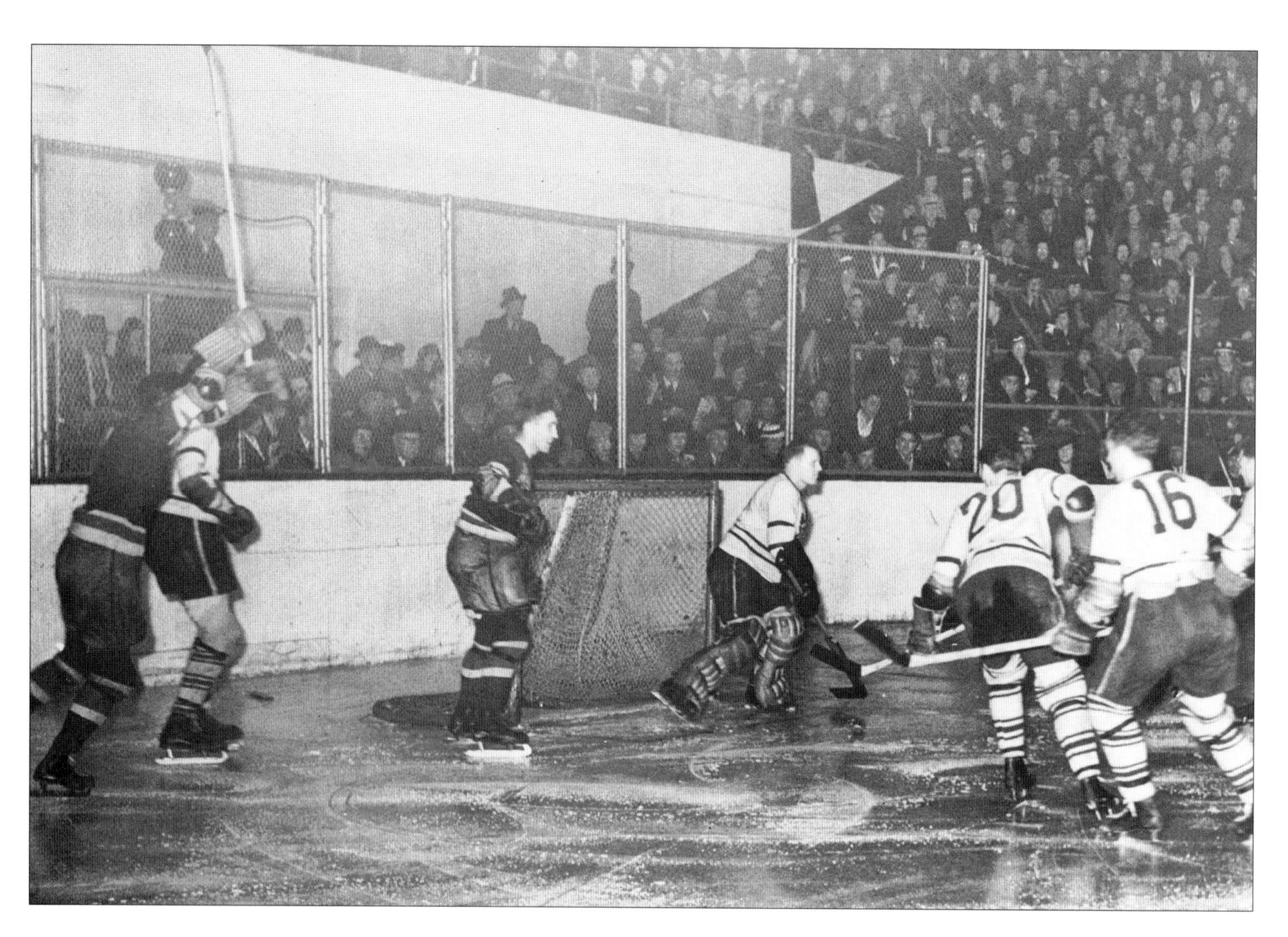

**High scorer Bryan Hextall raises his arms after scoring his most important goal yet, defeating Toronto in overtime to give the Rangers the 1940 Stanley Cup.**

Rangers squeaked out a 2–1 win in double-overtime when Muzz Patrick—who'd scored only twice all season—drove home his third goal of the postseason.

After such a huge win, the Rangers sighed in relief . . . one game too soon. In Game 6 on April 13, the Maple Leafs skated brilliantly and aggressively while the Rangers looked a bit lost, falling behind 1–0 in the first period after Watson lost the puck. Seeing such lax play, Lester Patrick visited the dressing room, telling his men, "Let's get down to business. I've made arrangements for a victory party. Don't let me down."

The Rangers responded, well, not at all. They allowed another goal in the second and continued meandering up and down the ice. But in the third, realizing their opportunity really was slipping away, the Rangers shoved their way back into the game, swarming around the puck and using energetic forechecking to keep the Leafs pinned at their own end for long stretches.

Finally, the Rangers' offense struck twice within two minutes to grab the momentum and silence the crowd. First Neil Colville took a pass from Shibicky and angled a tough shot in, then at 10:02, on a 4-on-4, Pike faked out Leaf goalie Turk Broda and lifted the puck past him for a 2–2 tie.

Five minutes later, the Rangers thought they had the championship clinched when Hextall sent the puck to a wide-open Watson, who flicked it toward the cage. The puck landed underneath Broda at the bottom of a pile of players; the red light flashed for a goal, and the Rangers started celebrating, but the officials ruled that Hextall was illegally in the crease and the goal did not count.

Like Game 5, this one went to overtime. This time, however, there was a quick resolution. Two minutes in, Hiller forced his way among several Leafs to get the puck behind Toronto's net. He flicked it to Watson near the blue line. Watson found Hextall about 10 feet from the net. Without pausing to aim, Hextall reared back and fired a hard backhander high and to the right, past a desperate Broda.

The Rangers were NHL champions. It would be a long while before they could say that again.

## 13. Allan Houston sinks Miami, May 16, 1999, Miami Arena

With just four and a half seconds to save the New York Knicks' season, Allan Houston caught the ball and took two dribbles. The Miami Heat's Dan Majerle was with him, Tim Hardaway was lurking, and Alonzo Mourning was looming. Perhaps two seconds elapsed. Houston went airborne from about 14 feet out. With his classic form and sweet touch, Houston was the Knicks' best pure shooter, but he lifted an ugly, running, leaning jumper, short-armed off the front rim. The Knicks watched the ball bounce—not away, toward doom, but up, where it floated as if deciding which team fate should smile upon before kissing the backboard and dropping through the net. 78–77, New York.

Houston's astonishing game-winner in the opening round of the playoffs earned the save but gave the big W—which made the Knicks the first eighth seed in the East ever to upset the top seed—to Patrick Ewing, whose brave and bravura performance was the highlight of the Knicks' soapiest and most improbable year of the decade. Drama may be integral to all sports classics, but the Knicks, 1990s edition, led the NBA in melodrama: the headline-grabbing rivalries with Chicago, Indiana, and Miami; the never-ending search for a point guard; the much-heralded arrival of Pat Riley and his overanalyzed resignation by fax; the disastrous but short-lived Don Nelson era.

Still, nothing could match 1998–99, when each key person seemed to come with the phrase "oft-maligned" attached to his name, among them: Patrick Ewing, the union president who showed up out of shape after rancorous and controversial negotiations led to a shortened season; Latrell Sprewell, the infamous coach-choker who cost the team sentimental favorite John Starks and whose early shooting sprees and inconsistent defense irked team officials and the media and who only worsened his reputation by yukking it up after a shameful loss in Chicago and letting his agent trash coach Jeff Van Gundy in the press; Van Gundy, whose status remained imperiled as the Knicks barely snuck into the playoffs; and president Dave Checketts, who drew heat for firing general manager Ernie Grunfeld over dessert after a two-hour dinner and for lying to Van Gundy about negotiating behind the coach's back with Phil Jackson.

Still, no matter how deep their wounds, the Knicks remained dangerous, especially as Sprewell came around late in the season, igniting the Knicks and electrifying the crowd, going from NBA Public Enemy Number One to number 8, the jersey worn by Spike Lee and countless other fans.

On the season's final day, Pat Riley, by then the head Heat honcho, even rested three players, hoping to lose and avoid New York in the first round.

But with a bitter rivalry built on two intense playoff series marred by headline-grabbing brawls—the 1997 bench-clearing fight that cost the Knicks that series and the 1998 scrum that ended up with Van Gundy wrapping around the ankle of Miami star Alonzo Mourning—and a simmering feud between two coaches who had once been mentor and protégé, New York–Miami was destiny.

The biggest surprise in 1999 was the lack of fisticuffs; certainly no one was shocked that the Knicks-Heat series went the distance for the third straight year: the Knicks grabbed the advantage with a 32–2 run in Game 3, but Miami trounced New York in Game 4, giving the Heat the home court edge for the finale.

In Game 5 on May 16, the Heat looked as though they would blow New York right out of the Miami Arena as they breezed to a 21–8 lead; after nailing a bank shot, Mourning even mimicked Larry Johnson's signature move of forming an "L" with his arms. Then the Knicks shoved back, metaphorically this time, as Chris Childs buried a jumper and Sprewell chipped in 11 first-half points.

The teams were deadlocked at 60 after three, but when Ewing, already hobbled by sore knees and a strained Achilles tendon, badly injured his rib cage in the third, his mobility was reduced to that of a wobbly statue. Still, he kept scoring, kept rebounding, kept leading, remaining in the game the entire fourth quarter. "You would have to take a stun gun and shoot him to get him off the court," Childs said.

Less than three minutes into the fourth, the Knicks trailed again, 69–62, but they clawed back once more. Houston, long castigated by fans and the press as too soft with the game on the line, had started just 1–7 and sat during the first-half comeback, but now he rose up with two jumpers to help tie the game.

Rugged defense, always central to these battles, then devoured whatever offensive opportunities remained. After the Knicks grabbed their first lead at 72–71 with 4:05 remaining, it took Miami three minutes to inch ahead just to 77–74.

One defensive stop by New York was an all-time classic. With about 1:20 left, Ewing found himself guarding Mourning to the left of the basket. Seven years Ewing's junior, Mourning was a fellow Georgetown alum who had once treated Ewing as a mentor, but with Ewing's legs deteriorating, Mourning had often treated him as chattel in this series—Miami had regained the lead 75–74 when he'd stomped past Ewing into the lane. So with the game, the series, and the season on the line, Mourning expected to have his way with the invalid before him and seize the destiny that awaited his generation and his team.

Mourning threw a fake. Ewing didn't bite. Mourning moved toward the hoop. Ewing managed to shift his feet laterally, cutting him off. The Knick center just would not give in. Finally, Mourning was forced to go baseline—what Ewing had wanted, demanded of the situation—and having frittered away his chance, Mourning began falling out of bounds and tried to pass as the 24-second clock buzzed. Ewing wasn't done. When Sprewell missed off the rim, Ewing grabbed a crucial offensive rebound to keep hope alive. Mourning fouled him with 39.7 seconds left. Two shots.

Despite Ewing's tremendous effort under extraordinary physical duress to keep the Knicks close throughout the game, in their souls most Knick fans groaned. For all Ewing had done for the team over the years, for all his scoring, his rebounds, his defense, Knick fans saw only his failures—the occasions when he displayed stone hands, refused to share the ball, clogged up a running offense, or fell for the head fake—and all those failures added up to one grand failure: the inability to win that elusive championship. Never mind that Michael Jordan never won without Scottie Pippen and that neither John Starks nor Allan Houston was a Scottie Pippen. The perception was that in these situations the Big Fella would come close but fall short. Right after stopping Mourning, hadn't he missed a jumper that would have put the Knicks back in front? Probably almost everyone expected him to miss one of the two shots.

For the third time in under a minute, Ewing came through, calmly sinking them both. 77–76, Miami.

After the Knicks recovered the ball with 19.9 seconds left, Van Gundy called a pick-and-roll for Sprewell. But these teams knew each other too well, and Sprewell got trapped, then had the ball knocked out of bounds by Terry Porter. From the bench, Van Gundy signaled for Triangle Down, a play in which Sprewell inbounded, ideally to Houston, whom Ewing should free with a high screen. Although Sprewell and Johnson would crisscross underneath to provide another option, there were only four and a half seconds left, so Houston didn't look for second choices. Instead, he finally shed his image as a player who disappeared at crunch time. (Call it "the $100 Million Shot," since it later helped persuade Knick management to foolishly pay him that sum.)

Eight-tenths of a second remained, but it was over—Terry Porter's desperation heave was too late, and the Knicks triumphed. Their momentum propelled them through a General Sherman–

**As the clock ticks down Allan Houston sinks his shot and sinks archrival Miami in the decisive Game 5.**

esque sweep of Atlanta and a memorable upset over Indiana that catapulted them back to the Finals, where their odd season but enchanted playoff run ended.

Houston's game-winning shot made it all possible, but Game 5 really was Ewing's final great moment as a Knick—he outscored Mourning 22–21, out-rebounded him 11–5, and made the biggest plays at the biggest moments, all while in excruciating pain that would have felled a less committed player. In other words, he pulled a Willis Reed but added results to the inspiration.

## 14. Leyritz powers a Yankees comeback, October 23, 1996, Fulton County Stadium, Atlanta

If the midcentury Yankees were like U.S. Steel, the 1996 New York Yankees were a ball club even a Mets fan or old Brooklyn Dodger fan could bring themselves to root for . . . almost. At least, in the history of Yankee domination, this team that faced the Atlanta Braves in the World Series was the hardest team to hate since Babe Ruth retired.

For this Yankee team, winning seemed fresh and surprising—the Mets had won as many World Series in the previous 30 years, and the Yankees hadn't worn the crown in 18 seasons—and for all the advantages their bloated budget and impetuous owner gave them (a bench with Tim Raines and Cecil Fielder), they entered the World Series as underdogs. Their core was immensely appealing, a mix of homegrown young talent (Derek Jeter, Bernie Williams, Andy Pettitte, Mariano Rivera) and unsung old-school guys (Joe Girardi, Paul O'Neill).

Additionally, the script of this Yankee journey was an exceedingly sentimental one. New manager Joe Torre hailed from Brooklyn and had played for and run the Mets; his success in 1996 was especially satisfying because he'd been considered by many to be a poor choice, with an un-Yankee-like record of 32 seasons and 4,110 games as a player or manager without reaching a World Series. His older brother Frank, who had played for the Braves against the Yankees in two World Series, was now gravely ill and awaiting a heart transplant. Bench coach Don Zimmer played on the 1955 Dodgers, and pitching coach Mel Stottlemyre was an ex-Yankee but more recently the Mets pitching coach in 1986.

The starters included popular ex-Met David Cone, who suffered an aneurysm in his arm in May but recovered to pitch well at crunch time, and Dwight Gooden, the erstwhile Met icon whose early-season pitching woes nearly led to his release before Cone's ailment granted him one last chance; he responded with a no-hitter and 11 wins. The lefty slugger picked up from the independent Northern League was Darryl Strawberry, a fallen ex-Met whom George Steinbrenner signed as much to give another chance as to bolster the roster.

So it was only fitting that the 1996 World Series was no clean and efficient thrashing in the style of Babe Ruth's Murderers' Row or Joe DiMaggio's Bronx Bombers but a cardiac-alert comeback that featured a Game 4 turning point seemingly lifted from the playbook of, say, the 1947 Dodgers or the 1986 Mets.

The Yankees had come back three times against the Texas Rangers in the ALDS, then twice against the Baltimore Orioles in the ALCS, before facing the Atlanta Braves, a team for which Torre had managed and played.

The defending champion Braves—the Microsoft of baseball with their monopoly on divisional titles—were not intimidated by the Yankees. After oohing and aahing about the thrill of playing in the Stadium, they stomped New York 12–1 in the opener and 4–0 in Game 2, the most lopsided two-game margin ever. In Game 1, 19-year-old Andruw Jones became the youngest player to homer in a Series and just the second (after Gene Tenace) to go yard in his first two Series at bats. In Game 2, Greg Maddux beat the Yankees with just 82 pitches in eight innings, only 20 of which were called balls—at one point, 11 straight Yankees failed to hit a ball out of the infield.

Counting their NLCS wins, the Braves had outscored opponents 48–2, the greatest postseason streak ever, and they had not trailed in 45 innings. They were cocky, and they were going home to Fulton County Stadium. It seemed pretty obvious which team was the dynasty in the making.

Cone gave New York a clutch performance in Game 3 to give New York a slim ray of hope, but on October 23, Game 4 starter Kenny Rogers was the antithesis of the gutsy Cone. He nibbled at the strike zone, became unnerved when no one covered first on a safety squeeze, and recorded just six outs while allowing five runs. By the fifth, the Yankees trailed 6–0 and faced a seemingly impossible task; only two teams had overcome such a deficit in World Series play: Philadelphia, down eight in 1929, and Brooklyn, down six in 1956. New York had only two hits (one by the departed Rogers), so overcoming the Braves seemed faintly ludicrous. A loss would give Atlanta a 3–1 edge with Cy Young winners John Smoltz, Maddux, and Tom Glavine locked and loaded.

But in the sixth, fate smiled on the Yankees just as it had in days of yore — and as in the olden days, the Yankees capitalized on the opportunity. An umpire inadvertently blocked right fielder Jermaine Dye as he chased Jeter's pop foul. Jeter singled, sparking a three-run rally (abetted by a subsequent error by Dye) that knocked out starter Denny Neagle, getting the Yankees into Atlanta's shaky bullpen.

Mike Bilecki got Atlanta out of the sixth, striking out the side with runners on first and second, and he pitched well in the seventh, but Braves manager Bobby Cox called on closer Mark Wohlers to pitch the eighth — just the second time he'd done that all year. The hard-throwing Wohlers was victimized by bad luck as a weak but well-placed roller and a botched double-play ball put two Yankees on base. Then he made a bad decision.

Jim Leyritz represented the tying run at the plate. Leyritz, who had come in only because the Yankees pinch-hit for Girardi, had walloped a game-winning homer in the 15th inning against Seattle in the 1995 ALDS but had just 14 homers in 529 total at-bats over the previous two years and was just 4-for-22 over two postseasons. Wohlers, meanwhile, had fanned 100 in $77^1/_3$ innings while reaping 39 saves during 1996, and he

## Honorable Mention: The Yankees Always Find a Way

**Jeremy Giambi doesn't slide, Derek Jeter makes the relay, October 13, 2001, Oakland Coliseum**

When Oakland's Terrence Long doubled into the right-field corner, Jeremy Giambi took off from first, expecting to score the tying run. On October 13, with New York desperately clinging to a seventh-inning 1–0 lead and just one defeat away from losing the 2001 ALDS to Oakland, the play looked potentially deadly.

Then Derek Jeter intervened.

Positioned near the pitcher's mound, Jeter saw right fielder Shane Spencer hurl the ball in and immediately realized the throw would fly right over both cutoff men, Alfonso Soriano and Tino Martinez.

So Jeter made a play only he could make. Some shortstops might have had the alertness and acuity to see the play unfolding, some might have been blessed with speed to react in time, and others might have had the skill, instinct, and grace under extreme pressure to complete the play in the innovative way that was the only possible way, but only Jeter had all those traits — only Jeter, the Joe DiMaggio of shortstops, could make the one play necessary to keep the Yankees alive.

Sprinting from the mound across the first-base line, Jeter scooped up the errant throw in foul territory 30 feet from home plate — as far from his normal position as he could possibly be — and, realizing he had no time to spin and throw, in one quick motion shoveled the ball laterally, like a quarterback, to Jorge Posada at home. Giambi was so stunned he forgot to slide, and Posada swiped him with the tag, ending the inning and turning the series around. Oakland had been baseball's best team since June, and winner of 17 straight at home, but the Yankees won that game and the next two as well.

**Jim Leyritz watches his eighth-inning blast off Mark Wohlers's slider leave the park for a game-tying three-run homer.**

had allowed just two hits in $7^1/_3$ innings in the postseason.

When Wohlers unleashed a 100-mph fastball, Leyritz got a surprisingly good rip, fouling it straight back. On a 98-mph blazer, Leyritz again fouled it straight back, meaning that, for all the velocity, he was timing Wohlers. Afraid to repeat himself, Wohlers went to his third-best pitch, his slider.

The selection fooled Leyritz, who expected another fastball, but there's a reason for sticking with what you do best—the slider was awful, a big, fat meatball. Leyritz clocked it over the wall in left, silencing the obnoxious tomahawk chop routine of the Braves fans.

"That was the hit," Torre said after the Yankees became the first team to win four straight games after losing the first two at home, "that made us believe we were going to win this thing."

Before they could win the Series, the Yankees had to win the game. They loaded the bases in the ninth, but Dye snagged Mariano Duncan's liner while nearly falling. They also almost lost in the ninth when Mariano Rivera yielded a one-out single and a walk, but Graeme Lloyd replaced the young setup man and coaxed a double-play grounder out of slugger Fred McGriff.

Finally, they did win, in bizarre fashion, in the 10th. With two outs and two on, Cox faced a decision: have lefty Steve Avery intentionally walk Bernie Williams — New York's most dangerous hitter — or bring in righty Brad Clontz to force Williams to bat from his far weaker left side. Cox walked Williams to face Andy Fox, who had pinch-run for Fielder in the ninth.

But thanks to his years of NL managing experience, Torre had saved one man on his bench. It was a lefty, but one with far more of a reputation than Fox, a rookie with zero at-bats in the postseason: Wade Boggs.

Boggs was a Hall of Fame singles hitter with a keen plate discipline. Avery's 1–2 pitch was so close that catcher Eddie Perez reacted as if the inning was over. But Boggs got the call. On 3–2, Avery missed with a slider, walking home the go-ahead run.

Cox then erred again, bringing on Clontz but making a double switch that put Ryan Klesko at first. Klesko promptly muffed Hayes's soft liner, and Clontz failed to cover first, allowing Jeter to score for an 8–6 lead. In their last licks, Atlanta got a single from Andruw Jones, and Terry Pendleton smashed a long drive to left off closer John Wetteland. Tim Raines slipped as he got near the wall but caught the ball just as he lost his balance, ending the game.

The Braves were crushed. The Yankees won Game 5, 1–0, then returned to New York to learn that Frank Torre, hospitalized since August, was finally getting a new heart — the donor had lived in the Bronx and the doctor's last name was Oz. This was a fairy-tale season after all.

"Destiny ends with N-Y," Tom Verducci wrote in *Sports Illustrated* after New York finished the Braves off at the Stadium in Game 6. They had won despite a .216 batting average, and they would win 12 of 13 more Series games by the end of 2000.

Sure, Wade Boggs's horseback ride around the Stadium brought up the bile again in Yankee-haters, and sure, Game 4 turned out to be the cornerstone of that new dynasty, but its twists and turns, its ups and downs, make it both a baseball classic and a truly happy ending.

## 15. The Jets intercept the Raiders, January 15, 1983, Los Angeles Coliseum

Jim Plunkett looked downfield. Cliff Branch curled on a down-and-in pattern. Plunkett fired, but linebacker Lance Mehl stepped in and intercepted the pass, preserving the New York Jets' upset of the Los Angeles Raiders.

Jim Plunkett looked downfield. Cliff Branch curled on a down-and-in pattern. Plunkett fired, but linebacker Lance Mehl stepped in and intercepted the pass, preserving the New York Jets' upset of the Los Angeles Raiders.

Really, it happened just like that. In the closing moments of the AFC playoff game on January 15, 1983, at the Los Angeles Coliseum, the Raider quarterback twice called the same play, only to be picked off by the same player both times. This strange sequence capped one of only four postseason Jets wins in their New York era, and one of their most exciting and emotional wins ever.

In 1982 big things were expected of the Jets,

who had returned to the postseason the previous year for the first time since 1969. After a labor strike disrupted the season, the Jets finished 6–3 and routed the favored Cincinnati Bengals 44–17 in the first playoff round, behind 202 yards from running back Freeman McNeil. But few expected them to beat the 8–1 Raiders in Los Angeles.

However, the only predictable thing about an important Jets-Raiders game was that it would be wild and, well, unpredictable. In the 1960s the two clubs had a nasty rivalry. In 1962 Al Davis was brought in to coach the Raiders and promptly fired defensive coach Walt Michaels, ordering him to leave his playbook behind. ("I had two words for him, and they weren't 'thank you,'" Michaels recalled years later.) Michaels went on to coach the Jets' defense under Weeb Ewbank. In 1968 Davis tried ordering his grounds crew to keep the tarp on the field to prevent the visiting New Yorkers from practicing; Michaels made him back down. That Raiders squad's defensive strategy consisted of playing dirty and trying to injure Joe Namath.

Now, in the Jets' Coliseum locker room, defensive tackle Marty Lyons got pumped up and punched what appeared to be a piece of wood but turned out to be glass painted to look like wood; it shattered, leaving Lyons bleeding and Michaels wondering whether Davis installed the piece for espionage purposes.

The Jets, however, did not appear especially rattled on the field. While L.A.'s rookie running back, Marcus Allen, managed only eight yards in the half (finishing with just 36 on 15 carries), Jet sophomore Freeman McNeil gained 75 (and would finish with 105). After Raider Chris Bahr bonked a 34-yard field goal attempt off the upright, Richard Todd zipped in a 20-yard touchdown pass to Wesley Walker, and Pat Leahy redeemed one field goal miss by making his next. At halftime, the Jets led 10–0 against a team that had not been held scoreless for a half all season.

Allen later admitted that his team spent the first half consumed by thoughts of cheap shots and dirty play—at one point Raider Lyle Alzado yanked off the helmet of Jet offensive tackle Chris Ward and hurled it at him. But the dirtiest trick apparently came while Michaels was on his way in for halftime. A security guard called out that Jet owner Leon Hess was on the phone. Michaels soon heard a voice telling him to tone down the antics of showboating defensive star Mark Gastineau. After a half-minute, Michaels realized the voice was not Hess's and hung up; he would immediately blame Al Davis for having someone place the call as a diversionary tactic.

The Jets seem distracted in the third, or maybe they were just worn out. Free safety Darrol Ray, defensive tackle Abdul Salaam, tackle Marty Lyons, and end Joe Klecko were also hobbled or sidelined by injuries, and at certain points the Jets were down to using third-stringers on the defensive line. The Raiders responded with a 14-play, 77-yard touchdown march that ate up seven minutes and then, on their next possession, a 57-yard touchdown reception by Malcolm Barnwell. In the third, the Raiders outgained the Jets 157 yards to 17, capturing a 14–10 lead.

After Lester Hayes intercepted Todd on New York's 42 with 43 seconds left in the quarter, the Jets defense was gasping for air, and grasping for hope. A touchdown would make it 21–10 and perhaps bury the Jets. L.A. steamed to New York's 19. But then Allen, who had made his name in the Coliseum starring for USC, was drilled by Jerry Holmes and coughed up the ball. Jet Joe Klecko recovered.

It was merely the first momentum swing in what became a dizzying final quarter.

The Jets moved quickly downfield until their ex-mate Burgess Owens intercepted a pass in the end zone. On the next possession, Todd lobbed a beauty to Walker, who journeyed 45 yards to the Raider 1. Scott Dierking plunged in, giving New York the lead back with 3:45 left, 17–14.

Here was where Plunkett made his two big mistakes . . . or rather, the same mistake twice. He looked to Branch, but Mehl read the play perfectly and picked the ball off on the Raider 35.

With their fantastic field position and the clock winding down, the game should have belonged to the Jets. But that would have been too easy. On

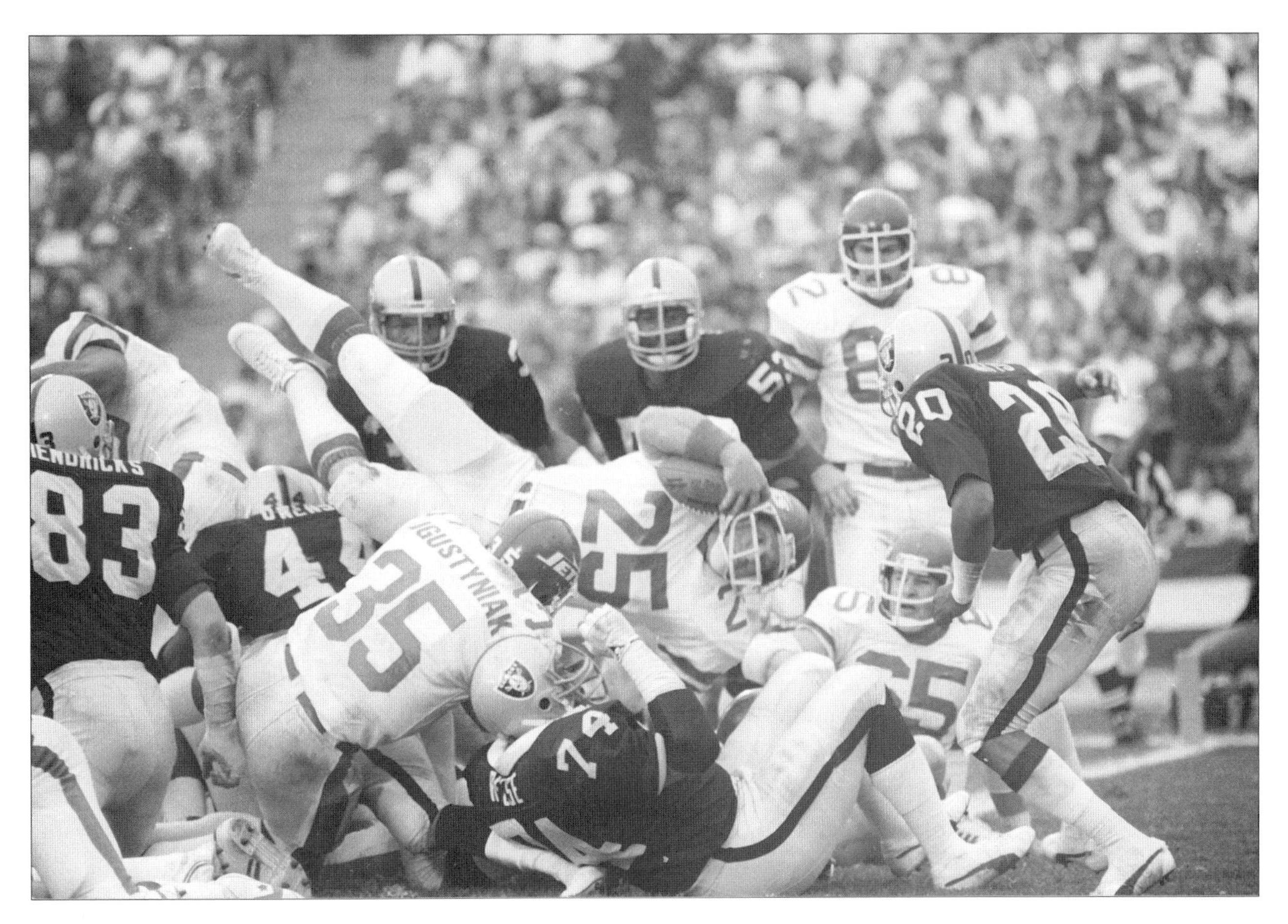


**Scott Dierking plunges ahead for the winning touchdown as the Jets fight their way past the Raiders to the 1983 AFC Finals.**

third down, McNeil, who had made his name in the Coliseum starring for UCLA, was drilled by Lyle Alzado and coughed up the ball. Raider Ted Hendricks recovered.

Raider ball, 2:26 on their own 33, down by three . . . Plunkett moved L.A. 25 yards in 36 seconds to the Jets' 42. The big mo had seemingly made its final move. "We were going in, I knew it, I could feel it," Raider coach Tom Flores said later. "I felt the game had turned for the last time."

On 2nd-and-2, instead of running, Plunkett sent Branch back on his down-and-in. Again, he was not open. Again, Plunkett tried looking Mehl off. Again, Plunkett failed to, but threw anyway. Again, Mehl intercepted. This one sealed the Raiders' tomb.

As if the Al Davis intrigue and hard-hitting thriller of a game weren't enough to stir up memories of Jets-Raiders matchups of yore, football fans in Joe Namath's native state of Pennsylvania endure what can only be called "the Ghost of Heidis Past." In the infamous 1968 game, NBC executives had decided the Jets couldn't possibly blow their 32–29 lead and switched at 7:00 P.M. to the kiddie movie *Heidi*. This time around, WICU, the NBC affiliate in Erie, cut away from the game after McNeil's fumble to show the state lottery drawing; the station desperately tried to stop the switching of feeds but couldn't because technological progress had empowered computers to control these things. The viewers' response, however, was no different than it had been a generation earlier. "The calls didn't stop," said program director John Ivan Tomcho afterwards. "They were irate calls. No, they weren't just irate, they were obscene. No, they were *very* obscene."

The game came back on in Erie just as the entire football nation watched Todd fall on the ball to end the game. Even that play featured fisticuffs as players went at it one last time.

Afterwards, Michaels was too busy ranting

about the halftime phone call to celebrate. Davis called him crazy and a bartender by the name of Larry Hammond at the Winfield Inn back in Woodside, Queens, confessed to the prank. It's unfortunate that Michaels was too wound up to savor the moment, though it was that level of intensity that fueled one of the biggest Jets victories ever.

## 16. The Silver Fox saves the day, April 7, 1928, Montreal Forum

New York Rangers coach Lester Patrick found himself in an unusual quandary. In 1928, New York's second NHL season, they'd reached the Stanley Cup finals but lost Game 1 to the heavily favored Montreal Maroons. Game 2 on April 7 was scoreless in the second period when Maroon star Nelson Stewart slammed a shot that caught Ranger netkeeper Lorne Chabot near the left eye (there were no masks then), giving him a severe concussion and rendering him useless for the rest of the series. Back then, teams could only afford to dress one goaltender, and Chabot, who'd made 15 first-period saves, had been it.

Without a goalie . . .

Following the tradition of the times, the teams called an early intermission while Patrick chose a new player from those sitting in the crowd. Usually some relatively qualified player would be hanging around just in case, the opposing team would approve the selection, and the appointed sub would hurry down and join the fray. But with the championship on the line, Montreal manager Eddie Gerard chucked aside the unwritten rules of politesse. Patrick may have been overreaching when he first picked Ottawa's Alex Connell, a top goaltender who was in attendance, but Gerard rejected not only Connell but also Patrick's second request, minor leaguer Hughie McCormack.

Without a goalie . . .

Patrick turned to his team and asked for volunteers. No hands went up.

Without a goalie . . .

"Why don't you do it?" Ranger leading scorer Frank Boucher joked. The 44-year-old Patrick had been a defenseman in his playing days but had not played competitive hockey for seven years. He occasionally donned the goalie pads while coaching scrimmages, but that was a long way from the Stanley Cup finals. Still, he was their leader, the man players looked to. What choice did he have? So the dapper Silver Fox shed his suit and put on the pads. (Imagine Pat Riley changing into uniform to play in place of John Starks in the 1994 NBA Finals.)

The Forum fans mocked him, and the Maroons attacked aggressively. But Patrick inspired his team to play defense like they never had before —they broke up nearly every play, permitting few shots near the net. One shot right at Patrick's face prompted him to duck, but the puck soared over the net. He caught another, blocked two more, and deflected one off his pads. The period ended still scoreless.

In the third, Ranger Bill Cook nailed a long shot for a 1–0 lead, but Stewart, after Patrick blocked one of his shots with his pads and another with his stick, finally faked the novice goalie out and lifted a shot over him to tie the game at 1–1. Still, the exhausted Patrick hung on and maintained the tie until the buzzer.

In the first overtime game in Ranger history, Stewart missed several more shots, and Patrick smothered a shot by Doug Munro for his 18th save before Boucher fired in the game-winner. As the Rangers hoisted their coach-turned-goalie onto their shoulders for a skate around the ice, Patrick —who played 46 superb minutes—wept with joy and relief, and even the Montreal fans stood and cheered.

The Rangers quickly signed Joe Miller, a rookie goalie from the last-place New York Americans; he lost his first game 2–1 but allowed only one goal over the last two games as the Rangers won their first Stanley Cup. Miller's contribution was vital, but it was Patrick's intrepid stand that infused his team with that championship spirit.

**Lester Patrick reflects on his three Rangers teams to win the Stanley Cup. For the first one in 1928, the legendary coach had to shed his suit and take over as goalie in Game 1.**

## 17. Mel Ott homers to win the Series, October 7, 1933, Griffith Stadium, Washington, D.C.

Mel Ott started and finished the 1933 World Series the same way: with a bang.

No one would mistake the 5'9", 170-pound Ott for Babe Ruth or Jimmie Foxx, but the diminutive Giant with the high leg kick at the plate proved nearly as prodigious in the power department. From 1929 through 1944, Ott—who'd finish with 512 four-baggers—finished first or second in home runs in the National League in all but three seasons. One of those off-years was 1933, when Ott slipped to third, but the Giants, led by Carl Hubbell's masterful pitching, still won their first pennant since 1924.

In the Series they faced the Washington Senators, who had beaten them back in 1924 and were favored again. But the Giants attacked aggressively, swinging at the first pitch as often as possible. In Game 1, Ott reasserted himself with a bang, smashing a two-run dinger and three singles and giving Hubbell a 4–2 win.

Over the next three games, Ott managed only another two hits, but Hubbell and Hal Schu-

**Mel Ott touches 'em all, and his homer wins the Series for New York.**

macher each stymied the Senators once, and the Giants headed into Game 5 up 3–1.

New York handed Schumacher a 3–0 lead, but with two down in the sixth, Washington's Fred Schulte evened matters with a three-run homer. Schumacher yielded two more hits, prompting a crisis: a loss would force the Giants to use Freddie Fitzsimmons, who'd been roughed up in Game 3, in Game 6. Bill Terry replaced his tiring 22-year-old starter with 43-year-old Dolf Luque, who'd first played in the big leagues back in 1914.

Luque escaped the jam, struck out the side in the seventh, then allowed just one hit through the ninth inning. But the Giants hit into a double play in the eighth and ran themselves out of a rally in the ninth.

In the 10th, Ott came up with two outs. He had struck out his first two at-bats, was 0-for-4 on the day, and had just two hits in his last 13 at-bats. But this time he drilled a hard line drive toward left-center. Schulte sped back, leaped at the bleachers, and fell into the stands. He climbed out with a limp, but without the ball.

Second-base umpire Charlie Pfirman stopped Ott in his tracks, calling a ground-rule double: he believed the ball had bounced off the railing, and the ball had to completely clear the fence to be a homer. The Giants went berserk, charging Pfirman en masse to argue their case. Pfirman turned to fellow ump George Moriarity, who declared that the ball had touched Schulte's glove but had reached the stands of its own momentum. A home run.

The Senators were enraged and protested, to no avail, as a jubilant Ott finally circled the bases. Washington made one last desperate threat, but Luque fanned Joe Kuhel with two on and two outs. For the first time since 1922, the Giants were champions. Their pitching had carried them, but Ott's power had vaulted them over the top.

## 18. Baseball's best team wins its 125th game, October 23, 1998, Jack Murphy Stadium, San Diego

Everybody loves a coronation. So, despite a distinctive lack of tension in the 1998 World Series, it was certainly a historic event as the New York Yankees completed their triumphal march into the record books.

The year had begun with a new general manager (31-year-old Brian Cashman), several new players (most notably third baseman Scott Brosius, who would go on to become the World Series MVP), and a renewed determination (after 1997, when they surrendered their divisional title and fell in the ALDS). After the Yankees stumbled to a 1–4 start, manager Joe Torre, known for his unruffled demeanor, lit into his players, providing the necessary spark for an unprecedented explosion. The Yankees won the next day . . . and the day after . . . and, it seemed, just about every day after that.

The Yankees remained ruthless until the finish line, compiling a 114–48 record, the most regular-season wins for a team since the 1906 Chicago Cubs won 116. But those Cubs, who had needed to win one postseason round to achieve immortality, couldn't do it, falling in the World Series to the White Sox. The Yankees knew their mission would be complete only if they got through the ALDS and ALCS and their final win ended the World Series.

The Yankees swept Texas in the first round, not even missing a step when Darryl Strawberry was diagnosed with a malignant colon tumor. The ALCS against Cleveland posed more of a challenge, but after falling behind 2–1, the Yankees ran the table. By Series time, the Yankees couldn't help but brim with confidence. Most were restrained and made noises about taking the San Diego Padres seriously, but David Wells, a direct descendant of Babe Ruth and Reggie Jackson, did not: "I'd like to wrap it up in four," he said. And they did.

In New York the Padres were overmatched from the start as the Yankees battered ace Kevin Brown, jumping to a 7–1 lead. Behind Wells, they won that first game 9–6 and rode their midseason addition, Cuban defector Orlando Hernandez, to a 9–3 win in the second. In San Diego, with David Cone starting and Brosius drilling two homers, the Yankees seized a 3–0 lead in games, having led every inning but one.

So Game 4 at Jack Murphy Stadium on October 23 was largely devoid of suspense. The biggest question was whether the Yankees would sweep for the first time since 1950, a necessarily grand gesture for this team to climb onto the same pedestal as the 1927 Murderers' Row Yankees and the equally dominant 1932 and 1939 clubs.

For five innings it was close, but only on the surface. It seemed unlikely that Andy Pettitte would crack, and if he lasted just another round or two, the Yankees' indomitable bullpen would arrive. The script played out perfectly. The Yankees carved out a run in the sixth as Derek Jeter singled, Paul O'Neill doubled, and Bernie Williams got the run home with a grounder. They added two more in the eighth in a similar fashion. Jeter walked. O'Neill singled. Williams advanced them with a grounder. Brosius, who'd finish with six RBIs and a .471 average, knocked one run home with a single, and Rickey Ledee, another surprising piece to the puzzle, who'd hit .600 in the Series, drove home another with a sacrifice fly.

San Diego threatened in the eighth, but it was too late. With two on and one out, Jeff Nelson came on to strike out Greg Vaughn, and then Mariano Rivera came on. After allowing a single by Ken Caminiti, Rivera got ex-Yankee Jim Leyritz to fly to center.

Just as it was apt, given the team spirit, that everyone on offense contributed — from the sole superstar Jeter to a star like Williams to a backup like Ledee — it was also fitting that Rivera, on his way to becoming the linchpin of this new dynasty and the Lou Gehrig of closers, was on the mound to complete the sweep. It was Rivera's 10th ap-

SPORTS ★ ★ ★ ★ FINAL

20-PAGE WORLD SERIES SPECIAL

# DAILY NEWS

50¢ www.nydailynews.com NEW YORK'S HOMETOWN NEWSPAPER Thursday, October 22, 19

# GREATEST!

KEITH TORRIE DAILY NE

YANKEES SWEEP SAN DIEGO PADRES

**The Yankees celebrate, with good cause, having swept the World Series and won their record 125th game of the year.**

pearance of the postseason, and he had maintained a steady 0.00 ERA. It remained there after he disposed of the Padres in the ninth.

Although the Yankees would replicate their sweep in 1999 and win a third straight Series in 2000, this unbeatable team had done something few Yankee teams could match. The extra round of playoffs added just three years earlier may have artificially inflated their record total of 125 total wins, but no one could deny that this accomplishment signified a team for the ages. After all, it was right there in their overall winning percentage, an archetypal Yankee number that defines baseball greatness: .714.

## 19. Bernard buries Detroit, April 27, 1984, Joe Louis Arena, Detroit

Up, up, and away.

Bernard King lifted off and, while still on the rise, fired away—zap—releasing the ball so quickly that no defender could stop him.

Swish.

And again. Swish.

And again. Swish.

In his prime, King's turnaround jump shot was a thing of explosive beauty—unconventional yet unstoppable, as thrilling as Earl Monroe's hip-shattering jukes yet as reliable as Patrick Ewing inside the paint. In his glory, King's shot lifted a distinctly mediocre Knicks squad up beyond its capabilities.

He was certainly in his glory at Detroit's Joe Louis Arena on April 27, 1984. Had New York's 127–123 overtime triumph over the Pistons in Game 5 transpired in the NBA Finals, it would have been hailed as one of the sport's greatest games, and King would forever be heralded for his gutsy, inspiring performance. King was so riveting that even though this game merely clinched the opening round and the Knicks were eliminated in the next series, it outshines every other game between New York's 1973 championship and 1994's Eastern Conference Finals Game 7 over Indiana.

The 6'7" King was a Brooklyn native whose early promise with the New York (later New Jersey) Nets was derailed by alcoholism. After bouncing to Utah and Golden State, he straightened out his life and career. Acquired by New York in 1982 for the talented but undisciplined Michael Ray Richardson, King led the Knicks that season to their first playoff series win since 1974.

And in 1983–84, everything clicked. Fueled by back-to-back 50-point games, King became an All-Star and finished fifth in the league with a 26.3 scoring average; he was the team's leading scorer in 51 of the 77 games he played.

Carrying the team took its toll, however, and by the Detroit series he had dislocated both middle fingers. He could play—he couldn't not play—but with his fingers splinted, he had to figure out how to catch passes with his palms and shoot with an altered motion to avoid banging and bending the damaged digits. (Dribbling on the run was nearly impossible.) He had to make the adjustments because he was the Knick offense. In Game 1, coach Hubie Brown ran the first 13 plays through King. He responded with 36 points in that game, which the Knicks won 94–93.

King would only get better. Although the Knicks lost Game 2 and King added leg cramps and a strained left knee to his woes, he dropped in 46, including an NBA record 23 consecutive points for his team during one mind-blowing 5:29 stretch. As *Sports Illustrated* noted, King scored on everyone, but in different ways—using his height against Kelly Tripucka, his explosive moves against Kent Benson, his fakes against Earl Cureton, and his quick release and forward momentum against Cliff Livingston. King poured in 46 more the next game, which New York won. He was remarkable again in Game 4, with 41 points, but Detroit's streaky young guard Isiah Thomas overshadowed King as he sparked Detroit to a win that forced a deciding game. By then, King was also hampered by the flu,

**Bernard King shoots and scores and shoots and scores while Detroit watches helplessly.**

replete with 102-degree temperature, and there was some question whether he'd even play in Game 5.

A scheduling conflict bumped the game from the Silverdome to downtown Detroit's old arena, a boiling building that gave the ensuing showdown between Thomas and King the feeling of a fever dream. Thomas later recalled that it felt a bit like "a summer league game where everyone is crammed into the gym, and it was a two-man shootout between me and Bernard."

King was too ill for the game-day shoot-around, and the stifling, smoky arena just made him feel worse; by halftime he was practically unconscious, and an IV feed was needed to resuscitate him. Yet nothing could stop him. "He looked like he was playing on an eight-foot basket," teammate Ernie Grunfeld said.

In the third quarter, King already had 26 points, but the physical stresses left him committing unnecessary fouls; his fourth forced him to the bench for the rest of the quarter. Still, with Bill Cartwright, who'd score 23 second-half points, leading the way, the Knicks maintained their lead.

But with 1:57 left and the Knicks cruising with a 106–98 advantage, Thomas—who'd been held to just 18 points per game by Rory Sparrow—exploded with a hot streak that nearly matched King's wild ride in Game 2. Sparrow was so befuddled that in the midst of Thomas's run he was reduced to fouling the pumping Piston three times in 30 seconds. Even with Darrell Walker, a stellar defender, helping out, Thomas could not be stopped. In just over a minute and a half, Thomas hit two jumpers, four foul shots, a lay-up with a free throw tacked on, and another jumper, and with 23 seconds left—after King gave the Knicks a 114–111 cushion with his 39th and 40th points—Thomas hit a three-point killer from way out around 26 feet to tie the game.

With the game and series slipping away, New York headed off disaster on the last play of regulation when Walker stripped the ball from Thomas before he could score the winning basket.

It was as if Walker had done more than save that one play—it was as if he'd pulled back the curtain and showed that the man behind it was no wizard but a vulnerable little guy. In overtime Thomas missed three shots, while King, whose scoring had been overlooked amid Thomas's razzle-dazzle, enjoyed a coronation. With the game tied at 116, King slammed home a dunk off an offensive rebound that sealed the game by sparking a 7–0 run. And when Thomas again closed the gap with a three-pointer, King immediately responded with his trademark jumper to maintain a safe distance. Thomas, meanwhile, fouled out and headed to the bench.

The Knicks won 127–123, and King finished with 44, giving him a 42.6 average for the series on 60 percent shooting; his 213 points broke Elgin Baylor's five-game playoff record, which had stood since 1961. King added to his legend with two 40-point games in the next round as the Knicks stretched Boston to its absolute limit. He would lead the league in scoring in 1984–85 with a 32.9 average—including a 60-point game the following Christmas—before being felled by a devastating knee injury. It makes sense in a way: if he was at his apex in '84–85, then this Detroit series showed that King was still on his way up . . . the moment when he was most deadly.

## 20. The Mets finally come out on top, October 1, 1973, Wrigley Field, Chicago

The 1973 New York Mets were just not that good.

But they were just good enough.

The team everyone wrote off, the injury-plagued team in last place until the last day of August, the offensively challenged team that scored the second-fewest runs in the major leagues . . . was the team that captured its second National League pennant in just its 12th season.

Needless to say, it was close.

Inspired by reliever Tug McGraw's new war

**You gotta believe that when Tug McGraw lets loose, good things happen for the Miracle Mets.**

cry, "You gotta believe," and his sudden rebirth on the mound, the Mets finished a torrid 21–8, scaling the lowly mountain known as the NL "Least." On September 21, the Mets reached .500 for the first time since May and simultaneously took over first place, something no team had ever done before. But the Chicago Cubs were in fifth place and they were just two and a half games back.

The Mets held on but could not escape the pack. The final weekend ranks among baseball's wildest. The Mets had four games at Wrigley Field but were rained out on Friday and Saturday, so a double-header was scheduled for the season's final day, and another the day after the season technically ended.

On Sunday, the Mets lost 1–0 but bounced back 9–2 in the nightcap to eliminate both the Cubs and Montreal Expos. New York was 81–79, the St. Louis Cardinals were 81–81, and the Pittsburgh Pirates were 80–81. If the Mets dropped two on Monday in "the Not-So-Friendly Confines" and the Pirates won, there'd be a three-way tie.

On October 1, Tom Seaver started for the 36th time. He scuffled along without his best stuff, but the Mets' offense had been on a hot streak: Cleon Jones (17 RBIs in the final month) homered, Wayne Garrett (.333, 17 RBIs in 23 games), Jerry Grote (.300, 18 RBIs in 18 games), and Felix Millan (14 multi-hit games in the final 28) chipped in two hits apiece, while Rusty Staub (riding a 15-game hitting streak) banged out four.

The Mets piled up a 6–2 lead, but in the seventh a weary Seaver allowed a two-run homer by Rick Monday. It was 6–4. There was only one thing to do.

Manager Yogi Berra called on Tug McGraw to save the Mets' season. McGraw pitched three brilliant innings, allowing one single and striking out four, to nail down the game and the pennant.

The New York Mets were Eastern Division champs . . . even if you didn't believe, now you could look it up.

## 21. The Knicks win at the buzzer in double-overtime in the deciding playoff game against the Celtics, March 26, 1952, Boston Garden

By the time the game at Boston Garden on March 26, 1952, was all over, both teams had staged comebacks and blown leads, the officials had spent 10 minutes defending one of their own calls and accusations that they'd been bought, seven players had fouled out, and two overtimes had come and gone. By the time it was all over, the New York Knicks and the Boston Celtics had fought a battle for the ages, an early highlight of the oft-heated rivalry that would rise and fall through the decades with the fortunes of these two original NBA teams.

Both teams had begun with the league's forerunner, the BAA. The Celtics were pathetic for the first few years until Red Auerbach became coach in 1950–51 and soon acquired the rights to a young guard named Bob Cousy after the Chicago Stags folded. (Nobody, including Auerbach and the Knicks, wanted him initially.) Boston finished second that year but was upset in the playoffs by the Knicks, en route to their first NBA Finals.

The two clubs met again in the opening round in 1952 after Boston, 39–27, had again finished second ahead of 37–29 New York. The teams split the first two games, setting the stage for this classic of a rubber match.

**Ernie Vandeweghe and New York manage to contain Boston's wizard Bob Cousy just enough to sneak by in the 1952 playoffs.**

The Celtics took an early nine-point lead over the woefully sloppy Knicks, who "made so many mistakes they resembled a high school quintet," the *New York Times* said. New York sharpened its form in the second quarter, took the lead in the third, and expanded it to 69–61 early in the fourth, led by veteran star Max Zaslofsky (whom they'd gotten from the Stags roster), Connie Simmons, and Ernie Vandeweghe—they'd finish as the team's three top scorers, with 21, 18, and 14 points, respectively.

But Cousy, who'd top everyone with 34 points, took over near the end and brought the Celtics within two. Then came a jump ball. The Knicks thought big man Nat "Sweetwater" Clifton should face off against Cousy, but the refs pointed to playmaker Dick McGuire. An argument ensued. The refs changed their mind and changed it back as players and coaches vociferously debated each decision. The call finally went against New York, Boston got the ball, Cousy got fouled, and, two free throws later, the game was tied. When Clifton's last-second shot bounced off the rim, the foes headed for overtime.

It had been a rough, physical game, and in overtime the mounting fouls took their toll. The Celtics and Knicks each lost three players. (Afterwards, angry Celtics fans jeered the officials, one fan attacked league president Maurice Podoloff, and Boston Garden president Walter Brown claimed the league used "New York referees.")

Offensive output slowed until it foreshadowed those low-scoring 1990s Knick wars against Indiana and Miami. The first OT began at 79-all and ended with a George Kaftan hook shot that brought the Knicks back to a tie at just 83-all. Harry Gallatin missed another potential gamewinner at the buzzer.

The second overtime was equally devoid of scoring and even more excruciating in tension. The Knicks went up one on a foul shot by Kaftan, but Cousy tied it. Then Kaftan, Gallatin, and Vandeweghe each added a free throw for an 87–84 bulge; since Cousy got called for his sixth foul with 2:20 left, that expanse must have felt like an ocean. But Bones McKinney, who hadn't scored the entire game, drained a set shot from the corner, and Bob Donham hit from the line. 87-all.

With 30 seconds left, Vandeweghe missed two free throws. The Knicks grabbed the rebound and ran the clock down to 17 seconds before running a play for Vandeweghe to get one last shot. He was fouled again, but this time he nailed his free throw and the Knicks had an 88–87 lead.

Boston had time for one last shot, but Clifton stepped in and intercepted a pass to end the game, send the Celtics to a harrowing defeat, and propel New York back to the NBA Finals for the second straight year.

## 22. The Rangers win their forgotten Cup, April 13, 1933, Maple Leaf Gardens, Toronto

1933 is the New York Rangers' forgotten Stanley Cup.

The 1928 trophy stands out because it was first and because of the dramatic Game 1 when coach Lester Patrick came out of retirement to play goalie. The 1940 win is remembered for the classic battle with Toronto, but also for the futility that followed—the Rangers became the team "that hadn't won since 1940." Similarly, 1994 was hailed as the end of a devastating drought.

But 1933, when the Rangers avenged their finals loss to Toronto from the previous year, gets overlooked. After a lackluster season in which the Blueshirts played below .500 in the second half, they entered the playoffs with low expectations—no third-place team had yet won the Cup. But the club had two potent weapons—original Ranger Bill Cook, whose 28 goals and 22 assists in 48 games gave him the scoring title at age 37, and a rookie goalie named Andy Aitkenhead.

New York topped both Montreal and Detroit to advance to the finals against the Maple Leafs, the Canadian Division winner.

**The Rangers receive their Stanley Cup trophy, the second in just five years.**

After the Rangers easily won Game 1 at home, 5–1, New York's road to the Cup got trickier when Madison Square Garden announced—to the derisive booing of Ranger fans—that the rest of the series would take place in Toronto to make way for the circus at the Garden. This was particularly unfortunate because the Rangers' bosses had maintained stronger fan support than most other clubs by cutting ticket prices by one-third to offset the effects of the Depression, giving the team a real home ice advantage.

After the Rangers won Game 2, the Leafs toughened up, pulling out a 3–2 victory in Game 3 in this best-of-five series. For Game 4 on April 13 at Maple Leaf Gardens, Aitkenhead was on the spot as his counterpart in the Toronto net, ex-Ranger Lorne Chabot, finally shut down the potent New York offense.

Despite a constant bombardment from an aggressive Toronto offense, Aitkenhead proved equal to the task, saving 48 shots over three periods. Regulation ended with the game still scoreless, the tension still excruciating.

In overtime, the Leafs committed not one but two costly penalties, sending two players to the box at once. Given this huge advantage, the Rangers finally broke through: Butch Keeling found Cook with a pass at 7:33, and Cook drove it past Chabot to win the game. The Rangers had become just the second NHL team to win two Cups.

## 23. St. John's wins down south, March 22, 1952, Reynolds Coliseum, Raleigh, North Carolina

In 1952 more than at any other time, New York needed a feel-good college basketball story. Frank McGuire's St. John's team delivered.

College basketball across the city had been badly tarnished by the point-shaving scandal the previous year in which virtually all of New York's powerhouses were implicated. St. John's escaped either because the program was clean or, some speculated, because of semidivine intervention — Cardinal Spellman pressured Frank Hogan, the Irish-Catholic Manhattan district attorney. With Madison Square Garden perceived as a den of iniquity, the NIT was badly wounded, and the expanding NCAA tournament fled New York, never to return. To redeem the city's reputation the 25–6 St. John's had to hit the road, which it did with a vengeance.

The team journeyed to Raleigh, North Carolina, for the first two rounds of the NCAA. St. John's had already had one unpleasant experience down south during the regular season. Kentucky coach Adolph Rupp had called McGuire asking that he leave Solly Walker, St. John's first black player, home when the Redmen visited Lexington. McGuire refused, and the nation's top-ranked team blew out St. John's 81–40, leaving a sour memory.

Now St. John's postseason started with another racial indignity. (CCNY had won two national championships in 1950 with three black starters, but outside New York integration was sporadic.) Upon arriving at their Raleigh hotel for breakfast, McGuire was told by the hotel manager, "Coach, I can't take care of that boy," referring to Walker. The chef agreed to feed Walker in the kitchen, so McGuire stood by his player, dining with him there.

St. John's started off the tournament with this chip on its shoulder and took pleasure in wiping

## Honorable Mention: St. John's Surprise

**Frank Viola outlasts Ron Darling's 11 no-hit innings, 1–0, May 21, 1981, Yale Field, New Haven**

Before Ron Darling drove Mets fans nuts as an overthinking nibbler, he was a Seaver-esque power pitcher for Yale. But in the NCAA Northeast Regional at Yale Field on May 21, 1981, he met his match in another future Met, Frank Viola.

Darling was 9–3 with a 2.42 ERA for an underwhelming 24–12–1 Yale team; Viola, 9–0, 1.00, was backed by 31–2 St. John's, with its .325 team average. With 50 scouts watching, Darling — on his way to 16 Ks — blew hitters away with high fastballs and sliders and even dove for a hard grounder in the fifth, keeping a potential no-hitter alive. He kept it going even into extra innings as Viola, who wasn't quite as sharp, kept slithering out of trouble, stranding seven runners in the first six innings and keeping pace in scoreless frames.

In the 11th, Yale loaded the bases, but Viola escaped once more. Finally, in the 12th, St. John's Steve Scafa blooped Darling's inside fastball to left. It was an aluminum bat dink, but it fell for a single. Everyone, including St. John's players, gave Darling a standing ovation. Scafa then thoroughly ruined Darling's day, stealing both second and third. Then, on a double steal, second baseman Jeremy Spear held the ball too long in a rundown, and Scafa raced home. Eric Stampful replaced Viola to close out St. John's 1–0 win.

Neither team reached the College World Series, but both participated in the greatest pitching duel in college baseball history.

**In his final season at St. John's, Frank McGuire leads the team on a magical journey down south and then to the Final Four.**

out hometown favorite North Carolina State 60–49 in the opening round. Waiting in the second round was the defending champ and tournament favorite, Kentucky, riding a 23-game win streak.

St. John's was ready for revenge. On March 22, the New Yorkers came out calm and focused, grabbing a 12–7 lead and never looking back. Center Bob Zawoluk's hook shot and McGuire's slow-down tactics neutralized the potent Wildcat fast-breakers. St. John's led 34–28 at the half thanks to Zawoluk's 16 points. In the locker room, St. John's players listened in as Rupp berated his players next door. When Kentucky closed the gap to 42–39, Zawoluk responded with two quick buckets to help build the lead back to nine. Kentucky got desperate, and soon center Cliff Hagan and two other Wildcats fouled out. The Redmen held on to win 64–57 as Zawoluk set an NCAA record with 32 points and grabbed 12 rebounds.

Afterwards, St. John's traveled to Seattle and squeaked past number two–ranked Illinois, 61–59, on Zawoluk's 24 points. The magical ride ended in the finals, however, when Kansas's Clyde Lovellette broke Zawoluk's record with 33 points and the Jayhawks prevailed, 80–63.

After the tournament, Kentucky was stunned when the widening point-shaving scandal shut its hoops program for a year. St. John's got a rude awakening from its dream season too. McGuire, the Coach of the Year, decided he needed quieter environs in which to raise his one-year-old son, who was afflicted with cerebral palsy. He moved, of all places, to the state that had seemed so hostile to New Yorkers, setting up at the University of North Carolina, where five years later he cemented his legend by finally winning an NCAA tourney.

## 24. The Mets outlast Atlanta, July 4–5, 1985, Fulton County Stadium

Imagine Abbott & Costello performing a baseball skit built on absurdities and impossibilities, but imagine that instead of their famous vaudeville number they found themselves stuck inside a Samuel Beckett script.

On July 4 (and July 5, for that matter), 1985, the New York Mets (and the Atlanta Braves) found themselves wandering through such a surreal blast of comic existentialism—a game for the ages that lasted for ages, one that had observers (make that survivors) asking all sorts of strange questions:

Why on earth was Rick Camp, who had batted .024, .077, and .111 in the three previous seasons (the lowest average of any active major leaguer), hitting with his Braves down a run with two outs in their last licks?

How did Met Tom Gorman, having surrendered one game-tying home run already, manage to allow a game-tying home run to Camp . . . on an 0–2 pitch no less?

And after all that, how did Gorman earn the win?

The early prognosis for this Independence Day affair was for a quick, well-pitched ball game—the unhittable Dwight Gooden in his "Dr. K" prime against Atlanta's steady junkballer Rick Mahler—and fireworks above Fulton County Stadium sometime between 10 and 11 P.M.

Things went awry from the start, which was a false one thanks to a 90-minute rain delay, fol-

## Honorable Mention: Baseball Marathon

**The Dodgers play a game without end, May 1, 1920, Braves Field, Boston**

Once upon a time, in a land without pitch counts, Brooklyn's Leon Cadore and Boston's Joe Oeschger endured perhaps the greatest pitching duel of all time. They each allowed just one run over the equivalent of almost three complete games . . . in a single afternoon.

The May 1 game at Braves Field didn't start until 3:00 P.M. because of rain, and only 3,000 fans braved the cold weather, but they got more than their money's worth.

Brooklyn scored in the fifth, and Boston retaliated in the sixth. But that was it. No more scoring. In the ninth, Cadore induced a double-play ball with the bases loaded. In the 17th, Brooklyn had a runner thrown out at the plate. After the 21st, neither pitcher bothered with warm-up tosses anymore . . . and neither allowed a hit.

At 6:50 P.M., after 26 innings (but only three baseballs), umpire Barry McCormick "remembered he had an appointment pretty soon with a succulent beefsteak," the *New York Times* quipped. "He wondered if it wasn't getting dark. He held out one hand as a test and decided that, in the gloaming, it resembled a Virginia ham."

Brooklyn's Ivy Olson—one of 15 men to play the whole game—requested one more inning to equal to three full games, but McCormick was done. It was a 1–1 tie.

Each pitcher faced 85 batters and threw perhaps 250 to 300 pitches. Neither man showed a definitive injury, yet neither was quite the same afterwards—Cadore's ERA climbed rapidly as his innings total plunged in the next three seasons; then he was out of baseball. Oeschger managed one more good year, than fell off precipitously.

Meanwhile, Brooklyn, which was riding its pitching to a second pennant in five seasons, continued its offensive struggles that May. They returned home the next day, and Burleigh Grimes pitched 13 innings in a loss to Philadelphia. Back in Boston the following day, Sherry Smith lost 2–1 in 19 innings. That's three pitchers throwing 58 innings in three days. This was dead ball baseball, but it was an era that was about to die—the 26 innings of Cadore-Oeschger were drowned out in the press as Babe Ruth hit his first home run as a Yankee. A new day dawned.

**After watching 18 innings of baseball, Ron Darling makes the first relief appearance of his career and nearly blows a five-run lead in the 19th before escaping with one of the wildest wins in Mets history.**

lowed by a 41-minute interruption in the third. Gooden didn't return after the second outburst, and Roger McDowell pitched the Mets to a 3–1 deficit. But the Mets mauled Mahler for four in the fourth when Wally Backman sank an RBI single into an outfield pond and Keith Hernandez picked up a triple because Claudell Washington slipped on the wet grass. (This piece of good luck later enabled the lead-footed Hernandez to hit for the cycle.) Hernandez's eighth-inning homer gave the Mets a damp but comfortable 7–4 lead. That's when the new scripts arrived and it became apparent that the 44,947 fans would be waiting for Godot, er, sorry, the fireworks for quite some time.

In the home eighth, the reliably unreliable Doug Sisk served up a two-out, three-run double to Dale Murphy that put Atlanta up 8–7. Needing three more outs, the Braves sent former great Bruce Sutter to the mound, where he promptly relinquished the tying run. This game would go on . . . and on . . . and on . . .

The promised pitchers' duel suddenly materialized from the 10th through the 12th, but in the 13th Howard Johnson blasted a two-run home run for a 10–8 lead. Now the Mets needed just three outs.

After a single, new reliever Tom Gorman got two of those outs on strikeouts. He got ahead 0–2 on Terry Harper. Time to waste a pitch, no? No. Eager to end it, Gorman grooved one, and Harper rocketed the ball fair by inches off the screen attached to the foul pole in left. Tied it at 10–10 . . . and on . . . and on. . . . Each team mustered just one hit in the next three innings, sending the game into the 17th.

Thanks to an innate penchant for bizarre occurrences, the Mets tended to slip down the rabbit hole into these long, strange ball games more than any other team. In only their 24th season, this game was their 18th trip through 17 innings or more. Why, less than 10 weeks earlier the Mets had played an 18-inning affair against Pittsburgh that resembled Jean Paul Sartre's *No Exit*: after Darryl Strawberry's first-inning grand slam, the Mets were shut out on just three hits for the next 16—count 'em, 16—frames, before scoring the winning run on an error in the 18th. That game lasted so long that the Mets were forced to deploy 41-year-old Rusty Staub—who had the shape and speed of a giant sea turtle—in the outfield, his first foray there in two years. (Gorman had pitched seven shutout innings for the win in that one, going longer than emergency starter Roger McDowell.)

On July 5, the 17th turned feisty when Darryl

# Honorable Mention: If Only We Knew for Sure

**Pee Wee comes to Jackie's side, 1947 . . . or 1948, Cincinnati . . . or Boston**

This is the story of a magnificent gesture—a famous symbol of integration, loyalty, and friendship—that may or may not have happened.

In May 1947, the Brooklyn Dodgers were in Cincinnati, and the fans were showering pioneering rookie Jackie Robinson with racist "abuse." Dodger shortstop and captain Pee Wee Reese, a southerner from nearby Louisville with friends and family in the stands, walked over to the first baseman and draped his arm around him, talking quietly. This thoughtful and brave gesture left the hecklers silenced, the Reds agog, and the Dodgers more accepting of Robinson as a teammate.

That's the legend, celebrated for years and commemorated in 2005 in a statue outside the Brooklyn Cyclones' Keyspan Park.

The truth is murkier. The story wasn't actually reported until much later, and it has numerous variations: it happened during batting practice, no, between innings, no, Reese called "time" and stopped play to make his stand.

Perhaps it didn't even happen in Cincinnati or in 1947. Carl Erskine said he witnessed it, and he didn't join Brooklyn until 1948. Robinson doesn't mention the incident in an autobiography published after his rookie year, and in both a 1952 magazine interview and his 1960 book *Wait Till Next Year* he placed it in 1948, in Boston, saying Reese responded to Brave players taunting Reese for playing alongside Robinson, who by then was a second baseman. If it happened in 1948, it is still a fine gesture, albeit a less heroic one.

A key figure for Robinson in 1947, Reese would move beyond defender and become his friend. In June, when Robinson and black writer Wendell Smith were playing golf near Reese and three other whites, Reese invited the two black men to join them.

Although the truth may be lost in the mists of time with each retelling in biographies, in Peter Golenbock's lovely picture book *Teammates* (which perpetuates the 1947 myth), and with the new statue (for which sculptor Will Behrends unfortunately played into the legend at the last minute by changing Robinson's glove from a fielder's glove to a first baseman's mitt), the image of Reese's arm around Robinson has ascended into folklore, frozen in time as a moment that—whenever and wherever it happened—has taught generations of children the value of tolerance, friendship, and taking a stand.

Strawberry and Davey Johnson were ejected for arguing a called third strike. Home plate umpire Terry Tata said, "There aren't any bad calls at 3 A.M." But Johnson insisted that baseball existed outside of time: "What has three o'clock in the morning got to do with whether or not it's a strike?"

In the 18th inning, the Mets inched ahead, again. Howard Johnson singled, went to third on Atlanta pitcher Rick Camp's error, then came home on Lenny Dykstra's fly-out. Ah, home. That was a place for which the players and the 7,000 remaining fans yearned.

Just three more outs. Gerald Perry grounded out. Two more. Gorman got Harper this time. One more. Gorman got two quick strikes on Camp. Why indeed was Camp up? Not up as in awake but up as in at bat? The Braves were completely out of position players—the two teams combined had used 43. Only Met Ronn Reynolds, poor Ronn Reynolds, failed to dent the box score, riding the pine on this slow journey through the night and early morning. (Gary Carter's reserve was kept in reserve in case the Met catcher got hurt.)

Why would Gorman throw a forkball over the fat part of the plate? For that, there's no satisfactory answer, but as Camp—who'd never homered before—jogged around the bases and into southern folklore, as the scoreboard registered the 11–11 tie, outfielder Danny Heep covered his head in despair and Dykstra threw his glove in disgust . . . and on . . . and on. . . .

However, the journey from home, around and back again, took something out of Camp. In the 19th inning, Carter—who'd catch 305 pitches—banged out his fifth hit of the night. Two batters later, Ray Knight, who had left nine men on base, doubled him home. Heep added some insurance—no lead could possibly be considered safe—with a two-run single. A third run scored when Washington misplayed his hit. Then, on the Mets' 28th hit, Backman drove home their 16th run for a five-run lead.

And still it wasn't over.

Ron Darling, who had started just two days earlier (well, three by this late hour), came in for the last of the 19th. After an error by Gold Glover Hernandez, Darling lost control, walking two batters. Harper then delivered his fifth hit of the night to cut the Mets' lead to 16–13.

Two outs and two on. The tying run at the plate. Ladies and gentlemen . . . Rick Camp.

Fortunately for the Mets, although unfortunately perhaps for baseball history, Camp did not have another homer long past the gloaming. Darling struck him out. At 3:55 A.M., after a record 6 hours and 10 minutes of baseball, the game was over. The Braves didn't want to cheat the loyal fans still there, so at 4:01 A.M. fireworks exploded, jolting awake hundreds if not thousands of residents, terrified that their city was under attack.

The Mets and Braves hadn't stuck around for the display. They knew they had to be back at the ballpark in just a few hours . . . for a day game.

## 25. The Jets beat the Giants in the biggest preseason game ever, August 17, 1969, Yale Bowl, New Haven

For the upstart New York Jets of the American Football League, winning the Super Bowl was all well and good, but beating the New York Giants, now that would mean something.

Sure, that's an exaggeration, but it's hard to overstate how strongly these cross-town teams and their fans felt about the August 17, 1969, preseason affair at the Yale Bowl in New Haven, Connecticut. Despite the impending AFL-NFL merger, which would be completed the following year, plenty of bad blood remained between the two leagues. And despite the fact that the Jets were the defending Super Bowl champions, while the Giants were coming off a 7–7 season that matched their best record in five years, plenty of snobbery remained among the Giants and their fans, who considered the Jets' win a lucky fluke. As Robert

**Joe Namath shows the Giants that the Jets are not only Super Bowl champs but the best team in New York.**

Lipsyte wrote in the *New York Times*: "For almost every year since 1925, the Giants have been football in New York, a bulwark of the National Football League and a symbol to the country of what football should be, how it should be coached and operated and played."

Beyond that, it was personal. Don Maynard recalled being cut by Giants coach Allie Sherman; Joe Namath resented Giants owner Wellington Mara for not drafting him; Mara disdained Namath and the Jets as a bunch of long-haired miscreants and complained (inaccurately) to the *New York Times* that the paper gave the Jets more press; and the three remaining Jets from the franchise's early days as the lowly Titans remembered being sneered at by the Giants, their fans, the press, the television networks . . . everybody.

To inspire his team, Jets coach Weeb Ewbank, who admitted that beating the Giants would make their success seem official, named those three originals—Maynard, Bill Mathis, and Larry Grantham—as captains for this game, which was dubbed—in glittering Gotham self-aggrandizement—"the World Championship of New York."

"I want to win even more than the Super Bowl," Mathis declared.

Heightening the circus atmosphere was Namath's off-season: he had dramatically retired rather than cut his ties to his celebrated bar, Bachelors III, and the unsavory characters hanging out there, and then, after busying himself with movies, he had unretired and returned to the Jets. This was not the sort of behavior one would have ever associated with the Giants' glory days. But those days were so far removed that this game seemed as much a referendum on the embattled Sherman—long taunted with "Good-bye, Allie" chants by frustrated fans—as on the uppity rebels from the AFL.

More than 70,000 fans, many from the city, endured horrific traffic to reach New Haven; they began arriving hours before game time. (An assistant coach at West Point drove over to root, strangely enough, for the anti-establishment Jets. His name was Bill Parcells.) It was so brutally hot that 75 people suffered heat exhaustion. None of them had as bad a day, however, as Mara, Sherman, and company.

Although Ewbank said later that he felt more confident before the Super Bowl, this game was a rout—it was over almost as soon as it started. Namath commandeered a quick five-play drive in the first, highlighted by a 28-yard touchdown pass to George Sauer. The Giants played supremely sloppy football, while the Jets sparkled—a bad punt by Dave Lewis set up a Jets field goal, and a Giant fumble on the subsequent kickoff practically handed the Jets another touchdown. Then, less than two minutes into the second quarter, Mike Battle returned a punt 86 yards for a touchdown and a 24–0 lead.

Fran Tarkenton rallied the Giants' hopes with a 92-yard drive and a 40-yard touchdown pass in the third. But Tarkenton was inconsistent and careless, finishing 9–21 for 139 yards with two interceptions, while Namath was crisp and controlled, going 14–16 for 188 yards. After the Giants pulled within 10, Namath coolly engineered a 66-yard drive, aided by three Giants penalties; he capped it with a 20-yard pass to Mathis, building the lead back up to 31–14. Despite the runaway score, Namath insisted on staying in until midway through the fourth, departing only after firing his third touchdown pass to make it 37–14. Both coaches kept almost all their regulars active until then too.

The most memorable fourth-quarter play transpired on the sidelines, where Maynard gleefully led the fans in another chorus of "Good-bye, Allie." Mara, who was devastated by this defeat, finally heard the message he should have heeded long before, and less than a month later Sherman was gone. But it was too late. As long as Namath's knees held up, the Jets would remain New York's team.

# Fearsome Foes The Top 10

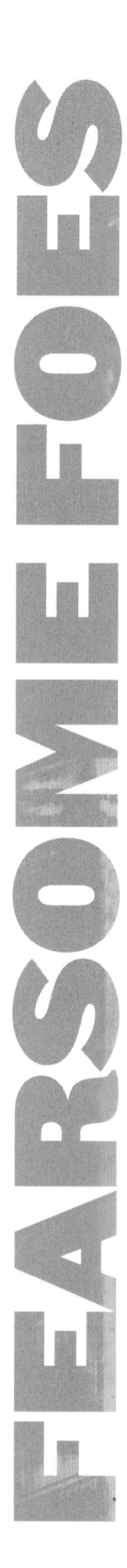


## The Top 10

1. *Johnny U. changes pro football, December 28, 1958, Yankee Stadium*
2. *Schilling socks it to the Yankees, October 19, 2004, Yankee Stadium*
3. *Red Grange saves the NFL and the Giants, December 6, 1925, Polo Grounds*
4. *Hank Luisetti revolutionizes the game, December 30, 1936, Madison Square Garden*
5. *Ol' Pete fans Tony Lazzeri, October 10, 1926, Yankee Stadium*
6. *Lew Burdette slays the mighty Yankees, October 10, 1957, Yankee Stadium*
7. *Reggie, Reggie, Reggie, May 7, 1995, Madison Square Garden*
8. *Home Run Baker earns his nickname, October 17, 1911, Polo Grounds*
9. *MJ gets the Double Nickel, March 28, 1995, Madison Square Garden*
10. *Johnny Vander Meer pitches a second straight no-hitter, June 15, 1938, Ebbets Field*

## On the Road: The Top 5

1. *Wilt reaches the century mark, March 2, 1962, Hershey Sports Arena, Hershey, Pennsylvania*
2. *Michael Jordan slices and dices the Knicks, May 17, 1992, Chicago Stadium*
3. *Babe Ruth displays his prowess . . . on the mound, October 9, 1916, Braves Field, Boston*
4. *David Ortiz bashes the Yankees twice in 24 hours, October 18, 2004, Fenway Park*
5. *Bird establishes "Larry Legend," May 13, 1984, Boston Garden*

# 1. Johnny U. changes pro football, December 28, 1958, Yankee Stadium

It's a classic fairy tale, a hardscrabble tale of rebuffs and failure in which perseverance and dedication are rewarded and the hero emerges to perform unimaginable feats of derring-do, growing overnight from man into legend.

It starts with a young quarterback turned away by his first choice, Notre Dame, for being too scrawny at 6', 138 pounds, then failing the entrance exam for the University of Pittsburgh, his hometown school, which had offered a scholarship.

After graduating from the University of Louisville, this crew-cut, hunch-shouldered kid is drafted by the Pittsburgh Steelers. One of four quarterbacks in camp, he never plays a down and is cut after five exhibition games; team officials deem him not bright enough for pro football.

The reject hitchhikes home and gets a job working construction but can't give up the game, playing semipro ball on a dirt field for $6 a week.

Given another shot, with the Baltimore Colts, he rides the pine until the fourth game, when starting quarterback George Shaw breaks his leg. On the rookie's first play, his pass is intercepted and run back for a touchdown. On his second, he botches a handoff, causing a fumble. The Colts lose 58–27. The newcomer finishes the 1956 season with more interceptions than touchdowns.

Thus begins the saga of Johnny U.

Unitas, of course, won the NFL's Most Valuable Player Award in 1957, then achieved immortality in the NFL Championship game against the New York Giants at Yankee Stadium on December 28, 1958, when he emblazoned the league in America's consciousness with his indelible performance in what became known as "the Greatest Game Ever Played."

Although football's following was already growing, few imagined this game would forever alter sports. At game time there were still several thousand seats unsold, something unimaginable today even during the regular season. And as it turned out, this game was flawed and downright sloppy at times — the Giants fumbled the ball away four times. But where previous championships had been yawn-inducing blowouts, this one locked the glamorous Giants — the proud original NFL franchise that played on sports' most hallowed ball field had become the golden boys of Madison Avenue after their 1956 championship — and the gritty Unitas, emerging as the archetype of the modern quarterback, in a riveting battle that produced the NFL's first sudden-death overtime. Television had undergone a concurrent boom, and when this dramatic game captivated the television audience — 45 million Americans watched on 11 million sets — it marked the beginning of the lasting and influential marriage between the sport and the medium. (Ironically, the game was blacked out in New York because NFL commissioner Bert Bell, still stuck in the old mindset, insisted that people at home should not get for free what they could be paying to see at the stadium.)

"That game is the reason why pro football is what it is today," Unitas said in 1998. (Had the Gi-

**From talented quarterback to American icon: Johnny Unitas guides the Colts to triumph and helps create "the Greatest Game Ever Played."**

ants pulled it out, this game would have ranked second or third in the top 100.)

In 1958 the Giants and Colts both finished the regular season 9–3, but the Giants, who rode in on the league's best defense, had needed five straight win-or-go-home games just to force a postseason tiebreaker, which they won over Cleveland.

The Colts, NFL newcomers, had earned their first winning season in 1957 as Unitas came into his own. In 1958 this collection of secondhand players had gelled as a team under coach Weeb Ewbank, racking up a league-leading 381 points. The game would hinge on the Giants defense versus the Colts offense.

The first quarter gave little indication of the drama to come, remaining close through ineptitude. Unitas fumbled on his first offensive series and was intercepted soon after; later he would admit that the Colts had been "a little intimidated" by the vaunted Giants and Yankee Stadium. Giants coach Jim Lee Howell, meanwhile, was overly conservative, sticking to his traditional strategy of starting backup quarterback Don Heinrich to preserve 37-year-old Charlie Conerly. But Heinrich was ineffective, and it wasn't until Conerly entered that the Giants scored a field goal for a 3–0 lead. The most telling play occurred moments before when Baltimore receiver Lenny Moore beat Jim Patton one-on-one for a 40-yard catch before running 20 more to New York's 25. Kicker Steve Myhra missed a field goal, and after a penalty, Giant linebacker Sam Huff blocked his second attempt, but the damage was done. The Giants defense remained wary of being burned again, keying extra coverage on Moore and on bombs, while Unitas picked, picked, picked, hitting Raymond Berry underneath.

In the second quarter, "Big Daddy" Lipscomb recovered a Frank Gifford fumble, and Alan Ameche and Moore pounded the ball in. Gifford fumbled again at Baltimore's 14, and Unitas made an 86-yard drive look easy, mixing running plays with midrange passes to Berry, including the 15-yard touchdown pass.

By halftime, the Colts had amassed a 14–3 lead and nearly 200 yards to the Giants' 86. The third quarter initially seemed like more of the same: the Colts, who had not been stopped all season inside their opponent's 10, got first down at New York's 3. But the Giants responded with ferocity and tenacity and kept the Colts at bay. The Colts went for it on fourth down, but amid the Yankee Stadium din, Ameche misheard the call for a fullback option pass and ran a sweep instead; Giant Cliff Livingston nailed him at the five-yard line.

Having rocked the Colts, the Giants opened up on offense. From the 13, Conerly hit Kyle Rote at the 40, and he scampered to Baltimore's 25, where he was drilled so hard that he fumbled the ball. But out of catastrophe came opportunity. Running back Alex Webster had trailed the play, and he scooped up the ball and rumbled to Baltimore's 1. Two plays later, the Giants scored. Soon after, Conerly helmed a quick strike—two passes netted 63 yards. Then Conerly exploited a weakness revealed in Polaroid photos that owner Wellington Mara had taken from the press box during the first half: they showed the Colts' secondary shifting to the strong side. So Conerly went weak side for Gifford, who lugged cornerback Milt Davis with him into the end zone. The Stadium erupted, and the press was stunned: with the fourth quarter just under way, the Giants had a 17–14 lead.

A mist settled over the field, a symbol of the gloom enveloping Baltimore. Bert Rechechar, who handled the Colts' long kicks, missed a 46-yard field goal; later, Unitas was sacked on consecutive plays. The clock was working for the Giants.

With less than two and a half minutes remaining—just around the time Conerly was voted Most Valuable Player in the press box—the Giants faced 3rd-and-less-than-4 near midfield. One more first down and the championship would be theirs. Gifford ran outside on a sweep, then cut back toward a hole. An off-balance Gino Marchetti, a Colt defensive lineman, dragged him down with a desperate lunge. Gifford appeared to have gained just enough, but a howl tore through the cluster of players, distracting everyone. The 288-pound Lipscomb had landed on Marchetti, shattering his right leg above the ankle. After Marchetti was carted off, the ref marked the ball inches shy of the first down. The Giants argued, but in vain, and then Howell had them punt rather than run against Marchetti's second-tier replacement. "We only needed four inches," said guard Jack Stroud later. "We would have run through a brick wall at that point."

The punt shoved Baltimore back to its 14. "I looked down the field, and the goal posts looked like they were in Baltimore," Berry said later.

Unitas stepped into the breach. He quarterbacked with an air of inevitability; even after two straight incompletions, he never let up. On 3rd-and-10, he stunned the Giants by switching to the run. Moore galloped through the opening for 11. After two more incompletions, Unitas hit Berry—the slow guy, the one with the contact lenses and the two different shoes to compensate for having one leg shorter than the other, the guy who never missed—for 25. Calling audibles on nearly every play, Unitas mixed it up by not mixing it up: he went back to Berry twice more, for 15 and 22 yards. Time was nearly gone, but Unitas had brought the Colts to New York's 13. Myhra nailed the field goal, and the game was tied.

For a moment, nobody was sure what would happen next. There was a rule on the books about sudden-death overtime, but it had only been implemented in an exhibition game.

The Giants were completely spent, almost beaten already, worn down by their consecutive survival tests. But the fans in the stands, the viewers at home, and the press were revved up and lusting for more football. After the fourth quarter's excitement, overtime added historic heft to the adventure.

The Giants won the toss but fell less than a

## Honorable Mention: Fearsome Foes

**1. Dean brothers do double duty, September 21, 1934, Ebbets Field**

Someone finally upstaged Ol' Diz, and wouldn't you know it, it was the other one of those Dean boys. With St. Louis stalking the New York Giants in a taut pennant race, the Gashouse Gang was in Brooklyn for a crucial double-header. Dizzy started the first game, his brother Paul the second.

Back in the spring, Dizzy's forecast was, "Me 'n Paul will win 45 games this year." It ain't boastin' if you can back it up—the Deans began this day with 26 and 17 wins, respectively, for a total of 43.

The dynamic duo had recently swept the Giants at the Polo Grounds, and before this twin bill Dizzy mouthed off to a sportswriter, saying Brooklyn would face "one-hit Dean and no-hit Dean today."

Then they backed up those words. In the opener, Dizzy pitched a no-hitter until the eighth before yielding three singles, but no runs, in a 13–0 rout.

Paul, the quiet brother, was even better, doing what Dizzy nearly managed—he allowed no hits and only eight balls out of the infield. In the ninth, with Brooklyn fans cheering him on, he retired two lefty pinch hitters. He was one out from a no-hitter, but the last batter was Ralph Boyle, who'd ruined Dizzy's bid. Boyle scorched one toward short, where the ball short-hopped into, then out of, Leo Durocher's glove. Durocher scooped it up and fired to first just in time. The Dean boys beat the Dodgers twice while simultaneously dealing a double blow to the Giants.

The Cards would need both wins—they wouldn't clinch the pennant until the season's final game nine days later when, one day after Paul won his 19th, Dizzy sealed the deal with his 30th.

Two dozen no-hitters or perfect games have been pitched against New York teams since 1900, but many of the most memorable were somewhat diluted by circumstance. Cy Young stopped the Highlanders at age 41 in 1908, but in those dead ball days there were 19 no-no's from 1905 to 1910. On Father's Day 1964, Jim Bunning, father of nine, pitched the NL's first perfect game against the woeful Mets, but in the pitcher-friendly expansion era of 1962 to 1965, there were 17 no-hitters. By contrast, the Deans pitched during a time of explosive offenses—only three no-hitters had been pitched in the previous eight years. Throw in Dizzy's comments, his opening-game effort, and the pennant race pressure, and "one-hit Dean and no-hit Dean" truly earned their place in the history books.

## Honorable Mention: Fearsome Foes

**2. Ray Nitschke stops the Giants, December 30, 1962, Yankee Stadium**

When the Brooklyn Dodgers left town, New York's football Giants assumed their role as the so-close heartbreak team. The Giants had won the NFL Championship in 1956, one year after Brooklyn's World Series triumph, but then lost the big game in 1958, 1959, and 1961. In 1962 against Green Bay, they were doubly desperate—the previous year's loss was a humiliating 37–0 rout at the hands of the Packers, coached by former Giant offensive coach Vince Lombardi.

But against the Packers again, the Giants ran into two unstoppable, omnipresent forces: freezing winds and middle linebacker Ray Nitschke. The Giants planned to ride quarterback Y. A. Tittle's vaunted aerial attack, but gusts of 40 mph and temperatures near 10 degrees severely hampered him. Ultimately, however, in what Arthur Daley of the *New York Times* called "a game of rugged violence," the real difference was Nitschke.

Nitschke's father died when he was three, and his mother died when he was 13. He lived on the streets and took his anger out on other kids. He'd grown up to be a gentle, loving family man, but on the gridiron he let loose those childhood demons, gleefully frightening foes. "You want the ball carrier to be a little shy," he'd say about his penchant for slamming players down with his forearm. "And a little shyer the next time."

Nitschke was everywhere. He blitzed relentlessly. He punished Giant runners with every tackle. He stunted at the line to keep Tittle off-balance. And he made the big play, not once or twice, but three times.

In the first quarter, Tittle, who'd set an NFL record with 33 touchdown passes, passed from the Packer 16 toward Joe Walton, alone at the goal line. Nitschke reached up, deflecting the pass toward Green Bay's Dan Currie, who intercepted it. In the second quarter, Nitschke helped cause and then snatched Phil King's fumble on the Giants' 28, setting up a touchdown. In the third quarter, with Green Bay clinging to a 10–7 lead, Nitschke helped out on special teams (talk about ubiquitous) and recovered a fumble on a punt return to set up a critical field goal.

The Packers won 16–7, but without Nitschke's three big plays, it's easy to envision the Giants winning 14–6. Not surprisingly, Nitschke was named Player of the Game, one of the few times a defensive player garnered such recognition in the title game. He was a "towering defensive hero in the middle," the *Washington Post* wrote.

The recognition was not universal. That night, dressed in civilian clothes and having transformed back into a mild-mannered Clark Kent kind of guy, Nitschke appeared on the television show *What's My Line*. No one could guess he had spent the day playing Superman against the Giants.

yard shy and punted. Unitas started at his own 20. "We're going to take the ball right down and score," Unitas said in the huddle.

He mixed a short pass with two runs to sail to the 43. On 3rd-and-15 after a sack, the Giants focused on Moore, so Unitas found his other weapon, Berry, for 21 yards. That play worked so well that Unitas called it again. But at the line he noticed Huff shifting to help Harland Svare on Berry; Unitas audibled a fullback trap for Ameche, who barreled for 23 yards. The Colts were in striking distance.

On CBS, Chuck Thompson decreed, "Something historic that will be remembered forever is happening here today, ladies and gentlemen."

With the Giants completely off-kilter, Unitas went back to Berry, who'd catch 178 of Unitas's 349 passing yards. Berry roped it in near the 8. Thompson said, "Berry makes a diving catch inside the 10. The ball is on about . . ."

Suddenly, across America, the picture went dark. Excited Colts fans in the stands had accidentally dislodged a power cable. After a brief timeout, Unitas was ready to roll when a crazed middle-aged drunk raced onto the field, weaving like Frank Gifford in the open field, cheered by the fans and finally chased down by the police. While the press called it a drunk's stunt, in reality the man was Stan Rotkiewicz, an NBC business manager doubling as a statistician on the sidelines, who improvised that desperation down-and-out pattern to buy precious moments for engineers working to repair the cable before the Colts' score. Rotkiewicz's ploy succeeded—Unitas ran one rushing play to gain a yard, but then the picture was restored in time for the nation to see his final two glorious plays.

Trusting no one but himself to win it, Unitas defied conventional wisdom and his coach, who had told Unitas to keep it on the ground and settle for a field goal if necessary. He floated a cross-field pass to Jim Mutscheller in the flat, where an interception would yield a long, possibly fatal runback. Mutscheller snared it, going out at the 1. This pass starkly contrasted with Howell's tentativeness and was a perfect made-for-TV play. But while nearly everyone in America thought it too risky, Unitas—who'd seen the Giants overshifting against Berry—coolly downplayed the dangers afterwards: "When you know what you're doing, you don't get intercepted."

Even on the final play, Unitas crossed up the Giants—he handed off to Ameche, but instead of running him through the left side and Jim Parker, Baltimore's best blocker, Unitas sent him through the right. Ameche poured through the enormous hole. Baltimore won 23–17.

*Sports Illustrated* headlined its story "The Best Football Game Ever Played," and in the *Daily News* Gene Ward wrote, "In years to come when our children's children are listening to stories about football, they'll be told about the greatest game ever played—the one between the Giants and Colts for the 1958 NFL Championship."

Even Giant founder Tim Mara appreciated what Unitas had done. Mara, who died soon after, proclaimed, "We're gonna sell out next year." And they did—in a year that again brought the Giants to the championship game, where Unitas again beat them. Unitas would remain the league's greatest star for more than a decade.

The league would never again average less than 40,000 a game, and by 1961 the increased demand prompted expansion from 12 to 14 games. The game also inspired young millionaire Lamar Hunt to pursue a football franchise; rebuffed by the old-school NFL, he formed the AFL, a rebel league that would ultimately have a huge impact on the pro game. The media also paid more attention: by 1960 *Sports Illustrated,* which had annually allotted just one NFL cover (but numerous college football covers), tripled its tally. More importantly, that year new commissioner Pete Rozelle replaced small-time local television deals with a national TV contract. He also helped launch NFL Films, which built on 1958's legacy by making every big game feel like the invasion of Normandy. In the 1950s pro football was fretting over challenges by the new National Basketball Association, but by the mid-'60s the sport was asserting its primacy over baseball as the nation's most popular sport. Soon would come *Monday Night Football,* the Super Bowl as a national holiday (seemingly to celebrate the launch of new advertising campaigns), and television deals reaching into the billions.

There was a happy ending of sorts for New Yorkers, although it was a long time coming: Hunt's upstart AFL made its mark when the New York Jets outspent NFL teams for a young quarterback hailing, like his idol Unitas, from Pennsylvania. This flamboyant newcomer, however, was the antithesis of the Colt legend. Joe Namath's signing helped force the leagues' merger, which modernized the NFL and greatly accelerated its national growth and appeal. That fate was sealed in 1969 in pro football's second-most important game, when the championship again pitted New York against Baltimore. Unitas again steered Baltimore to a dramatic late-game touchdown, but in 1969 Joe Namath was the quarterback with an air of inevitability. And in Super Bowl III, New York won.

# 2. Schilling socks it to the Yankees, October 19, 2004, Yankee Stadium

For the New York Yankees, the nights just kept getting longer and longer. Game 4 of the 2004 ALCS lasted 12 innings; Game 5 went 14. The sixth game lasted only nine frames, but it worked its way backwards through time, undoing decades of mystique and magic going all the way back to the fall of 1919.

That was the year the Boston Red Sox fixed the World Series. Not the 1919 Series, thrown by the Chicago White Sox, but virtually every Fall Classic after that, as they handed the Yankees the cornerstone of a dynasty, Babe Ruth. From then on, the fate of the Yankees and the Red Sox would be forever intertwined.

Boston had been the American League's best team from 1912 to 1918 but fell precipitously after Ruth's departure, sending New York many other players who proved crucial to its 1920s success. In the 1940s the rivalry flared as Ted Williams led Boston and seriously challenged Joe DiMaggio's Yankees. The bad blood was renewed in the 1970s when the Red Sox, as they had in the 1940s, won the American League first but failed to win a World Series and soon faded beneath a flowering Yankee dynasty.

But the latest round of chases and battles topped them all. It had begun in 1995 when Boston won its fourth divisional title in a decade and the Yankees captured the wild card to reach the postseason for the first time since 1981. Both teams lost in the playoffs that year, but the Yankees won the World Series in 1996 and 1998, beating the second-place Sox each year for the division. In 1999 New York routed Boston in five games in the ALCS. In 2003 Boston was on the verge of playoff victory, leading 5–2 in Game 7, when Grady Little froze, Pedro Martinez wilted, and Aaron Boone homered. That night Red Sox Nation wept the bitterest tears of all.

But the new Boston management team was finally as savvy and financially committed as New York's, and the historic 2004 ALCS boiled down to this: after the 2003 debacle, the Boston Red Sox traded for Curt Schilling specifically to beat the Yankees so that Boston could win the World Series; in Game 6 of the ALCS on October 19, he did just that, and he did it in heroic fashion.

Both Boston and New York had wanted Schilling, a fiercely competitive strikeout pitcher with impeccable credentials. Beyond his 20-win seasons and ability to eat innings, Boston really wanted the 37-year-old ace because he was baseball's ultimate money pitcher, a genuine Mr. October. In three postseasons, he'd hurled 86⅔ innings, allowing just 73 hits and walks and compiling a miserly 1.66 ERA while firing home 91 strikeouts. At the heart of that were his three starts for Arizona in 2001 when he and Randy Johnson had broken the Yankees' viselike grip on the World Series—in three starts he'd posted a 1.69 ERA with 26 strikeouts in 21⅓ innings.

The Yankees had a shot at Schilling too but would not trade Alfonso Soriano, so the Red Sox got him. Schilling, a fan of baseball history who had named his son Gehrig, declared, "I guess I hate the Yankees now."

Then Boston, which didn't need more offense, was publicly embarrassed when the players' union undid its trade for Alex Rodriguez on a technical-

**Red blood on a Red Sox white sock? It doesn't stop Curt Schilling from shutting down the Yankees.**

ity. So New York, which also didn't need more offense but liked the idea of rubbing Boston's nose in the infield dirt, acquired A-Rod . . . for Alfonso Soriano. But in midseason 2004, when Randy Johnson—the other Arizona ace and the one available pitcher able to go toe to toe with Schilling—was on the market, the Yankees no longer had Soriano and couldn't swing the deal.

In the divisional series against California, Schilling aggravated an ankle injury that had bothered him for much of the year, dislocating his tendon. Unable to push hard off that foot, Schilling was hammered in a 10–7 loss to the Yankees in Game 1 of the ALCS. After that, the series quickly unraveled for Boston. But just three outs from being swept, the Red Sox revived. In Game 4, Dave Roberts stole second and scored off Yankee closer Mariano Rivera in the ninth inning, and David Ortiz homered in the 12th to win. In Game 5, Ortiz drove home the game-winner in the 14th to send the ALCS back to New York.

The Yankees' lead had shrunk to 3–2. Still, they remained confident. No team had ever even forced a seventh game from down 3–0—it was one thing to win a game or two at home, but another to go into hostile territory and win at the Stadium where the Yankees reigned supreme.

Boston's medical staff had been working feverishly in a darkened underground laboratory (well, not really) to get Schilling onto the mound in one piece for Game 6. They'd tried a numbing medication, but it made him lose his feel for pitching; they'd tried a hightop cleat to stabilize the ankle, but that evoked the bad karma of Bill Buckner, who wore such footwear for a big Game 6 in New York once upon a time long ago—plus it put too much pressure on the stitches in Schilling's tendon. They tried a magic potion made from unicorn's blood . . . well, they would have if they could have.

Finally, before the fifth game, Dr. Bill Morgan tried an experimental technique—which he'd practiced on an amputated leg—attaching the skin around the tendon to deep tissue to improvise a sheath that would hold it in place.

It was just 49 degrees and misty when Schilling took the mound, but nothing short of a tornado would have kept him from his appointed rounds. Even when his stitches tore and the blood stained his sock red, Schilling remained undeterred.

In the first, Schilling, who in 2001 had famously dismissed the Yankees' "mystique" and "aura" as nothing but names for nightclub dancers, made a different statement by brushing back the second hitter, Alex Rodriguez. It was vintage old-school baseball. Schilling was brimming with confidence—and with a 94-mph heater as well. He followed his 1–2–3 first with a 1–2–3 second. He allowed a two-out hit in the third, but that was it.

The decisive inning was the fourth. With two outs, Boston's Kevin Millar scored when Jason Varitek singled after fouling off four two-strike pitches. After Orlando Cabrera also singled, Mark Bellhorn lifted a ball into the stands in left, where it bounced off a fan and landed back on the field. Umpire Jim Joyce said the ball hit the wall and was in play, but the other umpires persuaded him to reverse course and correct the call. It was a three-run homer. The Red Sox had their mojo working.

In the bottom of the fourth, the Yankees had two on and no out with Hideki Matsui, Bernie Williams, and Jorge Posada coming up, but Schilling shot down any notion of Yankee momentum by getting a pop out and two grounders to first. The threat was vanquished. Then Schilling retired another seven in a row before Bernie Williams homered in the seventh. Schilling's day was done after that inning, but so, for all intents and purposes, were the Yankees.

In the eighth, there would be one more controversial play, but it would only serve to reinforce the notion that Boston, not New York, made the right off-season acquisition. Boston reliever Bronson Arroyo allowed a one-out RBI single to Derek Jeter, which brought up Rodriguez with the score 4–2. In July, Arroyo had hit Rodriguez, inciting a mini-brawl. This time Rodriguez tapped the ball into the grass, and when Arroyo scooped it up and

## Honorable Mention: Fearsome Foes

**3. O.J. rushes to 2,000 yards, December 16, 1973, Shea Stadium**

Once upon a time, there was no murder trial, no white Ford Bronco on a freeway, no lackluster announcing, mediocre movie roles, or endless car rental commercials. Once upon a time, there was "the Juice," O. J. Simpson, the greatest running back football had seen since Jim Brown.

Simpson led the league in rushing in 1972, but in 1973, aided by his front line known as "the Electric Company," he'd transformed the lowly Buffalo Bills—with just 17 wins in six years—into a playoff contender. Simpson gained a record 250 yards the first week, then more than 100 in eight other games. After racking up 219 in the penultimate week, he came to freezing Shea Stadium with 1,803 yards, just 60 shy of Brown's single-season record.

This was Weeb Ewbank's final game as New York Jets coach, but the team had fallen so far since the 1969 Super Bowl that it was fitting that his departure would be overshadowed by the triumphant march of an invader.

Simpson broke the record on the Bills' second possession. The game stopped, Simpson's teammates congratulated him, and they gave him the ball as a keepsake. Then he fumbled on the very next play.

He resumed rolling, however, with a 13-yard touchdown run. With the game a rout (Buffalo won 34–14), the Bills offense focused solely on whether Simpson could reach 2,000 yards.

With 5:56 remaining and 193 yards for the day, Simpson slid off the left side for seven yards, becoming the first person to reach 200 yards twice in a row and three times in one season. Most importantly, he'd reached 2,003 for the season. He was again given the ball to keep, and as his teammates hoisted him on their shoulders and carried him off the field even the Jet fans wildly cheered their opponent.

went to tag him, Rodriguez flailed at the glove, knocking the ball away. Jeter alertly raced around to score, making it 4–3, but the Red Sox argued, the umpires again huddled, and again it was the Yankees suffering a reversal: not only was Jeter called back to first, not only was Rodriguez out for interference, but "the Slap," as it was soon called, stood in stark contrast to Schilling's gutsy performance. The next day, before the Sox routed the Yankees to complete the greatest comeback of all time, Schilling topped off his pitching effort in typical fashion by offering a long and loud critique of Rodriguez's actions, which he deemed "junior high school baseball" unworthy of Yankee pinstripes.

If only Schilling had been the one wearing pinstripes it might never have come to that. But unfortunately for the Yankees, he wasn't. He was proudly wearing a bloody red sock.

## 3. Red Grange saves the NFL and the Giants, December 6, 1925, Polo Grounds

Every culture has its creation myth, the story of its birth. The National Football League was born in 1920 as the American Professional Football Association, but it wasn't until Red Grange galloped onto the pro gridirons in 1925 that it seemed the league might have a future. Baseball and boxing ruled the sports world, and in pigskin perceptions college football was the superior sport. Then Grange, whose college exploits made him an equal of Babe Ruth and Jack Dempsey, joined the Chicago Bears and convinced fans and sportswriters to pay attention to this malnourished fledgling of a league that was largely mired in remote mill towns. His first trip to New York helped save the Mara family, the Giants, and the league.

Growing up in Illinois, Grange played a game where one kid tried to tackle any of the 10 racing past him; the tackled joined the tackler, and the defensive group grew and grew until just one runner tried evading them all. In high school, he scored 75 touchdowns but also lettered in baseball, basketball, and track. At the University of Illinois, he had to be prodded into going out for football; thinking there was too much competition, he thought he might instead focus on basketball and track. Once he joined the team, however, he shredded all competitors; in his first game he scored three touchdowns, including a 66-yard outburst.

Grange was remarkably quick and had great lateral movement and an unparalleled ability to change speeds; with his peripheral vision and knack for seeing holes opening ahead of him, he proved nearly unstoppable. His star power prompted the school to build a new stadium and people across the nation to buy those newfangled radios so they wouldn't have to wait to find out about the latest deeds of "the Galloping Ghost." His legend was assured in 1924 when he single-handedly demolished Michigan, a team riding a 20-game winning streak. He ran a kickoff back for 95 yards and had touchdown runs of 67, 56, and 44

**Red Grange leads Chicago to a 19–7 win over New York, but more importantly, he draws 70,000 fans to the Polo Grounds.**

yards . . . all in the first quarter. He finished the 39–14 rout with five touchdowns rushing and one passing for 402 yards of total offense.

While the football games of schools like Illinois drew upwards of 50,000, the NFL bumbled along with scant press coverage and attendance often in the low four figures for franchises in towns like Rochester, Dayton, and Pottsfield, Pennsylvania. Attaining legitimacy would require a franchise in New York, and in 1925 the league persuaded a successful bookmaker named Tim Mara to roll the dice. According to various tellings, Mara invested $500 or $2,500; either way, he famously told his son Wellington, "An empty store with two chairs in it in New York is worth more than that."

Throughout 1925, Mara's Giants hemorrhaged money — they handed out free tickets, but the stadium remained more than half-empty. Governor Al Smith, a family friend, advised, "This pro football will never amount to anything. Get rid of that team."

Mara would gladly have dumped the franchise, but "the only trouble was where would you find anyone crazy enough to buy it," he recalled later. The only way to save it was to go for broke, so he secretly journeyed by train to Chicago to offer Grange big bucks to join after graduation. Back then, most college stars didn't deign to play in the bush league pro game.

Grange was willing, but Mara was too late: C. C. Pyle, perhaps the first sports agent, had signed the star to a management deal. Immediately after his final game—but months before graduation—Grange turned pro. Technically, Pyle was leasing him to the Bears; Grange got 50 percent of the Bears' receipts (minus Pyle's cut), and after the regular season the team would go on a body-bruising barnstorming tour to fatten everyone's coffers. In total, there'd be 10 games in 18 days, followed by a nine-game tour out west.

Football, unlike baseball or basketball, had developed purely as a collegiate sport, and those who viewed the college game as a lofty undertaking played for the sport of it and to build character were scandalized by this mercenary move. (Never mind the huge stadiums being built around the country by college football receipts.) The NFL, by contrast, was a fringe sport, a fly-by-night operation run by undesirable characters; Mara, don't forget, was a bookie. Fans, sportswriters, Grange's college coach, and even many editorial pages away from the East Coast trashed his decision. "I'd have been more popular with the colleges if I had joined the Capone mob in Chicago," Grange said, while frankly acknowledging that money was the motivator. "I have to get the money now because people will forget all about me in a few years."

Grange brought the NFL credibility and a much-needed financial boost. His first game in Chicago drew 36,000, by far a new NFL record. (The Bears averaged closer to 5,000.) The second drew 28,000 in a snowstorm against the winless Columbus squad. The next game, in St. Louis, only drew 8,000, but it was played midweek in 12-degree weather against an ad hoc club sponsored by a mortician (a telling reminder of the pro game's status).

In college, Grange had played only once in the East, and in this pre-television era the chance to see a great icon in person generated tremendous excitement. On Saturday, December 5, the Bears drew 35,000 to Shibe Park in Philadelphia, where Grange scored two touchdowns. Then it was on to New York for another game in the same muddy uniforms the next day.

In a league where advance sales were virtually nonexistent, the Giants (whose losses had by then mounted to a staggering $45,000) had sold 40,000 tickets over three days of frenzied anticipation. The NFL was suddenly front-page news, even if it was all about the money.

Sunday fell sunny and mild. Mara had hoped for 50,000 to 55,000 people, but close to 70,000 crushed into the Polo Grounds. Extra seats were set up in the end zones and on the sidelines, thousands more were turned away, and 250 extra police could barely handle it all. (Grange was given a detail of 50 men just to protect him.) It was the largest crowd ever to see a pro game.

Equally important was the massive press contingent; nearly 100 reporters turned out. Sitting in a box seat watching the press mob number 77, Babe Ruth quipped, "I'll have to sue that bum. They're my photographers."

The game itself was almost anticlimactic, especially since the Giants—riding a seven-game winning streak—devoted all their energy to shutting down Grange. (All Chicago's foes did, often playing extra rough against the richest man in pro sports, while hometown refs rarely punished such dirty tactics.) They constantly put two men on him and shut down his running game, allowing him only 45 yards from scrimmage. (He did complete a pass.) But the double-teaming allowed Chicago's Joe Sternaman to score twice in the first quarter (once after a crucial block by Grange) for a 12–0 lead.

Suffering a torn muscle in his left arm and completely exhausted—this was his fifth pro game since his college season ended just 15 days before—Grange sat out the third quarter and the start of the fourth. But New Yorkers are a demanding bunch, and the crowd incessantly chanted, "Grange, Grange, we want Grange."

The superstar returned and intercepted a pass, galloping back 35 yards for a touchdown. The home team was beaten 19–7, but the fans got what they paid for. The press was blinded by dollar signs—the *New York Times* front-page headline didn't mention the score or Grange's interception, reading, "Grange Gets $30,000, Says It's Secondary"—but they were looking in the wrong wallet. The bigger news for New York and the league was that the Giants were suddenly in the black, and Mara was inspired to stick around.

There'd be financial struggles over the next few years, especially in 1926 when Grange and Pyle, angry at Chicago's stinginess, formed a rival league and Grange headed a New York squad that caused Mara significant monetary losses. (The league folded after one year, and Grange ultimately finished his career with the Bears.) The NFL would need plenty of time and several more watershed games over the next few decades before it could compete with baseball, but this game in 1925 demonstrated, thanks to Grange, that football was no longer just "the game of the colleges and for the colleges," Allison Danzig wrote in the *Times.* It was "the game of America."

Grange's earnings—he made six figures in a matter of months, especially with endorsements—encouraged other collegiate All-Americans to join the NFL. (The league mollified the colleges by promising that players would have to graduate first.)

Grange's arduous barnstorming trip was reminiscent of the thousands of miles traveled in 1869–70 by the Cincinnati Red Stockings, who helped spread the idea that professional baseball was morally acceptable as well as exciting for fans and profitable for athletes and entrepreneurs. The Red Stockings had had to prove themselves in the baseball world by playing against New York's best teams. In 1925 the New York game was again the most crucial, but this time around it was New York that needed outside help. Wellington Mara said later, "That game gave my father, and everyone else in the NFL, new hope."

# 4. Hank Luisetti revolutionizes the game, December 30, 1936, Madison Square Garden

On December 30, 1936, basketball became a whole new ball game. In the era of the stodgy set shot, Stanford's Hank Luisetti brought his running one-handers from the lonesome West to the capital of both hoopdom and media, hoping to prove himself before the royal court.

Luisetti, who'd developed his shooting technique in high school, was one of several players out west using this forerunner of the modern jump shot. But without television, no one who counted had seen the newfangled technique. Even after Stanford topped Temple, New Yorkers scoffed—that's Philly, man, let's see what Luisetti can do here, against Clair Bee's Long Island University squad, which had won 43 straight games. They'd school Luisetti.

They were wrong. Luisetti handled the ball, set up his teammates with crisp passes, and rotated between forward, guard, and center. But what mattered most was how he scored often and easily. His first bucket came on a fake and pivot near the foul line; LIU's big men sneeringly dismissed the unorthodox shot as lucky. But Luisetti repeated it—again and again—quieting his foes. "Some of his shots would have been declared foolhardy if attempted by any other player, but with Luisetti doing the heaving these were accepted as matter of course," the *New York Times* wrote.

**Hank Luisetti came from out west to teach New Yorkers a thing or two.**

Stanford opened a big lead in the second half, trouncing LIU 45–31, and when Luisetti left with 15 points, the New York crowd gave him a standing ovation. The LIU winning streak was over, but they knew they had seen a new future that day. It wasn't just the sellout crowd that was sold on the new style—so too were the powerful New York press and the city's players, who began imitating Luisetti. (Some skeptics remained: CCNY coach Nat Holman said, "That's not basketball. If my boys ever shot one-handed, I'd quit coaching.")

It didn't matter how many other people had been using this shot around the country. The immense power of New York basketball and its press made this day, when Luisetti made it in New York, the day the shot was born. After that, shooting suddenly meant flash and speed and hanging in the air as basketball took one giant, running leap toward the modern era.

## 5. Ol' Pete fans Tony Lazzeri, October 10, 1926, Yankee Stadium

Bases loaded, two out. A one-run game. Game 7 of the World Series. The quintessential pressure situation. In shambled an old man, tired and quite probably hung over, a man who'd been deemed washed up by his former employers earlier that summer. Grover Cleveland Alexander had already proved them wrong by beating the Yankees in Games 2 and 6 of the 1926 Series for St. Louis, but could he deliver another win when there was no room for error?

The 39-year-old Cardinal hurler faced rookie sensation Tony Lazzeri, who'd driven in 114 runs. Lazzeri had been eight years old when Alexander was a rookie sensation himself, winning 28 games for Philadelphia way back in 1911. In his prime, Alexander, with his concise three-quarters overhand delivery, lively fastball, and sharp curve, ranked among the game's elite pitchers, but heavy drinking, epilepsy, and 4,000 innings had worn him down. It had been three years since his last 20-win season, and when he started this season, 3–3 Chicago dumped him on the Cards.

Alexander went 9–7 for St. Louis, then resurrected his old form in October, striking out 10 Yankees in Game 2 and hurling a second complete-game win in Game 6. According to legend (which he denied), Alexander, figuring he wouldn't be called on the next day, celebrated his clutch performance in style that night, drinking as hard as he threw.

The deciding game took place on a wet and foggy October 10 at Yankee Stadium. The Cardinals overcame Babe Ruth's fourth homer of the Series, scaring up three unearned runs on sloppy defense. But Cardinal starter Jesse Haines developed a blister and began losing his grip on his tenuous lead. The Yankees scored one in the sixth and mounted a seventh-inning attack that seemed potentially fatal for St. Louis. Earle Combs singled and was bunted to second. Ruth was, naturally, walked intentionally. One out later, young Lou Gehrig patiently worked out a walk.

Up came Lazzeri. In came Alexander. The roaring fans fell silent in anticipation. St. Louis player-

**Young Tony Lazzeri whiffs with the bases loaded against ancient Grover Alexander in Game 7 of the World Series.**

manager Rogers Hornsby had sent Alexander out to the bullpen, which was out of sight and under the bleachers, to judge Willie Sherdel and Herman Bell as they warmed up. According to lore, Alexander was instead taking a nap. When the phone did ring, it rang instead for "Ol' Pete," as Alexander was known. He quickly tossed a few throws, unaware of the game situation. Starting in, he saw the bases packed and Lazzeri waiting, so he slowed down, saying to himself, *Lazzeri isn't feeling any too good up there. Let him stew.*

Lazzeri had just one hit in seven at-bats off Alexander in their two previous confrontations. Alexander tried a curve, which had stymied Lazzeri in Game 6. Lazzeri didn't bite. But he did on the next one, hitting nothing but air. Worried that Lazzeri might look curve, catcher Bob O'Farrell called for inside heat. That, it turned out, was what Lazzeri was sitting on, and he pounced, crushing the fastball, high and far and . . . hooking . . . foul, by about eight feet. He'd been too eager.

With the count 1–2, Alexander knew Lazzeri would be even more anxious. He also knew he was done throwing fastballs. He spun in a curve, one that started as a strike before tailing off the plate. Lazzeri committed, flailing feebly as the pitch went by.

Alexander shuffled off the mound. After his Houdini-esque escape, he retired the Yankees in order in the eighth, then got Combs and Koenig on meek grounders in the ninth. Ruth was next, and Alexander, afraid of a game-tying homer, nibbled and nibbled until he walked him. With the dangerous Bob Meusel up, Ruth inexplicably took off for second and was caught stealing, a play that Glenn Stout in *Yankees Century* dubbed "easily the worst play ever to end a World Series."

Even the odd, ugly finish couldn't stain the shine on Grover Cleveland Alexander, who was not supposed to play that day and may have been snoring through this taut ball game, but who roused himself and outdueled Tony Lazzeri for perhaps the most famous strikeout in World Series history.

# 6. Lew Burdette slays the mighty Yankees, October 10, 1957, Yankee Stadium

In 1951 the New York Yankees dealt one of many young farmhands to the Braves for a proven veteran. It was a shrewd short-term transaction: Johnny Sain won 31 and saved 38 in his three full seasons with the club. But the long-term price was steep: the kid, Lew Burdette, won 203 regular-season games and three games against the Yankees in the 1957 World Series.

The Yankees had started 1957 as the heaviest favorites ever to win it all, so the oddsmakers must have smiled when they beat Milwaukee Brave ace Warren Spahn in Game 1 and Burdette, a 17-game winner, allowed two runs in the first three innings of Game 2. But then Burdette shut New York down for a 4–2 win and shut them out completely in a 1–0 win in Game 5. He did it with his usual mix of screwballs, sliders, sinkers, and pitches suspected of being spitters. (Red Smith once wrote about Burdette's saliva-drenched reputation, "He is the only pitcher in the big leagues

**For the third time in the Series, and on just two days' rest, Milwaukee's Lew Burdette shuts down the Yankees.**

whose pitching records include three columns: won, lost and relative humidity.")

When Spahn was stricken with the flu and couldn't pitch Game 7, Burdette volunteered to pitch on just two days' rest. On October 10 at Yankee Stadium, New York's 1956 pitching hero Don Larsen was knocked out in Milwaukee's four-run third, while Burdette scattered seven hits (just one for extra bases) and walked only one. By the time he was through, the 30-year-old right-hander was being likened to Christy Mathewson: he had won his third complete game and compiled 24 consecutive scoreless innings, leading Milwaukee to its first World Series crown. It was the first time since 1948 that a team from outside the five boroughs had won a World Series. Even jaded New Yorkers knew they had seen something special, and Yankee fans actually cheered his peerless pitching during the later innings, booed the Yankees for asking to have a ball inspected, and at game's end gave Burdette a lengthy standing ovation.

# 7. Reggie, Reggie, Reggie, May 7, 1995, Madison Square Garden

Want to rile up Knick fans? Just mention Reggie Miller. Forget Michael Jordan — Miller was Public Enemy Number One. It sometimes seemed that Knick fans felt awed, even privileged, to watch Jordan. Never with Miller. "I love being booed," said Miller, who rooted for the bad guy in the movies he watched as a kid. He must have loved New York — this tabloid terror was, until John Rocker, Gotham's most lustily jeered athlete ever.

And no performance cut so deeply as Miller's stunning outburst in the closing seconds of Game 1 of the 1995 Eastern Conference Semifinals. Miller had set the bar high in 1994 by ravaging the Knicks for 25 fourth-quarter points in Game 5 of the Finals while taunting Spike Lee, the front-row stand-in for every rabidly partisan Knick fan. Yet the Knicks responded by beating the Pacers twice to reach the Finals. Miller's attack on May 7, 1995, by contrast, proved the margin of victory as the Pacers held off their nemesis in seven brutal games, bringing the Pat Riley era to an end in New York.

Miller was largely quiet throughout the game, in both scoring and trash-talking, shooting just 5–16, although he contributed 12 additional points from the line. It was center Rik Smits who carried the Pacers, scoring 34 points and holding a hobbled Patrick Ewing to just 11. Still, Smits didn't have what it took to drive the stake through the Knicks' heart, and after he fouled out with 1:40 remaining, New York snatched the lead. With 18.7 seconds to go, the Knicks thought they had the win locked up, 105–99, and the Garden fans were hooting and hollering.

"Realistically, I thought we had no chance," Pacers coach Larry Brown confessed afterwards.

Then Miller time arrived.

Miller got the rock and quickly buried a shot from downtown. Now it was 105–102. During the previous huddle, Brown had reminded his players that the Knicks had frittered away their timeouts (calling three while falling out of bounds

**Devastating the Knicks with eight points in the final seconds isn't enough, so Reggie Miller launches a verbal attack on New York's most vocal Knick fan, Spike Lee.**

with the ball), so on the inbounds play Indiana stepped up the pressure. Under the Knick basket, Anthony Mason looked and looked for an open man. His five seconds were evaporating, so Mason leaned forward, practically falling into the court, his body language betraying his desperation. Miller pounced — Mason's target was Greg Anthony, who ended up on the Garden floor, courtesy of Miller, but the refs were focused on Mason and there was no call. The pass came right to Miller.

Miller wasn't a great villain just because he

could shoot and play dirty — he was also remarkably shrewd, with a maturity the '90s Knicks often lacked. Just eight feet from the basket, he could have driven in and hoped for a dumb foul to accompany his quick bucket. But he knew the surest way to tie the game was to break basketball convention by forgoing an open shot and racing away from the basket. So Miller dribbled to about 24 feet away, out in three-point land. Then he let loose. Bam! Just like that the game was tied, 105–105. In just 3.1 seconds on the game clock, Miller had unleashed the most powerful 1–2 punch the Garden had seen since Ali-Frazier.

"I've never seen 20,000 people shell-shocked," Pacer Mark Jackson, a former St. John's and Knick star, said afterward.

But Miller couldn't be everywhere, and teammate Sam Mitchell nearly undid his magic — thinking Indiana was still down one, Mitchell fouled Knick John Starks to stop the clock with 13.2 seconds left.

Starks choked, missing both free throws. Patrick Ewing grabbed the rebound but missed a short jumper. Okay, so maybe Miller could be everywhere. There he was crashing the boards, about to grab the ball, when Mason fouled him over the back.

Miller went to the line. With every New Yorker wishing him ill, Miller calmly nailed both shots. Barely more than 10 seconds had elapsed since the Pacers got the ball down six points. Now they led 107–105.

As the clock wound down Greg Anthony, in the game only because Derek Harper had been ejected for a foolish scuffle, fell trying to push the ball upcourt. He lay on his back as the buzzer sounded. Miller raced off the court, cursing Spike Lee one last time and yelling that the Knicks were "choke artists." He told NBC the Pacers were looking to sweep and fueled the furor for days by spewing comments like, "The Knicks are the biggest prima donnas I know. They think they're God's gift to basketball." Although those head games didn't do him any good in Game 2 — New York would hold Miller to 10 points and even the series — it was too late. Miller had given Indiana a step up in this series, and they used it to step over the Knicks in seven brutal games.

## 8. Home Run Baker earns his nickname, October 17, 1911, Polo Grounds

Pitching and base running, that's what the 1911 World Series would revolve around — a classic "inside baseball," deadball-era matchup between John McGraw's New York Giants and Connie Mack's defending champion Philadelphia Athletics.

Frank "Bake" Baker proved everyone wrong: the 1911 World Series was about him. Baker's heroic performance defeated New York, pitted Giant against Giant, and earned Baker immortality, along with a new and catchier nickname.

The A's had an impeccable pitching staff, headed by Eddie Plank, Chief Bender, and Jack Coombs, plus a slick-fielding, strong-hitting "$100,000 Infield." Agile first baseman Stuffy McInnis hit .321 in his first full year; superstar second baseman Eddie Collins batted .365 and

## Honorable Mention: Fearsome Foes

**4. Tom Seaver wins his 300th, August 4, 1985, Yankee Stadium**

If there were any justice in the world . . . well, every New York Met fan knows better.

It makes sense to those fans—in a dark and perverse way—that Mets management not only traded Tom Seaver to Cincinnati in his prime for petty personal reasons but also, after bringing him back to finish out his career at Shea Stadium, let him get away again by incompetently failing to protect him in a free agent compensation draft in 1984.

So the man once known as "the Franchise" would not win his 300th game in a New York uniform. But Seaver did the next best thing—he won his 300th in New York, by beating the Yankees.

Just days after Dwight Gooden broke Seaver's Met record of 10 straight wins, Tom Seaver of the Chicago White Sox took the mound. Yankee manager Billy Martin had brashly predicted that his team would knock Seaver out; Phil Rizzuto, about to be overshadowed on Phil Rizzuto Day, declared that Seaver would have to claim his 300th elsewhere.

But number 41, just months shy of 41, was undeterred. He retired nine straight from the fifth through the seventh as Chicago leaped ahead by 4–1. With the crowd—many of them Met fans—cheering him on, Seaver reached back through the mists of time for that something extra that had made him, along with Christy Mathewson and Carl Hubbell, one of the three greatest pitchers in New York history.

With two on and two out in the eighth, slugger Dave Winfield represented the tying run. Seaver set him up perfectly: a curve, then a steady barrage of fastballs, and then, with the count full, a changeup, low and away. Winfield struck out swinging. With two on and two out in the ninth, Seaver did it again, getting Don Baylor to fly harmlessly to left on his 146th pitch of the afternoon. Truly Tom Terrific.

was, with the deft Jack Barry, a devastating double-play combo; and Baker, the third baseman, led the American League with 11 homers. Even then, that was far from overwhelming—the National League had seven guys who hit 11 or more—but the left-handed-hitting Baker also hit .334 and had 14 triples.

The Giants countered with ace hurlers Christy Mathewson and Rube Marquard and an aggressive style that produced a record 347 stolen bases. McGraw's men gleefully sharpened their spikes on the bench before Game 1, hoping to intimidate the A's. The manager also carefully went over how to pitch to the Athletics' dangerous hitters.

The Series started on its projected story line with Mathewson outdueling Bender 2–1. Having heard Baker was spike-shy, McGraw had his men test their opponent immediately. Fred Snodgrass tried stealing third and went in spikes high; Baker blocked the bag but was knocked over by Snodgrass and charged with an error. But Baker also singled in his first at-bat against Matty, scoring Philly's lone run, then added another single.

Game 2 seemed like more of the same, a 1–1 sixth-inning tie. But Marquard, who'd retired 13 straight batters, yielded a double to Eddie Collins. Then he fired a fastball on the inside part of the plate to Baker, leaving it up in his power zone—exactly what McGraw had warned him not to do. Baker turned on it, rifling it into the bleachers for a 3–1 lead, which was how the game ended.

The next day an article ran in the *New York Herald*—and was syndicated in other papers—that lambasted Marquard for his costly mental lapse. "Marquard made a poor pitch to Frank Baker. . . . There was no excuse for it. [We] knew what pitches were difficult for him to hit, and those he could hit for extra bases. Well, Rube threw him the kind of ball that Baker likes."

Sportswriter Jack Wheeler ghostwrote the words, but the byline read Christy Mathewson. Thus, Mathewson bore the responsibility for publicly blasting his teammate. Mathewson was beloved not just for his pitching skills but for his

**Frank Baker shows off the swing that earns him the nickname "Home Run" for his World Series long balls against the Giants.**

pure and gentlemanly college-boy persona, which stood in stark contrast to that of unseemly rough-and-tumble men like Ty Cobb. So the article echoed not just through the Giant clubhouse but through all of baseball. It also focused even greater attention on the next round of Mathewson-Baker matchups.

In Game 3 on October 17 at the Polo Grounds, Mathewson looked superb, allowing just three hits in the first seven innings while holding Baker hitless. The Giants headed into the ninth with a 1–0 lead.

Baker came up with one out. Mathewson knew what to do—after all, he'd attended the same meeting with McGraw that Marquard had been at. Yet this at-bat produced the same result: Mathewson threw a fat pitch the Athletic third baseman "could hit for extra bases," and Baker, proving the bat mightier than the pen, smashed the ball into the right-field stands, tying the game at 1–1.

"Home Run" Baker was born.

But Game 3 wasn't over, and Baker wasn't done.

In the 10th, Snodgrass again tested Baker, sliding into third spikes high, shredding Baker's pants from crotch to knee and cutting him open. Baker held the ball this time.

Baker was also central to the winning 11th-inning rally, following Collins's single with one of his own and later following Collins home for a 3–1 lead. Baker's tally proved decisive as the Giants pushed one run across in their last licks, falling 3–2.

The next day, Mathewson appeared contrite in print while Marquard, ghosted by Fred Menke, lashed back at his teammate in print; the controversy underscored the significance of Baker's blasts, carrying his newfound fame even further. Six days of rain followed, and the downtime ensured that the focus remained on Baker's long balls. He'd hit no more homers in this series, but he contributed two crucial doubles in Philadelphia's Game 4 win and two more hits in the Game 6 rout in which the A's wrapped up the Series.

Baker led all hitters in the Series with his .375 average, nine hits, five RBIs, and seven runs scored. But like Reggie "Mr. October" Jackson, he earned his nickname with the long ball. He'd lead the league in homers again for the next three years without ever hitting more than 12 in a season, prompting some observers in the post-Ruthian era of baseball to scoff at Baker's moniker as a dead ball farce. But as Marquard and Mathewson would have testified, when it comes to home runs, it's all in the timing.

## 9. MJ gets the Double Nickel, March 28, 1995, Madison Square Garden

Okay, so Superman probably couldn't hit the curveball either. No one really cared that Michael Jordan had failed at baseball. The real question in March 1995 was this: after nearly two years away from basketball, could Jordan still soar and score, or would the accumulated rust and the erosion caused by time and age reduce him to a mere mortal? If he came back at age 32 and was good or even great, it would be a disappointment. Michael Jordan had to be unique.

Jordan had shocked the sports world by leaving the game in 1993. In the midst of capturing his third straight NBA crown, he'd endured both a stain on his magnificent marketing image courtesy of his prodigious gambling habits and the death of his father James, who was killed during a robbery. In 1994 he surprised everyone by playing minor league baseball for the Chicago White Sox. After flopping there, Jordan wanted to restore his luster, so in March 1995 he returned to the Bulls. Jordan needed a few games to find himself, going just 7–28 in his initial effort. Fair enough—the first two games, against top contenders Indiana and Orlando, could be written off as an abbreviated preseason. He played better against lesser defenses in Boston and Atlanta, beating the Hawks with 32 points.

It all seemed like a tune-up for Broadway and the true test—the world's media capital, the home of the Bulls' toughest rivals, and the place Jordan loved playing most of all outside Chicago. Jordan thrived in New York, dating back to opening night 1986 when, in his return after a broken foot, he set a scoring mark for an opponent in the new Madison Square Garden by pouring in 50 points.

On March 28, 1995, the Garden did not host a basketball game but an event; to call the tingling buzz a "playoff atmosphere" was to do it injustice. There were 325 press credentials, more than twice the normal amount and far more than the Garden could seat; scalpers asked $1,000 for a $95 ticket, and countless celebrities flocked to the front rows—not just Spike and Woody and other 1990s regulars like Tom Brokaw and Connie Chung, but also Bill Murray, Diane Sawyer, Christopher Reeve, Lawrence Taylor, Itzhak Perlman, and even Earl Monroe.

Packed with Knick rooters, the Garden still cheered Jordan during introductions. "The fans wanted to see him have a great game," Bulls coach Phil Jackson said. "It was like they'd gone to a Broadway show."

With expectations so high, failure was not an option. Jordan staked out his territory early. He was no longer able to leap tall players in a single bound, but he was a more complete player than in his youth and certainly a better, savvier shooter. Seconds into the game, he nailed a jumper over John Starks. The next time down, he taunted Starks, waving the ball around before firing in another bucket. Having set Starks up, Jordan caught a baseline pass, arched his back, rocked back and forth, grooving the game to his own personal rhythm before spinning for a lay-up. He used the same spin the next time but shifted into a fallaway jumper. The Knicks were so flustered that they were called for illegal defense twice in the first five minutes.

*The New Yorker*'s David Remnick wrote that his notes were "a whacked-out mess—a stream of underlinings, exclamation points, hieroglyphs, each centered on another Jordanian amazement."

The Knicks tried six different men on Jordan. No one had an answer. At the end of one quarter, Jordan had 20 points on 9–11 shooting. He went 5–8 in the second, scoring 15 of the Bulls' 19 points.

Jordan tired noticeably in the second half, going 7–18 and scoring just six points in the final 12 minutes—the Bulls even enjoyed their best run when he sat for a breather, building a 99–90 edge. Still, down the stretch, after Patrick Ewing scored eight straight points to close the gap, Chicago turned to Jordan. A jumper made it 107–102; his first assist, on a pass to Scottie Pippen, made it 109–107, and his final two points pushed them to 111–109. He had set a record for the new Garden with 55 points, what Spike Lee would dub "the double nickel."

With 14.6 seconds left, Will Purdue became the second Bulls center to foul out, and New York tied it at 111. Everyone—not just on the floor but in the stands and watching on television in a record-setting audience for an NBA cable telecast—knew the last play would be called for Jordan. But the Bulls' coaching staff warned third-string center Bill Wennington to stay alert: after using single coverage nearly the whole game, the Knicks had begun sending Ewing out to help on Jordan; he'd even rejected one Jordan shot moments earlier.

Jordan let a few seconds tick off the clock, then

**The uniform number is different, but the skills are easy to recognize as Michael Jordan lights up the Garden with 55 points in his return.**

drove hard to the right before cutting so sharply to his left and toward the basket that Starks lost his footing, twisting his ankle. With five seconds left, Jordan went up to shoot, as planned, and Ewing leaped out to help, as expected.

In his early years, Jordan perennially led the league in scoring, but often at the expense of his teammates—disdained as "the Jordanaires"—and the team never won a championship. When Jackson became coach, however, he implemented the team-oriented Triangle Offense, which brought constant motion and more openings for other players. Jordan bought into it, and the Bulls became unbeatable. On this night, with Jackson's encouragement, Jordan had gone back to his free-shooting ways, but with the game on the line, he showed that he remembered not just how to score but how to win. In midair, amid the frenzy, he serenely slithered a pass to Wennington, who dunked. 113–111. For good measure, on the Knicks' final possession Jordan forced Starks to turn the ball over.

After this epic display, Jordan solemnly went to Jackson and deadpanned, "I've decided to quit. What else can I do?"

He didn't quit, of course, and would haunt the Knicks as he led the Bulls to three more championships while awing New Yorkers with more indelible performances. The Garden crowd would expect nothing less.

# 10. Johnny Vander Meer pitches a second straight no-hitter, June 15, 1938, Ebbets Field

It's history times two, doubled, as Johnny Vander Meer pitches lights out with the lights on . . . and with a daffy sentence like that, you just know the victims were the Brooklyn Dodgers. On June 15, 1938, Ebbets Field hosted New York's first pro night game, and the Cincinnati Reds' Vander Meer emblazoned his name in the record books as the only person in history to pitch back-to-back no-hitters.

And to think that Larry MacPhail felt he had to dress up the event with gimmicks. The Dodger president had brought night baseball to Cincinnati while working there, and this year MacPhail had borrowed $100,000 to install lights in Brooklyn. So he loaded up to ensure a sellout crowd.

The bleachers filled up by 6 P.M.; 28,000 of the 38,000 tickets sold were walk-ups, and another 10,000 were turned away. Babe Ruth and former Dodger Babe Herman were on hand. Three bands performed. A rocket shot into the air, and at 8:37, when a switch was flipped, 615 floodlights with 92 million candlepower illuminated the ballpark. It was enough, newspapers boasted, to light 9,000 city blocks. Jesse Owens tried breaking the world record in a long-jump demonstration and ran races with the ballplayers.

Those novelties would have faded to darkness had it not been for Vander Meer, a wild 23-year-old lefty who had nearly been a Dodger. In 1932 NL president John Heydler was making a promotional film to encourage young boys to play baseball. He

**Under the not-so-bright lights at Ebbets Field, Johnny Vander Meer dazzles the crowd with his second straight no-hitter.**

asked the Dodger organization to find "a lad who has a modest background. His people must be middle class, he must be clean cut, religious, and his father should have an industrial background." The Dodgers found Vander Meer, the teenage son of a Dutch immigrant stonemason, pitching in a church league near his home in the New Jersey suburb of Midland Park. Vander Meer didn't impress the Dodger brass during filming, but veteran southpaw Joe Shaute liked the kid and persuaded Brooklyn to give him a shot. After one year in the minors, Vander Meer was released; Shaute, then in the Reds' system, got him signed there. The man who signed Vander Meer in Cincy and later saved him from being released again was, of course, MacPhail.

In his previous start that June, Vander Meer had hurled a no-hitter against Boston; in fact, he'd allowed just one hit in his previous 17 innings. In Brooklyn, 500 friends and family members cheered from the start. By the end, Brooklyn's fans would be rooting too.

The moon rose at 9:16. The game began at 9:23. Cincy's hitters saw just fine under the lights, scoring four in the third and one each in the seventh and eighth, pounding 11 hits in all.

Vander Meer, using a deceptive pump-handle wind-up, had a vicious curve; no defensive gems were required—the closest call came in the first when second basemen Lonnie Frey fielded a grounder that ricocheted off Vander Meer's glove.

In the seventh, the pitcher, who had scattered three walks thus far, started thinking about the no-hitter and promptly walked two men before escaping. In the ninth, Vander Meer completely fell apart. With one down, he walked three straight men before manager Bill McKechnie calmed him down. Vander Meer got Ernie Koy to hit a two-hopper to third. Brooklyn got the runner at home, but Lew Riggs played it so cautiously that there was no chance for a double play.

It was all up to light-hitting Leo Durocher. Vander Meer had allowed fewer than a half-dozen balls out of the infield all night, but Durocher smacked a hard, high line drive . . . hooking . . . foul.

With the count 1–2, Durocher popped to center field for the final out. No other pitcher at that point had ever pitched two no-hitters in a season (Allie Reynolds and Virgil Trucks later would), much less two in a row. Brooklyn fans, quite used to losing, were thrilled to lose in such dramatic fashion. They stormed the field in celebration as the Reds shielded Vander Meer and helped him back to the clubhouse; Vander Meer's parents were trapped for another 15 minutes.

That night MacPhail, who would introduce television to baseball (and vice versa), had proven emphatically that baseball was for real, but it was Vander Meer—on his way to a 119–121 career record—who defied the odds and achieved greatness.

Nine years later, in a quirk of history, Cincinnati's Ewell "the Whip" Blackwell hurled a no-hitter against Boston in mid-June and then took a no-hitter against Brooklyn all the way to the ninth inning. History did not repeat itself, as he finally yielded two singles. That was the closest anyone has ever come to equaling Vander Meer's feat. To break it someone would need three straight no-hitters. Vander Meer's record, like Joe DiMaggio's hitting streak, looms as one of the few truly unbreakable marks in all sports.

## Honorable Mention: Fearsome Foes

**5. Sid Luckman passes for seven TDs on Sid Luckman Day, November 14, 1943, Polo Grounds**

Sid Luckman was the hometown boy made good. Too good. On the day New York celebrated his accomplishments, he paid the city back by beating the home team as it had never been beaten before.

A Brooklyn native, Luckman was Columbia University's star quarterback before going west to Chicago, where he'd already emerged as one of the greatest pro passers, leading his team to two straight championships (one over the Giants). On Sid Luckman Day, he received two $1,000 war bonds in a pregame ceremony, and in the midst of his greatest season—he'd lead the league in yardage and touchdowns—Luckman said thanks by treating the season-high crowd of 56,681 to an astonishing aerial attack.

His first touchdown pass came on the second drive. Then he flung a 54-yard TD bomb at the quarter's end. He also threw a 27-yard touchdown pass on 4th-and-20, a 38-yarder, and three more, ending with a 40-yarder that tied Sammy Baugh's high of seven touchdown passes while setting a new mark with 453 yards passing. The Giants suffered a 56–7 shellacking, but as Luckman departed with five minutes to go their fans stood and cheered him with unapologetic vigor. On his day, he could do no wrong.

"If they had added a broad jump or pole vault to the program he probably would have broken those marks also," the *New York Times* quipped.

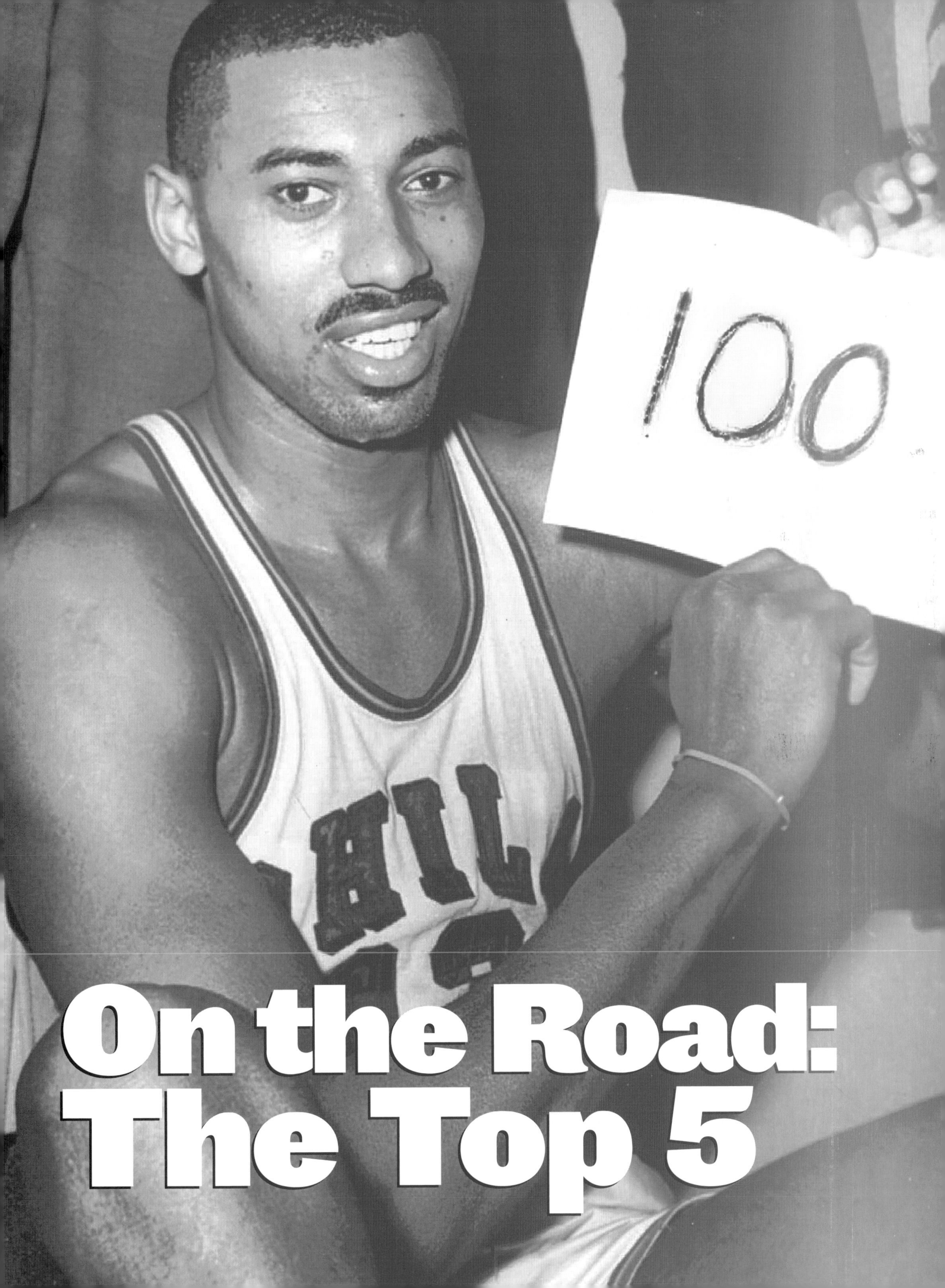


# On the Road: The Top 5

# 1. Wilt reaches the century mark, March 2, 1962, Hershey Sports Arena, Hershey, Pennsylvania

Wilt Chamberlain was out all night with a new lady friend the night before the Philadelphia Warriors game of March 2, 1962. Unconventional perhaps, but certainly not shocking for an NBA star, especially one who would achieve notoriety with his claim of bedding 20,000 women.

But Chamberlain was out in New York, even though the Warriors had a home game scheduled. Unconventional but not atypical: Chamberlain lived in New York, where the nightlife was fine—especially at his popular club, Big Wilt's Smalls Paradise—and where he was a big enough star to be allowed to commute for home games. After all, beginning with his very first NBA game—a 43-point, 28-rebound effort at Madison Square Garden in 1959—Chamberlain had revolutionized pro basketball: by muscularly yet elegantly hoisting the game up above the rim, he'd given the struggling league its first legitimate drawing card and helped it take an important step toward credibility. Although during this overpowering 1961–62 season Philadelphia's home attendance actually declined—as if Chamberlain's constant success was becoming a bore—the long-term impact was pivotal. "I believe Wilt Chamberlain single-handedly saved the league," Oscar Robertson once said.

***Previous page*: The simple piece of paper says it all: basketball's big man, Wilt Chamberlain, has posted the biggest number of all.**

The Warriors' home game was not even in Philadelphia, but at the Hershey Sports Arena 85 miles away. Once more, unconventional yet fairly common—back before the NBA became a billion-dollar business, many teams played "home" games in small arenas outside their city hoping to expand their fan base. The Warriors and New York Knicks were not much of an attraction—to bolster attendance there was a preliminary game between the Harlem Globetrotters and football players from the Philadelphia Eagles and Pittsburgh Steelers. The event still drew just 4,124 people, a number that may well have been inflated.

Hanging out at the Arena beforehand, Chamberlain broke the records on the pinball machines in the penny arcade. Then he went out and dropped in 41 first-half points in a meaningless game against the Knicks. This was perhaps the most predictable element of all—the Knicks were the league's worst team, regular center Phil Jordon was out with a hangover, and "the Big Dipper" had scored 67 (against New York), 65, and 61 points in his three previous games.

But something unconventional and downright unusual was indeed happening: Wilt Chamberlain was hitting his foul shots. Chamberlain was perhaps the world's worst free-throw shooter, so teams often resorted to a rotation of hackers to slow the scoring machine. He came into the game shooting just .506 from the line, and for his career he had a higher field-goal than free-throw percentage. This time, however, Chamberlain was 13 of 14 at the half and would finish 28 of 32 from the line—the most foul shots anyone ever made in one game. Such remarkable success enabled him to set a far grander record.

With a nine-point spurt in the final two minutes of the third quarter, Chamberlain finished the period with 69 points. He held the NBA regulation record of 73 and the overall record of 78, which had come in overtime. With 10:25 to go, Chamberlain tied the first mark; with nearly eight minutes left, he casually tossed in a 20-foot jumper to break the second. Suddenly, a new, more monumental goal seemed within reach—the magical, impossible-sounding 100.

The fans were already chanting, "Give it to Wilt," but with the record broken, Warrior PA man Dave Zinkoff loudly announced the Dipper's point total after each new tally; that, writes Gary Pomerantz in his definitive book *Wilt, 1962,* "intensified everything, the crowd's excitement, the Knicks' dread, the Warriors' curiosity. . . . The game had a new urgency, purpose, and meaning."

Knick star Richie Guerin and coach Eddie Donovan later complained that the game became a farce, especially when the Warriors let the Knicks score uncontested to get the ball back for Chamberlain. But the Knicks, frantic to keep Chamberlain from reaching the century mark, were equally guilty—as the total ascended, they'd pass up good shots to chew up the 24-second clock, quadruple-team the center, and commit mindless fouls to send other Warriors to the line and keep the ball from Chamberlain. The Warriors then retaliated by putting in subs who'd commit fouls of their own to stop the clock.

With 5:30 to go, Chamberlain had 87, but it took until 2:12 to reach 94. With 1:19 left, he dunked for 98. Then he tried too hard—after intercepting an errant pass, Chamberlain missed, then he missed his next. The Warriors got the rebound and got the ball to Chamberlain . . . who missed again.

Finally, with 46 seconds left, Chamberlain leaped in the air, caught an alley-oop, and threw it down. A Dipper Dunk for 100. Play stopped as fans stormed the court in a wild celebration. Chamberlain was so caught up in rejoicing that he later told people the game never resumed, not remembering anything after his last basket. There wasn't much to recall, since he avoided the ball, not wanting to add more points to a number he knew would resonate forever.

The Warriors won 169–147. Chamberlain was 36–63 from the field (the most shots ever attempted and made were also among his records set), while his teammates took only 52 shots. Chamberlain hitched a ride back to New York with several Knicks; two days later in New York, he managed "just" 58 points against them.

At the time, his accomplishment barely penetrated the national consciousness—the Hershey game had not been televised and there was no footage; the New York papers hadn't sent anyone, and neither had the *Philadelphia Inquirer.* The *Inquirer* asked Warrior PR man Harvey Pollack to file a story, as he would for AP and UPI. (*The New York Times* threw Pollack's coverage in with material about a track meet at Madison Square Garden.) Better than anything he wrote was Pollack's visual touch: he scribbled the number "100" on a piece of paper, then had Chamberlain hold it up for a photo that became the lasting memento of a performance that would gradually develop an aura of implausibility. The number on that paper was high, so impossibly high, that only the game's biggest big man could reach it.

## 2. Michael Jordan slices and dices the Knicks, May 17, 1992, Chicago Stadium

In his prime, Michael Jordan could not be stopped. It was just that simple. Sure, he could be bumped, slowed, and even temporarily shackled, but in the end he'd have his way and lead the Chicago Bulls to victory.

Throughout the 1992 Eastern Conference Semifinals, the New York Knicks wore Jordan down, holding him below 40 percent shooting in the fourth quarter. In Game 6, they stifled him, holding him to 9–25 shooting; afterwards he questioned the character of his own team, then, with Scottie Pippen, snuck away from practice without talking to the press. New York seriously thought the Knicks were ready to knock off the defending champions.

But from the opening moments of his first Game 7, Jordan seized control. "Jordan approached the game like a heavyweight boxer seeking a first-round knockout," Clifton Brown wrote in the *New York Times.* "Jordan was playing at a different level than anyone else, making jumpers, spinning left and right on driving moves like a ballet dancer and making the Knicks' head spin."

Jordan piled in 18 first-quarter points and 29 in the opening half, many coming inside the paint to show both friends and foes that the Bulls were not afraid. In that first quarter, when Knick Xavier McDaniel hassled the emotionally brittle Scottie Pippen, Jordan got in McDaniel's face, taking a technical foul just to show that the Bulls would not be intimidated. Pippen responded to Jordan's protection with a triple-double.

In the third, with the Knicks within six points at 63–57, Jordan put back a John Paxson miss, zigged, zagged, and zigged some more for a dizzying lay-up, then stole the inbound pass and, when it was stolen back by John Starks, raced down-court to block McDaniel's lay-up, setting up a back-breaking three-pointer by B. J. Armstrong that finished the Knicks. With Chicago safely en route to a 110–81 wipeout, Jordan left the game with 2:20 left. He'd done enough damage, scoring 42 points on 15–29 shooting.

Jordan had numerous stellar showings against New York, of course. The next year, against a stronger Knick team, Jordan responded to an 0–2 hole and controversy surrounding his late-night gambling excursions with a 54-point effort in Game 4 to even the series. But the 1992 performance was the defining one because it was lethal: in a Game 7, with the Bulls' title defense on the line, Jordan outplayed everyone in sight.

## 3. Babe Ruth displays his prowess . . . on the mound, October 9, 1916, Braves Field, Boston

Babe Ruth is one of the most *underrated* players in baseball history . . . as a pitcher. Celebrated in song and story for his slugging feats, Ruth probably would have reached Cooperstown as the premier left-handed pitcher of his generation even if he'd never hit a homer in his life. In Game 2 of the 1916 World Series, the Brooklyn Robins (as the Dodgers were called during Wilbert Robinson's managerial reign) learned that the hard way.

High off their first modern pennant, Brooklyn ran into the Red Sox. Boston manager Bill Carrigan inexplicably skipped Ruth in the opener, but Boston escaped with a 6–5 win and sent Ruth out in Game 2 hoping to take command of the Series. (The games were played at Braves Field to accommodate larger crowds.)

Ruth was the AL's best hurler, slightly better than the legendary Walter Johnson — Ruth had led the AL in ERA and hits-per-nine-innings and was third in wins (with 23), strikeouts, and innings pitched.

Brooklyn got a cheap run in the first on a ball that was misplayed into an inside-the-park home run, but Boston tied it in the third. After allowing four hits and a walk in the first five innings, Ruth got stronger and stronger — the game would extend until the 14th inning, and over the final six and two-thirds innings Ruth pitched a no-hitter, allowing one measly walk; in all, he pitched 13 straight shutout innings before Boston finally got its second run home on a pinch-hit single that the fans could barely see in the late-afternoon gloom.

The game was acclaimed as an instant classic, and it wasn't until 2005 that another Series game lasted 14 innings. To win that one, however, the Chicago White Sox used nine pitchers for the job Ruth performed by himself in 1916.

## 4. David Ortiz bashes the Yankees twice in 24 hours, October 18, 2004, Fenway Park

Technically speaking, David Ortiz's performance on October 18, 2004, might be the greatest single day any athlete ever experienced. The day began at midnight with Boston and New York still playing Game 4 of the ALCS, which started on October 17.

**Before he was a Yankee slugger, Babe Ruth was a Boston ace, as Brooklyn learned the hard way, over 14 innings in the 1916 World Series.**

With the Yankees on the verge of sweeping the Red Sox, Ortiz, already 7-for-16 in the series, walloped a 12th-inning, walk-off, two-run homer to give the Sox their first win.

Most Red Sox fans believed the team had lived just to die another day . . . later that same day in fact. But Ortiz, who had flourished in Boston after Minnesota let him walk before the 2003 season, made them see it wasn't so.

In Game 5, later on the 18th, Ortiz drove home one run, then scored himself. When the Yankees assumed command and built a 4–2 lead, Ortiz behaved like a true clutch player: in the eighth, after Alex Rodriguez failed to get New York an insurance run, Ortiz led off with a homer to halve Boston's deficit. Inspired, Boston manufactured a run to tie it.

Finally, in the bottom of the 14th, Ortiz came up, with two outs but two on. Down two strikes against Esteban Loaiza, Ortiz fouled off six pitches before hitting a little blooper off his fists into center. This dink of a shot shared one important trait with his long blast from nearly 24 hours earlier — it brought home the winning run. Adding in his

10th-inning walk-off homer to clinch the ALDS, Ortiz had just become the first person to produce three postseason walk-offs in his career.

Ortiz later added a first-inning, two-run blast in Game 7 en route to becoming the MVP for the series; then he kick-started the Red Sox World Series sweep of St. Louis with a three-run shot in the very first inning. For the cheering throngs in Red Sox Nation in that 2004 postseason, there was no question who their daddy was: Big Papi.

## 5. Bird establishes "Larry Legend," May 13, 1984, Boston Garden

Although the Boston Celtics had been a far superior team to the Knicks in 1984, the Knicks had ridden Bernard King's hot hand and forced a seventh game against the Celtics in the second round of the playoffs. But while King had scored at least 40 points in six of the Knicks' first 11 playoff games, there was one player on the court who was even better, and that proved the Knicks' undoing.

Larry Bird had been the 1979–80 Rookie of the Year, but he began his greatest stretch in this 1983–84 season; surrounded by teammates like Robert Parish, Dennis Johnson, and Kevin McHale, he won the first of three straight Most Valuable Player Awards while leading the Celtics to two championships in three years.

The Celtics built their defense around keeping the ball away from King or double- and triple-teaming him when he did touch it. Hounded, King missed his first five shots, while Bird poured in eight points during an early 16–8 run and finished the half with 28 as the Celtics led 67–52.

The Celtics romped 121–104. Bird finished with a career playoff high of 39 points, 15 more than King, essentially the margin of victory. "Larry Legend" also grabbed 12 rebounds—more than any Knick—and dished 10 assists as his outside shooting and savvy passing opened the floor for Parish, who scored 22, and Johnson, who added 21.

Bird's display left him with a higher scoring average for the series than King (30.4 to 29.1), and he finished with more than twice the rebounds. Afterwards, alluding to the as-yet-uncounted regular-season MVP votes and the Madison Square Garden cheers endorsing King, Bird's teammate McHale stated, "New York's MVP won it for the Knicks Friday night in New York, and the NBA's MVP won it for us today." For New Yorkers, it was hard to argue.

# Worst Days
## The 5 Worst Days

## The 5 Worst Days

1. *The Dodgers announce their move, October 8, 1957, Waldorf-Astoria Hotel*
2. *CCNY stars indicted in point-shaving scandal, February 18, 1951*
3. *Ray Chapman is killed by a pitch, August 16, 1920, Polo Grounds*
4. *Benny Paret dies at the hands of Emile Griffith, March 24, 1962, Madison Square Garden*
5. *Baseball loses its first big star, October 14, 1862, Brooklyn*

## The Worst Day on the Road

*The Yankees lose their captain, August 2, 1979, Canton, Ohio*

## More Days to Forget

*Heartbreaking Losses*
*Worst Blunders*
*Losing Ugly*
*Painful Plays*
*Bad Calls*
*Fans in the Game*
*Brawls Outside the Ring*
*Bad Behavior*
*Bad Behavior on the Court: Nasty, Jimbo, and the Brat*
*Billy and the Boss: 20 Classic Bad Behavior Disasters*
*The Antic Antidote: Casey at the Bat and in the Dugout*

# 1. The Dodgers announce their move, October 8, 1957, Waldorf-Astoria Hotel

Knowing in advance that you're going to get stabbed in the heart doesn't make it any less painful.

Brooklynites may not have known all the behind-the-scenes minutiae in Dodger owner Walter O'Malley's schemes, dreams, and negotiations, and they may not have understood that city parks commissioner and power broker Robert Moses deserved nearly as much blame for the Dodgers' departure from Brooklyn, but they had known for some time that news was coming and it would be grim. (And many of the Dodger fans had already fled themselves out to the suburbs, causing the attendance drop that justified O'Malley's decision.) Not only had the press been speculating about the situation, but the New York Giants had already announced their departure for the West Coast, even though they were actually riding the Dodgers' jet stream.

So the news on October 8, 1957, announced at the Waldorf-Astoria by PR men for the Dodgers and the National League in brief statements — O'Malley wasn't even there — was no surprise and, in a way, anticlimactic. The Dodgers' one paragraph was remarkably passive, beginning, "In view of the action of the Los Angeles City Council yesterday . . ." — as if the Dodgers were being pulled out west unwillingly.

Every franchise move has hurt, but this one cut the deepest. The Giants had fans but did not represent New York (the Yankees did that more convincingly) the way the Dodgers did their borough. The football Giants' move to the suburbs was a painful but fitting symbol of the city's dark days in the 1970s, but the Giants sucked so badly and stayed so close to home that it lessened the impact. (The Jets had spent only two decades in the city, so their 1980s move to the 'burbs caused minimal pain.)

But for those who remained loyal to Brooklyn, the day the Dodgers left would live in infamy as the day Brooklyn lost a vital piece of its soul.

**Walter O'Malley looks west for a new stadium and more money.**

## 2. CCNY stars indicted in point-shaving scandal, February 18, 1951

They were barely more than boys, but before they knew it, they were national heroes and local icons—the 1950 CCNY basketball team, a bunch of local kids proving the city game was the best by winning both the NIT and NCAA in one year.

From this highest high they fell, like Icarus, on February 18, 1951, when district attorney Frank Hogan had CCNY stars Ed Warner, Ed Roman, and Alvin Roth apprehended as they came into Penn Station on their return from a road game in Philadelphia. The three were indicted on charges of shaving points for money.

***Facing page*: Alvin Roth, second from left, is one of three CCNY stars busted in the first major wave of the 1951 point-shaving scandal.**

Every sport has gambling woes, especially in New York, America's capital of accumulating capital. Baseball in Gotham had its dark prince, Hal Chase, who probably threw numerous games as a Yankee and, as a Giant in 1919, was quite probably involved with the New York money men who fixed the World Series; John McGraw once tried bribing an umpire; Carl Mays may have slacked off in the 1921 Series; and Giants Jimmy O'Connell and Cozy Dolan were banned in 1924 for suspicious activity. Boxing long seemed corrupt at its mob-infested core, and countless fights aroused suspicion—fighters like Rocky Graziano and Willie Pep were believed to have tanked certain fights, and Jake LaMotta famously took a dive against Billy Fox in 1947.

But this was different. These guys were America's fresh-scrubbed youths and the hope of the city, the living proof that anyone really could make it here. And it was bigger than anyone had possibly imagined.

After the first CCNY arrests—Hogan had already nailed Manhattan College player and fixer Hank Poppe, along with several others in January—the conflagration spread through the city and beyond and even backward in time: at least 32 players from seven schools, including powerhouses like Kentucky, LIU, and Bradley, were implicated in 86 games going back to 1947. When four more CCNY players—Herb Cohen, Norman Mager, Irwin Dambrot, and Floyd Layne—were charged, the entire program was essentially condemned. Then it was revealed that even the championship season had been tainted—at least two regular-season losses were games in which the team shaved too closely—and that assistant coach Bobby Sands may have doctored transcripts to ensure eligibility while coach Nat Holman remained purposefully oblivious and the school turned a blind eye.

Its championships irrevocably tarnished, CCNY suspended its program (Holman nearly lost his job but was ultimately reinstated, albeit with his aura severely diminished); the other local schools banned themselves from Madison Square Garden, which it turned out was the mecca not only of college basketball but of gamblers as well. The NCAA title game never returned.

The players had thrown it all away for a few thousand dollars. Worse, there were no lessons learned. The Ivy League's leading scorer in 1951 was Columbia's Jack Molinas. Three years later, he would be barred from the NBA for gambling, and in 1961, when a new college scandal erupted, Molinas would be at the heart of it.

# 3. Ray Chapman is killed by a pitch, August 16, 1920, Polo Grounds

At the Polo Grounds on August 16, 1920, Yankee pitcher Carl Mays threw the most notorious inside pitch in baseball history.

Chasing Cleveland in the pennant race, the Yankees were trailing 3–0 in the fifth inning when Indian shortstop Ray Chapman came up.

Chapman was, by all accounts, a great guy, a genuine sportsman liked and admired by teammates and opponents, friends and family. Mays was an ill-tempered man who alienated everyone around him, including his teammates. Still, that contrast was merely a coincidence.

Given that Chapman had bunted twice already, it was logical that Mays would pitch him up and in, even though Mays had been so shaken by a teammate's beaning that spring that he'd been pitching inside less than usual.

Given that Mays, the game's only submariner,

sped the ball home with his knuckle scraping the dirt, it was natural that Chapman would have trouble picking the ball up — Mays always finished among the league leaders in hit batters not just because he dusted them but because the ball arrived from such an unusual angle.

Given that penny-pinching owners used as few balls per game as possible and that the one Mays was using was damp from an earlier rain and scuffed from use, it made sense that the pitch sailed a bit, although it was still near the strike zone.

Given how much Chapman crowded the plate, it was not surprising he got hit.

What nobody could anticipate was that this HBP would stand out among the thousands of others in major league baseball history. This one would be fatal.

The ball sped to the plate, and Chapman froze. Safe helmets would not be invented and worn for decades, and the ball smashed into his temple with what sportswriter Fred Lieb called a "sickening thud," then bounced back toward Mays. Thinking Chapman had hit it, Mays scooped it up and threw to first. Then everyone saw, as Mike Sowell wrote in his definitive book, *The Pitch That Killed,* "Chapman sinking slowly to the ground, his face twisted in agony."

**Ray Chapman, beloved by his teammates and community, becomes major league baseball's sole on-field fatality when he's beaned by a fastball in 1920.**

Umpire Tommy Connolly called for medical assistance, but Chapman allayed some of the immediate concerns when he stood and walked on his own toward the center-field clubhouse. Then, near second base, his legs buckled and he had to be helped off.

The game continued, with Cleveland scoring a fourth run in that inning, then holding on to win 4–3. Meanwhile, Chapman was taken to St. Lawrence Hospital, where he fell unconscious, his skull fractured, his brain damaged, his blood clotting, his pulse dropping. At 12:29 A.M., doctors began surgery, which seemed to improve his pulse at least. But at 4:40 A.M., Chapman died, the first, and only, major league player to ever be killed by a pitched ball. (There had been several minor league fatalities.)

Baseball implemented a new policy to introduce new white balls whenever the one in play got scuffed or stained. (Combined with the new rule banning spit and shine balls and Babe Ruth's stunning and immensely popular display of power, the new balls would transform the game by aiding an explosion of home runs.)

During and after the shock and the mourning that followed, controversy swirled as Mays was ostracized and vilified; the Indians and other teams threatened boycotts if he pitched. But while the Yankees skipped his next turn in Cleveland, Mays finished the season leading the AL in wins and innings and would pitch effectively as late as 1926. The Indians called up Joe Sewell to replace Chapman and went on to win their one and only World Series. But the Indians and Mays would be haunted by this one game for the rest of their lives.

## 4. Benny Paret dies at the hands of Emile Griffith, March 24, 1962, Madison Square Garden

Boxing is a sport so drenched in blood-lust that it is only natural that it would be haunted by the specter of death. Still, it's not just the power of a human fist pummeling another man senseless that causes such irrevocable damage. All too often, greed, desperation, or incompetence is central in the tragedy.

New York has seen its fair share of these deaths: heavyweight Ernie Schaaf died in 1933 after a fight with Primo Carnera, largely because he had just endured terrible beatings and a bout of influenza; Willie Claasen died after being beaten by Wilfred Scypion in 1979 because there was no ambulance on hand at Madison Square Garden; and Beethoven Scottland died at the hands of George Jones in 2001 in a fight that underscored the perils of an ineptly run state commission — no doctor visited Scottland's corner after the fourth round, and no one stopped the fight despite ESPN broadcaster Max Kellerman's desperate pleas.

But no fight more starkly depicted the dark forces driving life in the ring than the final fight between Emile Griffith and Benny Paret on March 24, 1962, at the Garden, and none have had ghosts that lingered as long. Paret had lost his welterweight title to Griffith in 1961 but regained it in a controversial split decision later that year. At that bout, Paret made disparaging remarks about Griffith's suspect sexuality. The third fight would be one of the first broadcast live on network television. It would also prove fatal. And it never should have happened.

In December, Paret had tried fighting middleweight champ Gene Fullmer and been thoroughly demolished. Then he had hinted at retirement, but manager Manny Alfaro squeezed him for one last payday. The odds against him were 4–1 — meaning that every betting man knew Fullmer had wrecked him.

But once in the game, Paret played the rivalry to the hilt — at the weigh-in, he called Griffith a "maricon" (homosexual) and mimed humping him. "I'm going to get you and your husband," he sneered. Griffith, who designed ladies' hats, worked in the Garment District, and, despite subsequent denials, seems to have been gay, was outraged. In

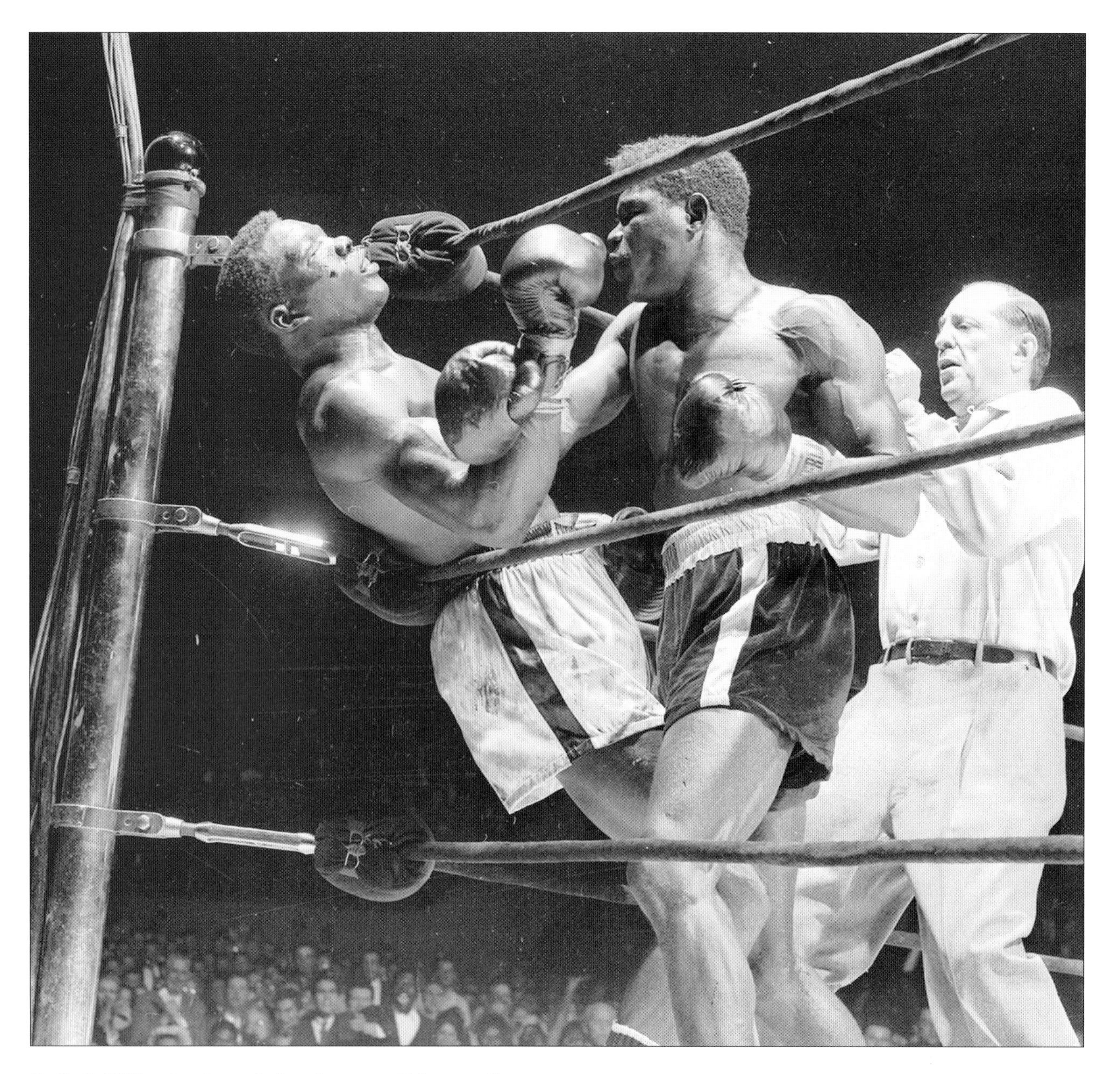

**Emile Griffith unleashes a furious barrage of blows on the helpless Benny Paret, who later dies from the beating.**

1962, and especially in the black and Latino culture and, of course, the world of boxing, this was considered the ultimate insult; being subjected to it in front of everyone was too much.

Paret endured until the 12th round, but when he finally sagged, Griffith unleashed all his fury —punch after punch, about 20 to the head in the space of five seconds, with Paret too weak to defend himself. Ref Ruby Goldstein, often criticized for halting fights too soon, was too slow to stop this one. Paret slid down the ropes, in a coma.

Although the initial attacks were aimed at the respected Goldstein (who retired soon after), attention soon shifted to Alfaro. There were investigations and calls for stricter rules and perhaps federal regulation, as well as cries for the abolition of what critics denounced as a primitive sport. Amid the commotion, Paret died on April 2.

Griffith would go on to fight more main event bouts at the Garden—26—than any other fighter. And boxing went on as always, with substantive changes not coming until more ring deaths 20 years later. Radical fixes, like federal regulation, remain elusive.

# 5. Baseball loses its first big star, October 14, 1862, Brooklyn

James Creighton of the Brooklyn Excelsiors was baseball's first star (helping popularize the sport in the Northeast), the inventor of the fastball (thanks to a then-illegal wrist snap of his underhand delivery), and most likely the first professional ballplayer (paid under the table). In 1862 he also became baseball's first tragic figure.

Against the Bronx-based Morrisiana's Union Club on October 14, Creighton took a huge swing, smashing a home run but rupturing his bladder at the same time. After scoring, he said, "I must have snapped my belt," then collapsed in agony. He died at home on Union Street four days later from internal hemorrhaging. He was not yet 22.

**James Creighton, the sport's and the city's first baseball star, ruptures his bladder while crashing a home run. He dies soon after.**

# The Worst Day on the Road

**The Yankees lose their captain, August 2, 1979, Canton, Ohio**

August 2, 1979, was an off day for the Yankees. Thurman Munson, feeling the years of catching taking their toll on his body, wanted to enjoy himself. Munson loved his family, and he loved to fly. He'd flown his new Cessna Citation home from Chicago to Canton, Ohio, the previous night. Now, after visiting with his family, he was practicing his takeoffs and landings.

But when the novice Munson—who had 516 flying hours but just 33 in this new, powerful plane—lost control of the plane, the most nondescript day on the Yankee calendar became the most unforgettable.

The plane plunged, hit trees, which sheared off the wings, and then slammed into the ground 1,000 feet from the runway, banging hard into a tree stump that damaged the main door on Munson's side. Munson asked his friend Jerry Anderson and instructor David Hall, "Are you guys okay?" then said, "I can't move, I can't move." They tried helping him, but Munson's neck was broken, and he was pinned to the seat. With flames consuming the cabin, they had to flee. The plane exploded in a fiery wreck, killing the soul of the Yankees.

The Yankees cried when they learned that the team's first captain since Lou Gehrig was dead, then broke down again the next day in the clubhouse. They were there to play the Baltimore Orioles—some players requested a postponement, but George Steinbrenner and Munson's widow Diana both said the curmudgeonly catcher would have wanted them to play.

The Stadium's flags flew at half-mast, and when the Yankees took the field, they left Munson's spot behind the plate empty while the message board showed Munson's face and the words, "Our captain and leader has not left us. Today, tomorrow, this year, next, our endeavors will reflect our love and admiration for him." There was supposed to be a moment of silence, but it transformed into an eight-minute, tear-filled ovation with the fans chanting their catcher's name. Then the Yankees played, but without much passion, and lost 1–0.

**When Thurman Munson's plane crashes in 1979, the Yankees lose not only their catcher but their captain and the cantankerous soul of the clubhouse.**

On August 6, Steinbrenner chartered a plane to fly everyone to Canton, Ohio, for the funeral and then back for a game that night. At the airport, they saw the burned-out shell of the plane; at the funeral home, hundreds of fans lined the streets in tribute.

Bobby Murcer, one of Munson's closest friends, delivered one of the eulogies; no longer a regular, he hadn't played since August 1, but he asked Billy Martin if he could start that night's game. On national television, Murcer smashed a three-run, seventh-inning homer and a two-run, ninth-inning single to lead the Yankees from a 4–0 deficit to a 5–4 win. Murcer gave his bat to Diana Munson. To this day, Munson's locker in the Yankee Stadium clubhouse remains empty.

# More Days to Forget

# HEARTBREAKING LOSSES

*Not all losses are created equal, and nothing hurts more than the close game, with everything on the line, that seems filled with high hopes but ends in crushing defeat.*

## 1. The Dodgers lose their shot at the pennant in extra innings on the final day, October 1, 1950, Ebbets Field

The Brooklyn Dodgers clinched the 1949 pennant on the season's final day by beating the Philadelphia Phillies in 10 innings. On October 1, 1950, at Ebbets Field, the Dodgers again met the Phillies on the final day. The game again went 10 innings. But there'd be no joy in Brooklyn this day.

In the final two weeks, the Dodgers had cut a nine-game deficit to just one. A win at home would force a playoff. And in the ninth, with the game tied 1–1, Brooklyn nearly made it happen.

With Cal Abrams on second and Pee Wee Reese on first, Philly shortstop Granny Hamner flashed a pickoff sign. Center fielder Richie Ashburn saw it and snuck in to back up the play, but pitcher Robin Roberts missed the sign and pitched to Duke Snider . . . who smacked a single to center.

With Abrams's speed and Ashburn's weak arm, the game should have ended, but Abrams had leaned back toward second because of the possible pickoff and also took too wide a turn. Meanwhile, Ashburn was in so close that his throw nailed Abrams by 15 feet. With two outs and the bases full, Gil Hodges's blast to deep right-center was caught at the wall.

In the 10th, Don Newcombe yielded two singles. Dick Sisler, son of Hall of Fame hitter George Sisler (the Dodgers' chief scout), lifted a fly to left that carried over Abrams's head and into the seats 348 feet away for a 4–1 Whiz Kid win.

***Previous page*: Dick Sisler's 10th-inning homer on the season's final day gives the Phillies Whiz Kids the 1950 pennant and deprives the Dodgers of their second straight pennant.**

Abrams was the fans' goat, but manager Burt Shotton and third-base coach Milt Stock were fired in the aftermath. To play in a tiebreaking playoff the Dodgers would have to wait till next year.

## 2. Dwight Gooden gives up a homer to Mike Scioscia to derail the Mets' dreams, October 9, 1988, Shea Stadium

Finally! After a disappointing 1987 and a sluggish start to 1988, the Mets finally seemed poised to fulfill their dynastic potential. They'd decimated their competition with a 29–8 stretch run to finish with 100 wins and captured two of the first three in the NLCS from Los Angeles, whom they'd also beaten 10 times in 11 tries during the season.

In the ninth inning of Game 4 on October 9, the Mets had a 4–2 lead, and Dwight Gooden was pitching a three-hitter with eight strikeouts. They were minutes away from a commanding 3–1 lead in games. It was almost World Series time. Ah, but those eggs never did hatch.

Never walk the leadoff hitter. A basic baseball lesson. Gooden, who had never won in five postseason starts, walked John Shelby. Catcher Mike Scioscia—who admittedly had just three homers on the year and no hits on the night—thus represented the tying run. Seconds later, he was indeed the tying run, crossing the plate after he smacked Gooden's first pitch just barely over the wall in right.

With two outs in the 12th, Kirk Gibson homered

off Roger McDowell for a 5–4 L.A. lead. But the Mets, who'd already left two on in the 11th, had more agony in store for their fans, who would watch them take three body blows in their last licks. With two on, Gregg Jeffries failed to bunt the runners over; then, with the bases loaded, ex-Met Jesse Orosco got Darryl Strawberry to meekly pop out. Finally, Orel Hershiser, who had thrown 111 pitches the previous day but volunteered for bullpen duty because Jay Howell had been suspended for scuffing the ball, retired Kevin McReynolds on a weak looper to center.

The Mets were finished, outscored 14–9 as they dropped two of the last three games and handed the pennant to the Dodgers. There'd be no dynasty. There wouldn't even be another playoff appearance for a decade.

## 3. The Knicks fall just short, April 19, 1971, Madison Square Garden

On April 19, 1971, Bill Bradley found himself backed into a corner with the Knicks' dynasty on the line and history against him.

Since the Knicks had edged the Baltimore Bullets in the 1970 playoffs en route to their NBA title, Baltimore's teams had won the World Series and the Super Bowl, two championships that had recently gone to New York at Baltimore's expense. So the Knicks may have been doomed from the start of their rematch with the Bullets in the Eastern Conference Finals.

Still, New York—which always easily handled Milwaukee, the finalist from the West—looked good halfway through Game 7 with a 47–43 lead. Baltimore rallied to grab a 73–68 lead, but the Knicks recaptured the lead again at 88–87 with 2:44 left. It was hold-your-breath time.

Baltimore snuck ahead 93–91, but with three seconds left, Bradley shot from the corner, hoping to tie. At the last second, however, Baltimore center Wes Unseld appeared out of nowhere and got his hand in the way, deflecting the shot and the Knicks' dreams.

"We never thought anyone could beat us at home," Walt Frazier said. "We never had any doubt that we would beat them. . . . When the game was over, the fans were still there, and we were all still on the court, mesmerized. We could not believe that it happened."

## 4. The Jets can't gain that final yard, December 20, 1969, Shea Stadium

At the Janis Joplin concert on December 19, 1969, the Madison Square Garden public address system told her roaring fans, "Miss Joplin would like to dedicate the entire set to the New York Jets for their victory over the Kansas City Chiefs tomorrow."

But the Jets took another piece of Joplin's heart out on a windy, frigid day at Shea Stadium.

In defending their Super Bowl crown New York went 10–4 but they hadn't beaten any clubs better than .500. They were wracked with injuries to key players, including Jim Hudson, Gerry Philbin, and especially Don Maynard, who barely played against the Chiefs.

The Jets still had one perfect opportunity. Trailing 6–3 in the third, the Jets found themselves with first down on Kansas City's 1-yard line thanks to a pass interference call. This was it, the moment when they'd assert themselves and return to the AFL Championship en route to the Super Bowl.

But Matt Snell was jammed up at the one-foot line. Bill Mathis was stopped there too. Joe Namath tried shaking things up with a play-action pass, faking a pitch to Snell and a handoff to Mathis, but linebacker Bobby Bell read it all the way. Namath's pass fell incomplete, and Jim Kearney and Jim Lynch hit him hard, leaving his hand throbbing and his head spinning. The golden opportunity had slipped away.

The Jets settled for a game-tying field goal, but Chief quarterback Len Dawson, aided by the wind at his back, completed a 61-yarder and a 19-yard touchdown pass for a two-play drive. The Jets trailed 13–6. One last drive fell apart as the wind forced Namath's passes down before he was finally intercepted in the Kansas City end zone. The Jets would not reach the postseason again until 1981.

## 5. The Knicks' chances roll off the rim, May 21, 1995, Madison Square Garden

As was so often the case, the Knicks had done everything they'd needed . . . almost. In the 1995 Eastern Conference Semifinals, the defending Eastern champs re-

## Heartbreaking Losses on the Road

**1. Bill Mazeroski homers his way into history, October 13, 1960, Forbes Field, Pittsburgh**

A 7–4 Yankee lead in the eighth inning of Game 7 evaporated when a double-play ball took a bad hop off shortstop Tony Kubek's larynx. Pittsburgh responded with five runs, capped by Hal Smith's three-run homer.

But the big shocker came in the ninth—after the Yankees rallied to tie the game at 9–9, Pirate second baseman Bill Mazeroski slammed Ralph Terry's second pitch for a game-winning, Series-clinching homer.

**2. Mariano Rivera is revealed to be human after all, November 4, 2001, Bank One Ballpark, Phoenix**

With the Yankees on the verge of their fourth straight title—one made more poignant by the recent tragic events in New York and the imminent departure of several aging stars—it all slipped away. Leading Arizona 2–1 in the ninth inning of Game 7, Mariano Rivera, who had 14 straight postseason saves, threw a bunted ball into center field, yielded a game-tying double, hit a batter, then watched a soft flare fall in behind the drawn-in infield as the Diamondbacks' winning run scored.

**3. Red Grange slams down the Giants' hopes, December 17, 1933, Wrigley Field**

Trailing 23–21 against Chicago in the first NFL Championship game, the Giants tried a trick play as time ran out, but just as receiver Red Badgro tried to lateral the ball to Dale Burnett, Chicago's Red Grange wrapped his arms around him, thwarting New York's final hope.

**4. The Knicks come all the way back . . . for naught, April 25, 1951, Edgerton Park Sports Arena, Rochester**

After losing the first three games of their first-ever NBA Finals to Rochester, the Knicks had shocked everyone by winning three straight to force a seventh game. They came back once more, erasing a 14-point deficit to tie the game at 75, but Rochester scored the final four points to end the Knicks' run.

**5. The Rangers get kicked out of the Garden and lose in one of the closest finals ever, April 23, 1950, Olympia Stadium, Detroit**

The Rangers may lead the league in heartbreaking losses—Game 1 of the 1972 finals when they rallied from 5–1 down against Boston for naught, Game 4 of the 1992 Eastern finals when Pittsburgh's Ron Francis snuck a soft 65-footer past Mike Richter, Game 7 of the 1971 semifinals against Chicago when they failed to capitalize on their triple-overtime win in Game 6, or Game 5 in the first round against the Islanders when their hopes of revenge dissipated in overtime—but none was worse than the last game of the 1950 Stanley Cup finals.

Forced to play the entire series on the road because the circus was at Madison Square Garden, the Rangers pushed favored Detroit to a seventh game. But they squandered a 2–0 lead and banged two shots off the post while tied 3–3 in OT before finally falling on a 35-foot shot at the start of the second overtime.

bounded from a 3–1 deficit against the hated Indiana Pacers to force a seventh game at Madison Square Garden on May 21, dug themselves out of a 15-point third-quarter hole, and with the season on the line got the ball in the hands of their leader, Patrick Ewing, who already had 29 points and 14 rebounds.

With his team down 97–95 with two seconds left, the 10-year veteran got the ball near the foul line. Although a step or two deeper than would be ideal, Ewing spun to his left and drove. Indiana's defense evaporated, and Ewing let go of his finger roll just a few feet from the hoop. It was a shot Ewing made almost every time, and he almost made it this time, but the ball hit the back rim and fell away. The series and the season were over, and when coach Pat Riley faxed in his resignation in the aftermath of the loss, an era ended as well.

# WORST BLUNDERS

*Sometimes it's not that the other team outplays your team—it's that someone on your team fails to execute the fundamentals of the game and presents the victory to your opponent on a platter, gift-wrapped, and with a ribbon on top.*

## 1. Fred Merkle fails to reach second base, September 23, 1908, Polo Grounds

The box score recorded a simple force play at second, but history books marked it down as "Merkle's Boner." On September 23, 1908, a crucial Giants win against the Chicago Cubs—and, most likely, the pennant—was taken away when a youngster's naiveté ran into a veteran's savvy.

Two outs, two on. Bottom of the ninth. The score tied 1–1. A single to center, and New York's winning run raced in from third. Nineteen-year-old Fred Merkle, the runner at first, saw the ball fall safely, stopped short of second, and headed for the clubhouse as fans rushed the field.

Players had done that for years, but Cub second baseman Johnny Evers had recently upended custom against Pittsburgh on a similar play by getting the ball and stepping on second. Umpire Hank O'Day ruled against him, refusing to nullify the run, but the resulting controversy prompted O'Day to subsequently acknowledge the argument's legitimacy . . . something Giant manager John McGraw should have warned his players about.

With O'Day umpiring the Giant-Cub game, Evers again called for the ball. Giant pitcher Joe McGinnity grabbed it and heaved it into the surging crowd. But Evers found another ball, and O'Day called Merkle out.

Since it was impossible to clear the field, the game was ruled a tie. The two clubs then finished the season deadlocked and had to replay the Merkle game, which Chicago won to capture the pennant.

## 2. Charles Smith tries, tries, and tries again, without success, June 2, 1993, Madison Square Garden

Losing hurts, but losing games you should have won really stings. And losing games you should have won because you failed to accomplish the most basic

**Fred Merkle never makes it to second base in a crucial game and spends the rest of his life haunted by this "boner," which cost New York the 1908 pennant.**

tasks haunts a team and its fans for a long, long time.

The Knicks' Game 5 loss in the 1993 playoffs against Chicago cut deeply into the club's psyche. Although this game is remembered as the Charles Smith game — the too-soft Knick forward achieved near-Bucknerian goathood for his endgame failures — it really was a team effort in the worst sense.

When Smith failed with the Knicks trailing 95–94, the club had already frittered away this pivotal game. Armed with the league's stingiest defense, the Knicks had won 60 games, earning them home court advantage, which meant that, with the series tied at 2–2, they needed this win to preserve everything they had fought for. And despite Michael Jordan's triple-double, they could have done it, but they choked at the line. The refs generously sent New York to the home stripe 35 times, but the Knicks made just 20 shots. That's 15 points carelessly tossed away. Patrick Ewing missed 6 of 14, and with the Knicks down 95–93 and 52.8 seconds left, Smith missed the first of his two free throws — had he made both, his blunders beneath the hoops would not have been so devastating.

But there Smith was, with 10 seconds left, the Knicks down 95–94, and Ewing tossing him the ball after stumbling in the lane.

Just three feet from the hoop, Smith went up for an easy shot — he should have at least earned a foul. But no, he failed to go strong, and Horace Grant blocked his shot.

Smith retained possession and went up again. Jordan blocked this shot.

Miraculously, Smith got it back, earning a chance at redemption. But Scottie Pippen came from behind and stripped the ball away.

Still, the ball landed back in Smith's hands. One more try. But there was Pippen again, and this time there'd be no recovery. B. J. Armstrong added a basket at the buzzer for a 97–94 final. The home court advantage gone, the Knicks went down for good in Game 6 in Chicago.

"You get the idea Smith could go under there Thursday morning, alone in the Garden, and try to make those shots, and Jordan and Pippen would come out of nowhere and block him again," Mike Lupica wrote. But who was making the Knicks miss all those free throws?

## 3. Strike three does not mean "yer out," October 5, 1941, Ebbets Field

Tommy Henrich flailed at the ball. "Strike three," shouted umpire Larry Goetz.

That was the ball game. The Dodgers had a crucial 4–3 win, evening the 1941 World Series against the Yankees at two games apiece . . . except. . . .

Catcher Mickey Owen had been fooled by Hugh Casey's sharp curve (or spitter). . . .

And had been lazy, stabbing at it instead of blocking it. . . .

And the ball bounded to the backstop. . . .

And Owen couldn't retrieve it as policemen rushed out to keep the fans off the field. . . .

And Henrich ran safely to first. . . .

And Brooklyn manager Leo Durocher froze in the dugout, failing to go out to calm or remove the high-strung Casey. . . .

And Casey unraveled, yielding three hits and a walk. . . .

And the Yankees won 7–4. . . .

And the deflated Dodgers folded the next day. . . .

And New York was again crowned champion.

# Worst Blunders on the Road

**1. Pat Riley lets John Starks fire away, June 22, 1994, the Summit, Houston**

In the fourth quarter of Game 7 of the NBA Finals, Knick coach Pat Riley let John Starks run wild. Despite a 1–8 performance through three periods, the ice-cold Starks chucked up 10 more shots, scoring just once as the Knicks fell just short to Houston. Had Riley replaced Starks with Rolando Blackman or called more plays for Hubert Davis or Patrick Ewing, the Knicks probably would have been 1994 NBA champions. Yet the dream eluded them as Riley, who was something of a control freak, inexplicably stood pat.

**2. Snodgrass, Meyers, Merkle, and Mathewson all blow the World Series, October 10, 1912, Fenway Park, Boston**

The Giants took a 2–1 lead into the last of the 10th inning of the deciding game of the 1912 World Series. Fred Snodgrass earned lasting infamy by muffing an easy fly ball, but then Christy Mathewson walked a man, and first baseman Fred Merkle and catcher Chief Meyers failed to catch Tris Speaker's easy foul pop. Speaker tied the game with a single, and two batters later, Boston finished off New York—ironically, with a sacrifice fly that was one of the few balls cleanly caught in that disastrous inning.

**3. The Giants' defense collapses, blowing the World Series, October 10, 1924, Griffith Stadium, Washington**

History highlights the bad-hop single over rookie Giant third baseman Fred Lindstrom in the 12th inning of the seventh game of the 1924 World Series, but that play only mattered because moments before catcher Hank Gowdy tripped over his mask and missed a pop foul, and shortstop Travis Jackson bobbled an easy roller. So instead of two outs there were two on when Earl McNeely hit a perfect double-play ball to Lindstrom that found a pebble and leaped into left as the winning run scored.

**Heinie Zimmerman and the Giants' infield defense gives away a crucial run and the World Series all in one botched rundown.**

## 4. Jack Chesbro throws away the pennant, October 10, 1904, Hilltop Park

Jack Chesbro won 41 games for the Highlanders (not yet the Yankees) in 1904, but all anyone remembered was one of the last pitches he threw in the last game he lost. On October 10 at Hilltop Park, Chesbro faced off against the Boston Pilgrims (not yet the Red Sox), who had recently overtaken New York for first place. It was the season's final day, and if New York won both games of the doubleheader, they'd win the pennant.

Chesbro was matched up in the opener against Boston's Bill Dinneen, who would later umpire the game when Babe Ruth hit his 60th home run for New York in 1927. But "the Curse of the Bambino" did not yet exist, and it was Chesbro, a Massachusetts native, who blew the 2–2 game in the ninth.

With a runner on third but two outs and two strikes, Chesbro's spitball produced the wildest of wild pitches. The saliva-drenched sphere flew well over catcher Red Kleinow's head and all the way to the backstop as Lou Criger trotted home with the run that clinched the pennant.

## 5. The Giants fail fundamentally, October 15, 1917, Polo Grounds

Good pitching beats good hitting, but bad fielding undermines just about everything. Seeking to force a seventh game against the Chicago White Sox in the 1917 World Series, the Giants made the fourth inning of Game 6 one of the worst ever seen on New York soil.

Third baseman Heinie Zimmerman threw away Eddie Collins's grounder. Man on second.

Outfielder Davey Robertson dropped Joe Jackson's fly ball. First and third.

Hap Felsch tapped back to pitcher Rube Benton, who ran at Collins, chasing him to third. Benton threw to Zimmerman. Collins reversed course.

Had Zimmerman thrown immediately to catcher Bill Rariden, Collins might have been out, but Rariden had meandered too far up the line, and Collins sped past him. Since neither Benton nor first baseman Walter Holke backed up Rariden, home plate was utterly unguarded, leaving Zimmerman in desperate and futile pursuit as Collins scored the game's first run. A dispirited Benton allowed two more runs in the inning as Chicago finished off New York, 4–2.

# LOSING UGLY

*Unlike the heartbreakingly close loss, certain games are so distressing and disgusting that they leave you with a bad taste in your mouth.*

## 1. The Yankees complete their collapse against Boston, October 20, 2004, Yankee Stadium

Perhaps the Yankees should simply have forfeited Game 7. It wouldn't have been worse than what actually transpired. After losing Games 4 and 5 to Boston on David Ortiz's clutch extra-inning walk-off hits and Game 6 to Curt Schilling in his bloody sock, it was obvious that the 2004 Yankees had choked away the ALCS and their final collapse was imminent.

Short on heart and talent, the Yankees strived for mystique, having Bucky Dent throw out the first pitch and forcing the Red Sox owners to sit in Yankee Stadium's Babe Ruth Suite. But there was no delaying the inevitable. Kevin Brown, who'd gone from disappointment to disaster in Game 3, gave up a leadoff hit to Johnny Damon, batting just .103. Even after Damon was thrown out trying to score on Manny Ramirez's single, David Ortiz made sure Yankee fans knew there was no stopping the Sox as he smashed a two-run homer—the first of four Boston bombs, all into the right-field seats, an area called "Ruthville" once upon a time.

When Boston loaded the bases in the second, Joe Torre pulled Brown for Javier Vazquez, who was not used to pitching in relief and entering a jam. Damon, who'd hit two homers off Vazquez on June 29, smacked the first pitch for a grand slam and a 6–0 lead. Two innings later, Damon bounced Vazquez from the game with a two-run blast that made it 8–1. The Yankee crowd was stunned into silence, revived only briefly to cheer when the Yankees scored twice off Pedro Martinez in the seventh and to boo Alex Rodriguez in his four fruitless at-bats. As the Red Sox completed their 10–3 rout, Babe Ruth's ghost finally left Boston, flying west to haunt Barry "Clear and the Cream" Bonds as he headed for homer number 714.

## 2. Evander Holyfield sticks around too long, November 13, 2004, Madison Square Garden

Evander Holyfield was always admired as a fighter with tremendous heart and an indefatigable spirit. But by 2004 that was all the champ seemed to have left. Like so many other greats, he didn't know when to quit. The nadir was his third straight loss, against the undistinguished Larry Donald at the Garden on November 13, 2004, a performance so woeful that Holyfield was put on indefinite medical suspension, which prevented him from fighting anywhere in the United States.

Facing Donald, Holyfield's footwork was nonexistent, and his fists were remarkable only in their sluggishness. He threw the fewest punches he ever had in a 12-round bout, landing just 78 of 264 punches, compared to Donald's 260–643. Only one judge gave the 42-year-old more than one round.

Unfortunately, while everyone else was convinced, Holyfield remained obstinate. In 2005 he took a battery of tests that persuaded the New York State Athletic Commission to lift the medical

**Johnny Damon's grand slam and subsequent two-run homer bury the Yankees early in the crucial Game 7 of the classic 2004 ALCS.**

suspension. Although he remained on administrative suspension in New York State for "poor performance and diminished skills," he was now free to fight elsewhere . . . if anyone would have him.

## 3. The worst loss among so many for Columbia, September 21, 1985, Wien Stadium at Baker Field

With 44 consecutive losses, Columbia's streak of football futility offers plenty of dark days from which to choose. Yet selecting the most dismal is actually easy because the on-field fiasco was followed by a despicable meltdown.

In 1985 new head coach Jim Garrett came to Columbia from the Cleveland Browns determined to inject a new attitude into a team that had lost 11 straight games (back when 11 seemed like a lot). And well into the third quarter of his first game, Garrett seemed a miracle worker as the Lions led Harvard 17–0. That lead, however, only made the way they lost more humiliating. Harvard scored a touchdown on a 15-yard double-reverse: 17–7. Next possession, another on an eight-yard run: 17–14. And another, a 25-yarder: 21–17. Make it four in a row, a 64-yard bomb: 28–17. And so on, and so on . . . in 21 minutes, seven straight possessions and seven straight touchdowns, for a 49–17 trouncing.

Afterwards, Garrett exploded: "They are drug-addicted losers," he said of his players, before singling out Pete Murphy, the senior punter (and perhaps the person least responsible for the devastation, since his three punts in the third quarter, though lacking in style and hang-time, averaged 39 yards each). "The punting killed us," Garrett said. "I just told the squad he'll never kick for me again. . . . I want to see him when he graduates and goes to work downtown on Wall Street and does three things that he did today. See how long he is gonna work for that company, how long Merrill Lynch or Smith Barney is gonna have him around."

There was an immediate backlash from players, fans, the media, and the Columbia administration, all dismayed at both Garrett's overall tone and his public attack on a single player.

Murphy quit the team, which went on to lose every game under Garrett, who was forced to resign at season's end.

## 4. The Saints can't beat anyone . . . except the Jets, December 14, 1980, Shea Stadium

If you didn't know any better, you'd think this was big-time football, not a miserable date with ignominy. After the New Orleans Saints overcame the Jets' 13–7 fourth-quarter lead with a touchdown drive, Richard Todd gave New York the lead back with a dynamic 31-yard touchdown run on a broken play. But Saints quarterback Archie Manning led a 73-yard march, and Tony Galbreath plunged home from the 1-yard line for a 21–20 lead with 4:49 left.

That brief spurt of quality drama could not disguise the game's true identity. On December 14, 1980, playing in arctic conditions at Shea Stadium — 46-mph wind gusts, wind chill below zero, and a light snow that undercut vision, grip, and traction — the New York Jets, winners of just three games on the year, were on the verge of becoming the first team to find a way to lose to 0–14 New Orleans, a team whose fans were wearing bags over their heads, a team so bad they were called the "Aints." Every other team scored at least 22 points against the Saints that season, and that was all it would take the Jets to send New Orleans into its final game still winless.

The Jets couldn't do it. First Todd got sacked twice, and the Jets had to punt the ball away. On their last chance, they moved downfield but failed to get into range as the clock ran out while they sat on the New Orleans 37.

The only bright side was that you couldn't get any lower than losing to the Saints. In the next two years, the Jets rebounded in style, putting together their best seasons since the heyday of Broadway Joe.

## 5. The Yankees plunge to a new low, September 22, 1966, Yankee Stadium

No one would have predicted the Yankees could sink so far, so fast. It had been bad enough in 1965 when the Yankees, winners of five straight AL pennants and 15 pennants in 18 years, fell to sixth for their first trip to the second division since Babe Ruth missed more than a third of the 1925 season. But 1966 would be worse, far worse.

Convinced that the tumble had been a fluke, the Yankees essentially stood pat — the starting lineup in 1966 was virtually identical to the one from the glory days of 1964. But those players were two years older and aging fast. Early on, general manager Ralph Houk fired skipper Johnny Keane — whom the players loathed — but nothing could right this ship. The Yankees would finish dead last for the first time since 1912, 26½ games out of first, while the Mets — last in the NL

# Losing Ugly on the Road

**1. The Giants get routed by the coach who got away, December 31, 1961, City Stadium, Green Bay**

In the 1950s the Giants' innovative offensive coordinator wanted nothing more than to become head coach for his hometown team, but when the Mara family failed to give him that opportunity, he headed west, where he resurrected the lowly Green Bay franchise. In 1961 Vince Lombardi got revenge against New York, thrashing the Giants in the NFL Championship with 24 second-quarter points in a humiliating 37–0 rout.

**2. Everything goes wrong for Brooklyn, October 10, 1920, Dunn Field, Cleveland**

Murphy's Law was born in Game 5 of the 1920 World Series when everything went wrong for Brooklyn's pitchers: starter Burleigh Grimes yielded the first World Series grand slam (to Elmer Smith) and the first Series homer hit by a pitcher (Jim Bagby) and also hit into a double play; his reliever, Clarence Mitchell, hit into what remains the only unassisted triple play in Series history (turned by second baseman Bill Wambsganss) and then hit into a double play as well. The pitchers made seven outs in three at-bats while losing 8–1.

**3. The Yankees' big-game pitcher gives up some big numbers, November 3, 2001, Bank One Ballpark, Phoenix**

The Yankees had won three straight games in dramatic fashion and hoped to clinch the World Series in Game 6, but what they didn't know was that their most battle-tested and trusted big-game starter, Andy Pettitte, was tipping his pitches. Arizona knew, however, and they struck for a run in the first and three in the second. Reliever Jay Witasick was even worse, yielding eight runs, and New York trailed 15–0 after four. Worse, thanks to the huge lead, Arizona starter Randy Johnson was able to leave early, a move that gave him just enough energy to pitch in relief the next day as the Diamondbacks finished off New York.

**4. Armando Benitez and Kenny Rogers give away the NLCS, October 19, 1999, Turner Field, Atlanta**

One year after watching their team lose five straight games to choke away the wild card, Met fans watched an amazing comeback crumble at the hands of two tentative pitchers. Down 3–0 in games, New York rallied to force a Game 6; then they recovered from a 5–0 first-inning deficit to tie the game. But when they took a 9–8 lead in the 10th, Armando Benitez showed he couldn't handle the pressure, issuing a walk and two hits to send the game to the 11th. In that inning, Kenny Rogers, who had previously been run out of New York by Yankee fans for his dismal performance in the spotlight, folded. After a double and a bunt, he walked two men intentionally; then, with the bases loaded, he nibbled at the strike zone, afraid to challenge Andruw Jones. His sixth pitch was *way* out of the strike zone, committing baseball's unforgivable sin: walking in the winning run.

**5. The Giants stop clawing and fall apart completely, October 26, 1911, Shibe Park, Philadelphia**

In a tight Series, the Giants had been outscored only 14–11 and knew that if they could win Game 6 they'd play the deciding game at home. But after a first-inning run, the Giants fell quickly into the red. With two men on, pitcher Red Ames fielded a sacrifice bunt, but his throw ricocheted off the batter. Right fielder Red Murray chased the ball but heaved it past everyone to the other foul line. There, left fielder Josh Devore fell trying to retrieve it. The result: a three-run bunt "homer." The Giants made a bad situation worse by allowing seven runs in the seventh, falling 13–2.

**6. Sam Huff rubs it in, November 27, 1966, Griffith Stadium, Washington**

When the insecure and offensive-minded Giant coach Allie Sherman broke up the team's vaunted defense by trading stars like Cliff Livingston, Dick Modzelewski, and Sam Huff, both the fans and the players were furious. As the once-great team collapsed the fans taunted Sherman by yelling, "Huff-Huff-Huff-Huff." Two years after the trade, Huff got his own revenge. The Redskins were crushing the Giants, 69–41, and running out the clock, but with just seconds left, Huff grabbed the reins, calling time out and sending the field goal unit out. The 72-point total remains the most the Giants' defense has ever allowed. "A linebacker is the one guy you don't want to get angry," Huff said nearly four decades later, still seething.

with a worse record—would outdraw the Yankees 1.9 million to 1.1 million.

The low came in September. The club fell into the cellar for good on the 18th with a 10-inning loss to first-place Minnesota as Mickey Mantle finished his season by striking out for the 1,500th time (the first player to achieve that dubious feat). The next day Dan Topping severed another link to the past when he resigned as president; the overwhelmed Michael Burke took over.

On September 22, after three days of rain, the Yankees returned to action against Chicago. Yes, it was a weekday afternoon, and yes, it was drizzly, so a small turnout was to be expected, but there's low and then there's low, and on this day the Yankees plummeted to new depths when only 413 people turned out. That is not a typo: the vast expanse of Yankee Stadium held just 413 fans. (Chicago's share of the gate receipts was a meager $101.51.)

Legendary broadcaster Red Barber asked his director to pan the empty seats, but a suit named Perry Smith vetoed the request and cropped all shots—the camera could not even follow foul balls into the stands. Barber told his audience that the game featured "the smallest crowd in the history of the Stadium. And that smallest crowd is the story, not the ball game." For this honest reporting, Burke fired Barber four days later.

On the field that day, a win would have pulled the Yankees even with the lowly Senators, but the Bombers fired duds, managing only one run on 10 hits as they left 12 on base. Trailing 4–1 in the ninth, they had the bases loaded, but Joe Pepitone struck out. There was no joy in the Bronx that day, but worse, no one really noticed.

## Losing Ugly on the Road (CONTINUED)

**7. The Jets get another shellacking up in New England, September 9, 1979, Foxboro Stadium**

In the worst Jet loss ever, they fumbled three balls away and endured three interceptions and seven sacks. New England outgained them 597 yards to 134 and outscored them 56–3. It would have been far worse, but fortunately the Patriots removed several regulars in the third quarter, including quarterback Steve Grogan after his fifth touchdown pass.

**8. The Rangers lose 15–0, January 23, 1944, Olympia Stadium, Detroit**

"We've got nothing to hope for this season except for it to end," Rangers general manager Lester Patrick said on January 22, 1944, about a season in which the Rangers would go 6–44 while many of their best players served in World War II. The next night their stand-in goalie, Ken McAuley, proved his point, turning a 2–0 first-period game into a 15–0 rout, the biggest shutout in NHL history.

**9. The Knicks reach a new low, December 25, 1960, Onondaga War Memorial, Syracuse**

From 1956–57 through 1965–66, the Knicks were the league's laughingstock, compiling a .379 winning percentage. Their Christmas 1960 loss to Syracuse summed it all up as they fell 162–100. It was then the worst NBA rout (there has been one 63-point blowout since) and remains the Knicks' worst loss ever.

**10. The Mets lose their 120th, September 30, 1962, Wrigley Field, Chicago**

The 1962 Mets were a seasonlong mishap. They'd gotten stuck in a hotel elevator the day before their first game. In their first inning of play, their pitcher balked home a run. In their home opener, the PA announcer gave the wrong lineup. They were nine and a half games out after just nine games and were—get this—mathematically eliminated on August 10. So it was fitting that their record 120th loss on the season's final day ended as it did. Trailing 5–1 in the eighth, the Mets got two men on with nobody out, but Joe Pignatano, in what would also be his final big league at-bat, hit the ball right to Chicago second baseman Ken Hubbs, who snagged it on a fly to start a triple play, the ultimate symbol of futility. Perfect.

**Joe Namath's final season in New York is a grim affair, ending in a horrible 42–3 rout.**

## 6. The Knicks quit on the court, January 21, 2002, Madison Square Garden

It's one thing to lose. It's another thing to be a bunch of losers. And by quitting on the court at Madison Square Garden on January 21, 2002, the Knicks showed themselves to be just that.

New coach Don Chaney hoped that the Knicks, dragging a seven-game skid behind them, could right themselves against the 18–21 Charlotte Hornets. Instead, New York made them look like the Boston Celtics of the Bill Russell era.

With the exception of one Charlotte hot streak, the Knicks actually outscored the Hornets 19–17 in the first quarter . . . but that streak was a 22–0 run that put the game permanently out of reach. Down 20, the Knicks just seemed to fold. As boos rained down from the Garden crowd, they turned that 20-point first-quarter deficit into a 60–33 halftime hole. The second half was worse: the Hornets built their lead to 92–51 after three. They could have run it up even higher had they tried, since the Knicks shot just 30 percent from the floor. Even Latrell Sprewell, whose middle name seemed to be "Fight" (in both the best and worst sense of the word), looked sapped of spirit, going 0–9 with four of those shots being blocked.

The loss gave the Knicks their longest losing streak since 1986, and the final score, 111–68, was the most lopsided home loss in Knick history. "They threw in the towel," Chaney said. "They gave up."

## 7. Joe Namath ends on an ugly note, December 12, 1976, Shea Stadium

In 1976 Joe Namath was not the Joe Namath of old. His knees were shot, his buddies were gone—new coach Lou Holtz had brought in 25 new players—and his team was wretched, scoring just 169 points while fumbling 44 times and mustering just 16 sacks. It would have been nice if the greatest football star the city had ever known could have gone out in a blaze of glory, but in that awful year, in that dismal era, it was simply too much to ask.

The only teams the Jets beat that year were the 2–12 Buffalo Bills (twice) and the hapless 0–14 Tampa Bay Buccaneers. For the finale on December 12, however, the Jets faced the Cincinnati Bengals, owners of the league's sixth-best offense and the conference's third-best defense. Namath's last game was the antithesis of his greatest moments —a hopeless cause in which the Jets managed only to perform even worse than expected.

Total attendance: 31,067, the smallest home crowd in Namath's career.

Total offensive yards: 72, a club record for futility.

Total first downs: 6, another negative team mark.

Namath's line: 4–15 for 28 yards, and four first-half interceptions before being replaced by rookie Richard Todd.

Final score: 42–3.

## 8. Phil Watson burns out the Blueshirts, February 15, 1959, Madison Square Garden

Phil Watson knew what it took to win—he had been a key player on the last Rangers championship team back in 1940—but he didn't know how to convey that to his players. Watson became the Rangers coach in 1955, and by 1959, after three years of losing in the first round of the playoffs, the martinet, after feuding in the press with goalie Louie Worsley and always riding his players too hard, had alienated the entire team.

On February 15, 1959, soon after a six-game losing streak that threatened their playoff hopes, the Rangers looked lost as Montreal hammered them 5–1. Watson pulled his players back out of the locker room afterwards for an extra practice. Well, not practice exactly. Torture and humiliation was more like it—in front of their foes and the remaining Garden fans, Watson forced his men to skate wind sprint after wind sprint. Disgusted, the team lost its will and won just five times in the last 20 games, falling from the playoff picture on the season's last day. They would not return to the postseason until 1966.

## 9. The Titans go down disastrously, September 17, 1960, Polo Grounds

Even before they spelled their name J-E-T-S, the Jets made a specialty out of agonizing defeats. In just their second game ever, the team then known as the Titans led the Boston Patriots 24–7 after three quarters. Boston scored twice in the fourth, but with seven seconds left, the Titans led 24–21 and simply had to run out the clock with one last play.

Coach Sammy Baugh elected to punt, but Rick Sapienza—who had been released by the Patriots after trying out at halfback, not punter—looked up at the defense and the snap bounced off his hands. He bent to pick it up and accidentally kicked it away, like a Keystone Cop slapstick artist. About a half-dozen players gave chase, grasping unsuccessfully at the bounding ball before Boston's Chuck Shonta scooped it up at the Titan 25 and raced for a game-winning touchdown.

Titans owner Harry Wismer publicly lambasted Baugh's decision to punt but also filed a protest with the league, claiming that since the Patriots' players, like Sapienza, had inadvertently kicked the ball while reaching for it, the play should have been dead. AFL officials supervisor Bob Austin reviewed the film and agreed, saying the double infraction should have produced a do-over down. Commissioner Joe Foss said that Austin was right, but that if this new league started off by changing games after the fact, they'd lose credibility. The loss stood.

Sapienza, meanwhile, was released that Wednesday. He returned home to North Attleboro, Massachusetts, where he reportedly made

**Phil Watson has his Rangers smiling in his early years as coach, but by 1959 the players and their martinet of a ruler are dragging each other down.**

more money playing semipro ball (while working as a teacher and coach) than he would have playing for the financially shaky Titans.

## 10. The Yankees lose 22–0, August 31, 2004, Yankee Stadium

The *Daily News* headline said it all: "Stinkees." In the midst of a heated pennant race with archrival Boston, the Yankees embarrassed themselves . . . badly. You could say they played the worst game in their history, but it hardly seemed as if they played. Cleveland spanked them repeatedly in a 22–0 humiliation, the most lopsided shutout in baseball since 1900.

The Yankees starters had just one win in the past 16 games, and Javier Vazquez gave up a bases-loaded triple in the first and three hits and a walk in the second. But Tanyon Sturtze also seemed to have been hired by the Indians for batting practice purposes — he gave up three in the third and three more in the fifth, leaving with a man on — whom C. J. Nitkowski graciously allowed to score as well.

Nitkowski was charged with three more runs by the end of the sixth. Meanwhile, former Yankee farmhand Jake Westbrook allowed no hits through four and just five hits overall.

Trailing 16–0, the Yankees turned to Esteban Loaiza, who managed to strand two runners in the seventh and two runners in the eighth. His good fortune vanished in the ninth, the most horrific of innings, when the Indians twice more put two men on. This time Loaiza surrendered two three-run homers as the Yankees sank 22–0.

George Steinbrenner went into motivator mode, trotting out platitudes like "Quitters never win, and winners never quit," but while the Yankees managed to stave off the Red Sox and win another pennant, this game presaged their historic postseason choke.

# PAINFUL PLAYS

## 1. Mickey Mantle twists his knee, October 5, 1951, Yankee Stadium

Willie Mays was handed the keys to center field as soon as he arrived in New York in 1951. But Mickey Mantle, a rookie that same year, found himself shuttled off to right because the Yankees already had a center fielder, a guy by the name of Joe DiMaggio. The move nearly crippled Mantle.

In Game 2 of the World Series, Mays lifted an easy fly to right-center. Mantle hustled over, but DiMaggio, though old, slow, and nearly done, still ruled the field and called the kid off. Mantle was within 10 feet of DiMaggio and stopped short, catching his cleat on a drain cover hidden in the grass. Mantle crumpled to the ground, his cartilage torn, his season done.

Already plagued by osteomyelitis and not disciplined enough to stick with his postsurgery physical therapy, Mantle permanently lost some of his speed and durability. He would be plagued by pain in virtually every game in his long career.

**As Joe DiMaggio camps under a routine fly ball, Mickey Mantle takes one wrong step and goes down with a devastating knee injury.**

## 2. Frank Gifford gets knocked out, November 20, 1960, Yankee Stadium

On November 20, 1960, Frank Gifford, the fleet-footed golden boy of the New York Giants, caught a pass over the middle at Yankee Stadium. It was nearly the last pass he ever caught.

Gifford was a symbol for all that was great and glamorous about New York and its football team—which had reached the championship three times in four years—while Chuck Bednarik, a gritty, hard-hitting linebacker for the Philadelphia Eagles, a team that was having its first good season in years, was the antithesis.

Bednarik slammed Gifford from the blind side, and Gifford, seeing him at the last second, tried a quick move that left him off-balance. He crumpled to the ground, fumbling the ball. When the Eagles recovered his fumble, Bednarik pumped his fist in celebration—which made him look like a ruthless villain given that Gifford was lying on the ground with a deep brain concussion and an injured leg. Gifford looked, according to Fredrick Exley's brilliant book *A Fan's Notes*, "like a small, broken, blue-and-silver manikin."

Gifford came to in the locker room, lying next to a security guard who'd just died of a heart attack. When Gifford's wife Maxine, who was outside the room, heard people talking about the tragic death, she thought it was her husband who was dead.

Bednarik actually sent Gifford a telegram, a get-well card, flowers, and a basket of fruit in the hospital, but he milked the role of bad guy on the rubber chicken circuit—unjustifiably, Gifford believed, since it was a clean hit—making this a career-defining play for both men. The Giants had come into the game 5–1–1, the Eagles 6–1. With Gifford out, the Giants stumbled to their worst finish since 1955, while the Eagles won the NFL crown. Gifford announced his retirement, although he'd return as a flanker in 1962, becoming the first Pro Bowler at three positions and the Comeback Player of the Year.

## 3. Dennis Potvin draws the ire of Ranger fans, February 24, 1979, Madison Square Garden

"Potvin sucks!"

It's a sound that after three-plus decades still echoes down from the blue seats no matter who is playing at Madison Square Garden—the chant has been known to burst out even at Knick games. And yet, the reality is that Denis Potvin was probably not to blame for Ulf Nilsson's broken ankle, suffered after the Islander defenseman checked him in the corner on February 24, 1979.

Nilsson, a newcomer helping spark the Rangers with 27 goals and 66 points, said later that his foot simply got stuck in the ice and Potvin didn't do anything wrong. Still, try explaining that to fans who saw the Rangers' season end with a finals loss and then watched Nilsson play without any of his former pizzazz in subsequent seasons while the Islanders won four Stanley Cups in a row. Their answer, in all likelihood, would still be "Potvin sucks!"

## 4. Pete Reiser crashes into yet another wall, June 4, 1947, Ebbets Field

Brooklyn's Pete Reiser ran into outfield walls more often and faster than anyone else. This habit shortened his career, and on June 4, 1947, it nearly got him killed.

Chasing a blast to deep center, Reiser forgot the Dodgers had shortened Ebbets Field's fence from 420 to 390 feet. Catching the ball midstride, he smashed full speed and head-first into the concrete wall. While Reiser was carried off on a stretcher—one of 11 such trips overall—the umpire pulled the ball out of his glove and signaled an out. (Left fielder Gene Hermanski later admitted that Reiser had dropped the ball and he'd stuck it back in.)

In the clubhouse, the doctor called for a priest, who gave the unconscious player last rites. Reiser came to, but quickly collapsed again. He woke up in the hospital and was paralyzed for over a week. After the season, Brooklyn padded the walls with one-inch foam, but it was too late: Reiser's career was ruined—after ringing up 457 at-bats annually and a .312 average for four years despite his assorted crashes, Reiser managed only 122 at-bats a year in his last five seasons, hitting just .246.

# Painful Plays on the Road

**1. Bernard King goes down in a heap, March 23, 1985, Kansas City**

Bernard King was leading the NBA with a 32.8 scoring average when he tore cartilage and the anterior cruciate ligament in his right knee while trying to stop Kansas City's Reggie Theus from driving past him in a meaningless regular-season game. After losing their leading man, the Knicks lost their last 12 games but got a 7' consolation prize in number-one draft pick Patrick Ewing. Then, after King rehabbed for two years, the Knicks let him walk away, only to spend the entire Ewing era vainly searching for a second scorer while King became an All-Star, scoring as many as 28.4 points per game.

**2. Joe Namath fails to make it out of preseason, August 7, 1971, Tampa**

After leading the Jets to the Super Bowl and then in the 1969 playoffs, Namath missed the last nine games of 1970 with a fractured wrist, and the Jets sagged to 4–10.

Namath's comeback was cut short in 1971 when, in a meaningless exhibition game in Tampa, he went for a tackle after a fumble. The cruciate and medial ligaments and cartilage in his left knee were all shredded on the play, and he suffered nerve damage down to his foot. Namath would return by midseason . . . but he would never be the same.

**3. Pete Reiser smashes up, July 19, 1942, Sportsman's Park, St. Louis**

On July 19, 1942, Brooklyn led the NL by eight games thanks to Pistol Pete Reiser's .380 average. But when the speedy and reckless center fielder chased a long blast by St. Louis's Enos Slaughter straight into the Sportsman's Park wall, he fractured his skull for his third severe concussion within a year. Still, manager Leo Durocher and president Larry MacPhail soon coaxed Reiser back onto the bench and into action. As a pinch hitter in Pittsburgh, Reiser smashed a hit but collapsed again rounding first. After recovering, he was rushed back into action once more, but dizziness, double vision, and tentativeness caused him to misplay fly balls, while his average plummeted by 70 points. Without a healthy Reiser, Brooklyn collapsed and lost the pennant to St. Louis by two games. Without proper care, Reiser never fulfilled his potential.

**4. Y. A. Tittle sags, a model of pain and suffering, September 20, 1964, Pitt Stadium, Pittsburgh**

In the second quarter of the second game of the 1964 season, quarterback Y. A. Tittle, the Giants' biggest star, saw Pittsburgh's 270-pound defensive end John Baker closing fast. Having just been sacked by Baker, Tittle hurried his pass, which was picked off. But Tittle never saw that as Baker smashed him so hard that his helmet popped off. Tittle had a concussion and bruised ribs; rocking on his haunches, he was too stunned to rise, his bald, bloodied head filled with cobwebs.

*Pittsburgh Post-Gazette* photographer Morris Berman captured the moment, and though his editors didn't even use it, the image became a football classic. It also symbolized the demise of the Giants. When Tittle returned two weeks later, he had lost his touch, and the Giants fell from 11–3 to 2–10–2. Years of lousy football had begun.

**5. Mike Cameron and Carlos Beltran collide, August 11, 2005, Petco Park, San Diego**

Gold Glove center fielder Mike Cameron grudgingly moved to right field to accommodate high-priced free agent Carlos Beltran, but he let it be known that he would play like a center fielder, going for everything he could reach. On August 11, both Cameron and Beltran went all-out for a short fly, racing at top speed, then diving for the ball. They smashed head-on. Beltran hobbled off the field with assistance, having suffered a concussion and a broken bone in his face. He was the lucky one. Cameron lay prone, blood oozing from his mouth, for 10 minutes before being carried off on a stretcher. He was hospitalized for six days with broken bones in his nose, cheek, and orbital socket, along with a concussion. In the aftermath, he lost 11 pounds and suffered headaches and blurry vision. His season was over.

## 5. Freddie Fitzsimmons takes one on the knee, October 4, 1941, Ebbets Field

In their first Subway Series in 1941, the Dodgers appeared every bit the Yankees' equal, and with the Series at 1–1, Game 3 was tied 0–0 in the seventh inning. Then Brooklyn's luck ran out.

Yankee pitcher Marius Russo rapped a line drive up the middle and off pitcher Freddie Fitzsimmons's kneecap. Astonishingly, the ball ricocheted high in the air and was caught for an out, but Fitzsimmons's kneecap was chipped and his season ended... as were the Dodgers after reliever Hugh Casey gave up two runs in the eighth, then came in the next day and threw a third strike that Mickey Owen famously failed to catch. Fitzsimmons later developed arthritis in that knee as a result of the injury.

## 6. Jean Ratelle is nailed by friendly fire, February 29, 1972, Madison Square Garden

The 1971–72 Rangers looked like Stanley Cup champions. They had a great defenseman in Brad Park, and they had the unstoppable goal-a-game line of Jean Ratelle, Vic Hadfield, and Rod Gilbert. Then their season was undermined by friendly fire.

On February 29, Ranger Dale Rolfe smacked a hard shot that never reached the net, smashing instead into the ankle of the league's leading scorer, Ratelle. He had lifted his skate to get it out of the way but instead put it right in the puck's path, and his ankle was broken. Ratelle missed six weeks, and though he came back for the NHL finals against Boston, he was out of playing shape and the Rangers lost in six games.

## Painful Plays: A New York Welcome

**1. Bump Hadley ends Mickey Cochrane's career, May 25, 1937, Yankee Stadium**

Mickey Cochrane was widely considered the greatest catcher of his time, but his time ended too soon when he became the most famous ballplayer ever to have his career ended by a bean ball. On May 25, 1937, at Yankee Stadium, Detroit's player-manager, a two-time MVP with a .320 lifetime average, homered off New York's Bump Hadley to break a 1–1 tie in the third. When Cochrane batted again in the fifth, Hadley fired a fastball that sailed up and in. Cochrane lost it in the shadows, and the pitch fractured his skull in three places. He lay in a coma for 10 days. Upon recovering, he acquitted Hadley of any blame but retired immediately and was bothered afterwards by headaches and night sweats. A year later, the Tigers fired him as manager.

**2. It's all fun and games until someone gets hit in the eye, April 28, 1974, Madison Square Garden**

Barry Ashbee played the 1973–74 season in constant pain from a pinched nerve in his neck and a chipped vertebrae, yet he was still a second-team All-Star for the Philadelphia Flyers. Then, in the overtime of Game 4 of the playoffs against the Rangers, Ashbee suffered an injury from which there'd be no recovery—New York's Dale Rolfe fired off a shot that accidentally hit Ashbee right in the eye, badly damaging his retina, permanently harming his vision, and ending his career.

**Pete Reiser's great hitting is undone by his penchant for running headfirst into walls.**

## 7. Without Rusty, the Mets have no one to lend a hand, June 3, 1972, Shea Stadium

On April 5, 1972, the Mets, realizing they were one big bat shy of contending for a pennant, traded Ken Singleton, Mike Jorgensen, and Tim Foli to Montreal for Rusty Staub, a three-time .300 hitter who had averaged 26 homers and 90 RBIs over the previous three years. "Le Grande Orange" immediately proved his worth.

By June, Staub was hitting .313 with a .395 on-base percentage, seven homers, and 27 RBIs. The Mets, armed with Tom Seaver and rookie Jon Matlack, were in first place by five games with a dazzling 31–12 record. But on June 3, Atlanta's George Stone hit Staub with a pitch, breaking bones in his hand. Staub, who'd only missed seven games in the previous four seasons, tried playing through the pain, but his average and productivity plunged . . . as did the Mets. On June 18, Staub had to leave the game. That day the Mets slipped from the top spot. By the time Staub returned in mid-September, the Mets, who had no one else who managed to finish with more than 17 homers or 52 RBIs, were out of the running, their pennant lost on one misplaced pitch.

Don Zimmer's Brooklyn Dodger career is derailed when he suffers the second dreadful beaning of his young career.

## 8. The Cardinals get their man so that Brooklyn doesn't, June 18, 1940, Ebbets Field

When the Brooklyn Dodgers acquired Ducky Joe Medwick from St. Louis in 1940, he had averaged 127 RBIs for the previous six years, and his aggressive persona had made him one of baseball's most feared hitters. But on June 18, six days after he arrived in Brooklyn, an ex-teammate damaged his career.

Medwick and new Brooklyn manager Leo Durocher (also an ex-Card) got into an argument with former teammate Bob Bowman in a hotel elevator, which ended with Bowman allegedly yelling, "I'll take care of both you guys!"

That day Bowman beaned Medwick, hitting him in the temple; as Medwick was carried off unconscious, Durocher nearly attacked Bowman, while Brooklyn president Larry MacPhail challenged the Cardinal bench to a fight. Although he missed little time, Medwick was never the same hitter. He pulled off the plate and averaged only 85 RBIs over the next four years.

## 9. Don Zimmer suffers a second brutal beaning, June 23, 1956, Ebbets Field

When Brooklyn's Don Zimmer came to bat at Ebbets Field on June 23, 1956, he had plenty of potential—he'd hit 15 homers in just 280 at-bats in 1955. But he also had a scarred past—in 1953 a minor league beaning left him unconscious for two weeks and unable to speak for six; four titanium buttons in his head were a permanent souvenir.

Then a fastball from Cincinnati's Hal Jeffcoat smashed Zimmer in the face, fracturing his cheekbone, detaching his retina, ending his season, and depriving the Dodgers of a crucial extra bat in the seven-game 1956 World Series. Zimmer would have productive seasons in 1958 and 1961, but his career never fully recovered. In 1957 the National League made batting helmets mandatory, and the American League followed in 1958.

**Zach Wheat gives his all for Brooklyn's fans for 18 years, most dramatically with his final home run.**

## 10. Zach Wheat's mind is willing, but his legs are unable, August 5, 1926, Ebbets Field

Zach Wheat hit the longest home run in baseball history . . . time-wise.

On August 5, 1926, the 18-year Brooklyn veteran was nursing an injured heel when he blasted a pinch-hit home run at Ebbets Field. Trotting slowly to first, Wheat felt his leg suddenly clench up with a charley horse. Favoring that leg, he pulled a muscle in the other and could only hobble to second, where he sat on the bag. Manager Wilbert Robinson and the umpires gathered round. Robinson offered a pinch runner, but Wheat wanted the homer. Finally, he arose and—with great encouragement from the fans—dragged himself, limping and wincing, the final 180 feet home. The journey took five full minutes.

# BAD CALLS

## 1. Billy Martin incites "the Pine Tar Incident," July 24, 1983, Yankee Stadium

There's nothing complicated about the long ball. It is a simple and definitive statement. Except, that is, in the case of "the Pine Tar Incident." On July 24, 1983, George Brett's ninth-inning, two-out, two-run homer off Yankee closer Goose Gossage was barely out of the park before Yankee manager Billy Martin stirred up the most famous baseball rules controversy since Merkle's Boner in 1908.

Martin persuaded crew chief Joe Brinkman and home plate umpire Tim McClelland that the Kansas City star's bat had pine tar (the sticky substance used for grip enhancement) on it beyond the allowable 18-inch area.

The umpires bought Martin's story and undid the homer, giving the Yankees the win but making a mistake of epic proportions. First they faced Brett's now-famous explosion of volcanic rage. Then they were publicly humiliated as the controversy became a national story and league president Lee MacPhail overturned their decision.

According to rule 1.10b, a pine tar violation should prompt only the removal of a bat, not the nullification of a hit. Rule 6.06d permits umpires to call batters out if they alter bats "to improve distance or to make the ball do funny things when it leaves the bat," but pine tar, unlike cork or super balls, does not give the hitter any advantage. MacPhail saw no justification for taking away Brett's home run.

The game had to be finished from the point after which the homer had given the Royals a 5–4 lead, but the Yankees, trying to be difficult, protested MacPhail's August 18 date. George Steinbrenner's lawyer, Roy Cohn (yes, that Roy Cohn, the former acolyte of Senator Joe McCarthy apparently had a thing for self-aggrandizing bullies), sought an injunction to prevent the game.

Steinbrenner, who also announced a day game when the league was planning an evening game, was fined $300,000 for his outrageous tactics, but Martin's maneuvers were worse. First, he turned the final four outs into a farce by putting pitcher Ron Guidry in center field and first baseman Don Mattingly at second base. Then, because the league used an umpire crew that was close at hand instead of flying in the original umpires, he tried an appeal play, saying Brett had failed to touch the bases. But MacPhail outwitted Martin by arming umpire Dave Phillips with a signed affidavit from the July 24 crew testifying that Brett had touched them all. Martin stubbornly announced a protest, but he'd been beaten. Twelve minutes later, the Royals' win was finally, officially, in the books.

## 2. Joe Louis "wins" over Jersey Joe Walcott, December 5, 1947, Madison Square Garden

To dethrone the heavyweight champ you have to knock him out or at least really stick it to him—otherwise, judges tend to play favorites, especially with the most iconic figures. Muhammad Ali's win over Ken Norton at Yankee Stadium in 1976 was largely attributed to judges being seduced by the Greatest's aura or sense of style. But the most egregious example came on December 5, 1947, at Madison Square Garden when unheralded Jersey Joe Walcott twice knocked down Joe Louis yet still

**Billy Martin provokes the infamous "Pine Tar Incident" when he insists that the umpires measure the sticky stuff on George Brett's bat.**

came up short on two judges' cards in rounds. It was in part Walcott's fault for fighting defensively at the end to avoid a late knockout like the one Louis administered to Billy Conn in 1941. (Oddly, one judge, along with referee Ruby Goldstein, gave Walcott the win in points, but back then it was rounds that counted.)

Louis, who was booed by the fans for his lackluster showing, was so sure he'd lost that he was climbing out of the ring when he was announced as the winner. He went over to Walcott and said, "Joe, I'm sorry." Louis did redeem himself by knocking Walcott out in a rematch.

## 3. Don Gerhmann wins the Wanamaker — no, wait, Fred Wilt does, no wait . . . January 28, 1950, Madison Square Garden

In 1950 it took 4 minutes and 9.3 seconds to run the Wanamaker Mile at the Millrose Games at Madison Square Garden. But it took 314 days, 12 hours, and 33 minutes to resolve who won.

**This run will not matter in the end. Why? Because the umpires inexplicably call this World Series game on account of darkness—when there's 45 minutes of daylight left.**

With a late surge by Don Gerhmann, he and Fred Wilt had what should have been a photo finish, but the officials clustered around the finish line blocked the camera. The officials, meanwhile, couldn't agree on what they had seen with the naked eye.

The first-place judge thought Wilt won, as did the alternate. But the second-place judge saw Wilt finish second. Still, it was 2–1 in Wilt's favor. Then, as an afterthought, someone asked the third-place judge what he thought. It shouldn't have counted—and he later testified that he'd given a private opinion, not a judge's statement—but he thought Wilt was second. Chief Judge Asa Bushnell, who had no voting rights, staged a coup and declared that he was breaking the tie and voting Gerhmann as the winner.

It didn't last. The Metropolitan Amateur Athletic Union registration committee held a two-and-a-half-hour debate two weeks later, overturned the decision, and fixed the mistake, making Wilt the champion. But Gerhmann appealed this appeal to the full Metropolitan AAU, and they reversed the reversal, reinstating Bushnell's power to bend the rules and Gerhmann as champion. Still, it wasn't over. That December the national AAU convention took up the case in a special committee. On December 9, they finalized matters with a vote supporting the Metropolitan AAU and Gerhmann.

The race became known as "the Marathon Mile."

## 4. Game called for darkness during daylight, October 5, 1922, Polo Grounds

Talk about a costly mistake. Game 2 of the 1922 World Series set a record with a $120,000 gate, but the Giant and Yankee owners pocketed none of it. After 10 innings of tense, exciting baseball, umpire George Hildebrand suddenly called the game, claiming a haze had descended. But at 4:45 on October 5, at least 45 minutes of sunlight remained, and the fans—suspecting the owners had ordered this move to get an extra day's worth of receipts—rebelled, staging an impromptu protest in front of the press box and commissioner Kenesaw Mountain Landis's seat and jeering him when he refused to overrule the umpire. Waving his cane and surrounded by police protectors, Landis beat a hasty retreat. But Landis's actions belatedly admitted both Hildebrand's and his error—he ordered the money donated to local veterans' charities and forbade any other interruptions, so Game 4 was played till the messy end in rain that turned the field into a mud pit.

## 5. Bad calls cost Serena Williams the match and Mariana Alves her umpire chair, September 7, 2004, National Tennis Center

Most players can live with one bad call, even with a terrible overrule by an inept chair umpire. But combine that overrule with three more egregious mistakes and

## Bad Calls on the Road

**1. NBC drops football for *Heidi*, November 17, 1968, Oakland Coliseum**

With just 65 seconds left and the Jets winning 32–29, NBC figured the game was over and it was safe to cut away to start the kiddie movie *Heidi* at its scheduled time for East Coast audiences. Boy, were they wrong. Oakland scored two touchdowns in those final thrilling seconds, and NBC was deluged with irate calls, overloading the system. (Some viewers even called the police to complain.) The network was forced to grovel in the press, but the game did show both how popular the AFL had become and how deeply ingrained pro football as a television event had become in the American psyche. The rules were changed dictating that networks could not switch away during games unless there was a national disaster. The Jets, meanwhile, would avenge the loss with a dramatic win in the AFL Championship on their way to winning their only Super Bowl.

**2. The Jets bog down in the Mud Bowl, January 23, 1983, Orange Bowl, Miami**

The 1982 New York Jets looked like a Super Bowl–bound team after routing the Cincinnati Bengals and holding off the Los Angeles Raiders in the first two rounds of the playoffs. But the Jets' season was undone by bad weather and bad decisionmaking.

Miami was deluged with three and a half inches of rain in the week leading up to the AFC Championship game, yet the Dolphins made no effort to cover the field. As a result, the turf looked like surf, with pond-sized puddles and swampy areas that raised suspicions among New Yorkers that Miami coach Don Shula was trying to bog down the Jets' high-flying offense. The NFL official in charge of making sure the field was in good condition, Al Ward (a former Jet general manager), declared that since the turf in question was guaranteed to drain, Miami was not required to have provided a tarp. That was fine in theory, but Ward somehow ignored the reality on the ground, which was that the field was a mess. The Jets offense went nowhere, and the team fell 14–0.

**Serena Williams argues in vain against another bad call in her 2004 Open match against Jennifer Capriati.**

the player is bound to feel "cheated" and "robbed," as Serena Williams did in her 2–6, 6–4, 6–4 quarterfinal loss to Jennifer Capriati at the U.S. Open on September 7, 2004.

Williams — who also admitted she should have finished Capriati off in the second set — was serving to start the third when she blasted a backhand winner past her foe. The lineswoman called it in, which it was, by several inches. Then, out of nowhere, chair umpire Mariana Alves overruled the call. Williams was irate because the shot was as far from the chair as possible and not particularly close, but Alves was obstinate. Capriati broke serve.

Up 5–4, Capriati got three more gifts to finish off Williams: one second serve was so deep that the Cyclops machine that beeps for out serves didn't go off, yet the linesperson failed to make the call. Williams, expecting a double fault, hit the ball back into the net, and Capriati got a free point; in that same game, two of Williams's shots hit the line but were called out. On those, Alves remained silent. Capriati won the game, set, and match.

Open officials apologized to Williams and made sure Alves wasn't used for the rest of the tournament, but they failed to push ahead on discussions of using instant-replay challenges. Had they been in effect in 2004, Williams, not Capriati, would have reached the semis.

# FANS IN THE GAME

## 1. Jeffrey Maier gives the Yankees an unfair advantage, October 9, 1996, Yankee Stadium

Here's the way destiny works. When a fan got in the way of a fly ball at a turning point in the 2003 playoffs for the Chicago Cubs, for whom Ernie Banks always smiled but fate never did, they lost, and the fan had to go underground to escape harassment. When a fan interfered with a fly ball at a turning point in the 1996 playoffs for the New York Yankees, a team that has almost always gotten the breaks from the baseball gods, they won the game, the series, and the championship, while the fan was feted on national television.

The Yankees trailed Baltimore 4–3 with one out in the eighth inning of Game 1 of the ALCS on October 9, 1996, when rookie shortstop Derek Jeter — with three hits already — lofted a shot to the short porch in right. Tony Tarasco, just inserted into the game for defensive purposes, camped under it, ready to make the catch. But the ball disappeared into a black glove swooping in out of nowhere. It wasn't a teammate's mitt — it was a glove belonging to Jeffrey Maier, a 12-year-old fan who blatantly interfered with play by reaching onto the field to swipe a souvenir, another reminder of how lax security in Yankee Stadium often is when it comes to misbehaving fans. Fortunately for the Yankees — but unfortunately for fairness — umpire Rich Garcia blew the call, as he later confessed, ruling it a home run instead of an automatic out. (Garcia even said the game should be replayed from that point, which didn't happen.) The Yankees won in 11 innings on Bernie Williams' homer, which proved crucial when Baltimore won the second game. Without Maier's assistance, the last Yankee dynasty might not have been born in 1996. (Maier would go on to set a school record at Wesleyan for hits.)

Some in the media castigated Maier, and even manager Joe Torre said he shouldn't be glorified. But whereas Cubs fan Steve Bartman would be vilified by his fellow rooters for his intrusion (despite the fact that the Cubs deserved most of the blame), Maier — who felt "pretty good" about helping his team win with an illegal maneuver — ended up with a publicist, was celebrated on the morning and late-night shows, and was given free tickets to Game 2, where he was treated as a hero by Yankee fans, for whom a win was a win.

## 2. The fans get their way at the U.S. Open, September 5, 1977, West Side Tennis Club

Power to the people. The genteel days of the proper tennis club were long gone by the U.S. Open's last year at the West Side Tennis Club in Forest Hills. The tennis fans at the 1977 tourney had lived through an era of antiwar protests and radical anti-authoritarianism, and it showed.

The crowd for the daytime session on September 5 expected matches featuring Wimbledon champ Virginia Wade, young Tracy Austin, Vitas Gerulaitis, and Guillermo Vilas.

But when the evening session's star attraction, Chris Evert, had her match postponed because of her opponent's fever, referee Mike Blanchard knew he couldn't feed those fans just one doubles match. So at 4:40, after Gerulaitis was upset by Harold Solomon, the public address system informed spectators that Vilas's match was being

**Baltimore's Tony Tarasco thinks he has a play—until Jeffrey Maier interferes and gives the Yankees an unintended boost.**

rescheduled until the evening session. There was nothing more to see, so would everybody please move along?

The answer, it turned out, was no. The fans would not leave. They stayed in their seats chanting, "We won't go," and, "We want Vilas," stomping their feet and clapping their hands in protest. Some even threw garbage onto the court.

The PA announcer tried reasoning with them: "Ladies and gentlemen, you've had wonderful tennis since 11 A.M., there is a crowd lining up outside, it is physically impossible to put on another match."

He even tried bribing them—"Ladies and gentlemen, the tournament committee is attempting to put on another match, but not the Vilas match"—but while this act of civil disobedience was for a relatively selfish cause, it was unstoppable.

"The people have spoken," Blanchard finally admitted. And he asked Vilas and Jose Higueras to change their plans again and come out and play, requesting only that the remaining fans move to seats not belonging to evening ticket-holders. (Back in those days, the evening sessions didn't sell out.) Vilas demolished Higueras 6–3, 6–1, and went on to win the tournament.

## 3. Andrew Golota, and everyone else, resorts to dirty tactics, July 11, 1996, Madison Square Garden

When chaos consumed Madison Square Garden on July 11, 1996, there was plenty of blame to go around. Everyone was guilty: the fighters, their handlers, Madison Square Garden and the New York State Athletic Commission, and, most definitely, the fans.

Andrew Golota had been destroying Riddock Bowe in a major upset that should have been the high point of his career before he resorted to one low blow too many. Golota, who'd been guilty of head butts and biting in past bouts, slammed the bloated Bowe below the belt in the second, fourth, sixth, and seventh rounds. When he did it a second time in the seventh, Bowe fell down and began writhing in agony — although some observers believed he was faking it so as to escape certain defeat with some pride intact.

As Golota was being disqualified by referee Wayne Kelly the fallen fighter's handlers, led by the volatile and controversial Rock Newman, charged into the ring. Newman claimed he was just going to protect Bowe, but one entourage member slammed Golota with a walkie-talkie, cutting his scalp (13 stitches were later required), while 74-year-old trainer Lou Duva was pinned in a corner and knocked down — he was eventually taken out on a stretcher and needed an oxygen mask.

The state commission under Governor George Pataki was in disarray and failing to properly oversee events — for example, by allowing the Garden to cut corners by providing less security than necessary. As a result, life in the ring quickly spun out of control. Some fans, seeing an opportunity for unrestrained mayhem, cut loose. Soon there were 50 people in the ring (Bowe was still on the canvas), and fists and chairs were flying. New York City police on traffic detail came to help, but it wasn't until a half-hour later, when 100 police in riot gear arrived, that order was fully restored and the building evacuated. Sixteen people were arrested, and 22 were treated for injuries, while the sport of boxing and the Garden's fight plans both sustained black eyes.

## 4. Ty Cobb goes on the attack, May 15, 1912, Hilltop Park

Sic the brashest, rudest fans on the meanest, dirtiest player, and this is what you get.

During batting practice at intimate Hilltop Park on May 15, 1912, a loudmouth Highlander fan (predecessor of the loudmouth Yankee fan) started taunting the volatile Ty Cobb with old chestnuts like "Your mother is a whore."

Four innings into the game, as the berating continued unabated, Cobb started yelling back. He also asked the Highlanders to kick the heckler out. Finally, Cobb could stand no more. He vaulted the railing, smashed people out of his way, then began pummeling the man, Claude Lueker, with a dozen blows while kicking him with his spikes. According to instant legend, Lueker's neighbors shouted, "He has no hands" (he'd lost all but two fingers in an accident), to which Cobb retorted, "I don't care if he has no legs."

Cobb's fellow Tigers — who loathed him almost as much as Highlander fans did — came to his defense, climbing in behind Cobb or staying at the railing with bats raised as Cobb fought his way back to the field. American League president Ban Johnson suspended Cobb indefinitely, but 16 Tigers telegraphed Johnson saying they would not play without him, and even a *New York American* poll found that local fans voted 3,013–1,167 in favor of Cobb, saying Lueker had gone too far.

Cobb's teammates, feeling their honor was at stake and wanting organized baseball to treat them better and protect them, decided to boycott; the Tigers sent out a bunch of amateurs for their next game and lost 24–2. Cobb tried talking his teammates out of it, but they relented only when Johnson threatened permanent banishment. But the first baseball strike was essentially a success: Johnson also backed down and let Cobb back after 10 days.

## 5. A knife hurtles down from the sky, August 26, 1986, Yankee Stadium

All too frequently, Yankees fans justify their reputation as the most brutish, boorish hooligans this side of a European soccer pitch. All too often through the years, the "Bleacher Creatures" and their fellow drunkards have pelted opposing players with crude commentary and blunt objects. Meanwhile, George Steinbrenner has implicitly permitted this intimidation by failing to provide enough security at big moments.

In the 1977 World Series, fans threw whiskey bottles, cups of beer, and even firecrackers. Dodger Reggie Smith was hit with a hard rubber ball. In 1978 the fans hurled batteries. This behavior has remained a pathetic constant—in the 1995 ALDS, Seattle manager Lou Piniella pulled his players after maniacs hurled onto the field a shot glass, a working Walkman, a golf ball, and a piggy bank's worth of loose change. In 1997, Jose Canseco was pelted with bottles and baseballs. (Okay, so maybe that one was justified.)

But never have Yankee fans behaved in a manner more depraved, more subhuman, than on August 26, 1986. (At least regarding the players—the previous year a pregnant woman was shot in the hand, and throughout the mid-'80s, muggings were reportedly common inside the Stadium.)

That was the day that mild-mannered California Angel Wally Joyner headed to the mound to congratulate Mike Witt on his pitching performance and felt something hit him in the shoulder. He thought it was a comb at first, but actually someone had thrown a bowie knife with a five-inch blade from the upper deck down at the mound. Fortunately, only the side of the blade nicked Joyner's shoulder. He was lucky to escape from New York alive.

## 6. Babe Ruth snaps, May 25, 1922, Polo Grounds

This was no ordinary slump. When Babe Ruth came to bat on May 25, 1922, nothing had gone right since the previous October, when his Yankees lost their first World Series. Commissioner Kenesaw Mountain Landis had suspended the Yankee superstar for six weeks at the start of 1922 for cashing in on his popularity with an illicit barnstorming trip, and the media had jumped on Ruth for his mammoth $52,000-a-year contract (more than three times his next-highest-paid teammate). While sidelined, he'd had his tonsils and adenoids removed. Upon his return on May 20, an anxious Ruth barely hit, managing just two hits in his first five games to a steady downpour of derision. On May 24 he went 0-for-5, twice failing with the bases loaded and the game on the line.

On May 25 at the Polo Grounds, Ruth tried stretching a single into a double but was called out. In response, he hurled dirt in umpire George Hildebrand's eyes, earning him his first ejection as a Yankee. The crowd unleashed its venom. Ruth bowed to them.

But according to Robert Creamer's *Babe*, one final heckler pushed him over the edge. When a man yelled loudly, "You goddamned big bum, why don't you play ball?" Ruth leaped into the stands and chased the man, who scrambled away. Irate, Ruth challenged him and everyone else in the crowd to a fight. Then he stormed off. Ruth was immediately suspended again (although just for one day because Washington owner Clark Griffith, eager to have Ruth drawing crowds in D.C., pleaded with AL president Ban Johnson), fined, and stripped of his brand-new captaincy. But worse, his public reputation was in tatters and would remain that way until the following year.

## 7. Fans are a pain in the neck for Frank Chance, worse for Jake Pfeister, October 8, 1908, Polo Grounds

In the ugliest end to a pennant race in history, the Giants crumbled, manager John McGraw snapped, and the fans behaved worst of all.

On October 8, 1908, the Giants and Chicago Cubs, tied for first place, met at the Polo Grounds to decide the pennant by playing the infamous "Merkle's Boner" tie game. The controversy drew an overflow crowd—thousands of whom smashed down part of the back fence trying to get in. (One man watching from a viaduct pillar fell to his death.)

Before the game, McGraw reportedly tried bribing umpire Bill Klem, to no avail. Giant pitcher Joe McGinnity tried—also to no avail—picking a fight with his friend, Cub player-manager Frank Chance, in the hope of injuring Chance.

In the third inning, center fielder Cy Seymour ignored Christy Mathewson's request that he back up, and Joe Tinker belted the exhausted Matty's pitch over Seymour for a triple that sparked a pennant-clinching four-run rally.

But nothing was worse than the aftermath as fans swarmed the field attacking the Cubs. Chance was punched in the neck, damaging cartilage, while Jake Pfeister was stabbed in the shoulder. The police had to brandish revolvers and guard the clubhouse door to save the players from the angry mob.

**Chicago's Frank Chance has the smile wiped off his face when, after winning the 1908 pennant, he and his teammates are brutally attacked by Giants fans after the season's final game.**

## 8. Giant fans are sore winners, December 6, 1959, Yankee Stadium

Sure, the game was over . . . in the sense that the Giants were routing the Cleveland Browns 48–7 en route to clinching the conference title. But the game wasn't literally over—nearly four minutes remained when fans started invading the Yankee Stadium field on December 6, 1959. They couldn't wait to party, and the celebration turned ugly in a hurry.

Fans rushed the field, fighting each other, tearing down a goal post, surrounding the Browns' bench, and hassling the players. With 1:53 left, Cleveland coach Paul Brown removed his team, getting punched and clawed at along the way.

"I had never seen so many crazed expressions," Frank Gifford wrote afterwards. Public address announcer Bob Shepherd tried calming the crowd by saying the Giants might have to forfeit, but Brown, enraged by what he called "the worst crowd behavior" ever, demanded that New York finish the game. Charlie Conerly refused to return, but the rest of the Giants trudged back out and ran out the clock while fans milled about on the field. On the last play, Giant Mel Triplett took a handoff and vanished into the crowd.

## 9. The Rangers and the Bruins fight and find they have company, December 23, 1979, Madison Square Garden

Ranger fans have always enjoyed watching a good fight, but on December 23, 1979, they found themselves in the middle of one. After Boston beat New York 4–3, a skirmish broke out when New York goalie John Davidson went after Boston's Al Secord because he believed that the Bruin had sucker-punched Ulf Nilsson at the buzzer. With the two teams starting to brawl, a fan hit Bruin Stan Jonathan, then grabbed his stick. When teammate Terry O'Reilly saw that, he hurdled the glass into the stands with his fellow Bruins behind him.

The brawl lasted 10 minutes, four fans were arrested, and three Bruins were suspended, including Mike Milbury, who earned lasting notoriety when he rushed back from the dressing room, grabbed one fan's shoe, and began beating him with it. "It was a cheap penny loafer," Milbury said, "befitting a man of his lack of stature."

## 10. Reggie! bars rain down on the field, April 13, 1978, Yankee Stadium

If ever there was a day for Yankee fans to shower the field with debris, this was it. Reggie Jackson had finally gotten his wish—he'd had a candy bar named after him. Standard Brands Confectionary introduced its new Reggie! bars by handing out thousands of free samples at the Yankees' home opener on April 13, 1978. In the first inning, on his first swing, Jackson smashed a three-run homer off Chicago pitcher Wilbur Wood's knuckleball. It was his fifth consecutive homer on five swings in five at-bats dating back to Game 5 of the 1977 World Series.

As the crowd chanted, "Reggie! Reggie!" someone decided the celebration would be more festive if he threw his candy bar down to Jackson. Hundreds, then thousands, followed suit as the orange-and-blue squares soared onto the field for nearly five minutes. While some of the White Sox moaned about the interruption, Jackson savored the experience. "It was a nice gesture," he said afterwards.

**Reggie! bars hurtle to earth by the hundreds, then the thousands, after Jackson homers to start the 1978 season.**

## 11. Jimmy Piersall fights back, September 10, 1961, Yankee Stadium

You'd have to be crazy to fight a bunch of out-of-control Yankee fans, but Jimmy Piersall never made any great claims on sanity. So when two fans jumped onto the field in the seventh inning on September 10, 1961, and charged the Cleveland center fielder, he didn't run, he didn't hide, and he didn't try making peace with the enemy. He launched an attack of his own. (A year later, while with Washington, Piersall would climb into the stands to physically silence a heckler.)

The first to arrive was the recipient of a knockdown punch from Piersall's gloved hand. The second hastily retreated, but Piersall was on the warpath—he chased him down and threw a flying kick that narrowly missed. The cavalry arrived in the form of teammates Johnny Temple and Walt Bond, who landed a few punches before the police arrived. When play resumed, Piersall made a leaping catch at the wall, crashing into teammate Willie Kirkland but stealing a homer from Yankee Johnny Blanchard. His toughness and talent earned him a rare ovation from the Yankee fans.

## 12. Nothing comes between Calvin Klein and Latrell Sprewell, except maybe security, March 24, 2003, Madison Square Garden

Latrell Sprewell was about to inbound the ball in the final minutes of a game against Toronto when somebody suddenly grabbed him by the arm. It wasn't an official, a teammate, or even an opponent. It was, of all people, Calvin Klein. The designer, who would enter rehab two weeks later, had reportedly been drinking and started muttering at the Knick guard before security pulled him away. Afterwards, the City Council passed "the Calvin Klein law," levying fines and punishments on fans who interrupt sporting events.

# Fans in the Game on the Road

**1. Whitey Witt catches more than just a fly ball, September 16, 1922, Sportsman's Park, St. Louis**

In the ninth inning of a crucial game, a St. Louis Browns fan vainly tried to help his team by hurling a bottle off the head of center fielder Whitey Witt as he chased a fly ball. Witt was carried, bleeding and unconscious, to the bench, and though no one came forward to claim the $1,000 reward for information on the culprit, Browns fans redeemed themselves the next day by cheering the bandaged Witt. In the series' rubber game, Witt had the last word, singling home the winning runs in the ninth inning.

**2. Washington fans give the Yankees a win, September 30, 1971, RFK Stadium**

With two outs in the ninth inning, the Yankees were about to lose their season-ender to the Washington Senators. But this was no ordinary finale—it was the end of the Senators, who for the second time were leaving town. The few fans remaining decided to take part in the farewell and suddenly swarmed the field, forcing umpires to forfeit the game in the Yankees' favor. Instead of finishing 81–81, New York ended 82–80.

# BRAWLS OUTSIDE THE RING

## 1. Buddy Harrelson stands up to Pete Rose, October 8, 1973, Shea Stadium

There are few brawls truly worth celebrating. But when the little guy stands up to the bully, when the Miracle Mets showed the Big Red Machine that it couldn't shove them around, well, that was worth fighting for.

On October 8, 1973, the Mets were battering the Reds 9–2 in the fifth inning, poised to take a 2–1 advantage in their best-of-five NLCS, when the 200-pound Pete Rose barreled hard into the 146-pound shortstop Buddy Harrelson at second base trying to break up a double play. "I was trying to knock him into left field," Rose admitted after. Harrelson told Rose he didn't like such treatment, and soon Rose was punching Harrelson, who held his own as his teammates charged out in support. The under-card featured Cincinnati's Pedro Borbon sucker-punching Met Buzz Capra and then Capra exacting revenge while Duffy Dyer pinned Borbon. The highlight came when Borbon realized he'd somehow ended up wearing a Mets hat, which he then bit and tore in half.

The melee finally ended, but emotions remained high, and when Rose returned to left field, fans began throwing the hard stuff—including a whiskey bottle—at the obnoxious outfielder. He, of course, provoked more outrage by firing stuff back into the box seats. Red manager Sparky Anderson pulled his team off the field, and the Mets had to send out fan favorites Yogi Berra, Tom Seaver, Cleon Jones, Rusty Staub, and Willie Mays as emissaries to plead for peace. For most fans, the brawl—with the subsequent ROSE IS A REED banners—became the defining moment of the 1973 season.

## 2. Willis Reed fights back, October 18, 1966, Madison Square Garden

No matter what you've heard, Willis Reed didn't fight the entire Los Angeles Laker team. But once he got going on October 18, 1966, at the Garden, he did administer multiple whuppings.

Reed had been complaining vainly to the refs that Laker Rudy LaRusso was mugging him. Finally, Reed, who generally played power forward while Walt Bellamy played center, reclaimed his territory under the board with some liberal use of his elbows. LaRusso threw a haymaker in retaliation. Laker Darrel Imhoff grabbed Reed in a bear hug and LaRusso readied himself to hurl another blow when Reed exploded. He unleashed several long left hooks, connecting hard on LaRusso. Because the action began near the Laker bench, Reed found himself surrounded by enemies, so he kept going, flattening the 6'10", 220-pound Imhoff with a shot to the eye and fracturing the nose of rookie John Block. Although Reed (along with LaRusso) was ejected, he had established himself as the team's leader and warrior in a way the passive Bellamy never would. Soon the center position, and indeed the Knick franchise, belonged to Reed.

## 3. Lou Fontinato loses big-time to a big name, February 1, 1959, Madison Square Garden

Lou Fontinato was the Rangers' tough guy, their enforcer. Then he ran into one of the fiercest players in NHL history. But it wasn't a goon, it was one of the all-time greats, Gordie Howe. In one of the most famous fights in league history, the Detroit Red Wing legend leveled the Ranger roughneck, and how.

The 1958–59 Rangers were still in the running for the playoffs on February 1 when, in the middle of a fight between two other players, Fontinato tried sticking it to Howe. Both players landed blows, but when Fontinato bent over, Howe unleashed one nasty uppercut after another. When they were pulled apart, Howe wrote later, "Fontinato was a bloody mess, with his nose spread around his face."

*Life* magazine gave the brawl a three-page spread. Fontinato was out of action for weeks and was never the same player; as for Howe, his reputation was secured. "I never had to fight again," he wrote.

## 4. Bad blood stirs up a big brawl, May 20, 1976, Yankee Stadium

The Red Sox were defending AL champs in 1976, and the Yankees were on their way to their first pennant in 12 years. There was also plenty of bad blood dating to a 1973 brawl between rival catchers Thurman Munson and Carlton Fisk in Fenway Park.

So when the hotheaded Lou Piniella bowled over the hotheaded Fisk at home plate, Fisk showed Piniella up, shoving the ball in his face. Piniella responded with a sharp right to the face. In the brawl that followed, Mickey Rivers punched Boston's Bill Lee, and Graig Nettles—looking to make a point about what the Yankees thought of the free-spirited, loudmouthed pitcher—body-slammed Lee to the ground, badly damaging his pitching arm. Lee then charged Nettles, who gave him a black eye with a right hook. (Lee would pitch with shoulder pain for over a year.)

It made for good theater, landing Fisk and Piniella on the cover of *Sports Illustrated* under the headline "Head-on Collision in the East." Thirty years later, the teams are still bumping heads.

## 5. Mike Tyson bites again, January 22, 2002, Hudson Theatre

That whole thing about history repeating itself, first as tragedy and then as farce? Well, when it came to Mike Tyson and biting, the ex-champ went straight to the farce part, although given his pathetic self-destruction, there was a touch of tragedy too.

Even when he was being talked about as the greatest heavyweight since Muhammad Ali, Tyson had a penchant for trouble. In 1988 he got into a late-night street fight in Harlem with Mitch "Blood" Green, a boxer and former gang leader whom Tyson had previously beaten in the ring. (Green later won $45,000 in a civil suit over the street brawl.) But in the 1990s Tyson unraveled completely, losing to a nobody named Buster Douglas, then going to jail for rape, then being consumed by one controversy after another. When he achieved lasting infamy for biting Evander Holyfield in the ring, everyone presumed that was a onetime fiasco.

But on January 22, 2002, Tyson strode across the stage right at WBC champ Lennox Lewis. Tyson had once challenged Lewis, saying, "I want your heart. I want to eat your children. Praise be to Allah." Now the two were at the Millennium Hotel's Hudson Theatre on West 44th Street to promote their upcoming Las Vegas bout, which was contingent on Nevada's athletic commission granting Tyson a new license, which they had not done since 1999.

Trouble had been dogging Tyson yet again—in the previous week he'd fired his trainer, his wife had filed for divorce, and police in Nevada had

**Buddy Harrelson stands up to Cincinnati's bigger, stronger Pete Rose in the 1973 NLCS.**

given evidence to prosecutors claiming Tyson had committed sexual assault in 2001. Once on the stage he quickly settled any questions about his mental fitness, although it's possible he was subconsciously looking to derail a matchup against a clearly superior fighter.

Tyson went nose to nose with Lewis in a traditional macho photo op. But Lewis's bodyguard, thinking (quite reasonably) that an attack was imminent, overreacted and pushed Tyson away. Tyson threw a punch at him, and Lewis unleashed a right at Tyson. A security-free fracas followed in which WBC president Jose Sulaiman was briefly knocked out while the two boxers grappled on the floor.

Tyson allegedly resorted to his inner two-year-old once more and bit Lewis on the leg. No reporter ever saw the bite marks, and one of Tyson's trainers gamely claimed that Lewis had bitten himself, but given Tyson's track record, the myth was instantly hailed as truth. Afterwards, Tyson spewed an expletive-laced tirade at someone from the audience who'd shouted, "Put him in a straitjacket."

Tyson was deemed boxer non grata in Nevada, but the fight found a home that June in Memphis, where Lewis, showing his opponent how a true champion works, methodically sliced and diced Tyson before an eighth-round knockout.

## 6. Jeff Van Gundy gets a little too involved, April 30, 1998, Madison Square Garden

It was fight night at the Garden. Unfortunately for Jeff Van Gundy, it was also a Knicks game. On April 30, 1998, one year after Van Gundy's Knicks brawled their way out of the playoffs against his former mentor Pat Riley's Miami Heat, the two clubs went at it again. With just 1.4 seconds left in Game 4 of the opening round, New York's Larry Johnson punched Miami's Alonzo Mourning.

The two ex-teammates (who'd never liked each other much) started swinging. Mostly they missed, but what elevated this from a routine rhubarb to a notorious night in Knick annals was that Van Gundy leapt into the fray. Well, actually he fell, and soon the diminutive coach was wrapped around Mourning's leg, holding on like a little terrier while the Heat center tried shaking him off.

(Van Gundy had gotten black eyes breaking up a 1994 fight between Derek Harper and Jo Jo

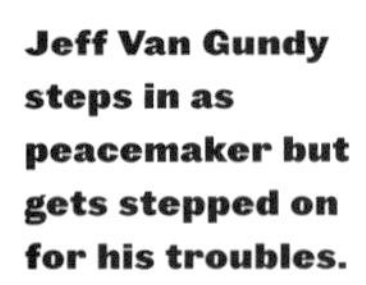
Jeff Van Gundy steps in as peacemaker but gets stepped on for his troubles.

English, and in 2001 he would need 15 stitches after being head-butted by his own player, Marcus Camby, during another peacekeeping effort.)

Johnson and Mourning were suspended from the next game, which gave the Knicks the decisive edge, but the lingering—and embarrassing—image was of Van Gundy getting in over his head.

## 7. Mark Gastineau enrages Jackie Slater, September 25, 1983, Shea Stadium

Mark Gastineau loved his "sack dance." Everyone else, well . . . not so much. Gastineau's teammates thought him a shameless spotlight hog, while his opponents found his antics insulting and infuriating. On September 25, 1983, at Shea Stadium, Los Angeles Ram Jackie Slater got so fed up that he took matters into his own hands, with historic repercussions.

With the game tied at 14 and the Rams on the New York 6-yard line, Gastineau surged past Slater, the right tackle, and dropped quarterback Vince Ferragamo for a nine-yard loss. When Gastineau jumped up and did his icky shuffle, Slater attacked him from behind. "One lousy tackle and he puts on a big act," Slater said afterwards. "Why don't I dance every time I block him out?"

Dozens of players charged into the action. Gastineau said it warmed his heart to see his teammates back him up, although Ram Bill Bain claimed later that during the melee one Jet told him that Gastineau was "an ass" and that some of his teammates were out there hoping to see him get rocked.

Gastineau's sack forced Los Angeles to settle for three points, and the revved-up Jets came back to win 27–24. The NFL fined a record 37 players for taking part in the punch-up, but more importantly, the league introduced new "anti-taunt" legislation that penalized teams yardage for "prolonged, excessive, or premeditated" celebrations by a performer after a play. The rule was only inconsistently and intermittently enforced.

Meanwhile, just days later, Gastineau found trouble in a different environment. His involvement in a brawl at Studio 54 led to a misdemeanor assault conviction and a sentence of 90 days of community service.

## 8. Muzz Patrick needs only one punch to beat the Bruin bully, March 28, 1939, Madison Square Garden

Eddie Shore was one of the league's top players, but also a well-known tough customer. When the Boston Bruin defenseman crosschecked Ranger Phil Watson so hard that he knocked Watson unconscious, he got what was coming to him. Before he knew it, Ranger Muzz Patrick, who'd once won the Canadian Amateur heavyweight title and fought in the Garden under traditional fight circumstances, skated onto the scene. Shore threw a punch and missed. The future Ranger coach and general manager threw one punch and connected, flooring Shore, breaking his nose and bloodying his mug so badly that he landed in *Look* magazine as an example of the perils of playing rough. Later Shore and Patrick became pals, and Shore would introduce the Ranger as the guy who made him famous.

## 9. Carl Furillo goes after Leo Durocher, September 6, 1953, Polo Grounds

Charging the mound is predictable. Charging the dugout makes headlines.

Dodger right fielder Carl Furillo had hated Giant manager Leo Durocher since 1949 because Durocher had ordered his beaning, caus-

# Brawls Outside the Ring, on the Road

**1. The Knicks brawl their way out of the playoffs, May 14, 1997, Miami Arena**

Poised to threaten the defending champion Chicago Bulls, the volatile and immature Knicks instead self-destructed against the less talented, less experienced Miami Heat.

At the end of a Game 5 loss against former coach Pat Riley's new club, guard Charlie Ward tried boxing out low for a rebound against Miami's P. J. Brown, who was nearly a foot taller. Brown, the winner of the league's citizenship award, picked up the Knicks' Bible study leader and flipped him over his hip, body-slamming him to the floor.

It wasn't the fight that mattered but the fact that Patrick Ewing, John Starks, Larry Johnson, and Allan Houston all violated the rules by leaving the Knick bench to intercede. Brown was banned for two games and Ward for one, but because New York had such a rough reputation, the league treated them as strictly as possible—Houston and Ewing (who'd gone just three steps beyond the bench) were suspended for Game 6, and Johnson and Starks were out of Game 7. Shorthanded and demoralized, the Knicks lost the final two games.

**2. Dave Schultz bullies the Rangers, May 5, 1974, Philadelphia Spectrum**

In 1974 the Rangers were mugged en route to the finals. The Rangers were favored in the semifinals over the Philadelphia Flyers, but the Broad Street Bullies beat them by beating them up, setting a record with 252 penalty minutes, led by 101 for goon Dave Schultz. In Game 7, Schultz pounded Dale Rolfe and, through him, the Rangers into submission—he fired 15 punches into Rolfe, then threw in a head-butt for good measure. Not a single player came to Rolfe's defense; nor did New York retaliate. They seemed shaken as the Flyers turned a scoreless game into a 3–1 edge and ultimately outshot the Rangers 46–15 in their 4–3 win.

**3. Don Zimmer charges into action, October 11, 2003, Fenway Park**

A pitcher against a 72-year-old coach. Two ballplayers against a groundskeeper. It doesn't get any weirder, or uglier, than the infamous Yankees–Red Sox brawl in the 2003 ALCS.

First Boston's Pedro Martinez hit Karim Garcia. Garcia later snarled at Martinez, prompting a bit of jawing but no fisticuffs . . . yet. Then Roger Clemens threw an inside fastball to Manny Ramirez in the next inning, and Ramirez went after him. That emptied the dugouts again, led by Yankee bench coach Don Zimmer, who went straight for Martinez. Martinez slammed the beach ball–shaped old-timer to the ground, earning himself enmity in the public and media. Even that rhubarb wasn't the end of it—later, Yankee reliever Jeff Nelson started fighting a Boston groundskeeper, Paul Williams, in the bullpen, and Garcia jumped the fence to gang up on him. By the time it was over, this game had pacifists thinking a Rangers-Bruins game would be a healthy alternative.

**4. Photo Day becomes Fight Day, March 2, 1989, Port St. Lucie, Florida**

When the Mets congregated for Photo Day on March 2, 1989, they were a veteran team gearing up for one last pennant run, but they'd also already been pegged by many as hubristic underachievers dissipating their legacy in late-night partying. The photo shoot symbolized the end of an era, as a temper tantrum by Darryl Strawberry revealed a team on the verge of imploding.

When Strawberry was assigned to sit next to Keith Hernandez, who had angered Strawberry by criticizing him in the media, the immature outfielder loudly commented in front of reporters and photographers, "I only want to sit next to my real friends." After a brief verbal exchange, Strawberry suddenly launched a punch that grazed Hernandez's cheek, prompting jokes that it was the first time in years Strawberry had hit the cutoff man. After both men were restrained, Strawberry yelled, "Don't hold him back," then told Hernandez, "I've been tired of you for years," and sneered at Gary Carter, "You're next."

The stars finally sat for the photo (separated by Carter and manager Davey Johnson), and later everything was declared settled. But Strawberry went into a tailspin, which killed the team's chances and prompted management to trade many holdovers from the fabled 1986 squad. By season's end, the team photo was filled with ghosts, a haunting reminder of

## Brawls Outside the Ring, on the Road (CONTINUED)

the thin line between dynasty and disappointment.

**5. Carlton Fisk and Thurman Munson go at it, August 1, 1973, Fenway Park**

When Thurman Munson barreled full force into Carlton Fisk at home plate on a missed suicide squeeze, there had already been trouble brewing—Fisk had tripped another Yankee the previous day, and then he had been hit in the head with a pitch in this game. Plus, neither catcher particularly liked his rival. Now Fisk held on to the ball and dumped Munson on his head. Munson came up swinging . . . and connecting; Fisk punched Munson with ball in hand. In the huge pileup that followed, Fisk was on the bottom crushing Gene Michael and punching Munson. Afterwards, Boston's Bill Lee sneered that the Yankees fought "like a bunch of hookers, swinging their purses." The animosity between the Yankees and Red Sox—which had tapered off somewhat in the 1950s and 1960s when first the Red Sox and then the Yankees had fallen from contention—was reborn.

ing a concussion. But things came to a head—or rather a rib, a neck, and a finger—on September 6, 1953.

Under orders from Durocher, Ruben Gomez plunked Furillo in the ribs. When Furillo, leading the league with a .344 average, looked toward the Giant dugout, Durocher taunted him, signaling, "Come on." So Furillo charged in and grabbed the manager by the throat. Monte Irvin stepped in to break it up but accidentally stepped on and broke Furillo's pinky. That ended Furillo's season and inadvertently helped him clinch the batting crown, since he had no more at-bats—and thus no more outs.

## 10. The Rangers and the Canadiens lose control, March 16, 1947, Madison Square Garden

Most hockey fights are somewhat predictable, but one 1947 brawl at the Garden drew in the Rangers, the Montreal Canadiens, the fans, and the police in one of the wildest scenes in NHL history.

With just 30 seconds left in the game, Ranger Bryan Hextall hit Montreal's Kenny Reardon in the face with a stick; Reardon would require 10 stitches.

While being led off the ice, Reardon started arguing with players on the New York bench, then attacked them.

Soon everyone from both teams was swinging fists and sticks—the main event came when Montreal's Maurice Richard slid behind a kneeling Bill Juzda and smashed him in the head with his stick, snapping it (the stick, not the head) in two. Juzda pulled himself up and threw Richard to the ice. A fan punched a Canadien, who walloped said fan in the noggin with his stick. The refs and the Garden's special police force could not stop the fracas and instead got caught up in it; organist Gladys Gooding played "The Star-Spangled Banner," but no one came to attention. Finally, after 10 minutes, the players wore themselves out. A half-minute later, the Rangers lost and were eliminated from playoff contention.

# BAD BEHAVIOR

## 1. Babe Ruth gets a bellyache, April 8, 1925

Babe Ruth never behaved particularly well by normal societal standards. Usually he got away with it. But on April 8, 1925, everything—the food, the booze, the women—caught up to him all at once in what became known as "the Bellyache Heard 'Round the World."

Ruth had ballooned to 256 pounds that winter and arrived in spring training with a fever. When his wife Helen headed back to New York, Ruth went on a three-pronged bender, inhaling every burger, drink, and dame in sight as the team barnstormed its way back north. Although his fever returned, accompanied by chills, Ruth was walloping homers and batting .447, so he kept on going. Then in Asheville, North Carolina, on April 7, Ruth collapsed on the train platform. He was taken to a hotel and told to rest. As the team went on ahead without him, rumors spread that Ruth had died, making his illness a national sensation. Ruth was alive, of course, but he really did almost die: when he vomited and then fainted in the train's washroom, he banged his head hard as he fell. Arriving in New York on the ninth, Ruth was lifted, unconscious and wrapped in blankets, through the train window and lowered onto a rolling stretcher. He came to, passed out, awoke delirious, and writhed about before being sedated. The whole process was repeated before he was finally taken to St. Vincent's Hospital, convulsing several times in the ambulance.

Though venereal disease was rumored, it was more likely the hot dogs and beer: a week later, Ruth had abdominal surgery to remove an intestinal abscess. He didn't fully recover the entire year, playing just 98 games and hitting 25 homers.

**Nineteen twenty-five becomes a dark and unhappy year for Babe Ruth when he implodes with "the Bellyache Heard 'Round the World."**

## 2. Ben Chapman gives voice to the ugliest kind of racism, April 22, 1947, Ebbets Field

"Hey, nigger, why don't you go back to the cotton field where you belong?"

"They're waiting for you in the jungles, black boy."

Managers lead their teams, and no skipper ever set a more malicious tone than Philadelphia's Ben Chapman, a southerner trying to break Brooklyn rookie Jackie Robinson and ruin Branch Rickey's integration efforts.

It nearly worked.

Beginning April 22, 1947, three games' worth of vitriol — including aiming bats machine gun-style at Robinson — made Robinson "wild and rage-crazed" internally. It was as close as he ever came to abandoning the noble experiment for a full-out attack. But instead, Robinson held everything in. He also scored the lone run in the first game and watched his Dodger teammates step up as Alabama native Eddie Stanky challenged Chapman: "Why don't you guys go to work on somebody who can fight back? There isn't one of you has the guts of a louse."

The press and commissioner Happy Chandler also came to Robinson's defense, with Chandler issuing a cease-and-desist order. But Rickey actually believed this trial-by-insult helped, saying later, "Chapman did more than anybody to unite the Dodgers."

**After launching vicious racial attacks on rookie Jackie Robinson, Phillie manager Ben Chapman is forced to pose for this goodwill publicity photo. Robinson is none too happy about it either.**

## 3. Roger Clemens pitches a bat at Mike Piazza, October 22, 2000, Yankee Stadium

Roger Clemens had already demonstrated that he lacked class. In July 2000 the truculent Yankee fireballer had knocked the most valuable Met, Mike Piazza, unconscious with a fastball to the head, which was bad enough, but then he had failed to offer even a token apology, saying only that it was an inside pitch that got away. So when the teams faced off that year in the Subway Series, everyone eagerly anticipated the Clemens-Piazza showdown. While Joe Torre took flak for arranging his rotation to avoid pitching Clemens at Shea Stadium (where he'd not only be booed mercilessly but also have to bat), controversy and Clemens found each other anyway.

In the first inning of Game 2, on October 22, Clemens blazed a 1–2 fastball in tight to Piazza. The Met could only manage to punch the ball foul, but he broke his bat on the swing, and as he took his first few steps toward first, the bat head bounced toward the mound. Clemens grabbed the bat head and hurled it within inches of Piazza. Piazza showed remarkable restraint: he barked, "What's your problem?" but did not charge the mound.

Clemens claimed he thought he fielded the ball, and when he saw it was the bat he merely tossed it aside. Admittedly, his adrenaline was flowing, and he was acting not with malicious intent but

**Roger Clemens, who already knocked Mike Piazza unconscious with a beanball earlier in 2000, ratchets up the crosstown hostilities by throwing a broken bat at him in the World Series.**

on instinct, but his instincts seemed pretty primitive to the national television audience that witnessed his behavior. The fact that he made no effort to clear the air or alleviate the tension and never reached out to Piazza only further cemented his image as a fierce competitor whose humanity took a backseat when he was on the field.

## 4. M. Donald Grant humiliates Cleon Jones, May 14, 1975, Shea Stadium

For a man in charge of a baseball team, Mets chairman M. Donald Grant had three enormous strikes against him: he lacked baseball expertise; he treated players not as people but as subordinates at best, chattel at worst; and he was overly concerned with the team's image even as his mishandling of situations did more to tarnish it than anything else.

While the 1977 trade of Tom Seaver did the most damage to the franchise, Grant revealed his worst instincts in 1975 after Cleon Jones was arrested during extended spring training for being naked in a van parked on a public street with a woman who wasn't his wife. The indecent exposure charge was dropped, but Grant's sanctimonious pigheadedness turned a minor display of bad judgment on Jones's part into a major public relations disaster for the Mets. After suspending and fining Jones, Grant locked him in the public stockade and flogged him before the villagers. Actually, the event Red Smith described as "an exercise in medieval torture" was a press conference in New York—the best hitter in Mets history to that point had to fly in and publicly apologize, with his wife Angela by his side.

(It wasn't just the righteous indignation. It was the hypocrisy. Grant had excused a more dangerous spring training incident when general manager Joe McDonald smashed his car into a parked city bus in St. Petersburg by claiming that McDonald was not coming home drunk but was up early and "had gone out looking for some blueberries for his breakfast." Really.)

Before Jones could read his canned statement, Grant—so concerned about not alienating the team's imagined target audience—issued a condescending "tongue lashing worthy of a plantation owner," Pete Axthelm wrote in *Newsweek*.

Having emasculated his player, Grant then showed his manliness by telling the press a joke about a man who wanted 11 women in one night. A class act all the way around.

## 5. Rosie Ruiz "runs" the Marathon, October 21, 1979

Preparing for a marathon requires days, weeks, months of training. But preparing to cheat in a marathon, well, that's a bit easier. Rosie Ruiz earned lasting infamy in 1980 when she won the Boston Marathon in 2:31:56, only to be uncovered as a fake who popped up near the finish line and sauntered across it. But running in the Boston Marathon requires qualifying for it, and Ruiz had earned her number by running the 1979 New York City Marathon in 2:56:29.

Except, of course, she didn't. What she actually did was drop out early on, take the subway up to Columbus Circle, wait for the right moment, then jog into Central Park as a finisher. Because her time was much more pedestrian in New York (she finished 24th among women), no one gave it a second thought until after her Boston ruse was discovered. Fred Lebow then angrily invalidated her New York time. Ruiz was later arrested twice, once for selling large amounts of cocaine and once, perhaps not surprisingly, on larceny and forgery charges. She has steadfastly maintained to this day that she completed both marathons.

## 6. Earl Cochell goes way too far, August 31, 1951, West Side Tennis Club

John McEnroe had nothing on Earl Cochell, a player with a reputation for immature outbursts who, in his fourth-round match against Gardner Mulloy at Forest Hills in 1951, set the gold standard for boorish behavior.

Unhappy with a line call, Cochell smashed a ball far out of the court. When he argued another call, the crowd began booing. Cochell yelled at them to shut up. The petulant player then tanked a game by playing left-handed, and the jeering escalated. When he served underhand lollipops, the fans really let him have it. Finally, Cochell lost control and tried climbing into the umpire's chair to grab the microphone to yell at his hecklers—since the mike was on, everyone heard him say, "Let me talk to those no-good sons of bitches." When he was turned away, he continued his monologue sans amplification. When chair ump Ellsworth Davenport later tried cooling Cochell down, the super-brat allegedly retorted, "Go shit in your hat," along with other obscenities. Mulloy won the match, and two days later Cochell was suspended indefinitely. He never played in another tournament.

## 7. Willie Pep and Sandy Saddler break all the rules, September 26, 1951, Polo Grounds

The first fight between Willie Pep and Sandy Saddler was a dramatic and surprising upset as Saddler dethroned the reigning champ in 1948. The second fight, the following year, was a classic as Pep outpointed his

# Bad Behavior on the Road

**1. Vince Coleman throws a firecracker, July 24, 1993, Dodger Stadium, Los Angeles**

The 1993 Mets were so loathsome that they became national news for their misdeeds: Bobby Bonilla threatened a reporter; Bret Saberhagen threw a firecracker near reporters and sprayed bleach at them on another occasion, lying about his guilt in both cases; and manager Dallas Green responded to questions about their horrific play by quipping, "I just beat the hell out of [my wife] Sylvia."

But July 24 had an unmatched combination of on- and off-field fiascos: Anthony Young lost his record 27th consecutive game 5–4, walking in the winning run, and Vince Coleman, while leaving the park in a car, threw an M-100 firecracker—the equivalent of a quarter-stick of dynamite (some reports called it an M-80, 1/16 of a stick of dynamite)—near a crowd of fans, injuring three people, including a young girl who sustained second-degree burns to her cheek, damage to an eye, and a finger injury.

Worse, Coleman didn't apologize, and Green blamed the news media for the fact that he had to bench Coleman during the resulting furor. Days later, Coleman finally made a lame statement at what the Associated Press called a "carefully staged press conference with his family" during which "he never used the word 'apologize.'" Over a month after the incident, the Mets finally declared Coleman's tenure over. It was too little too late.

**2. Jake Powell gives an honest answer, July 29, 1938, Chicago**

In 1936 the Yankees traded Ben Chapman, a hotheaded racist and all-around toxic presence, for Jake Powell, who had a bad reputation of his own. Powell outdid even Chapman two years later during a pregame interview on a Chicago radio station: when asked how he kept fit during the off-season, Powell offhandedly remarked that as a policeman he stayed in shape by "cracking niggers over the head" with his nightstick.

Attempts to shrug the comment off by the mainstream press failed as the black press erupted. Commissioner Kenesaw Mountain Landis (a racist and hard-line segregationist himself) felt compelled to suspend Powell for 10 days without pay, one of the harshest non-gambling-related penalties of his long, iron-fisted reign, while the Yankees sent Powell on a humiliating apology tour of the bars, businesses, and newspapers of Harlem. When he returned to action, fans threw bottles at him.

Although few noted it at the time—and few have corrected the misconception since—Powell was not only a racist but a résumé-padding liar: he never actually fulfilled his dream of becoming a policeman. He did finally make it to a police station in 1948, when he was arrested in Washington for writing bad checks. In the precinct house, he killed himself with a gun.

**3. St. John's basketball players get called for a bad move, February 5, 2004, Pittsburgh**

The St. John's basketball program was already in disarray when several Johnnies picked up one very drunk 38-year-old flight attendant at a strip club in Pittsburgh. The woman, Sherri Ann Urbanek-Bach, offered to have sex with them for money, then falsely accused them of rape. Although they were cleared immediately (and Bach was charged with filing a false report and extortion), the badly embarrassed university suspended two players and expelled one. Two more withdrew rather than be expelled, but one, Abe Keita, further stained the school's reputation by going public with the school's under-the-table payments to him. The team was barred from postseason play the following year, a minor price considering the dismal state of St. John's basketball.

**4. The Yankees take up wife-swapping, March 5, 1973**

On March 5, 1973, a trade captured headlines around the nation. Yankee pitchers Fritz Peterson and Mike Kekich had swapped wives.

The deal had been consummated the previous fall—Peterson not only sent over wife Marilyn but two kids and a poodle for Kekich's wife Susanne, two kids, and a terrier—but it didn't become public until the players arrived for spring training. Then everything changed. Both men were castigated by virtually every-

**Take my wife, please. Fritz Peterson (*left*) and Mike Kekich (*above*) make headlines in 1973, not for their pitching but for their off-season wife-swapping.**

one in sight, and their careers were soon ruined. Kekich's new marriage ended almost immediately, and he was soon shipped to Cleveland, where he pitched only eight more times. Peterson was shell-shocked by the backlash and slumped badly before also being dumped on Cleveland the following year. On the bright side, Peterson and Susanne remained married and had four kids together.

### 5. The Rangers party away a shot at the championship, May 15, 1979, Montreal

After the Rangers won Game 1 of the Stanley Cup finals in Montreal, superstar Phil Esposito pleaded with rookie coach Fred Shero to move the team to a Montreal suburb to keep them out of trouble. Espo knew that the Rangers, already depleted because of injuries, had little room for error and that many key players had a well-earned reputation for enjoying the nightlife. But Shero said no, and the Rangers went out and said yes to all Montreal's wondrous diversions. Four drunken players were spotted wrestling in the hotel hallway at 4 A.M., and later that day the team ran out of steam, blowing a 2–0 lead. Their momentum gone, the Rangers were overrun in three straight.

foe to regain the crown. But Pep-Saddler III in 1950 was marred by nasty behavior — Saddler won but was accused of illegal punching and arm twisting; he called Pep a quitter and accused Pep of stepping on his foot before swinging.

Like a Hollywood studio, these fighters kept returning for one more sequel. The fourth and final bout was one of the dirtiest street fights ever to find its way into the ring. Today the fight would have been stopped early and both men disqualified for their sordid tactics, which included spitting, gouging, heeling, head-butting, wrestling, and even choking. At one point, they actually worked together to hurl the referee to the canvas to stop him from separating them. The fight was finally stopped after nine rounds because Pep's eye was swollen.

Rocky Marciano called it the "roughest, dirtiest fight I have ever seen." Saddler was suspended for 60 days by the state athletic commission and Pep for life, although he was reinstated after two years. Fortunately, there was no rematch.

## 8. John L. Sullivan shows up drunk, June 30, 1884, Madison Square Garden

John L. Sullivan preferred drinking to training. For a boxer, that's a bit problematic. This early king of the heavyweights had overwhelmed a fighter named Charley Mitchell at Madison Square Garden in 1883, sparking interest in the sport of boxing and fueling demand for a rematch. The date was set for June 30, 1884, with the Garden raking in as much as $25 for box seats.

Unfortunately, up in his native Boston five days before the fight, Sullivan went for a drink . . . and never stopped, going on a five-day bender that reportedly featured two informal brawls in Boston pubs. By the time he showed up at the Garden, the binge had taken its toll — he was bloated and unshaven and could barely keep his eyes open. The crowd immediately recognized that he was drunk, and as he apologized by saying, "Gentlemen, I am sick and not able to box," he was chased out of the arena by a deluge of catcalls. Then he fled back to Boston.

## 9. Dan Rather storms off the set as the Open runs late, September 11, 1987

The Steffi Graf–Lori McNeil semifinal in the 1987 U.S. Open ran long, going until 6:32 P.M. No one at the National Tennis Center thought anything of it. Everyone watching at home, however, soon noticed something amiss. Something very big — like an entire television network.

When Dan Rather, in Miami covering the pope's visit, was informed at 6:15 that his *CBS Evening News* 6:30 broadcast might be delayed, he threw a tantrum worthy of John McEnroe, storming off and calling CBS News president Howard Stringer to inform him that if he couldn't start on time, then CBS Sports should fill the entire half-hour. At 6:30, the women were still at it, so Rather left the set once more to hound Stringer. Two minutes later play ended, and CBS Sports threw over to CBS News. But Rather was nowhere to be found. Chaos consumed the control room. Instead of running a taped segment or a "Please Stand By" announcement, the network simply went completely blank . . . for more than six minutes. Irate affiliates called to complain, while viewers clicked off in droves.

Finally, at 6:39, Rather returned and began an abbreviated newscast as if nothing had happened.

Rather had already attracted attention for unusual behavior, most famously for being beaten up in 1986 by assailants shouting, "What's the frequency, Kenneth," and for closing his newscast by saying, "Courage." This walk-off prompted questions from the press (the London *Times* wondered if he was "losing his marbles"), jokes from Johnny Carson (the blank six minutes gave CBS its "highest ratings of the year"), and a scathing attack from venerated predecessor Walter Cronkite ("I would have fired him").

The ultimate price came in February 1988 when Rather was trying vainly to elicit honest answers from presidential candidate George H. W. Bush about his involvement in the Iran-Contra scandal. Bush zinged him back with the interview's most memorable line: "It's not fair to judge my whole career by a rehash of Iran. How would you like it if I judged your career by those seven minutes when you walked off the set?"

## 10. Bret Saberhagen sprays and lies, July 27, 1993, Shea Stadium

It wasn't just that Bret Saberhagen sprayed bleach at reporters in the Mets' clubhouse on July 27, 1993. And it wasn't just that he lied about it. It was that he lied about it even after closed-door meetings with Mets officials and union head Donald Fehr about the team's relationship with the media . . . and that he lied about it all while admitting to throwing a firecracker at reporters' feet earlier in the month. "I consider myself a role model, unlike some professionals," he said about the firecrackers. "I'm saying to fans who took offense to it, or parents with children, that it won't happen again."

It wasn't until August 10 that Saberhagen confessed to the bleach incident. The Mets then made matters worse by failing to discipline him sufficiently, suspending him for just one start. Saberhagen's incessant dishonesty earned him immortality for immorality in Mets' annals.

**Heavyweight champ John L. Sullivan humiliates himself when he shows up at the Garden too drunk to fight.**

# BAD BEHAVIOR ON THE COURT: NASTY, JIMBO, AND THE BRAT

## 1. Nastase challenges McEnroe and the system, August 30, 1979, National Tennis Center

Nasty versus the Brat. Fight Night in Flushing. When those emotive heavyweights John McEnroe and Ilie Nastase climbed into the ring, er, walked onto the court for the second round of the 1979 U.S. Open, everyone expected tennis with an accompaniment of verbal fireworks. They got more than they bargained for.

The match itself was fairly one-sided, with Nastase, 33, long past his prime and McEnroe, 21, just entering his; on his way to winning the tournament, Mac won easily in four sets. But the score was secondary.

In their previous match, Nastase had reportedly rubbed ash on his nose to poke fun of a spot on McEnroe's. This time around, with the crowd cheering for Nastase—and for McEnroe's errors—the youngster slowed the pace of the match to try to retain control. Nastase seized on this and began chatting up spectators; he even taunted his foe by lying down behind the baseline for a nap.

At one point, McEnroe called Nastase a "son of a bitch," and Nastase requested that chair umpire Frank Hammond "make him call me Mister Son of a Bitch."

Hammond, normally a well-respected players' favorite, warned Nastase to behave and finally lost his temper, yelling at the star and assessing him a point penalty, which incurred the wrath of the fans. Nastase, of course, did not reform, and in the fourth set Hammond penalized him a full game. Nastase screamed and refused to continue. Finally, Hammond declared a default: "Game, set, match, McEnroe."

But the crowd was having none of it, and Grand Prix supervisor Frank Smith overruled him. Hammond spoke with tournament ref Mike Blanchard, who grabbed the microphone and said, "Ladies and gentlemen, unless we have some quiet so the players can continue, this match will be discontinued until tomorrow."

When they tried to restart play, the crowd chanted, "Two to one," trying to undo the defaulted game. Some fans let loose not just with verbal abuse but with beer cans and debris; some of them fought among themselves, while others vaulted onto the court, bringing out armed police.

But before Flushing Meadow could erupt, tournament director Bill Talbert emerged to make a pragmatic but unethical decision: Nastase could keep playing, while Hammond was evicted from the umpire's chair. The Romanian rebel had won the battle, although several games later he lost the match.

## 2. Jimmy Connors crosses the line, September 10, 1977, West Side Tennis Club

The final U.S. Open tournament at Forest Hills was, without doubt, the strangest tournament that ever took place there, reflecting the terrible turmoil consuming the city in that era almost too well.

First a judge ruled that the USTA had to let transsexual Dr. Renee Richards play in the women's tournament without taking a sex chromosome test. There were two bomb scares; one spectator was struck by a bullet from a sniper who was never caught; a near-riot by fans forced offi-

**Ilie Nastase and John McEnroe wreaked plenty of havoc individually, but pit them against each other and anything could happen—as it does during this controversial match.**

cials to back down from plans to reschedule a match; anti-apartheid protests were aimed at South African players; and a racial controversy erupted after West Side official William McCullough warned that the neighborhoods surrounding the new National Tennis Center at Flushing Meadows were "95 percent Negro" and Open officials "will not only have trouble in making the tennis fans come but in getting the community to work with them."

Jimmy Connors, the defending champ and reigning troublemaker, contributed more than his share to the bad vibes that year, and he particularly earned the wrath of sportsmanship aficionados in the first set of his semifinal victory over Corrado Barazzutti.

With the score tied at 3–3, Barazzutti argued that a Connors backhand had been long and asked the chair umpire to come investigate the mark in the clay. Instead, it was Connors who raced over and scuffed out the evidence before strutting away. When umpire Jack Stahr tried reprimanding him, Connors refused to look. Stahr finally said over the microphone, "You really had no right to do that, although you meant it in fun." And when the fans booed, Connors shouted, "I'm the last [American] you've got left, so you'd better pull for me."

When the fans began cheering each Connors miss, Stahr felt compelled to announce, "It is contrary to the spirit of the game, even in these days, to applaud faults."

Connors would continue his own lack of good spirit in the finals. After Guillermo Vilas beat Connors, the winner's Latin American supporters, acting as if they were at a soccer match, poured onto the court to lift the new champ on their shoulders for a victory lap. Connors angrily pushed and shoved his way through the crowd (hitting one fan, according to some reports), then left immediately, not sticking around for the awards ceremony or a scheduled press conference.

Fortunately for Connors, he didn't have to worry about such problems the next year when he once again won it all.

## 3. Connors and Nastase ignore the umpire, September 7, 1982, National Tennis Center

When the 1982 U.S. Open draw pitted Jimmy Connors against Ilie Nastase, it featured a man who once mooned fans while on a practice court (Connors) versus a man who once brought a chimp to a match (Nastase). And these two rascals were good friends. This one would be anything goes.

The first sign of strange times came when chair umpire Don Wiley—clearly expecting the worst—leveled a "code misconduct" violation against Connors, only to have to take it back when he realized he'd misinterpreted Connors's "okay" signal to a linesman as something more malevolent.

But when Nastase argued over not getting an extra serve on a disputed play, Wiley heard every obscenity clearly and nailed him for a penalty point. (A $1,000 fine was added on later.)

So after a sprinkle of rain, when a tournament official told Wiley to stop play, the two anti-authoritarians, who had once played doubles together at Wimbledon and who brought umbrellas onto the court when it started drizzling, were in no mood to listen. They staged a mini-rebellion.

Nastase hurled his towel at the umpire, then strode back out. Connors, relishing the chance to defy conventions and please his fans simultaneously, gladly joined him, holding an umbrella to ward off the rain. And so, after play had officially been stopped, Connors and Nastase finished the match. Connors won easily, but the fans cheered for both competitors.

## 4. McEnroe melts down, September 5, 1987, National Tennis Center

When John McEnroe was good, he was very, very good. Unbeatable in fact. But when he was bad, he was very, very bad. Incorrigible, to be precise.

In the third round of the 1987 U.S. Open, McEnroe was unbeatable and incorrigible all at once. He came back to beat hard-serving Slobodan Zivojinovic in five sets but cursed loudly and screamed continually, aiming his invective at linesmen, at the man holding the CBS microphone courtside, and at chair umpire Richard Ings, who, in the second set, gave McEnroe a warning, docked him a point, and then penalized him a game.

Once he was within a tantrum of disqualification, McEnroe behaved himself, but still, the player who'd been suspended and fined more than anyone else earned himself his stiffest penalties to date: a fine of $17,500 and a two-month suspension.

## 5. Connors marks his territory, September 9, 1978, National Tennis Center

In 1978, Jimmy Connors still reigned supreme at the U.S. Open, winning for the third time in five years. But in 15th-seeded teenager John McEnroe he recognized a new challenger. To defeat him in the semifinals Connors felt compelled not only to play his best but to intimidate the youngster, to show he was still king. He did it with a physical display that showed he and McEnroe spoke the same primitive language.

After cruising through the first two sets, Connors fell behind 5–1 in the third. Then he dismantled the youngster physically and psychologically with punishing backhands. At 5–3, Connors hit one with such pace that McEnroe ended up sprawled on the ground, his racket bouncing away, while Connors strutted around playing to the crowd. Then he drilled a forehand past McEnroe on the next point and exulted again, both arms reaching for the stars. But his finishing touch came after he won that game.

During the changeover, Connors popped up from his seat while McEnroe was still resting. As Connors sauntered past his foe's chair he brazenly spit water at McEnroe's feet. Take that, kid.

Then he went out and ended the match by winning the set 7–5.

# BILLY AND THE BOSS: 20 CLASSIC BAD BEHAVIOR DISASTERS

## 1. Martin's birthday brawl, May 16, 1957, Copacabana Hotel

At the end of Billy Martin's 29th birthday celebration, the Yankee "Rat Pack"—Martin, Yogi Berra, Mickey Mantle, Whitey Ford, Gil McDougald, Johnny Kucks, and Hank Bauer—were watching Sammy Davis Jr. perform at the Copacabana at 2 A.M. Staying out late drinking never caused a problem. But when a local bowling team acted rowdy and a brawl broke out—ex-Marine Bauer allegedly broke one bowler's jaw and nose—that was real trouble. The tabloids pushed the story, and several players were benched and fined a total of $5,500. But general manager George Weiss pinned the blame on Martin, a good scapegoat because he was a well-known instigator and he'd lost his starting job to Bobby Richardson. Two weeks later, Weiss exiled Martin to the lowly Kansas City A's. It would take George Steinbrenner to put Martin back in pinstripes.

## 2. Steinbrenner illegally hires Dick Williams, December 13, 1973

Ralph Houk resigned as manager of the Yankees. Dick Williams resigned as manager of the Oakland A's. George Steinbrenner wanted Williams, but he was technically still under contract; Oakland owner Charlie Finley didn't like the Yankees, so he refused the rookie owner's request. In a giant F-you to Finley, Steinbrenner hired Williams anyway, holding a big press conference to announce it. But the Boss lost this pissing match to the maverick when the AL office KO'd the deal.

## 3. Steinbrenner gets suspended over felony charge, November 27, 1974

After George Steinbrenner admitted his cover-up and changed his plea regarding illegal campaign contributions to Richard Nixon's reelection campaign to guilty, commissioner Bowie Kuhn declared Steinbrenner "ineligible and incompetent" to run a team. Kuhn suspended him from taking part in baseball operations for two years. (Kuhn reinstated Steinbrenner after 15 months.) That's not to say Steinbrenner didn't maybe call the front office once or twice with suggestions.

## 4. Martin and Reggie Jackson have it out on national TV, June 18, 1977, Fenway Park, Boston

Martin hadn't wanted Reggie Jackson and seethed with resentment until Jackson badly botched a fly ball against Boston. Choosing to interpret the gaffe as loafing and hoping to humiliate his egotistical star, Martin pulled Jackson off the field in the middle of the inning. As the stunned right fielder entered the dugout, Martin (whom Jackson later

***Right*:** **Billy Martin on one of those days when George Steinbrenner hasn't yet fired him.**

***Far right*:** **George Steinbrenner is opening his mouth to speak, meaning he's probably about to fire—or rehire—Billy Martin.**

claimed was drunk) attacked him, first verbally and then, after provoking the desired reaction, physically, although coach Yogi Berra restrained Martin. But this was no ordinary scrap — the game was on NBC's *Game of the Week*, and TV cameras beamed the incident out to the nation.

When the two later met to work things out, Martin called Jackson "boy," confirming Jackson's view that Martin was racist. The only good thing to come from this was that Steinbrenner meddled in a positive way: in August he told Martin to bat Jackson cleanup or lose his job. Jackson helped carry the Yankees to the pennant.

## 5. Martin says what he thinks about Jackson and Steinbrenner, July 23, 1978

First Martin inexplicably asked Jackson to bunt a runner over. Then he changed his mind, but Jackson defied the new orders. Martin fined and suspended the insubordinate Jackson, who returned sans apology. Angry at his star's attitude (and everything else in the world), and drunk (as usual), Martin ripped both his player and his boss in a single, unforgettable quote: "The two of them deserve each other. One's a born liar, the other's convicted."

The next day a sober and sorrowful Martin resigned.

## 6. Steinbrenner rehires the manager he just fired, July 29, 1978

Of all Steinbrenner's Martin-related maneuvers, this was the strangest and most illogical. Five days after Martin resigned and Steinbrenner had hired Bob Lemon, the Boss rendered his new manager a lame duck. At Old-Timers' Day, PA announcer Bob Sheppard informed the crowd that Lemon would return in 1979 and then become general manager, but that "the manager for the 1980 season, and hopefully for many years after, will be number one, Billy Martin."

As Martin raced out, the fans cheered wildly.

Then Lemon led the club in one of baseball's greatest comebacks in 1978. But Steinbrenner couldn't even wait until 1980—65 games into 1979, Lemon was gone and Martin was back.

## 7. Martin punches out a sportswriter, November 10, 1978, Reno, Nevada

Martin was manager-in-waiting when he proved he was also disaster-in-waiting. Young journalist Ray Hagar made the mistake of interviewing Martin in a bar, and the longer they talked (and drank), the more paranoid Martin got. Finally, he demanded to see Hagar's notes. When Hagar put his notes behind his back, Martin slugged the defenseless writer in the face, chipping three teeth and bruising his eye. Martin was charged with assault but reached an out-of-court settlement; the following spring, under pressure from Steinbrenner, he publicly apologized.

## 8. Martin fights a marshmallow salesman, October 23, 1979, Bloomington, Minnesota

After less than a season back in New York, Martin lost his temper . . . again, and lost his job . . . again. In a Minnesota hotel, Billy the Kid sucker-punched Joseph Cooper, then had his tough-guy image tainted when it turned out Cooper was a real softie—a marshmallow salesman. Worse, Steinbrenner didn't buy Martin's sweet-talking efforts—"As I walked through the lobby I heard a noise. I turned around and saw a guy lying on the floor."—and fired him. The A's hired Martin, but in his first trip to Minnesota the next season he nearly jumped into the stands when fans tossed marshmallows at him.

## 9. Steinbrenner has a "phantom elevator" fight, October 25, 1981, Los Angeles

At least Billy Martin fought flesh-and-blood people. When Steinbrenner emulated his once-and-future manager, the Boss fought phantoms. Diverting attention from the Yankees' third straight World Series loss to the Dodgers, Steinbrenner flaunted a puffy lip and left hand in a cast as he told reporters he'd been accosted in an elevator by two drunk and violent Los Angeles twenty-somethings. He boasted that he'd punched both out and left the elevator while both were still down for the count. While many suspected he'd punched a wall in frustration, especially since neither man ever materialized, Steinbrenner found another way to steal headlines just days later.

## 10. Steinbrenner humiliates his team and undercuts the Dodgers' triumph, October 28, 1981

Game 6 of the 1981 World Series was a debacle for New York. The Yankees lost their fourth straight game. Bob Lemon made several questionable moves, George Frazier set a Series record with his third loss, and Dave Winfield made a fuss by asking to keep the ball after his first hit, although he'd gone a disastrous 1-for-22 overall. But still, the Yankees played hard, and the fans, though disappointed, knew it.

Then Steinbrenner snatched the spotlight with a press release that, in a few simple words, managed to undermine the Dodgers' achievement, patronize Yankee fans, and question the integrity of his players in yet another classless act.

"I want to sincerely apologize to the people of

New York and to the fans of the New York Yankees everywhere for the performance of the Yankee team in the World Series." Apology not accepted.

## 11. Steinbrenner returns to Billy Brawl after firing three men in less than 12 months, January 11, 1983

By the time Steinbrenner hired Martin for Round 3, it was fair to wonder who was less stable. In the midst of his manic hiring-firing spree that cycled through 17 skippers in 17 seasons, he'd fired Martin in 1978 for Bob Lemon, dumped Lemon in 1979 for Martin, then Martin for Dick Howser in 1980, then Howser for Gene Michael in 1981. Then he replaced Michael midseason with Lemon before replacing Lemon in early 1982 with Michael, before ditching Michael for Clyde King, and finally King for Martin.

Ironically, Martin became the first man to last a full season, despite getting suspended for kicking dirt on an umpire, fighting in a California bar, smashing a urinal in Cleveland's clubhouse, verbally attacking a newspaper researcher, calling an umpire a "stone liar" (he was suspended again and later sued for defamation), and turning the Pine Tar Incident replay into a farce with players out of position and bogus protests. But the cumulative effect was too much, and finally, on December 16, 1983, Martin was fired . . . again.

## 12. Steinbrenner has someone else tell Yogi Berra he's fired, then rehires Martin, April 28, 1985

Before Donald Trump, no one said, "You're fired," more than George Steinbrenner. Yet when it came time to dump Berra—whom he'd publicly promised would manage all of 1985—just 16 games into the season, even the master of amorality must have sensed he was doing something wrong. So he made the descent from wrong to unconscionable and called general manager Clyde King during a game to tell him to ax Berra after the game. Only later did Steinbrenner phone Berra, who swore not to return to Yankee Stadium for as long as Steinbrenner remained. A mere 14 years later, Steinbrenner apologized.

## 13. Steinbrenner calls Winfield "Mr. May," September 14, 1985

The Yankees had gone 30–6 to climb within one and a half games of Toronto. But as the team dropped its second straight to the Blue Jays the Boss went into panic mode, which meant lashing out indiscriminately and harmfully—in the press box he trashed everyone from Don Baylor ("not a money player") to Ken Griffey ("a Little Leaguer does better"). But what rang loudest was his diatribe against Dave Winfield, with whom he'd had a tempestuous relationship: "Where is Reggie Jackson?" he said. "'We need a Mr. October or a Mr. September. . . . Dave Winfield is Mr. May."

Steinbrenner was wrong on several counts: what he needed was pitching, someone like Doyle Alexander, whom he had treated badly and then run out of town. Alexander beat the Yankees on the very next night on his way to a 17-win season. Winfield, meanwhile, was quite the satisfactory Mr. September, batting .303 with 34 hits and 22 RBIs that month. Still, the nickname stuck, an embarrassment for Winfield but a source of shame for Steinbrenner . . . if he'd been capable of feeling such an emotion.

## 14. Martin gets beaten up by Ed Whitson, early morning, September 22, 1985, Baltimore

Four rounds of fighting with pitcher Ed Whitson undid Martin's fourth round as Yankee manager. On Friday night, Martin had nearly gotten into a bar fight (for calling a man's wife "fat"), but on Saturday night—or early Sunday morning—he took "nearly" out of the equation. How the fight with unhappy pitcher Ed Whitson began is disputed (Whitson said Martin sucker-punched him), but once it began it didn't stop, sprawling from the hotel bar to the lobby (where Whitson broke Martin's arm), to outside (where Whitson bounced Martin's head off the pavement), to the third floor. Along the way, Martin also got two broken ribs, and in the aftermath he also lost his job. Whitson was shipped out the following season.

## 15. Martin gets into a fight in a topless bar, early morning, May 7, 1988, Arlington, Texas

Why Steinbrenner ditched Lou Piniella after just one year we may never know, but why he rehired Martin for a fifth time doesn't deserve an answer since nothing could excuse this disastrous idea. One month into the season, Martin kicked dirt on an umpire, then after the game went out to wind down in an Arlington topless bar. He ended up in the hospital and the headlines, claiming he was assaulted, although police said Martin provoked the altercation and threw the lone punch; the gash and bruises on his head came when said skull slammed into a wall upon his ejection from the club. Martin somehow lasted nearly seven more weeks as manager. Then Steinbrenner rehired Piniella.

## 16. Steinbrenner gets suspended over Howard Spira extortion, July 30, 1990

Steinbrenner had been tyrannical, petty, and capricious, but after his lesson with Watergate, he had avoided real trouble. Then his dislike for Dave Winfield drove the Yankee despot to a new low. When Winfield sued Steinbrenner for failure to pay money owed to the outfielder's charitable foundation, Steinbrenner was outraged. So he found someone to dig up dirt on Winfield. Worse, he picked the wrong guy—given that Pete Rose had just been kicked out of baseball for betting, Steinbrenner's choice of gambler Howie Spira was foolish, to say the least. When commissioner Fay Vincent found all this out, he kicked Steinbrenner out of baseball for life . . . which turned out to be only two years.

## 17. Steinbrenner fires Rob Butcher for missing a press conference, December 22, 1995

In 1995 Steinbrenner finally made the right call on managers, replacing Buck Showalter with the unflappable Joe Torre—although he did it with a press release saying Showalter had resigned and then, in the face of the negative reaction from the public and the press, reportedly flew to Florida and told Showalter he'd ditch Torre at the altar to bring Showalter back.

Needing someone else to fire, he turned on media relations director Rob Butcher. The offense? Wanting to be home for the holidays. Butcher had permission to travel home to Ohio for a family reunion, but Steinbrenner made it contingent on his being available if pitcher David Cone re-signed. Cone agreed to a deal three hours after Butcher left, so the PR man worked the phones from home. Steinbrenner told him that wasn't enough—he was through. Having heard these threats before, Butcher returned on December 22 in time for Cone's press conference, only to find out that Scroogebrenner was serious: Butcher was given the proverbial lump of coal and sent away.

Less than two weeks later, Steinbrenner—looking for the lucky 13th media director of his reign—tried hiring . . . Rob Butcher. Wisely, Butcher refused.

## 18. Steinbrenner starts calling names, April 1, 1999

This was no April Fool's joke. With three days left in the exhibition season, Steinbrenner was frustrated by Japanese import Hideki Irabu's mental mistakes in pitching and fielding. Steinbrenner lashed out, calling Irabu a "fat pussy toad." For that one, Steinbrenner was forced to apologize.

## 19. Steinbrenner goes after the little people, November 8, 2002

Steinbrenner used the new labor agreement and its luxury tax as an excuse to fire scouts and 25 other employees while cutting hours for the Stadium's elevator operators. But on November 8, *Newsday* broke a story that he planned to cut the dental plan for front-office employees such as secretaries and janitors. This would save $100,000—right when he was signing Hideki Matsui to a multimillion-dollar deal. Lacerated by public criticism, Steinbrenner backed down.

## 20. Steinbrenner tells YES not to mention or show Don Zimmer, May 28, 2003

Steinbrenner spent the whole year sniping at Joe Torre and his coaches. In spring training, he held back Don Zimmer's rental car. In mid-May, he told his lackeys at the YES network to make sure its analysts and reporters got tough with Torre. Then, at the end of the month, when Zimmer defended Torre and his coaches on air, Steinbrenner issued a new edict: Zimmer was not to be shown on the YES network cameras. Out of sight (Zimmer) and out of mind (Steinbrenner) added up to out of town—at season's end, Zimmer quit, blasting the bullying Boss on his way out the door.

# THE ANTIC ANTIDOTE: CASEY AT THE BAT AND IN THE DUGOUT

*George Steinbrenner and Billy Martin have earned countless demerits for bad behavior through the years, but New York had one character with enough charm to offset the two of them. Casey Stengel spent parts of nine seasons as a player for the Dodgers and the Giants and then 19 more as manager for the Dodgers, Yankees, and Mets. Although he was a talented hitter and an innovative manager, he was also never anything less than wildly entertaining.*

## 1. Casey and the Dodgers, May 25, 1919, Ebbets Field

When Casey Stengel, former Brooklyn favorite, returned in a Pittsburgh uniform and struggled at the plate and in the field, the Ebbets Field faithful mocked him relentlessly. But Stengel knew how to win them back. Seeing ex-teammate Leon Cadore capture a sparrow in the Brooklyn bullpen, he surreptitiously borrowed it.

Then it was Casey at the bat. The heckling continued, so he gave a low, sweeping bow, doffing his hat . . . and out flew the sparrow.

Stengel had given the fans "the bird." The jeers turned to laughter and cheers.

## 2. Casey and the Giants, October 10 and October 12, 1923, Yankee Stadium

At 33, Stengel was a part-timer for John McGraw's Giants, but in the World Series he garnered nearly as many headlines as Babe Ruth. In the ninth inning of Game 1, with the score tied, Stengel pummeled a full-count pitch to deep left-center at Yankee Stadium and began sprinting around the bases. After second base, his gait changed noticeably, as if age were suddenly overtaking him. The real culprit was a loose shoe pad that made him worry that the shoe would fly off midstride. To hear the great (over)writers of the day tell it, Stengel, "gimpy, crooked-fingered, spavined, halt, squint-eyed and mebbe a grandfather" (Hype Igoe), staggered with his "eyes bulging and mouth wide open" (Joe Vila), with "very little breath left in his body" (Frank Graham) and "his arms flying back and forth like

**Casey Stengel, who began his playing career with Brooklyn, attained his greatest success as a player with the Giants in the 1923 World Series.**

those of a man swimming with a crawl stroke. His flanks heaving, his breath whistling, his head far back" (Damon Runyon). By the time Stengel staggered and slid across the plate for an inside-the-park homer, he was a modern folk hero.

In Game 3, Stengel's seventh-inning homer made him the first player to break up a 0–0 Series game with a roundtripper and the first to win two games in one Series with long balls. With plenty of time to round the bases, he delighted the crowd by thumbing his nose and blowing kisses at the Yankee dugout. Yankee owner Jacob Ruppert complained to commissioner Kenesaw Mountain Landis, but his players enjoyed Stengel's antics. "Casey's a lot of fun," Ruth said.

## 3. Casey and the Yankees, June 17, 1960, Comiskey Park, Chicago

On the first trip to Chicago, Stengel was irritated by Bill Veeck's show-offy and gimmicky scoreboard, which set off fireworks for every hometown homer. On the next trip to the Windy City, Stengel was ready. When Yankee Clete Boyer hit a homer, Stengel and his players ascended to the edge of the field, where they surprised the crowd by dancing around waving sparklers. For one of the only times in his life, Veeck was left speechless.

## 4. Casey and the Mets, June 17, 1962, Polo Grounds

With two men on against Chicago at the Polo Grounds, Marv Throneberry lashed a triple, only to be called out for missing first base. When Stengel came to argue, first-base coach Cookie Lavagetto explained that Marvelous Marv missed second base too. So when Charlie Neal followed with a home run, Stengel took no chances. He emerged from the dugout, stopped Neal, and pointed to first base, then to each of the other bases along the way, melodramatically making sure Neal didn't miss one. The crowd loved it, roaring as if Neal had hit a game-winner. In actuality, the Mets lost by one run, 8–7.

Extra
Innings
33

EXTRA INNINGS

# Wheeling and Dealing

## THE BEST DEALS: The Top 10

**1. The Yankees get Babe Ruth from Boston for $125,000 and a $300,000 loan, 1919**
It's Babe Ruth. Enough said.

**2. The Giants get Christy Mathewson from Cincinnati for Amos Rusie, 1900**
Rusie never won another game. Mathewson won 372 for New York.

**3. The Knicks get Dave DeBusschere from Detroit for Walt Bellamy and Howard Komives, 1968**
This deal not only added DeBusschere but moved Willis Reed from forward to center and made Walt Frazier the main man at guard.

**4. The Rangers get Mark Messier and Jeff Beukeboom from Edmonton for Bernie Nicholls, David Shaw, Steven Rice, and Louie DeBrusk and $1.5 million, 1991**
The Rangers had plenty of talent, but in Messier they got the leader they needed.

**5. The Dodgers get Pee Wee Reese from Boston for $75,000 and five prospects, 1939**
Boston player-manager Joe Cronin was afraid he'd lose his shortstop job to this young kid, so he had Reese shipped to Brooklyn, where player-manager Leo Durocher was perfectly content to groom his replacement, who became the heart of the Dodgers for an entire generation.

**6. The Giants get Andy Robustelli from Los Angeles for a first-round draft pick, 1956**
The Rams wouldn't let Robustelli report late when his wife was pregnant back east, so Wellington Mara engineered a deal. Robustelli anchored the Giants defense as they won the championship in 1956 and reached the title game six times in nine years.

**7. The Mets get Keith Hernandez from St. Louis for Neil Allen and Rick Owenby, 1983**
With Hernandez's four straight years of a declining batting average, the rumors of cocaine use, and his disdain for the lowly Mets, this deal looked questionable . . . until Hernandez showed up and helped transform the Mets into winners.

**8. The Mets get Donn Clendenon from Montreal for Steve Renko, Kevin Collins, and two minor leaguers, 1969**
Needing some pop to contend, the Mets made a deadline deal for Clendenon, who went on to smack 12 homers in 202 at-bats. More importantly, he hit three crucial blasts in the World Series, earning MVP honors.

**9. The Knicks get Earl Monroe from Baltimore for Mike Riordan, Dave Stallworth, and cash, 1971**
The Knicks deprived their archrivals of their most dangerous weapon, and when Monroe surprised everyone by adapting his dazzling game to Red Holzman's team ethic, he became a crucial component in the Knicks' 1972–73 championship.

**10. The Giants get Y. A. Tittle from San Francisco for Lou Cordileone, 1961**
Tittle was already 35 in 1961 but drank from some secret fountain: his record-setting passing stats actually improved from 1961 to 1963 as he shared NFL Player of the Year or MVP honors each season and led the Giants to three straight NFL Championship games.

## THE BEST DRAFT PICKS: The Top 10

**1. The Jets pick Joe Namath, 1965**
The Jets made Namath the top pick in the AFL. The St. Louis Cardinals made him the top NFL pick. But the Jets splurged, lavishing $400,000 and a new car to double the Cards' offer and land the man who'd become Broadway Joe. The bidding war helped compel the leagues to move to a shared draft en route to an ultimate merger, while Namath's presence gave the new league both glamour and credibility. More significantly, of course, he brought the Super Bowl to New York.

**2. The Knicks pick Willis Reed, 1964**
The lowly Knicks had the top pick in the 1964 draft, and they needed a big man. They picked Jim "Bad News" Barnes. But there was good news too: no one else picked Grambling star Willis Reed in the first round, and the Knicks snatched him in the second.

**3. The Yankees pick Derek Jeter, 1992**
Baseball drafts are often a crapshoot, but the 1992 draft was deep and productive,

with the first round featuring future All-Stars like top pick Phil Nevin, Preston Wilson (taken by the Mets), Jason Kendall, and Charles Johnson. But only the Yankees got a future Hall of Famer when—after watching the likes of Paul Shuey, Billy Wallace, and Chad Mottola get called—they used the sixth pick on Derek Jeter.

### 4. The Giants pick Roosevelt Brown, 1953

Down in the 27th round of the draft, you don't expect much. So no one in the Giants organization objected when someone with the club tossed out a name he'd seen in an article about an unknown black All-American from little Morgan State College: Roosevelt Brown. The Giants had never seen him play, and Brown had never seen a pro game, never seen a white college team, and never played with or against whites. But the young Virginian came to New York, became one of only four players from that draft to make the Giants, and remained as the starting tackle until 1965—and the linchpin of the offense during the glory years of the franchise.

### 5. The Yankees pick Thurman Munson, 1968

In 1968 the once-proud Yankees were foundering, heading for their fourth straight year out of the running. Their starting catcher was one Jake Gibbs, who had little to recommend him. So the Yankees used the fourth overall pick in the draft on Munson, whose rise to the majors two years later began the rebirth of the Yankee franchise.

### 6. The Rangers pick Brad Park, 1966

Yes, Bobby Orr was great, the best defenseman there ever was. But Brad Park, chosen second overall by the Rangers in 1966, was, outside of Orr, the best of their generation, and his arrival in New York coincided with one of the finest eras in Rangers hockey.

### 7. The Knicks pick Patrick Ewing, 1985

The Big Fella never seemed entirely comfortable with New York, its fans, and its media hordes, and he never brought the team that elusive NBA championship. But from the day the Knicks exulted upon winning the right to pick him in the first NBA draft lottery, Ewing did just about everything else—score, rebound, and turn the Knicks into annual contenders throughout the 1990s.

### 8. The Rangers pick Brian Leetch, 1986

With the ninth overall pick of the 1986 draft, the Rangers got their best defenseman since Brad Park: Leetch became the first Garden denizen to win the Calder Trophy (for best rookie), won two Norris Trophies as best defenseman, was just the fifth defenseman in history (and the only American defenseman) to notch 100 points in a season, and was the first non-Canadian and only American to earn the Conn Smythe Trophy as playoff MVP. He even became captain after Mark Messier left, a sure sign of his stature in New York.

### 9. The Knicks pick Walt Frazier, 1967

Back in college, Walt Frazier didn't know how to catch people's attention with his clothes or vocabulary, but he was always dazzling on the court. When unheralded Southern Illinois romped through the 1967 NIT at Madison Square Garden and upset Marquette in the finals, Knick officials couldn't help but notice the team's guard, who scored, passed, rebounded, and played defense. They made sure to pick Frazier in the first round so that he could keep on doing those things on the Garden floor.

### 10. The Rangers pick Mike Richter, 1985

In 1985 the Rangers chose Ulf Dahlen seventh overall. Dahlen proved a solid player, but it was down in the second round at the 28th pick that the Rangers made the steal of the draft, uncovering goalie Mike Richter, who would go on to play an integral part in the 1994 championship and become possibly the Rangers' greatest goalie of all time.

## THE BEST FREE-AGENT SIGNINGS: The Top 5

### 1. The Mets luck into Tom Seaver, 1966

Tom Seaver arrived before traditional free agency, but his original contract with Atlanta, which drafted him, was voided on a technicality. Seaver was made a free agent, and the commissioner's office ruled that teams willing to spend $50,000 to match the Braves' offer could drop their names in a hat. Only the Phillies, Indians, and Mets thought Seaver worth the investment. The Mets were picked, and voilà, their future was rewritten.

### 2. The Yankees hitch up with Reggie Jackson, 1976

The Boss wanted a big name, a splashy player who could mash the ball. He got all that and more by signing Jackson for

## Honorable Mention—Best Free-Agent Signings: Three More from the Sports World's Biggest Spender

1. **Steinbrenner springs for a second closer, Goose Gossage, 1977**
2. **Steinbrenner imports Hideki Matsui, 2002**
3. **The Boss buys David Wells, 1996**

## Honorable Mention: The Best Deals

**1. The Mets get Mike Piazza from Florida for Preston Wilson, Ed Yarnall, and Geoff Goetz, 1997**

**2. The Rangers get Stephane Matteau, Brian Noonan, Glenn Anderson, and Craig MacTavish at the 1994 trading deadline**

**3. The Yankees get Roger Maris from Kansas City for Hank Bauer, Don Larsen, Norm Siebern, and Marv Throneberry, 1959**

**4. The Mets get Gary Carter from Montreal for Hubie Brooks, Mike Fitzgerald, Herm Winningham, and Floyd Youmans, 1984**

**5. The Dodgers get Dolf Camilli from Philadelphia for Eddie Morgan and $45,000, 1938**

$2.96 million over five years. Jackson produced 144 homers for the Yankees and an equal number of headlines. He also helped the club win the World Series in his first two seasons.

### 3. The Rangers splurge on Adam Graves, 1991

Edmonton knew Adam Graves was going to be good, very good. But they didn't feel like throwing an extra $500,000 his way during negotiations. Neil Smith, the Rangers' general manager, had no such compunction, and he wooed away the Oiler, who would lead the league in points in two of the next three seasons, including the Rangers' championship year. Graves was more than just very good. He was great. And worth every penny.

### 4. The Knicks take a chance on John Starks, 1991

John Starks was an undrafted reject, a CBA nobody, an undersized guard of limited skills. After the Knicks were able to sign him cheap, he impressed them with his emotion and his drive. Soon enough he was an inspiration, the crowd favorite, the league's best sixth man, and even an All-Star. Not bad for a scrub.

### 5. The Yankees, of course, grab the first free agent, Catfish Hunter, 1974

After arbitrator Peter Seitz revolutionized baseball and settled Hunter's contract dispute with Oakland by setting him loose as the game's first free agent, a frenzied two-week bidding war erupted. Fifteen clubs sent people to woo the ace down home in North Carolina. George Steinbrenner outspent them all—naturally—giving Hunter a $1 million bonus plus around $2.5 million over five years. Hunter only had one great and one good year before injuries set in, but he revitalized the franchise.

## THE WORST DEALS: The Top 10

### 1. The Mets trade Tom Seaver to Cincinnati for Pat Zachary, Steve Henderson, Doug Flynn, and Dan Norman, 1977

Chairman of the board M. Donald Grant liked to show who was boss, and he didn't like it when the little people—the players—stood up to him. Seaver had been outspoken in a 1976 labor dispute, then criticized the Mets' lack of improvement that off-season, all while asking for more money. Grant called Seaver an "ingrate" and planted stories with the vituperative but widely read *Daily News* columnist Dick Young, whose son-in-law had been hired by the Mets sales department. When Young's smear jobs extended to Seaver's wife Nancy, the superstar demanded a trade. At the trade deadline on June 15, 1977, he was shipped to Cincinnati. Grant was forced out the next year, but the fans and the franchise would not recover until the mid-1980s.

### 2. The Giants trade Sam Huff to Washington for defensive tackle Andy Stynchula and running back Dick James, 1964

Offensive-minded head coach Allie Sherman was insecure about the praise heaped on the Giants' famous defensive unit, so he dismantled it, trading Rosey Grier, Dick Modzelewski, and, most notoriously, the outspoken Sam Huff. Huff would play five strong seasons for the Redskins while the Giants plummeted into what became essentially an 18-year funk.

### 3. The Mets trade Nolan Ryan and three players to California for Jim Fregosi, 1971

An epic mistake. Fregosi's best days were past while Ryan's best were still to come . . . and would last two decades.

### 4. The Giants deal Edd Roush, Christy Mathewson, and Bill McKechnie to Cincinnati for Buck Herzog and Red Killefer, 1916

Christy Mathewson wanted to manage, so Giant manager John McGraw traded him to Cincinnati, which had just fired player-manager Buck Herzog. But the Reds wanted another player, so McGraw threw in outspoken young Edd Roush, with whom he had clashed. Roush was

## More Mets Messes Through the Decades

**1. The 1960s: The Mets trade Harry Chiti for himself, 1962**

No move better symbolized the endearing ineptitude of the early Mets than the Harry Chiti trade. The Mets acquired the catcher from Cleveland in April for a player to be named later. In 41 at-bats, Chiti batted .195, far worse than the five other catchers the Mets auditioned. So on June 15 the team announced the player being sent to Cleveland was Chiti himself. Thanks, but no thanks.

**2. The 1970s: The Mets trade Rusty Staub (and prospect) to Detroit for Mickey Lolich (and prospect), 1975**

The Amos Otis–for–Joe Foy trade damaged the Mets slightly more in the 1970s, but took place in late 1969. Meanwhile, Staub (who had cost the Mets Ken Singleton and Mike Jorgensen) was the Mets' best hitter, having set a club record with 105 RBIs in 1975, and he was also immensely popular with teammates and fans. But the Mets, believing they had a cheap replacement in prospect Mike Vail, traded Staub for Mickey Lolich, an overweight, out-of-shape has-been three years removed from his last good season. Lolich gave the Mets one bad season and Vail was a dud, while Staub drove in 318 runs over the next three years.

**3. The 1980s: The Mets dump Kevin Mitchell (with four others) for Kevin McReynolds (and two prospects), 1986**

Kevin Mitchell came from a notoriously difficult background and was perceived by the Mets front office as a potential bad influence on impressionable Doc Gooden and Darryl Strawberry, even though Mitchell really was better trained to deal with whatever life dealt, while Gooden and Strawberry found trouble on their own. So shortly after the 1986 World Series, the Mets traded Mitchell for McReynolds. Although their RBI totals and batting averages were comparable over the next five years, Mitch was an exuberant fan favorite, while McReynolds was a loner who preferred hunting to baseball and played like it. The Mets' bland-ification had begun.

**4. The 1990s: The Mets acquire and get rid of Jeff Kent, 1992 and 1996**

First the Mets dealt outspoken free-agent-to-be David Cone for Jeff Kent and Ryan Thompson. Cone would win the 1994 Cy Young and finish in the top 10 in ERA and strikeouts six more times and the top 10 in wins three times. Then the Mets gave up on Kent, who, despite a mediocre glove, had developed into a solid hitter. They traded him to Cleveland (with Jose Vizcaino) for Carlos Baerga and gloated about their heist. Baerga proved an even bigger liability defensively, and his once-vaunted offensive skills evaporated completely, while Kent landed in San Francisco and posted Hall of Fame–caliber numbers. It was, for the Mets, a lose-lose situation—as was virtually the entire decade.

**5. The 2000s: The Mets trade Jason Bay and Bobby Jones to San Diego for Steve Reed and Jason Middlebrook, 2002**

As bad as the headline-conscious deals were that brought Mo Vaughn and Roberto Alomar to the Mets, they didn't cost the team much. Far worse are the ones that get away. Although trading Scott Kazmir may haunt New York more in the long run, so far the loss of Jason Bay for a mediocre middle reliever hurts most of all. Bay won the 2004 Rookie of the Year Award, then followed up with a 32-homer, 101-RBI, .306-BA season in 2005, and he did it all for the lowly Pirates (who acquired him from San Diego). Imagine him in a Met uniform alongside Jose Reyes and David Wright.

among the league's top five batters in seven of the next eight seasons and hit over .300 12 times overall.

### 5. The Yankees trade Jay Buhner and two prospects to Seattle for Ken Phelps, 1988

In the 1980s George Steinbrenner unloaded prospects Willie McGee, Fred McGriff, Doug Drabek, and Bob Tewksbury for more established players. But he reached a new low in trading Jay Buhner for Ken Phelps. Phelps hit .224 and was gone a year later; Buhner averaged 32 homers and 99 RBIs from 1991 to 1997 and hit .458 in the 1995 ALDS against the Yankees.

### 6. The Yankees trade Vic Power to Kansas City in an 11-player deal, 1953

Vic Power was born in Puerto Rico, but to George Weiss, the racist Yankees general manager, the dark-skinned Power was black. And there was no way the first black Yankee was going to be flashy or flamboyant. So Power, who violated segregation rules down south during spring training, dated white women in the minors, and caught the ball one-handed on the field, was just too much. Although he tore up Triple A in 1952, Weiss refused to promote him; when Power did it again in 1953, Weiss buried him in an 11-player deal designed to hide the fact that he was giving up such a top talent. Power hit .300 four times and won seven Gold Gloves while being acknowledged as the best fielding first baseman of his era.

### 7. The Rangers give away Rick Middleton to Boston for Ken Hodge, 1976

The Rangers recognized Rick Middleton's talent, making him a first-round draft choice. Yet they surrendered him for someone whose stats and star were rapidly fading. Ken Hodge would score 23 goals and have 45 assists for the Rangers over two years; Middleton gave Boston over 400 goals and 500 assists through 1988.

### 8. The Mets trade Lenny Dykstra and Roger McDowell to Philadelphia for Juan Samuel, 1989

In the late 1980s, the disillusioned Mets front office became determined to purge the club of its feistiest personalities, and in so doing discarded two fan favorites in one terrible stroke. They sent McDowell, who'd pitch effectively for five more years, and Dykstra, who'd crush NL pitching for the next four, to Philadelphia for Samuel, a second baseman the Mets inexplicably believed could be their new center fielder (thus prompting another dubious deal—Mookie Wilson to Toronto for reliever Jeff Mussleman). Samuel hit just .228 with three homers in New York and looked utterly lost in center. The Mets quickly disposed of Samuel and spent six years looking for a new center fielder.

### 9. The Giants unload Rogers Hornsby to Boston for Shanty Hogan and Jimmy Welsh, 1928

One year after trading New York–born star Frankie Frisch for the legendary but cantankerous Rogers Hornsby, the Giants unloaded Hornsby for the eminently forgettable Shanty Hogan and Jimmy Welsh. Hornsby hit .387 with 21 homers and 94 RBIs for Boston in 1928, then went .380, 39, 149 in his MVP year in Chicago in 1929. Frisch, meanwhile, hit .300 or better seven times for St. Louis.

## Honorable Mention—Worst Free-Agent Signings: The Ones That Got Away

**1. The Mets don't sign Alex Rodriguez, 2000**

**2. The Knicks let Bernard King leave, 1987**

**3. The Jets let John Riggins walk free, 1976**

### 10. Isiah Thomas trades everyone, 2003

The Knicks were already a mess when Isiah Thomas came along, but the Knick executive's whirlwind of activity suggested a man without a plan and possibly without a clue. In under two years, he traded 19 players plus draft picks . . . including Moochie Norris, Tim Thomas, and Nazr Mohammed, players he had only recently acquired and proclaimed part of the solution. Although only some of the trades (not to mention player waivings, free-agent signings, and coach hirings and firings) have been distinctively bad and others may prove worthwhile, the addition of players with huge, long-term deals has prevented rebuilding, and the constant turnover has undermined any hope for the cohesion that was a trademark of the 1970s and 1990s Knicks.

## THE WORST DRAFT PICKS: The Top 10

### 1. The Mets make Steve Chilcott the country's number-one pick, 1966

Given the nation's number-one pick, the Mets and the Yankees almost always blow it big-time: the Yankees took Ron Blomberg over Jon Matlack, Ted Simmons, Vida Blue, and Dusty Baker, and the Mets selected Tim Foli over Thurman Munson, Greg Luzinski, Gary Mathews, and Bill Buckner.

But no mistake was more grievous than the Mets' selection of Chilcott, a catcher who bounced around the minors for six years before retiring. (Only one other top pick has ever failed to reach the majors, the Yankees' Brien Taylor.) Here's the real killer: the second pick in the draft was a guy who would have thrived in New York. Imagine the 1969 Mets with Reggie Jackson.

### 2. Showing their colors, the Knicks pick Ronnie Shavlik over K. C. Jones, 1956

An awful choice that also revealed the Knicks' priorities—they annually picked lackluster white players over more talented blacks. In 1957 it was Brendan McCann over Sam Jones; in 1958 they had two first-round choices and went with Mike Farmer and Pete Brennan over Hal Greer; in 1960 they selected Darrell Imhoff over Brooklyn's own Lenny Wilkens. By that time, of course, the Knicks were the laughingstock of the league. They only began improving after drafting Willis Reed and acquiring Dick Barnett.

### 3. The Jets pick Paul Seiler, 1967

Seiler, a lineman who'd play just 13 games for the Jets (and just 39 in the NFL), was picked ahead of four future Hall of Famers: Alan Page, Gene Upshaw, Lem Barney, and Willie Lanier.

**4. The Giants don't know Jack, 1971**
The Giants picked running back Rocky Thompson, converted him into a wide receiver, then bumped him down to kick returner for two years. They passed over Jack Youngblood, Jack Tatum, and Jack Ham, not to mention Kenny Anderson, Lyle Alzado, and Mel Gray.

**5. The Mets pick Rich Puig, 1971**
Rich Puig went 0-for-10 in his major league career. The Mets could have had Jim Rice, George Brett, Keith Hernandez, Ron Guidry, or Mike Schmidt. Given the Mets' chronic instability at third base, passing over Brett and Schmidt was particularly painful.

**6. The Yankees fork over $1.55 million for Brien Taylor, 1991**
Taylor's 99-mph rocket inspired a signing bonus that tripled the old record. (Thank you, agent Scott Boras.) But two years later, Taylor got into an off-season fight at a bar and fell on his shoulder. He never recovered and never reached the majors. Plenty of players picked after him did, however, including Manny Ramirez, Cliff Floyd, and Shawn Green.

**7. The price is not right for the Knicks, 1970**
The Knicks chose University of Illinois guard Mike Price; the next two teams, San Diego and Cincinnati, took future Hall of Fame guards Calvin Murphy and Nate Archibald (a native New Yorker), respectively.

**8. The Mets and the Yankees both blow it, 1993**
The Mets took Kirk Presley, and the Yankees took Matt Drews. Neither reached the majors. The Mets passed over Billy Wagner, Chris Carpenter, Derrek Lee, and Jason Varitek, while the Yankees had a shot at the latter three.

**9. The Jets pick Chris Ward, 1978**
The Jets used the fourth selection overall for Ward, an offensive tackle, instead of picking James Lofton, John Jefferson, or Ozzie Newsome.

**10. The Mets, going first, pick Shawn Abner, 1984**
The Mets took Abner over Bill Swift, Cory Snyder, Jay Bell, and, most infamously, USC slugger Mark McGwire.

## Honorable Mention—Worst Free-Agent Signings: The Steinbrenner Special

1. **Kenny Rogers folds in the Bronx, 1995**
2. **The Yankees revamp, briefly, with Dave Collins, 1981**
3. **The Evil Empire hauls in Jose Contreras, 2003**
4. **The Yankees give Spike Owen millions for no apparent reason, 1992**
5. **The Boss gets seduced by Carl Pavano and Jaret Wright, lets Pedro go to the Mets, 2004**

# THE WORST FREE-AGENT SIGNINGS

**1. Ed Whitson falls apart on the Yankees, 1985**
Ed Whitson is the ultimate symbol of Steinbrennerian misspending on players signed for a good-walk year without thought of whether they could handle the bubbling cauldron of the Bronx with its stew of feral fans, rabid reporters, and bombastic boss. After flourishing in San Diego, Whitson buckled under the abuse and pressure heaped on him here. His ERA skyrocketed, his outlook collapsed, and finally he was shipped back to the Padres, where he again pitched well. Now, if only Steinbrenner had learned a lesson.

**2. The Mets sign Vince Coleman, 1990**
Trying to make a splash, the Mets started the 1990s off by signing Vince Coleman, a one-tool player Met fans had loathed when he played with the rival St. Louis Cardinals. Familiarity would breed further contempt. With his hitting in decline, Coleman was a defensive liability and stood out only by being the least fan- and media-friendly player on baseball's most misanthropic team. After only 235 lackluster games over three years, the Mets shed this albatross. By then, there were plenty of others weighing them down.

**3. The Rangers sign Theo Fleury, Valeri Kamensky, Sylvain Lefebvre, Stephane Quintal, Kirk McLean, and Tim Taylor, 1999**
The Rangers' spending binge of the late 1990s and early 2000s produced one fiasco after another. In 1999 Neil Smith dashed off huge checks for a half-dozen free agents—Theo Fleury, Valeri Kamensky, Sylvain Lefebvre, Stephane Quintal, Kirk McLean, and Tim Taylor—all of whom were over the hill (with the possible exception of Fleury, who was known to have substance abuse issues). Instead of improving the Rangers' fortunes, this high-priced squadron annihilated them, ultimately costing Smith his job.

# Schoolboy Heroics

*Nearly every child dreams of growing up to win the big game, but some attain that fantasy while still a kid. Little League and high school sports have smaller players and smaller audiences, but on occasion they provide major league dramatics.*

## THE TOP 3 SCHOOLBOY GAMES

**1. Roger Brown**

Wingate High's Roger Brown poured in 39 points and outshone Boys High's already legendary star Connie Hawkins, but even after Hawkins fouled out, Boys High held on to win 62–59 in the Public School Athletic League semifinals on March 17, 1960, in Madison Square Garden.

**2. Stephon Marbury**

After his three brothers failed to win the PSAL, and after he fell just short twice himself, on March 18, 1995, in Madison Square Garden, Stephon Marbury scored 26 points and finally led Lincoln to its long-awaited championship.

**3. Kenny Anderson**

Archbishop Molloy freshman guard Kenny Anderson averaged 25 points per game in the playoffs. In the statewide Catholic High School Athletic Association title game at Rose Hill Gymnasium at Fordham University on March 15, 1986, with his team trailing 88–86 and four seconds left in overtime, he won it all by grabbing a rebound, scoring over a 7'2" center, and hitting the and-one foul shot.

## A SCHOOLBOY CLASSIC ON THE ROAD

**Danny Yacarino**

At Howard J. Lamade Field in Williamsport, Pennsylvania, on August 29, 1964, Danny Yacarino of Staten Island's Midland Little League single-handedly won the city's first Little League World Series title by hitting a first-inning homer, then pitching an eight-strikeout no-hitter.

## THE MOST HEARTBREAKING SCHOOLBOY LOSS

**Lew Alcindor**

After winning 71 straight games over two-plus seasons, Power Memorial seven-footer Lew Alcindor finally met his match in DeMatha High, whose coach, Morgan Wootten, held a tennis racquet above his head in practice to teach his kids to alter the trajectory of their shots. On January 30, 1965, at Cole Field House in Maryland, DeMatha won 46–43 in what many consider the greatest high school game ever.

## FANS IN THE GAME

**The PSAL championship, March 17, 1964, Madison Square Garden**

Bottles flew, fights broke out in the stands, and 500 fans swarmed the court afterwards while another large and hostile crowd surged into the streets of midtown after the PSAL championship, prompting Madison Square Garden to ban the tournament for a quarter-century.

## BAD BEHAVIOR

**Danny Almonte**

On August 31, 2001, after becoming a celebrity by striking out 48 batters over three starts—a no-hitter, the Little League World Series' first perfect game in 34 years, and a one-hitter—12-year-old Danny Almonte was revealed to in fact be 14, and to have joined his team, the Bronx-based Rolando Paulino All-Stars, after the official deadline. His performance and that of his team in the Little League World Series in Williamsport, Pennsylvania, were erased, and his father and team officials were banned from Little League for life.

# Movin' Out

*Even though the Giants and Jets play in New Jersey, they still call themselves New York teams, and admittedly, even the most diehard New Yorker pays attention to what goes on outside the city limits—at least in terms of sports. So it only seems fair to give those who perform just beyond the border their moment of glory.*

## THE BEST OF THE 'BURBS

### 1. Belmont Park, 1973

Secretariat won the Triple Crown by 31 lengths at the Belmont Stakes, covering the one-and-a-half-mile race in a record 2:24.

### 2. Giants Stadium, January 4, 1987

Joe Morris ran for one TD, Phil Simms passed for another, and Lawrence Taylor recovered a fumble and rumbled in for a third . . . all in the second quarter as the Giants destroyed the 49ers 49–3 in the playoffs en route to their first Super Bowl.

### 3. Nassau Coliseum, May 24, 1980

After five years of just falling short, the Islanders finally silenced their doubters by winning their first of four straight Stanley Cups when Bobby Nystrom, one of the last original Islanders, scored in overtime.

### 4. Nassau Coliseum, May 13, 1976

With a behind-the-glass, switch-hands, reverse-direction, under-the-backboard scoop and two devastating dunks, Julius Erving led the Nets back from 22 points down in the third quarter to finish off the favored Denver Nuggets in the final ABA Finals.

### 5. Belmont, June 10, 1978

In racing's greatest rivalry, Affirmed, ridden by Steve Cauthen, edged Alydar for the third straight race—by just a half-neck, in the sixth-fastest and fourth-closest Belmont Stakes ever—to finish off the Triple Crown.

### 6. Giants Stadium, January 13, 1991

With Phil Simms injured, the conservative Bill Parcells surprised everyone by turning Jeff Hostetler loose, while coordinator Bill Belichick switched up the defense as the Giants strangled Chicago, 31–3, in the playoff run to their second Super Bowl.

### 7. Continental Airlines Arena, June 9, 2003

Martin Brodeur came up with the NHL's first Game 7 finals shutout since 1965, leading the Devils to their third Stanley Cup in nine years.

### 8. Continental Airlines Arena, May 2, 2002

Jason Kidd scored 20 points across the fourth quarter and two overtimes as he turned back Reggie Miller's Pacers, leading the Nets out of the first round and on toward the NBA Finals.

### 9. Giants Stadium, January 10, 1999

Keyshawn Johnson caught a touchdown pass, scored on a reverse, recovered a fumble, and even grabbed an interception, while Curtis Martin and Vinny Testaverde also had big games. Bill Parcells's Jets, just two years removed from a 1–15 embarrassment, shot down Jacksonville in the playoffs, 34–24.

### 10. Nassau Coliseum, May 12, 1975

After upsetting the Rangers in the opening round and becoming just the second team in any sport to recover from being down 3–0, against Pittsburgh in the second round, the Islanders nearly did it again, falling behind the defending champion Philadelphia Flyers 3–0, then winning Games 4 and 5 and even Game 6, when Gerry Hart broke a 1–1 tie in the third period.

## THE WORST DAYS IN THE 'BURBS

### 1. Giants Stadium, November 20, 1978

Just seconds away from a seemingly certain victory, Joe Pisarcik fumbled it away, inspiring fans to fly an airplane toting the infamous banner: 15 Years of Lousy Football . . . We've Had Enough.

### 2. Giants Stadium, December 20, 2003

During a live sideline interview, a drunken Joe Namath told ESPN sideline reporter Suzy Kolber . . . twice . . . that he really wanted to kiss her.

### 3. Giants Stadium, December 23, 1995

Giant fans hurled snowballs and ice chunks, knocking out San Diego's equipment manager and injuring 15 fans and 10 security officers.

### 4. Giants Stadium, October 17, 1988

During a Monday Night Football game, drunken Jet fans set fire to their seats and brawled endlessly, producing 56 ejections, 15 arrests, and five hospitalizations.

### 5. Continental Airlines Arena, March 21, 1997

The Nets acknowledged playing prerecorded tapes of crowd noise during games to make it seem as if their fans really cared.

# Timeline The BEST of EACH YEAR

**1898** Charles Miller wins the last solo six-day bicycle race at the Garden.

**1899** Jim Jeffries beats Tom Sharkey in the first sporting event successfully filmed with artificial lights.

**1900** Jim Jeffries and Jim Corbett slug it out at Coney Island.

**1903** "Iron Man" Joe McGinnity wins both ends of a double-header three times in a month.

**1904** Jack Chesbro wild-pitches away the pennant for New York.

**1905** Christy Mathewson wins the Series with his third shutout.

**1908** Fred Merkle fails to touch second base.

**1909** Henri St. Yves wins the Marathon Derby.

**1911** "Home Run" Baker earns his nickname in the World Series.

**1912** Rube Marquard wins his 19th straight.

**1915** The Astor Cup brings big-time auto racing to Brooklyn.

**1916** Boston's Babe Ruth shuts down Brooklyn for 14 innings in the World Series.

**1917** The Giants' defense throws away the World Series on a botched rundown.

**1919** The Yankees get Babe Ruth.

**1920** Man o' War turns back one last challenge from John P. Grier at Aqueduct.

**1921** The Giants win the first "Subway Series."

**1922** Game 2 of the World Series is called for darkness despite plenty of daylight.

**1923** Babe Ruth christens "the House That Ruth Built" with a homer.

**1924** "The Four Horsemen" of Notre Dame beat Army at the Polo Grounds.

**1925** Red Grange joins the NFL and helps save the Giants' franchise.

**1926** Grover Alexander strikes out Tony Lazzeri with the bases loaded in Game 7.

**1927** Babe Ruth hits his 60th homer.

**1928** Notre Dame wins one for the Gipper.

**1929** Notre Dame beats Army again, this time on a 96-yard interception return.

**1930** The Giants beat Notre Dame's All-Stars to raise $100,000 for Depression victims.

**1932** Babe Ruth calls his homer shot.

**1933** Glenn Cunningham wins the Wanamaker Mile at the Millrose Games.

**1934** The Giants win the NFL Championship in "the Sneaker Game."

**1935** Jim Braddock, a.k.a. "Cinderella Man," wins the heavy-weight title.

**1936** Hank Luisetti brings the jump shot to New York.

**1937** Seabiscuit wins by a nose at Aqueduct.

**1938** Joe Louis defeats Max Schmeling.

**1939** Lou Gehrig proclaims himself "the luckiest man on the face of this earth."

**1940** The Rangers win their third Stanley Cup.

**1941** Joe DiMaggio sets a new hitting streak record.

**1942** Sugar Ray Robinson wins the first of his fights with Jake "Raging Bull" LaMotta.

**1943** Sid Luckman passes for seven TDs on Sid Luckman Day.

**1944** St. John's wins its second straight NIT.

**1946** "The Battle of the Century" between Army and Notre Dame ends 0–0.

**1947** Jackie Robinson breaks the color barrier.

**1948** Babe Ruth makes a final appearance at the Stadium.

**1949** The Yankees beat the Red Sox on the season's final day, giving birth to a new dynasty.

**1950** CCNY wins the NIT and NCAA.

**1951** Bobby Thomson hits "the Shot Heard 'Round the World."

**1952** Billy Martin's lunging catch saves Game 7 for the Yankees.

**1953** Billy Martin's 12th hit gives the Yankees their fifth straight crown.

**1954** Willie Mays makes "the Catch."

**1955** "Next year" finally arrives for Brooklyn.

**1956** Don Larsen achieves perfection.

**1957** The Dodgers move to the West Coast.

**1958** Johnny Unitas leads the Colts over the Giants in "the Greatest Game Ever Played."

**1959** Ingemar Johansson floors Floyd Patterson.

**1960** Wingate High's Roger Brown scores 39 points to outplay Boys High's superstar Connie Hawkins, but Boys High pulls off a 62–59 win in the PSAL semifinals.

**1961** Roger Maris hits his 61st homer.

**1962** The Mets bring NL baseball back to New York City.

**1964** Staten Island's Danny Yaccarino pitches a no-hitter to win the Little League World Series.

**1965** The Jets draft Joe Namath.

**1966** The Mets get Tom Seaver when their name is picked out of a hat.

**1967** Walt Frazier sparks Southern Illinois's surprising NIT win and inspires the Knicks to draft him.

**1968** Arthur Ashe wins the first U.S. Open.

**1969** The Amazin' Mets win the World Series.

**1970** Willis Reed limps and Walt Frazier soars as the Knicks win Game 7.

**1971** Ali-Frazier I at the Garden.

**1972** The Knicks storm back with 19 straight points to beat Milwaukee, 87–86.

**1973** The Mets complete their last-to-first comeback, clinching the pennant on the last day of the season.

**1974** Jimmy Connors topples the tennis establishment and caps off his year with a U.S. Open win.

**1975** Pele becomes a Cosmo, and suddenly New York watches soccer.

**1976** The New York Marathon goes citywide.

**1977** Reggie Jackson hits three homers to win the World Series.

**1978** Bucky Dent lifts one over the Green Monster.

**1979** The Rangers beat the Islanders to reach the Stanley Cup finals.

**1980** John McEnroe gets revenge against Bjorn Borg in the U.S. Open.

**1981** St. John's Frank Viola outlasts Yale's Ron Darling.

**1982** Ilie Nastase and Open champion-to-be Jimmy Connors defy the umpires and play in the rain.

**1983** St. John's wins the Big East.

**1984** Every match goes the distance on Super Saturday.

**1985** Tom Seaver wins his 300th at Yankee Stadium.

**1986** Mookie Wilson hits a slow roller to first.

**1987** Eamonn Coghlan breaks Glenn Cunningham's record for most Wanamakers won.

**1988** Columbia finally ends its losing streak.

**1989** The Mets disintegrate as Darryl Strawberry swings at Keith Hernandez on Photo Day and the front office trades away Lenny Dykstra, Roger McDowell, and Mookie Wilson.

**1990** George Steinbrenner gets suspended "for life" for conspiring with gambler Howie Spira against Dave Winfield.

**1991** Jimmy Connors makes his last stand at the U.S. Open.

**1992** Fred Lebow overcomes cancer to run his marathon.

**1993** John Starks dunks over Michael Jordan.

**1994** After 54 years, the Rangers finally win.

**1995** Michael Jordan returns to the Garden and scores 55.

**1996** Jim Leyritz sparks the Yankee dynasty with his homer off Mark Wohlers.

**1997** The Mets get Mike Piazza.

**1998** The Yankees capture the World Series with their 125th win.

**1999** Allan Houston finishes Miami at the buzzer.

**2000** The Subway Series returns to New York.

**2001** Mike Piazza gives the city a lift after 9/11.

**2002** Pete Sampras beats Andre Agassi in his final Open final.

**2003** Aaron Boone sinks the Red Sox.

**2004** Curt Schilling carries Boston on his back despite his bloodied ankle.

**2005** Andre Agassi comes back against James Blake.

# Calendar The BEST of EACH DAY

| JANUARY 1 | JANUARY 2 | JANUARY 5 | JANUARY 9 | JANUARY 11 | JANUARY 12 | JANUARY 14 |
|---|---|---|---|---|---|---|
| Columbia beats Stanford in the Rose Bowl, 1934. | The Jets sign number-one pick Joe Namath, 1965. | The Yankees publicly announce their acquisition of Babe Ruth, 1920. | Oscar Robertson breaks out at the Garden, 1958. | George Steinbrenner hires Billy Martin for the third time, 1983. | The Jets win Super Bowl III, 1969. | Benny Leonard bloodies Ritchie Mitchell, 1921. |
| **JANUARY 15** | **JANUARY 21** | **JANUARY 22** | **JANUARY 23** | **JANUARY 27** | **JANUARY 28** | **JANUARY 30** |
| Lance Mehl's interceptions carry the Jets to the AFC Championship, 1983. | The Knicks play like quitters, 2002. | The Giants draft Roosevelt Brown in the 27th round, 1953. | The Jets lose the "Mud Bowl" in the AFC Championship in Miami, 1983. | Carl Lewis leaps into history, 1984. | Don Gehrmann and Fred Wilt finish in a virtual dead heat in the Wanamaker Mile, 1950. | Eamonn Coghlan wins his seventh Wanamaker Mile, 1987. |
| **JANUARY 31** | **FEBRUARY 1** | **FEBRUARY 4** | **FEBRUARY 5** | **FEBRUARY 11** | **FEBRUARY 15** | **FEBRUARY 18** |
| John Thomas high-jumps into the record book, 1959. | Lou Fontinato gets his face smashed in by Gordie Howe, 1959. | Glenn Cunningham wins his first Wanamaker Mile, 1933. | Gunnar Nielsen beats the battling boys behind him in the Wanamaker, 1955. | Willie Pep gets revenge against Sandy Saddler, 1949. | Coach Phil Watson humiliates his Rangers, 1959. | CCNY stars indicted, 1951. |
| **FEBRUARY 21** | **FEBRUARY 24** | **FEBRUARY 29** | **MARCH 2** | **MARCH 5** | **MARCH 6** | **MARCH 8** |
| Iona stuns number-two Louisville in prime time at the Garden, 1980. | Dennis Potvin checks Ulf Nilsson, breaking his ankle and inspiring a new cheer, 1979. | Jean Ratelle gets his ankle broken by a teammate's shot, 1972. | Wilt Chamberlain scores 100 against the Knicks, 1962. | Mike Kekich and Fritz Peterson make headlines with their wife-swapping, 1973. | The Dodgers get Dolf Camilli for a spare part and cash, 1938. | Ali-Frazier I at the Garden, 1971. |
| **MARCH 12** | **MARCH 14** | **MARCH 15** | **MARCH 16** | **MARCH 17** | **MARCH 18** | **MARCH 20** |
| St. John's wins the first Big East at the Garden, 1983. | Ernie Calverly hits the most famous shot in NIT history, a 55-foot, game-tying buzzer beater, 1946. | Freshman Kenny Anderson scores three points in OT's final seconds to give Archbishop Molloy the state Catholic School title, 1986. | The Rangers and Canadiens brawl with each other, fans, and Garden police, 1947. | Wingate's Roger Brown scores 39 to outshine Boys High star Connie Hawkins, but Boys High wins 62–59, 1960. | CCNY wins NIT, 1950. | Joe Lapchick wins fourth NIT in last game, 1965. |

| | | | | | | |
|---|---|---|---|---|---|---|
| **MARCH 21** George Mikan pours 53 points against Rhode Island in the NIT, 1945. | **MARCH 22** Frank McGuire's St. John's squad gets revenge on Adolph Rupp's Kentucky and advances to the Final Four, 1952. | **MARCH 23** Bernard King tears up his knee, 1985. | **MARCH 24** Emile Griffith fatally injures Benny Paret in a fight at the Garden, 1962. | **MARCH 26** The Knicks win over the Bullets in double-overtime in Game 1 of the playoffs, 1970. | **MARCH 27** The Americans stun the Rangers in quadruple-overtime, 1938. | **MARCH 28** CCNY wins its second title in three weeks, 1951. |
| **MARCH 30** The Rangers edge Detroit in a goal game on their way to the Stanley Cup, 1933. | **APRIL 1** George Steinbrenner calls Hideki Irabu a "fat pussy toad," 1999. | **APRIL 3** The Mets get the rights to Tom Seaver when the team's name is picked out of a hat, 1966. | **APRIL 4** The Knicks stun Syracuse with a fourth-quarter comeback in the deciding game, 1951. | **APRIL 7** Secretariat wins big at the Gotham, 1973. | **APRIL 8** Babe Ruth gets the "bellyache heard 'round the world," 1925. | **APRIL 9** The Rangers' Smurfs stomp the Broad Street Bullies, 1983. |
| **APRIL 12** The Mets get a ticker-tape parade before they've ever won a game, 1962. | **APRIL 13** The Rangers win the Stanley Cup, 1940. | **APRIL 15** Jackie Robinson breaks the color barrier, 1947. | **APRIL 17** Mickey Mantle hits the first "tape measure" homer, 1953. | **APRIL 18** Babe Ruth christens "the House That Ruth Built" with a homer, 1923. | **APRIL 19** The Knicks' last shot falls just short, as does their effort to repeat as champs, 1971. | **APRIL 22** Tom Seaver strikes out 19, including 10 in a row, 1970. |
| **APRIL 23** Wayne Gretzky pulls out one last hat trick, 1997. | **APRIL 24** "The Great Footrace" popularizes a new sport, 1835. | **APRIL 25** The Rangers pick up Brad Park in the draft, 1966. | **APRIL 26** The hapless expansion Mets acquire Harry Chiti for a player to be named, only to later return Chiti to sender, 1962. | **APRIL 27** Bernard pours in another 40-pointer to bury Detroit, 1984. | **APRIL 28** George Steinbrenner angers Yogi Berra by using a go-between to fire him, 1985. | **APRIL 29** The Knicks win Game 7 of the Eastern Conference Finals in Boston, 1973. |
| **APRIL 30** Jeff Van Gundy wraps himself around Alonzo Mourning's leg, 1998. | **MAY 1** Brooklyn goes 26 innings in a tie, 1920. | **MAY 3** The Knicks pick Walt Frazier in the draft, 1967. | **MAY 4** Willis Reed goes down, but the Knicks bounce back to win in Game 5, 1970. | **MAY 5** Dave Schultz bullies the Rangers into submission, 1974. | **MAY 7** Reggie Miller shoots down the Knicks, 1995. | **MAY 8** Willis Reed limps and Walt Frazier soars as the Knicks win Game 7, 1970. |
| **MAY 11** Jim Corbett has his finest hour in a loss to Jim Jeffries, 1900. | **MAY 12** The Knicks tear off a 32–2 run to stop Miami, 1999. | **MAY 13** Peytona versus Fashion draws a huge crowd at Union Course, 1845. | **MAY 14** John L. Sullivan brings boxing to the Garden, 1883. | **MAY 15** Ty Cobb attacks a New York heckler, 1912. | **MAY 16** Allan Houston sinks Miami, 1999. | **MAY 17** David Wells pitches a perfect game, 1998. |
| **MAY 20** Lou Piniella and Carlton Fisk incite a major Yankees–Red Sox brawl, 1976. | **MAY 21** The Dodgers pound the Reds for 15 runs in first inning, 1952. | **MAY 22** The Mets trade for Mike Piazza, 1998. | **MAY 25** John Starks dunks over Michael Jordan, 1993. | **MAY 26** Andy Payne wins the Bunyon Derby, 1928. | **MAY 27** The Rangers finally get past the Devils in OT in Game 7, 1994. | **MAY 28** George Steinbrenner orders YES network not to show Don Zimmer, 2003. |

| | | | | | | |
|---|---|---|---|---|---|---|
| **MAY 31**<br>Henry Armstrong collects another belt, 1938. | **JUNE 1**<br>The Yankees pick Derek Jeter in the first round, 1992. | **JUNE 2**<br>Charles Smith can't get the ball in from underneath, 1993. | **JUNE 3**<br>Lou Gehrig becomes the first modern player to homer four times in a game, 1932. | **JUNE 4**<br>Pete Reiser receives last rites after yet another crash into the outfield wall, 1947. | **JUNE 5**<br>Patrick Ewing lifts the Knicks into the NBA Finals, 1994. | **JUNE 7**<br>The Yankees take Thurman Munson with their first pick, 1968. |
| **JUNE 8**<br>In draft, the Mets take Rich Puig over Jim Rice, George Brett, Keith Hernandez, Ron Guidry, and Mike Schmidt, 1971. | **JUNE 10**<br>Triple dead heat at Aqueduct, 1944. | **JUNE 13**<br>Babe Ruth makes one final appearance at Yankee Stadium, 1948. | **JUNE 14**<br>The Rangers finally win, 1994. | **JUNE 15**<br>Johnny Vander Meer pitches his second straight no-hitter, 1938. | **JUNE 17**<br>Ron Guidry fans 18, 1978. | **JUNE 18**<br>The Knicks take Patrick Ewing with the number-one pick in the draft, 1985. |
| **JUNE 21**<br>The Rangers select Brian Leetch in the draft, 1986. | **JUNE 22**<br>Joe Louis defeats Max Schmeling, 1938. | **JUNE 23**<br>Don Zimmer suffers a brutal beaning, 1956. | **JUNE 25**<br>Baseball returns to Brooklyn, 2001. | **JUNE 26**<br>Seabiscuit wins by a nose, 1937. | **JUNE 30**<br>The Mets pound Atlanta with a 10-run eighth, 2000. | **JULY 2**<br>Joe DiMaggio sets the all-time hitting streak mark, 1941. |
| **JULY 3**<br>Rube Marquard wins his 19th straight, 1912. | **JULY 4**<br>Lou Gehrig proclaims himself the "luckiest man," 1939. | **JULY 5**<br>At 3:55 A.M., the Mets finish a 19-inning game they started on July 4, 1985. | **JULY 10**<br>Man o' War turns back John P. Grier, 1920. | **JULY 11**<br>Jesse Owens leads American track stars in a rousing show at the Olympic trials, 1936. | **JULY 17**<br>Rocky Marciano and Ezzard Charles go the distance, 1954. | **JULY 18**<br>David Cone pitches a perfect game, 1999. |
| **JULY 19**<br>Pete Reiser crashes into the wall in St. Louis, ruining his .380 average and the Dodgers' pennant hopes, 1942. | **JULY 20**<br>The Giants trade away Edd Roush, who would then top .300 12 times, 1916. | **JULY 21**<br>The Yankees trade Jay Buhner for Ken Phelps, 1988. | **JULY 23**<br>Billy Martin says of Reggie Jackson and George Steinbrenner, "One's a born liar, the other's convicted," 1978. | **JULY 24**<br>Billy Martin incites "the Pine Tar Incident," 1983. | **JULY 27**<br>Bret Saberhagen sprays bleach at reporters, then lies about it, 1993. | **JULY 29**<br>Jake Powell dispenses some virulent racism in a radio interview, 1938. |
| **JULY 30**<br>George Steinbrenner gets suspended "for life" over his association with gambler-extortionist Howie Spira, 1990. | **JULY 31**<br>Mets trade prospect Jason Bay for mediocre relief help, 2002. | **AUGUST 1**<br>Thurman Munson and Carlton Fisk duke it out, 1973. | **AUGUST 2**<br>Thurman Munson dies in a plane crash, 1979. | **AUGUST 4**<br>Tom Seaver wins his 300th game, at Yankee Stadium, 1985. | **AUGUST 5**<br>Zack Wheat's legs give out as he crawls around the bases, 1926. | **AUGUST 7**<br>Joe Namath rips up his knee during the preseason, 1971. |
| **AUGUST 11**<br>Mike Cameron and Carlos Beltran collide, 2005. | **AUGUST 15**<br>The Giants swipe Y. A. Tittle from the 49ers, 1961. | **AUGUST 16**<br>Ray Chapman is fatally wounded by a pitched ball at Yankee Stadium, 1920. | **AUGUST 17**<br>The Jets beat the Giants in the biggest preseason game ever, 1969. | **AUGUST 18**<br>The "Pine Tar" game is finally finished, 1983. | **AUGUST 26**<br>A Yankee fan hurls a knife onto the field, striking Wally Joyner, 1986. | **AUGUST 29**<br>Yankee Sullivan outlasts William Bell, 1842. |

| | | | | | | |
|---|---|---|---|---|---|---|
| **AUGUST 30** Ilie Nastase nearly causes a riot in his loss to John McEnroe, 1979. | **AUGUST 31** Joe McGinnity wins his third double-header in a month, 1903. | **SEPTEMBER 2** Jimmy Connors defeats Aaron Krickstein and Father Time, 1991. | **SEPTEMBER 4** Chris Evert emerges as a force with her comeback win, 1971. | **SEPTEMBER 5** Pete Sampras shows his guts against Alex Corretja, 1996. | **SEPTEMBER 6** Bill Tilden wins the U.S. Nationals and becomes the first tennis superstar, 1920. | **SEPTEMBER 7** John McEnroe gets revenge against Bjorn Borg, 1980. |
| **SEPTEMBER 8** Every match goes the distance on Super Saturday, 1984. | **SEPTEMBER 9** Arthur Ashe wins the first U.S. Open, 1968. | **SEPTEMBER 10** Steffi Graf wins the Grand Slam, 1988. | **SEPTEMBER 11** Dan Rather storms off the CBS News set when the U.S. Open runs overtime, 1987. | **SEPTEMBER 12** Dr. K fans 16 and sets a rookie strikeout record, 1984. | **SEPTEMBER 14** Jack Dempsey and Luis Firpo slug each other, 1923. | **SEPTEMBER 16** Yankee Whitey Witt is knocked unconscious when a St. Louis fan beans him with a bottle during a crucial game, 1922. |
| **SEPTEMBER 17** Phil Rizzuto's suicide squeeze knocks out the Indians, 1951. | **SEPTEMBER 20** The Miracle Mets win in a miracle finish in the 13th inning, 1973. | **SEPTEMBER 21** Mike Piazza lifts New York's spirits with a home run, 2001. | **SEPTEMBER 22** The Yankees fall to a new low, land in basement, then draw just 413 fans, 1966. | **SEPTEMBER 23** Sugar Ray Robinson and Carmen Basilio slug each other senseless, 1957. | **SEPTEMBER 24** Don Budge becomes the first to win the Grand Slam, 1938. | **SEPTEMBER 25** Mark Gastineau's "sack dance" incites a brawl that leads to "anti-taunt" rules, 1983. |
| **SEPTEMBER 26** Babe Ruth hits homers 57 and 58 to spark a crucial win en route to the Yankees' first pennant, 1921. | **SEPTEMBER 27** Tony Zale drops Rocky Graziano, 1946. | **SEPTEMBER 29** Willie Mays makes "the Catch," 1954. | **SEPTEMBER 30** Babe Ruth hits his 60th, 1927. | **OCTOBER 1** Roger Maris hits his 61st, 1961. | **OCTOBER 2** The Yankees and the Dodgers both clinch on the final day of the season, 1949. | **OCTOBER 3** Bobby Thomson hits "the Shot Heard 'Round the World," 1951. |
| **OCTOBER 4** "Next year" finally arrives for Brooklyn, 1955. | **OCTOBER 5** The Yankees win their fifth straight Series, 1953. | **OCTOBER 7** Mel Ott's 10th-inning homer wins the World Series for the Giants, 1933. | **OCTOBER 8** Don Larsen achieves perfection, 1956. | **OCTOBER 9** Babe Ruth hits three homers to complete the Yankees' sweep of St. Louis, 1928. | **OCTOBER 10** Grover Alexander fans Tony Lazzeri with the bases loaded in Game 7, 1926. | **OCTOBER 11** Lenny Dykstra rolls a ninth-inning homer in the NLCS, 1986. |
| **OCTOBER 12** Casey Stengel becomes the first player to break up a scoreless World Series game with a homer, then thumbs his nose at Babe Ruth and the Yankees, 1923. | **OCTOBER 13** The Giants win 1–0 to win the first Subway Series, 1921. | **OCTOBER 14** Mathewson shuts out the A's again, 1905. | **OCTOBER 15** The Yankees win their first Series, 1923. | **OCTOBER 16** The Amazin' Mets win it all, 1969. | **OCTOBER 17** Robin Ventura hits a grand-slam single, 1999. | **OCTOBER 18** Reggie, Reggie, Reggie, 1977. |
| **OCTOBER 19** Grantland Rice's "Four Horsemen" column appears after Notre Dame beats Army, 1924. | **OCTOBER 20** The Yankees complete their collapse against Boston, 2004. | **OCTOBER 21** The Subway Series returns to New York, 2000. | **OCTOBER 22** Roger Clemens throws half a bat at Mike Piazza, 2000. | **OCTOBER 23** Dixon exults, Smith collapses at the end of the Marathon, 1983. | **OCTOBER 24** First five-borough Marathon, 1976. | **OCTOBER 25** Mookie Wilson hits a slow roller to first, 1986. |

| **OCTOBER 26** Alberto Salazar wins the New York Marathon on his first try, 1980. | **OCTOBER 27** The Mets come back once more to win Game 7, 1986. | **OCTOBER 28** Y. A. Tittle throws for seven TDs, 1962. | **NOVEMBER 1** Fred Lebow runs his own NYC Marathon while battling brain cancer, 1992. | **NOVEMBER 2** Margaret Okayo sets a women's Marathon record, 2003. | **NOVEMBER 3** Jim Jeffries beats Tom Sharkey under the blazing lights, 1899. | **NOVEMBER 4** Mariano Rivera proves human in the ninth inning of Game 7, 2001. |
|---|---|---|---|---|---|---|
| **NOVEMBER 6** German Silva makes a wrong turn, 1994. | **NOVEMBER 7** Paula Radcliffe wins the closest women's Marathon, 2004. | **NOVEMBER 9** Notre Dame 0, Army 0, 1946. | **NOVEMBER 10** Notre Dame wins one for the Gipper, 1928. | **NOVEMBER 11** Army humiliates Notre Dame. 59–0, 1945. | **NOVEMBER 13** Evander Holyfield fights despite his badly diminished skills, 2004. | **NOVEMBER 14** Sid Luckman passes for seven TDs on Sid Luckman Day, 1943. |
| **NOVEMBER 17** The Jets blow the game and NBC blows the coverage in the *Heidi* fiasco, 1968. | **NOVEMBER 18** Down 86–68, the Knicks score 19 straight to beat the Bucks, 87–86, 1972. | **NOVEMBER 20** Frank Gifford gets hit so hard that he temporarily retires, 1960. | **NOVEMBER 22** Richard Todd leads the Jets past Miami, 1981. | **NOVEMBER 23** The Giants clinch the Eastern Division with a last-minute comeback, 1941. | **NOVEMBER 24** Ken Strong leads NYU as it thrashes Carnegie Tech, 1928. | **NOVEMBER 26** NYU topples Fordham's "Seven Blocks of Granite," 1936. |
| **NOVEMBER 27** Yale routs Princeton before 32,000 in Brooklyn on Thanksgiving Day, showing off the growing popularity of football, 1890. | **NOVEMBER 28** Joe Namath makes a memorable comeback, 1971. | **NOVEMBER 29** The Yankees sign Reggie Jackson, 1976. | **NOVEMBER 30** Notre Dame slides past Army 7–0 on a 96-yard touchdown return, 1929. | **DECEMBER 4** The Rangers acquire Mark Messier, 1991. | **DECEMBER 5** Joe Louis wins over Joe Walcott on a bad decision, 1947. | **DECEMBER 6** "The Galloping Ghost" rides into town, saves the Giants and the NFL, 1925. |
| **DECEMBER 9** The Giants win the NFL Championship in "the Sneaker Game," 1934. | **DECEMBER 10** Charles Miller breaks the six-day bike record and gets married, 1898. | **DECEMBER 11** The Giants hold off the Packers for their second championship, 1938. | **DECEMBER 12** Joe Namath goes out on an ugly note, 1976. | **DECEMBER 13** George Steinbrenner illegally hires Dick Williams as manager, 1973. | **DECEMBER 14** Pat Summerall kicks a field goal in the snow to send the Giants into a tiebreaker playoff, 1958. | **DECEMBER 15** The Giants acquire young Christy Mathewson for washed-up Amos Rusie, 1900. |
| **DECEMBER 16** O. J. Simpson rushes for 2,000 yards, 1973. | **DECEMBER 17** Red Grange slams down the Giants' NFL Championship hopes, 1933. | **DECEMBER 19** The Knicks get Dave Debusschere in a trade, 1968. | **DECEMBER 20** Sugar Ray Robinson wins the welterweight title, 1946. | **DECEMBER 21** The Giants hold Jim Brown to eight yards in their tiebreaker playoff, 1958. | **DECEMBER 22** George Steinbrenner fires a publicist for missing a press conference right before Christmas, 1995. | **DECEMBER 23** The Rangers and the Bruins fight and the fans join in, 1979. |
| **DECEMBER 25** The Knicks win on their "one-second play," 1969. | **DECEMBER 26** The Yankees and the Red Sox privately seal the deal on the Babe Ruth sale, 1919. | **DECEMBER 27** The Jets avenge their *Heidi* loss and win the AFL title, 1968. | **DECEMBER 28** Johnny Unitas leads the Colts over the Giants in "the Greatest Game Ever Played," 1958. | **DECEMBER 29** Ned Irish debuts the Garden double-header, 1934. | **DECEMBER 30** The Giants crush the Bears for the NFL Championship, 1956. | **DECEMBER 31** The Yankees sign the first free agent in history, Catfish Hunter, 1974. |

# Acknowledgments

Of all the thank-yous I have to proffer, there are five that matter most, for they go to the people without whom this book would not have been.

First, my uncle, Jay Kriegel. Not only did he take me to my first baseball game and pass on his Jackie Robinson autograph to me, but he also laughed at the enormity of my original book idea—an "Encyclopedia of New York City Sports"—and sagely suggested something a bit more pragmatic. Of course, his suggestion was that I cover the top 25 days in New York City sports, which I couldn't resist expanding into this more encyclopedic tome. But that's entirely my problem.

Next was Luke Cyphers, who brainstormed with me on ideas for the top 100 list and the book proposal before bowing out with the wise realization that a project like this would consume far too much of a normal person's life.

Then came Susan Canavan, my editor at Houghton Mifflin, who believed in the project and thus transformed a mere idea into the book you now hold in your hands. (Thanks also for letting me tinker with the list up until and even after the last possible minute.)

And of course, Linda Lowenthal, who came on in relief at Houghton Mifflin and did an amazing job of slicing away all my excess verbiage and unnecessary trivia. (Any that remains is entirely due to my intransigence.)

Finally, the biggest thanks go to my wife Sharon and my boys, Caleb and Lucas. Once Susan gave me the go-ahead, it was my family that had to live with the insanity of the whole thing—my constant ramblings about obscure events, mumblings about moving things on and off the list, and of course, the crazy, round-the-clock work schedule it took to get this done.

I also owe a great debt to all the reporters, columnists, authors, and others who came before me, leaving behind such vivid (albeit occasionally contradictory) descriptions. And while I thank the New York and Brooklyn library systems for giving me access to all that material, I'd also like to urge everyone who enjoys reading nonfiction books of any kind to keep the pressure on our local politicians to fund our public libraries, which are cornerstones of our civilization.

Society has also changed, of course, and I offer my gratitude to the people who have created such astonishing research conveniences on the Internet as retrosheet.org, baseballlibrary.com, baseball-reference.com (and similar sites for basketball, football, and hockey), and jt-sw.com (a football treasure trove)—they are largely accurate, incredibly detailed, always available, and completely free.

I also had numerous sounding boards—people who were willing to give me their feedback about my rankings, suggestions about events I might have omitted, and insights and information about the games and athletes I was writing about.

For tennis, my rallies with Joel Drucker, Mary Carillo, and Peter Bodo were particularly helpful, but I also had coaching from Bud Collins and Gene Scott. Special thanks also to Chris Widmaier at the USTA for filling in the fact gaps. When it came to fisticuffs, I received championship-caliber consultations from Herb Boyd, Herb Goldman, Thomas Hauser, Harold Lederman, and Bert Sugar, who naturally also provided an earful of wonderful ideas on every sport imaginable.

In the worlds of marathons and track events, Peter Gambaccini, Allan Steinfeld, and Howard Schmertz helped bring me up to speed. Stanley Cohen provided an education on the CCNY basketball championships, while Dennis D'Agostino gets an assist for his thoughts on the Knicks.

Bill Shannon, Marty Appel, Doug Drotman, and Greg Prince each came up big with ideas or advice in the baseball realm; I also relied on some of my oldest friends, particularly David Schwartzberg, to help put the Mets highlights in perspective.

Others provided research help in different ways—John Rawlings and Steve Geitscher opened the doors at the marvelous *Sporting News* archives to me, and Tim Wiles and others at the Baseball Hall of Fame Library guided me through their voluminous material. Cecile Cross-Plummer and Ray Stallone at HBO and Josh Krulewitz at ESPN dug out hard-to-find tapes for me. And I owe a big thanks to everyone—particularly at Corbis and AP—who helped me find the photos I needed and tracked down all my endless (and constantly changing) photo requests.

Last, I'd like to thank everyone at Houghton Mifflin, especially Will Vincent, for guiding the endless flow of material and questions, and the book's designer, Lisa Diercks, for her superb work.

# Index

*Page numbers in italics refer to illustrations.*

## Illustration Credits

**Author's collection:** xi. **Associated Press / Wide World Photos:** 1, 13, 20, 37, 70, 85, 92, 106, 109, 121, 130, 135, 155, 158, 168, 170, 205, 208, 210, 229, 238, 258, 268, 279, 289, 291, 300, 303, 322, 326, 351, 354, 359, 363, 373, 376, 379, 386, 395, 416, 421, 431, 474, 476, 485, 492, 497. **Corbis:** x, 10, 17, 27, 45, 49, 65, 73, 89, 102, 112, 119, 132, 138, 141, 150, 152, 166, 175, 177, 180, 186, 189, 193, 196, 200, 213, 218, 221, 224, 226, 233, 245, 249, 262, 264, 274, 277, 284, 287, 297, 306, 313, 318, 329, 336, 339, 344, 348, 356, 361, 365, 368, 370, 381, 382, 388, 389, 393, 398, 413, 419, 441, 456, 460, 462, 471, 491, 499, 509. **Getty:** 58, 62, 161, 184, 252, 254, 404, 427. **Keeneland:** 146, 202, 295. **Library of Congress:** 144, 331. **National Baseball Hall of Fame Library, Cooperstown, New York:** 9, 32, 55, 78, 82, 95, 116, 418, 424, 429, 435, 439, 442, 445, 446, 447, 452, 454, 456, 463, 467, 468, 469, 472, 479, 481, 490, 495, 502 left and right, 507. **National Museum of Racing and Hall of Fame:** 236. ***New York Daily News:*** 41, 163, 272, 384, 391, 437, 444, 486. ***New York Times:*** 310. **University of Notre Dame Archives:** 98, 127, 242, 308. **ZUMA Press:** 401, 410